fifth canadian edition

Essentials of
Business Communication

fifth canadian edition

Essentials of
Business Communication

> MARY ELLEN GUFFEY
Professor of Business Emerita
Los Angeles Pierce College

> RICHARD ALMONTE
George Brown College

Jen 67

THOMSON

✦

NELSON

Australia   Canada   Mexico   Singapore   Spain   United Kingdom   United States

THOMSON
NELSON

**Essentials of Business Communication,
Fifth Canadian Edition**

by Mary Ellen Guffey and Richard Almonte

**Associate Vice President,
Editorial Director:**
Evelyn Veitch

Publisher:
Joanna Cotton

Marketing Manager:
Sandra Green

Senior Developmental Editor:
Rebecca Rea

Developmental Editor:
Linda Sparks

Permissions Coordinator:
Mary Rose MacLachlan

Senior Production Editor:
Natalia Denesiuk

Copy Editor:
Lisa Berland

Proofreader:
Karen Rolfe

Indexer:
Andrew Little

Senior Production Coordinator:
Hedy Sellers

Design Director:
Ken Phipps

Interior Design Modifications:
Fernanda Pisani

Cover Design:
Liz Harasymczuk

Cover Image:
Linda Bleck/Stock Illustration
Source

Compositor:
Carol Magee

Printer:
Quebecor World

**Library and Archives Canada
Cataloguing in Publication Data**

Guffey, Mary Ellen

    Essentials of business communication / Mary Ellen Guffey, Richard Almonte. — 5th Canadian ed.

Includes bibliographical references and index.

ISBN 0-17-641503-3

    1. Business writing—Textbooks. 2. English language—Business English—Textbooks. 3. Business communication—Textbooks.

I. Almonte, Richard II. Title.

HF5718.3.G84 2006   808'.06665
C2005-907514-7

Brief Contents

UNIT 6

Communicating for Employment 355

Contents

UNIT 3

Corresponding at Work 93

5 E-Mails and Memos 94

6 Routine Letters and Goodwill Messages 124

7 Persuasive Messages 162

8 Negative Messages 192

UNIT 4

Reporting Data 221

14 Employment Interviews and Follow-Up Messages 394

Preface

Today's graduates enter working environments with ever-increasing demands. As a result of growing emphasis on team management and employee empowerment, they will be expected to gather data, solve problems, and make decisions independently. They will be working with global trading partners and collaborating with work teams in an increasingly diverse workplace. And they will be using sophisticated technologies to communicate.

Surprisingly, writing skills are becoming more and more important. In the past, businesspeople may have written a couple of business letters a month, but now they receive and send hundreds of e-mail messages weekly. Their writing skills are showcased in every message they send. To help students develop the skills they need to succeed in today's technologically enhanced workplace, we have responded with a thoroughly revised Fifth Canadian Edition.

Effective Features That Remain Unchanged

The Fifth Canadian Edition maintains the streamlined, efficient approach to communication that has equipped past learners with the skills needed to be successful in their work. It is most helpful to postsecondary and adult learners preparing themselves for new careers, planning a change in their current careers, or wishing to upgrade their writing and speaking skills. The aim of this edition is to incorporate more of the comments, suggestions, and insights provided by adopters and reviewers over the last few years. For those new to the book, some of the most popular features include the following:

- **Text/Workbook Format.** The convenient text/workbook format presents an all-in-one teaching-learning package that includes concepts, workbook application exercises, writing problems, and a combination handbook/reference manual. Students work with and purchase only one volume for efficient, economical instruction.
- **Comprehensive but Concise Coverage.** An important reason for the enormous success of *Essentials of Business Communication* is that it practises what it preaches. The Fifth Canadian Edition follows the same strategy, concentrating on essential concepts presented without wasted words.
- **Writing Plans and Writing Improvement Exercises.** Step-by-step writing plans structure the writing experience so that novice writers get started quickly—without struggling to provide unknown details to unfamiliar, hypothetical cases. Many revision exercises build confidence and skills.
- **Wide Coverage of Communication Technology.** All relevant chapters build technology skills by including discussions and applications involving e-mail,

instant messaging, PDAs, cell phones, Web research, contemporary software, online employment searches, and electronic presentations.

- **Grammar/Mechanics Emphasis.** Each chapter features a systematic review of the Grammar/Mechanics Handbook. Readers take a short quiz to review specific concepts, and they also proofread business documents that provide a cumulative review of all concepts previously presented.

Revision Highlights

The following new features update the Fifth Canadian Edition:

- **New Technological Emphasis.** Recognizing that communication technologies such as e-mail, instant messaging, PDAs, online research databases, and cell phones have fundamentally changed business communication tasks, this new edition emphasizes the importance of e-mails over memos in Chapter 5, and of online research in general, leading to a more up-to-date presentation of the realities of business communication today.

- **New Definition of Routine Correspondence.** Persuasive writing is the kernel of most business writing, and as such, it has been added to a new expanded unit called Correspondence at Work. Similarly, the ability to write and speak bad news has been judged to be a routine occurrence, and it also appears in the new unit on everyday correspondence.

- **Expanded Focus on Oral Communication Skills.** Following the suggestions of our reviewers, we have split coverage of oral communication into separate new chapters. Chapter 11 looks at oral interpersonal skills: person-to-person conversations, telephone communication (including cell phone etiquette), and business meeting skills, while Chapter 12 specifically discusses business presentation skills.

- **More Concentrated Grammar/Mechanics Handbook.** The Grammar/Mechanics Checkups exercises have been moved from the end of each chapter to the Grammar/Mechanics Handbook section at the end of the book. This amalgamation allows instructors to offer a more concentrated and varied amount of review exercises at the end of each handbook section.

- **New Activities and Cases.** On average, 25 percent of the activities and cases are new. A number of the new cases recognize the importance of scripting, role play, and performance as effective means of practising business communication skills. The new cases are also more closely tied to the Canadian economy, with many of the new cases including a real company.

- **More Challenging Cases.** The reality of the work world is that communication situations will not always easily fit the models provided in a business communication textbook. As a result, we have threaded ambiguity and complexity into the tasks so that students have a chance to use their critical thinking skills as well as their business communication skills regularly.

- **Collection Letters.** Recognizing the importance of the small business sector to the Canadian economy, and the fact that small business owners often have to take the collections function in to their own hands, we have added a section on how to write collection letters.

- **Updated Documentation.** The fact that many students today almost solely use the Internet for their research has led to documentation challenges. While recognizing that the basics of documentation remain the same, we have introduced a number of documentation situations (e.g., Web site without author; online company report) that closely mirror the reality of today's classrooms.

- **Plagiarism.** An unfortunate reality of the Internet age is the difficulty today's students have in understanding the need for proper citation and documentation, as well as the difficulty in understanding the seriousness of plagiarism and its difficult repercussions. We have added a discussion of plagiarism as well as exercises to help students spot and eradicate it.

- **More Writing Improvement Exercises.** This edition includes four new writing improvement exercises that tackle realistic workplace situations.
- **New epigraphs and cartoons.** Most of the epigraphs have been changed with this edition, and all of the new epigraphs come from Canadian businesspeople, commenting on how business communication skills impact their own job. A number of new cartoons have been added that reflect the sometimes humorous reality of multitasking and communication overload in today's workplace.

Other Features That Enhance Teaching and Learning

Although the Fifth Canadian Edition of *Essentials of Business Communication* packs considerable information into a small space, it covers all of the critical topics necessary in a comprehensive business communication course; and it also features many teaching-learning devices to facilitate instruction, application, and retention.

- **Focus on Writing Skills.** Most students need a great deal of instruction and practice in developing basic and advanced writing techniques, particularly in view of today's increased emphasis on communication by e-mail. Writing skills have returned to the forefront since so much of today's business is transacted through written messages.
- **E-Mail Emphasis.** *Essentials* devotes an entire chapter to the writing of e-mail, which have become the most used communication channels in the business world.
- **Listening, Speaking, and Nonverbal Skills.** Employers are increasingly seeking well-rounded individuals who can interact with fellow employees as well as represent the organization effectively. *Essentials* provides professional tips for managing nonverbal cues, overcoming listening barriers, developing speaking skills, planning and participating in meetings, and making productive telephone calls.
- **Coverage of Formal and Informal Reports.** Two chapters develop functional report-writing skills. Chapter 9 provides detailed instruction in the preparation of six types of informal reports, while Chapter 10 covers proposals and formal reports. For quick comprehension all reports contain marginal notes that pinpoint writing strategies.
- **Employment Communication Skills.** Successful résumés, cover letters, and other employment documents are among the most important topics in a good business communication course. *Essentials* provides the most realistic and up-to-date résumés in the field. The models show chronological, functional, combination, and computer-friendly résumés.
- **Employment Interviewing.** *Essentials* devotes an entire chapter to effective interviewing techniques, including a discussion of screening interviews and hiring interviews. Chapter 14 also teaches techniques for fighting fear, answering questions, and following up.
- **Models Comparing Effective and Ineffective Documents.** To facilitate speedy recognition of good and bad writing techniques and strategies, *Essentials* presents many before-and-after documents. Marginal notes spotlight targeted strategies and effective writing. We hope that instructors turn this before-and-after technique into effective pedagogy whereby all their students' written assignments undergo the scrutiny of an editing and revising process before being handed in as final products.
- **Variety in End-of-Chapter Activities.** An amazing array of review questions, critical-thinking questions, writing improvement exercises, revision exercises,

activities, and realistic case problems hold student attention and help them apply chapter concepts meaningfully.

- **Diagnostic Test.** An optional grammar/mechanics diagnostic test helps students and instructors systematically determine specific student writing weaknesses. Students may be directed to the Grammar/Mechanics Handbook for remediation.
- **Grammar/Mechanics Handbook.** A comprehensive Grammar/Mechanics Handbook supplies a thorough review of English grammar, punctuation, capitalization style, and number usage. Its self-teaching exercises may be used for classroom instruction or for supplementary assignments. The handbook also serves as a convenient reference throughout the course and afterwards.

Unparalleled Instructor Support

The Fifth Canadian Edition of *Essentials* continues to set the standard for business communication support. Classroom success is easy to achieve because of the many practical ancillary items that supplement Guffey textbooks. No other author matches her level of support.

The following time-saving ancillaries and resources accompany the Fifth Canadian Edition of *Essentials*:

- **Instructor's Manual with Test Banks and Solutions Masters** (0-17-622492-0). The IM supplies general suggestions for teaching business communication, lesson plans for each chapter, test banks with 50 questions for each chapter, three unit tests, keys for all cumulative editing quizzes, and solutions transparency masters. In addition to ideas for course organization and evaluation, the IM provides many supplementary lectures on relevant topics not covered in the text.
- **PowerPoint® Slides** (0-17-622414-9). Summaries of important chapter concepts are professionally rendered in PowerPoint®. Instructors can use our chapter presentations or alter them for custom lectures. Our unique interactive program not only introduces concepts but also engages students in a dialogue that reviews and reinforces what they are seeing. This dynamic program captures attention, creates lively lectures, and, most important, enhances learning and retention.
- **Computerized Test Bank** (0-17-622494-7). All items from the printed test bank are available through this automated testing program. Create exams by selecting provided questions, modifying existing questions, and adding questions. Provided free to adopters of the text.
- **BusinessLink Video Cases** (0-324-01364-7). Featuring real companies with real communication issues that managers and employees face, seven new videos (each about eight minutes long) require student analysis, problem-solving skills, and application of communication concepts from the text. We've tried hard to provide a practical application for each video. For example, in the Hudson video students compare customer profiles with those developed by the trainees in the film. And your students will be as astonished as the Hudson trainees at the outcome!
- **Canadian Web Site for Students and Instructors.** This complete learning environment can be found at <**www.guffeyessentials5e.nelson.com**>. Instructors will find PowerPoint slides and other teaching aids. Instructors should contact their Nelson sales representative for more information. Students will find book-specific learning tools such as chapter quizzes and learning objectives as well as general resources such as study tips and career resources.
- **Mary Ellen Guffey's WestWords.** Dr. Guffey has created a rich Web site called WestWords for instructors and students in the United States. Canadian

adopters of her titles are also invited to visit at <**www.westwords.com**>. Passwords can be requested from your local Nelson sales representative.

- **Web Tutor** (0-17-622517-X). Web Tutor on WebCT is a content rich, Web-based teaching and learning aid that reinforces and clarifies complex concepts. Web Tutor delivers innovative learning aids such as chapter reviews, flashcards, writing improvement exercises, spelling and vocabulary quizzes, and more. It also provides rich communication tools to instructors and students including a course calendar, chat, and e-mail. Instructors can incorporate Web Tutor as an integral part of the course, or students can use it on their own as a study guide.
- **Print Newsletter.** *Business Communication News,* a twice-yearly newsletter, brings relevant business communication news, teaching tips, and announcements of new free materials. Instructors who have adopted *Essentials* may be put on the mailing list by sending their names and addresses to their local Nelson sales representative or to the Marketing Manager for Business Communication at Nelson.
- **E-Mail Newsletter.** *The Online Guffey Report* is a monthly electronic newsletter sent directly to instructors' e-mail boxes. Instructors may sign up at Mary Ellen Guffey's Instructor Web site <**www.westwords.com/instructor.html**>. The newsletter provides relevant news nuggets, classroom teaching tips, lecture ideas, and bonus case-study problems. Dr. Guffey remains the number one business communication author when it comes to accessibility, complimentary teaching materials, and online resources.
- **Distance Learning Resources.** Numerous distance learning instructors have made *Essentials* their textbook choice because of its comprehensive learning/testing system, its technologically savvy approach, and its many online resources. Distance learning students have direct access to PowerPoint slides, interactive chapter review questions, interactive skill builders, electronic citation formats, and many other student-oriented electronic resources.

Acknowledgments

The Fifth Canadian Edition of *Essentials of Business Communication* includes many of the constructive suggestions and timely advice provided by professional communicators, educators and students who use the book across Canada. These dedicated reviewers include: LaRoyce Batchelor, Red River College; Judy Johnson, North Island College; Gord Mackie, Red River College; Kathleen Moran, Conestoga College; Paula Pedwell, Georgian College; Mary Ryan, Cambrian College; Alberta Smith, Algonquin College; Catherine Walsh, Compu College; and Karen Weinstein, CDI College of Business, Technology and Health Care.

A new edition like this would not be possible without the development team at Thomson Nelson. Special thanks go to Rebecca Rea, Natalia Denesiuk, Maya Bahar, Heather Leach, and Mike Thompson. Thanks also go to the copy editor, Lisa Berland.

—Mary Ellen Guffey
Richard Almonte

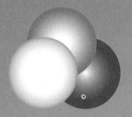

Communication Foundations

Today's Communication Challenges

CHAPTER

We live in a time of unbridled change. Computers are taking us in bold directions never foreseen—in business, communication and society…. For years, companies have been told that their future lies in product innovation [but] tomorrow's winners will be those firms that become innovators in how they do business—not in what they make or sell.[1]

Rick Spence, *Profit Magazine*

LEARNING OBJECTIVES

1. Understand the importance of becoming an effective business communicator in today's changing workplace.
2. Examine the process of communication.
3. Discuss how to become an effective listener.
4. Analyze nonverbal communication and explain techniques for improving nonverbal communication skills.
5. Explain how culture affects communication and describe methods for improving cross-cultural communication.
6. Identify specific techniques that improve effective communication among diverse workplace audiences.

Becoming an Effective Business Communicator

People with different backgrounds bring varied views to decision making. As Rick Spence implies in his *Profit* article, improving vital processes like decision making and communication is what will lead to business success in the knowledge economy of tomorrow. Businesses must rely on their employees' ability to work with a highly diverse group of people who are located across international borders. The more effectively employees work together, the more successful their company is. In this age of information, career success is directly related to good communication, a skill that is made more challenging by tremendous changes in technology, the workforce, work environments, and the globalization of business.

Through e-mail, instant messaging, and other technology-based communication channels, business communicators today are doing more writing than ever before. Their writing is also having a more immediate impact. This book focuses on developing business writing skills. But you will also learn to improve your listening, nonverbal, and speaking skills.

Quick Check

The information revolution has made communication skills extremely important.

While you are born with the ability to acquire language and to listen, effective business communication skills are learned. Good communicators are not born; they are made. Your ability to thrive in the dynamic and demanding contemporary world of work will depend on many factors, some of which you cannot control. One factor that you do control, however, is how well you communicate.

The goals of this book are to teach you basic business communication skills, such as how to write an effective e-mail, memo, or letter and how to make a presentation. Anyone can learn these skills with the help of effective instructional materials and good model documents, all of which you'll find in this book. You also need practice—with meaningful feedback. You need someone such as your instructor to tell you how to modify your responses so that you can improve.

We've designed this book to provide you with everything necessary to make you a successful business communicator in today's dynamic workplace. Given the increasing emphasis on communication, Canadian corporations are paying millions of dollars to communication coaches and trainers to teach employees the very skills that you are learning in this course. For example, Ottawa-based Backdraft Corporation, a leading provider of corporate writing training, and the first writing services company in the world to be granted ISO 9000 registration, lists among its clients the Royal Bank of Canada, Siemens Canada, the National Gallery of Canada, and the Government of Alberta.[2] Your coach is your instructor. Get your money's worth! Pick his or her brains.

Once you've had a couple of years of business experience, you will look back on this course and this textbook as the most important in your entire postsecondary education. To get started, this first chapter presents an overview. You'll take a look at (1) the changing workplace, (2) the communication process, (3) listening, (4) nonverbal communication, (5) culture and communication, and (6) workplace diversity. The remainder of the book is devoted to developing specific writing and speaking skills.

Because communication skills are learned, you control how well you communicate.

This book and this course might well be the most important in your postsecondary education.

Succeeding in the Changing World of Work

The entire world of work is changing dramatically. The kind of work you'll do, the tools you'll use, the form of management you'll work under, the environment in which you'll work, the people with whom you'll interact—all are undergoing a pronounced transformation. Many of the changes revolve around processing and communicating information. As a result, the most successful players in this new world of work will be those with highly developed communication skills. The following business trends illustrate the importance of excellent communication skills.

✓ **Quick Check**

Trends in the new world of work emphasize the importance of communication skills.

- **Innovative communication technologies.** E-mail, instant messaging, the Web, mobile technologies, audio- and videoconferencing—all of these technologies mean that you will be communicating more often and more rapidly than ever before. Your writing and speaking skills will be showcased and tested as never before.
- **Flattened management hierarchies.** To better compete and to reduce expenses, businesses have for years been trimming layers of management. This means that as a frontline employee, you will have fewer managers. You will be making decisions and communicating them to customers, to fellow employees, and to executives.
- **More participatory management.** Gone are the days of command-and-control management. Now, even new employees will be expected to understand and contribute to the success of the organization. Improving productivity and profitability will be everyone's job, not just management's.
- **Increased emphasis on self-directed work and project teams.** Businesses today are often run by cross-functional teams of peers. You can expect to work

with a team in gathering information, finding and sharing solutions, implementing decisions, and managing conflict. Good communication skills are extremely important in working together successfully in a team environment.

- **Heightened global competition.** Because Canadian companies are required to move beyond local markets, you may be interacting with people from many different cultures. At the same time, because of increased immigration, you may be expected to interact with people from many cultures in your local market as well as in your organization.[3] As a successful business communicator, you will want to learn about other cultures. You'll also need to develop interpersonal skills including sensitivity, flexibility, patience, and tolerance.
- **New work environments.** Mobile technologies and the desire for better work/family balance have resulted in flexible working arrangements. You may become part of the 1.5 million Canadians engaged in full- or part-time telecommuting.[4] Working away from the office requires exchanging even more messages in order to stay connected.
- **The move to a knowledge economy.** As Statistics Canada researchers Desmond Beckstead and Tara Vinodrai show in their paper "Dimensions of Occupational Changes in Canada's Knowledge Economy, 1971–1996," the decrease in the importance of sectors like manufacturing and agriculture has taken place at the same time as "the importance of knowledge occupations has continuously increased over the last three decades."[5] By definition, such "knowledge occupations," many of which are in business, require excellent communication skills.

Examining the Communication Process

As you can see, in today's workplace you can expect to be communicating more rapidly, more often, and with greater numbers of people than ever before. Since good communication skills are essential to your success, we need to take a closer look at the communication process.

Just what is communication? For our purposes communication is the transmission of information and meaning from one individual or group (the sender) to another (the receiver). The crucial element in this definition is meaning. Communication has as its central objective the transmission of meaning. The process of communication is successful only when the receiver understands an idea as the sender intended it. This classic theory of communication was first articulated by theorist Harold Lasswell (1947) and later expanded upon by Claude E. Shannon and Warren Weaver (1949). A succinct summary and critique of the work of these major theorists is available on the Communication, Culture and Media Studies Web site, <www.ccms-infobase.com>, by searching under "Shannon-Weaver model." This theoretical process generally involves five steps, discussed here and shown in Figure 1.1.

1. **Sender forms an idea.** The idea may be influenced by the sender's mood, frame of reference, background, and culture, as well as the context of the situation. (For example, an accountant realizes income tax season is about to begin.)
2. **Sender encodes the idea in a message.** Encoding means converting the idea into words or gestures that will convey meaning. A major problem in communicating any message is that words have different meanings for different people. That's why skilled communicators try to choose familiar words with concrete meanings on which both senders and receivers agree. (For example, an accountant writes a letter asking all her clients to begin scheduling income tax appointments.)

Quick Check

Communication is the transmission of information and meaning from one individual or group to another.

Quick Check

The communication process has five steps: idea formation, message encoding, message transmission, message decoding, and feedback.

FIGURE 1.1 Communication Process

Communication barriers may cause the communication process to break down.

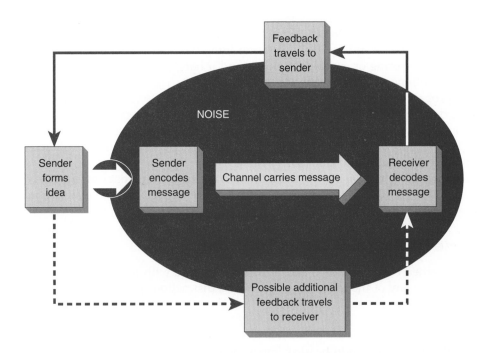

3. **Message travels over a channel.** The medium over which the message is transmitted is the channel. Messages may be sent by computer, telephone, fax, portable handheld device like a BlackBerry, traditional mail, or Web site blog. Because both verbal and nonverbal messages are carried, senders must choose channels carefully. Any barrier that disrupts the transmission of a message in the communication process is called noise. Channel noise ranges from static that disrupts a telephone conversation to spelling and grammar errors in an e-mail message, to e-mails that are not sent because of firewalls. Such errors can damage the credibility of the sender. (For example, an accountant's assistant sends letter to 125 clients via traditional mail in early January.)

4. **Receiver decodes message.** The person for whom a message is intended is the receiver. Translating the message into meaning involves decoding. Successful communication takes place only when a receiver understands the meaning intended by the sender. Such success is often hard to achieve because barriers and noise may disrupt the process. (For example, client opens letter, reads it, decides to do taxes himself this year.)

5. **Feedback travels to sender.** The response of the receiver creates feedback, a vital part of the entire communication process. Feedback helps the sender know that the message was received and understood. Senders can encourage feedback by including statements such as *Please let me know what you think as soon as possible.* Senders can further improve feedback by delivering the message at a time when receivers can respond. Senders should also provide only as much information as a receiver can handle. Receivers can improve the process by paraphrasing the sender's message. They might say, *Thanks for your e-mail explaining the new safe procedure.* (For example, client calls accountant, leaves voice mail thanking her for letter but letting her know he's going to do his taxes himself this year.)

An important part of the communication process is listening. By many accounts, however, most of us are not very good listeners. Do you ever pretend to be listening when you're not? Do you know how to look attentive in class when your mind wanders far away? How about losing interest in people's messages when their ideas are boring or complex? Do you find it hard to focus on ideas when a speaker's clothing or mannerisms are unusual?

You probably answered yes to one or more of these questions because many of us have developed poor listening habits. In fact, some researchers suggest that we listen at only 25 percent efficiency. Such poor listening habits are costly in business. Letters must be rewritten, shipments reshipped, appointments rescheduled, contracts renegotiated, and directions restated.

To improve listening skills, we must first recognize barriers that prevent effective listening. Then we need to focus on specific techniques that are effective in improving listening skills.

Quick Check

Most individuals listen at only 25 percent efficiency.

Barriers to Effective Listening

As you learned earlier, barriers and noise can interfere with the communication process. Have any of the following barriers and distractions prevented you from hearing what's said?

- **Physical barriers.** You cannot listen if you cannot hear what is being said. Physical impediments include hearing impairments, poor acoustics, and noisy surroundings. It's also difficult to listen if you're ill, tired, uncomfortable, or worried.
- **Personal barriers.** Everyone brings to the communication process a different set of cultural, ethical, and personal values. Each of us has an idea of what is right and what is important. If another person's ideas run counter to our preconceived thoughts, we tend to lose interest in his or her message and thus fail to hear.
- **Language problems.** Unfamiliar words can destroy the communication process because they lack meaning for the receiver. In addition, if a speaker's oral communication skills are compromised by a thick accent or pronunciation mistakes, listeners may be unable to understand what follows.
- **Nonverbal distractions.** Some of us find it hard to listen if a speaker is different from what we are expecting. Unusual clothing, speech mannerisms, body twitches, or a radical hairstyle or colour sometimes cause enough distraction to prevent us from hearing what the speaker has to say.
- **Thought speed.** Because we can process thoughts over three times faster than speakers can say them, we can become bored and allow our minds to wander.
- **Faking attention.** Most of us have learned to look as if we are listening even when we're not. Faked attention seriously threatens effective listening because it encourages the mind to engage in flights of unchecked fancy. Those who practise faked attention often find it hard to concentrate even when they want to.
- **Grandstanding.** Would you rather talk or listen? Naturally, many of us would rather talk. Since our own experiences and thoughts are most important to us, we want the attention in conversations. We sometimes fail to listen carefully because we're just waiting politely for the next pause so that we can have our turn to speak.

Quick Check

Barriers to listening may be physical, personal, verbal, or nonverbal.

Quick Check

Most North Americans speak at about 125 words per minute. The human brain can process information at least three times as fast.

Tips for Becoming an Active Listener

You can reverse the harmful effects of poor listening habits by making a conscious effort to become an active listener. This means becoming involved and taking responsibility for understanding. The following techniques will help you become an active and effective listener.

- **Stop talking.** The first step to becoming a good listener is to stop talking. Let others explain their views. Learn to concentrate on what the speaker is saying, not on what your next comment will be.
- **Control your surroundings.** Whenever possible, remove competing sounds. Close windows or doors, turn off radios and noisy appliances, and move away from loud people or engines. Choose a quiet time and place for listening.
- **Establish a receptive mindset.** Expect to learn something by listening. Strive for a positive and receptive frame of mind. If the message is complex, think of it as a mental challenge. It's hard work but good exercise to stretch and expand the limits of your mind.
- **Keep an open mind.** We all sift and filter information through our own biases and values. For improved listening, discipline yourself to listen objectively. Be fair to the speaker. Hear what is really being said, not what you want to hear.
- **Listen for main points.** Concentration is enhanced and satisfaction is heightened when you look for and recognize the speaker's central themes.
- **Capitalize on lag time.** Make use of the quickness of your mind by reviewing the speaker's points. Anticipate what's coming next. Evaluate evidence the speaker has presented. Don't allow yourself to daydream.
- **Listen between the lines.** Focus both on what is spoken and what is unspoken. Listen for feelings as well as for facts.
- **Judge ideas, not appearances.** Concentrate on the content of the message, not on its delivery. Avoid being distracted by the speaker's looks, voice, or mannerisms.
- **Be patient.** Force yourself to listen to the speaker's entire argument or message before reacting. Such restraint may enable you to understand the speaker's reasons and logic before you jump to false conclusions.
- **Take selective notes.** For some situations thoughtful note taking may be necessary to record important facts that must be recalled later. Select only the most important points so that the note-taking process does not interfere with your concentration on the speaker's total message.
- **Provide feedback.** Let the speaker know that you are listening. Nod your head and maintain eye contact. Ask relevant questions at appropriate times. Getting involved improves the communication process for both the speaker and the listener.

Quick Check

To become an active listener, stop talking, control your surroundings, develop a positive mindset, listen for main points, and capitalize on lag time.

Quick Check

Listening actively may mean taking notes and providing feedback.

Improving Your Nonverbal Communication Skills

Understanding messages often involves more than listening to spoken words. Nonverbal clues, in fact, can speak louder than words. These clues include eye contact, facial expression, body movements, space, time, distance, and appearance. All these nonverbal clues affect how a message is interpreted, or decoded, by the receiver.

Just what is nonverbal communication? It includes all unwritten and unspoken messages, whether intended or not. These silent signals have a strong effect on receivers. But understanding them is not simple. Does a downward glance indicate modesty? Fatigue? Does a constant stare reflect coldness? Dullness? Do crossed arms mean defensiveness? Withdrawal? Or do crossed arms just mean that a person is cold?

Messages are even harder to decipher when the verbal and nonverbal codes do not agree. What would you think if Scott says he's not angry, but he slams the door when he leaves? Or what if Alicia assures her server that the meal is excellent, but she eats very little? The nonverbal messages in these situations speak more loudly than the words.

When verbal and nonverbal messages conflict, research shows that receivers put more faith in nonverbal cues. In one study speakers sent a positive message

Quick Check

Nonverbal communication includes all unwritten and unspoken messages, intended or not.

Quick Check

When verbal and nonverbal messages clash, listeners tend to believe the nonverbal message.

but averted their eyes as they spoke. Listeners perceived the total message to be negative. Moreover, they thought that averted eyes suggested lack of affection, superficiality, lack of trust, and nonreceptivity.[6]

Successful communicators recognize the power of nonverbal messages. Although it's unwise to attach specific meanings to gestures or actions, some cues broadcast by body language are helpful in understanding the feelings and attitudes of senders.

How the Eyes, Face, and Body Send Silent Messages

Words seldom tell the whole story. Indeed, some messages are sent with no words at all. The eyes, face, and body can convey a world of meaning without a single syllable being spoken.

Quick Check

The eyes are thought to be the best indicator of a speaker's true feelings.

Eye Contact. The eyes have been called the "windows of the soul." Even if they don't reveal the soul, the eyes are often the best indicator of a speaker's true feelings. Most of us cannot look another person straight in the eyes and lie. As a result, in Canada we tend to believe people who look directly at us. Sustained eye contact suggests trust and admiration; brief eye contact signals fear or stress. Good eye contact enables the message sender to see if a receiver is paying attention, showing respect, responding favourably, or feeling distress. From the receiver's viewpoint, good eye contact reveals the speaker's sincerity, confidence, and truthfulness.

Facial Expression. The expression on a person's face can be almost as revealing of emotion as the eyes. Experts estimate that the human face can display over 250,000 expressions.[7] To hide their feelings, some people can control these expressions and maintain "poker faces." Most of us, however, display our emotions openly. Raising or lowering the eyebrows, squinting the eyes, swallowing nervously, clenching the jaw, smiling broadly—these voluntary and involuntary facial expressions can add to or entirely replace verbal messages.

Quick Check

Nonverbal messages often have different meanings in different cultures.

Posture and Gestures. A person's posture can convey anything from high status and self-confidence to shyness and submissiveness. Leaning toward a speaker suggests attraction and interest; pulling away or shrinking back denotes fear, distrust, anxiety, or disgust. Similarly, gestures can communicate entire thoughts via simple movements. However, the meanings of these movements differ in other cultures. Unless you know local customs, they can get you into trouble. In Canada, for example, forming the thumb and forefinger in a circle means everything's OK. But in Germany and parts of South America, the gesture is obscene.

Understanding body language, gestural literacy, and other nonverbal messages requires that you be aware that they exist and that you value their importance. To take stock of the kinds of messages being sent by your body, ask a classmate to critique your use of eye contact, facial expression, and body movements. Another way to analyze your nonverbal style is to videotape yourself making a presentation and study your performance. This way you can make sure your nonverbal cues send the same message as your words.

How Time, Space, and Territory Send Silent Messages

In addition to nonverbal messages transmitted by your body, three external elements convey information in the communication process: time, space, and distance.

Time. How we structure and use time tells observers about our personality and attitudes. For example, if a financial planner sets aside one-hour blocks of time for client meetings, he is signalling respect for, interest in, and approval of the visitor or the topic to be discussed. If however he schedules only a 15-minute meeting, the client may feel less important.

Space. How we order the space around us tells something about ourselves and our objectives. Whether the space is a bedroom, a classroom, an office, or a department, people reveal themselves in the design and grouping of their furniture. Generally, the more formal the arrangement, the more formal the communication. The way office furniture is arranged sends cues on how communication is to take place. An instructor who arranges chairs informally in a circle rather than in straight rows conveys her desire for a more open exchange of ideas. A manager who creates an open office space with few partitions separating workers' desks seeks to encourage an unrestricted flow of communication and work among areas.

Territory. Each of us has certain areas that we feel are our own territory, whether it's a specific spot or just the space around us. Family members may have a favourite living-room chair, students who sit in a chair during their first class may return to that chair throughout the term, a cook might not tolerate intruders in his or her kitchen, and veteran employees may feel that certain work areas and tools belong to them.

We all maintain zones of privacy in which we feel comfortable. Figure 1.2 categorizes the four classic zones of social interaction among North Americans, as formulated by anthropologist Edward T. Hall.[8] Notice that North Americans are a bit standoffish; only intimate friends and family may stand closer than about 45 cm (1.5 feet). If someone violates that territory, North Americans feel uncomfortable and defensive and may step back to re-establish their space.

How Appearance Sends Silent Messages

The physical appearance of a business document, as well as the personal appearance of an individual, transmits immediate and important nonverbal messages.

Appearance of Business Documents. The way an e-mail, letter, memo, or report looks can have either a positive or a negative effect on the receiver. Sloppy e-mail messages send a nonverbal message that says you are in a terrific hurry or that the reader or message is not important enough for you to care. Envelopes— through their postage, stationery, and printing—can suggest routine, important,

FIGURE 1.2 Four Space Zones for Social Interaction

Zone	Distance	Uses
Intimate	0 to 45 cm (1.5 feet)	Reserved for members of the family and other loved ones.
Personal	45 cm to 123 cm (1.5 to 4 feet)	For talking with friends privately. The outer limit enables you to keep someone at arm's length.
Social	123 cm to 360 cm (4 to 12 feet)	For acquaintances, fellow workers, and strangers. Close enough for eye contact yet far enough for comfort.
Public	360 cm and over (12 feet and over)	For use in the classroom and for speeches before groups. Nonverbal cues become important as aids to communication.

or junk mail. Letters and reports can look neat, professional, well organized, and attractive—or just the opposite. In succeeding chapters you'll learn how to create documents that send positive nonverbal messages through their appearance, format, organization, readability, and correctness.

Appearance of People. The way you look—your clothing, grooming, and posture—sends an instant nonverbal message about you. On the basis of what they see, viewers make quick judgments about your status, credibility, personality, and potential. Because appearance is such a powerful force in business, some aspiring professionals are turning for help to image consultants. For example, Kingston, Ontario–based image consultant Catherine Bell's company Prime Impressions offers corporate training in the areas of professional attire, dining protocol, and interview coaching among many others. Bell even offers a "telecoaching" service that provides training over the phone.[9]

"Here come the suits."

Tips for Improving Your Nonverbal Skills

Nonverbal communication can outweigh words in the way it influences how others perceive us. You can harness the power of silent messages by reviewing the following tips for improving nonverbal communication skills:

Because nonverbal clues can mean more than spoken words, learn to use nonverbal communication positively.

- **Establish and maintain eye contact.** Remember that in Canada appropriate eye contact signals interest, attentiveness, strength, and credibility.
- **Use posture to show interest.** Encourage communication interaction by leaning forward, sitting or standing erect, and looking alert.
- **Improve your decoding skills.** Watch facial expressions and body language to understand the complete verbal and nonverbal message being communicated.
- **Probe for more information.** When you perceive nonverbal cues that contradict verbal meanings, politely seek additional clues (*I'm not sure I understand, Please tell me more about …*, or *Do you mean that …*).
- **Avoid assigning nonverbal meanings out of context.** Make nonverbal assessments only when you understand a situation or a culture.

- **Associate with people from diverse cultures.** Learn about other cultures to widen your knowledge and tolerance of intercultural nonverbal messages.
- **Appreciate the power of appearance.** Keep in mind that the appearance of you, your business documents, and your business space sends immediate positive or negative messages to receivers.
- **Observe yourself on videotape.** Ensure that your verbal and nonverbal messages agree by taping and evaluating yourself making a presentation.
- **Enlist friends and family.** Ask them to monitor your conscious and unconscious body movements and gestures to help you become a more effective communicator.

Understanding How Culture Affects Communication

Comprehending the verbal and nonverbal meanings of a message is difficult even when communicators are from the same culture. But when they are from different cultures, special sensitivity and skills are necessary.

✓ Quick Check

Verbal and nonverbal meanings are even more difficult to interpret when people are from different cultures.

Negotiators for a Canadian company learned this lesson when they were in Japan looking for a trading partner. The Canadians were pleased after their first meeting with representatives of a major Japanese firm. The Japanese had nodded assent throughout the meeting and had not objected to a single proposal. The next day, however, the Canadians were stunned to learn that the Japanese had rejected the entire plan. In interpreting the nonverbal behavioural messages, the Canadians made a typical mistake. They assumed the Japanese were nodding in agreement as fellow Canadians would. In this case, however, the nods of assent indicated comprehension—not approval.

Every country has a common heritage, joint experience, and shared learning that produce its culture. These elements give members of that culture a complex system of shared values and customs. The system teaches them how to behave; it conditions their reactions. Comparing Canadian values with those in other cultures will broaden your world view. This comparison should also help you recognize some of the values that shape your actions and judgments of others.

Comparing Key Cultural Values

While it may be difficult to define a typical Canadian, one poll found that Canadians are convinced that a unique national identity exists—even if they are unable to agree on what it is. When asked what makes Canadian individuals distinct, respondents highlighted the tendency toward nonviolence and tolerance of others. When asked what makes Canada as a country distinct, respondents cited social programs and a nonviolent tradition as the two leading factors that make Canada different from the United States and other countries.[10]

Research shows that Canadians tend to be more collective, conforming, and conservative than their U.S. neighbours. Canadians are more supportive of civil and political institutions and collective decision making. Americans on the other hand, tend to be much more supportive of individual decision making and questioning of collective decisions.[11]

Despite the differences outlined above, most Canadians have habits and beliefs similar to those of other members of Western, technologically advanced societies. It's impossible to fully cover the many habits and beliefs of Western culture here, but we can look at four of the crucial ones that characterize the Canadian context.

✓ Quick Check

While Canadians value both individualism and collectivism, as well as personal responsibility, other cultures emphasize group- and team-oriented values.

Individualism versus Collectivism. One of the most identifiable characteristics of Western culture is its built-in tension between individualism, an attitude of independence and freedom from control, and collectivism, the idea that the group or nation is more important than its individual citizens. Political scientist Seymour Martin Lipset has persuasively argued that Canadians are more collectivist than Americans (e.g., they support universal health care).[12] Today, however, regional tensions over health care, for example, between some parts of Western Canada and Central Canada, demonstrate that Canadians' collectivist past may not be as assured in the future. Some non-Western cultures are even more collectivist than Canada. They encourage membership in organizations, groups, and teams and acceptance of group values, duties, and decisions. Members of these cultures sometimes resist independence because it fosters competition and confrontation instead of consensus.

Formality. A second significant dimension of Canadian culture is its attitude toward formality. Canadians place less emphasis on tradition, ceremony, and social rules than do people in some other cultures. We dress casually and are soon on a first-name basis with others. Our lack of formality is often characterized by directness in our business dealings. Indirectness, we feel, wastes time, a valuable commodity.

Communication Style. A third important dimension of our culture relates to communication style. We value straightforwardness, are suspicious of evasiveness, and distrust people who might have a "hidden agenda" or who "play their cards too close to the chest." Canadians also tend to be uncomfortable with silence and impatient with delays. Moreover, we tend to use and understand words literally.

Time Orientation. A fourth dimension of our culture relates to time orientation. Canadians consider time a precious commodity to be conserved. We equate time with productivity, efficiency, and money. Keeping people waiting for business appointments wastes time and is also rude. In other cultures, time may be perceived as an unlimited and never-ending resource to be enjoyed.

Controlling Ethnocentrism and Stereotyping

The process of understanding and accepting people from other cultures is often hampered by two barriers: ethnocentrism and stereotyping. These two barriers, however, can be overcome by developing tolerance, a powerful and effective aid to communication.

Ethnocentrism. The belief in the superiority of one's own culture is known as ethnocentrism. This attitude is found in all cultures. If you were raised in Canada, the values just described probably seem "right" to you, and you may wonder why the rest of the world doesn't function in the same sensible fashion. A Canadian businessperson in a foreign country might be upset at time spent over coffee or other social rituals before any "real" business is transacted. In many cultures, however, personal relationships must be established and nurtured before earnest talks may proceed.

Ethnocentrism causes us to judge others by our own values. We expect others to react as we would, and they expect us to behave as they would. Misunderstandings naturally result. A Canadian who wants to set a deadline for completion of a deal may be considered pushy overseas. Similarly, a foreign businessperson who prefers a handshake to a written contract is seen as naive and possibly untrustworthy by a Canadian. These ethnocentric reactions can be reduced through knowledge of other cultures and development of flexible, tolerant attitudes.

Stereotypes. Our perceptions of other cultures sometimes cause us to form stereotypes about groups of people. A stereotype is an oversimplified behavioural pattern applied to entire groups. For example, the Swiss are hard working, efficient, and neat; Germans are formal, reserved, and blunt; Americans are loud, friendly, and impatient; Canadians are polite, trusting, and tolerant; Asians are gracious, humble, and inscrutable. These attitudes may or may not accurately describe cultural norms. But when applied to individual business communicators, such stereotypes may create misconceptions and misunderstandings. Look beneath surface stereotypes and labels to discover individual personal qualities.

Tolerance. Working among people from other cultures demands tolerance and flexible attitudes. As global markets expand and as our multicultural society continues to develop, tolerance becomes critical. Tolerance does not mean "putting up with" or "enduring," which is one part of its definition. Instead, tolerance is used in a broader sense. It means having sympathy for and appreciating beliefs and practices differing from our own.

One of the best ways to develop tolerance is by practising empathy. This means trying to see the world through another's eyes. It means being nonjudgmental, recognizing things as they are rather than as they "should be." It includes the ability to accept others' contributions in solving problems in a culturally appropriate manner. When a few Canadian companies began selling machinery in China, an Asian advisor suggested that the companies rely less on legal transaction and more on creating friendships. Why? In China, the notion of friendship implies a longer-term relationship of trust and loyalty where business obligations are transacted. Instead of insisting on what "should be" (contracts and binding agreements), these companies adopted successful approaches by looking at the challenge from another cultural point of view.[13]

Making the effort to communicate with sensitivity across cultures can be very rewarding in both your work life and your personal life. The suggestions below provide specific tips for preventing miscommunication in oral and written transactions across cultures.

Quick Check

Developing intercultural tolerance means practising empathy, being nonjudgmental, and being patient.

Tips for Minimizing Oral Miscommunication Among Cross-Cultural Audiences

When you have a conversation with someone from another culture, you can reduce misunderstandings by following these tips:

- **Use simple English.** Speak in short sentences (under 15 words) with familiar, short words. Eliminate puns, specific cultural references, slang, and jargon (special business terms). Be especially alert to idiomatic expressions that can't be translated, such as *burn the midnight oil* and *under the weather*.
- **Speak slowly and enunciate clearly.** Avoid fast speech, but don't raise your voice. Overpunctuate with pauses. Always write numbers for all to see.
- **Encourage accurate feedback.** Ask probing questions, and encourage the listener to paraphrase what you say. Don't assume that a yes, a nod, or a smile indicates comprehension or assent.
- **Check frequently for comprehension.** Avoid waiting until you finish a long explanation to request feedback. Instead, make one point at a time, pausing to check for comprehension. Don't proceed to B until A has been grasped.
- **Observe eye messages.** Be alert to a glazed expression or wandering eyes. These tell you the listener is lost.
- **Accept blame.** If a misunderstanding results, graciously accept the blame for not making your meaning clear.
- **Listen without interrupting.** Curb your desire to finish sentences or to fill out ideas for the speaker. Keep in mind that Canadian listening and speaking habits may not be familiar to other cultures.
- **Remember to smile.** Roger Axtell, international behaviour expert, calls the smile the single most understood and most useful form of communication in either personal or business transactions.

Quick Check

You can improve cross-cultural oral communication by using simple English, speaking slowly, enunciating clearly, encouraging feedback, observing eye messages, accepting blame, and listening without interruption.

- **Follow up in writing.** After conversations or oral negotiations, confirm the results and agreements with follow-up letters or e-mails. For proposals and contracts, engage a translator to prepare copies in the local language.

Tips for Minimizing Written Miscommunication Among Cross-Cultural Audiences

When you write to someone from a different culture, you can improve your chances of being understood by following these tips:

- **Adopt local styles.** Learn how documents are formatted and how letters are addressed and developed in the intended reader's country. Use local formats and styles.
- **Consider hiring a translator.** Engage a translator if (1) your document is important, (2) your document will be distributed to many readers, or (3) you must be persuasive.
- **Use short sentences and short paragraphs.** Sentences with fewer than 15 words and paragraphs with fewer than 5 lines are most readable.
- **Avoid ambiguous wording.** Include relative pronouns (*that, which, who*) for clarity in introducing clauses. Stay away from contractions (especially ones like *Here's the problem*). Avoid idioms (*once in a blue moon*), slang (*my presentation really bombed*), acronyms (*ASAP* for *as soon as possible*), abbreviations (*DBA* for *doing business as*), and jargon (*input, output, bottom line*). Use action-specific verbs (*purchase a printer* rather than *get a printer*).
- **Cite numbers carefully.** Use figures (*15*) instead of spelling them out (*fifteen*). Always convert dollar figures into local currency. Avoid using figures to express the month of the year. In Canada, for example, March 5, 2006, might be written as 3/5/06, while in Europe the same date might appear as 5.3.06. For clarity, always spell out the month.

Capitalizing on Workforce Diversity

As global competition opens world markets, Canadian businesspeople will increasingly interact with customers and colleagues from around the world. At the same time, the Canadian workforce is also becoming more diverse—in race, ethnicity, age, gender, national origin, physical ability, and countless other characteristics.

No longer, say the experts, will the workplace be predominantly male or oriented toward Western cultural values alone. The majority of new entrants to the workforce are women, First Nations, new Canadians, and other visible-minority groups. The Canadian workforce is getting older as the baby boom generation ages. By the year 2016 half of the Canadian population will be over 40 and 16 percent over 65. At the same time, the proportion of people under 15 will shrink to 19 percent from the current 25 percent.[14]

While the workforce is becoming more diverse, the structure of many businesses across Canada is also changing. As you learned earlier, workers are now organized by teams. Organizations are flatter, and employees are increasingly making decisions among themselves and being asked to manage relationships with customers, suppliers, and others along the supply chain. What does all this mean for you as a future business communicator? Simply put, your job may require you to interact with colleagues and customers from around the world. Your work environment will probably demand that you cooperate effectively with small groups of coworkers. And these coworkers may differ from you in race, ethnicity, gender, age, and other ways.

A diverse work environment has many benefits. Customers want to deal with companies that reflect their values and create products and services tailored to their needs. Organizations that hire employees with different experiences and backgrounds are better able to create the customized products these customers desire. In addition, businesses with diverse workforces suffer fewer human rights complaints, fewer union clashes, and less interpersonal conflict. That's why diversity is viewed by a growing number of companies as a critical bottom-line business strategy to improve employee relationships and to increase productivity. For some businesses, diversity also makes economic sense. As Virginia Galt reports in *The Globe and Mail*, "There is one token Canadian on Western Union's national marketing team in Canada. The rest come from China, India, Colombia, Poland, the Philippines." According to Galt, while "Western Union may be further along than most employers in diversifying its work force … others are planning to follow suit, driven by a competitive need to expand into international markets and serve the increasingly diverse population at home."[15]

Tips for Effective Communication with Diverse Workplace Audiences

Capitalizing on workplace diversity is a challenge for most organizations and individuals. Harmony and acceptance do not happen automatically when people who are dissimilar work together. The following suggestions can help you become a more effective communicator as you enter a rapidly evolving workplace with diverse colleagues and clients.

- **Understand the value of differences.** Diversity makes an organization innovative and creative. Sameness fosters "groupthink," an absence of critical thinking sometimes found in homogeneous groups. Diversity in problem-solving groups encourages independent and creative thinking.
- **Don't expect conformity.** Gone are the days when businesses could demand that new employees or customers simply conform to the existing organization's culture. Today, the value of people who bring new perspectives and ideas is recognized. But with those new ideas comes the responsibility to listen and to allow those new ideas to grow.
- **Create zero tolerance for bias and stereotypes.** Cultural patterns exist in every identity group, but applying these patterns to individuals results in stereotyping. Assuming that Canadians of African descent are good athletes or that women are poor at math fails to admit the immense differences in people in each group. Check your own use of stereotypes and labels. Don't tell sexist or ethnic jokes at meetings. Avoid slang, abbreviations, and jargon that imply stereotypes. Challenge others' stereotypes politely but firmly.
- **Practise focused, thoughtful, and open-minded listening.** Much misunderstanding can be avoided by attentive listening. Listen for main points; take notes if necessary to remember important details. The most important part of listening, especially among diverse communicators, is judging ideas, not appearances or accents.
- **Invite, use, and give feedback.** As you learned earlier, a critical element in successful communication is feedback. You can encourage it by asking questions such as *Is there anything you don't understand?* When a listener or receiver responds, use that feedback to adjust your delivery of information. Does the receiver need more details? A different example? Slower delivery? As a good listener, you should also be prepared to give feedback. For example, summarize your understanding of what was said or agreed on.
- **Make fewer assumptions.** Be careful of seemingly insignificant, innocent workplace assumptions. For example, don't assume that everyone wants to

observe the holidays with a Christmas party and a decorated tree. Celebrating only Christian holidays in December and January excludes those who honour Hanukkah, Chinese New Year, and Ramadan. Moreover, in workplace discussions don't assume that everyone is married or wants to be or is even heterosexual, for that matter. For invitations, avoid phrases such as "managers and their *wives*." *Spouses* or *partners* is more inclusive. Valuing diversity means making fewer assumptions that everyone is like you or wants to be like you.

- **Learn about your cultural self.** Knowing your own cultural biases helps you become more objective and adaptable. Begin to recognize the reactions and thought patterns that are automatic to you as a result of your upbringing. Become more aware of your own values and beliefs. That way you can see them at work when you are confronted by differing values.

- **Seek common ground.** Look for areas where you and others not like you can agree or share opinions. Be prepared to consider issues from many perspectives, all of which may be valid. Accept that there is room for different points of view to coexist peacefully. Although you can always find differences, it's much harder to find similarities. Look for common ground in shared experiences, mutual goals, and similar values. Professor Nancy Adler of McGill University offers three useful methods to help diverse individuals find their way through conflicts made more difficult by cultural differences: (1) Look at the problem from all participants' points of view, (2) uncover the interpretations each side is making on the basis of their cultural values, and (3) create cultural synergy by working together on a solution that works for both sides.[16] Looking for common ground and mutual goals can help each of you reach your objectives even though you may disagree on how.

Summing Up and Looking Forward

This chapter described the importance of becoming an effective business communicator in the knowledge economy. Many of the changes in today's dynamic workplace revolve around processing and communicating information. Flattened management hierarchies, participatory management, increased emphasis on work teams, heightened global competition, and innovative communication technologies are all trends that increase the need for good communication skills. To improve your skills, you should understand the communication process. Communication doesn't take place unless senders encode meaningful messages that can be decoded by receivers.

One important part of the communication process is listening. You can become a more active listener by keeping an open mind, listening for main points, capitalizing on lag time, judging ideas and not appearances, taking selective notes, and providing feedback.

The chapter also described ways to help you improve your nonverbal communication skills.

You learned the powerful effect that culture has on communication, and you became more aware of key cultural values. Finally, the chapter discussed ways that businesses and individuals can capitalize on workforce diversity.

The following chapters present the writing process. You will learn specific techniques to help you improve your written expression. Remember, communication skills are not inherited. They are learned.

1. Why should business students and professionals alike strive to improve their communication skills, and why is it difficult or impossible to do so without help?
2. Recall a time when you experienced a problem as a result of poor communication. What were the causes of and possible remedies for the problem?
3. How are listening skills important to employees, supervisors, and executives? Who should have the best listening skills?
4. What arguments could you give for or against the idea that body language can be interpreted accurately by specialists?
5. Since English is becoming the preferred language in business globally, why should Canadians bother to learn about other cultures?

Chapter Review

6. Are communication skills acquired by *nature* or by *nurture*? Explain.

7. List seven trends in the workplace that affect business communicators. How might they affect you in your future career?

8. Give a brief definition of the following words:
   a. Encode

   b. Channel

   c. Decode

9. List and explain 11 techniques for improving your listening skills.

10. What is nonverbal communication? Give several examples.

11. Why is good eye contact important for communicators?

12. What is the difference between individualism and collectivism? Can you think of evidence to support the argument that Canadians are more collectivist than Americans?

13. What is ethnocentrism, and how can it be reduced?

14. List and explain seven suggestions for enhancing comprehension when you are talking with people for whom English is a second language.

15. List and explain eight suggestions for becoming a more effective communicator in a diverse workplace.

Activities and Cases

1.1 Getting to Know You. Since today's work and class environments often involve cooperating in teams or small groups, getting to know your fellow classmates is important. To learn something about the people in this class and to give you practice in developing your communication skills, your instructor may choose one of the following techniques.
   a. For larger classes your instructor may divide the class into groups of four or five. Take one minute to introduce yourself briefly (name, major interest, hobbies, goals). Spend five minutes in the first group session. Record the first name of each individual you meet. Then informally regroup. In new groups, again spend five minutes on introductions. After three or four sessions, study your name list. How many names can you associate with faces?
   b. For smaller classes your instructor may ask each student to introduce himself or herself in a two-minute oral presentation to the class. Where were you born? What are your educational goals? What are your interests? This informal presentation may serve as the first of two or three oral presentations correlated with Chapter 12.

1.2 Class Listening. Observe the listening habits of the students in one of your classes for a week. What barriers to effective listening did you observe? How many of the suggestions described in this chapter are being implemented by listeners in the class? Write a memo or an e-mail message to your instructor describing your observations. (See Chapter 5 to learn more about memos and e-mails.)

1.3 Role Play: What Was That You Said? Think of a recent situation in your life that matches one of these situations: someone wouldn't stop talking so you stopped listening; there was so much noise around you that you stopped listening; you didn't agree with someone's opinions or didn't like the way he or she looked so you stopped listening; or someone was talking and you didn't provide feedback. With a partner, write a three-minute skit that dramatizes one of the above "before" situations. Then, write another three-minute skit that dramatizes an "after" situation where the poor listening situation was improved so that you could listen actively. Perform the two skits for your class.

1.4 Research: What Do the Experts Say about Listening? You are the customer service training manager for CIBC in Vancouver. Your boss, Cara Stanley, the regional director of marketing for CIBC in British Columbia, is unhappy. According to recent surveys, CIBC's customer service rating is not as high as the rating of B.C. credit unions, such as VanCity. Your boss has decided that the bank's customer service training must be lacking something, and she suspects what's missing is a focus on listening skills. She asks you to research (using the Web as well as library databases) best practices in business listening skills, and to e-mail her what you've found out. From past experience, you know that while she likes knowing about "big picture" solutions, she also doesn't like spending too much money on these solutions.

Related Web site: <www.vancity.com/MyCommunity/AboutUs/MediaCentre/MediaArchive2003/Jan15VancityBeatOutBigBank>

1.5 Silent Messages. Analyze the kinds of silent messages you send your instructor, your classmates, and your employer. How do you send these messages? Group them into categories, as suggested by what you learned in this chapter. What do these messages mean? Be prepared to discuss them in small groups or in a memo to your instructor.

1.6 Role Play: You're in My Space. Working in groups of three or four, test the findings of anthropologist Edward T. Hall (page 9) by writing a couple of short skits in which you turn his findings upside down. Begin by choosing a zone of social interaction (e.g., intimate), then write a one-minute skit where instead of standing at the correct distance (45 centimetres), a person communicating something intimate stands at an inappropriate distance (e.g., 4 metres) from his or her audience. Perform your short skits for your class, and after each skit, ask the class what was wrong with the situation as you presented it. Can you or your classmates dramatize any situations where Hall's findings don't hold up?

1.7 Body Language. What attitudes do the following body movements suggest to you? Do these movements always mean the same thing? What part does context play in your interpretations?
a. Whistling, wringing hands
b. Bowed posture, twiddling thumbs
c. Steepled hands, sprawling sitting position
d. Rubbing hand through hair

Activities and Cases

e. Pacing back and fourth, twisting fingers through hair

f. Wringing hands, tugging ears

1.8 The True Meaning of Diversity. You are the new human resources manager of a fast-growing sports apparel company, Proforme Ltee., headquartered in Laval, Quebec. The company manufactures T-shirts and baseball caps as well as more specialized clothing for soccer, tennis, and hockey players. Due to increased immigration to the Montreal area (see endnote 3), Proforme's CEO has asked you to propose a plan for diversifying the workforce. He says to you that this "should be easy as it's just a matter of hiring a few immigrants, right?" You want to please your new boss, but you quickly realize that his understanding of diversity issues needs to be updated. A good friend of yours works for the Laurentian Bank, a company that has an advanced diversity policy. You can learn some information from his company's Web site. Also research some other companies with strong diversity policies. Write your boss an e-mail that clears up his misconception about diversity (without offending him), and that proposes some positive steps Proforme can take.

Related Web site: <www.career.laurentianbank.com>

1.9 Anne of Green Gables Travels to Tokyo. Jacques Guay represents a Winnipeg company that builds circus sets and theme park attractions. The owners of a Japanese theme park asked Guay's creative team to develop a theme attraction for their Tokyo park. The Japanese company requested final approval over all designs. Jacques and his team recently travelled to Japan to make an important presentation to the company. His team had worked for the past year developing the concept of a small nineteenth-century Canadian village, modelled on the "Avonlea" of Lucy Maud Montgomery's *Anne* novels. The jobs of his entire team depended on selling the idea of this new attraction (including restaurants and gift shops) to the owners of the Tokyo park. Because the owners smiled and nodded throughout the presentation, Jacques assumed they liked the idea. When he pushed for final approval, the owners smiled and said that an outdoor village attraction might be difficult in their climate. Jacques explained away that argument. He was hoping for a straightforward yes or no, but the Japanese answered, "We will have to study it very carefully." Thinking he had not made himself clear, Jacques began to review the strong points of the presentation. Over dinner that evening with his translator, Keiji Matsumoto (who wants to retain Jacques as a client even though he thinks Jacques did a poor job at the meeting), Jacques mentions that he doesn't think things went that well. What cultural elements may be interfering with communication in this exchange, according to Jacques' translator?

1.10 Soup's On. As a junior manager at Florenceville, New Brunswick–based McCain Foods Limited, you have been sent to Hong Kong to work on the development of new regional food varieties to appeal to two billion Asian consumers. The Chinese are among the highest per capita soup eaters in the world, consuming an average of one bowl a day. In the Hong Kong taste kitchen, you are currently working on cabbage soup, scallop broth, and a special soup that combines watercress and duck meat. You've even tested exotic ingredients like shark's fin and snake.[17] The supervisor of the taste kitchen understands English, but sometimes her eyes glaze over when you discuss procedures with her. In your hotel room that evening, you analyze what happened that day. What could you do to improve comprehension and minimize misunderstandings?

1.11 Translating Idioms. Explain in simple English what the following idiomatic expressions mean. Assume that you are explaining them to people for whom English is a second language.

a. let the cat out of the bag
b. take the bull by the horns
c. he is a tightwad
d. putting the cart before the horse
e. to be on the road
f. lend someone a hand
g. with flying colours
h. turn over a new leaf

Role Play: Walking a Fine Line with a New Client. You are an account manager at an up-and-coming advertising agency in Calgary named Crane & Kim. You've recently landed a new client, IPCO Petroleum, one of Canada's best-known oil and gas producers. IPCO has hired you to perk up its image, which hasn't changed much in the last 20 years. As part of your mandate, you are to design and produce a television commercial and a series of newspaper advertisements promoting IPCO as a progressive company. Your design and production staff has come up with an energetic new campaign that features people of various ethnicities and racial backgrounds. When Frank Pekar, director of marketing at IPCO, sees the campaign materials for the first time, he is anxious. He tells you that the blatant diversity in the materials is not really what he's looking for. Keeping in mind that you need to balance your personal belief in diversity and your belief in the strengths of diversity as a marketing tactic alongside Pekar's reservations and his importance as a client, script a five-minute skit between yourself and Pekar where you try to settle the issue. Perform your skit with a partner for your class.

Grammar/Mechanics Review—1

The following exercise includes a variety of errors based on the grammar, punctuation, number style, capitalization, spelling words, and confusing words discussed in the Grammar/Mechanics Handbook. In the space provided write a corrected version of each sentence. Your instructor has the key for this exercise.

Example: Before eating sixteen members of the Committee met in the sabin centre.

Revision: Before eating, 16 members of the committee met in the Sabin Centre.

1. At last Sundays graduation ceremonys Jennifer Riddock who uses a wheelchair, was honoured because she was the only graduate who had never missed a day of classes.
2. If its not to late to register my brother and myself plan to take courses in History, Management, and English.
3. In just two hours time I was able to locate 9 excelent Web sites, containing relevant information for my report.
4. Mistakes are a fact of life, however it is the response to the error that really counts.
5. Complicating the problem is inefficent legislation, and lack of enforcement personel.
6. We cannot procede with the mailing, until the list of names and address are verified.
7. My new Sport Utility Vehicle came equiped with: antilock brakes, alloy wheels and a trip computer.
8. My bosses biggest computer worry is the possibility of us being hacked, and not knowing it.
9. Beside your résumé and cover letter you must submit a seperate employment application form.

10. Elizabeth was suprised that the Ingles who once owned 2 popular resterants were now her neighbour.
11. Although the manufacture promised excelent milage my wife and me get only fifteen miles to the gallon.
12. Your bill of two hundred dollars is now ninety days overdue, therefore we are submitting it to a agency for collection.
13. If you have all ready sent your payment please disregard this notice.
14. Of the 350 letters mailed only five were returned as reported by Ms. Sandhus assistant.

Grammar/Mechanics Challenge—1

Document for Revision

The following memo has many faults in grammar, spelling, punctuation, capitalization, word use, and number form. Study the guidelines in the Grammar/ Mechanics Handbook to sharpen your skills. When you finish, your instructor can show you a revised version of this memo.

Memo

To: Tran Nguyen

From: Rachel Stivers, Manager

CC:

Date: May 14, 2006

Re: WORK AT HOME GUIDELINES

Since you will be completeing most of your work at home for the next 4 months. Follow these guidelines;

1. Check your message bored daily and respond promptly, to those who are trying to reach you.

2. Call the office at least twice a day to pick up any telephone messages, return these calls promply.

3. Transmit any work you do, via e-mail to Jerry Jackson in our computer services department, he will analyze each weeks accounts, and send it to the proper Departments. .

4. Provide me with monthly reports' of your progress.

We will continue to hold once a week staff meetings on Friday at 10 a.m. in the morning. Do you think it would be possible for you to attend 1 or 2 of these meeting. The next one is Friday May 17th.

I know you will work satisfactory at home Tran. Following these basic guidelines should help you accomplish your work, and provide the office with adequate contact with you.

Using the Net to Boost Your Career Search

As a business communicator in today's workplace, you must be able to effectively use the Internet. When searching for information on the Web, it's far too easy to waste time and money while roaming through cyberspace. Whether you're a novice or a surfing pro, this workshop will help you sharpen your Internet skills so that your searches are done quickly and accurately.

Getting Started

Go to <www.learnthenet.com>. Click on "Find Information" and then on "Advanced Web Searching." Read the entire article, paying special attention to the section on Boolean logic. Then try a few web searches using Boolean logic; for example, a search on jobs in Canada, jobs in your city or town or province, workplace literacy in Canada, or workplace diversity in Canada. What's the difference between a Google search that uses the search term "workplace diversity in Canada" and a search that uses Boolean logic in its search term, e.g., "workplace" "diversity" "Canada"?

Career Application

Assume that you are about to finish your program, and you are now looking for a job. The easiest way to job search today is on the Web. A terrific selection of Web job-search sites is available to students using Nelson textbooks. At the direction of your instructor, conduct a survey of electronic job advertisements in your field. What's available? What are the salaries? What are the requirements?

Your Task

Go to <www.workopolis.ca>. This is the largest job site in Canada. Click on "Search Jobs." Search for a job by typing in a keyword. Now go through the following steps:

- **Study the first page.** Use your scroll bar to run up and down the page. Notice how jobs are located on the page and how they are hyperlinked to additional information.
- **Conduct another practice search.** Scroll back up to the top of the page. Click on "Fast Track" and search for a job by job category. Then try another search by "Locations." Just for fun, try a location different from your home and an unusual career choice.
- **Conduct a real search.** Now conduct a job search in your career area and in geographical areas of your choice. Select five ads and print them. If you cannot print, make notes on what you find.
- **Analyze the skills required.** How often do the ads mention communication, teamwork, and computer skills? What other tasks do the ads mention? Is a salary given? Your instructor may ask you to submit your findings and/or report to the class.

Web   **Related Web sites: You may also consider <www.monster.ca> for this workshop.**

Writing and Revising Skills

Writing for Business Audiences

CHAPTER

I write for a number of different business audiences and I always consider my audience before starting. The content, tone, and level of detail varies depending on whether I'm writing to clients, financial advisors or other stakeholders.[1]

John DeGoey, *financial advisor, Assante Wealth Management Office Team*

LEARNING OBJECTIVES

1. Understand that business writing should be audience oriented, purposeful, and economical.
2. Identify and implement the three phases of the writing process.
3. Appreciate the importance of analyzing the task and profiling the audience for business messages.
4. Create messages that spotlight audience benefits and cultivate a "you" view.
5. Develop a conversational tone and use positive language.
6. Explain the need for inclusive language, plain expression, and familiar words.
7. List seven ways in which technology helps improve business writing.

Basics of Business Writing

An Ipsos-Reid study conducted among Canadian CEOs indicated that CEOs devote half of their time (49 percent) to communicating with a variety of audiences including both external stakeholders, such as investors, government, the media, and customers, and internal audiences, such as employees and management.[2] All members of the organization, from the CEO to front-line staff, must concern themselves with their audience.

Audience awareness is one of the basics of business communication, as John DeGoey indicates above. This chapter focuses on writing for business audiences. Business writing may be different from other writing you have done. High school

Quick Check

Excellent communicators concentrate on the audience for their messages.

or college compositions and term papers may have required you to describe your feelings, display your knowledge, or prove a thesis or argument. Business writing, however, has different goals. In preparing business messages and oral presentations, you'll find that your writing needs to be:

- **Audience oriented.** You will concentrate on looking at a problem from the receiver's perspective instead of seeing it from your own.
- **Purposeful.** You will be writing to solve problems and convey information. You will have a definite purpose to fulfil in each message.
- **Economical.** You will try to present ideas clearly but concisely. Length is not rewarded.

Business writing is audience oriented, purposeful, and economical.

These distinctions actually ease the writer's task. You won't be searching your imagination for creative topic ideas. You won't be stretching your ideas to make them appear longer. In business writing, longer is not better. Conciseness is what counts.

The ability to prepare concise, audience-centred, and purposeful messages does not come naturally. Very few people, especially beginners, can sit down and compose an effective letter or report without training. But following a systematic process, studying model messages, and practising the craft can make nearly anyone a successful business writer or speaker.

Writing Process for Business Messages and Oral Presentations

Whether you are preparing an e-mail message, memo, letter, or oral presentation, the process will be easier if you follow a systematic plan. Our plan breaks the entire task into three separate phases: prewriting, writing, and revising as shown in Figure 2.1.

Following a systematic process helps beginning writers create effective messages and presentations.

To illustrate the writing process, let's say that you own a popular local fast food restaurant franchise. At rush times, you've got a big problem. Customers complain about the chaotic, multiple waiting lines to approach the service counter. You once saw two customers nearly get into a fight over who was first in line. And customers often are so intent on looking for ways to improve their positions in line that they fail to look at the menu. Then they don't know what to order when their turn arrives. You want to convince other franchise owners that a single-line (serpentine) system would work better. You could telephone the owners, but you want to present a serious argument with good points that they will remember and be willing to act on when they gather for their next district meeting. You decide to write a letter that you hope will win their support.

The writing process has three parts: prewriting, writing, and revising.

FIGURE 2.1 **The Business Writing Process**

Writing Process for Business Messages and Oral Presentations

Prewriting

The first phase of the writing process prepares you to write. It involves analyzing the audience and your purpose for writing. The audience for your letter will be other franchise owners who represent a diverse group of individuals with varying educational backgrounds. Your purpose in writing is to persuade them that a change in policy would improve customer service. You are convinced that a single-line system, such as that used in banks, would reduce wait times and make customers happier because they would not have to worry about where they are in line.

Prewriting also involves anticipating how your audience will react to your message. You're sure that some of the other owners will agree with you, but others might fear that customers seeing a long single line might go elsewhere. In adapting your message to the audience, you try to think of the right words and the right tone that will win approval.

Writing

The second phase involves researching, organizing, and then composing the message. In researching information for this letter, you would probably investigate other kinds of businesses that use single lines for customers. You might check out your competitors. What are other fast food outlets doing? You might do some telephoning to see if other franchise owners are concerned about customer lines. Before writing to the entire group, you might generate ideas with a few owners to increase the number of potential solutions to the problem.

Once you have collected enough information, you would focus on organizing your letter. Should you start out by offering your solution? Or should you work up to it slowly, describing the problem, presenting your evidence, and then ending with the solution? The final step in the second phase of the writing process is actually composing the letter. Naturally, you'll do it at your computer so that you can make revisions easily.

Revising

The third phase of the process involves revising, proofreading, and evaluating your letter. After writing the first draft, you'll spend time revising the message for clarity, conciseness, tone, and readability. Could parts of it be rearranged to make your point more effectively? This is the time when you look for ways to improve the organization and sound of your message. Next, you'll spend time proofreading carefully to ensure correct spelling, grammar, punctuation, and format. The final phase involves evaluating your entire message to decide whether it accomplishes your goal.

Scheduling the Writing Process

Although the business writing process described above shows the three phases equally, the time you spend on each varies depending on the complexity of the task, the purpose, the audience, and your schedule. Here are some rough estimates for scheduling a project:

- Prewriting—25 percent
- Writing—25 percent
- Revising—50 percent (30 percent revising and 20 percent proofreading)

These are rough guides, yet you can see that good writers spend most of their time on the final phase of revising and proofreading. Much depends, of course, on your project, its importance, and your familiarity with it. What's critical to remember, though, is that revising is a major component of the writing process.

Chapter 2 Writing for Business Audiences

It may appear that you complete one phase of the business writing process and progress to the next, always following the same order. Most business writing, however, is not that rigid. Although writers perform the tasks described, the steps may be rearranged, abbreviated, or repeated. Some writers revise every sentence and paragraph as they go. Many find that new ideas occur after they've begun to write, causing them to back up, alter the organization, and rethink their plan.

Analyzing the Purpose for Writing and the Audience

We've just taken a look at the total writing process. As you develop your business writing skills, you should expect to follow this process closely. With experience, though, you'll become like other good writers and presenters who alter, compress, and rearrange the steps as needed. But following a plan is helpful at first. The remainder of this chapter covers the first phase of the writing process. You'll learn to analyze the purpose for writing, anticipate how your audience will react, and adapt your message to the audience.

Identifying Your Purpose

As you begin to compose a message, ask yourself two important questions: (1) Why am I sending this message? and (2) What do I hope to achieve? Your responses will determine how you organize and present your information.

Your message may have primary and secondary purposes. For college work your primary purpose may be merely to complete the assignment; secondary purposes might be to make yourself look good and to get a good grade. The primary purposes for sending business messages are typically to inform and to persuade. A secondary purpose is to promote goodwill: you and your organization want to look good in the eyes of your audience.

Quick Check

The primary purpose of most business messages is to inform or to persuade; the secondary purpose is to promote goodwill.

Selecting the Best Channel

After identifying the purpose of your message, you need to select the most appropriate communication channel. Some information is most efficiently and effectively delivered orally. Other messages should be written, and still others are best delivered electronically. Whether to set up a meeting, send a message by e-mail, or write a report depends on some of the following factors:

Quick Check

Choosing an appropriate channel depends on the importance of the message, the feedback required, the need for a permanent record, the cost, the formality needed, and best practices of your company.

- Importance of the message
- Amount and speed of feedback required
- Necessity of a permanent record
- Cost of the channel
- Degree of formality desired
- Best practices in your company

These six factors will help you decide which of the channels shown in Figure 2.2 is most appropriate for delivering a message.

Switching to Faster Channels

Technology and competition continue to accelerate the pace of business today. As a result, communicators are switching to ever-faster means of exchanging information. In the early to mid-twentieth century, business messages within organizations were delivered largely by hard-copy memos. Responses would typically

FIGURE 2.2 Choosing Communication Channels

Channel	Best Use
Written	
E-mail	When you wish to deliver routine or urgent messages quickly and inexpensively across time zones or borders. Appropriate for small, large, local, or dispersed audiences. Quickly becoming preferred channel replacing hard-copy memos and many letters. Printout provides permanent record.
Instant message	When you need to have a brief conversation with a trusted colleague or customer at a distance. The question does not warrant a telephone call and should be about something you are working on at that moment. Expected to overcome e-mail as the most preferred channel within organizations for exchanging routine messages.
Fax	When your message must cross time zones or international boundaries, when a written record is significant, or when speed is important.
Memo	When you want a written record to explain policies clearly, discuss procedures, or collect information within an organization.
Letter	When you need a written record of correspondence with customers, the government, suppliers, or others outside an organization.
Report or proposal	When you are delivering considerable data internally or externally.
Spoken	
Telephone call	When you need to deliver or gather information quickly, when nonverbal cues are unimportant, and when you cannot meet in person.
Voice mail message	When you wish to leave important or routine information that the receiver can respond to when convenient.
Face-to-face conversation	When you want to be persuasive, deliver bad news, or share a personal message.
Face-to-face group meeting	When group decisions and consensus are important. Inefficient for merely distributing information.
Video- or teleconference	When group consensus and interaction are important but members are geographically dispersed.

take a couple of days. But that's too slow for today's communicators. Cell phones, faxes, Web sites, e-mail, and instant messaging can deliver that information much faster than traditional channels of communication. In fact, according to business writer Don Tapscott, within some organizations and between colleagues at different organizations, instant messaging is being added to e-mail as a popular channel choice. Tapscott even names some large companies like IBM that have abandoned e-mail in favour of instant messaging.[3] Instant messaging software alerts colleagues in distant locations that a coworker is prepared to participate in an online exchange. Once signed in, individuals or entire groups can carry on and manage two-way discussions. Instant messaging resembles a conversation where a sender types a one- or two-sentence note followed by the receiver who types his or her response to the note. Responses appear next to the original message for both sender and receiver to see. Through instant messaging, an entire conversation can be completed online without the time delay that can occur when sending and responding to e-mail. A few years ago, *The Globe and Mail* reported that instant messaging would soon surpass e-mail as the primary way in which people interact electronically. While this prediction has not yet come true, experts like Tapscott signal that instant messaging is certainly a force to be reckoned with, especially because it is already so much a part of many young people's personal lives.[4]

Within many organizations, hard-copy memos are still written, especially for messages that require persuasion, permanence, or formality. But the channel of choice for corporate communicators today is clearly e-mail. It's fast, cheap, and easy. Thus, fewer hard-copy memos are being written. Fewer letters are also being written. That's because many customer service functions are now being served through Web-based customer relationship management tools or by e-mail. Interestingly, the fact that fewer memos and letters are being written does not make knowing how to write one less important. In fact, it makes it more important. This is because novice business communicators often assume business e-mails can be as informal as their personal e-mails. The reality is that business e-mails should be nearly as structured as memos and letters have always been.

Whether your channel choice is e-mail, a hard-copy memo, or a report, you'll be a more effective writer if you spend sufficient time in the prewriting phase.

Anticipating the Audience

A good writer anticipates the audience for each message: What is the reader like? How will the reader react to the message? Although you can't always know exactly who the reader is, you can imagine some characteristics of the reader. Even writers of direct mail sales letters have a general idea of the audience they wish to target. Picturing a typical reader is important in guiding what you write. By profiling your audience and shaping a message to respond to that profile, you are more likely to achieve your communication goals.

Profiling the Audience

Visualizing your audience is a pivotal step in the writing process. The questions in Figure 2.3 will help you profile your audience. How much time you devote to answering these questions depends on your message and its context. An analytical report that you compose for management or an oral presentation before a big group would, of course, demand considerable audience anticipation. On the other hand, an e-mail message to a coworker or a letter to a familiar supplier might require only a few moments of planning. No matter how short your message,

FIGURE 2.3 **Asking the Right Questions to Profile Your Audience**

Primary Audience

Who is my primary reader or listener?
What is my personal and professional relationship with that person?
What position does the individual hold in the organization?
How much does that person know about the subject?
What do I know about that person's education, beliefs, culture, and attitudes?
Should I expect a neutral, positive, or negative response to my message?

Secondary Audience

Who might see or hear this message in addition to the primary audience?
How do these people differ from the primary audience?

though, spend some time thinking about the audience so that you can adjust your words appropriately for your readers or listeners. "The most often unasked question in business and professional communication," claims a writing expert, "is as simple as it is important: *Have I thought enough about my audience?*"[5]

Responding to the Profile

Profiling your audience helps you make decisions about shaping the message. You'll discover what kind of language is appropriate, whether you're free to use specialized technical terms, whether you should explain everything, and so on. You'll decide whether your tone should be formal or informal, and you'll select the most desirable channel. Imagining whether the receiver is likely to be neutral, positive, or negative will help you determine how to organize your message.

Another advantage of profiling your audience is considering the possibility of a secondary audience. For instance, you might write a report that persuades your boss to launch a Web site for customers. Your boss is the primary reader, and he is familiar with many of the details of your project. But he will need to secure approval from his boss, and that person is probably unfamiliar with the project details. Because your report will be passed along to secondary readers, it must include more background information and more extensive explanations than you included for the primary reader, your boss. Analyzing the task and anticipating the audience assists you in adapting your message so that it will accomplish what you intend.

Adapting to the Task and Audience

After analyzing your purpose and anticipating your audience, you must convey your purpose to that audience. Adaptation is the process of creating a message that suits your audience.

One important aspect of adaptation is tone. Tone, conveyed largely by the words in a message, determines how a receiver feels upon reading or hearing it. Skilled communicators create a positive tone in their messages by using a number of adaptive techniques, some of which are unconscious. These include spotlighting audience benefits, cultivating a polite "you" attitude, sounding conversational, and using inclusive language. Additional adaptive techniques include using positive expression and preferring plain language with familiar words.

Audience Benefits

Smart communicators know that the chance of success of any message is greatly improved by emphasizing reader benefits. This means making readers see how the message affects and benefits them personally.

It is human nature for individuals to be most concerned with matters that relate directly to themselves. This is a necessary condition of existence. If we weren't interested in attending to our own needs, we could not survive.

Adapting your message to the receiver's needs means temporarily putting yourself in that person's shoes. This skill is known as empathy. Empathic senders think about how a receiver will decode a message. They try to give something to the receiver, solve the receiver's problems, save the receiver money, or just understand the feelings and position of that person. Which of the following messages is more appealing to the audience?

Sender focus   To enable us to update our shareholder records, we ask that the enclosed card be returned.

Audience focus So that you may promptly receive dividend cheques and information related to your shares, please return the enclosed card.

Sender focus	Our warranty becomes effective only when we receive an owner's registration.
Audience focus	Your warranty begins working for you as soon as you return your owner's registration.
Sender focus	We offer evening language courses that we have complete faith in.
Audience focus	The sooner you enrol in our evening language courses, the sooner the rewards will be yours.
Sender focus	The Human Resources Department requires that the online survey be completed immediately so that we can allocate our training resource funds.
Audience focus	By filling out the online survey, you can be one of the first employees to sign up for the new career development program.

Polite "You" View

Notice how many of the previous audience-focused messages included the word *you*. In concentrating on receiver benefits, skilled communicators naturally develop the "you" view. They emphasize second-person pronouns (*you, your*) instead of first-person pronouns (*I/we, us, our*). Whether your goal is to inform, persuade, or promote goodwill, the most attention-getting words you can use are *you* and *your*. Compare the following examples.

Quick Check

Because receivers are most interested in themselves, emphasize *you* whenever possible.

"I/We" View	I have scheduled your vacation to begin May 1.
"You" View	You may begin your vacation May 1.
"I/We" View	We have shipped your order by courier, and we are sure it will arrive in time for the sales promotion January 15.
"You" View	Your order will be delivered by courier in time for your sales promotion January 15.
"I/We" View	As a financial planner, I care about my clients' well-being.
"You" View	Your well-being is the most important consideration for financial planners like me.

To see if you're really concentrating on the reader, try using the "empathy index." In one of your messages, count all the second-person references; then count all the first-person references. Your empathy index is low if the *I*'s and *we*'s outnumber the *you*'s and *your*'s.

The use of *you* is more than merely a numbers game. Second-person pronouns can be overused and misused. Readers appreciate genuine interest; on the other hand, they resent obvious attempts at manipulation. Some sales messages, for example, become untrustworthy when they include *you* dozens of times in a direct mail promotion. Furthermore, the word can sometimes create the wrong impression. Consider this statement: *You cannot return merchandise until you receive written approval.* The word *you* appears twice, but the reader feels singled out for criticism. In the following version the message is less personal and more positive: *Customers may return merchandise with written approval.* In short, avoid using *you* for general statements that suggest blame and could cause ill will.

In recognizing the value of the "you" attitude, however, writers do not have to sterilize their writing and totally avoid any first-person pronouns or words that show their feelings. Skilled communicators are able to convey sincerity, warmth, and enthusiasm by the words they choose. Don't be afraid to use phrases such as *I'm happy* or *We're delighted*, if you truly are. When speaking face to face, communicators show sincerity and warmth with nonverbal cues such as a smile and pleasant voice tone. In letters, memos, and e-mail messages, however, only expressive words and phrases can show these feelings. These phrases suggest

Quick Check

Emphasize you but don't eliminate all I and we statements.

hidden messages that say to readers and customers "You are important, I am listening, and I'm honestly trying to please you."

Conversational but Professional

✓ Quick Check

Strive for conversational expression, but also remember to be professional.

Most business e-mails, letters, memos, and reports are about topics that would otherwise be part of a conversation. Thus, they are most effective when they convey an informal, conversational tone instead of a formal, pretentious tone. But messages should not become so conversational that they sound overly casual and unprofessional. With the increasing use of e-mail, a major problem has developed. Sloppy, unprofessional expression appears in many e-mail messages. You'll learn more about e-mail in Chapter 5. At this point, though, we urge you to strive for a warm, conversational tone that does not include slang or overly casual wording. The following examples should help you distinguish between three levels of diction.

Unprofessional (low-level diction)	Conversational (mid-level diction)	Formal (high-level diction)
badmouth	criticize	denigrate
guts	nerve	courage
pecking order	line of command	dominance hierarchy
ticked off	upset	provoked
rat on	inform	betray
rip off	steal	embezzle/appropriate

Unprofessional	If we just hang in there, we can snag the contract.
Conversational	If we don't get discouraged, we can win the contract.
Formal	If the principals persevere, they can acquire the contract.

Your goal is a warm, friendly tone that sounds professional. Talk to the reader with words that are comfortable to you. Avoid long and complex sentences. Use familiar pronouns such *I*, *we*, and *you* and an occasional contraction, such as *we're* or *I'll*. Stay away from third-person constructions such as *the undersigned*, *the writer*, and *the affected party*. Also avoid legal terminology and technical words. Your writing will be easier to read and understand if it sounds like the following conversational examples:

Formal	All employees are herewith instructed to return the appropriately designated contracts to the undersigned.
Conversational	Please return your contracts to me.
Formal	Pertaining to your order, we must verify the sizes that your organization requires prior to consignment of your order to our shipper.
Conversational	We'll send your order as soon as we confirm the sizes you need.
Formal	The writer wishes to inform the above-referenced individual that subsequent payments may henceforth be sent to the address cited below.
Conversational	Your payments should now be sent to us in Sudbury.
Formal	To facilitate ratification of this agreement, your negotiators urge that the membership respond in the affirmative.
Conversational	We urge you to approve the agreement by voting yes.

Positive Language

The clarity and tone of a message are considerably improved if you use positive rather than negative language. Positive language generally conveys more information than negative language. Moreover, positive messages are uplifting and pleasant to read. Positive wording tells what is and what can be done rather than what isn't and what can't be done. For example, *Your order cannot be shipped by January 10* is not nearly as informative as *Your order will be shipped January 20.* Notice in the following examples how you can revise the negative tone to reflect a more positive impression.

Negative	We are unable to send your shipment until we receive proof of your payment.
Positive	We look forward to sending your shipment as soon as we receive your payment.
Negative	We are sorry that we must reject your application for credit at this time.
Positive	At this time we can serve you on a cash basis only.
Negative	You will never regret opening a charge account with us.
Positive	Your new charge account enables you to purchase high-quality clothing at reasonable prices.
Negative	If you fail to pass the exam, you will not qualify.
Positive	You'll qualify if you pass the exam.
Negative	Although I've never had a paid position before, I have completed a work placement in a law office as an administrative assistant while completing my diploma.
Positive	My work placement experience in a lawyer's office and my recent training in legal procedures and computer applications can be assets to your organization.

Positive language creates goodwill and gives more options to receivers.

Inclusive Language

A business writer who is alert and empathic will strive to create messages that include rather than exclude people. Words, phrases, and images that reflect stereotypes reinforce mistaken assumptions about certain groups or individuals. Referring to a letter carrier as a *mailman*, for example, reinforces the stereotype that mail delivery is carried out only by men. This stereotype creates a barrier for women who want to be letter carriers and can exclude them from a career delivering mail. By using inclusive language such as *letter carrier*, we battle an inappropriate stereotype and show we are aware that a person who delivers the mail could be either a woman or a man.

Sensitive communicators avoid language that excludes people.

Stereotypes also inject bias into our communication. Women, First Nations, people with disabilities, and visible minorities have traditionally been most affected by the negative effects of stereotyping. Biased language not only hampers communication but also alienates some individuals and excludes others entirely. All of your written, oral, electronic, and visual communication should be inclusive, unbiased, and fair for all individuals and groups.

When creating your messages, identify or address people first as individuals, then mention the group to which they belong only if that information is relevant. Job titles should describe the role rather than who is best to assume the role. Using terms such as *manager, sales clerk,* or *flight attendant* suggests that anyone can be considered an appropriate candidate for these roles.

Some words have been called sexist because they seem to exclude women or refer to women in ways the sender would not use to refer to a man. Notice the use of the masculine pronouns *he* and *his* in the following sentences:

If a physician is needed, he will be called.
Every homeowner must read his insurance policy carefully.

These sentences illustrate an age-old grammatical rule called "common gender." When a speaker or writer did not know the gender (sex) of an individual, masculine pronouns (such as *he* or *his*) were used. Masculine pronouns were understood to indicate both men and women. Today, however, writers and speakers striving for clarity replace common-gender pronouns with inclusive constructions. You can use any of four alternatives.

Sexist   Every lawyer has ten minutes for his summation.

Alternative 1   All lawyers have ten minutes for their summations. (Use a plural noun and plural pronoun.)

Alternative 2   Lawyers have ten minutes for summations. (Omit the pronoun entirely.)

Alternative 3   Every lawyer has ten minutes for a summation. (Use an article instead of a pronoun.)

Alternative 4   Every lawyer has ten minutes for his or her summation. (Use both a masculine and a feminine pronoun.)

Note that the last alternative, which includes a masculine and a feminine pronoun, is wordy. Don't use it too frequently.

Other words are considered sexist because they suggest stereotypes. For example, the nouns *fireman* and *mailman* suggest that only men hold these positions. Use neutral job titles or functions. Consider the following: *firefighter, letter carrier, salesperson, flight attendant, department head, committee chair,* and *technician.*

Some word constructions are considered sexist because they make assumptions about gender, such as *women's intuition, ladylike, his better half,* or describe women in ways that a man would not be described in the same situation, such as *an assertive man, a strident or shrill woman.*

Plain Language

Business communicators who are conscious of their audience try to use plain language that expresses clear meaning. They do not use showy words and ambiguous expressions in an effort to dazzle or confuse readers. They write to express ideas, not to impress others.

Some business, legal, and government documents are written in an inflated style that obscures meaning. This style of writing has been given various terms, such as *legalese, federalese, bureaucratese, doublespeak,* and *the official style.* It may be used intentionally to mask meaning. It may be an attempt to show off the writer's intelligence and education. It may be the traditional or accepted way of writing in that field. Or it may result from lack of training. What do you think the manager's intention is in the following message?

Quick Check

Inflated, unnatural writing that is intended to impress readers often confuses them.

> Personnel assigned vehicular space in the adjacent areas are hereby advised that access will be suspended temporarily Friday morning.

Employees will probably have to read that sentence several times before they understand that they are being advised not to park in the lot next door on Friday morning.

To overcome this pretentious style, the federal government requires public servants to use plain language to inform the public about government policies, programs, and services. This means a clear, simple style that uses everyday words. But the plain-English movement goes beyond word choice. It can also mean writing that is easy to follow and organized into segments with appropriate headings.

The important thing to remember is not to be impressed by important-sounding language and legalese, such as *herein, thereafter, hereinafter, whereas,* and similar expressions. Your writing will be better understood if you use plain language.

Familiar Words

Clear messages contain words that are familiar and meaningful to the receiver. How can we know what is meaningful to a given receiver? Although we can't know with certainty, we can avoid long or unfamiliar words that have simpler synonyms. Whenever possible in business communication, substitute short, common, simple words. Don't, however, give up a precise word if it says exactly what you mean.

Less Familiar Words	Simple Alternatives	Less Familiar Words	Simple Alternatives
ascertain	find out	perpetuate	continue
conceptualize	see	perplexing	troubling
encompass	include	reciprocate	return
hypothesize	guess	stipulate	require
monitor	check	terminate	end
operational	working	utilize	use
option	choice	leverage	make use of

Technology Improves Your Business Writing

Thus far, we've concentrated on the basics of business writing, especially the prewriting phase of analyzing, anticipating, and adapting to the intended audience. Another basic for beginning business communicators is learning to use technology to enhance their writing efforts. Although computers and software programs cannot actually do the writing for you, they provide powerful tools that make the entire process easier and the results more professional. Here are seven ways your computer can help you improve written documents, oral presentations, and Web pages.

1. **Fighting writer's block.** Because word processors enable ideas to flow almost effortlessly from your brain to a screen, you can expect fewer delays resulting from writer's block. You can compose rapidly, and you can experiment with structure and phrasing, later retaining and polishing your most promising thoughts. Many authors begin by recording unedited ideas quickly to start the composition process and also to brainstorm for ideas on a project. Then, they tag important ideas and use the outlining function in word processing or presentation software to organize those ideas into logical sequences.

2. **Collecting information electronically.** Much of the world's information is now accessible by computer. Through a library's online databases you can locate many full-text articles from magazines, newspapers, and government publications. Massive amounts of information are available from the Internet, CD-ROMs, and online services. Through specialized library online databases such as ABI-INFORM and CBCA Reference you can have at your fingertips the latest business, legal, scientific, and scholarly information.

3. **Using templates.** One of the most useful and time-saving features of today's word processing software for the business writer is templates. As Figure 2.4 demonstrates, templates are pre-formatted documents into which business writers simply have to add content. Any time you open up a new document in Microsoft Word, for example, on the right-hand side of your document you will see the option to choose a template. Typical templates include memos, letters, résumés, and reports. For the purposes of your business communication

 Quick Check

Powerful writing tools can help you fight writer's block, collect information, outline and organize ideas, improve correctness and precision, add graphics, and design professional-looking documents.

DILBERT © United Feature Syndicate. Reprinted by permission.

course, you should always choose a "professional" template, such as Word's Professional Letter template. Templates save time for business writers because instead of memorizing the various parts of a letter (e.g., how many spaces from the top the date and address should be placed), they can now concentrate on the more important things, such as making sure grammar and style are perfected. This is not to say that knowing the parts of a letter is unimportant (please see Appendix A), only that most of us don't have time to think about these features every time we sit down to write. In many large companies, templates have been customized for that company's needs, and few people write letters from "scratch" any more.

4. **Improving correctness and precision.** Word processing programs today provide features that catch and correct spelling and typographical errors. Poor spellers and weak typists universally bless their spell checkers for repeatedly saving them from humiliation. Most popular word processing programs today also provide grammar checkers that are markedly improved over earlier versions. They now detect many errors in capitalization, word use (such as *it's/its*), double negatives, verb use, subject-verb agreement, sentence structure, number agreement, number style, and other writing faults. However, grammar programs don't actually correct the errors they detect. You must know how to do that. Similarly, spell checkers don't catch all misspelled

FIGURE 2.4 Microsoft Templates That Outline and Organize Ideas

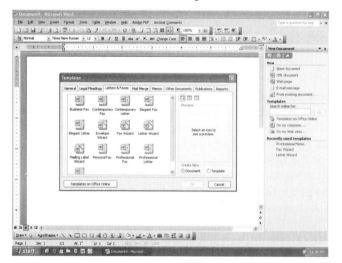

words. This is especially important in Canada because most spell checkers use American spelling. For example if you have written the word *traveling* in your memo and your spell checker hasn't caught the mistake, this is because *traveling* is the correct American spelling, whereas *travelling* is the correct Canadian spelling. You must know how to correct your own spelling mistakes.

5. **Adding graphics for emphasis.** Your letters, memos, and reports may be improved by the addition of graphs and artwork to clarify and illustrate data. You can import charts, diagrams, and illustrations created in database, spreadsheet, and graphics programs. Moreover, ready-made pictures, called clip art, can be used to symbolize or illustrate ideas.

6. **Designing and producing professional-looking documents, presentations, and Web pages.** Most popular word processing programs today include a large selection of scalable fonts (for different character sizes and styles), italics, boldface, symbols, and styling techniques to aid you in producing consistent formatting and professional-looking results. Moreover, today's presentation software, such as Microsoft's PowerPoint, enables you to incorporate animated slide effects, colour, sound, pictures, and even movies into your talks for management or customers. Web document builders also help you design and construct Web pages. These tools can be used effectively to help you reinforce your message and help your audience understand and remember your message.

7. **Using software for team writing.** As part of today's team-based work environment, you can expect to work with others on projects. Word processing programs usually have an editing feature with commenting and strikeout that allows you to revise easily, to identify each team member's editing, and to track multiple edits. E-mail and instant messaging programs allow group members to share documents and information freely and work on the same document from several remote locations at the same time. While collaboration between team and group members is a positive aspect of computer-based writing, such collaboration also entails an extra responsibility. When a number of people are working on an assignment and using computers to piece together the various parts they've worked on, there is often a temptation not to revise the document sufficiently.

Remember to build in enough time to edit and proofread the document that has been created by pasting together the work of numerous people, so that it reads as if it was written by one person. Another danger in collaborative writing is plagiarism. Plagiarism is the stealing of another writer's words or ideas by putting them in one's own assignment without crediting the original author. Plagiarism is the most serious of academic offences, usually leading to a failing grade on the assignment, if not the course. When proven in the work world, plagiarism leads to the firing of the guilty person.[6] Plagiarism is discussed in greater detail in Chapter 10.

Summing Up and Looking Forward

In this chapter you learned that good business writing is audience centred, purposeful, and economical. To achieve these results, business communicators typically follow a systematic writing process. This process includes three phases: prewriting, writing, and revising. In the prewriting phase, communicators analyze the task and the audience. They select an appropriate channel to deliver the message, and they consider ways to adapt their message to the task and the audience. Effective techniques include spotlighting audience benefits, cultivating the "you" view, using conversational language, and expressing ideas positively. Good communicators also use inclusive language, plain expressions, and familiar words. Today's computer software provides wonderful assistance for business communicators. Technological tools help you fight writer's block, collect information, pour content into templates, improve correctness and precision, add graphics, design professional-looking documents and presentations, and collaborate on team writing projects.

The next chapter continues to examine the writing process. It presents additional techniques to help you become a better writer. You'll learn how to eliminate repetitious and redundant wording, as well as how to avoid wordy prepositional phrases, long lead-ins, needless adverbs, and misplaced modifiers. You'll also take a closer look at spell checkers and grammar checkers.

Critical Thinking

1. As a business communicator, you are encouraged to profile or "visualize" the audience for your messages. How is this possible if you don't really know the people who will receive a sales letter or who will hear your business presentation?
2. If adapting your tone to your audience and developing reader benefits are so important, why do we see so much writing that fails to reflect these suggestions?
3. Discuss the following statement: "The English language is a minefield—it is filled with terms that are easily misinterpreted as derogatory and others that are blatantly insulting."
4. Why is writing in a natural, conversational tone difficult for many people?
5. If computer software is increasingly able to detect writing errors, can business communicators stop studying writing techniques? Why?

Chapter Review

6. Name three ways in which business writing differs from other writing.

7. List the three phases of the business writing process and summarize what happens in each phase. Which phase requires the most time?

8. What five factors are important in selecting an appropriate channel to deliver a message?

9. How does profiling the audience help a business communicator prepare a message?

10. What is meant by audience benefit? Give an original example.

11. List three specific techniques for developing a warm, friendly, and conversational tone in business messages.

12. Why does positive language usually tell more than negative language? Give an original example.

13. List five examples of sexist pronouns and nouns.

14. What does plain language mean in relation to its expected use in government communications?

15. Name seven ways your computer can help you improve written documents.

Writing Improvement Exercises

Selecting Communication Channels. Using Figure 2.2, suggest the best communication channels for the following messages. Assume that all channels shown are available. Be prepared to explain your choices.

16. As department manager, you wish to inform four members of a training session scheduled for three weeks from now.

17. As assistant to the vice-president, you are to investigate the possibility of developing work placement programs with several nearby colleges and universities.

18. You wish to send price quotes for a number of your products in response to a request from a potential customer in Taiwan.

19. You must respond to a notice from the Canada Revenue Agency insisting that you did not pay the correct amount for last quarter's employee remittance.

20. As a manager, you must inform an employee that continued tardiness is jeopardizing her job.

21. Members of your task force must meet to discuss ways to improve communication among 500 employees at 12 branches of your company. Task force members are from Toronto, Winnipeg, Calgary, Regina, and Halifax.

22. You need to know whether Davinder in Printing can produce a special pamphlet for you within two days.

Audience Benefits and the "You" View. Revise the following sentences to emphasize the perspective of the audience and the "you" view.

23. To prevent us from possibly losing large sums of money, our bank now requires verification of any large cheque presented for immediate payment.

24. We take pride in announcing daily flights to Singapore.

25. So that we may comply with new federal privacy legislation, we are asking you to complete the enclosed waiver.

26. For just $1195 (CDN) per person, we have arranged a seven-day trip to Las Vegas that includes deluxe accommodations, a Cirque du Soleil performance, and selected meals.

27. I give my permission for you to attend the two-day workshop.

28. We're requesting all employees to complete the enclosed questionnaire so that we may develop a master schedule for summer vacations.

29. I think my background and my education match the description of the manager trainee position you advertised.

30. We are offering an in-house training program for employees who want to improve their writing skills.

31. We are pleased to announce an arrangement with Hewlett-Packard that allows us to offer discounted computers in the student bookstore.

32. We have approved your application for credit, and the account may be used immediately.

33. We are pleased to announce that we have selected you to join our trainee program.

34. Our safety policy forbids us from renting power equipment to anyone who cannot demonstrate proficiency in its use.

35. We will reimburse you for all travel expenses.

36. To enable us to continue our policy of selling name brands at discount prices, we cannot give cash refunds on returned merchandise.

Conversational, Professional Tone. Revise the following sentences to make the tone conversational yet professional.

Example: As per your recent request, the undersigned is happy to inform you that we are sending you forthwith the brochures you requested.

Revision: I'm happy to send you the brochures you requested.

37. Kindly inform the undersigned whether or not your representative will be making a visitation in the near future.

38. Pursuant to your letter of the 12th, please be advised that your shipment was sent 9 June 2006.

39. She was pretty ticked off because the manager accused her of ripping off office supplies.

40. Kindly be informed that your vehicle has been determined to require corrective work.

41. He didn't have the guts to badmouth her to her face.

42. The undersigned respectfully reminds affected individuals that employees desirous of changing their benefits package must do so before December 30.

Positive Expression. Revise the following statements to make them more positive.

43. If you fail to pass the examination, you will not qualify.

44. In your e-mail message, you claim that you returned a defective headset.

45. We can't process your application because you neglected to insert your social insurance number.

46. Construction cannot begin until the building plans are approved.

47. It is impossible to move forward without community support.

48. Customers are ineligible for the 10 percent discount unless they show their membership cards.

49. Titan Insurance Company will not process any claim not accompanied by documented proof from a physician showing that the injuries required physiotherapy.

Inclusive Language. Revise the following sentences to eliminate terms that are considered sexist or that suggest stereotypes.

50. Any applicant for the position of fireman must submit a medical report signed by his physician.

51. Every employee is entitled to see his personnel file.

52. All conference participants and their wives are invited to the banquet.

53. At most hospitals in the area, a nurse must provide her own uniform.

Chapter 2 Writing for Business Audiences

54. Representing the community are a businessman, a lady attorney, and a female doctor.

55. A salesman would have to use all his skills to sell those condos.

56. Every doctor is provided with a parking spot for his car.

Plain Language and Familiar Words. Revise the following sentences to use plain expression and familiar words.

57. Profits are declining because our sales staff is not cognizant of our competitor's products.

58. He hypothesized that the vehicle was not operational because of a malfunctioning gasket.

59. Because we cannot monitor all cash payments, we must terminate the contract.

60. The contract stipulates that management must maintain in perpetuity the retirement plan.

Plain, Positive Language. Can you make the following understandable?

61. If your evidence is not received before June 18, 2006, which is one year from the date of our first letter, your claim, if entitlement is established, cannot be processed before the date of the receipt of the evidence.

Grammar/Mechanics Review—2

The following sentences contain errors in grammar, punctuation, capitalization, number style, usage, and spelling. Below each sentence write a corrected version.

1. In the evening, each of the female nurses are escorted to their car.

2. It must have been him who received the highest score although its hard to understand how he did it.

3. The Manager asked Hilary and I to fill in for him for 4 hours on Saturday morning.

4. Working out at the Gym and jogging twenty miles a week is how she stays fit.

5. 3 types of costs must be considered for proper inventory control, holding costs, ordering costs, and stocking costs.

6. If I was him I would fill out the questionaire immediately so that I would qualify for the prize.

7. Higher engine revolutions per kilometre mean better acceleration, however lower revolutions mean better fuel economy.

8. Our teams day to day operations include: setting goals, improvement of customer service, manufacturing quality products and hitting sales targets.

9. If I had saw the shippers bill I would have payed it immediately.

10. Salary, hours, and benefits, these are 3 items about which most all job candidates ask.

11. Do you think it was him who left the package on the boss desk.

12. About 1/2 of Pizza to Gos sixty outlets makes deliverys, the others concentrates on walk in customers.

13. Every thing accept labour is covered in this 5 year warranty.

14. Our Director of Human Resources felt nevertheless that the applicant should be given a interview.

15. When Keisha completes her degree she plans to apply for employment in: Moose Jaw, Regina, or Saskatoon.

Grammar/Mechanics Challenge—2

The sample e-mail that follows has many faults in grammar, spelling, punctuation, capitalization, word use, and number form. Pay attention to developing a conversational but professional tone, using familiar words, and striving for positive expression. Use standard proofreading marks (see Appendix B) to correct the errors. When you finish, your instructor can show you the revised version of this e-mail.

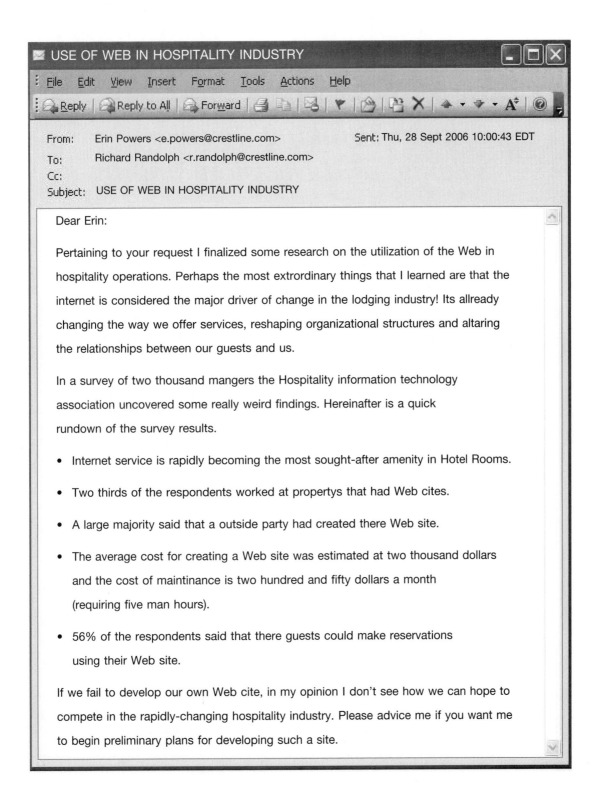

USE OF WEB IN HOSPITALITY INDUSTRY

File   Edit   View   Insert   Format   Tools   Actions   Help

Reply | Reply to All | Forward

From: Erin Powers <e.powers@crestline.com>   Sent: Thu, 28 Sept 2006 10:00:43 EDT
To: Richard Randolph <r.randolph@crestline.com>
Cc:
Subject: USE OF WEB IN HOSPITALITY INDUSTRY

Dear Erin:

Pertaining to your request I finalized some research on the utilization of the Web in hospitality operations. Perhaps the most extrordinary things that I learned are that the internet is considered the major driver of change in the lodging industry! Its allready changing the way we offer services, reshaping organizational structures and altaring the relationships between our guests and us.

In a survey of two thousand mangers the Hospitality information technology association uncovered some really weird findings. Hereinafter is a quick rundown of the survey results.

- Internet service is rapidly becoming the most sought-after amenity in Hotel Rooms.

- Two thirds of the respondents worked at propertys that had Web cites.

- A large majority said that a outside party had created there Web site.

- The average cost for creating a Web site was estimated at two thousand dollars and the cost of maintinance is two hundred and fifty dollars a month (requiring five man hours).

- 56% of the respondents said that there guests could make reservations using their Web site.

If we fail to develop our own Web cite, in my opinion I don't see how we can hope to compete in the rapidly-changing hospitality industry. Please advice me if you want me to begin preliminary plans for developing such a site.

Sharpening Your Skills for Critical Thinking, Problem Solving, and Decision Making

Gone are the days when management expected workers to follow the leader blindly and do only what they were told. Today, you'll be expected to think critically. You'll be solving problems and making decisions. Much of this book is devoted to helping you solve problems and communicate those decisions to management, fellow workers, clients, governments, and the public. Faced with a problem or an issue, most of us do a lot of worrying before making a decision. All that worrying can become directed thinking by channelling it into the following procedure.

1. Identify and clarify the problem. Your first task is to recognize that a problem exists. Some problems are big and unmistakable, such as failure of a courier service to get packages to customers on time. Other problems may be continuing annoyances, such as regularly running out of toner for an office copy machine. The first step in reaching a solution is pinpointing the problem area.

2. Gather information. Learn more about the problem situation. Look for possible causes and solutions. This step may mean checking files, calling suppliers, or brainstorming with fellow workers. For example, the courier service would investigate the tracking systems of the airlines carrying its packages to determine what is going wrong.

3. Evaluate the evidence. Where did the information come from? Does it represent various points of view? What biases could be expected from each source? How accurate is the information gathered? Is it fact or opinion? For example, it is a fact that packages are missing; it is an opinion that they are merely lost and will turn up eventually.

4. Consider alternatives and implications. Draw conclusions from the gathered evidence and pose solutions. Then weigh the advantages and disadvantages of each alternative. What are the costs, benefits, and consequences? What are the obstacles, and how can they be handled? Most important, what solution best serves your goals and those of your organization? Here's where your creativity is especially important.

5. Choose and implement the best alternative. Select an alternative and put it into action. Then, follow through on your decision by monitoring the results of implementing your plan. The courier company decided to give its unhappy customers free delivery service to make up for the lost packages and downtime. Be sure to continue monitoring and adjusting the solution to ensure its effectiveness over time.

Career Application

Let's return to the fast food franchise problem (discussed earlier in this chapter) in which some franchise owners are unhappy with the multiple lines for service. Customers don't seem to know where to stand to be next in line. Tempers flare when aggressive customers cut in line, and other customers spend so much time protecting their places in line that they fail to study the menu. Then they don't know what to order when they approach the counter. As a franchise owner, you would like to find a solution to this problem. Any changes in procedures, however, must be approved by all the franchise owners in a district. That means you'll have to get a majority to agree. You know that management feels that the multi-line system accommodates higher volumes of customers more quickly than a single-line system. Moreover, the problem of perception is important. What happens when customers open the door to a restaurant and see a long, single line? Do they stick around to learn how fast the line is moving?

Your Task

- Individually or with a team, use the critical thinking steps outlined here. Begin by clarifying the problem.
- Where could you gather information to help you solve this problem? Would it be wise to see what your competitors are doing? How do banks handle customer lines? Airlines? Sports events?
- Evaluate your findings and consider alternatives. What are the pros and cons of each alternative?
- Choose the best alternative. Present your recommendation to your class and give your reasons for choosing it.

Related Web site: Visit the Canadian Franchise Association's Web site <www.cfa.ca> to learn the recommended ethical requirements of franchisers and franchisees in Canada. Do the opinions of franchisees really count?

3

Improving Writing Techniques

Write with your target audience in mind. Ask yourself what information your audience requires and ensure you present the key messages in a clear and concise way. People don't take time to read lots of jargon and flowery words.[1]

Shelly Chagnon, *publicist, Rogers Television*

LEARNING OBJECTIVES

1. Contrast formal and informal methods of researching data and generating ideas for messages.
2. Specify how to organize information into outlines.
3. Compare direct and indirect patterns for organizing ideas.
4. Distinguish components of complete and effective sentences.
5. Emphasize important ideas and de-emphasize unimportant ones.
6. Use active voice, passive voice, and parallelism effectively in messages.
7. Develop sentence unity by avoiding imprecise writing, mixed constructions, and misplaced modifiers.
8. Identify strategies for achieving paragraph coherence and composing the first draft of a message.

Writing naturally, as Shelly Chagnon advises, may seem easy. But it's not. It takes instruction and practice. You've already learned some techniques for writing naturally (using a conversational tone, positive language, plain expression, and familiar words). This chapter presents additional writing tips that make your communication not only natural but also effective.

Figure 3.1 reviews the entire writing process. In Chapter 2 we focused on the prewriting stage. This chapter addresses the second stage, which includes researching, organizing, and composing.

Researching

No smart businessperson would begin writing a message before collecting the needed information. We call this collection process research. For simple documents, the process of research can be quite informal. Research is necessary before

FIGURE 3.1 The Writing Process

beginning to write because the information you collect helps shape the message. Discovering significant information after a message is completed often means starting over and reorganizing. To avoid frustration and inaccurate messages, collect information that answers this primary question:

• What does the receiver need to know about this topic?

When the message involves action, search for answers to secondary questions:

• What is the receiver to do?
• How is the receiver to do it?
• When must the receiver do it?
• What will happen if the receiver doesn't do it?

Whenever your communication problem requires more information than you have in your head or at your fingertips, you must conduct research. This research may be formal or informal.

Formal Research Methods

Long reports and complex business problems generally require some use of formal research methods. Let's say you are a market specialist for a major soft drink manufacturer, and your boss asks you to evaluate the impact on cola sales of generic ("no name") soft drinks. Or let's assume you must write a term paper for a college class. Both tasks require more data than you have in your head or at your fingertips. To conduct formal research, you could:

• **Search manually.** You'll find helpful background and supplementary information through manual searching of resources in public and college libraries. These traditional sources include books and newspaper, magazine, and journal articles. Other sources are encyclopedias, reference books, handbooks, dictionaries, directories, and almanacs.
• **Search electronically.** Much of the printed material just described is now contained in searchable databases available through the Internet. College and public libraries subscribe to retrieval services that permit you to access most periodical literature. You can also find extraordinary amounts of information, though not always of the best quality, by searching the Web. You'll learn more about using electronic sources in Chapter 10.
• **Go to the source.** For firsthand information, go directly to the source. For the cola sales report, for example, you could find out what consumers really think by conducting interviews or surveys, by putting together questionnaires, or by organizing focus groups. Formal research includes structured sampling and controls that enable investigators to make accurate judgments and valid predictions.

The second stage of the writing process involves research, which means collecting the necessary information to prepare a message.

Formal research may include searching libraries and electronic databases or investigating primary sources.

Good sources of primary information are interviews, surveys, questionnaires, and focus groups.

- **Conduct scientific experiments.** Instead of merely asking for the target audience's opinion, scientific researchers present choices with controlled variables. Let's say, for example, that the brand-name cola manufacturer wants to determine at what price and under what circumstances consumers would switch from the brand name to a generic brand. The results of such experimentation would provide valuable data for managerial decision making.

Because formal research techniques are particularly necessary for reports, you'll study them more extensively in Chapters 9 and 10.

Informal Research and Idea Generation

Most routine tasks—such as composing e-mails, memos, letters, informational reports, and oral presentations—require data that you can collect informally. Here are some techniques for collecting informal data and for generating ideas:

- **Search company files.** If you are responding to an inquiry, you often can find the answer by investigating your company's files or by consulting colleagues.
- **Talk with your boss.** Get information from the individual making the assignment. What does that person know about the topic? What slant should be taken? What other sources would he or she suggest?
- **Interview the target audience.** Consider talking with individuals at whom the message is aimed. They can provide clarifying information that tells you what they want to know and how you should shape your remarks.
- **Conduct an informal survey.** Gather unscientific but helpful information via questionnaires or telephone surveys. In preparing a memo report predicting the success of a proposed fitness centre, for example, circulate a questionnaire asking for employee reactions.
- **Brainstorm for ideas.** Alone or with others, discuss ideas for the writing task at hand, and record at least a dozen ideas without judging them. Small groups are especially fruitful in brainstorming because people spin ideas off one another.

Organizing Data

Once you've collected data, you must find some way to organize it. Organizing includes two processes: grouping and patterning. Well-organized messages group similar items together; ideas follow a sequence that helps the reader understand relationships and accept the writer's views. Unorganized messages proceed without structure or pattern, jumping from one thought to another. Such messages fail to emphasize important points. Puzzled readers can't see how the pieces fit together, and they become frustrated and irritated. Many communication experts regard poor organization as the greatest failing of business writers. A simple technique can help you organize data: the outline.

Outlining

A simple way to organize data is the outline.

In developing simple messages, some writers make a quick ideas list of the topics they wish to cover. They then compose a message at their computers directly from the list.

Most writers, though, need to organize their ideas—especially if the project is complex—into a hierarchy, such as an outline. The beauty of preparing an outline is that it gives you a chance to organize your thoughts before you start to choose specific words and sentences. Figure 3.2 shows a format for an outline.

FIGURE 3.2 Sample Outline

Awards Ceremony Costs

I. Venue
   A. Rentals
      1. Microphone
      2. Screen projector
      3. Tablecloths
   B. Extra staff
      1. Security guard
      2. Set-up, clean-up staff
II. Food
   A. Pre-awards
      1. Nonalcoholic beverages
      2. Appetizers
   B. Post-awards
      1. Alcohol
      2. Dinner
      3. Dessert
III. Awards
   A. Certificates
   B. Cash prizes

Tips for Writing Outlines

- Define the main topic in the title.
- Divide the topic into major components, preferably three to five.
- Break the components into subpoints.
- Use details, illustrations, and evidence to support subpoints.
- Don't put a single item under a major component if you have only one subpoint; integrate it with the main item above it or reorganize.
- Strive to make each component exclusive (no overlapping).

The Direct Pattern

After preparing an outline, you will need to decide where in the message you will place the main idea. Placing the main idea at the beginning of the message is called the direct pattern. In the direct pattern the main idea comes first, followed by details, explanation, or evidence. Placing the main idea later in the message (after the details, explanation, or evidence) is called the indirect pattern. The pattern you select is determined by how you expect the audience to react to the message, as shown in Figure 3.3.

✓ **Quick Check**

Business messages typically follow either (1) the direct pattern, with the main idea first or (2) the indirect pattern, with the main idea following explanation and evidence.

FIGURE 3.3 Audience Response Determines Pattern of Organization

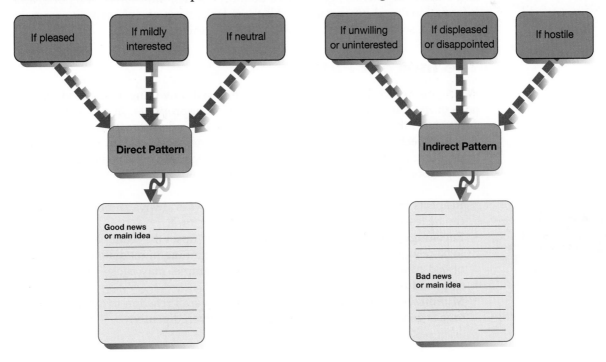

Organizing Data

In preparing to write any message, you need to anticipate the audience's reaction to your ideas and frame your message accordingly. When you expect the reader to be pleased, mildly interested, or, at worst, neutral—use the direct pattern. That is, put your main point—the purpose of your message—in the first or second sentence. Compare the direct and indirect patterns in the following memo openings. Notice how long it takes to get to the main idea in the indirect opening.

Indirect opening   Bombardier is seeking to improve the process undertaken in producing its annual company awards ceremony. To this end, the Marketing Department, which is in charge of the event, has been refining last year's plan, especially as it regards the issue of rental costs and food and beverage costs.

Direct opening   The Marketing Department at Bombardier suggests cutting costs for the annual awards ceremony by adjusting the way we order food and the way we handle rentals.

Explanations and details should follow the direct opening. What's important is getting to the main idea quickly. This direct method, also called *frontloading*, has at least three advantages:

- **Saves the reader time.** Many businesspeople can devote only a few moments to each message. Messages that take too long to get to the point may lose their readers along the way.
- **Sets a proper frame of mind.** Learning the purpose up front helps the reader put the subsequent details and explanations in perspective. Without a clear opening, the reader may be thinking, Why am I being told this?
- **Prevents frustration.** Readers forced to struggle through excessive text before reaching the main idea become frustrated. They resent the writer. Poorly organized messages create a negative impression of the writer.

This direct strategy works best with audiences that are likely to be receptive to or at least not likely to disagree with what you have to say. Typical business messages that follow the direct pattern include routine requests and responses, orders and acknowledgments, nonsensitive memos, e-mails, informational reports, and informational oral presentations. All these tasks have one element in common: none has a sensitive subject that will upset the reader.

The Indirect Pattern

When you expect the audience to be uninterested, unwilling, displeased, or perhaps even hostile, the indirect pattern is more appropriate. In this pattern you don't reveal the main idea until after you have offered explanation and evidence. This approach works well with three kinds of messages: (1) bad news, (2) ideas that require persuasion, and (3) sensitive news, especially when being transmitted to superiors. The indirect pattern has these benefits:

- **Respects the feelings of the audience.** Bad news is always painful, but the pain can be lessened when the receiver is prepared for it.
- **Encourages a fair hearing.** Messages that may upset the reader are more likely to be read when the main idea is delayed. Beginning immediately with a piece of bad news or a persuasive request, for example, may cause the receiver to stop reading or listening.
- **Minimizes a negative reaction.** A reader's overall reaction to a negative message is generally improved if the news is delivered gently.

Typical business messages that could be developed indirectly include letters and memos that refuse requests, deny claims, and disapprove credit. Persuasive requests, sales letters, sensitive messages, and some reports and oral presentations also benefit from the indirect strategy. You'll learn more about how to use the indirect pattern in Chapters 7 and 8.

In summary, business messages may be organized directly, with the main idea first, or indirectly, with the main idea delayed. Although these two patterns cover many communication problems, they should not be considered universal. Every business transaction is distinct. Some messages are mixed: part good news, part bad; part goodwill, part persuasion. In upcoming chapters you'll practise applying the direct and indirect patterns in typical situations. Then, you'll have the skills and confidence to evaluate communication problems and vary these patterns depending on the goals you wish to achieve.

Effective Sentences

After deciding how to organize your message, you are ready to begin composing it. As you create your first draft, you'll be working at the sentence level of composition. Although you've used sentences all your life, you may be unaware of how they can be shaped and arranged to express your ideas most effectively. First, let's review some basic sentence elements.

Complete sentences have subjects and verbs and make sense.

SUBJECT VERB
This report is clear and concise.

Clauses and phrases, the building blocks of sentences, are related groups of words. Phrases don't have subjects and verbs, while clauses do.

SUBJECT   PHRASE 1   VERB   PHRASE 2
The CEO of that organization sent a letter to our staff.

Clauses can be divided into two groups: independent and dependent. Independent clauses are grammatically complete, while dependent clauses depend for their meaning on independent clauses. In the example below, the clause beginning with *Because* does not make sense by itself, while the clause beginning with *Tracy* does make sense by itself.

VERB 1   SUBJECT VERB 2
Because she writes well, Tracy answers most customer letters.

DEPENDENT CLAUSE   INDEPENDENT CLAUSE

Here's a final example.

VERB 1   SUBJECT VERB 2
When she writes to customers, Naomi uses straightforward language.

DEPENDENT CLAUSE   INDEPENDENT CLAUSE

By learning to distinguish phrases, independent clauses, and dependent clauses, you'll be able to punctuate sentences correctly and avoid three basic sentence faults: the fragment, the run-on sentence, and the comma splice.

Sentence Fragment

✔ Quick Check

Fragments are broken-off parts of sentences and should not be punctuated as sentences.

One of the most serious errors a writer can make is punctuating a fragment as if it were a complete sentence. A fragment is a broken-off part of a sentence that is missing either a subject or a verb.

Fragment	Because most transactions require a permanent record. Good writing skills are critical.
Revision	Because most transactions require a permanent record, good writing skills are critical.
Fragment	The interviewer requested a writing sample. Even though the candidate seemed to communicate well.
Revision	The interviewer requested a writing sample, even though the candidate seemed to communicate well.

Fragments can often be identified by the words that introduce them—words such as *although, as, because, even, except, for example, if, instead of, since, so, such as, that, which,* and *when.* These words introduce dependent clauses. Make sure such clauses always connect to independent clauses.

Run-On (Fused) Sentence

✔ Quick Check

When two independent clauses are run together without punctuation or a coordinating conjunction, a run-on (fused) sentence results.

A sentence with two independent clauses must be joined by a coordinating conjunction (*and, or, nor, but*) or by a semicolon (;). Without a conjunction or a semi-colon, the result is a run-on sentence.

Run-on	Most job seekers present a printed résumé some are also using Web sites as electronic portfolios.
Revision 1	Most job seekers present a printed résumé, but some are also using Web sites as electronic portfolios.
Revision 2	Most job seekers present a printed résumé; some are also using Web sites as electronic portfolios.

Comma-Splice Sentence

✔ Quick Check

When two independent clauses are joined by a comma without a conjunction, a comma splice results.

A comma splice results when a writer joins two independent clauses with a comma. Independent clauses should be joined with a coordinating conjunction (*and, or, nor, but*) or a conjunctive adverb (*however, consequently, therefore,* and others). Notice that clauses joined by coordinating conjunctions require only a comma. Clauses joined by a coordinating adverb, however, require a semicolon. Here are three ways to rectify a comma splice:

Comma splice	Some employees responded by e-mail, others picked up the telephone.
Revision 1	Some employees responded by e-mail, and others picked up the telephone.
Revision 2	Some employees responded by e-mail; however, others picked up the telephone.
Revision 3	Some employees responded by e-mail; others picked up the telephone.

Sentence Length

✔ Quick Check

Sentences of 20 or fewer words have the most impact.

Because your goal is to communicate clearly, you're better off limiting your sentences to 20 or fewer words. Nicholas Russell, a writer, editor, and lecturer in Victoria, B.C., has said, "If your lead sentence is more than 20 words long, it had

Chapter 3 Improving Writing Techniques

better be damn good!"[2] Thus, in crafting your sentences, think about the relationship between sentence length and comprehension:

Sentence Length	Comprehension Rate
8 words	100%
15 words	90%
19 words	80%
28 words	50%

Instead of grouping clauses with *and*, *but*, and *however*, break some of your sentences into separate segments. Business readers want to grasp ideas immediately. They can do that best when thoughts are separated into short sentences. On the other hand, too many monotonous short sentences will sound unprofessional and may bore or even annoy the reader. Strive for a balance between longer sentences and shorter ones.

Emphasis

When you are talking with someone, you can emphasize your main ideas by saying them loudly or by repeating them slowly. You could pound the table if you want to show real emphasis. Another way you could signal the relative importance of an idea is by raising your eyebrows or by shaking your head or whispering in a low voice. But when you write, you must rely on other means to tell your readers which ideas are more important than others. Emphasis in writing can be achieved in two ways: mechanically or stylistically.

Emphasis through Mechanics

To emphasize an idea, a writer may use any of the following devices:

Underlining	<u>Underlining</u> draws the eye to a word.
Italics and boldface	Use *italics* or **boldface** for special meaning and emphasis.
Font changes	Changing from a large font to a smaller font or to a different font adds interest and emphasis.
All caps	Printing words in ALL CAPS is like shouting them.
Dashes	Dashes—if used sparingly—can be effective in capturing attention.
Tabulation	Listing items vertically makes them stand out:

    1. First item
    2. Second item
    3. Third item

Quick Check

You can emphasize an idea mechanically by using underlining, italics, boldface, font changes, all caps, dashes, and tabulation.

Other means of achieving mechanical emphasis include the arrangement of space, colour, lines, boxes, columns, titles, headings, and subheadings. Today's software and colour printers provide a wide choice of capabilities for emphasizing ideas.

Emphasis through Style

Although mechanical means are occasionally appropriate, more often a writer achieves emphasis stylistically. That is, the writer chooses words carefully and constructs sentences skillfully to emphasize main ideas and de-emphasize minor or negative ideas. Here are four suggestions for emphasizing ideas stylistically:

Quick Check

You can emphasize ideas stylistically by using vivid words, labelling the main idea, and positioning the main idea strategically.

- **Use vivid words.** Vivid words are emphatic because the reader can picture ideas clearly.

Emphasis

| General | One business uses personal selling techniques. |
| Vivid | Avon uses face-to-face selling techniques. |

| General | A customer said that he wanted the contract returned soon. |
| Vivid | Mr. LeClerc insisted that the contract be returned by July 1. |

- **Label the main idea.** If an idea is significant, tell the reader.

| Unlabelled | Explore the possibility of leasing a site, but also hire a consultant. |
| Labelled | Explore the possibility of leasing a site; but most important, hire a consultant. |

- **Place the important idea first or last in the sentence.** Ideas have less competition from surrounding words when they appear first or last in a sentence. Observe how the concept of productivity is emphasized in the first and second examples:

Emphatic	Productivity is more likely to be increased when profit-sharing plans are linked to individual performance rather than to group performance.
Emphatic	Profit-sharing plans linked to individual performance rather than to group performance are more effective in increasing productivity.
Unemphatic	Profit-sharing plans are more effective in increasing productivity when they are linked to individual performance rather than to group performance.

- **Place the important idea in a simple sentence or in an independent clause.** Don't dilute the effect of the idea by making it share the spotlight with other words and clauses.

Emphatic	You are the first trainee whom we have hired for this program. (Use a simple sentence for emphasis.)
Emphatic	Although we considered many candidates, you are the first trainee whom we have hired for this program. (Independent clause contains main idea.)
Unemphatic	Although you are the first trainee whom we have hired for this program, we had many candidates and expect to expand the program in the future. (Main idea is lost in a dependent clause.)

De-emphasize. To de-emphasize an idea, such as bad news, try one of the following stylistic devices:

- **Use general words.**

| Vivid | Our records indicate that you were recently fired. |
| General | Our records indicate that your employment status has changed recently. |

- **Place the bad news in a dependent clause connected to an independent clause with something positive.** In sentences with dependent clauses, the main emphasis is always on the independent clause.

| Emphasizes bad news | We cannot issue you credit at this time, but we do have a plan that will allow you to fill your immediate needs on a cash basis. |
| De-emphasizes bad news | We have a plan that will allow you to fill your immediate needs on a cash basis since we cannot issue credit at this time. |

Quick Check

You can de-emphasize ideas through word choice and placement.

Chapter 3 Improving Writing Techniques

Active and Passive Voice

In sentences with active-voice verbs, the subject is the doer of the action. In passive-voice sentences, the subject is acted upon.

Active verb   Mr. Wong completed the tax return before the April 30 deadline. (The subject, *Mr. Wong*, is the doer of the action.)

Passive verb   The tax return was completed before the April 30 deadline. (The subject, *tax return*, is acted upon.)

In the first sentence, the active-voice verb emphasizes *Mr. Wong*. In the second sentence, the passive-voice verb emphasizes *tax return*. In sentences with passive-voice verbs, the doer of the action may be revealed or left unknown. In business writing, and in personal interactions, some situations demand tact and sensitivity. Instead of using a direct approach with active verbs, we may prefer the indirectness that passive verbs allow. Rather than making a blunt announcement with an active verb (*Gunnar made a major error in the estimate*), we can soften the sentence with a passive construction (*A major error was made in the estimate*).

Here's a summary of the best use of active- and passive-voice verbs:

- **Use the active voice for most business writing.** It clearly tells what the action is and who is performing that action.
- **Use the passive voice to emphasize an action or the recipient of the action.** *You have been selected to represent us.*
- **Use the passive voice to de-emphasize negative news.** *Your watch has not been repaired.*
- **Use the passive voice to conceal the doer of an action.** *A major error was made in the estimate.*

How can you tell if a verb is active or passive? Identify the subject of the sentence and decide whether the subject is doing the acting or being acted upon. For example, in the sentence *An appointment was made for January 1*, the subject is *appointment*. The subject is being acted upon; therefore, the verb (*was made*) is passive. Another clue in identifying passive-voice verbs is that they generally include a *to be* helping verb, such as *is, are, was, were, being,* or *been*.

Parallelism

Parallelism is a writing technique that creates balanced writing. Sentences written so that their parts are balanced or parallel are easy to read and understand. To achieve parallel construction, use similar structures to express similar ideas. For example, the words *computing, coding, recording,* and *storing* are parallel because they all end in *-ing*. To express the list as *computing, coding, recording,* and *storage* is disturbing because the last item is not what the reader expects. Try to match nouns with nouns, verbs with verbs, and clauses with clauses. Avoid mixing active-voice verbs with passive-voice verbs. Your goal is to keep the wording balanced in expressing similar ideas.

Lacks parallelism   The market for industrial goods includes manufacturers, contractors, wholesalers, and those concerned with the retail function.

Revision   The market for industrial goods includes manufacturers, contractors, wholesalers, and retailers. (Parallel construction matches nouns.)

Lacks parallelism	Our primary goals are to increase productivity, reduce costs, and the improvement of product quality.
Revision	Our primary goals are to increase productivity, reduce costs, and improve product quality. (Parallel construction matches verbs.)
Lacks parallelism	We are scheduled to meet in Toronto on January 5, we are meeting in Montreal on the 15th of March, and in Burlington on June 3.
Revision	We are scheduled to meet in Toronto on January 5, in Montreal on March 15, and in Burlington on June 3. (Parallel construction matches phrases.)
Lacks parallelism	Mrs. Chorney audits all accounts lettered A through L; accounts lettered M through Z are audited by Mr. Faheem.
Revision	Mrs. Chorney audits all accounts lettered A through L; Mr. Faheem audits accounts lettered M through Z. (Parallel construction matches active-voice verbs in balanced clauses.)

All items in a list should be expressed in parallel constructions.

In presenting lists of data, whether shown horizontally or tabulated vertically, be certain to express all the items in parallel form.

Parallelism in vertical list	Three primary objectives of advertising are as follows:
	1. Increase the frequency of product use.
	2. Introduce complementary products.
	3. Enhance the corporate image.

Unity

Unified sentences contain only related ideas.

Unified sentences contain thoughts that are related to only one main idea. The following sentence lacks unity because the first clause has little or no relationship to the second clause:

Lacks unity	Our insurance plan is available in all provinces, and you may name anyone as a beneficiary for your coverage.
Revision	Our insurance plan is available in all provinces. What's more, you may name anyone as a beneficiary for your coverage.

The ideas in a sentence are better expressed by separating the two dissimilar clauses and by adding a connecting phrase. Three writing faults that destroy sentence unity are imprecise writing, mixed constructions, and misplaced modifiers.

Imprecise Writing

Imprecise sentences often should be broken into two sentences.

Sentences that twist or turn unexpectedly away from the main thought are examples of imprecise writing. Such confusing writing may result when too many thoughts are included in one sentence or when one thought does not relate to another. To rectify a imprecise sentence, revise it so that the reader understands the relationship between the thoughts. If that is impossible, move the unrelated thoughts to a new sentence.

Imprecise writing	I appreciate the time you spent with me last week, and I have purchased a computer and software that generate graphics.
Revision	I appreciate the time you spent with me last week. As a result of your advice, I have purchased a computer and software that generate graphics.

Imprecise writing	The stockholders of a corporation elect a board of directors, although the chief executive officer is appointed by the board and the CEO is not directly responsible to the stockholders.
Revision	The stockholders of a corporation elect a board of directors, who in turn appoints the chief executive officer. The CEO is not directly responsible to the stockholders.

Mixed Constructions

Writers who fuse two different grammatical constructions destroy sentence unity and meaning.

 Quick Check

Mixed constructions confuse readers.

Mixed construction	The reason I am late is because my car battery is dead.
Revision	The reason I am late is that my car battery is dead. (The construction introduced by *the reason is* should be a noun clause beginning with *that*, not an adverbial clause beginning with *because*.)
Mixed construction	When the stock market index rose five points was our signal to sell.
Revision	When the stock market index rose five points, we were prepared to sell. OR: Our signal to sell was an increase of five points in the stock market index.

Dangling and Misplaced Modifiers

For clarity, modifiers must be close to the words they describe or limit. A modifier dangles when the word or phrase it describes is missing from its sentence. A modifier is misplaced when the word or phrase it describes is not close enough to be clear. In both instances, the solution is to position the modifier closer to the word(s) it describes or limits. Introductory verbal phrases are particularly dangerous; be sure to follow them immediately with the words they logically describe or modify.

Quick Check

Modifiers must be close to the words they describe or limit.

Dangling modifier	To win the lottery, a ticket must be purchased. (Purchased by whom? The verbal phrase must be followed by a subject.)
Revision	To win the lottery, you must purchase a ticket.
Dangling modifier	Driving through Tetrahedron Plateau, the ocean suddenly came into view. (Is the ocean driving through Tetrahedron Plateau?)
Revision	Driving through Tetrahedron Plateau, we saw the ocean suddenly come into view.

Try this trick for detecting and remedying dangling modifiers. Ask the question "Who or what?" after any introductory phrase. The words immediately following should tell the reader who or what is performing the action. Try the test on the previous danglers.

Misplaced modifier	Seeing his error too late, the envelope was immediately resealed by Adrian. (Did the envelope see the error?)
Revision	Seeing his error too late, Adrian immediately resealed the envelope.
Misplaced modifier	A wart appeared on my left hand that I want removed. (Is the left hand to be removed?)
Revision	I want to remove the wart that appeared on my left hand.

Misplaced modifier	The busy human resources director interviewed only candidates who had excellent computer skills in the morning. (Were the candidates skilled only in the morning?)
Revision	In the morning the busy human resources director interviewed only candidates who had excellent computer skills.

Paragraph Coherence

A paragraph is a group of sentences with a controlling idea, usually stated first. Paragraphs package similar ideas into meaningful groups for readers. Effective paragraphs are coherent; that is, they hold together. But coherence does not happen accidentally. It is achieved through effective organization and (1) repetition of key ideas, (2) use of pronouns, and (3) use of transitional expressions.

Quick Check

Three ways to create paragraph coherence are (1) repetition of key ideas, (2) use of pronouns, and (3) use of transitional expressions.

- **Repetition of key ideas or key words.** Repeating a word or key thought from a preceding sentence helps guide a reader from one thought to the next. This redundancy is necessary to build cohesiveness into writing.

Effective repetition	Quality problems in production are often the result of inferior raw materials. Some companies have strong programs for ensuring the quality of incoming production materials and supplies.

The second sentence of the preceding paragraph repeats the key idea of *quality*. Moreover, the words *incoming production materials and supplies* refer to raw materials mentioned in the preceding sentence. Good writers find similar words to describe the same idea, thus using repetition to clarify a topic for the reader.

Quick Check

Pronouns with clear antecedents can improve coherence.

- **Use of pronouns.** Pronouns such as *this, that, they, these,* and *those* promote coherence by connecting the thoughts in one sentence to the thoughts in a previous sentence. To make sure that the pronoun reference is clear, consider joining the pronoun with the word to which it refers, thus making the pronoun into an adjective.

Pronoun repetition	Xerox has a four-point program to assist suppliers. *This program* includes written specifications for production materials and components.

Be very careful, though, in using pronouns. A pronoun without a clear antecedent can be annoying. That's because the reader doesn't know precisely to what the pronoun refers.

Faulty	When company profits increased, employees were given either a cash payment or company stock. *This* became a real incentive to employees. (Is *This* the cash or the stock or both?)
Revision	When company profits increased, employees were given either a cash payment or company stock. *This profit-sharing plan* became a real incentive to employees.

Quick Check

Transitional expressions build paragraph coherence.

- **Use of transitional expressions.** One of the most effective ways to achieve paragraph coherence is through the use of transitional expressions. These expressions act as road signs: they indicate where the message is headed, and they help the reader anticipate what is coming. Here are some of the most effective transitional expressions. They are grouped according to use.

Time Association	Contrast	Illustration
before, after	although	for example
first, second	but	in this way
meanwhile	however	
next	instead	
until	nevertheless	
when, whenever	on the other hand	

Cause, Effect	Additional Idea
consequently	furthermore
for this reason	in addition
hence	likewise
therefore	moreover

Paragraph Length

Although no rule regulates the length of paragraphs, business writers recognize the value of short paragraphs. Paragraphs with eight or fewer printed lines look inviting and readable. Long, solid chunks of print appear formidable. If a topic can't be covered in eight or fewer printed lines (not sentences), consider breaking it into smaller segments.

Quick Check
The most readable paragraphs contain eight or fewer printed lines.

Composing the First Draft

Once you've researched your topic, organized the data, and selected a pattern of organization, you're ready to begin composing. Communicators who haven't completed the preparatory work often suffer from "writer's block" and sit staring at the computer screen. It's easier to get started if you have organized your ideas and established a plan. Composition is also easier if you have a quiet environment in which to concentrate. Businesspeople with messages to compose often set aside a given time and do not allow calls, visitors, or other interruptions. This is a good technique for students as well.

Quick Check
Create a quiet place in which to write.

As you begin composing, keep in mind that you are writing the first draft, not the final copy. Experts suggest that you write quickly (sprint writing). According to one university writing centre, "The purpose of the initial draft is to produce raw material, not to dazzle the critics with your finely shaped prose."[3] As you take up each idea, imagine that you are talking to the reader. Don't let yourself get bogged down. If you can't think of the right word, insert a substitute or type "find perfect word later."[4] Sprint writing works especially well for those composing on a computer, because it's simple to make changes at any point of the composition process. If you are handwriting the first draft, double-space so that you have room for changes.

Summing Up and Looking Forward

This chapter explained the second phase of the writing process including researching, organizing, and composing. Before beginning a message, every writer collects data, either formally or informally. For most simple messages, writers look in their company's files, talk with their boss, interview the target audience, or possibly conduct an informal survey. Information for a message is then organized into a list or an outline. Depending on the expected reaction of the receiver, the message can be organized directly (for positive reactions) or indirectly (for negative reactions or when persuasion is necessary).

Summing Up and Looking Forward

In composing the first draft, writers must be sure that sentences are complete. Emphasis can be achieved through mechanics (underlining, italics, font changes, all caps, and so forth) or through style (using vivid words, labelling the main idea, and positioning the important ideas). Important writing techniques include skillful use of active- and passive-voice verbs, developing parallelism, and achieving unity while avoiding imprecise writing, mixed constructions, and misplaced modifiers. Coherent paragraphs result from planned repetition of key ideas, proper use of pronouns, and inclusion of transitional expressions.

In the next chapter you'll learn helpful techniques for the third phase of the writing process, which includes revising and proofreading.

Critical Thinking

1. Why is audience analysis so important in choosing the direct or indirect pattern of organization for a business message?
2. In what ways do you imagine that writing on the job differs from the writing you do in your academic studies?
3. How are speakers different from writers in the manner in which they emphasize ideas?
4. Why are short sentences and short paragraphs appropriate for business communication?
5. When might it be unethical to use the indirect method of organizing a message?

Chapter Review

6. What three steps are included in the second phase of the writing process?

7. Distinguish between formal and informal methods of researching data for a business message.

8. What is the difference between a list and an outline?

9. What is frontloading, and what are its advantages?

10. When is the indirect method appropriate, and what are the benefits of using it?

11. List five techniques for achieving emphasis through mechanics.

Chapter 3 Improving Writing Techniques

12. List four techniques for achieving emphasis through style.

13. What is parallelism? Give an original example.

14. List three techniques for developing paragraph coherence.

15. What environment should you establish if you have something important to write? Why?

Writing Improvement Exercises

Revising Sentences. Revise the following sentences. Identify whether the mistake is a sentence fragment, run-on sentence, or comma splices.

16. When McDonald's tested pizza, Pizza Hut fought back. With aggressive ads ridiculing McPizza.

17. Companies sometimes sue their rivals they also may respond with counterattacks.

18. Aggressive advertisements can backfire that's why marketing directors consider them carefully.

19. Although Tim Hortons is the country's number one doughnut chain. Robin's is popular in western Canada.

20. About half of Swiss Chalet's outlets make deliveries, the others concentrate on walk-in customers.

Emphasis. For each of the following sentences, circle (a) or (b). Be prepared to justify your choice.

21. Which is more emphatic?
    a. We need a faster, more efficient distribution system.
    b. We need a better distribution system.
22. Which is more emphatic?
    a. Increased advertising would improve sales.
    b. Adding $50,000 in advertising would double our sales.
23. Which is more emphatic?
    a. The committee was powerless to act.
    b. The committee was unable to take action.
24. Which sentence puts more emphasis on product loyalty?
    a. Product loyalty is the primary motivation for advertising.
    b. The primary motivation for advertising is loyalty to the product, although other purposes are also served.
25. Which sentence places more emphasis on the seminar?
    a. An executive training seminar that starts June 1 will include four candidates.
    b. Four candidates will be able to participate in an executive training seminar that we feel will provide a valuable learning experience.
26. Which sentence puts more emphasis on the date?
    a. The deadline is December 30 for applications for overseas jobs.
    b. December 30 is the deadline for applications for overseas jobs.
27. Which is less emphatic?
    a. Lily Takahashi said that her financial status had worsened.
    b. Lily Takahashi said that she had lost her job and owed $2000.
28. Which sentence de-emphasizes the credit refusal?
    a. We are unable to grant you credit at this time, but we will reconsider your application later.
    b. Although we welcome your cash business, we are unable to offer you credit at this time; but we will be happy to reconsider your application later.
29. Which sentence gives more emphasis to judgment?
    a. He has many admirable qualities, but most important is his good judgment.
    b. He has many admirable qualities, including good judgment and patience.
30. Which is more emphatic?
    a. Three departments are involved: (1) Legal, (2) Accounting, and (3) Distribution.
    b. Three departments are involved:
       1. Legal
       2. Accounting
       3. Distribution

Active-Voice Verbs. Business writing is more forceful if it uses active-voice verbs. Revise the following sentences so that verbs are in the active voice. Put the emphasis on the doer of the action. Add subjects if necessary.

Example: The computers were powered up each day at 7:00 a.m.
Revision: Kamal powered up the computers each day at 7:00 a.m.

31. Initial figures for the bid were submitted before the June 1 deadline.

32. New spices and cooking techniques were tried by Lick's to improve its hamburgers.

33. Substantial sums of money were earned by employees who enrolled early in our stock option plan.

34. A significant financial commitment has been made by us to ensure that our customers can take advantage of our discount pricing.

Passive-Voice Verbs. When indirectness or tact is required, use passive-voice verbs. Revise the following sentences so that they are in the passive voice.

Example: Sade did not submit the accounting statement on time.
Revision: The accounting statement was not submitted on time.

35. Andreas made a computational error in the report.

36. We cannot ship your order for 10 monitors until June 15.

37. The government first issued a warning regarding the use of this pesticide over 15 months ago.

38. We will notify you immediately if we make any changes in your travel arrangements.

39. We cannot allow a cash refund unless you provide a receipt.

Parallelism. Revise the following sentences so that their parts are balanced.

40. (*Hint:* Match verbs.) Some of our priorities include linking employee compensation to performance, keeping administrative costs down, the expansion of computer use, and the improvement of performance review skills of supervisors.

41. (*Hint:* Match active voice of verbs.) Yin Huang, of the Red River office, will now supervise our Western Division; and the Eastern Division will be supervised by our Ottawa office manager, David Ali.

42. (*Hint:* Match nouns.) Word processing software is used extensively in the fields of health care, by lawyers, by secretaries in insurance firms, for scripts in the entertainment industry, and in the banking field.

43. If you have decided to cancel our service, please cut your credit card in half, and the card pieces should be returned to us.

44. We need more laboratory space, additional personnel is required, and we also need much more capital.

45. The application for a grant asks for this information: funds required for employee salaries, how much we expect to spend on equipment, and what is the length of the project.

46. To lease a car is more expensive than buying one.

47. To use the copier, insert your account card, the paper trays must be loaded, indicate the number of copies needed, and your original sheet should be inserted through the feeder.

Sentence Unity. The following sentences lack unity. Rewrite, correcting the identified fault.

Example: (Dangling modifier) By advertising extensively, all the open jobs were filled quickly.

Revision: By advertising extensively, we were able to fill all the open jobs quickly.

48. (Dangling modifier) To open a money market account, a deposit of $3000 is required.

49. (Mixed construction) The reason why Ms. Rutulis is unable to travel extensively is because she has family responsibilities.

50. (Misplaced modifier) Identification passes must be worn at all times in offices and production facilities showing the employee's picture.

51. (Misplaced modifier) The editor-in-chief's rules were to be observed by all staff members, no matter how silly they seemed.

52. (Imprecise sentence) The business was started by two engineers, and these owners worked in a garage, which eventually grew into a million-dollar operation.

Coherence. Revise the following paragraphs to improve coherence. Be aware that the transitional expressions and key words selected depend largely on the emphasis desired. Many possible revisions exist.

Example: Computer style checkers rank somewhere between artificial intelligence and artificial ignorance. Style checkers are like clever children: smart but not wise. Business writers should be cautious. They should be aware of the usefulness of style checkers. They should know their limitations.

Revision: Computer style checkers rank somewhere between artificial intelligence and artificial ignorance. For example, they are like clever children: smart but not wise. For this reason, business writers should be cautious. Although they should be aware of the usefulness of these software programs, business writers should also know their limitations.

53. Our computerized file includes all customer data. It provides space for name, address, and other vital information. It has an area for comments. The area for comments comes in handy. It requires more time and careful keyboarding, though.

54. No one likes to turn out poor products. We began highlighting recurring problems. Employees make a special effort to be more careful in doing their work right the first time. It doesn't have to be returned to them for corrections.

55. Service was less than perfect for many months. We lacked certain intangibles. We didn't have the customer-specific data that we needed. We made the mistake of removing all localized, person-to-person coverage. We are returning to decentralized customer contacts.

Grammar/Mechanics Review—3

The following sentences contain errors in grammar, punctuation, capitalization, number style, usage, and spelling. Pay special attention to sentence fragments. Below each sentence write a corrected version. Check with your instructor for the solutions.

1. Although most of our capitol is tied up in equipment. We expect to purchase 2 vans in Febuary.

2. During the Fall Elisas schedule included classes in: Management, Marketing, and French.

3. A list of resterants with dinners costing less than six dollars were given to my friend and I.

4. Although we normally hire only experienced programmers. We occasionally consider well trained individuals who lack experience.

5. All houses accept your's has to be inspected for termite damage.

6. The following 3 employees are indispensible Max, Gabrielle, and Tyler.

7. Every classified employee, as well as all certified employees and members of management are eligible for new health benefits.

8. The 4 announcements from our human resources department surprised management as much as us.

9. Just between you and I, we expect to raise over two thousand dollars during the four-week campaign.

10. Of course all of we homeowners are upset over this latest increase in property taxs.

11. Nick Foster a writer for Channel Business e-zine quoted a mathematician as saying "On average, people are average."

12. If the President and Manager agree that next years sales campaign should emphasize customer service. Then we can procede.

13. Considering total sales Nicola is more of a team player than him. Which explains her recent promotion.

14. We trust that the New Year will be profitable for you, and that we may have many opportunitys to serve you.

15. Microsoft says, that they makes computing more accessable for every one because they offer: new ideas, new products, and services that are new for customers.

Grammar/Mechanics Challenge—3

Document for Revision

The following memo has many faults in grammar, spelling, punctuation, capitalization, word use, and number form. Use standard proofreading marks (see Appendix B) to correct the errors. Study the guidelines in the Grammar/Mechanics Handbook to sharpen your skills. When you finish, your instructor can show you the revised version of this memo.

Title Guaranty Co.

Memo

To: Jamal Warner, Vice President
From: Roxanne Crosley, Manager, Payroll
CC:
Date: July 24, 2006
Re: Departmental Error

This is to inform you that last month our central accounting department changed it's computer program for payroll processing. When this computer change was operationalized some of the stored information was not transfered to the new information database. As a consequence of this maneuver several errors occured in employee paycheques (1) health benifits were not deducted (2) RSP deductions were not made and (3) errors occured in Federal with-olding calculations.

Each and every one of the employees effected have been contacted; and this error has been elucidated. My staff and myself has been working overtime to replace all the missing data; so that corrections can be made by the August 30th payroll run.

Had I made a verification of the true facts before the paycheques were ran this slip-up would not have materialized. To prevent such an error in the future I decided to take the bull by the horns. At this point in time I have implemented a rigorous new verification system. I am of the firm opinion that utilization of the new system will definitely prevent this perplexing event from reoccuring

---

Using Ethical Tools to Help You Do the Right Thing

In your career you will face times when you are torn by conflicting loyalties. Should you tell the truth and risk your job? Should you be loyal to your friends even if it means bending the rules? Should you be tactful or totally honest? Is it your duty to help your company make a profit, or should you be socially responsible?

Being ethical, according to the experts, means doing the right thing given the circumstances. Each set of circumstances requires analyzing issues, evaluating choices, and acting responsibly. Resolving ethical issues is never easy, but the task can be made less difficult if you know how to identify key issues. The following questions may be helpful.

- **Is the action you are considering legal?** No matter who asks you to do it or how important you feel the result will be, avoid anything that is prohibited by law. Giving remuneration to a buyer for a large order is illegal, even if you suspect that others in your field do it and you know that without the remuneration you will lose the sale.
- **How would you see the problem if you were on the opposite side?** Looking at all sides of an issue helps you gain perspective. Consider the issue of mandatory drug testing among employees. From management's viewpoint such testing could stop drug abuse and improve job performance. From the employees' viewpoint mandatory testing reflects a lack of trust of employees and constitutes an invasion of privacy. By weighing both sides of an issue, you can arrive at a more equitable solution.
- **What are the alternative solutions?** Consider all dimensions of other options. Would the alternative be more ethical? Under the circumstances, is the alternative feasible? Can an alternative solution be implemented with a minimum of disruption and with a high degree of probable success?
- **Can you discuss the problem with someone whose opinion you value?** Suppose you feel ethically bound to report accurate information to a client—even though your boss has ordered you not to do so. Talking about your dilemma with a coworker or with a colleague in your field might give you helpful insights and lead to possible alternatives.
- **How would you feel if your family, friends, employer, or coworkers learned of your action?** If the thought of revealing your action publicly produces fear, your choice is probably not a wise one. Losing the faith of your friends or the confidence of your customers is not worth whatever short-term gains might be realized.

Career Application

After six months of job hunting, you land a job with Company X, but it's in a city 700 kilometres from your home. A week after starting work, you receive a job offer from Company Y that would increase your salary by 10 percent and would move you to a location closer to your home. You want very much to leave Company X to accept Company Y's offer. However, you are troubled because Company X has begun to train you. You feel particularly guilty because many nice people have made a special effort to welcome you and get you started in your new position.

Your Task

- In teams or individually, decide on an action to take. Begin by asking whether the action you are considering is legal.
- Looking at the problem from Company X's perspective, how much harm would be done by your leaving? What will Company X lose if you leave?
- What are alternative solutions? Is it entirely a money issue? Would you be happy with a higher salary at Company X?
- Can you discuss the problem with someone whose opinion you value? Should you consult someone at Company X? Your family? Friends?
- How would you feel if your family, friends, employer, or coworkers learned of your action?
- Present your decision in class discussion or in a memo to your instructor. Support your decision with your reasons.

Related Web site: Visit the Canadian Centre for Ethics & Corporate Policy site <www.ethicscentre.ca>.

4

Revising and Proofreading Business Messages

The importance of the written word in business—whether in an e-mail, proposal, or promotional piece—cannot be underestimated. It is often what a client sees first, and it becomes a living, tangible reflection of the company itself. Grammatical slip-ups can suggest to a client a lack of professionalism and inattention to detail. Believe me, it's and its can negatively impact a company's bottom line, and even jeopardize its position and branding in the marketplace.[1]

Stephanie Mikelbrencis, *director of marketing, Brock Solutions*

LEARNING OBJECTIVES

1. Understand the third phase of the writing process, revision.
2. Revise messages to achieve concise wording by eliminating wordy prepositional phrases, outdated expressions, long lead-ins, and needless adverbs.
3. Revise messages to eliminate fillers, repetitious words, and redundancies.
4. Revise messages to use jargon sparingly and avoid slang and clichés.
5. Revise messages to include precise verbs, concrete nouns, and vivid adjectives.
6. Describe effective techniques for proofreading routine and complex documents.

Understanding the Process of Revision

The best business writing is clear, vigorous, and free of errors. In this chapter you'll concentrate on techniques to achieve those qualities. These techniques are part of the third phase of the writing process, which centres on revising and proofreading. Revising means improving the content and sentence structure of your message. It may include adding to, cutting, and changing what you've written. Proofreading involves correcting the grammar, spelling, punctuation, format, and mechanics of your messages.

Both revising and proofreading require a little practice to develop your skills. That's what you will be learning in this chapter. Take a look at Figure 4.1. Notice how the revised version of this paragraph is clearer, more concise, and more vig-

 Quick Check

The third phase of the writing process includes revision, proofreading, and evaluating.

FIGURE 4.1 Revising for Conciseness

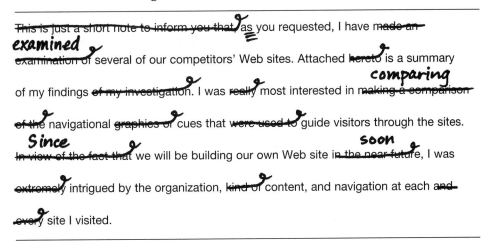

orous because we removed a lot of extra words that were not adding to the message. Major ideas stand out when they are not covered up by unnecessary words.

Rarely is the first or even the second version of a message satisfactory. The revision stage is your chance to make sure your message says what you mean. It's also your chance to project a good image of yourself.

Many professional writers compose the first draft quickly without worrying about language, precision, or correctness. Then they revise and polish extensively. Other writers prefer to revise as they go—particularly for shorter business documents. Whether you revise as you go or do it when you finish a document, you'll want to focus on concise wording. Such a focus includes eliminating wordy prepositional phrases, long lead-ins, outdated expressions, needless adverbs, fillers, and repetitious and redundant words. You'll also decide whether to include jargon, slang, and clichés. And you'll be looking for precise words that say exactly what you mean.

 Quick Check

Some communicators write the first draft quickly; others revise and polish as they go.

Concise Wording

In business, time is money. Translated into writing, this saying means that concise messages save reading time and, thus, money. In addition, messages that are written directly and efficiently are easier to read and comprehend. In the revision process look for shorter ways to say what you mean. Examine every sentence you write. Could the thought be conveyed in fewer words? Notice how the following wordy expressions could be said more concisely.

Quick Check

Main points are easier to understand in concise messages.

Wordy	Concise	Wordy	Concise
at a later date	later	fully cognizant of	aware of
at this point in time	now	in addition to the above	also
afford an opportunity	allow	in spite of the fact that	even though
are of the opinion that	believe, think that	in the event that	if
at the present time	now, currently	in the amount of	for
despite the fact that	though	in the near future	soon
due to the fact that	because, since	in view of the fact that	because
during the time	while	inasmuch as	since
feel free to	please	more or less	about
for the period of	for	until such time as	until

 **Quick Check**

A wordy phrase can often be reduced to a single word.

Wordy Prepositional Phrases

Quick Check

Replace wordy prepositional phrases with adverbs whenever possible.

Some wordy prepositional phrases may be replaced by single adverbs. For example, *in the normal course of events* becomes *normally* and *as a general rule* becomes *generally*.

Wordy	DCI approached the merger *in a careful manner*.
Concise	DCI approached the merger carefully.

Wordy	The merger will *in all probability* be effected.
Concise	The merger will probably be effected.

Wordy	We have taken this action *in very few cases*.
Concise	We have seldom taken this action.

Long Lead-Ins

Quick Check

Avoid long lead-ins that delay the reader from reaching the meaning of the sentence.

Delete unnecessary introductory words and phrases. The main idea of the sentence often follows the words *that* or *because*.

Wordy	*I am sending you this announcement to let you all know that* the office will be closed Monday.
Concise	The office will be closed Monday.

Wordy	*You will be interested to learn that* you can now be served at our Web site.
Concise	You can now be served at our Web site.

Wordy	*I am writing this letter because* Dr. Rahib Peshwar suggested that your organization was hiring trainees.
Concise	Dr. Rahib Peshwar suggested that your organization was hiring trainees.

Outdated Expressions

Quick Check

Replace outdated expressions with modern, concise phrasing.

The world of business has changed greatly in the past century. Yet some business writers continue to use antiquated phrases and expressions borrowed from a period when the language of business was exceedingly formal. In the 1800s, letter writers "begged to state" and "trusted to be favoured with" and assured their readers that they "remained their humble servants." Such language was current in the 1800s but it is now out of fashion. Replace outdated expressions such as those shown here with more modern phrasing:

Outdated Expressions	Modern Phrasing
are in receipt of	have received
as per your request	at your request
attached hereto	attached
enclosed please find	enclosed is/are
pursuant to your request	at your request
thanking you in advance	thank you
I trust that	I think, I believe
under separate cover	separately

Chapter 4 Revising and Proofreading Business Messages

Needless Adverbs

Eliminating intensifying adverbs such as *very, definitely, quite, completely, extremely, really, actually, somewhat,* and *rather* streamlines your writing. Omitting these intensifiers generally makes you sound more credible and businesslike.

Wordy   We *actually* did not *really* give his plan a *very* fair trial.
Concise   We did not give his plan a fair trial.

Wordy   Professor Anna Pictou offers an *extremely* fine course that students *definitely* appreciate.
Concise   Professor Anna Pictou offers a fine course that students appreciate.

Fillers

Good writers avoid crowding sentences with excess words. Beginning an idea with *there is* usually indicates that writers are having a hard time deciding what the main idea of the sentence should be. Used correctly, *there* indicates a specific place (*I placed the box there*). Used as fillers, *there* and occasionally *it* merely take up space.

Wordy   There are three vice-presidents who report directly to the president.
Concise   Three vice-presidents report directly to the president.

Wordy   It is the client who should make application for licensing.
Concise   The client should apply for licensing.

Repetitious Words

Communicators who want to create vibrant sentences vary their words to avoid unintentional repetition. Notice how monotonous the following personnel announcement sounds:

Quick Check

Avoid the monotony of unintentionally repeated words.

Employees will be able to elect an additional six employees to serve with the four previously elected employees who currently comprise the employees' board of directors. To ensure representation, shift employees will be electing one shift employee as their sole representative.

In this example the word *employee* is used six times. In addition, the last sentence begins with the word *representation* and ends with the similar word *representative*. An easier-to-read version follows:

Employees will be able to elect an additional six representatives to serve with the four previously elected members of the employees' board of directors. To ensure representation, shift workers will elect their own board member.

In the second version, synonyms (*representatives, members, workers*) replaced *employee*. The last sentence was reworked by using a pronoun (*their*) and by substituting *board member* for the repetitious *representative*. Variety of expression can be achieved by searching for appropriate synonyms and by substituting pronouns.

Good writers are also alert to the overuse of the articles *a, an,* and particularly *the*. Often the word *the* can simply be omitted, particularly with plural nouns.

Wordy   The committee members agreed on many rule changes.
Improved   Committee members agreed on many rule changes.

Redundant Words

Repetition of words to achieve emphasis or effective transition is an important writing technique discussed in the previous chapter. The needless repetition, however, of words whose meanings are clearly implied by other words is a writing fault called *redundancy*. For example, in the expression *final outcome*, the word *final* is redundant and should be omitted, since *outcome* implies finality. Learn to avoid redundant expressions such as the following:

absolutely essential	*final* outcome
adequate *enough*	*grateful* thanks
advance warning	*mutual* cooperation
basic fundamentals	*necessary* prerequisite
big *in size*	*new* beginning
combined *together*	*past* history
consensus *of opinion*	reason *why*
continue *on*	red *in colour*
each *and every*	refer *back*
exactly identical	repeat *again*
few *in number*	*true* facts

Jargon

Except in certain specialized contexts, you should avoid jargon and unnecessary technical terms. Jargon is special terminology that is peculiar to a particular activity or profession. For example, geologists speak knowingly of *exfoliation*, *calcareous ooze*, and *siliceous particles*. Engineers are familiar with phrases such as *infrared processing flags*, *output latches*, and *movable symbology*. Telecommunica-

"FYI, Cc: R & D Re: B2B IPO ASAP."

© Mark Anderson

tion experts use such words and phrases as *protocol*, *mode*, and *asynchronous transmission*. Business professionals are especially prone to using jargon, with words and phrases such as *leverage*, *ramp up*, *in the pipeline*, *cascade*, *pushback*, and *bullish* or *bearish* being just a few of the many you may find in the business section of the newspaper or in your local office.

Every field has its own special vocabulary. Using that vocabulary within the field is acceptable and even necessary for accurate, efficient communication. Don't use specialized terms, however, if you have reason to believe that your reader or listener may misunderstand them.

Slang

Slang is composed of informal words with arbitrary and extravagantly changed meanings. Slang words quickly go out of fashion because they are no longer appealing when everyone begins to understand them. Consider the following excerpt from an e-mail sent by a ski resort company president to his executive team: "Well guys, the results of our customer survey are in and I'm massively stoked by what I'm hearing. Most of our customers are totally happy with the goods, and I just want to congratulate all my peeps on a job well done!"

The meaning here, if the speaker really intended to impart any, is considerably obscured by the use of slang. Good communicators, of course, aim at clarity and avoid unintelligible slang.

Clichés

Clichés are expressions that have become exhausted by overuse. These expressions lack not only freshness but also clarity. Some have no meaning for people who are new to our culture. The following partial list contains representative clichés you should avoid in business writing.

Clichés are dull and sometimes ambiguous.

below the belt	keep your nose to the grindstone
better than new	last but not least
beyond the shadow of a doubt	make a bundle
easier said than done	pass with flying colours
exception to the rule	quick as a flash
fill the bill	shoot from the hip
first and foremost	stand your ground
hard facts	true to form
	one in a million

Precise Verbs

Effective writing creates meaningful images in the mind of the reader. Such writing is marked by robust, concrete, and descriptive words. Ineffective writing is often dulled by insipid, abstract, and generalized words. The most direct way to improve lifeless writing is through using precise verbs. Precise verbs describe action in a way that is understandable for the reader. These verbs deliver the force of the sentence. Select verbs that will help the reader see precisely what is happening.

Precise verbs make your writing forceful, clear, and lively.

General   Our salesperson will *contact* you next week.
Precise   Our salesperson will (*telephone*, *fax*, *e-mail*, *visit*) you next week.

| General | The CEO *said* that we should contribute. |
| Precise | The CEO (*urged, pleaded, demanded*) that we contribute. |

| General | We must *consider* this problem. |
| Precise | We must (*clarify, remedy, rectify*) this problem. |

| General | The newspaper was *affected* by the strike. |
| Precise | The newspaper was (*crippled, silenced, demoralized*) by the strike. |

The power of a verb is diminished when it is needlessly converted to a noun. This happens when verbs such as *acquire, establish,* and *develop* are made into nouns (*acquisition, establishment,* and *development*). These nouns then receive the central emphasis in the sentence. In the following pairs of sentences, observe how forceful the original verbs are compared with their noun forms.

| Weak | *Acquisition* of park lands was made recently by the provincial government. (Noun-centred) |
| Strong | The provincial government *acquired* park lands recently. (Verb-centred) |

| Weak | The webmaster and the designer had a *discussion* concerning graphics. (Noun-centred) |
| Strong | The webmaster and the designer *discussed* graphics. (Verb-centred) |

| Weak | Both companies must grant *approval* of the merger. (Noun-centred) |
| Strong | Both companies must *approve* the merger. (Verb-centred) |

Concrete Nouns

Quick Check

Concrete nouns help readers visualize the meanings of words.

Nouns name persons, places, and things. Abstract nouns name concepts that are difficult to visualize, such as *automation, function, justice, institution, integrity, form, judgment,* and *environment.* Concrete nouns name objects that are more easily imagined, such as *desk, car,* and *light bulb.* Nouns describing a given object can range from the very abstract to the very concrete—for example, *object, motor vehicle, car, convertible, Mustang.* All of these words or phrases can be used to describe a Mustang convertible. However, a reader would have difficulty envisioning a Mustang convertible when given just the word *object* or even *motor vehicle* or *car.*

In business writing, help your reader "see" what you mean by using concrete language.

| General | a *change* in our budget |
| Concrete | a *10 percent reduction* in our budget |

| General | *that company's product* |
| Concrete | *Motorola's Ultra Express* pager |

| General | a *person* called |
| Concrete | *Mrs. Tomei, the administrative assistant,* called |

| General | we *improved* the assembly line |
| Concrete | we *installed 26 advanced Unimate robots* on the assembly line |

Vivid Adjectives

Including highly descriptive, dynamic adjectives makes writing more vivid and concrete. Be careful, though, neither to overuse them nor to lose objectivity in selecting them.

General	The report was on time.
Vivid	The *detailed 12-page report* was submitted on time.

General	Clayton needs a better truck.
Vivid	Clayton needs a *rugged*, *four-wheel-drive Dodge* truck.

General	We enjoyed the movie.
Vivid	We enjoyed the *entertaining* and *absorbing* movie.
Overkill	We enjoyed the *gutsy*, *exciting*, *captivating*, and *thoroughly marvellous* movie.

A thesaurus (on your computer or in a book) helps you select precise words and increase your vocabulary.

The Process of Proofreading

Once you have the message in its final form, it's time to proofread. Don't proofread earlier because you may waste time checking items that are eventually changed or omitted.

What to Watch for in Proofreading

Careful proofreaders check for problems in these areas:

- **Spelling.** Now's the time to consult the dictionary. Is *recommend* spelled with one or two *c*'s? Do you mean *affect* or *effect*? Use your computer spell checker, but don't rely on it. See the Communication Workshop section on pages 90–91 to learn more about the benefits and hazards of computer spell checkers.
- **Grammar.** Locate sentence subjects. Do their verbs agree with them? Do pronouns agree with their antecedents? Review the principles in the Grammar/Mechanics Handbook if necessary. The Communication Workshop discusses grammar checkers more extensively, but we recommend not using them until you've mastered grammar, mechanics, and punctuation on your own.
- **Punctuation.** Make sure that introductory clauses are followed by commas. In compound sentences put commas before coordinating conjunctions (*and*, *or*, *but*, *nor*). Double-check your use of semicolons and colons.
- **Names and numbers.** Compare all names and numbers with their sources, because inaccuracies are not immediately visible. Especially verify the spelling of the names of individuals receiving the message. Most of us immediately dislike someone who misspells our name.
- **Format.** Be sure that letters, printed memos, and reports are balanced on the page. Compare their parts and format with those of standard documents shown in Appendix A. If you indent paragraphs, be certain that all are indented.
- **Consistency.** Make sure all words are spelled and formatted the same way throughout your document. For example, spelling *cheque* the Canadian way three times and then twice the American way (*check*) reduces your credibility as a business writer and confuses readers.

Good proofreaders check spelling, grammar, punctuation, names, numbers, format, and consistency.

How to Proofread Routine Documents

Most routine messages, including e-mails, require proofreading. Use the down arrow to reveal one line at a time, focusing your attention at the bottom of the screen. Read carefully for faults such as omitted or doubled words.

For routine messages such as printed letters or memos, a safer proofreading method is reading from a printed copy. You're more likely to find errors and to observe the tone. Your words convey status. In fact, recent research shows that lower-status employees tend to write longer, wordier e-mails, while higher-status

Routine documents need proofreading.

employees write short messages, often with poor grammar and spelling. It is generally only the higher-status employees who can get away with poor grammar and spelling.[2] Use standard proofreading marks, shown in Figure 4.2, to indicate changes.

How to Proofread Complex Documents

Quick Check

For both routine and complex documents, it's best to proofread from a printed copy, not from a computer screen.

Long, complex, or important documents demand more careful proofreading using the following techniques:

- Print a copy, preferably double-spaced, and set it aside for some time. You'll be more alert after a breather.
- Allow adequate time to proofread carefully. A common excuse for sloppy proofreading is lack of time.
- Be prepared to find errors. One student confessed, "I can find other people's errors, but I can't seem to locate my own." Psychologically, we don't expect to find errors, and we don't want to find them. You can overcome this obstacle by anticipating errors and congratulating, not criticizing, yourself each time you find one.
- Read the message at least twice—once for word meanings and once for grammar/mechanics. For very long documents (book chapters and long articles or reports), read a third time to verify consistency in formatting.
- Reduce your reading speed. Concentrate on individual words rather than ideas.
- For documents that must be perfect, have someone read the message aloud. Spell names and difficult words, note capitalization, and read punctuation.
- Use standard proofreading marks, shown in Figure 4.2, to indicate changes. A more complete list of proofreading marks appears in Appendix B.

FIGURE 4.2 Proofreading Marks

Quick Check

Proofreaders use these standard marks to indicate revisions.

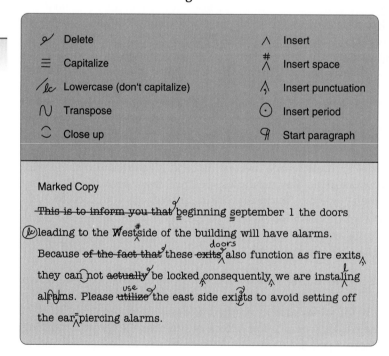

Chapter 4 Revising and Proofreading Business Messages

NEL

Your word processing program may include a style or grammar checker. These programs generally analyze aspects of your writing style, including readability level and use of passive voice, trite expressions, split infinitives, and wordy expressions. Most programs use sophisticated technology (and a lot of computer memory) to identify significant errors. In addition to finding spelling and typographical errors, grammar checkers can find subject–verb nonagreement, word misuse, spacing irregularities, punctuation problems, and many other faults. But they won't find everything, as you will see in the Communication Workshop below. While grammar and spell checkers can help you a great deal, you are the final proofreader.

Summing Up and Looking Forward

Revision is the most important part of the writing process. To revise for clarity and conciseness, look for wordy phrases that can be shortened (such as *more or less*). Eliminate wordy prepositional phrases (*in all probability*), long lead-ins (*This is to inform you that*), outdated expressions (*pursuant to your request*), needless adverbs (*definitely, very*), and fillers (*there are*). Also watch for repetitious words and redundancies (*combined together*). Use jargon only when it is clear to receivers, and avoid slang and clichés altogether. The best writing includes precise verbs, concrete nouns, and vivid adjectives. After revising a message, you're ready for the last step in the writing process: proofreading. Watch for irregularities in spelling, grammar, punctuation, names and numbers, and format. Although routine messages may be proofread on the screen, you will have better results if you proofread from a printed copy. Complex documents should be printed, put away for a while, and then proofread several times.

In Chapters 2, 3, and 4 you've studied the writing and revision process. You've also learned many practical techniques for becoming an effective business communicator. Now it's time for you to put these techniques to work. Chapter 5 introduces you to writing e-mails and memos, the most frequently used forms of communication for most businesspeople. Later chapters present letters and reports.

Critical Thinking

1. "A real writer can sit down at a computer and create a perfect document the first time." Do you agree or disagree? Why?
2. Carefully written short messages often take longer to write than longer messages. Do you agree or disagree? Why?
3. Because clichés are familiar and have been used for long periods of time, do they help clarify writing?
4. If your boss writes in a flowery, formal tone and relies on outdated expressions, should you follow that style also?
5. Is it unethical to help a friend revise a report when you know that the friend will be turning that report in for a grade?

Chapter Review

6. How is revising different from proofreading?

7. Why is conciseness especially important in business?

8. What is a long lead-in? Give an original example.

9. What's wrong with using adverbs such as *very*, *really*, and *actually*?

10. What is a redundancy? Give an example.

11. What is jargon? When can it be used? What are examples in your field?

12. What happens when a verb (such as *describe*) is converted to a noun expression (*give a description*)? Provide an original example.

13. Should you proofread when you are writing or after you finish? Why?

14. What six areas should you especially pay attention to when you proofread?

15. How does the proofreading of routine and complex documents differ?

Writing Improvement Exercises

Wordiness. Revise the following sentences to eliminate wordy phrases, wordy prepositional phrases, outdated expressions, and long lead-ins.

Example: This is to notify you that at a later date we may be able to submit the report.

Revision: We may be able to submit the report later.

16. In the event that the response is at all favourable, we will in all probability start our Web site in the month of January.

17. This is to advise you that beginning with the date of April 1 all charges made after that date will be charged to your new credit card number.

18. Pursuant to your request, enclosed please find a copy of your August statement.

19. In view of the fact that our sales are increasing in a gradual manner, we must secure a loan in the amount of $50,000.

20. This is to let you know that you should feel free to use your credit card for the purpose of purchasing household items for a period of 60 days.

Needless Adverbs, Fillers, Repetitious Words. Revise the following sentences to eliminate needless adverbs, fillers (such as *there is* and *it is*), and unintentional repetition.

21. It is Web-based technology that is really streamlining administrative processes and reducing business costs for businesses.

22. It is certainly clear that there are many younger managers who are very eager but who are actually unprepared to assume management or leadership roles.

23. There are four employees who definitely spend more time in Internet recreational uses on the Internet than they spend on business-related Internet work.

24. There are definitely five advantages that computers have over a human decision maker.

Redundancies, Jargon, Slang, Clichés. Revise the following sentences to eliminate redundancies, jargon, slang, clichés, and any other wordiness.

Example: Last but not least, Tobias collected together as much support material as possible to avoid getting burned in cash losses or bottom-line profits.

Revision: Finally, Tobias collected as much support material as possible to avoid losing cash or profits.

25. First and foremost, we plan to emphasize an instructional training program.

26. It was the consensus of opinion of members of the committee that the committee should meet at 11 a.m. in the morning.

27. If you will refer back to the contract, you will definitely find that there are specific specifications to prevent anyone from blowing the budget.

28. This memorandum serves as an advance warning that all books and magazines borrowed from the library must be taken back to the library by June 1.

29. In view of the fact that our last presentation failed, we are at this point in time convinced that we must include only the most absolutely essential selling points this time.

30. In the normal course of events, we would wait until such time as we had adequate enough credit reports.

Precise Verbs. Revise these sentences, centring the action in the verbs.

Example: Ms. Tulita gave an appraisal of the Web site.
Revision: Ms. Tulita appraised the Web site.

31. The webmaster made a description of the project.

32. Can you bring about a change in our company travel policy?

33. Web-based customer service will produce the effect of reduction in overall costs.

34. In writing this proposal, we must make application of new government regulations.

35. The board of directors made a recommendation affirming abandonment of the pilot project.

36. An investigator made a determination of the fire damages.

37. We hope to have production of our new line of products by January.

38. The duty of the comptroller is verification of departmental budgets.

39. Please make a correction in my account to reflect my late payment.

Vivid Words. Revise the following sentences to include vivid and concrete language. Add appropriate words.

Example: They said it was a long way off.
Revision: Management officials announced that the merger would not take place for
                two years.

40. Our new copier is fast.

41. An employee from that company notified us about the change in date.

42. Please contact them soon.

43. They said that the movie they saw was good.

44. Workers improved when they saw the big picture.

45. The report was weak.

Grammar/Mechanics Review—4

The following sentences contain errors in grammar, punctuation, capitalization, number style, usage, and spelling. Pay special attention to eliminating wordiness. Below each sentence write a corrected version.

Example: Inasmuch as our sales dropped fifty thousand dollars we are now fully cog-
               nizant of our competition.
Revision: Because our sales dropped $50,000, we are now aware of our competition.

1. This is to inform you that for a period of 2 weeks we must place a restriction on parking.

2. We made a plan to keep all our customers names and addresses in Mr. Betz database.

3. There are three laptop problems that have been solved, weight, size, and power consumption.

4. In view of the fact that the envelope was addressed to Manuel and I, him and me should receive the free gift.

5. Pursuant to your e-mail message of the 15th please be advised that your shipment was sent June 9.

6. Acting as President the budget was immediately signed by Rashida.

7. Although I'm sure it was him who sent the e-mail message the C.E.O. doesn't seem to care.

8. I am writing this e-mail to let you know that the meeting is May 15th.

9. The companys principle office is in Bella Coola however, most shipments come from Powell River.

10. If you are looking for a laptop that is small in size try the datapro superslim 505 model.

11. We expect 17 employees to attend the 2 meetings on november 2nd.

12. To improve you're language skills the rules of grammar must be applied.

13. The Vice-President and the Human Resources Director made a distribution of complementary tickets to the concert.

14. New corporate taxes will effect all corporations in the near future.

15. Dr. Erek M. Sheps who is one of the principle researchers sighted considerable evidence to support his arguement.

Grammar/Mechanics Challenge—4

Document for Revision

The following e-mail has faults in grammar, punctuation, conversational language, outdated expressions, sexist language, concise wording, long lead-ins, and many other problems. Use standard proofreading marks (see Appendix B) to correct the errors. Study the guidelines in the Grammar/Mechanics Handbook to sharpen your skills. When you finish, your instructor may show you the revised version of this letter.

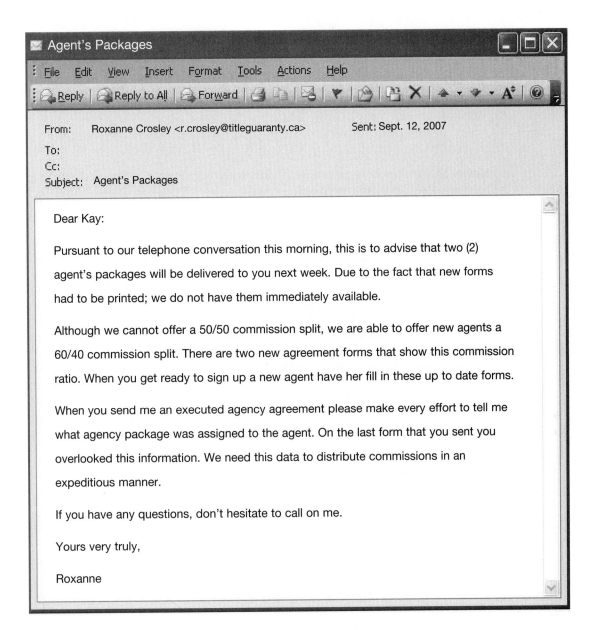

Agent's Packages

File　Edit　View　Insert　Format　Tools　Actions　Help

Reply　｜　Reply to All　｜　Forward

From: Roxanne Crosley <r.crosley@titleguaranty.ca>　Sent: Sept. 12, 2007

To:

Cc:

Subject: Agent's Packages

Dear Kay:

Pursuant to our telephone conversation this morning, this is to advise that two (2) agent's packages will be delivered to you next week. Due to the fact that new forms had to be printed; we do not have them immediately available.

Although we cannot offer a 50/50 commission split, we are able to offer new agents a 60/40 commission split. There are two new agreement forms that show this commission ratio. When you get ready to sign up a new agent have her fill in these up to date forms.

When you send me an executed agency agreement please make every effort to tell me what agency package was assigned to the agent. On the last form that you sent you overlooked this information. We need this data to distribute commissions in an expeditious manner.

If you have any questions, don't hesitate to call on me.

Yours very truly,

Roxanne

Grammar and Spell Checkers

Nearly all word processing programs now include grammar and spell checkers to help writers with their proofreading tasks.

Grammar Checkers

When first introduced, grammar and style checkers were not too helpful. They were limited in scope, awkward to use, and identified many questionable "errors." But today's grammar checkers detect a considerable number of legitimate writing lapses. Microsoft Word finds faults in word use (such as *there, their*) capitalization, punctuation, subject-verb agreement, sentence structure, singular and plural endings, repeated words, wordy expressions, gender-specific expressions, and many other problems.

How does a grammar checker work? Let's say you typed the sentence *The office and its equipment is for sale.* You would see a wavy green line appear under *is*. When you point your cursor at "Tools" in the tool bar and click on "Spelling and Grammar," a box opens up. It identifies the subject-verb agreement error and suggests the verb *are* as a correction. When you click on "Change," the error is corrected.

Spell Checkers

Spell checkers compare your typed words with those in the computer's memory. Microsoft Word uses a wavy red line to underline misspelled words as you type them. Although some writers dismiss spell checkers as an annoyance, most of us are only too happy to have our typos and misspelled words detected. What's annoying is that spell checkers don't find all the problems. In the following poem, for example, only two problems were detected (*your* and *it's*).

I have a spell checkers
    That came with my PC.
It plainly marks four my review
    Mistakes I cannot sea.
I've run this poem threw it,
    I'm sure your pleased too no.
Its letter perfect in it's weigh
    My checker tolled me sew.
            —Anonymous

The lesson to be learned here is that you can't rely totally on any spell checker. Homonyms—words that sound the same but are spelled differently—may not be highlighted because the spell checker doesn't know what meaning you have in mind. That's why you're wise to print out important messages and proofread them word by word.

Career Application

Your boss, Serena Simkus, is developing an in-service training program on word processing. She wants you to analyze the effectiveness of your computer's grammar and spell checkers. Your brief report will become part of a presentation to new employees.

Your Task

- You decide to try out your software with a set of test sentences. At a computer that has grammar and spell checking software, type the following four sentences, including all the errors. Print the sentences.
  1. Is the companys office located on riverside drive in new york city.
  2. The manger adviced her to make a consciensous effort to improve.
  3. There house and it's furniture was allready sold before they moved to saskatoon.
  4. My friend and me was going to apply for the job in june but we were to late.
- For each sentence, underline the errors the software identified. Then circle the errors that the software missed. (A word may contain only one error.) Total your underlines and circles. Make notes on the kinds of errors identified and the kinds missed. *Tip:* You should find 20 errors.
- On the basis of your findings, as well as some Web and library research into the pros and cons of grammar and spelling checkers, how would you rate the usefulness of your computer's grammar and spell checkers? What are the strengths and weaknesses?
- What advice would you give to employees about relying on these programs for proofreading?
- Stage an in-class debate on the topic "Resolved that grammar and spell checkers should not be relied upon by business writers."
- Depending on your own opinion, write a memo to your boss, Serena Simkus, suggesting what kind of policy she should adopt on the use of grammar and spell checkers.

Related Web site: Check out the following documents from the University of Manitoba and Blogos for a sampling of opinions on the efficacy and ethics of grammar and spell-checking software: <writing.umn.edu/docs/home/ write@uFall_2001.pdf> and <www.multilingualblog.com/index.php/weblog/ the_ethics_of_grammar_checkers>

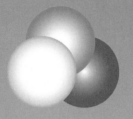

Corresponding at Work

5 E-Mails and Memos

E-mail isn't just the message you write, it's also a powerful way to distribute information. It's a cost-efficient way for people with colleagues and clients in far-flung locations to stay in immediate contact. For example, last week instead of couriering a 40-page contract to one of my overseas clients, I just e-mailed it and she got it immediately.[1]

Peter Schneider, *lawyer, Gowling Lafleur Henderson LLP*

LEARNING OBJECTIVES

1. Explain the importance of internal communication.
2. Analyze the writing process as it applies to e-mails and memos.
3. Describe how to use e-mail effectively and safely.
4. Explain and demonstrate a writing plan for e-mails and memos.
5. Demonstrate several ways to improve readability by using listing techniques and graphic highlighting.
6. Write e-mails and memos that inform.
7. Write e-mails and memos that make requests.
8. Write e-mails and memos that respond.

The Importance of Internal Communication

Electronic mail has become an important tool in reducing barriers created by size and distance. Employees can almost instantly communicate with each other whether they are working in separate rooms, in separate buildings, or on separate continents. As Peter Schneider alludes to above, the other revolutionary aspect of e-mail is its capacity as a channel of communication. The act of writing e-mails is not so much what's significant (though as you'll see there are important differences between letter writing and e-mail writing) as is the ability to do things with e-mails, such as send attachments. In fact, e-mail is becoming so popular that more traditional channels of communication like the telephone and fax are becoming less widely used.

At many companies today internal communication has become increasingly important. Organizations are flattening chains of command, building collaborative work teams, and expecting all employees to make decisions and take action. Today's knowledge workers find that they must collect, exchange, and evaluate information about the products and services they offer. Management also needs input from employees to respond rapidly to global market realities.

This growing demand for information means increasing use of e-mail. Until the early 1990s hard-copy memos were the most common channel for exchanging internal communication. Now, however, e-mail is the favoured medium.

Canadians are "world-class click potatoes," logging more time online than users in any other country. We spend an average of 15 hours per month online using the Internet and sending e-mail.[2] Businesspeople are writing more messages than ever before, and using e-mail to distribute those messages more often. Although routine, e-mails and memos require preparation because they may travel farther than you expect. A novice market researcher in Calgary, for example, was eager to please her boss. When asked to report on the progress of her project, she quickly e-mailed a summary of her work. It contained numerous grammatical mistakes. Later that week a vice-president asked her boss how the project was progressing. Her boss forwarded the market researcher's hurried e-mail memo. Unfortunately, the resulting poor impression was difficult for the new employee to overcome.

Developing skill in writing e-mails and memos brings you two important benefits. First, well-written documents are likely to achieve their goals. Second, such documents enhance your image within the organization. Individuals identified as competent, professional writers are noticed and rewarded; most often, they are the ones promoted into management positions.

This chapter concentrates on routine e-mails and memos. You'll study the writing process, as well as how to organize and format messages that inform, request, and respond. These straightforward messages follow the direct strategy because their topics are not sensitive and require little persuasion.

The Writing Process

Careful e-mail and memo writing takes time—especially at first. By following a systematic plan and practising your skill, however, you can speed up your efforts and greatly improve the product. The effort you make to improve your communication skills can pay big dividends. Frequently, your speaking and writing abilities determine how much influence you'll have in your organization. To make the best impression and to write the most effective messages, follow the three-phase writing process.

Phase 1: Analysis, Anticipation, and Adaptation

In Phase 1 you'll need to spend some time analyzing your task. It's amazing how many of us put our pens or computers into gear before engaging our minds. Ask yourself three important questions:

- **Do I really need to write this memo or e-mail?** A phone call or a quick visit to a nearby coworker might be more effective—and save the time and expense of a written message. On the other hand, some written messages are needed to provide a permanent record. Another decision is whether to write a hard-copy memo or send an e-mail. Familiarize yourself with your organization's preferred method. Deviating from the preferred method might signal a degree of seriousness or importance that you may not intend. Consider as well that an important message sent as e-mail could become lost among the many light-hearted and inconsequential e-mails people receive during a typical work day.

- **Why am I writing?** Determine why you are writing and what you hope to achieve. Deciding your goals for writing will help you recognize what the important points are and where to place them.
- **How will the reader react?** Visualize the reader and the effect your message will have. Consider ways to shape the message to benefit the reader.

Phase 2: Research, Organization, and Composition

In Phase 2 you'll first want to gather and review any information you may have on your subject such as previous messages, meeting minutes or other notes you may keep in a work file. Make an outline of the points you wish to cover. If you are responding to a message, you can write your notes on the document you are answering. For e-mails consider printing the message and adding notes to the printed copy.

Phase 3: Revision, Proofreading, and Evaluation

Careful writers revise their messages, proofread the final copy, and try to evaluate the success of their communication before clicking the send button.

- **Revise for clarity.** Viewed from the receiver's perspective, are the ideas clear? Do they need more explanation? If the e-mail is forwarded on to others, will those receivers need further explanation? Consider having a colleague critique your message if it is an important one.
- **Proofread for correctness.** Are the sentences gramatically correct and punctuated properly? Did you overlook any typos or misspelled words?
- **Plan for feedback.** How will you know if this message is successful? You can improve feedback by asking yourself questions such as *Do these suggestions meet our needs? Have I concluded my message by soliciting feedback?*

Developing a Writing Plan for E-Mails and Memos

In this book you will be shown a number of writing plans appropriate for different messages. These plans provide a skeleton; they are the bones of a message. Writers provide the flesh. Simply plugging in phrases or someone else's words won't work. Good writers provide details and link their ideas with transitions to create fluent and meaningful messages. However, a writing plan helps you get started and gives you ideas about what to include. At first, you will probably rely on these plans considerably. As you progress, they will become less important. Later in the book no plans are provided.

Here is a general writing plan for a routine e-mail or memo that is not expected to create displeasure or resistance.

 ### Writing Plan for Routine E-Mails and Memos

- **Subject line.** Summarize contents.
- **Opening.** State the main idea.
- **Body.** Provide background information and explain the main idea.
- **Closing.** Request action, summarize message, or present closing thought.

Writing the Subject Line

Probably the most important part of an e-mail or memo is the subject line. It should summarize the central idea and provide quick identification. It is usually written in an abbreviated style, often without articles (*a*, *an*, *the*). It need not be a complete sentence, and it does not end with a period. E-mail subject lines are particularly important, since meaningless ones may cause readers to delete a message without ever opening it. Good subject lines, such as the following, are specific, eye-catching, and talking (that is, they contain a verb form):

✓ Quick Check

A subject line must be concise but meaningful.

Subject: Funding Sources for Youth Health and Safety Internship Program
Subject: Recommendations to Improve Network Security
Subject: Staff Meeting to Discuss Summer Vacation Schedules

Opening with the Main Idea

Most memos and e-mails cover routine, nonsensitive information that can be handled in a straightforward manner. Begin by frontloading; that is, reveal the main idea immediately. Even though the purpose of a memo or e-mail is summarized in the subject line, that purpose should be restated—and amplified—in the first sentence. Some readers skip the subject line and plunge right into the first sentence. Notice how the following indirect memo openers can be improved by frontloading.

✓ Quick Check

Frontloading means revealing the main idea immediately.

Indirect Opening

This is to inform you that for the past six months we have been examining benefits as part of our negotiation package under a contract that expires soon.

As you may know, employees in Document Production have been complaining about eye fatigue as a result of the overhead fluorescent lighting in their centre.

Direct Opening

Please review the following four changes in our benefits package and let us know your preference by January 1.

To improve lighting in Document Production, I recommend that we purchase high-intensity desk lamps.

Explaining Clearly in the Body

In the body of the message, explain the main idea. If you are asking for detailed information, arrange your questions in logical order. If you are providing information, group similar information together. When a considerable amount of information is involved, use a separate paragraph for each topic. Use effective transitions between paragraphs.

Design your data for easy comprehension by using bulleted lists, headings, and tables. You'll learn more about writing lists shortly. All these techniques make readers understand important points quickly. Compare the following two versions of the same message. Notice how the graphic devices of bullets, columns, headings, and white space make the main points easier to comprehend.

✓ Quick Check

Organize the message logically, keeping similar information grouped together.

Hard-to-Read Paragraph

Effective immediately are the following air travel guidelines. Between now and December 31, only account executives may take company-approved trips. These individuals will be allowed to take a maximum of two trips per year, and they are to travel economy class or discount airline only.

Improved with Graphic Highlighting

Effective immediately are the following air travel guidelines:

- Who may travel: Account executives only
- How many trips: A maximum of two trips yearly
- By when: Between now and December 31
- Air class: Economy or discount airline only

In addition to highlighting important information, pay attention to the tone of your message. Although memos are generally informal, they should also be professional. Remember that e-mail messages are not telephone conversations. Don't be overly casual, jocular, or blunt. Do attempt to establish a conversational tone by using occasional contractions (*won't, didn't, couldn't*) and personal pronouns (*I, me, we*).

Closing the Message

Generally, end an e-mail or memo with (1) action information, dates, or deadlines; (2) a summary of the message; or (3) a closing thought. Here again the value of thinking through the message before actually writing it becomes apparent. The closing is where readers look for deadlines and action language. An effective e-mail or memo closing might be *Please submit your report by June 1. We need to review your recommendations before our July planning session.*

In more complex messages a summary of main points may be an appropriate closing. If no action request is made and a closing summary is unnecessary, you might end with a simple concluding thought (*I'm happy to provide answers to your questions* or *This project sounds like a good idea*). Although you needn't close messages to coworkers with goodwill statements such as those found in letters to customers or clients, some closing thought is often necessary to prevent a feeling of abruptness.

Closings can show gratitude or encourage feedback with remarks such as *Thanks for your help on this project* or *Do you have any suggestions on this proposal?* Other closings look forward to what's next, such as *How would you like to proceed?* Avoid trite expressions, such as *Please let me know if I may be of further assistance.* Whenever possible, the closing paragraph of a request should be end-dated. An end date sets a deadline for the requested action and gives a reason for this action to be completed by the deadline. Such end-dating prevents procrastination and allows the reader to plan a course of action to ensure completion by the date given. Giving a reason adds credibility to a deadline.

> Please submit your order by December 1. We need to know the number of labels required for mailing the year-end reports January 15.

Putting It All Together

The memo shown in Figure 5.1 is the first draft of a message Cynthia Chomsky wrote to her team leader. Although it contains solid information, the first version is so wordy and poorly organized that the reader has trouble grasping its significance. Cynthia's revised message opens directly. Both the subject line and the first sentence explain the purpose for writing. Notice how much easier the revised version is to read. Bullets and boldfaced headings emphasize the actions necessary to solve the database problems. Notice, too, that the revised version ends with a deadline and refers to the next action to be taken.

FIGURE 5.1 Revising a Draft Memo

Before

TO: Susan Hsu

This is in response to your recent inquiry about our customer database. Your message of May 9 said that you wanted to know how to deal with the database problems.

I can tell you that the biggest problem is that it contains a lot of outdated information, including customers who haven't purchased anything in five or more years. Another problem is that the old database is not compatible with the new Access database that is being used by our mailing service, and this makes it difficult to merge files.

I think I can solve both problems, however, by starting a new database. This would be the place where we put the names of all new customers. And we would have it entered into the Access database. The problem with outdated information could be solved by finding out if the customers in our old database wish to continue receiving our newsletter and product announcements. Finally, we would rekey the names of all active customers into the new database.

Fails to reveal purpose quickly and concisely

Does not help reader see the two problems or the three recommendations

Forgets to conclude with next action and end date

After

Design Source

Memo

To: Susan Hsu, Team Leader

From: Cynthia Chomsky, Marketing Associate

CC:

Date: May 15, 2006

Re: IMPROVING OUR CUSTOMER DATABASE

Subject line summarizes and identifies purpose

Opening states purpose concisely

As you requested, here are my recommendations for improving our customer database. The database has two major problems. First, it contains many names of individuals who have not made purchases in five or more years. Second, the format is not compatible with the new Access database used by our mailing service. The following procedures, however, should solve both problems:

Body organizes main points for readability

- **Start a new database.** Effective immediately, enter the names of all new customers in a new Access database.

- **Determine the status of customers in our old database.** Send out a mailing asking whether recipients wish to continue receiving our newsletter and product announcements.

- **Rekey the names of active customers in the new database.** Enter the names of all responding customers in our new database so that we have only one active database.

Closing mentions key benefit, provides deadline, and looks forward to next action

These changes will enable you, as team leader, to request mailings that go only to active customers. Please respond by May 20 with suggestions or other alternatives I could review. I will then investigate costs.

Because e-mail is an evolving communication channel, its formatting and usage conventions are still fluid. On the other hand, formatting memos has become much easier because of software templates. Whereas students used to learn how to create memos from scratch (see Appendix A for details), today students are just as often encouraged to choose a template in their word processing program (e.g., Microsoft Word's Professional Memo template) and begin filling in their content. Once in the workforce, people are usually encouraged to use a company memo template. While memo formatting is standard and rarely varies, e-mail users and authorities, for instance, do not always agree on what's appropriate for salutations and closings. The following suggestion can guide you in formatting most e-mail messages, but always check with your organization to observe its practices.

Guide Words. Following the guide word *To*, some writers insert just the recipient's e-mail address, such as *pwyatt@accountpro.com*. Other writers prefer to include the receiver's full name plus the e-mail address, as shown in Figure 5.2. By including full names in the *To* and *From* slots, both receivers and senders are better able to identify the message. The order of *Date, To, From, Subject,* and other guide words varies depending on your e-mail program and whether you are sending or receiving the message.

> ✓ **Quick Check**
>
> Although e-mail formatting style is still developing, all messages contain *To, From, Date,* and *Subject* lines.

Most e-mail programs automatically add the current date after *Date*. On the *Cc* line (which stands for *carbon* or *courtesy copy*) you can type the address of anyone who is to receive a copy of the message. Remember to send copies only to those people directly involved with the message. Most e-mail programs also include a line for *Bcc* (*blind carbon copy*); this sends a copy without the addressee's knowledge. Many savvy writers today use *Bcc* for the names and addresses of a list of receivers, a technique that avoids revealing the addresses to the entire group. On the *Subject* line, identify the subject of the memo. Be sure to include enough information to be clear and compelling.

Salutation. Many e-mail writers omit a salutation because they consider the message a memo. In the past, hard-copy memos were sent only to company insiders, and salutations were omitted. However, when e-mail messages travel to outsiders, omitting a salutation seems curt and unfriendly. Because the message is more like a letter, a salutation is appropriate (such as *Dear Jake; Hi Jake; Greetings;* or just *Jake*). Including a salutation is also a visual cue to where the message begins. Many messages are transmitted or forwarded with such long headers that finding the beginning of the message can be difficult. A salutation helps, as shown in Figure 5.2. Other writers do not use a salutation; instead, they use the name of the recipient in the first sentence.

> ✓ **Quick Check**
>
> Salutations may be omitted in messages to close colleagues, but they are generally used in messages to others.

Body. The body of a business e-mail should be typed with upper- and lowercase characters—never in all-uppercase or all-lowercase characters. Cover just one topic, and try to keep the total message as concise as possible. To assist you, many e-mail programs have basic text-editing features, such as cut, copy, paste, and word wrap. Avoid boldface and italics unless you know the recipient's computer can display them. Often, boldface and italics can create a string of control characters that may cause chaos on the recipient's computer. Finally, any time you have more than two points to make, get into the habit of using graphic highlighting (bullets, numbering, extra spaces). Graphic highlighting helps to distinguish between your points and makes your e-mail easier on the reader's eyes.

> ✓ **Quick Check**
>
> Closing lines (or a signature block) should name the writer and provide sufficient information for identification.

Closing Lines. Writers of e-mail messages sent within organizations may omit closings and even skip their names at the end of messages. They can omit these items because receivers recognize them from identification in the opening lines.

FIGURE 5.2 Typical E-Mail Request Message

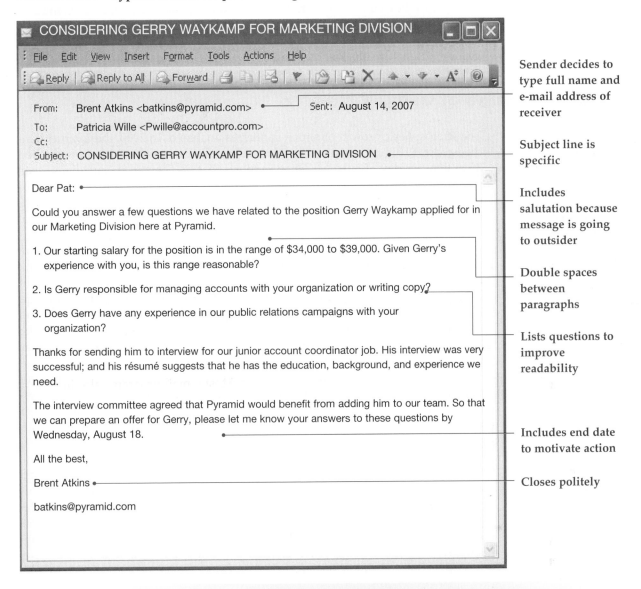

Sender decides to type full name and e-mail address of receiver

Subject line is specific

Includes salutation because message is going to outsider

Double spaces between paragraphs

Lists questions to improve readability

Includes end date to motivate action

Closes politely

Tips for Formatting E-mail

- After *To*, type the receiver's e-mail address. If you include the receiver's name, enclose the address in angle brackets <like this>.
- After *From*, type your name and e-mail address, if your program does not insert it automatically.
- After *Subject*, provide a specific description of your message.
- Insert the addresses of anyone receiving carbon or blind copies.
- Include a salutation (such as *Dear Pat, Hi Pat, Greetings*) or weave the receiver's name into the first line. Some writers omit a salutation.
- Set your line length for no more than 80 characters. If you expect your message to be forwarded, set it for 60 characters.
- Use word wrap rather than pressing Enter at line ends.
- Double-space between paragraphs.
- Do not type in all caps or in all lower-case letters.
- Include a complimentary close, your name, and (if you wish) your address.

But for outside messages, a writer might include a closing such as *Cheers* or *Best* or *Regards* followed by the writer's name and e-mail address (because some systems do not transmit your address automatically). If the recipient is unlikely to know you, it's wise to include your title and organization. Veteran e-mail users include a signature block containing their contact information.

The Challenge of Using E-Mail

Quick Check

E-mail has become an essential means of communication within organizations as well as with customers and suppliers.

The stratospheric growth of e-mail continues unabated. In 2000, the Internet handled about 10 billion e-mails a day. Estimates indicate e-mail use has now reached 35 billion per day.[3] Statistics Canada reports that 60 percent of Canadians use a computer in their job with the majority (78 percent) using one daily. A full 54 percent of those workers used their computer for Internet access and e-mail.[4] Suddenly, companies find that e-mail has become an indispensable means of internal communication as well as an essential link to customers and suppliers.

At the same time, as a recent high-profile case demonstrates, companies are also finding the widespread use of e-mail problematic. A major Canadian bank recently sued ten of its former employees for what it claimed was illegal use of BlackBerrys it had assigned these employees.[5] The employees used the communication devices to send e-mails to each other discussing the setting up of a new and rival company to the bank. The employees obviously didn't realize that the e-mails sent using the BlackBerrys were not private, but rather that the bank was fully within its rights to store these e-mails.

Today, the average e-mail message may remain in the company's computer system for several years. And, in an increasing number of cases, the only impression a person has of the e-mail writer is from a transmitted message; they never actually meet. That's why it's important to take the time to organize your thoughts, compose carefully, and ensure correct grammar and punctuation.

Savvy e-mail business communicators are also learning its dangers. They know that their messages can travel (intentionally or unintentionally) to unexpected destinations. A quickly drafted note may end up in the boss's mailbox or forwarded to an unintended receiver. Making matters worse, computers—like elephants—never forget. Even erased messages can remain on disk drives. The case involving the bank discussed above is a cautionary tale for any company-employed business writer naive enough to assume e-mail is a simple, private, two-way communication system.

Smart E-Mail Practices

Despite its dangers and limitations, e-mail is increasingly the channel of choice for sending routine business messages. In large part, this increased popularity is a result of the advent of personal digital assistants (PDAs—BlackBerry and Palm Pilot are the best-known brands) that make it possible for people to carry their e-mail with them wherever they go. However, other channels of communication are still more effective for complex data or sensitive messages.

Getting Started. The following pointers will help you get off to a good start in using e-mail safely and effectively.

Quick Check

Composing with your word processing program generally produces better e-mail messages.

- **Compose offline.** Instead of dashing off hasty messages or worse, mistakenly sending a half-finished message, take the time to compose offline. Consider word processing and then cutting and pasting your message to your e-mail program. This method can help you avoid losing all your writing through some technical glitch or pressing the Send button before your message is complete.

- **Get the address right.** E-mail addresses can be long and complex, often including letters, numbers, dashes, and underscores. As with an address on an envelope, e-mail addresses are also unforgiving. Omit one character or misread the letter *l* for the number *1*, and your message will be returned. Solution: use your electronic address book frequently and use the reply feature in your e-mail program. Most e-mail programs include the correct e-mail address from the original message in the reply message. And double-check every address that you key in manually.
- **Avoid misleading subject lines.** With an abundance of "spam" (junk e-mail) clogging inboxes and the fear of computer viruses that are spread by e-mail attachments, many e-mail users ignore or delete messages with unclear subject lines. Make sure your subject line is specific and helpful. Generic tags such as "HELLO" and "GREAT DEAL" may cause your message to be deleted before it is opened.

Content, Tone, and Correctness. Although e-mail seems as casual as a telephone call, it's not. A telephone call has its own set of rules, as does a letter, but neither of these sets of rules applies to e-mail. Concentrating on tone, content, and correctness will help to reduce the potential for misinterpretation of e-mail messages. As well, since e-mail also produces a permanent record, think carefully about what you say and how you say it.

- **Be concise.** Don't burden readers with unnecessary information. Many e-mail recipients read dozens or even hundreds of e-mails every day. A concise message is appreciated. Organized and compelling messages will help to hold the reader's interest even if the e-mail contains many ideas.

Avoid sending e-mail messages that are longer than one screen.

- **Send only appropriate information.** Because e-mail seems like a telephone call or a person-to-person conversation, writers sometimes send sensitive, confidential, inflammatory, or potentially embarrassing messages. Information you consider appropriate, funny, or appealing may not be interpreted the same way by your audience. By sending an inappropriate message, you are also creating a permanent record that often does not go away even when deleted. Every message sent at work is a corporate communication for which both you and your employer are responsible.
- **Don't use e-mail to avoid contact.** Breaking bad news or resolving an argument through e-mail is not recommended. With e-mail you cannot rely on nonverbal communication, active listening techniques, and other face-to-face communication methods to ensure correct understanding of emotion and meaning. Imagine being fired by e-mail or having your job performance evaluated through e-mail. It's also not a good channel for dealing with conflict with supervisors, subordinates, or others. If there's any possibility of hurt feelings, pick up the telephone or pay the person a visit.

E-mail should not be used for bad news or angry messages.

- **Never respond when you're angry.** Always allow some time to compose yourself before responding to an upsetting message. You often come up with different and better alternatives after thinking about what was said. If possible, iron out differences in person.
- **Care about correctness.** People are still judged by their writing, whether electronic or paper-based. Sloppy e-mail messages (with missing apostrophes, haphazard spelling, and stream-of-consciousness writing) make readers work too hard. Readers quickly lose respect for writers of poor e-mails.
- **Resist humour and personal jokes.** Without the nonverbal cues conveyed by your face and your voice, humour can easily be misunderstood.

Avoid humorous or facetious expressions that may be misunderstood.

Netiquette. Although e-mail is an evolving communication channel, a number of rules of polite online interaction apply.

- **Limit the tendency to copy to your distribution list.** Send copies only to people who really need to see a message. It is unnecessary to document every business decision and action with an electronic paper trail.
- **Limit the tendency to reply to the entire cc list.** You should think carefully about whether your reply needs to be seen by everyone or just the person who sent you the message.
- **Don't automatically forward junk e-mail.** Internet jokes and other unnecessary messages such as warnings about new viruses, chain letters, or unusual fundraising campaigns are tiresome and valueless.
- **Consider using identifying labels.** When appropriate, add one of the following labels to the subject line: "ACTION" (action required, please respond); "FYI" (for your information, no response needed); "RE" (this is a reply to another message); "URGENT" (please respond immediately). These labels should be agreed upon among employees.
- **Use capital letters only for emphasis or for titles.** Avoid writing entire messages in all caps, which is equivalent to shouting.
- **Announce attachments.** If you're sending a lengthy attachment, tell your receiver. Consider summarizing or highlighting important aspects of the attachment briefly in the e-mail. Make sure the receiver can open the attachment you send. Some file formats cannot be opened on all computers.
- **Consider asking for permission before forwarding.** For messages containing private or project specific information, obtain approval before forwarding to others.

Replying to E-Mail. The following tips can save you time and frustration when answering messages.

"Have a seat. There are 342 email messages ahead of you."

- **Scan all messages in your inbox before replying to each individually.** Because subsequent messages often affect the way you respond, read them all first, especially all those from the same sender.
- **Don't automatically return the sender's message.** When replying, cut and paste the relevant parts. Avoid irritating your recipients by returning the entire "thread" or sequence of messages on a topic, unless the thread needs to be included to provide context for your remarks.
- **Revise the subject line if the topic changes.** When replying or continuing an e-mail exchange, revise the subject line as the topic changes.
- **Respond to messages quickly and efficiently.** Read them, then answer, delete, or file into a project-specific folder.

Personal Use. Remember that office computers are meant for work-related communication.

- **Don't use company computers for personal matters.** Unless your company specifically allows it, never use your employer's computers for personal messages, personal shopping, or entertainment.
- **Assume that all e-mail is monitored.** Employers can and do monitor e-mail.

Other Smart E-Mail Practices. Depending on your messages and audience, the following tips promote effective electronic communication.

- **Use graphic highlighting to improve readability of longer messages.** When a message is longer, help the reader with headings, bulleted lists, and perhaps an introductory summary that describes what will follow. Although these techniques lengthen a message, they shorten reading time.
- **Consider cultural differences.** When using this global tool, be especially clear and precise in your language. Remember that figurative clichés (*pull up stakes*, *playing second fiddle*), sports references (*hit a home run*, *play by the rules*), and slang (*cool*, *stoked*) can cause confusion abroad.
- **Double-check before hitting the Send button.** Have you included everything? Avoid the necessity of sending a second message, which makes you look careless. Edit for grammar and style and reread for fluency before sending.

Improving E-Mail and Memo Readability with Listing Techniques

Because readers of e-mail and memos are usually in a hurry, they want important information to stand out. One of the best ways to improve the readability of any message is by listing items. The information in e-mail and memos often lends itself to listing. A list is a group or series of related items, usually three or more. Since lists require fewer words than complete sentences, they can be read and understood quickly and easily. In writing lists, keep these general points in mind.

- **Make listed items parallel.** Listed items must all relate to the same topic, and they must be balanced grammatically. If one item is a single word but the next item requires a paragraph of explanation, the items are not suitable for listing.
- **Use bullets, numbers, or letters appropriately.** Numbers (1, 2, 3) and letters (a, b, c) suggest a hierarchy or sequence of operation; bullets merely separate.
- **Use generally accepted punctuation.** Most writers use a colon following the introduction to most lists. However, they don't use a colon if the listed items follow a verb or a preposition (for example, *the colours are red, yellow, and blue*). Use end punctuation only after complete sentences, and capitalize the first word of items listed vertically.

 Quick Check

You can improve the readability of a message by listing parallel items.

Parallelism

Instead of This

She likes *sleeping*, *eating*, and *to work*.

We are hiring the following: *sales clerks, managers who will function as supervisors,* and *people to work in offices.*

Try This

She likes *sleeping*, *eating*, and *working*.

We are hiring the following: *sales clerks, supervising managers,* and *office personnel.*

Instructions

Instead of This

Here are the instructions for operating the copy machine. First, you insert your copy card in the slot. Then you load paper in the upper tray. Last, copies are fed through the feed tray.

Try This

Follow these steps to use the copy machine:
1. *Insert* your copy card in the slot.
2. *Load* paper in the upper tray.
3. *Feed* copies through the feed tray.

Listed Items with Headings

Instead of This

On May 16 we will be in Regina, and Dr. Susan Dillon is the speaker. On June 20, we will be in Saskatoon and Dr. Diane Minger is the speaker.

Try This

Date	City	Speaker
May 16	Regina	Dr. Susan Dillon
June 20	Saskatoon	Dr. Diane Minger

Listed Items for Emphasis within Sentences

Instead of This

To keep exercising, you should make a written commitment to yourself, set realistic goals for each day's workout, and enlist the support of a friend.

Try This

To keep exercising, you should (a) make a written commitment to yourself, (b) set realistic goals for each day's workout, and (c) enlist the support of a friend.

Bulleted Items

Instead of This

Our goal
- is to recruit intensely competitive sales reps
- is to use reps who know our products
- recruit intelligent reps who are quick to learn

Try This

Our goal is to recruit sales reps who are
- Intensely competitive
- Familiar with our products
- Intelligent and quick to learn

E-Mails and Memos That Inform

You've now studied a basic plan for writing e-mails and memos, and you've learned how to highlight ideas with listing techniques. Now, you'll see how these techniques can be applied to specific situations. Most memos and e-mail messages can be divided into four groups: (1) those that inform, (2) those that request, (3) those that respond, and (4) those that persuade. In this chapter we will be concerned with the first three groups because they use the direct strategy.

The fourth group, persuasive messages, uses the indirect strategy. They will be discussed in Chapter 7.

Memos that inform generally explain organization policies, procedures, and guidelines. As policy-making documents, these messages must be particularly clear and concise.

The e-mail shown in Figure 5.3 (p. 108) informs department managers of a change in job-hiring procedures. The ineffective version begins negatively with an explanation of what went wrong with a new hiring procedure. Instead of starting directly, this message wanders through a maze of blame and incoherent explanation. The new procedure is stated negatively (*Do not submit your advertisements …*) and is hidden inside two hard-to-read paragraphs.

The effectively revised version begins directly by telling readers immediately what the e-mail is about. The next paragraph explains why the change is necessary. A list enumerates step-by-step procedures, thus making it easy for the reader to understand and follow the steps. The final paragraph restates the primary benefits of the new procedure and tells how more information may be obtained if necessary.

✓ **Quick Check**

E-mails and memos that inform often consist of policies, procedures, and guidelines.

E-Mails and Memos That Request

Messages that make requests are most effective when they use the direct approach. The reader learns immediately what is being requested. However, if you have any reason to suspect that the reader may resist the request, then an indirect approach would probably be more successful.

Requests should be courteous and respectful, as illustrated in Figure 5.4 (p. 109). They should not be demanding or dictatorial. The tone of the following request would likely antagonize its recipient:

✓ **Quick Check**

The tone of a request message should encourage cooperation.

> I want you to find out why the Davis account was not included in this report, and I want this information before you do anything else.

Requests should be considered carefully and written clearly so that in the intent of the message is not misunderstood. What may seem clear to the writer may not always be clear to a reader. That's why it's always a good idea to have a fellow worker read an important message for clarity before it is sent out.

Notice in Figure 5.4 that the writer ends by asking that the responses be made before May 5 because the information will be used for a Management Team meeting May 8. Providing an end date helps the reader know how to plan a response so that action is completed by the date given. Expressions such as "do it whenever you can" or "complete it as soon as possible" make little impression on procrastinators or very busy people. It's always wise to provide a specific date for completion. Dates can be entered into calendars to serve as reminders.

E-Mails and Memos That Respond

Much office correspondence reacts or responds to memos, e-mail messages, and other documents. When responding to a document, follow these preparatory steps:

1. Collect whatever information is necessary.
2. Organize your thoughts.
3. Make a brief outline of the points you plan to cover.

Begin the e-mail or memo with a clear statement of the main idea, which often is a summary of the contents of the memo. Avoid wordy and dated openings such

FIGURE 5.3 E-Mail That Informs

Before

Vague, negative subject line

Fails to pinpoint main idea in opening

Rambling, negative explanation

New procedure is hard to follow

Uses threats instead of showing benefits to reader

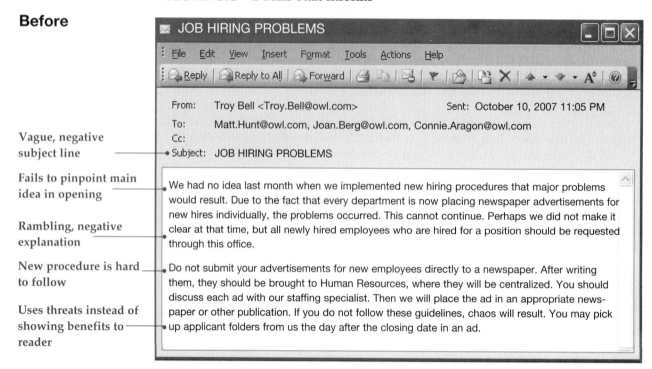

JOB HIRING PROBLEMS

File Edit View Insert Format Tools Actions Help

Reply | Reply to All | Forward

From: Troy Bell <Troy.Bell@owl.com>   Sent: October 10, 2007 11:05 PM
To: Matt.Hunt@owl.com, Joan.Berg@owl.com, Connie.Aragon@owl.com
Cc:
Subject: JOB HIRING PROBLEMS

We had no idea last month when we implemented new hiring procedures that major problems would result. Due to the fact that every department is now placing newspaper advertisements for new hires individually, the problems occurred. This cannot continue. Perhaps we did not make it clear at that time, but all newly hired employees who are hired for a position should be requested through this office.

Do not submit your advertisements for new employees directly to a newspaper. After writing them, they should be brought to Human Resources, where they will be centralized. You should discuss each ad with our staffing specialist. Then we will place the ad in an appropriate news-paper or other publication. If you do not follow these guidelines, chaos will result. You may pick up applicant folders from us the day after the closing date in an ad.

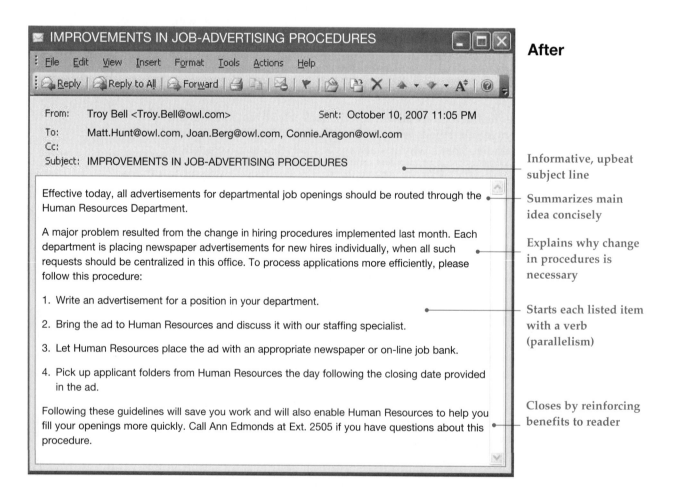

IMPROVEMENTS IN JOB-ADVERTISING PROCEDURES

File Edit View Insert Format Tools Actions Help

Reply | Reply to All | Forward

From: Troy Bell <Troy.Bell@owl.com>   Sent: October 10, 2007 11:05 PM
To: Matt.Hunt@owl.com, Joan.Berg@owl.com, Connie.Aragon@owl.com
Cc:
Subject: IMPROVEMENTS IN JOB-ADVERTISING PROCEDURES

Effective today, all advertisements for departmental job openings should be routed through the Human Resources Department.

A major problem resulted from the change in hiring procedures implemented last month. Each department is placing newspaper advertisements for new hires individually, when all such requests should be centralized in this office. To process applications more efficiently, please follow this procedure:

1. Write an advertisement for a position in your department.

2. Bring the ad to Human Resources and discuss it with our staffing specialist.

3. Let Human Resources place the ad with an appropriate newspaper or on-line job bank.

4. Pick up applicant folders from Human Resources the day following the closing date provided in the ad.

Following these guidelines will save you work and will also enable Human Resources to help you fill your openings more quickly. Call Ann Edmonds at Ext. 2505 if you have questions about this procedure.

After

Informative, upbeat subject line

Summarizes main idea concisely

Explains why change in procedures is necessary

Starts each listed item with a verb (parallelism)

Closes by reinforcing benefits to reader

FIGURE 5.4 E-Mail That Requests

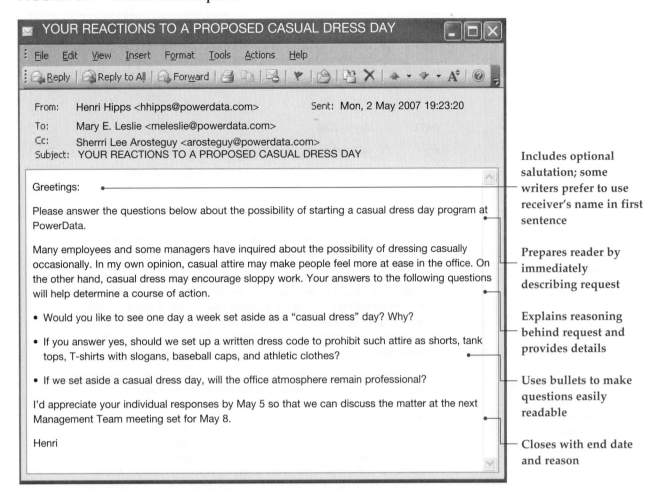

YOUR REACTIONS TO A PROPOSED CASUAL DRESS DAY

File   Edit   View   Insert   Format   Tools   Actions   Help

Reply   Reply to All   Forward

From: Henri Hipps <hhipps@powerdata.com>   Sent: Mon, 2 May 2007 19:23:20
To: Mary E. Leslie <meleslie@powerdata.com>
Cc: Sherrri Lee Arosteguy <arosteguy@powerdata.com>
Subject: YOUR REACTIONS TO A PROPOSED CASUAL DRESS DAY

Greetings:

Please answer the questions below about the possibility of starting a casual dress day program at PowerData.

Many employees and some managers have inquired about the possibility of dressing casually occasionally. In my own opinion, casual attire may make people feel more at ease in the office. On the other hand, casual dress may encourage sloppy work. Your answers to the following questions will help determine a course of action.

- Would you like to see one day a week set aside as a "casual dress" day? Why?

- If you answer yes, should we set up a written dress code to prohibit such attire as shorts, tank tops, T-shirts with slogans, baseball caps, and athletic clothes?

- If we set aside a casual dress day, will the office atmosphere remain professional?

I'd appreciate your individual responses by May 5 so that we can discuss the matter at the next Management Team meeting set for May 8.

Henri

Includes optional salutation; some writers prefer to use receiver's name in first sentence

Prepares reader by immediately describing request

Explains reasoning behind request and provides details

Uses bullets to make questions easily readable

Closes with end date and reason

as *Pursuant to your request of January 20, I am herewith including the information you wanted.* Although many business messages actually sound like this, they waste time and say little.

Notice in Figure 5.5 (p. 110) that Bill Leslie, manager of Legal Support Services, uses a straightforward opening in responding to his boss's request for information. He refers to her request, announces the information to follow, and identifies the date of the original message. Bill decides to answer with a standard hard-copy memo because he considers his reactions private and because he thinks that Vice-President Milowski would like to have a permanent record of each manager's reactions to take to the Management Team meeting. He also knows that he is well within the deadline set for a response.

The body of a response memo provides the information requested. Its organization generally follows the sequence of the request. In Bill's memo he answers the questions as his boss presented them. However, he further clarifies the information by providing summarizing headings in bold type. These headings emphasize the groupings and help the reader see immediately what information is covered. The memo closes with a reassuring summary.

FIGURE 5.5 Memo That Responds

IntraData Associates
Interoffice Memo

DATE: May 4, 2006

TO: Tamara Milowski, Vice-President, Employee Relations

FROM: Bill E. Leslie, Manager, Legal Support Services *BEL*

SUBJECT: REACTIONS TO PROPOSED CASUAL DRESS DAY PROGRAM

Here are my reactions to your inquiry about a casual dress day program made in your e-mail message of May 2.

- **Establish a casual dress day?** Yes, I would like to see such a day. In my department we now have a number of employees with flex schedules. They perform part of their work at home, where they can be as casual as they wish. Employees located here in the office are a little resentful. I think a casual dress day could offer some compensation to those who come to the office daily.

- **Implement a dress code?** By all means! We definitely need a written dress code not only to establish standards but also to project a professional image of the company to our customers.

- **Professional office atmosphere?** I would hope that casual dress would not promote casual work attitudes as well. We must establish that professionalism is non-negotiable. For example, we can't allow two-hour lunches or entire afternoons spent gossiping instead of working. Moreover, I think we should be careful in allowing casual dress only on the designated day, once a week.

I think a casual dress program can be beneficial and improve morale. But we definitely need a dress code in place at the beginning of the program. Let me know if I may assist in implementing a casual dress day program.

Annotations (left margin):

Announces main idea

Summarizes main idea and refers to previous message

Arranges responses in order of original request and uses boldface headings to emphasize and clarify groupings

Closes with reassuring remark and offer of further assistance

Summing Up and Looking Forward

E-mails and memos serve as vital channels of information within business offices. They use a standardized format to request and deliver information. Because e-mail messages are increasingly a preferred channel choice, this chapter presented many techniques for sending safe and effective e-mail messages. You learned to apply the direct strategy in writing messages that inform, request, and respond. You also learned to use bullets, numbers, and parallel form for listing information so that main points stand out. In the next chapter you will extend the direct strategy to writing letters that make requests and respond to requests.

Critical Thinking

1. How can the writer of a business e-mail or memo develop a conversational tone and still be professional? Why do e-mail writers sometimes forget to be professional?

2. What factors would help you decide whether to send an e-mail, write a memo, make a telephone call, leave a voice mail message, or deliver a message in person?

3. Why are lawyers and technology experts warning companies to store, organize, and manage computer data, including e-mail, with greater diligence?

4. Discuss the ramifications of the following statement: "Once a memo or any other document leaves your hands, you have essentially published it."

5. Ethical Issue: Should managers have the right to monitor the e-mail messages of employees? Why or why not? What if employees are warned that e-mail could be monitored? If a company sets up an e-mail policy, should only in-house transmissions be monitored? Only outside transmissions?

Chapter Review

6. What three questions should a writer ask before beginning an e-mail or memo?

7. Why are subject lines such as *Hello* or *Meeting* inappropriate?

8. Since e-mail messages are almost like telephone calls, why should one bother about correct spelling, grammar, punctuation, and style?

9. In formatting e-mails, when should you include a salutation (*Dear Mark*)?

10. Should writers of e-mails include their names at the ends of messages?

11. What are the four parts of the writing plan for a routine e-mail or memo? What is included in each?

12. How can listed or graphically highlighted items improve e-mails and memos?

13. When are numbers appropriate for listing items? When are bullets appropriate?

14. What are the main kinds of business e-mails and memos? Which require a direct strategy?

15. What is end-dating?

Writing Improvement Exercises

Message Openers. Compare the following sets of message openers. Circle the letter of the opener that illustrates a direct opening. Be prepared to discuss the weaknesses and strengths of each.

16. A letter to a security company inquiring about costs:
    a. We are considering keeping our facility open 24 hours a day because we can increase our profitability by running three shifts a day. We need some information.
    b. Please answer the following questions about the cost of adding security guards and electronic cameras to enable 24-hour operation of our facility.

17. An e-mail message announcing a professional development program:
    a. Employees interested in improving their writing and communication skills are invited to a training program beginning October 4.
    b. For the past year we have been investigating the possibility of developing a communication skills training program for some of our employees.

18. An e-mail message announcing a study:
    a. We have noticed recently a gradual but steady decline in the number of customer chequing accounts. We are disturbed by this trend, and for this reason I am asking our Customer Relations Department to conduct a study and make recommendations regarding this important problem.
    b. Our Customer Relations Department will conduct a study and make recommendations regarding the gradual but steady decline of customer chequing accounts.

19. A memo announcing a new procedure:
    a. Some customer representatives in the field have suggested that they would like to enter their reports from the field instead of coming back to the office to enter them in their computers. That's why we have made a number of changes. We would like you to use the following procedures.
    b. Customer representatives may now enter their field reports using the following procedures.

Opening Paragraphs. The following opening paragraphs to memos are wordy and indirect. After reading each paragraph, identify the main idea. Then, write an opening sentence that illustrates a more direct opening. Use a separate sheet if necessary.

20. Several staff members came to me and announced their interest in learning more about severance plans and separation policies. As most of you know, these areas of concern are increasingly important for most Human Resources

professionals. A seminar entitled "Severance & Separation Benefits" is being conducted February 11. The following employees are attending the seminar: Dave Neufeld, Tayreez Mushani, and Gail Switzer.

21. Your employee association has secured discounts on auto repair, carpet purchases, travel arrangements, and many other services. These services are available to you if you have a Buying Power Card. All employees are eligible for their own private Buying Power Cards.

Lists. Write lists as indicated below.

22. Use the following information to compose a single sentence that includes an introductory statement and a list with letters (a, b, c). Do not list the items vertically.

   The home page of a Web site should orient readers. This page should tell them what the site is about. It should also tell about the organization of the site. Finally, it should tell them how to navigate the site.

23. Use the following information to compose a bulleted vertical list with an introductory statement.

   To use the conventional inline skate heel brake, you should do these things. First, you should move one leg slightly forward. Then the ball of your foot should be lifted. Finally, the heel should be dragged to complete the braking action.

24. Use the following information to compose a sentence containing a list.

   Your equipment lease will mature in a month. When it does, you must make a decision. Three options are available to you. If you like, you may purchase the equipment at fair market value. Or the existing lease may be extended, again at fair market value. Finally, if neither of these options is appealing, the equipment could be sent back to the leasing company.

Activities and Cases

5.1 Memo That Informs: Sky-High Printing Bills. As Patricia Isaac, director of operations for DPI, a small software company, you are disturbed about some very large printing bills you've been receiving. DPI hires outside printers to prepare software manuals, marketing brochures, and sales materials. Printing is a necessary part of your business. Although the bills seem high, a recent bill from Print-Masters is particularly suspicious.

You don't want to blame anyone, but you do want to inform all staff members that no printing bills will be paid in the future without careful scrutiny. In talking it over with Sylvie Marchand, your colleague, you say, "We've got to make some changes. I can't plan my budget or control costs when these outrageous printing bills keep popping up. We're going to have to come up with some standardized procedure. Any ideas?" Sylvie responds, "One of the reasons that costs are so high is that some departments just don't think through their printing specifications before sending a job out. Maybe we should make departments write out their exact specifications and then get estimates and approvals—before they order any printing job."

You and she decide that two written estimates should be secured for any proposed printing job. You also decide that these estimates should be submitted to Sylvie for authorization. Only then can a department order any outside printing job. And this new procedure must start immediately. As Sylvie leaves, you remark, "You know, these new procedures mean that we'll probably get more competitive pricing. And they could even mean that departments will find better, more creative printing options!"

Your Task. Think through the process involved in creating a memo to the staff announcing the changes. To help you apply the principles you have learned in this chapter, read the options suggested here. Circle the most appropriate response for each question. Then compose the message as a memo addressed to all staff members or as an e-mail addressed to your instructor.

Developing the Memo

1. What is the main idea in this memo?
   a. You are outraged at the high printing bills being received lately.
   b. You can't plan budgets or control costs when these unexpected bills keep coming in.
   c. The bills from PrintMasters are particularly suspicious.
   d. A new procedure for submitting requests for outside printing jobs is being instituted immediately.
2. An effective opening sentence for your memo might be
   a. Sylvie Marchand and I have been concerned about the high printing bills we have received lately.
   b. Please follow the new procedures listed below in submitting requests for outside printing jobs.
   c. Very large expenditures for printing jobs have been submitted recently, some of which are quite suspicious.
   d. Henceforth, no employee may send out a printing job without prior written approval.
3. The body of the memo should
   a. Explain why the new procedure is necessary and how to follow it.
   b. Recount the highlights of your conversation with Sylvie.
   c. Identify the bills of the most offending printers, particularly PrintMasters.
   d. Identify the departments and employees who have been responsible for most of the high costs.
4. In explaining the new procedure, you will probably want to list each step. Which of the following statements illustrates the best way to list a step?
   a. Submission of all written estimates should be made to Sylvie Marchand.
   b. Written estimates should be submitted to Sylvie Marchand.
   c. Submit written estimates to Sylvie Marchand.
   d. Sylvie Marchand will expect all written estimates to be submitted to her.
5. An effective closing for your memo might be
   a. These procedures are effective immediately. Thank you for your cooperation in this matter.
   b. Following these new procedures, which are effective immediately, will result in more competitive pricing and perhaps may even provide you with new creative printing options. If you have any questions, call Sylvie Marchand at Ext. 556.
   c. These procedures are effective immediately. By the way, don't forget to send me your ideas for equipping the new fitness centre.
   d. If I may be of assistance to you in any way, do not hesitate to call on me.

5.2 E-Mail That Requests: Making the Best of Temps. Analyze the following poorly written e-mail. List its faults in the space provided. Outline an appropriate plan for an e-mail that requests. Then, on a separate sheet or as an e-mail message, write an improved version.

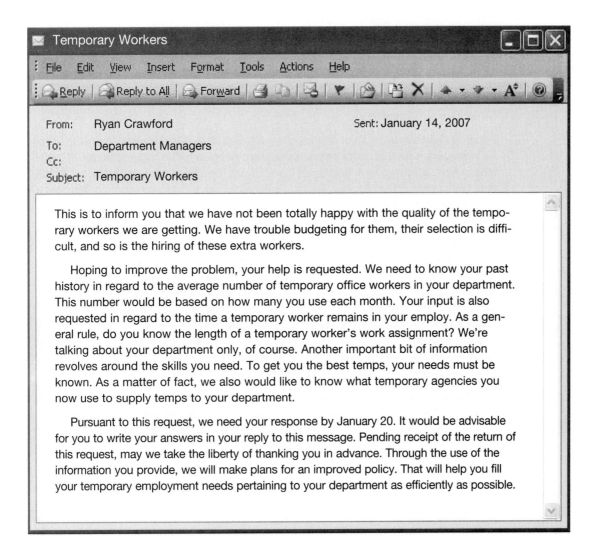

Temporary Workers — File Edit View Insert Format Tools Actions Help

Reply | Reply to All | Forward

From: Ryan Crawford   Sent: January 14, 2007

To: Department Managers

Cc:

Subject: Temporary Workers

This is to inform you that we have not been totally happy with the quality of the temporary workers we are getting. We have trouble budgeting for them, their selection is difficult, and so is the hiring of these extra workers.

Hoping to improve the problem, your help is requested. We need to know your past history in regard to the average number of temporary office workers in your department. This number would be based on how many you use each month. Your input is also requested in regard to the time a temporary worker remains in your employ. As a general rule, do you know the length of a temporary worker's work assignment? We're talking about your department only, of course. Another important bit of information revolves around the skills you need. To get you the best temps, your needs must be known. As a matter of fact, we also would like to know what temporary agencies you now use to supply temps to your department.

Pursuant to this request, we need your response by January 20. It would be advisable for you to write your answers in your reply to this message. Pending receipt of the return of this request, may we take the liberty of thanking you in advance. Through the use of the information you provide, we will make plans for an improved policy. That will help you fill your temporary employment needs pertaining to your department as efficiently as possible.

1. List at least five faults in this e-mail.

2. Outline a general writing plan for this e-mail.
   Subject line:

   Opening:

   Body:

   Closing:

5.3 Memo That Informs: Time Management Tips. Read the following poorly written memo, analyze its faults, outline a general writing plan, and then revise it.

DATE: Nov. 15, 2006

TO: Staff Members

FROM: Phil Kleeson, Manager

SUBJECT: Suggestions

Recently I had the pleasure of attending an excellent time management seminar in which we managers were told about some interesting strategies for managing the glut of information from which we all suffer. Since many of you have been complaining about all the time you spend on e-mail and voice mail, I thought I would send you some of the best pointers we were given. These might help you increase your productivity and decrease your frustration.

When it comes to e-mail, we were urged to practise e-mail "triage." This means glancing through all incoming mail quickly and separating the messages you need to answer immediately, as well as determining which messages can wait and which ones can be deleted. Generally, you can do this by checking subject lines and the names of senders. To cut down on the amount of time you spend on your e-mail, you should check e-mail messages only once or twice each day and at specific times so that you develop a routine. This simple practice can save you a lot of wasted time. Another technique involves time management but also courtesy. Be sure to respond briefly to all important e-mails, even if you can say only that you are looking into a matter.

When it comes to voice mail, check it at least three times a day. This prevents "message bump"—having the same person call you several times with the same request. Another idea for saving time with voice mail is to use the functions on your telephone to skip to the end of a message or past recorded messages to the beep when you want to leave a message.

By the way, we need a volunteer to attend a conference on preventing violence in the workplace. Thank you for your cooperation.

1. List at least five faults in this memo.

2. Outline a general writing plan for this memo.
    Subject line:

    Opening:

    Body:

    Closing:

5.4 Memo That Informs: Change in Insurance Premiums. You are the benefits manager for a national furniture retail chain, The Home Centre, headquartered in Richmond, British Columbia. Most of the full-time employees who work for the chain pay into an employee benefits plan. This plan includes dental and vision

Chapter 5 E-Mails and Memos   NEL care, prescription drug coverage, and other benefits. One of the most expensive benefits employees pay for is long-term disability insurance. Recently, your insurance provider, Cansafe, has informed you that due to the high number of recent long-term disability claims, premiums for long-term disability insurance will have to rise substantially, on the order of 15 percent. For the average employee, this means an increase of more than $20 per month.

Your Task. Your job requires you to write a well-organized memo informing The Home Centre employees about the impending increase. From past experience, you know that employees who are closer to retirement are big supporters of long-term disability insurance, whereas younger employees tend to be frustrated by the high premiums.

Related Web site: Sun Life Financial's site has a brief description of LTD insurance: <www.sunlife.ca/canada/cda/level2_page_v2/ 0,2330,1-982-1,00.html>.

5.5 Memo That Informs/Requests: Dress Code Controversy. As the Vancouver-based director of Human Resources at Sensational, you have not had a good week. The national media recently reported about the fact that Sensational—a leading woman's fashion chain—has been taken before the Nova Scotia Human Rights Commission to defend against a claim by a young woman. The young woman recently applied for a job at a Halifax Sensational location and was told in a pre-interview with a manager that "she'd never be hired if she wore her headdress to work." Citing the Commission's Web site claim that "It's against the law to fire an employee because he wears clothing that is required by his religion," the young woman lodged a complaint.[6] Head office in Vancouver has been in damage control mode ever since.

Your Task. Quickly realizing the effects the negative media reporting will have, you draft a memo to all employees. The purpose of the memo is to re-affirm that Sensational abides by and supports all Canadian human rights legislation, and at the same time, that employees should not talk to any media that may ask them for comments. You realize that these two messages are somewhat contradictory (one positive, one negative), but you feel time is of the essence.

Related Web site: Nova Scotia Human Rights Commission: <www.gov.ns.ca/ humanrights>.

5.6 Reply Memo: Someone's Going to Get Stung. The IS (Information Systems) network manager at Lionel Packaging in Peterborough, Ontario, worries that his company will have to upgrade its Internet connection because operations are noticeably slower than in the past. Upon checking, however, he discovers that extensive recreational Web surfing among employees is the real reason for the slowdown.

Since the company needs a good policy on using e-mail and the Internet, he assigns your team the task of investigating existing policies. Your team leader, Mary Richard, who has quite a sense of humour, says, "Developing an Internet policy is a lot like taking care of a beehive; too much activity and you can get stung, not enough and the bees do whatever they want." No one is going to like having e-mail and Internet use restricted.

Your Task. Develop a company policy on using e-mail and the Internet. Your team should first check Web sites to locate examples or models of company e-mail and Internet policies. For best results use Boolean logic (see p. 264) and try variations on the search term "company e-mail policy." Print any helpful material.

Then meet as a group and select six to eight major topics that you think should be covered in a company policy. Your investigation will act as a starting point in the process of developing a policy that provides safeguards but is not overly restrictive. You are not expected to write the policy at this time, but you could attach copies of anything interesting. Your boss would especially like to know where he could see or purchase model company policies. As Jason Tucker send an e-mail to Mary Richard, your team leader.

5.7 E-Mail Request: Can You Help Me with My New Small Magazine? After graduating from college you decide to combine your interest in business with your interest in music by starting a new magazine called *Toons*. You live in Burnaby, B.C., and you think a young, fresh, and irreverent monthly look at Vancouver's wide-ranging music scene (from classical to clubs) would be a sure-fire seller. You've already recruited friends who can write stories, friends who can design layout, a couple of fellow business grads who are willing to sell advertising, and one friend who has inherited a van and is willing to help you with distribution around the city. What you're missing is a subscriber base. You've done your homework, and you realize that newsstand sales will not be enough to keep your magazine afloat. A friend of yours from college has been working for just under a year at a local magazine, and you figure he might be able to help you out by sharing the electronic database containing names and addresses of his magazine's subscribers.

Your Task. You decide to write your friend an e-mail requesting his help with your new magazine subscriber base.

Related Web site: The Canadian Magazine Publisher's Association <www.cmpa.ca> has lots of information for people who want to start small magazines.

5.8 E-Mail Response: No, I Can't Help You! You are the friend referred to in Case 5.7. You work at *Geist*, a well-respected general-interest magazine published in Vancouver. Even though you can see why your friend would ask you to share subscriber information, you're surprised at how naive and uninformed he is. You recently attended a seminar about PIPEDA, the Personal Information Protection and Electronic Documents Act, so you know that in Canada, it is against the law for businesses to share the private information of their clients unless the clients have agreed in writing to this sharing of information. Furthermore, you're surprised at your friend because as a recent business graduate, you think he should have a greater sense of business ethics than he has demonstrated.

Your Task. Respond to your friend's e-mail denying his request to share your database of subscriber names and addresses.

Related Web sites: The government of Canada's PIPEDA site provides background for this case: <www.privcom.gc.ca/legislation/02_06_01_e.asp>. You may also find <www.geist.com> informative.

Web

5.9 Memo That Responds: What's New at Canada Post. Assume you are Maria Lopez and you work for MagicMedia, Inc., a large software manufacturer. The office manager, Rachel Wilder, asks you to seek two kinds of information from Canada Post. First, she wants to learn exactly how envelopes should be addressed according to Canada Post guidelines. Second, she wants to know the air and surface rates for sending packages to the United States. She expects to be sending plenty of parcels to a U.S. client in the spring.

Your Task. To obtain both sets of information, visit the Canada Post Web site. Write a one-page memo summarizing your findings.

Related Web site: <www.canadapost.ca>.

5.10 Memo That Informs: Corporate Team Building in Alberta. You are the coordinator of staff development for Imperial Oil. It has been recently announced that Imperial Oil is moving its headquarters from Toronto to Calgary. The news has been greeted positively by employees, but a few are unhappy while others already working in the Calgary office are unsure how well the amalgamation of the two offices with their different cultures will go. Recognizing this feeling of uncertainty, you decide to hold a series of corporate teambuilding retreats shortly after the headquarters move to Calgary. The retreat will be led by the Great Canadian Adventure Company. Employees will meet in downtown Calgary at 8:00 a.m. and buses will pick them up and take them to the Sylvan Lake area. There, they will spend the day on teambuilding activities like map-reading exercises that will require employee teams to find their way through a wooded area to a "home base" where lunch will be served. The group will return to downtown Calgary by 7:00 p.m.

Your Task. As the coordinator of staff development, write a memo to all employees announcing the retreat. You recognize the fact that there may be some friction between the "new" people from Toronto and the long-time Calgary employees.

Related Web sites: The *Calgary Sun*'s take on Imperial Oil's move to Calgary can be found at: <www.calgarysun.com/cgi-bin/ niveau2 .cgi?s=generic&p=92663.html&a=1> and The Great Canadian Adventure Company's Web site is <http://www.adventures.ca>.

Grammar/Mechanics Review—5

The following sentences contain errors in grammar, punctuation, capitalization, number style, usage, and spelling. Below each sentence write a corrected version.

1. As a matter of fact the italian alphabet has only twenty one letters.

2. About one hundred of Tim Hortons seven hundred forty canadian resterants is serving the new toffee donut.

3. Meanwhile the highly-advertised McDonald's 1.99 hamburger promotion which was pushed heavy by its Canadian Headquarters turned out to be a major dissappointment.

4. A powerful reason for Burger Kings new success is, a hefty 2 patty burger thats being promoted as an extra big Big Mac.

5. Experts say the 2 smartest dogs are scottish border collies and golden retrievers, on the other hand the dumbest are afghan hounds.

6. After listening carefully to your advise we paid several months rent in advance.

7. 2 sizes of batteries see Page Sixteen in the instruction booklet may be used in this flashlight.

8. When convenent will you please send me 3 copys of the companys color logo?

9. The first book ever wrote on a typewriter was: "Tom Sawyer."

10. A tacky tee shirt in the Niagara falls souvenir shop reads "my parents went to niagara falls and all I got was this t-shirt.

11. In Maclean's I saw an article titled How to develop the exercise habit.

12. Appearing next is the President and Sales Manager both of whom were personally invited by myself.

13. Production cost and markup is important to the manufacturer and to we vendors.

14. That stack of papers have been laying on your desk for at least three week's.

15. The only canadian Prime Minister to win a Nobel peace prize is Lester B. Pearson in 1957.

Document for Revision

The following memo has faults in grammar, punctuation, spelling, capitalization, number form, repetition, wordiness, and other areas. Use standard proofreading marks (see Appendix B) to correct the errors. When you finish, your instructor can show you the revised version of this memo.

DATE: March 2, 2007

TO: Department Heads, Managers, and Supervisors

FROM: James Robbins, Director, Human Resources

SUBJECT: Submitting Appraisals of Performance by April 15th

Please be informed that performance appraisals for all you're employees' are due, before April 15th . These appraisal are esspecially important and essential this year. Because of job changes, new technologys and because of office re-organization.

To complete your performance appraisals in the most effective way, you should follow the procedures described in our employee handbook, let me briefly make a review of those procedures;

1. Be sure each and every employee has a performance plan with 3 or 4 main objective.

2. For each objective make an assessment of the employee on a scale of 5 (consistently excedes requirements) to 0 (does not meet requirements at all).

3. You should identify 3 strengths that he brings to the job.

4. Name 3 skills that he can improve. These should pertain to skills such as Time Management rather then to behaviors such as habitual lateness.

5. The employee should be met with to discuss his appraisal.

6. Finish the appraisal and send the completed appraisal to this office.

We look upon appraisals like a tool for helping each worker assess his performance. And enhance his output. If you would like to discuss this farther, please do not hessitate to call me.

Whose Computer or BlackBerry or Palm Pilot Is It Anyway?

Many companies today provide their employees with computers and/or PDAs with Internet access. Should employees be able to use those devices for online shopping, personal messages, personal work, and listening to music or playing games?

But It's Harmless

According to a recent poll, one-third of Canadian workers have Internet access at work and four out of five of these say they log on for personal reasons, such as sending personal e-mails, checking out news or sports headlines, comparison shopping, checking investments, and making online purchases. While the poll did not determine whether this activity occurred during work or in the employee's spare time, the potential for abuse and evidence of abuse has led a growing number of employers in Canada to consider developing policies governing Internet use and also to monitor the online activities of employees.[7] To justify much of this personal activity, workers claim that pursuing personal online activities is performance-enhancing as it keeps them at their desk rather than in the shopping malls or at the water cooler.

Companies Cracking Down

Employers are less happy about increasing use of bandwidth for personal online activities. The growth of electronic monitoring has been significant since 1998 in both Canada and the United States. In fact, the number of companies in the United States reviewing e-mail and computer files stored on hard drives has doubled from the late 1990s.[8]

What's Reasonable?

Some companies try to enforce a "zero tolerance" policy, prohibiting any personal use of company equipment, while others allow some personal activity. In Canada under the Privacy Act and Charter of Rights and Freedoms, employees have a "reasonable expectation" of privacy in the workplace, but that expectation can be met simply by notifying employees that they are being monitored.[9] Currently many employers provide no guidelines on reasonable Internet use. As well, what some employers regard as a firing offence others view as acceptable personal use. As Paul Kent-Snowsell, a Vancouver lawyer specializing in Internet cases, warns: "It has always been cause for dismissal if you're not using company time to do company work."[10] At the same time, Robert Lendvai, marketing director for Ottawa's Kyberpass Corporation, a maker of network security software, indicates that while Canadian corporations use the security features of his company's software, only about one in five activates the monitoring capabilities.[11]

Career Application

As an administrative assistant at Big C Technologies in Vancouver, you have just received an e-mail from your boss asking for your opinion. It seems that many employees have been shopping online; one person actually received four personal packages couriered to him in one morning. Although reluctant to do so, management is considering installing monitoring software that not only tracks Internet use but also allows extensive blocking of Web sites, such as porn, hate, and game sites.

Your Task

- In teams or as a class, research and discuss the problem of workplace abuse of e-mail and the Internet.
- Should full personal use be allowed?
- In terms of equipment, are computers and their links to the Internet similar to office telephones?
- Should employees be allowed to access the Internet for personal use if they use their own private e-mail accounts?
- Should management be allowed to monitor all Internet use?
- Should employees be warned if e-mail is to be monitored?
- What specific reasons can you give to support an Internet crackdown by management?
- What specific reasons can you give to oppose a crackdown?

Decide whether you support or oppose the crackdown. Explain your views in an e-mail or a memo to your boss, Roberta Everson <reverson@bigc.com> or in a traditional in-class debate.

Related Web sites: Visit the Web Spy Software site <www.webspy.com> for an inner look at Internet surveillance software. For information on Canada's privacy laws and regulations, visit the Web site of the Office of the Privacy Commissioner of Canada <www.privcom.gc.ca>.

6

Routine Letters and Goodwill Messages

CHAPTER

Who cares about composing well crafted business letters today? Didn't that mode of communication start to die in the 1980s when the fax machine began to rule our lives? Surely after the advent of sophisticated voice mail systems in the early 1990s, the mailed business letter was destined for obsolescence! If nothing else, the explosion of email users must have put this archaic form of correspondence out of its misery by now! Think again. Believe it or not, there is at least one group of people who are still impressed when they receive a well written letter in the ordinary mail. They are called prospective clients/customers.[1]

Reg Pirie, lead partner, Pirie Management Consultants Inc.

LEARNING OBJECTIVES

1. Write letters requesting information and action.
2. Write letters making claims.
3. Write letters ordering merchandise.
4. Write letters complying with requests.
5. Write letters responding to customer orders.
6. Write letters granting claims.
7. Write letters of recommendation.
8. Write goodwill messages.

Letters that fail to get to the point or are badly written are a concern for employees and managers everywhere. For example, a bank's profitability can depend on the quality of information it provides to its customers. Without clear, well-written messages that transmit information concisely, banks and insurance companies risk alienating current customers and losing potential customers. This fact was demonstrated by the work of the Government of Canada's Task Force on the Future of the Canadian Financial Services Sector. In one of its research reports, "Assessing Financial Documents for Readability," the task force concluded that based on "readability scores, almost all the documents assessed in these studies are Difficult and Complex."[2] Since then, financial services companies have strived to use plain language in both their internal and external messages.

Messages that meander slowly toward their point have little appeal for most of us. Readers want to know why a message was written and how it involves them. And they want that information up front.

Writing Everyday Business Letters

This chapter focuses on written messages that travel outside an organization. These messages generally take the form of letters. Although as Reg Pirie implies, businesspeople today are writing fewer letters and more e-mail messages, you will still find many occasions when letters are required. When you need a formal record of an inquiry, response, or complaint, letters are the best communication channel.

Most business correspondence consists of routine letters. These everyday messages go to suppliers, government agencies, other businesses, and, most important, customers. Customer letters are given high priority because these messages encourage product feedback, project a favourable image of the company, and promote future business.

Like memos, letters are easiest to write when you have a plan to follow. The plan for letters, just as for e-mails and memos, stems from the content of the message and its expected effect on the receiver. Letters delivering bad news require an indirect approach, which you will learn about in Chapter 8. Most letters, however, carry good or neutral news. Because such letters will not produce a negative effect on their reader, they follow the direct strategy. You will recall that the main idea comes first in the direct strategy.

In this chapter you'll learn to apply the direct strategy in writing requests for information and action. You'll also learn how to respond to such requests. Finally, you'll learn how to write typical goodwill letters.

Quick Check

Letters communicate with outsiders and produce a formal record.

Quick Check

The content of a message and its anticipated effect on the reader determine the strategy you choose.

Information and Action Requests

Many business messages are written to request information or action. Although the specific subject of each inquiry may differ, the similarity of purpose in routine requests enables writers to use the following writing plan.

 Writing Plan for an Information or Action Request

- **Opening**—Ask the most important question first or express a polite command.
- **Body**—Explain the request logically and courteously. Ask other questions if necessary.
- **Closing**—Request a specific action with an end date, if appropriate, and show appreciation.

Opening Directly

The most emphatic positions in a letter are the openings and closings. Readers tend to look at them first. The writer should capitalize on this tendency by putting the most significant statement first. The first sentence of an information request is usually a question or a polite command. It should not be an explanation or justification, unless resistance to the request is expected. When the information requested is likely to be forthcoming, immediately tell the reader what you want. This saves the reader's time and may ensure that the message is read. A busy executive who skims the mail, quickly reading subject lines and first sentences only, may grasp your request rapidly and act on it. A request that follows a lengthy explanation, on the other hand, may never be found.

A letter inquiring about hotel accommodations, shown in Figure 6.1 (p. 126), begins immediately with the most important idea. Can the hotel provide meeting rooms and accommodations for 250 people? Instead of opening with an explanation

Quick Check

Readers find the openings and closings of letters most valuable.

FIGURE 6.1 Letter That Requests Information

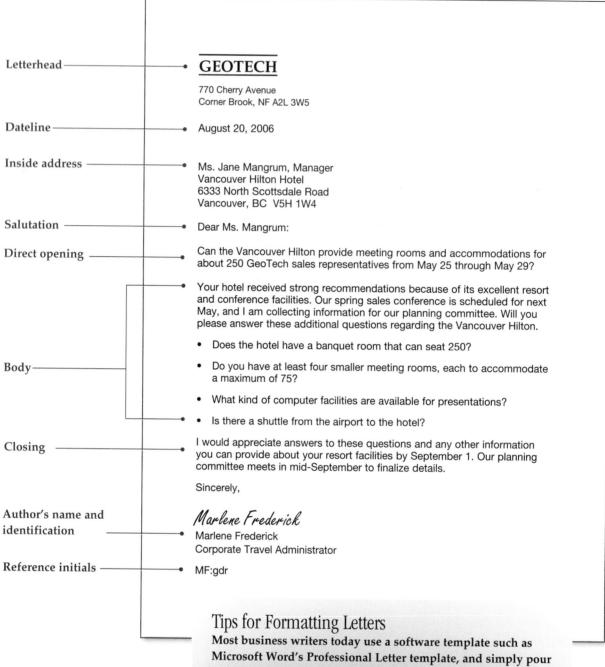

Letterhead ⎯⎯⎯⎯⎯⎯⎯⎯⎯•

GEOTECH

770 Cherry Avenue
Corner Brook, NF A2L 3W5

Dateline ⎯⎯⎯⎯⎯⎯⎯⎯• August 20, 2006

Inside address ⎯⎯⎯⎯⎯• Ms. Jane Mangrum, Manager
Vancouver Hilton Hotel
6333 North Scottsdale Road
Vancouver, BC V5H 1W4

Salutation ⎯⎯⎯⎯⎯⎯⎯• Dear Ms. Mangrum:

Direct opening ⎯⎯⎯⎯⎯• Can the Vancouver Hilton provide meeting rooms and accommodations for
about 250 GeoTech sales representatives from May 25 through May 29?

Your hotel received strong recommendations because of its excellent resort
and conference facilities. Our spring sales conference is scheduled for next
May, and I am collecting information for our planning committee. Will you
please answer these additional questions regarding the Vancouver Hilton.

• Does the hotel have a banquet room that can seat 250?

Body ⎯⎯⎯⎯⎯• • Do you have at least four smaller meeting rooms, each to accommodate
a maximum of 75?

• What kind of computer facilities are available for presentations?

• Is there a shuttle from the airport to the hotel?

Closing ⎯⎯⎯⎯⎯⎯• I would appreciate answers to these questions and any other information
you can provide about your resort facilities by September 1. Our planning
committee meets in mid-September to finalize details.

Sincerely,

Marlene Frederick

Author's name and ⎯⎯• Marlene Frederick
identification Corporate Travel Administrator

Reference initials ⎯⎯⎯• MF:gdr

Tips for Formatting Letters

**Most business writers today use a software template such as
Microsoft Word's Professional Letter template, and simply pour
in their content. If you don't have access to a template, follow
the steps below.**

- **Start the date on line 13 or 1 blank line below the letterhead.**
- **For block style like the letter above, begin all lines at the
  left margin.**
- **For modified block style like the letter on page 132, begin
  the date and closing lines at the centre.**
- **Leave side margins of 2.5 to 3 cm (1 to 1.5 inches)
  depending on the length of the letter.**
- **Single-space the body and double-space between
  paragraphs.**

of who the writer is or how the writer happens to be writing this letter, the letter begins directly.

If several questions must be asked, you have two choices. You can ask the most important question first, as shown in Figure 6.1. An alternative opening begins with a summary statement, such as *Will you please answer the following questions about providing meeting rooms and accommodations for 250 people from May 25 through May 29.* Notice that the summarizing statement sounds like a question but has no question mark. That's because it's really a command disguised as a question. Rather than bluntly demanding information (*Answer the following questions*), we often soften commands by posing them as questions. Such statements, called rhetorical questions, should not be punctuated as questions because they do not require answers.

Details in the Body

The body of a letter that requests information should provide necessary details and should be easy to read. Remember that the quality of the information obtained from a request letter depends on the clarity of the inquiry. If you analyze your needs, organize your ideas, and frame your request logically, you are likely to receive a meaningful answer that doesn't require a follow-up message. Whenever possible, itemize the information to improve readability. Notice that the questions in Figure 6.1 are bulleted, and they are parallel. They demonstrate an excellent use of graphic highlighting.

The body of a request letter may contain an explanation or a list of questions.

Closing with an Action Request

Use the final paragraph to ask for specific action, to set an end date if appropriate, and to express appreciation. As you learned in working with e-mails and memos, a request for action is most effective when an end date and reason for that date are supplied, as shown in Figure 6.1.

It's always appropriate to end a request letter with appreciation for the action taken. However, don't fall into a cliché trap, such as *Thanking you in advance, I remain …* or the familiar *Thank you for your cooperation.* Your appreciation will sound most sincere if you avoid mechanical, tired expressions.

The ending of a request letter should tell the reader what you want done and when.

Simple Claim Requests

In business many things can go wrong—promised shipments are late, warranted goods fail, or service is disappointing. When you as a customer must write to identify or correct a wrong, the letter is called a *claim.* Straightforward claims are those to which you expect the receiver to agree readily. But even these claims often require a letter. While your first action may be a telephone call or a visit to submit your claim, you may not get the results you seek. Written claims are generally taken more seriously, and they also establish a record of what happened. Claims that require persuasion are presented in Chapter 7. In this chapter you'll learn to apply the following writing plan for a straightforward claim that uses a direct approach.

Claim letters register complaints and usually seek correction of a wrong.

 Writing Plan for a Simple Claim

- **Opening**—Describe clearly the desired action.
- **Body**—Explain the nature of the claim, explain the claim is justified, and provide details regarding the action requested.
- **Closing**—End pleasantly with a goodwill statement and include end date if appropriate.

Opening with Action

If you have a legitimate claim, you can expect a positive response from a company. Smart businesses today want to hear from their customers. That's why you should open a claim letter with a clear statement of the problem or with the action you want the receiver to take. You might expect a replacement, a refund, a new order, credit to your account, correction of a billing error, free repairs, free inspection, or cancellation of an order.

When the remedy is obvious, state it immediately (*Please send us 24 Royal hot-air popcorn poppers to replace the 24 hot-oil poppers sent in error with our order shipped January 4*). When the remedy is less obvious, you might ask for a change in policy or procedure or simply for an explanation (*Because three of our employees with confirmed reservations were refused rooms at your hotel on September 16, would you please clarify your policy regarding reservations and late arrivals*).

Explaining in the Body

In the body of a claim letter, explain the problem and justify your request. Provide the necessary details so that the difficulty can be corrected without further correspondence. Avoid becoming angry or trying to lay blame. Bear in mind that the person reading your letter is seldom responsible for the problem. Instead, state the facts logically, objectively, and unemotionally; let the reader decide on the causes.

Include copies of all pertinent documents such as invoices, sales receipts, catalogue descriptions, and repair records. (By the way, be sure to send copies and not your originals, which could be lost.) When service is involved, cite names of individuals spoken to and dates of calls. Assume that a company honestly wants to satisfy its customers—because most do. When an alternative remedy exists, describe it (*If you are unable to send 24 Royal hot-air popcorn poppers immediately, please credit our account now and notify us when they become available*).

Closing Pleasantly

Conclude a claim letter with a courteous statement that promotes goodwill and expresses a desire for continued relations. If appropriate, include an end date (*We realize that mistakes in ordering and shipping sometimes occur. Because we've enjoyed your prompt service in the past, we hope that you will be able to send us the hot-air poppers by January 15*).

Finally, in making claims, act promptly. Delaying claims makes them appear less important. Delayed claims are also more difficult to verify. By taking the time to put your claim in writing, you indicate your seriousness. A written claim also starts a record of the problem, should later action be necessary. Be sure to keep a copy of your letter.

Putting It All Together

Figure 6.2 shows a hostile claim letter that vents the writer's anger but accomplishes little else. Its tone is belligerent, and it assumes that the company intentionally overcharged the customer. Furthermore, it fails to tell the reader how to remedy the problem. The revision tempers the tone, describes the problem objectively, and provides facts and figures. Most important, it specifies exactly what the customer wants done.

Notice that the letter in Figure 6.2 is shown with the return address typed above the date. This personal business style may be used when typing on paper without a printed letterhead. Notice, too, that this letter uses modified block style. The return address, date, and closing lines start at the centre.

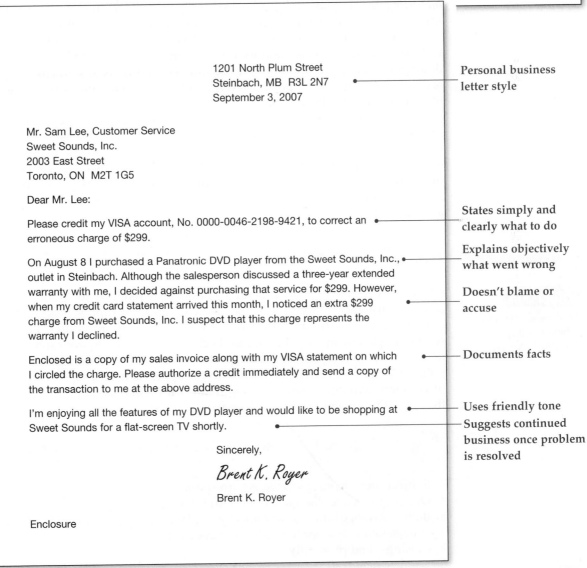

Sounds angry; jumps to conclusions

Forgets that mistakes happen

Fails to suggest solution

After

Dear Sweet Sounds:

You call yourselves Sweet Sounds, but all I'm getting from your service is sour notes! I'm furious that you have your salespeople slip in unwanted service warranties to boost your sales.

When I bought my Panatronic DVD player from Sweet Sounds, Inc., in August, I specifically told the salesperson that I did NOT want a three-year service warranty. But there it is on my credit card statement this month! You people have obviously billed me for a service I did not authorize. I refuse to pay this charge.

How can you hope to stay in business with such fraudulent practices? I was expecting to return this month and look at flat-screen TVs, but you can be sure I'll find an honest dealer this time.

Sincerely,

Brent K. Royer

1201 North Plum Street
Steinbach, MB R3L 2N7
September 3, 2007

Mr. Sam Lee, Customer Service
Sweet Sounds, Inc.
2003 East Street
Toronto, ON M2T 1G5

Dear Mr. Lee:

Please credit my VISA account, No. 0000-0046-2198-9421, to correct an erroneous charge of $299.

On August 8 I purchased a Panatronic DVD player from the Sweet Sounds, Inc., outlet in Steinbach. Although the salesperson discussed a three-year extended warranty with me, I decided against purchasing that service for $299. However, when my credit card statement arrived this month, I noticed an extra $299 charge from Sweet Sounds, Inc. I suspect that this charge represents the warranty I declined.

Enclosed is a copy of my sales invoice along with my VISA statement on which I circled the charge. Please authorize a credit immediately and send a copy of the transaction to me at the above address.

I'm enjoying all the features of my DVD player and would like to be shopping at Sweet Sounds for a flat-screen TV shortly.

Sincerely,

Brent K. Royer

Brent K. Royer

Enclosure

Personal business letter style

States simply and clearly what to do

Explains objectively what went wrong

Doesn't blame or accuse

Documents facts

Uses friendly tone
Suggests continued business once problem is resolved

✓ Quick Check

To order merchandise, you may occasionally have to write a letter.

Most people order merchandise by telephone, catalogue order form, fax, or through a Web site. Sometimes, though, you may not have a telephone number, order form, or Web address—only a street address. Other times you may wish to have a written record of the date and content of your order. When you must write a letter to order merchandise, use the direct strategy, beginning with the main idea.

 ## Writing a Plan for an Order Request

- **Opening**—Authorize purchase and suggest method of shipping.
- **Body**—List items vertically; provide quantity, order number, description, and unit price; and show total price of order.
- **Closing**—Request shipment by a specific date, discuss method of payment, and express appreciation.

To order items by letter, supply the same information that an order form would require. In the opening let the reader know immediately that this is a purchase authorization and not merely an information inquiry. Instead of *I saw a number of interesting items in your catalogue,* begin directly with order language such as *Please send me by courier the following items from your fall merchandise catalogue.*

If you're ordering many items, list them vertically in the body of your letter. Include as much specific data as possible: quantity, order number, complete description, unit price, and total price. Show the total amount, and figure out the tax and shipping costs if possible. The more information you provide, the less likely a mistake will be made.

In the closing say how you plan to pay for the merchandise. Enclose a cheque, provide a credit card number, or ask to be billed. Many business organizations have credit agreements with their regular suppliers that enable them to send goods without prior payment. In addition to payment information, mention when the merchandise should be sent and express appreciation. The letter from the human resources department of a business in Figure 6.3 illustrates the pattern of an order letter.

Information Response Letters

✓ Quick Check

Before responding to requests, gather facts, check figures, and seek approval if necessary.

Often, your messages will respond favourably to requests for information or action. A customer wants information about a product. A supplier asks to arrange a meeting. Another business inquires about one of your procedures. But before responding to any inquiry, be sure to check your facts and figures carefully. Any letter written on company stationery is considered a legally binding contract. If a policy or procedure needs authorization, seek approval from a supervisor or executive before writing the letter. In complying with requests, you'll want to apply the same direct pattern you used in making requests.

 ## Writing Plan for an Information Response Letter

- **Subject line**—Identify previous correspondence.
- **Opening**—Deliver the most important information first.
- **Body**—Arrange information logically, explain and clarify it, provide additional information if appropriate, and build goodwill.
- **Closing**—End pleasantly.

FIGURE 6.3   Order Request Letter

SPRUCE VALLEY LODGE

September 14, 2006

Randall's Office Supplies
1401 Second Ave.
Whitehorse, YK
Y1A 1B2

Dear Sir or Madam:

Please send by priority post the following items from your 2006–2007 ●————— Opens directly with authorization for purchase, method of delivery, and catalogue source
catalogue.

Quantity	Catalogue Number	Description	Price
250	OG44-18	Payroll cards	$102.99
250	OG31-22	Payroll card envelopes	$ 21.99
100	OM22-01	Performance cards	$ 79.99
		Shipping	$ 25.00
		SUBTOTAL	$229.97
		GST	$ 16.10
		TOTAL	**$246.07**

Uses columns to make quantity, catalogue number, description, and price stand out

Calculates totals to prevent mistakes

My company would appreciate receiving these cards immediately since ●————— Expresses appreciation and tells when items are expected; identifies method of payment
we are starting an employee recognition program this fall. Enclosed is our cheque for $246.07. If additional charges are necessary, please invoice us using the enclosed address.

Sincerely,

Tom McLaughlin
Operations Manager

Subject Line Efficiency

An information response letter should contain a subject line, which helps the reader recognize the topic immediately. Knowledgeable business communicators use a subject line to refer to earlier correspondence so that in the first sentence, the most important spot in a letter, they are free to emphasize the main idea. Notice in Figure 6.4 (p. 132) that the subject line identifies the subject completely.

Quick Check
Use the subject line to refer to previous correspondence.

Opening Directly

In the first sentence of an information response, deliver the information the reader wants. Avoid wordy, drawn-out openings (*I have before me your letter of February 6, in which you request information about ...*). More forceful and more efficient is an opener that answers the inquiry (*Here is the information you wanted about ...*). When agreeing to a request for action, announce the good news promptly (*I will be happy to speak to your business communication class on the topic of ...*).

FIGURE 6.4 Information Response Letter

TRG MEDIATION SERVICES

930 Taylor Avenue
Regina, Saskatchewan
S4A 2Y4

February 6, 2007

Ms. Irene McKenzie
The Regina Leader-Post
4980 Washington Avenue
Regina, Saskatchewan
S4L 4W6

Dear Ms. McKenzie:

Identifies previous correspondence

SUBJECT: YOUR FEBRUARY 1 LETTER REQUESTING INFORMATION ON THE ROLE OF MEDIATION SERVICES COMPANIES IN THE LABOUR-MANAGEMENT RELATIONSHIP

Here are answers to your questions about mediation services. We are eager to supply you with this information so that you can publish accurate news about the role mediators play in the labour-management relationship.

1. TRG is a mediation services company that provides assistance to businesses and individuals during labour disputes. Agencies such as ours provide professional mediators to help both sides in labour-management disputes reach acceptable settlement terms. Without mediation services, many of these disputes would undoubtedly proceed to job action. Our mediators deal with disputes of all sorts from harassment complaints to wage and contract negotiations.

Answers each inquiry fully and logically in list form

2. We do not handle mediation services for person-to-person disputes such as divorce or automobile accident insurance.

3. Many collective agreements include mediation as a required step in the negotiation process once contract talks have broken down. We do not, however, make decisions about the outcome of a settlement as an arbitrator would.

4. TRG uses the methods of principled negotiation as articulated by the Harvard School of Business and others. Principled negotiation urges the participants in a dispute to search for ways that each participant can win rather than dwelling on win-lose scenarios. Our mediators are trained to help participants find the "win-win."

Builds goodwill by providing extra information and ends cordially without clichés

You'll find additional information in the enclosed booklet, "Understanding and Using Mediation Services." To speak with me personally, just call (306) 598-2300. We look forward to seeing your article in print.

Sincerely,

Debbie Wills-Garcia

Debbie Wills-Garcia
Vice-President

DWG:rio
Enclosure

Arranging Information Logically in the Body

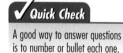

When answering a group of questions or providing considerable data, arrange the information logically and make it readable by using lists, tables, headings, bold-face, italics, or other graphic devices. When customers or prospective customers inquire about products or services, your response should do more than merely supply answers. You'll also want to promote your organization and products. Be sure to present the promotional material with attention to the "you" view and to reader benefits (*You can use our standardized tests to free you from time-consuming employment screening*). You'll learn more about special techniques for developing sales and persuasive messages in Chapter 7.

Closing Pleasantly

To avoid abruptness, include a pleasant closing remark that shows your willingness to help the reader. Provide extra information if appropriate. Tailor your remarks to fit this letter and this reader. Since everyone appreciates being recognized as an individual, avoid form-letter closings such as *If we may be of further assistance, ...*

Customer Order Responses

Some companies acknowledge orders by sending a printed postcard that informs the customer that the order has been received. Other companies take advantage of this opportunity to build goodwill and to promote new products and services. A personalized letter responding to an order is good business, particularly for new accounts, large accounts, and customers who haven't placed orders recently. An individualized letter is also necessary if the order involves irregularities, such as delivery delays, back-ordered items, or missing items.

Quick Check

Letters that follow up orders create excellent opportunities to improve the company image and to sell products.

Letters that respond to orders should deliver the news immediately; therefore, the direct strategy is most effective. Here's a writing plan that will achieve the results you want in acknowledging orders.

 ### Writing Plan for an Order Response

- **Opening**—Tell when and how the shipment will be sent.
- **Body**—Explain the details of the shipment, discuss any irregularities in the order, include resale information, and promote other products and services if appropriate.
- **Closing**—Build goodwill and use a friendly, personalized closing.

Giving Delivery Information in the Opening

Customers want to know when and how their orders will be sent. Since that news is most important, put it in the first sentence. An inefficient opener such as *We have received your order dated June 20* wastes words and the reader's time by providing information that could be inferred from more effective openers. Instead of stating that an order has been received, imply it in a first sentence that provides delivery details, as shown in Figure 6.5 on page 134 (*The books requested in your Order No. 2980 will be shipped ...*).

Quick Check

The first sentence should tell when and how an order will be sent.

Putting Details in the Body

You should include details relating to an order in the body of a letter that acknowledges the order. You will also want to discuss any irregularities about the order. If, for example, part of the order will be sent from a different location or prices have changed or items must be back-ordered, present this information.

The body of an order response is also the appropriate place to include resale information. *Resale* refers to the process of reassuring customers that their choices were good ones. You can use resale in an order letter by describing the product favourably, as shown in Figure 6.5 (*The volumes you have ordered are among our best-selling editions*). You might mention its features or attributes, its popularity among customers, or its successful use in certain applications.

Resale information confirms the good judgment of your customers and encourages repeat business. After an opening statement describing delivery information,

Quick Check

When a sales clerk tells you how good you look in the new suit you just purchased, the clerk is practising "resale."

FIGURE 6.5 Customer Order Response

Before

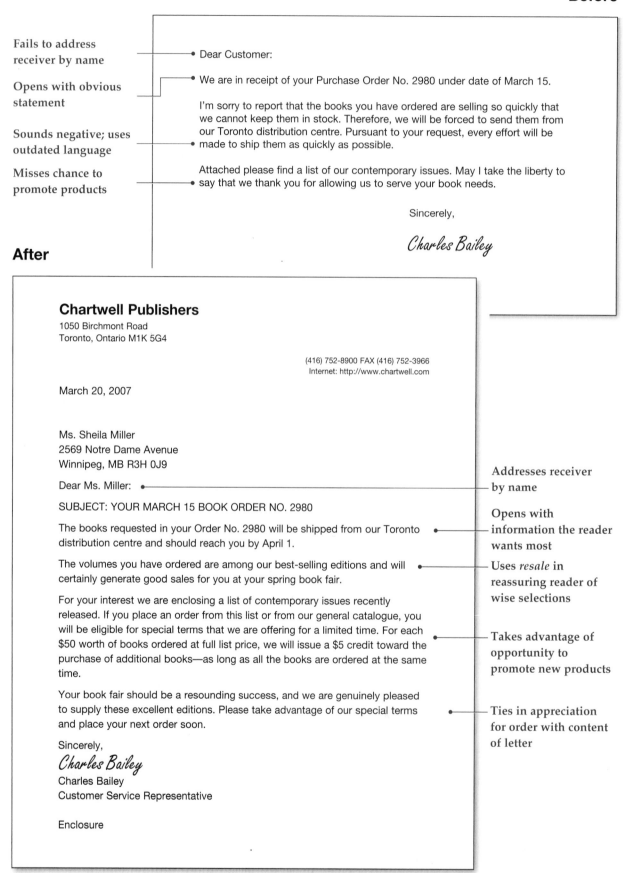

Fails to address receiver by name

Opens with obvious statement

Sounds negative; uses outdated language

Misses chance to promote products

Dear Customer:

We are in receipt of your Purchase Order No. 2980 under date of March 15.

I'm sorry to report that the books you have ordered are selling so quickly that we cannot keep them in stock. Therefore, we will be forced to send them from our Toronto distribution centre. Pursuant to your request, every effort will be made to ship them as quickly as possible.

Attached please find a list of our contemporary issues. May I take the liberty to say that we thank you for allowing us to serve your book needs.

Sincerely,

Charles Bailey

After

Chartwell Publishers

1050 Birchmont Road
Toronto, Ontario M1K 5G4

(416) 752-8900 FAX (416) 752-3966
Internet: http://www.chartwell.com

March 20, 2007

Ms. Sheila Miller
2569 Notre Dame Avenue
Winnipeg, MB R3H 0J9

Dear Ms. Miller:

SUBJECT: YOUR MARCH 15 BOOK ORDER NO. 2980

The books requested in your Order No. 2980 will be shipped from our Toronto distribution centre and should reach you by April 1.

The volumes you have ordered are among our best-selling editions and will certainly generate good sales for you at your spring book fair.

For your interest we are enclosing a list of contemporary issues recently released. If you place an order from this list or from our general catalogue, you will be eligible for special terms that we are offering for a limited time. For each $50 worth of books ordered at full list price, we will issue a $5 credit toward the purchase of additional books—as long as all the books are ordered at the same time.

Your book fair should be a resounding success, and we are genuinely pleased to supply these excellent editions. Please take advantage of our special terms and place your next order soon.

Sincerely,

Charles Bailey
Charles Bailey
Customer Service Representative

Enclosure

Addresses receiver by name

Opens with information the reader wants most

Uses *resale* in reassuring reader of wise selections

Takes advantage of opportunity to promote new products

Ties in appreciation for order with content of letter

resale information such as the following is appropriate: *The multipurpose cheques you have ordered allow you to produce several different cheque formats, including accounts payable and payroll. Customers tell us that these computerized cheques are the answer to their cheque-writing problems.*

Order acknowledgment letters are also suitable vehicles for sales promotion material. An organization often has other products or services that it wishes to highlight and promote. For example, a bed-and-breakfast establishment might include the following sales feature in a booking confirmation letter: *While staying with us next month, why not take advantage of our in-house spa. We offer services ranging from esthetics to massage, for women and men. We offer a 15 percent discount on spa services for our guests. Please book your spa services a week before you arrive to be eligible for the discount.* Sales promotion material should be used in moderation because too much of it may irritate the reader.

Quick Check

Resale emphasizes a product already sold; promotion emphasizes additional products to be sold.

Showing Appreciation in the Closing

The closing should be pleasant, forward-looking, and appreciative. Above all, it should be personalized. That is, it should relate to the particular customer whose order you are acknowledging. Don't use all-purpose form-letter closings such as *We appreciate your interest in our company* or *Thank you for your order* or *We look forward to your continued business.*

Quick Check

The best closings are personalized; they relate to one particular letter.

Customer Claim Responses

As you learned earlier, when an organization receives a claim, it usually means that something has gone wrong. In responding to a claim, you have three goals:

- To rectify the wrong, if one exists
- To regain the confidence of the customer
- To promote future business and goodwill

Quick Check

Responding to customer claims means rectifying the wrong, regaining customer confidence, and promoting future business.

If you decide to grant the claim, your response letter will represent good news to the reader. Use the direct strategy described in the following writing plan.

 Writing Plan for Granting a Claim

- **Subject line (optional)**—Identify the previous correspondence.
- **Opening**—Grant request or announce the adjustment immediately. Include resale or sales promotion if appropriate.
- **Body**—Provide details about how you are complying with the request. Try to regain the customer's confidence, and include resale or sales promotion if appropriate.
- **Closing**—End positively with a forward-looking thought, express confidence in future business relations, and avoid referring to unpleasantness.

Revealing Good News in the Opening

Instead of beginning with a review of what went wrong, present the good news immediately. When Amy Hopkins responded to Electronic Warehouse's claim about a missing shipment, her first draft, shown at the top of Figure 6.6, was angry. No wonder. Electronic Warehouse had apparently provided the wrong shipping address, and the goods were returned. But once Amy and her company decided to send a second shipment and comply with the customer's claim, she had to give up

Quick Check

Readers want to learn the good news immediately.

FIGURE 6.6 Customer Claim Response

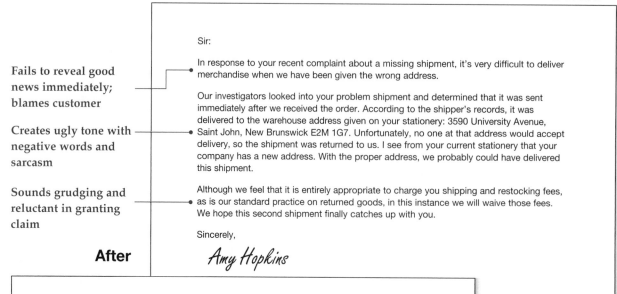

Before

Sir:

In response to your recent complaint about a missing shipment, it's very difficult to deliver merchandise when we have been given the wrong address.

Our investigators looked into your problem shipment and determined that it was sent immediately after we received the order. According to the shipper's records, it was delivered to the warehouse address given on your stationery: 3590 University Avenue, Saint John, New Brunswick E2M 1G7. Unfortunately, no one at that address would accept delivery, so the shipment was returned to us. I see from your current stationery that your company has a new address. With the proper address, we probably could have delivered this shipment.

Although we feel that it is entirely appropriate to charge you shipping and restocking fees, as is our standard practice on returned goods, in this instance we will waive those fees. We hope this second shipment finally catches up with you.

Sincerely,

Amy Hopkins

Fails to reveal good news immediately; blames customer

Creates ugly tone with negative words and sarcasm

Sounds grudging and reluctant in granting claim

After

E
W ELECTRONIC WAREHOUSE
930 Abbott Park Place
Saint John, New Brunswick E3L 0T7

February 21, 2007

Mr. Jeremy Garber
Sound, Inc.
2293 Second Avenue
Saint John, NB E3M 2R5

Dear Mr. Garber:

SUBJECT: YOUR FEBRUARY 20 LETTER ABOUT YOUR PURCHASE ORDER

You should receive by February 28 a second shipment of the speakers, VCRs, headphones, and other electronic equipment that you ordered January 20.

The first shipment of this order was delivered January 28 to 3590 University Avenue, Saint John, NB. When no one at that address would accept the shipment, it was returned to us. Now that I have your letter, I see that the order should have been sent to 2293 Second Avenue, Saint John, New Brunswick E3M 2R5. When an order is undeliverable, we usually try to verify the shipping address by telephoning the customer. Somehow the return of this shipment was not caught by our normally painstaking shipping clerks. You can be sure that I will investigate shipping and return procedures with our clerks immediately to see if we can improve existing methods.

As you know, Mr. Garber, our volume business allows us to sell wholesale electronics equipment at the lowest possible prices. However, we do not want to be so large that we lose touch with valued customers like you. Over the years our customers' respect has made us successful, and we hope that the prompt delivery of this shipment will earn yours.

Sincerely,

Amy Hopkins
Amy Hopkins
Distribution Manager

c David Cole
Shipping Department

Uses customer's name in salutation

Announces good news immediately

Regains confidence of customer by explaining what happened and by suggesting plans for improvement

Closes confidently with genuine appeal for customer's respect

Chapter 6 Routine Letters and Goodwill Messages

the anger and strive to retain the goodwill and the business of this customer. The improved version of her letter announces that a new shipment will arrive shortly.

If you decide to comply with a customer's claim, let the receiver know immediately. Don't begin your letter with a negative statement (*We are very sorry to hear that you are having trouble with your Sno-Flake ice crusher*). This approach reminds the reader of the problem and may rekindle the heated emotions or unhappy feelings experienced when the claim was written. Instead, focus on the good news. The following openings for various letters illustrate how to begin a message with good news.

> You may take your Sno-Flake ice crusher to Ben's Appliances at 310 First Street, Moose Jaw, where it will be repaired at no cost to you.

> Thanks for your letter about your new Snow Crusher tires. You are certainly justified in expecting them to last more than 12,000 km.

> We agree with you that the warranty on your Turbo programmable calculator Model AI 25C should be extended for six months.

> The enclosed cheque for $325 demonstrates our desire to satisfy our customers and earn their confidence.

In announcing that you will grant a claim, be sure to do so without a grudging tone—even if you have reservations about whether the claim is legitimate. Once you decide to comply with the customer's request, do so happily. Avoid half-hearted or reluctant responses (*Although the Sno-Flake ice crusher works well when it is used properly, we have decided to allow you to take yours to Ben's Appliances for repair at our expense*).

> ✔ **Quick Check**
> Be enthusiastic, not grudging, when granting a claim.

Explaining Compliance in the Body

In responding to claims, most organizations sincerely want to correct a wrong. They want to do more than just make the customer happy. They want to stand behind their products and services; they want to do what's right.

> ✔ **Quick Check**
> Most businesses comply with claims because they want to promote customer goodwill.

In the body of the letter, explain how you are complying with the claim. In all but the most routine claims, you should also seek to regain the confidence of the customer. You might reasonably expect that a customer who has experienced difficulty with a product, with delivery, with billing, or with service has lost faith in your organization. Rebuilding that faith is important for future business.

How to rebuild lost confidence depends on the situation and the claim. If procedures need to be revised, explain what changes will be made. If a product has defective parts, explain how the product is being improved. If service is faulty, describe genuine efforts to improve it. Notice in Figure 6.6 that the writer promises to investigate shipping procedures to see if improvements might prevent future mishaps.

Sometimes the problem is not with the product but with the way it's being used. In other instances customers misunderstand warranties or inadvertently cause delivery and billing mix-ups by supplying incorrect information. Remember that rational and sincere explanations will do much to regain the confidence of unhappy customers.

In your explanation avoid emphasizing negative words such as *trouble, regret, misunderstanding, fault, defective, error, inconvenience,* and *unfortunately.* Keep your message positive and upbeat.

> ✔ **Quick Check**
> Because negative words suggest blame and fault, avoid them in letters that attempt to build customer goodwill.

Deciding Whether to Apologize

Whether to apologize is a debatable issue. Some writing experts argue that apologies remind customers of their complaints and are therefore negative. These writers avoid apologies; instead they concentrate on how they are satisfying the customer. Real letters that respond to customers' claims, however, often include apologies.[3] If you feel that your company is at fault and that an apology is an appropriate goodwill gesture, by all means include it. Be careful, though, not to admit negligence. You'll learn more about responding to negative letters in Chapter 8.

Showing Confidence in the Closing

End your letter by looking ahead positively.

End positively by expressing confidence that the problem has been resolved and that continued business relations will result. You might mention the product in a favourable light, suggest a new product, express your appreciation for the customer's business, or anticipate future business. It's often appropriate to refer to the desire to be of service and to satisfy customers. Notice how the following closings illustrate a positive, confident tone.

> Your Sno-Flake ice crusher will help you remain cool and refreshed this summer. For your additional summer enjoyment, consider our Smoky Joe tabletop gas grill shown in the enclosed summer catalogue. We genuinely value your business and look forward to your future orders.

> We hope that this refund cheque convinces you of our sincere desire to satisfy our customers. Our goal is to earn your confidence and continue to justify that confidence with quality products and matchless service.

> You were most helpful in telling us about this situation and giving us an opportunity to correct it. We sincerely appreciate your cooperation.

> In all your future dealings with us, you will find us striving our hardest to earn your confidence by serving you with efficiency and sincere concern.

Letter of Recommendation

✔ Quick Check

You may write letters recommending people for awards, membership in organizations, or employment.

Letters of recommendation may be written to nominate people for awards and for membership in organizations. More frequently, though, they are written to evaluate present or former employees. The central concern in these messages is honesty. Thus, you should avoid exaggerating or distorting a candidate's qualifications to cover up weaknesses or to destroy the person's chances. Ethically and legally, you have a duty to the candidate as well as to other employers to describe that person truthfully and objectively. You don't, however, have to endorse everyone who asks. Since recommendations are generally voluntary, you can—and should—resist writing letters for individuals you can't truthfully support. Ask these people to find other recommenders who know them better.

Some businesspeople today refuse to write recommendations for former employees because they fear lawsuits. Other businesspeople argue that recommendations are useless because they're always positive. Despite the general avoidance of negatives, well-written recommendations do help match candidates with jobs. Hiring companies learn more about a candidate's skills and potential. As a result, they are able to place a candidate properly. Therefore, you should learn to write such letters because you will surely be expected to do so in your future career.

For letters of recommendation, use the direct strategy as described in the following writing plan.

Writing Plan for a Letter of Recommendation

- **Opening**—Identify the applicant, the position, and the reason for writing. State that the message is confidential. Establish your relationship with the applicant. Describe the length of employment or relationship.
- **Body**—Describe job duties. Provide specific examples of the applicant's professional and personal skills and attributes. Compare the applicant with others in his or her field.
- **Closing**—Summarize the significant attributes of the applicant. Offer an overall rating. Draw a conclusion regarding the recommendation.

Identifying the Purpose in the Opening

Begin an employment recommendation by identifying the candidate and the position sought, if it is known. State that your remarks are confidential, and suggest that you are writing at the request of the applicant. Describe your relationship with the candidate, as shown here:

Ms. Cindy Rosales, whom your organization is considering for the position of media trainer, requested that I submit confidential information on her behalf. Ms. Rosales worked under my supervision for the past two years in our Video Training Centre.

Letters that recommend individuals for awards may open with more supportive statements, such as *I'm very pleased to nominate Robert Walsh for the Employee-of-the-Month award. For the past sixteen months, Mr. Walsh served as staff accountant in my division. During that time he distinguished himself by . . . .*

 Quick Check

The opening of a letter of recommendation should establish the reason for writing and the relationship of the writer.

Describing Performance in the Body

The body of an employment recommendation should describe the applicant's job performance and potential. Employers are particularly interested in such traits as communication skills, organizational skills, people skills, ability to work with a team, ability to work independently, honesty, dependability, ambition, loyalty, and initiative. In describing these traits, be sure to back them up with evidence. One of the biggest weaknesses in letters of recommendation is that writers tend to make global, nonspecific statements (*He was careful and accurate* versus *He completed eight financial statements monthly with about 99 percent accuracy*). Employers prefer definite, task-related descriptions:

As a training development specialist, Ms. Rosales demonstrated superior organizational and interpersonal skills. She started as a Specialist I, writing scripts for interactive video modules. After six months she was promoted to team leader. In that role she supervised five employees who wrote, produced, evaluated, revised, and installed 14 computer/ videodisc training courses over a period of eighteen months.

Quick Check

A good recommendation describes general qualities ("organizational and interpersonal skills") backed up by specific evidence that illustrates those qualities.

Be especially careful to support any negative comments with verification (not *He was slower than other customer service reps* but *He answered 25 calls an hour, while most service reps average 40 calls an hour*). In reporting deficiencies, be sure to describe behaviour (*Her last two reports were late and had to be rewritten by her supervisor*) rather than evaluate it (*She is unreliable and her reports are careless*).

Evaluating in the Conclusion

In the final paragraph of a recommendation, you should offer an overall evaluation. Indicate how you would rank this person in relation to others in similar positions. Many managers add a statement indicating whether they would rehire the applicant, given the chance. If you are strongly supportive, summarize the candidate's best qualities. In the closing you might also offer to answer questions by telephone. Such a statement, though, could suggest that the candidate has weak skills and that you will make damaging statements orally but not in print. Here's how our sample letter might close:

Ms. Rosales is one of the most productive employees I have supervised. I would rank her in the top 10 percent of all the media specialists with whom I have worked. Were she to return to Waterloo, we would be pleased to rehire her. If you need additional information, call me at (519) 555-3019.

General letters of recommendation, written when the candidate has no specific position in mind, often begin with the salutation TO PROSPECTIVE EMPLOYERS. More specific recommendations, to support applications to known positions, address an individual. When the addressee's name is unknown, consider using the simplified letter format, shown in Figure 6.7, which avoids a salutation.

Figure 6.7 illustrates a complete employment letter of recommendation and provides a summary of writing tips. After naming the applicant and the position sought, the letter describes the applicant's present duties. Instead of merely naming positive qualities (*He is personable, possesses superior people skills, works well with a team, is creative, and shows initiative*), these attributes are demonstrated with specific examples and details.

Writing Goodwill Messages

Goodwill messages, which include thanks, recognition, and sympathy, seem to intimidate many communicators. Finding the right words to express feelings is sometimes more difficult than writing ordinary business documents. Writers tend to procrastinate when it comes to goodwill messages, or else they send a ready-made card or pick up the telephone. Remember, though, that the personal sentiments of the sender are always more expressive and more meaningful to readers than are printed cards or oral messages. Taking the time to write gives more importance to our well-wishing. Personal notes also provide a record that can be reread, and treasured.

In expressing thanks, recognition, or sympathy, you should always do so promptly. These messages are easier to write when the situation is fresh in your mind. They also mean more to the recipient. And don't forget that a prompt thank-you note carries the hidden message that you care and that you consider the event to be important. You will learn to write four kinds of goodwill messages—thanks, congratulations, praise, and sympathy. Instead of writing plans for each of them, we recommend that you concentrate on the five Ss. Goodwill messages should be:

- **Selfless.** Be sure to focus the message solely on the receiver not the sender. Don't talk about yourself; avoid such comments as *I remember when I . . . .*
- **Specific.** Personalize the message by mentioning specific incidents or characteristics of the receiver. Telling a colleague *Great speech* is much less effective than *Great story about RIM marketing in Washington.* Take care to verify names and other facts.

FIGURE 6.7 Employment Recommendation Letter

Illustrates
simplified
letter style

Identifies
applicant and
position

Supports
general
qualities
with specific
details

Summarizes
main points and
offers
evaluation

Mentions
confidentiality
of message

Tells
relationship
to writer

Describes and
interprets
accomplish-
ments

Kelowna Health Sciences Centre

2404 Euclid Avenue   Kelowna, BC V1Y 4S3   Phone: 250 768-3434 www.khsc.bc.ca

March 2, 2007

Vice President, Human Resources
Healthcare Enterprises
1200 Riel Blvd. N.
Winnipeg, MB R3C 2X4

RECOMMENDATION OF LANCE W. OLIVER

At the request of Lance W. Oliver, I submit this confidential information in support of his application for the position of assistant director in your Human Resources Department. Mr. Oliver served under my supervision as assistant director of Patient Services at Kelowna Health Sciences Centre for the past three years.

Mr. Oliver was in charge of many customer service programs for our 770-bed hospital. A large part of his job involved monitoring and improving patient satisfaction. Because of his personable nature and superior people skills, he got along well with fellow employees, patients, and physicians. His personnel record includes a number of "Gotcha" citations, given to employees caught in the act of performing exemplary service.

Mr. Oliver works well with a team, as evidenced by his participation on the steering committee to develop our "Service First Every Day" program. His most significant contributions to our hospital, though, came as a result of his own creativity and initiative. He developed and implemented a patient hotline to hear complaints and resolve problems immediately. This enormously successful telephone service helped us improve our patient satisfaction rating from 7.2 last year to 8.4 this year. That's the highest rating in our history, and Mr. Oliver deserves a great deal of the credit.

We're sorry to lose Mr. Oliver, but we recognize his desire to advance his career. I am confident that his resourcefulness, intelligence, and enthusiasm will make him successful in your organization. I recommend him without reservation.

Mary E. O'Rourke

MARY E. O'ROURKE, DIRECTOR, Patient Services

MEO:rtd

Tips for Writing Letters of Recommendation

- Identify the purpose and confidentiality of the message.
- Establish your relationship with the applicant.
- Describe the length of employment and job duties, if relevant.
- Provide specific examples of the applicant's professional and personal skills.
- Compare the applicant with others in his or her field.
- Offer an overall rating of the applicant.
- Summarize the significant attributes of the applicant.
- Draw a conclusion regarding the recommendation.

Quick Check

Goodwill messages are most effective when they are selfless, specific, sincere, spontaneous, and short.

- **Sincere.** Let your words show genuine feelings. Rehearse in your mind how you would express the message to the receiver orally. Then transform that conversational language to your written message. Avoid pretentious, formal, or flowery language (*It gives me great pleasure to extend felicitations on the occasion of your firm's 20th anniversary*).
- **Spontaneous.** Keep the message fresh and enthusiastic. Avoid canned phrases (*Congratulations on your promotion, Good luck in the future*). Strive for directness and naturalness, not creative brilliance.
- **Short.** Although goodwill messages can be as long as needed, try to accomplish your purpose in only a few sentences. What is most important is remembering an individual. Such caring does not require documentation or wordiness. Individuals and business organizations often use special note cards or stationery for brief messages.

Thanks

Quick Check

Send letters of thanks to customers, hosts, and individuals who have performed kind acts.

When someone has done you a favour or when an action merits praise, you need to extend thanks or show appreciation. Letters of appreciation may be written to customers for their orders, to hosts and hostesses for their hospitality, to individuals for kindnesses performed, and especially to customers who complain. After all, complainers are actually providing you with "free consulting reports from the field." Complainers who feel that they were listened to often become the greatest promoters of an organization.[4]

Because the receiver will be pleased to hear from you, you can open directly with the purpose of your message. The letter in Figure 6.8 thanks a speaker who addressed a group of marketing professionals. Although such thank-you notes can be quite short, this one is a little longer because the writer wants to lend importance to the receiver's efforts. Notice that every sentence relates to the receiver and offers enthusiastic praise. And, by using the receiver's name along with contractions and positive words, the writer makes the letter sound warm and conversational.

Written notes that show appreciation and express thanks are significant to their receivers. In expressing thanks, you generally write a short note on special notepaper or heavy card stock. The following messages provide models for expressing thanks for a gift, for a favour, and for hospitality.

Quick Check

Identify the gift, tell why you appreciate it, and explain how you will use it.

To Express Thanks for a Gift

Thanks, Laura, to you and the other members of the department for honouring me with the elegant Waterford crystal vase at the party celebrating my twentieth anniversary with the company.

The height and shape of the vase are perfect to hold roses and other bouquets from my garden. Each time I fill it, I'll remember your thoughtfulness in choosing this lovely gift for me.

Quick Check

Tell what the favour means using sincere, simple statements.

To Send Thanks for a Favour

I sincerely appreciate your filling in for me last week when I was too ill to attend the planning committee meeting for the spring exhibition.

Without your participation much of my preparatory work would have been lost. It's comforting to know that competent and generous individuals like you are part of our team, Mark. Moreover, it's my very good fortune to be able to count you as a friend. I'm grateful to you.

FIGURE 6.8 Thank-You for a Favour

The Canada-Japan Society of British Columbia

302-1107 Homer Street, Vancouver, BC V6B 2Y1 www.canadajapansociety.bc.ca 604 681-0295

March 20, 2007

Mr. Bryant Huffman
Marketing Manager
Ballard Power Systems
4343 North Fraser Way
Burnaby, BC V5J 5J9

Dear Bryant:

You have our sincere gratitude for providing The Canada-Japan Society of B.C. with one of the best presentations our group has ever heard.

Your description of the battle Ballard Power waged to begin marketing products in Japan was a genuine eye-opener for many of us. Nine years of preparation establishing connections and securing permissions seems an eternity, but obviously such persistence and patience pay off. We now understand better the need to learn local customs and nurture relationships when dealing in Japan.

In addition to your good advice, we particularly enjoyed your sense of humour and jokes—as you must have recognized from the uproarious laughter. What a great routine you do on faulty translations!

We're grateful, Bryant, for the entertaining and instructive evening you provided our marketing professionals. Thanks!

Cordially,

Judy Hayashi

Judy Hayashi
Program Chair, CJSBC

JRH:grw

Tells purpose and delivers praise

Personalizes the message by using specifics rather than generalities

Spotlights the reader's talents

Concludes with compliments and thanks

To Extend Thanks for Hospitality

Jeffrey and I want you to know how much we enjoyed the dinner party for our department that you hosted Saturday evening. Your charming home and warm hospitality, along with the lovely dinner and sinfully delicious chocolate dessert, combined to create a truly memorable evening.

Most of all, though, we appreciate your kindness in cultivating togetherness in our department. Thanks, Jennifer, for being such a special person.

✓ Quick Check

Compliment the fine food, charming surroundings, warm hospitality, excellent host and hostess, and good company.

"It's a thank you letter from our office supply vendor. It used up all our fax paper."

© Ted Goff, www.tedgoff.com

Response

 ✓ Quick Check

Take the time to respond to any goodwill message you may receive.

Should you respond when you receive a congratulatory note or a written pat on the back? By all means. These messages are attempts to connect personally; they are efforts to reach out, to form professional and/or personal bonds. Failing to respond to notes of congratulations and most other goodwill messages is like failing to say "You're welcome" when someone says "Thank you." Responding to such messages is simply the right thing to do. Avoid minimizing your achievements with comments that suggest you don't really deserve the praise or that the sender is exaggerating your good qualities.

To Answer a Congratulatory Note

Thanks for your kind words regarding my award, and thanks, too, for sending me the newspaper clipping. I truly appreciate your thoughtfulness and warm wishes.

To Respond to a Pat on the Back

Your note about my work made me feel good. I'm grateful for your thoughtfulness.

Sympathy

 ✓ Quick Check

Sympathy notes should refer to the misfortune sensitively and offer assistance.

Most of us can bear misfortune and grief more easily when we know that others care. Notes expressing sympathy are probably more difficult to write than any other kind of message. Commercial "In sympathy" cards make the task easier—but they are far less meaningful. Grieving friends want to know what you think—not what Hallmark's card writers think. To help you get started, you can always glance through cards expressing sympathy. They will supply ideas about the kinds of thoughts you might wish to convey in your own words. In writing a sympathy note, (1) refer to the death or misfortune sensitively, using words that show you understand what a crushing blow it is; (2) in the case of a death, praise the deceased in a personal way; (3) offer assistance without going into excessive detail; and (4) end on a reassuring, forward-looking note. Sympathy messages may be typed, although handwriting seems more personal. In either case, use notepaper or personal stationery.

To Express Condolences

We are deeply saddened, Gayle, to learn of the death of your husband. Warren's kind nature and friendly spirit endeared him to all who knew him. He will be missed.

Although words seem empty in expressing our grief, we want you to know that your friends at QuadCom extend their profound sympathy to you. If we may help you or lighten your load in any way, you just have to call.

We know that the treasured memories of your many happy years together, along with the support of your family and many friends, will provide strength and comfort in the months ahead.

Quick Check

In condolence notes mention the loss tactfully and recognize the good qualities of the deceased. Assure the receiver of your concern. Offer assistance. Conclude on positive, reassuring note.

Summing Up and Looking Forward

In this chapter you learned to write letters that respond favourably to information requests, orders, and customer claims. You also learned to write effective responses to these letters. Finally, you learned how to write recommendation and goodwill messages. Virtually all of these routine letters use the direct strategy. They open immediately with the main idea followed by details and explanations. But not all letters will carry good news. Occasionally, you must deny requests and deliver bad news. In the next chapter you will learn to use the indirect strategy in conveying negative news.

Critical Thinking

1. What is wrong with using the indirect pattern for writing routine requests and replies? If the reader understands the message, why make a big fuss over the organization?
2. Since brevity is valued in business writing, is it ever wise to respond with more information than requested? Why or why not?
3. Is it insensitive to include resale or sales promotion information in a letter that responds to a claim letter from a customer?
4. Which is more effective in claim letters—anger or objectivity? Why?
5. Why is it important to regain the confidence of a customer when you respond to a claim letter?
6. Is it appropriate for businesspeople to write goodwill messages expressing thanks, recognition, and sympathy to business acquaintances? Why or why not?

Chapter Review

7. Why do businesspeople still write letters when e-mail is so much faster?

8. What determines whether you write a letter directly or indirectly?

9. What are the two most important positions in a letter?

10. List two ways that you could begin an inquiry letter that asks many questions.

11. What three elements are appropriate in the closing of a request for information?

12. What is a claim letter? Give an original example.

13. What are the three goals when responding to a customer claim letter?

14. Why do some companies comply with nearly all claims?

15. What information should the opening in a letter of recommendation include?

16. The best goodwill messages include what five characteristics?

Writing Improvement Exercises

Letter Openers. Which of the following entries represents an effective direct opening?

_____ 17. a. Permit me to introduce myself. I am Alexa Alexander, and I represent TelCom. With the travel season approaching quickly, have you thought about upgrading your telecommunications system to meet the expected increased demand?

   b. Have you thought about upgrading your telecommunications system to meet the expected increased demand in the upcoming travel season?

_____ 18. a. Thank you for your letter of December 2 in which you inquired about the availability of No. 19 bolts of fabric.

   b. We have an ample supply of No. 19 bolts in stock.

_____ 19. a. Yes, the Princess Cruise Club is planning a 15-day Mediterranean cruise beginning October 20.

   b. This will acknowledge receipt of your letter of December 2 in which you ask about our Mediterranean cruise schedule.

_____ 20. a. Your letter of July 9 requesting a refund has been referred to me because Mr. Halvorson is away from the office.

   b. Your refund cheque for $175 is enclosed.

_____ 21. a. We sincerely appreciate your recent order for plywood wallboard panels.

   b. The plywood wallboard panels that you requested were shipped today by GoFast Express and should reach you by August 12.

Direct Openings. Revise the following openings so that they are more direct. Add information if necessary.

22. Hello! My name is Nalini Tomei, and I am the assistant manager of Body Trends, a fitness equipment centre in Montreal. My manager has asked me to inquire about the upright and semi-recumbent cycling machines that we saw advertised in the June issue of *Your Health* magazine. I have a number of questions.

23. Because I've lost your order form, I have to write this letter. I hope that it's all right to place an order this way. I am interested in ordering a number of things from your summer catalogue, which I still have although the order form is missing.

24. Pursuant to your letter of January 15, I am writing in regard to your inquiry about whether we offer our European-style patio umbrella in colours. This unique umbrella is a very popular item and receives a number of inquiries. Its 3-metre canopy protects you when the sun is directly overhead, but it also swivels and tilts to virtually any angle for continuous sun protection all day long. It comes in two colours: off-white and forest green.

25. I am pleased to receive your inquiry regarding the possibility of my acting as a speaker at the final meeting of your business management club on April 30. The topic of online résumés interests me and is one on which I think I could impart helpful information to your members. Therefore, I am responding in the affirmative to your kind invitation.

26. We have just received your letter of March 12 regarding the unfortunate troubles you are having with your Magnum DVD player. In your letter you ask if you may send the flawed machine to us for inspection. Although we normally handle all service requests through our local dealers, in your circumstance we are willing to take a look at your unit here at our plant in Edmonton. Therefore, please send it to us so that we may determine what's wrong.

Closing Paragraph. The following concluding paragraph to a claim letter response suffers from faults in strategy, tone, and emphasis. Revise and improve.

27. As a result of your complaint of June 2, we are sending a replacement shipment of laser printers by Excellent Express. Unfortunately, this shipment will not reach you until June 5. We hope that you will not allow this troubling

incident and the resulting inconvenience and lost sales you suffered to jeopardize our future business relations. In the past we have been able to provide you with quality products and prompt service.

Activities and Cases

6.1 Information Request: Can I Do a Co-op Placement at Your Firm? You are a second-semester interior design student at Algonquin College in Ottawa. As part of your four-year applied degree program, you are required to complete a 20-week co-op term. Rather than using the services of the college's co-op office, which normally helps students find co-op positions, you've decided to strike out on your own. Being fluently bilingual, you decide you'd like to move to Montreal for your co-op term. You've narrowed your search down to one well-known design firm, Leroux + Smythe, and you have a lot of questions. For example, has the firm used co-op students before? If so, what typical tasks did the students perform? Another question you'd like answered is whether the firm can pay a salary or at least an honorarium for your 20-week placement. Also, you'd like to know what kinds of clients the firm has for its design services. Finally, you're interested in the amount of French you'll have to write and speak during your placement. You decide to write the company a letter requesting information.

1. What should you include in the opening of this information request?

2. What should the body of your letter contain?

3. How can your phrase your questions most effectively?

4. How should you close this letter?

Your Task. Using your own return address, write a personal business letter requesting information about a co-op placement to Claudette Garneau, Manager Human Resources, Leroux + Smythe, 1450 rue Maclennan, Montreal, QC H3X 2Y4.

Related Web site: Information on Algonquin College's program in interior design is available at <www.algonquincollege.com/acad_menus/current/6148X3FWO.html>. Information on co-op placements is available at <www.algonquincollege.com/coop>.

6.2 Claim Request: Free Samples Are Surprisingly Costly. As marketing manager of Caribou Mountain Ranch, you are very ticked off at Quantum Enterprises. Quantum provides imprinted promotional products for companies. Your resort was looking for something special to offer in promoting its vacation packages. Quantum offered free samples of its promotional merchandise, under its "No Surprise" policy.

You figured, what could you lose? So on January 11 you placed a telephone order for a number of samples. These included three kinds of jumbo tote bags, a square-ended barrel bag with fanny pack, as well as a deluxe canvas attaché case and two colours of garment-dyed sweatshirts. All items were supposed to be free. You did think it odd that you were asked for your company's MasterCard number, but Quantum promised to bill you only if you kept the samples.

When the items arrived, you weren't pleased, and you returned them all on January 21 (you have a postal receipt showing the return). But your February credit statement showed a charge of $239.58 for the sample items. You called Quantum in February and spoke to Lane, who assured you that a credit would be made on your next statement. However, your March statement showed no credit. You called again and received a similar promise. It's now April and no credit has been made. You decide to write and demand action. Circle the correct choice in the following items.

1. To open this claim letter, you should
   a. Provide a complete chronology of what happened with all the dates and facts.
   b. Tell Quantum how sick and tired you are of this game it is playing.
   c. Explain carefully how much of your valuable time you have spent on trying to resolve this matter.
   d. Describe the action you want taken.

2. In writing this claim letter, you should assume that Quantum
   a. Regularly uses this trick to increase its sales.
   b. Made an honest mistake and will rectify the problem.
   c. Has no intention of crediting your account.
   d. Reacts only when threatened seriously.

3. In the body of this claim letter, you should
   a. Describe briefly what has taken place.
   b. Refer to specific dates and names of people contacted.
   c. Enclose copies of any relevant documents.
   d. All of the above.

4. The closing of this claim letter should
   a. Refer to your lawyer, whom Quantum will hear from if this matter is not settled.
   b. Explain what action you want taken and by when.
   c. Make sure that Quantum knows that you will never use their products again.
   d. Threaten to spread the word among the travel industry that Quantum can't be trusted.

Your Task. After circling your choices, write a claim letter that documents the problem and states the action you want taken. Add any information you feel is necessary. Address your letter to Ms. Kayla Tutshi, Customer Service, Quantum Enterprises, 1505 Victory Drive, Kamloops, BC V2C 4X3.

6.3 Order Request: Indian Pottery Not Available Online. You are the owner of Swank, a home decor shop in Toronto. Each year, you travel to India and Thailand to purchase goods for your shop. In Jaipur, India, you recently met for the first time Mr. Ajit Haryana, president of Blue Pottery Industries, the leading maker of pottery in India. Mr. Haryana gave you his card, which includes his e-mail and Web site addresses, and you promised to be in touch with him once you got back to Canada. Once back in Canada, however, you find that neither the e-mail nor the Web address on Mr. Haryana's card functions. His card doesn't have a phone number on it, only a mailing address. You ask your shop assistant to write an order letter to Mr. Haryana, requesting the shipment of a number of his pottery products. Your assistant comes back ten minutes later with a draft letter, which she asks you to approve. The letter is reproduced below.

Dear Mr. Haryana,

My boss saw a number of items in your Jaipur showroom recently that she would like to order for our shop. She is particularly interested in ordering 50 of the yellow and green 12" vases that you retail for 1,000 rupees. What is the wholesale cost to us? She would also like to order 50 of the 6" turquoise candlestick holders which retail for 750 rupees. Please also include in our shipment 25 of the brown monkey tiles and 25 of the blue elephant tiles. Finally, my boss would like you to send 50 of the 5" yellow-flower soap dishes that retail for 300 rupees.

We are interested in having these items charged to our credit card. The more quickly you can turn this order around the better, as our busiest season of the year starts in a month.

Sincerely,

Your Task. Analyze the above letter and list the reasons why it is ineffective. Rewrite the above order letter following an effective writing plan for an order letter. Use full block style, and write the letter on Swank letterhead. Send the letter to Mr. Ajit Haryana, President, Blue Pottery Industries, Friends Colony, 303904, Jaipur, India.

6.4 Information Request: Culture Vultures Seeking Adventure. You just saw a great television program about cheap travel in Europe, and you think you'd like to try it next summer. The program described how some people want to get away from it all; others want to see a little of the world. Some want to learn a different language; some want to soak up a bit of culture. The "get-away" group, the program advised, should book a package trip to a Contiki resort where they relax and soak up the sun. But "culture vultures" and FITs (free independent travellers) should select the countries they want to visit and plan their own trips. You decide to visit France, Spain, and Portugal.

Begin planning your trip by gathering information from the country's tourist office or Web site. Many details need to be worked out. What about visas? How about inoculations? Since your budget will be limited, you need to stay in hostels whenever possible. Where are they? Are they private? Some hostels accept only people who belong to their organization. You really need to get your hands on a list of hostels for every country before departure. You are also interested in any special transport passes for students, such as a Eurail Pass. And while you are at it, find out if they have any special guides for student travellers. All this information can be secured from a tourist office.

Your Task. Using the Internet, you found an address for information: Tourist Office of Spain in Canada, 3402–2 Bloor Street West, Toronto, ON M4W 3E2 <www.tourspain.toronto.on.ca/English/index.html>. Write a letter requesting information. If you prefer another country, find its tourist office address. Because this is a personal business letter, include your return address above the date.

6.5 Information Request: Meeting in Haines Junction at the Dalton Trail Lodge. Your company, Software Solutions, has just had an enormously successful two-year sales period. The CEO has asked you, as marketing manager, to arrange a fabulous conference/retreat as a thank-you gift for all 20 engineers, product managers, and salespeople. She wants the company to host a four-day combination sales conference/vacation/retreat at some spectacular location. She suggests that you start by inquiring at the Dalton Trail Lodge in Haines Junction, Yukon.

You check its Web site and get some good information. However, you decide to write a letter so that you can have a permanent, formal record of all the resorts you investigate. You estimate that your company will require about 20 rooms. You'll also need about three conference rooms for one and a half days. You want to know room rates, conference facilities, and outdoor activity possibilities for families. You have two times that would be possible: September 18–22 or October 4–8. You know that these are off-peak times, and you wonder if you can get a good room rate. What is the most economical way to get to Haines Junction from Software Solutions' headquarters in Prince George, B.C.? One evening you will want to host a banquet for about 140 people. The CEO wants a report from you by April 1.

Your Task. Write a well-organized information request to Dalton Trail Lodge, c/o Grayling Camp Enterprises, Box 5331, Haines Junction, Yukon Y0B 1L0.

Related Web site: <www.daltontrail.com>.

6.6 Information Request: Computer Code of Conduct. As an assistant in the campus computer centre, you have been asked by your supervisor to help write a code of conduct for use of the centre facilities. This code will spell out what behaviour and activities are allowed in your centre. The first thing you are to do is conduct a search of the Internet to see what other college or university computing centres have written as conduct codes.

Web

Your Task. Using at least two search engines, search the Web employing variations of the keywords "computer code of conduct." Print two or three codes that seem appropriate. Write a letter (or e-mail message, if your instructor agrees) to the director of an educational computer centre asking for further information about its code and its effectiveness. Include at least five significant questions. Attach your printouts to your letter.

6.7 Information Request: Backpacking Cuisine. Assume that you are Marc Vannault, manager of a health spa and also an ardent backpacker. You are organizing a group of hikers for a wilderness trip to Yukon. One item that must be provided is freeze-dried food for the three-week trip. You are unhappy with the taste and quality of backpacking food products currently available. You expect to have a group of hikers who are older, affluent, and natural-food enthusiasts. Some are concerned about products containing preservatives, sugar, and additives. Others are on diets restricting cholesterol, fat, and salt.

You heard that Outfitters, Inc., offers a new line of freeze-dried products. You want to know what they offer and whether they have sufficient variety to serve all the needs of your group. You need to know where their products can be purchased and what the cost range is. You'd also like to try a few of their items before placing a large order. You are interested in how they produce the food products and what kinds of ingredients they use. If you have any items left over, you wonder how long they can be kept and still be usable.

Your Task. Write an information request letter to Karie Osborne, Outfitters, Inc., 1169 Willamette Street, Canmore, Alberta T0L 2P2.

6.8 Order Confirmation Letter: A Rail Link to Pearson International Airport. You are the director of purchasing for the City of Toronto. After a multi-year process including requests for proposals from qualified suppliers and public meetings across the city, the city has decided to hire SNC-Lavalin to design and build a high-speed rail link from Union Station in downtown Toronto to Pearson International Airport in the suburb of Mississauga. While there have been intense negotiations between the Mayor of Toronto and SNC-Lavalin for months, it looks as if an agreement has been reached. SNC-Lavalin will conduct a transit study, conduct environmental testing, and design and build the rail link and rail cars. The total budget for the services is $860 million: $90 million for the transit study, $98 million for the environmental testing, and the balance for the design and building of the link and the cars. The project is expected to take five years to complete, and the city's payments will be phased over that time period.

Your Task. As the director of purchasing for the City of Toronto, you have been instructed by city council to write an official order confirmation letter to SNC-Lavalin. Address your letter to Jim Burke, Senior Vice-President and General Manager, Rail Services, SNC-Lavalin, 1075 West Georgia St., Vancouver, BC V6E 3C9.

Related Web site: Information on SNC-Lavalin's rail services is available at <www.snclavalin.com/en/2_0/2_13_1.aspx>.

6.9 Claim Letter: Undersized French Doors. As Julie Chen, owner of Smart Interiors, you recently completed a kitchen remodel that required double-glazed, made-to-order oak French doors. You ordered them by telephone on July 2 from Custom Wood, Inc. When they arrived on July 25, your carpenter gave you the bad news: the doors were cut too small. Instead of measuring a total of 3.23 square metres, the doors measured 3.13 square metres. In your carpenter's words, "No way can I stretch those doors to fit these openings!" You waited three weeks for these doors, and your clients wanted them installed immediately. Your carpenter said, "I can rebuild this opening for you, but I'm going to have to charge you for my time." His extra charge came to $455.50.

You feel that the people at Custom Wood should reimburse you for this amount, since it was their error. In fact, you actually saved them money by not returning the doors. You decide to write to Custom Wood and enclose a copy of your carpenter's bill. You wonder whether you should also include a copy of Custom Wood's invoice, even though it does not show the exact door measurements. You are a good customer of Custom Wood, having used their quality doors and windows on many other jobs. You're confident that it will grant this claim.

Your Task. Write a claim letter to Jay Brandt, Marketing Manager, Custom Wood, Inc., 401 Main Street, Vancouver, BC V1L 2E6.

6.10 Claim Letter: The Real Thing. Have you ever bought a product that didn't work as promised? Have you been disappointed in service at a bank, video store, restaurant, or department store? Have you had ideas about how a company or organization could improve its image, service, or product? Remember that smart companies want to know what their customers think, especially if a product could be improved.

Your Task. Select a product or service that has disappointed you. Write a claim letter requesting a refund, replacement, explanation, or whatever seems reasonable. For claims about food products, be sure to include bar-code identification from the package, if possible. Your instructor may ask you to actually mail this letter. When you receive a response, share it with your class.

6.11 Claim Letter: Deep Desk Disappointment. Assume that you are Monica Keil, President, Keil Consulting Services, 423 Lawrence Avenue, Montreal, Quebec H5L 2E3. Since your consulting firm is doing very well, you decide to splurge and purchase a fine executive desk for your own office. You order an expensive desk described as "North American white oak embellished with hand-inlaid walnut cross-banding." Although you do not ordinarily purchase large, expensive items by mail, you are impressed by the description of this desk and by the money-back guarantee promised in the catalogue.

When the desk arrives, you know that you have made a mistake—it is not the high-quality product that you had anticipated. The wood finish is rough, the grain looks splotchy, and many of the drawers do not pull out easily. The advertisement has promised "full suspension, silent ball-bearing drawer slides." You are disappointed with the desk and decide to send it back, taking advantage of the money-back guarantee.

Your Task. Write a letter to Rodney Harding, Marketing Manager, Big Spruce Wood Products, P.O. Box 488, Sandpoint, British Columbia V5N 7L8. You want your money refunded. You're not sure whether the freight charges can be refunded, but it's worth a try. Supply any details needed.

6.12 Information Response: Avoiding Employee Gifts That Are Re-gifted.

Web

A friend of yours, Megan Stowe, is an executive with a large insurance company. One day in late October you see her at an industry conference in St. John's, Newfoundland. Afterward, you decide to head down to Water Street for a coffee at a nearby café. After the usual small talk, she says, "You know, I'm beginning to hate the holidays. Every year it gets harder to choose presents for our staff. Once we gave fruitcakes, which I thought were tasty and elegant, but it turns out a lot of our people re-gifted them to other people before Christmas." As an executive training coach, you say, "Well, what's your gift goal? Do you want to encourage your employees? Are you just saying thanks? Or do you want your gifts to act as a retention tool to keep good people on your team?" Megan responds, "I never thought of it that way. Our company doesn't really have a strategy for holiday gifts. It's just something we do every year. Do you have any ideas?"

As it turns out, you have a lot of ideas. You've developed a gift list based on the reasons talented people stay in organizations. Megan asks you to get in touch next week explaining some of the gift ideas. She thinks she will be able to retain your services for this advice.

Your Task. Using your library databases and the Web, research articles and information on corporate gift giving. As a consultant, prepare a letter with a sampling of gift-giving ideas addressed to Megan Stowe, Vice President, Human Resources, London Life Insurance Company, 255 Dufferin Ave., London, ON N6A 4K1.

6.13 Information Response Request: Scannable Résumés.

Team

Critical
Thinking

As part of a team of interns at a Precision Shoes catalogue store, you have been asked to write a form letter to send to job applicants who inquire about your résumé-scanning techniques. The following poorly written response to an inquiry was pulled from the file.

Dear Mr. Chouxfleur:

Your letter of April 11 has been referred to me for a response. We are pleased to learn that you are considering employment here at Precision Shoes, and we look forward to receiving your résumé, should you decide to send same to us.

You ask if we scan incoming résumés. Yes, we certainly do. Actually, we use Smart-Track, an automated résumé-tracking system. SmartTrack is wonderful! You know, we sometimes receive as many as 30 résumés a day, and SmartTrack helps us sort, screen, filter, and separate the résumés. It also processes them, helps us organize them, and keeps a record of all of these résumés. Some of the résumés, however, cannot be scanned, so we have to return those—if we have time.

The reasons that résumés won't scan may surprise you. Some applicants send photocopies or faxed copies, and these can cause misreading, so don't do it. The best plan is to send an original copy. Some people use coloured paper. Big mistake! White paper (8 1/2 × 11-inch) printed on one side is the best bet. Another big problem is unusual type fonts, such as script or fancy gothic or antique fonts. They don't seem to realize that scanners do best with plain, readable fonts such as Helvetica, Arial, or Times New Roman in a 10-to-14-point size.

Other problems occur when applicants use graphics, shading, italics, underlining, horizontal and vertical lines, parentheses, and brackets. Scanners like plain résumés! Oh yes, staples can cause misreading. And folding of a résumé can also cause the scanners to foul up. To be safe, don't staple or fold, and be sure to use wide margins and a quality printer (no dot matrixes!!).

When a hiring manager within Precision Shoes decides to look for an appropriate candidate, he is told to submit keywords to describe the candidate he has in mind for his opening. We tell him (or sometimes her) to zero in on nouns and phrases that best describe what they want. Thus, my advice to you is to try to include those words that highlight your technical and professional areas of expertise.

If you do decide to submit your résumé to us, be sure you don't make any of the mistakes described herein that would cause the scanner to misread it.

Sincerely,

Your Task. As a team, discuss how this letter could be improved. Decide what information is necessary to send to potential job applicants. Search for additional information that might be helpful. Then, submit an improved version to your instructor. Although the form letter should be written so that it can be sent to anyone who inquires, address this one to Rene Chouxfleur, 629 Cathedral Street, Vancouver, BC V3L 2F3.

6.14 Information Response Request: Backpacking Cuisine. As Karie Osborne, owner of Outfitters, Inc., producer of freeze-dried backpacking foods, answer the inquiry of Marc Vannault (described in Activity 6.7). You are eager to have Mr. Vannault sample your new all-natural line of products containing no preservatives, sugar, or additives. You want him to know that you started this company two years ago after you found yourself making custom meals for discerning backpackers who rejected typical camping fare. Some of your menu items are excellent for individuals on restricted diets. Some dinners are cholesterol-, fat-, and salt-free, but he'll have to look at your list to see for himself.

You will send him your complete list of dinner items and the suggested retail prices. You will also send him a sample "Saturday Night on the Trail," a four-course meal that comes with fruit candies and elegant appetizers. All your food products are made from choice ingredients in sanitary kitchens that you supervise personally. They are flash-frozen in a new vacuum process that you have patented. Although your dried foods are meant to last for years, you don't recommend that they be kept beyond 18 months because they may deteriorate. This could happen if a package were punctured or if the products became overheated.

Your Task. Respond to Marc Vannault, 322 East Drive, Penticton, BC V2A 1T2. By the way, your products are currently available at High-Country Sports Centre, 19605 Rocky Mountain Highway, Calgary, AB T8L 1Z8. Large orders may be placed directly with you, and you offer a 5 percent discount on direct orders.

6.15 Order Response: Unfortunately We're Fully Booked... As the sales manager of the Dalton Trail Lodge in Haines Junction, Yukon, you sometimes wish you had an infinite number of rooms to offer prospective guests. Realistically, what often happens is that people all want to stay at the lodge at similar times. You recently received a letter from Software Solutions in Prince George, B.C. (Activity 6.5). Unfortunately, you have to tell Software Solutions that both dates it requested are already fully booked at the Lodge. That's the bad news. The good news as you see it is that the periods immediately after the ones requested by Software Solutions are free (i.e., September 25–29 and October 11–15). You are very eager to make the sale, despite the fact that the dates of the Lodge's availability don't exactly match up with Software Solutions' request.

Your Task. Because the original request came by letter, you decide to respond in an equally formal way by writing a letter on Lodge letterhead. In your letter, you encourage Software Solutions to be in touch via telephone or e-mail so that a solution to the situation can be reached more quickly.

6.16 Claim Response: Undersized French Doors. As Jay Brandt, manager of Custom Wood, Inc., you have a problem. Your firm manufactures quality pre-cut and custom-built doors and frames. You have received a letter dated August 3 from Julie Chen (described in Activity 6.9). Ms. Chen is an interior designer, and she complains that the oak French doors she recently ordered for a client were made to the wrong dimensions. Critical Thinking

Although they were the wrong size, she kept the doors and had them installed because her clients were without outside doors. However, her carpenter charged an extra $455.50 to install them. She claims that you should reimburse her for this amount, since your company was responsible for the error. You check her July 2 order and find that the order was filled correctly. In a telephone order, Ms. Chen requested doors that measured 3.13 square metres and that's what you sent. Now she says that the doors should have been 3.23 square metres.

Your policy forbids refunds or returns on custom orders. Yet, you remember that around July 2 you had two new people working the telephones taking orders. It's possible that they did not hear or record the measurements correctly. You don't know whether to grant this claim or refuse it. But you do know that you must look into the training of telephone order takers and be sure that they verify all custom order measurements. It might also be a good idea to have your carpenters call a second time to confirm custom measurements.

Ms. Chen is a successful interior designer and has provided Custom Wood with a number of orders. You value her business but aren't sure how to respond. You'd like to remind her that Custom Wood has earned a reputation as a premier manufacturer of wood doors and frames. Your doors feature prime woods, meticulous craftsmanship, and award-winning designs. And the engineering is ingenious.

Your Task. Decide how to treat this claim and then respond to Julie Chen, Smart Interiors, 3282 Richmond Road, Vancouver, BC V5Y 2A8. You might mention that you have a new line of greenhouse windows that are available in three sizes. Include a brochure describing these windows.

6.17 Claim Response: Deep Desk Disappointment. As Rodney Harding, Marketing Manager, Big Spruce Wood Products, it is your job to reply to customer claims, and today you must respond to Monica Keil, President, Keil Consulting Services (described in Activity 6.11). You are disturbed that she is returning the executive desk (Invoice No. 3499), but your policy is to comply with customer wishes. If she doesn't want to keep the desk, you will certainly return the purchase price plus shipping charges. Desks are occasionally damaged in shipping, and this may explain the marred finish and the sticking drawers.

You want Ms. Keil to give Big Spruce Wood Products another chance. After all, your office furniture and other wood products are made from the finest hand-selected woods by master artisans. Since she is apparently furnishing her office, send her another catalogue and invite her to look at the traditional conference desk on page 10-E. This is available with a matching credenza, file cabinets, and accessories. She might be interested in your furniture-leasing plan, which can produce substantial savings.

Your Task. Write to Monica Keil, President, Keil Consulting Services, 423 Lawrence Avenue, Montreal, Quebec H5L 2E3. In granting her claim, promise that you will personally examine any furniture she may order in the future.

6.18 Recommendation Letter: Telling It Like It Is. You are a business communication professor at a community college. Your students do a co-op semester from May to August as part of their program. In March, some of your students start asking for recommendation letters. This spring in particular has been heavy with requests, and one sticks in your mind. Jeff Brown, a second-year student, who has been in two of your classes, asks for a recommendation letter. He is applying for entry-level customer service jobs in the banking industry. You are Jeff's business communication professor, and you've got little to complain about. Jeff has been averaging an A in your two courses, his writing and speaking skills are superior, he thinks critically, solves problems in original ways, and is a good team player. Unfortunately, he's managed to demonstrate all of these strong skills and maintain his high average while continually skipping classes and arriving late for the classes he does show up to. You want to give Jeff a good recommendation, but you realize that in the work world, absenteeism and showing up late aren't treated as lightly as at college.

Your Task. Write a general letter of recommendation for Jeff Brown.

6.19 Thanks for the Favour: I Got a Job! You are Jeff Brown from Activity 6.18 above. It took you only three weeks of co-op job hunting and you landed a great job with Scotiabank. You'd like to thank your business communication professor for the recommendation letter s/he wrote you in early March. You're busy with end of term and final exams, though, so you put writing the thanks letter off till late April, more than six weeks since the recommendation letter was written.

Your Task. Write a letter thanking your professor.

6.20 Response to Thanks: Congratulations on Your New Job. As the professor from Activity 6.18 above, you've just received Jeff Brown's handwritten letter of thanks. You're off for your vacation at this point, and only checking in at the office once a week. You don't have Jeff's mailing address, but you do have his e-mail address.

Your Task. Send Jeff an e-mail responding to his letter of thanks.

6.21 Sympathy Message: For a Friend Who Can't Work Anymore. Your best friend at work, Alice Palumbo, was diagnosed with breast cancer some months ago. Her treatments appeared to be effective at first, and she continued to work even though her hair had fallen out and she was feeling weak. It's now six months since her original diagnosis and Alice has begun to miss first whole days and then whole weeks of work. Your supervisor sends an e-mail memo one day informing everyone on your team that Alice is taking a long-term leave of absence.

Your Task. Write Alice a sympathy message.

The following sentences contain errors in grammar, punctuation, capitalization, number style, usage, and spelling. Below each sentence write a corrected version.

1. Every secretaries desk will be equipped with the most latest computer and printer.

2. We ordered new stationary about 2 months ago but I can find no correspondance or invoice related to our order.

3. Anyone of the Vice-Presidents are authorized to sign cheques, however for amounts that are over 10 thousand dollars 2 signatures are required.

4. To be admitted an application must be submitted before April 1st.

5. Although twenty percent of the Companys sales now come from outside North America the Company expects to increase that number to thirty percent, by 2002.

6. The sierra club recommend investing in "socially responsible" companys such as the mountain equipment coop.

7. Some organizations worry that valueable company information may be stole over the internet.

8. Did you know that an ostriches eye is bigger than it's brain.

9. Jennifer completed a b.com. degree in Accounting, before taking a job with the boeing company.

10. Because she had took many computer courses Erin had numerous job opportunitys from which to chose.

11. The number of students taking Second Language courses are increasing everyyear.

12. To ensure valid survey results each of the fortune 500 companies were sent a questionnaire by the researchers.

13. When Doreen Sparx became Vice-President of Customer Support the customer contact centre was receiving more than ten thousand calls a month.

14. Amy miller president of quad graphics met privately with her director of marketing.

15. Some of my business electives Courses includes marketing, small business management, and Mandarin for business.

Grammar/Mechanics Challenge—6

Document for Revision

The following fax has faults in grammar, punctuation, spelling, number form, and wordiness. Use standard proofreading marks (see Appendix B) to correct the errors. When you finish, your instructor can show you the revised version of this fax.

January 20, 2006

FAX TRANSMISSION

Mr. Benjamin Spring

322 East Chapman St.

North Hatley, QC

Dear Mr. Spring:

SUBJECT: Your January 11 Letter Requesting Information About New All Natural Products

We have received your letter of January 11 in which you inquire about our all-natural products. Needless to say, we are pleased to be able to answer in the affirmative. Yes, our new line of freeze dried back packing foods meet the needs of older adults and young people as well. You asked a number of questions, and here are answers to you're questions about our products.

• Our all natural foods contains no perservatives, sugars or additives. The inclosed list of dinner items tell what foods are cholesterol-, fat-, and salt-free.

- Large orders recieve a five percent discount when they're placed direct with Outfitters, Inc. You can also purchase our products at Malibu Sports Center, 19605 Pacific Coast Highway Malibu CA, 90265.

- Outfitters, Inc., food products are made in our sanitary kitchens which I personally supervise. The foods are flash froze in a patented vacum process that retain freshness, texture and taste.

- Outfitters, Inc. food products are made from choice ingredients that combines good taste and healful quality.

- Our foods stay fresh and tasty for up to 18 months.

Mr. Spring I started Outfitters, Inc., two years ago after making custom meals for discerning back packers who rejected typical camping fare. What a pleasure it is now to share my meals with back packers like you.

I hope you'll enjoy the enclosed sample meal, "Saturday Night on the Trail" is a four-coarse meal complete with fruit candys and elegant appetizers. Please call me personally at (213) 459-3342 to place an order, or to ask other questions about my backpacking food products.

Sincerely,

Retailer Cleans Up Its Act

For years companies have been aware of the corporate social responsibility (CSR) movement. This movement requires that companies attempt to "operate in an economically and environmentally sustainable manner, while acknowledging the interests of all… stakeholders."[5] In a recent high-profile case in Saskatoon, a women's clothing retailer, Sensational, was picketed by local community members for what they claimed was "a lack of responsibility" around environmental issues. Apparently, in a bid to distinguish itself from the competing stores in the area, the store wrapped all its customers' purchases in multiple layers of tissue paper, and then put this package inside a huge plastic carrying bag with its name printed on the side. Soon, local sidewalk garbage cans began to overflow with the unnecessary packaging offered by this retailer. A vigilant community group wrote a letter to the retailer asking that it reconsider its packaging practices, but never heard anything back. Five months later, the protest took place, and the media covered the protest. The retailer was unhappy, to say the least, about the negative media coverage.

Career Application

In class discussion, consider these questions:
- Why are companies increasingly interested in social responsibility?
- Should employees be encouraged to report suspected irresponsible behaviour of their employers?
- What are the advantages and disadvantages of detailed codes of social responsibility for companies?

Your Task

You are the assistant manager of Sensational. Your boss, the manager, asks you to research corporate social responsibility and draft a memo summary of the most important points by next week. She also implies that if she likes what she sees, she'll send it to head office in Vancouver. Using library databases and the Web, research corporate social responsibility and write a memo to your boss, Sherry Cardinal, as instructed.

Related Web site: For a good example of a corporate social responsibility code, visit the Canadian Business for Social Responsibility (CBSR) Web site at <www.cbsr.bc.ca> and look for GoodCompany Guidelines under CSR Resources.

CHAPTER

Persuasive Messages

Information overload and the need to reprioritize are being experienced across all sectors in business today—it's the new normal. Persuading others to buy into your priorities is best done by looking for common interests and aligning collective goals. Acknowledge and provide support to those who are critical to your success and your agenda will become their agenda.[1]

Jose Ribau, *director, Partner Negotiations & Management*
Sales Effectiveness, Branch Banking, CIBC

LEARNING OBJECTIVES

1. Use the indirect strategy to persuade.
2. Write convincing claim request letters.
3. Request favours persuasively.
4. Present new ideas in persuasive memos.
5. Analyze techniques used in sales letters.
6. Compose carefully planned sales letters.

Quick Check

The ability to persuade is a primary factor in personal and business success.

Persuasion is the ability to make people think or do what you would like them to think or do. Developing the ability to persuade is a key factor in the success you achieve in your business messages, in your career, and in your interpersonal relations. As Jose Ribau implies, persuasive individuals are highly valued in today's successful organizations. He suggests that everyone make persuasive communication skills a priority. Persuasive individuals become decision makers, managers, executives, and entrepreneurs because their ideas generally prevail. This chapter will examine techniques for presenting ideas persuasively.

Using the Indirect Pattern in Persuasive Requests

Persuasion is necessary when resistance is anticipated or when ideas require preparation before they can be presented effectively. For example, asking for a favour implies that you want someone to do something for nothing—or for very little. Common examples are requests for the donation of time, money, energy, a name, resources, talent, skills, or expertise. On occasion, everyone needs to ask a favour. Small favours, such as asking a coworker to lock up the office for you on Friday, can be straightforward and direct. Little resistance is expected. Larger favours, though, require careful planning and an indirect strategy. A busy executive is asked to serve on a committee to help disadvantaged children. A florist is asked to donate table arrangements for a charity fundraiser. A well-known author is asked to speak before a local library group. In each instance persuasion is necessary to overcome natural resistance.

The letters shown in Figure 7.1 (p. 164) illustrate two versions of a favour request. Joanne North works for an organization without funds hoping to entice a well-known authority to speak before its regional conference. Such a request surely requires indirectness and persuasion, but the ineffective version begins with a direct appeal. Even worse, the reader is given an opportunity to refuse the request before the writer has a chance to present reasons for accepting. Moreover, this letter fails to convince the reader that she has anything to gain by speaking to this group. Finally, the closing suggests no specific action to help her accept, should she be so inclined.

A favour request is doomed to failure if the writer does not consider its effect on the reader. In the more effective version, notice how the writer applies the indirect strategy. The opening gains the reader's attention and makes her want to read more regarding the reaction to her article. By showing how Dr. Kasdorf's interests are related to the organization's, the writer builds interest before presenting the request. The request is then followed by language that reduces resistance, showing Dr. Kasdorf how she will benefit from accepting this invitation. This successful letter concludes with a specific action closing. A writing plan for a persuasive request is shown below:

 Writing Plan for a Persuasive Request

- **Gain attention** in the opening
- **Build interest** in the body
- **Reduce resistance** in the body
- **Motivate action** in the closing

The Components of an Indirect Persuasive Request

The indirect pattern described above contains separate strategies, but in a successful persuasive message all four appear together as a unified whole. And the order of the four strategies is not set in stone. Not every persuasive situation will require you to build interest before you reduce resistance, for example. However, the majority of persuasive messages begin by gaining attention and end by motivating action.

Gain Attention. In the opening of the message, which is usually brief, you gain the reader's attention through a strategy such as describing a problem, making an unexpected statement, mentioning a reader benefit, paying the reader a compliment, or posing a stimulating question. For example, in a persuasive request letter sent by a local seniors' investment club to a financial planner, the writer might begin by paying the planner a compliment: *A number of our club's members have used your services in the past and have had nothing but praise for your professionalism.*

FIGURE 7.1 Persuasive Favour Request

Before

Provides easy excuse
for refusal

Sounds writer-centred
instead of reader-
centred

Closes negatively and
fails to tell how to
respond

Dear Dr. Kasdorf:

Although your research, teaching, and consulting must keep you extremely busy, we hope that your schedule will allow you to be the featured speaker at the Canadian Association of Human Resource Managers' regional conference in Vancouver on March 23.

We are particularly interested in the article that appeared in the *Harvard Business Review*. A number of our members indicated that your topic, "Cost/Benefit Analysis for Human Resources," is something we should learn more about.

We have no funds to pay you, but we would like to invite you and your spouse to be our guests at the banquet following the day's sessions. We hope that you will be able to speak before our group.

Sincerely,

After

Canadian Association of Human Resource Managers
196 West 4th Avenue
Vancouver, BC V6R 3T4
(604) 543-8922

January 4, 2007

Professor Beverly J. Kasdorf
University College of the Cariboo
200 Mountain Way
Kamloops, BC V1L 2R4

Dear Dr. Kasdorf:

Cost/benefit analysis applied to human resources is a unique concept. Your recent article on that topic in the *Harvard Business Review* ignited a lively discussion at the last meeting of the Vancouver chapter of the Canadian Association of Human Resource Managers.

Many of the managers in our group are experiencing the changes you describe. Functions in the personnel area are now being expanded to include a wide range of salary, benefit, and training programs. These new programs can be very expensive. Our members are fascinated by your cost/benefit analysis that sets up a formal comparison of the costs to design, develop, and implement a program idea against the costs the idea saves or avoids.

The members of our association have asked me to invite you to be the featured speaker March 23, when we hold our annual conference in Vancouver. About 150 human resource specialists will attend the all-day conference at the Parkland Hotel. We would like you to speak at 2 p.m. on the topic of "Applying Cost/Benefit Analysis in Human Resources Today."

Although an honorarium is not provided, we can offer you an opportunity to help human resource managers apply your theories in solving some of their most perplexing problems. You will also meet managers who might be able to supply you with data for future research into personnel functions. In addition, the conference includes two other sessions and a banquet, to which you and a guest are invited.

Please call me at (604) 543-8922 to allow me to add your name to the program as the featured speaker before the Canadian Association of Human Resource Managers on March 23.

Respectfully,

Joanne North

Joanne North
Executive Assistant

Gains attention of
reader by appealing to
her interests

Builds interest by
persuading reader that
her expertise is valued

Makes direct request

Reduces resistance by
softening negative
aspects of request with
reader benefits

Motivates specific
action confidently

Build Interest. The message's body is intended to keep the reader's attention and persuade him or her that the request is reasonable. This section is often the longest part of the message, as it includes strategies such as the use of facts and statistics, expert opinion, listing of direct benefits to the receiver, examples and specific details, as well as indirect benefits to the receiver. In the seniors' investment club example, the writer may begin building interest by stating, *You may be interested to know that while five of our twenty-five members have used your services before, the other twenty members of the club are either without a financial planner or else considering changing planners.*

Reduce Resistance. A crucial part of a persuasive message's body, yet one that is often left out by unsophisticated writers, is the writer putting himself or herself in the receiver's shoes and asking, What kinds of problems might the receiver have with my request? For example, the seniors' investment club letter writer may guess that the financial planner is a busy person with many engagements. This is his most likely source of resistance. In order to counter this perceived resistance, the writer adds a short section where he or she anticipates and names this resistance and then counters it with a benefit. For example, the letter may read: *Even though we understand you have a busy schedule of daily meetings with clients, we believe an hour spent talking to us about trends in retirement planning could lead to a new client base.*

Motivate Action. Finally, no persuasive message is complete without the sender closing by telling the receiver exactly what he or she wants, and when he or she wants it. The trick in this section is to sound confident but not pushy, to motivate the reader to say yes. In essence, a persuasive message should end with a specific request that is confident but not pushy. In the seniors' investment club example, the letter might end, *The club meets at 1:00 pm on the last Friday of each month, in this case the 31st. Lunch is included. We would be grateful if you responded by the end of next week confirming your acceptance of our invitation. Please call Mr. David Taylor at (613) 686-3704.*

Persuasive Claims and Complaint Messages

Let's say you bought a new car and the transmission repeatedly required servicing. When you finally get tired of taking it in for repair, you decide to write to the car manufacturer's district office asking that the company install a new transmission in your car. You know that your request will be resisted. You must convince the manufacturer that replacement, not repair, is needed. Routine claim letters, such as those you wrote in Chapter 6, are straightforward and direct. Persuasive claims, on the other hand, are generally more effective when they are indirect.

The organization of an effective persuasive claim or complaint message centres on the closing and the persuasion. First, decide what action you want taken to satisfy the claim. Then, decide how you can prove the worth of your claim. Plan carefully the line of reasoning you will follow in convincing the reader to take the action you request. If the claim is addressed to a business, the most effective appeals are generally to the organization's pride in its products and its services. Refer to its reputation for integrity and your confidence in it. Show why your claim is valid and why the company will be doing the right thing in granting it. Most organizations are sincere in their efforts to produce quality products that gain consumer respect.

Although claim letters are often complaint letters, try not to be angry. Hostility and emotional threats toward an organization do little to achieve the goal of a claim letter. Claims are usually referred to a customer service department. The representative answering the claim probably had nothing to do with the design, pro-

Quick Check

Use persuasion when you must change attitudes or produce action.

Quick Check

The most successful appeals are to a company's pride in its products and services.

Claim letters should avoid negative and emotional words and should not attempt to fix blame.

duction, delivery, or servicing of the product or service. An abusive letter may serve only to offend, thus making it hard for the representative to evaluate the claim rationally.

A writing plan for an indirect claim follows the pattern below.

 ## Writing Plan for a Persuasive Request

- **Gain attention** in the opening by paying the receiver a compliment.
- **Build interest** in the body by explaining and justifying the claim or complaint with convincing reasons and without anger.
- **Reduce resistance** in the body by subtly suggesting the responsibility of the receiver. Appeal to the receiver's sense of fairness or desire for customer satisfaction.
- **Motivate action** in the closing by explaining exactly what action you want taken and when.

Observe how the claim letter shown in Figure 7.2 illustrates the preceding suggestions. When AMS Limitée bought several new enhanced telephones, it discovered that they would not work when the fluorescent lights were on. The company's attempt to return the telephones had been refused by the retailer. Notice that the opening statement gains attention with a compliment about the product. The second paragraph builds interest by describing the problem without animosity or harsh words. The letter reduces resistance by suggesting the responsibility of the manufacturer while stressing the disappointment of the writer. The final paragraph motivates action by stating exactly what action should be taken.

Persuasive Suggestions

Presenting reasons first avoids premature rejection of a new idea.

Within an organization the indirect strategy is useful when persuasion is needed in presenting new ideas to management or to colleagues. It's also useful in requesting action from employees and in securing compliance with altered procedures. Whenever resistance is anticipated, a sound foundation of reasoning should precede the main idea. This foundation prevents the idea from being rejected prematurely.

You should expect new ideas to meet with resistance. It doesn't matter whether the ideas are moving downward as orders from management, moving upward as suggestions to management, or moving laterally between coworkers. Resistance to change is natural. When asked to perform differently or to try something new, some individuals resist because they fear failure. Others resist because they feel threatened—the proposed changes may encroach on their status or threaten their security. Some people resist new ideas because they don't understand a proposed idea or are cautious of the person making the proposal.

Offering counterarguments helps overcome resistance.

Whatever the motivation, resistance to new ideas and altered procedures should be expected. You can prepare for this resistance by anticipating objections, offering counterarguments, and emphasizing benefits. Don't assume that the advantages of a new idea are obvious and therefore may go unmentioned. Use concrete examples and familiar illustrations in presenting arguments.

In the e-mail shown in Figure 7.3 (p. 168), Megan Wong, supervisor, argues for the purchase of a new scanner and software. She expects the director to resist this request because the budget is already overextended. Megan's memo follows the writing plan for a persuasive request. It gains attention by describing a costly

FIGURE 7.2 Persuasive Claim

AMS *Limitée*

309 rue du la Morenie, Sherbrooke, Quebec J1H 4E6 (819) 690-3500

November 21, 2006

Customer Service
D. Gerard, Inc.
594 avenue Montmorency
Montreal, Quebec H2L 2E9

SUBJECT: CODE-A-PHONE MODEL 100S

Your Code-A-Phone Model 100S answering unit came well recommended. We liked our neighbour's unit so much that we purchased thirty for different departments in our business.

After the thirty units were unpacked and installed, we discovered a problem. Apparently our office fluorescent lighting interferes with the electronics in these units. When the lights are on, heavy static interrupts every telephone call. When the lights are off, the static disappears.

We can't replace the fluorescent lights; thus we tried to return the Code-A-Phones to the place of purchase (Chauffage Saint-Laurent, 2560 Taschereau Boulevard, Brossard, QC J4W 3J8). A salesperson inspected the units and said they could not be returned since they were not defective and they had been used.

Because the descriptive literature and instructions for the Code-A-Phones say nothing about avoiding use in rooms with fluorescent lighting, we expected no trouble. We were quite disappointed that this well-engineered unit—with its time/date stamp, room monitor, and auto-dial features—failed to perform as we hoped it would.

If you have a model with similar features that would work in our offices, give me a call. Otherwise, please authorize the return of these units and refund the purchase price of $1038 (see enclosed invoice). We're confident that a manufacturer with your reputation for excellent products and service will want to resolve this matter quickly.

Reva A. Barat

Reva A. Barat, PRESIDENT

RAB:jkb
Enclosure

Uses simplified letter style when name of receiver is unknown

Gains attention with compliment

Builds interest by describing problem calmly

Reduces resistance by subtly suggesting responsibility

Stresses disappointment

Motivates action by stating what steps to take

Appeals to company's desire to preserve good reputation

Tips for Making Claims

- Begin with a compliment, point of agreement, statement of the problem, or brief review of action you have taken to resolve the problem.
- Provide identifying information.
- Prove that your claim is valid; explain why the receiver is responsible.
- Enclose document copies supporting your claim.
- Appeal to the receiver's fairness, ethical and legal responsibilities, and desire for customer satisfaction.
- Describe your feelings and your disappointment.
- Avoid sounding angry, emotional, or irrational.
- Close by telling exactly what you want done.

FIGURE 7.3 Persuasive Suggestion

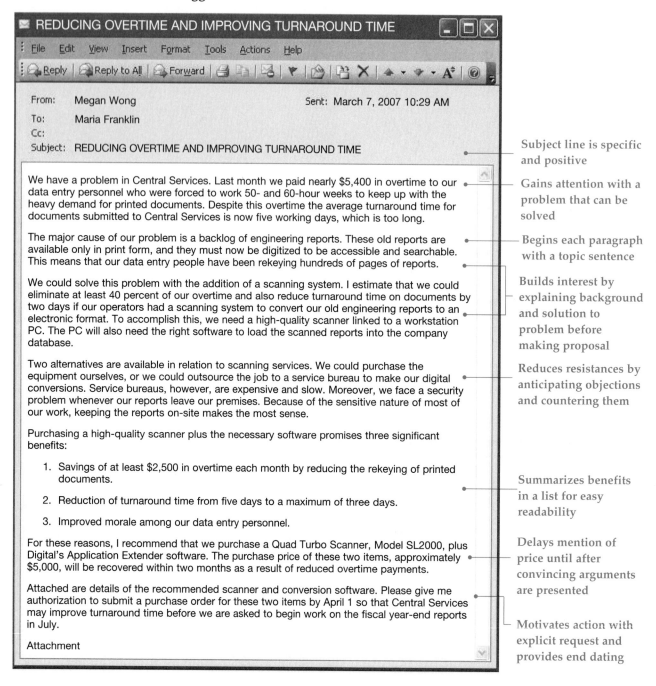

REDUCING OVERTIME AND IMPROVING TURNAROUND TIME

File   Edit   View   Insert   Format   Tools   Actions   Help

Reply | Reply to All | Forward

From: Megan Wong   Sent: March 7, 2007 10:29 AM
To: Maria Franklin
Cc:
Subject: REDUCING OVERTIME AND IMPROVING TURNAROUND TIME

We have a problem in Central Services. Last month we paid nearly $5,400 in overtime to our data entry personnel who were forced to work 50- and 60-hour weeks to keep up with the heavy demand for printed documents. Despite this overtime the average turnaround time for documents submitted to Central Services is now five working days, which is too long.

The major cause of our problem is a backlog of engineering reports. These old reports are available only in print form, and they must now be digitized to be accessible and searchable. This means that our data entry people have been rekeying hundreds of pages of reports.

We could solve this problem with the addition of a scanning system. I estimate that we could eliminate at least 40 percent of our overtime and also reduce turnaround time on documents by two days if our operators had a scanning system to convert our old engineering reports to an electronic format. To accomplish this, we need a high-quality scanner linked to a workstation PC. The PC will also need the right software to load the scanned reports into the company database.

Two alternatives are available in relation to scanning services. We could purchase the equipment ourselves, or we could outsource the job to a service bureau to make our digital conversions. Service bureaus, however, are expensive and slow. Moreover, we face a security problem whenever our reports leave our premises. Because of the sensitive nature of most of our work, keeping the reports on-site makes the most sense.

Purchasing a high-quality scanner plus the necessary software promises three significant benefits:

1. Savings of at least $2,500 in overtime each month by reducing the rekeying of printed documents.

2. Reduction of turnaround time from five days to a maximum of three days.

3. Improved morale among our data entry personnel.

For these reasons, I recommend that we purchase a Quad Turbo Scanner, Model SL2000, plus Digital's Application Extender software. The purchase price of these two items, approximately $5,000, will be recovered within two months as a result of reduced overtime payments.

Attached are details of the recommended scanner and conversion software. Please give me authorization to submit a purchase order for these two items by April 1 so that Central Services may improve turnaround time before we are asked to begin work on the fiscal year-end reports in July.

Attachment

Subject line is specific and positive

Gains attention with a problem that can be solved

Begins each paragraph with a topic sentence

Builds interest by explaining background and solution to problem before making proposal

Reduces resistances by anticipating objections and countering them

Summarizes benefits in a list for easy readability

Delays mention of price until after convincing arguments are presented

Motivates action with explicit request and provides end dating

problem in which Megan knows the reader is interested. To convince the director of the need for these purchases, Megan builds interest by explaining the background and providing a possible solution to the problem. Because Megan knows that the director values brevity, she tries to focus on the main points. To further improve readability, Megan begins every paragraph with a topic sentence.

After reviewing background information and the cause of the problem, Megan brings up the request for a new scanning system. She reduces resistance by discussing it in terms of benefits to the reader and the company (eliminating 40 percent of overtime and reducing turnaround time). Megan also anticipates objections (outsourcing as an alternative) but counters this possible objection by pointing out that outsourcing is expensive, slow, and insecure. In the closing Megan motivates action by asking for authorization to go ahead and for providing support documentation to speed the request. She also includes end-dating, which prompts the director to act by a certain date.

Sales Letters

Sales letters are usually part of direct mail marketing efforts that many people consider "junk mail." However, advertising in Canada is growing at an annual rate of 5.5 percent, while direct marketing is growing at an annual rate of 8.8 percent. Direct marketing is an $8.48 billion industry.[2] This includes all sales letters, packets, brochures, and catalogues sent directly to consumers.

The professionals who specialize in direct mail marketing have made a science of analyzing a market, developing an appropriate mailing list, studying the product, preparing a comprehensive presentation that appeals to the needs of the target audience, and motivating the reader to act. This carefully orchestrated presentation typically concludes with a sales letter accompanied by a brochure, a sales list, illustrations of the product, testimonials, and so forth.

We are most concerned here with the sales letter: its strategy, organization, and appeals. You'll want to learn the secrets of these messages for many reasons. Although the sales letters of large organizations are usually written by professional copywriters, many smaller companies cannot afford such specialized services. Entrepreneurs and employees of smaller businesses may be called on to write their own sales messages. For example, one recent graduate started a graphic design firm and immediately had to write a convincing letter offering her services. Another graduate went to work for a small company that installs security systems. Because of his recent diploma (other employees were unsure of their skills), he was asked to draft a sales letter outlining specific benefits for residential customers.

From a broader perspective nearly every letter we write is a form of sales. We sell our ideas, our organizations, and ourselves. Learning the techniques of sales writing will help you be more effective in any communication that requires persuasion and promotion. Moreover, recognizing the techniques of selling will enable you to respond to such techniques more rationally. You will be a better-educated consumer of ideas, products, and services if you understand how sales appeals are made.

Quick Check

Sales letters are written by professional copywriters in large firms, but in small firms employees must write their own.

Quick Check

Recognizing and applying the techniques of sales writing can be helpful even if you never write a sales letter.

Analyzing the Product and the Reader

Before writing a sales letter, it's wise to study the product and the target audience so that you can emphasize features with reader appeal.

Know Your Product. To sell a product effectively, learn as much as possible about how it was created, including its design, its parts, and the process of production and distribution. Study its performance, including ease of use, efficiency, durability, and applications. Consider warranties, service, price, and special appeals. Know your own product but also that of your competitor. In this way, you can emphasize your product's strengths against the competitor's products' weaknesses.

Know the Culture. If a product is being developed and marketed for consumers in different cultures, learn as much as possible about the targeted cultures. Although companies would like to use the same products and advertising campaigns as they push into global markets, most find that using a single approach for every local market falls flat. They may think globally, but they must execute locally. In producing and selling frozen yogurt to the world, Canadian company Yogen Früz makes learning about the host country's culture a priority. For example, at the grand opening of its first franchise in Guatemala, a country with a strong religious tradition, the company ensured that a priest was on hand to bless the proceedings.[3]

Knowing the audience and adapting your message to it is important for any communication. But it's especially true for sales letters. That's why the most effective sales letters are sent to targeted audiences. Mailing lists for selected groups can be purchased or compiled. For example, the manufacturer of computer supplies would find an appropriate audience for its products in the mailing list of subscribers to a computer magazine.

Target the Audience. By using a selected mailing list, a sales letter writer is able to make certain assumptions about the readers. Readers may be expected to have similar interests, abilities, needs, income, and so forth. The sales letter can be adapted to appeal directly to this selected group. In working with a less specific audience, the letter writer can make only general assumptions and must use a catch-all approach, hoping to find some appeal that motivates the reader.

The following writing plan for a sales letter attempts to overcome anticipated reader resistance by creating a desire for the product and by motivating the reader to act.

 ### Writing Plan for a Sales Letter

- **Gain attention** in the opening by standing out from the competition.
- **Build interest** in the body by emphasizing a central selling point and appealing to the reader's needs.
- **Reduce resistance** in the body by creating a desire for the product and introducing price strategically.

Gaining the Reader's Attention by Standing Out from the Competition

Gaining the attention of the reader is essential in unsolicited or uninvited sales letters. In solicited sales letters, individuals have requested information; thus, attention-getting devices are less important.

Attention-getting devices are especially important in unsolicited sales letters.

Provocative messages or unusual formats may be used to attract attention in unsolicited sales letters. These devices may be found within the body of a letter or in place of the inside address.

Offer	Your free calculator is just the beginning!
Product feature	Your vacations—this year and in the future—can be more rewarding thanks to an exciting new book from *Canadian Geographic*.
Inside-address opening	We Wonder, Mrs. Crain, If You Would Like to Know How to Retire in Style with Mutual Funds.
Startling statement	Extinction is forever. That's why we need your help in preserving many of the world's endangered species.
Story	On a beautiful late spring afternoon, 25 years ago, two young men graduated from the same college. They were very much alike, these two young men.... Recently, these men returned to their college for their 25th reunion. They were still very much alike.... But there was a difference. One of the men was manager of a small department of [a manufacturing company]. The other was its president.

Other effective openings include a bargain, a proverb, a solution to a problem, a quotation from a famous person, an anecdote, and a question.

Building Interest by Appealing to the Reader and Emphasizing Central Selling Points

Persuasive appeals generally fall into two broad groups: emotional appeals and rational appeals. Emotional appeals are those associated with the senses; they include how we feel, see, taste, smell, and hear. Strategies that arouse anger, fear, pride, love, and satisfaction are emotional.

Emotional appeals relate to the senses; rational appeals relate to reasoning and intellect.

Rational strategies are those associated with reason and intellect; they appeal to the mind. Rational appeals include references to making money, saving money, increasing efficiency, and making the best use of resources. Generally, use rational appeals when a product is expensive, long lasting, or important to health and security. Use emotional appeals when a product is inexpensive, short lived, or nonessential.

Banks selling chequing and savings services frequently use rational appeals. They emphasize saving money in chequing fees, earning interest on accounts, receiving free personalized cheques, and saving time in opening the account. In contrast, a travel agency selling a student tour to Mexico uses an emotional strategy by describing the "sun, fun, and partying" to be enjoyed. Many successful selling campaigns combine appeals, emphasizing perhaps a rational appeal while also including an emotional appeal in a subordinated position.

In sales letters build interest by developing one or two central selling points and stressing them.

Although a product may have a number of features, concentrate on just one or two of those features. Don't bewilder the reader with too much information.

Analyze the reader's needs and tailor your appeal directly to the reader. The letter selling a student tour to Mexico emphasized two points:

1. We see to it that you have a great time. Let's face it. By the end of the term, you've earned your vacation. The books and jobs and stress can all be shelved for a while.
2. We keep our trips affordable. Mazatlan 1A is again the lowest-priced adventure trip offered in Canada.

The writer analyzed the student audience and elected to concentrate on two appeals: (1) an emotional appeal to the senses (having a good time) and (2) a rational appeal to saving money (paying a low price).

Reducing Resistance by Creating a Desire for the Product and Introducing Price Strategically

In convincing readers to purchase a product or service, you may use a number of techniques:

Quick Check

Reduce resistance by creating a desire for a product through reader benefit, concrete and objective language, product confidence, or testimonials.

- **Reader benefit.** Discuss product features from the reader's point of view. Show how the reader will benefit from the product:

  You'll be able to extend your summer swim season by using our new solar pool cover.

- **Concrete language.** Use concrete words instead of general or abstract language:

  Our Mexican tour provides more than just a party. Maybe you've never set eyes on a giant saguaro cactus … or parasailed high above the Pacific Ocean … or watched a majestic golden sunset from your own private island.

- **Objective language.** Avoid language that sounds unreasonable. Overstatements using words like *fantastic, without fail, foolproof, amazing, astounding,* and so forth do not ring true. Overblown language and preposterous claims may cause readers to reject the entire sales message.

- **Product confidence.** Build confidence in your product or service by assuring customer satisfaction. You can do this by offering a free trial, money-back guarantee, free sample, or warranty. Another way to build confidence is to associate your product with respected references or authorities:

  Our concept of economical group travel has been accepted and sponsored by three major airlines. In addition, our program has been featured in *Maclean's*, the *Toronto Star*, *The Globe and Mail*, and the *National Post*.

- **Testimonials.** The statements of satisfied customers are effective in creating a desire for the product or service:

  A student returning from one of our cruises last year said, "I've just been to paradise."

Quick Check

Introduce price early if it is a sales feature; otherwise, delay mentioning it.

If product price is a significant sales feature, use it early in your sales letter. Otherwise, don't mention price until after you have created the reader's desire for the product. Some sales letters include no mention of price; instead, an enclosed order form shows the price. Other techniques for de-emphasizing price include the following:

- **Show the price in small units.** For instance, instead of stating the total cost of a year's subscription, state the magazine's price when calculated per issue. Or describe insurance premiums by their cost per day.
- **Show how the reader is saving money by purchasing the product.** In selling solar heating units, for example, explain how much the reader will save on heating bills.
- **Compare your prices with those of competitors.** Describe the savings to be realized when your product is purchased.
- **Make your price a bargain.** For instance, point out that the special introductory offer is one-third off the regular price. Or say that the price includes a special discount if the reader acts immediately.
- **Associate the price with reader benefits.** Note, for example, that for as little as $3 a month, you'll enjoy emergency road and towing protection, emergency trip-interruption protection, and nine other benefits.

Notice in Figure 7.4 (p. 174) how price is directly linked to customer benefits. New Western Bank opens its promotional letter by telling the reader how much money can be saved on its chequing account. This central selling feature is then emphasized throughout the letter, although other selling points are also mentioned.

Motivating Action by Stimulating the Reader to Buy

The closing of a sales letter has one very important goal: stimulating the reader to act. A number of techniques help motivate action:

- **Make the action clear.** Use specific language to tell exactly what is to be done:

Submit your request at our Web site.

Call this toll-free number.

Send the enclosed reservation card along with your cheque.

> ✓ **Quick Check**
>
> Motivate action in a sales letter by telling the reader exactly what to do.

FIGURE 7.4 Sales Letter

New Western Bank

3200 Portage Avenue, Winnipeg, MB R3H 8L9

Dianne Ladd
AVP & Manager
Personal Financial Centre

April 3, 2007

Mr. Chen Xian
1045 Cuthbert Drive
Winnipeg, MB R3L 2H3

Dear Mr. Xian:

Gains attention with appealing offer — Why pay $50, $100, or even $150 a year in chequing account service charges when New Western has the right price for chequing—FREE!

Builds interest by emphasizing central selling point but also introduces other — At New Western Bank we want your business. That's why we're offering "Totally Free Chequing." Compare the cost of your present chequing account. We know you'll like the difference. We also have six other personalized chequing plans, one of which is certain to be right for you.

Focuses on rational appeals — In addition to the best price on chequing accounts, we provide a variety of investment opportunities and two convenient credit-line programs. Once you qualify, you can use your credit line at any time without applying for a new loan each time you need money. With one of our credit-line programs, you can write a cheque for just about anything, including a vacation, home improvements, major purchases, unexpected bills, or investment opportunities.

Suggests specific reader benefits — If you have not yet heard about New Western Bank, you'll find that we have eight convenient locations to serve you.

Reduces resistance by making it easy for reader to open account — Check out the details of our services described in the enclosed pamphlets or at our Web site <www.newwesternbank.com>. Then check us out by stopping in to open your free chequing account at one of our eight convenient locations. You can also open your account by simply filling out the enclosed postage-paid card and returning it to us.

Motivates action by offering incentive before given date — If you open your New Western chequing account before June 15, we'll give you 200 free cheques and we'll buy back any unused cheques you have from your present chequing account. Act now to start saving money. We look forward to serving you.

Sincerely,

Dianne Ladd

Dianne Ladd
Accounts Vice-President

DL:egh
Enclosures

- **Make the action easy.** Highlight the simple steps the reader needs to take:

  Just fill in your credit card number and indicate the amount of your gift. Drop the postage-paid form in the mail, and we'll handle the details.

- **Offer an inducement.** Encourage the reader to act while low prices remain in effect. Offer a gift or a rebate for action:

  Now is a great time to join the Can-West Travel Club. By joining now, you'll receive a sleek and sophisticated cell phone case.

- **Limit the offer.** Set a specific date by which the reader must act in order to receive a gift, a rebate, benefits, low prices, or a special offer:

Act quickly, because I'm authorized to make this special price on solar greenhouses available only until May 1.

- **Make payment easy.** Encourage the reader to send a credit card number or to return a card and be billed later.

The sales letter for the Workplace Equity Institute shown in Figure 7.5 (p. 176) sounds quite casual. However, it actually required considerable planning on the part of the writer. This letter announces a newsletter containing tips to help managers avoid conduct that might result in unfair treatment of employees. The letter concentrates on a central selling point (the need for current and useful information) as it leads up to the action to be taken (returning a reservation form). Notice how the writer uses both emotional and rational appeals. Emotional appeals refer to a fear that managers might accidentally stumble into messy situations leading to claims against the company. Rational appeals centre on the cost of lawyers' fees compared with the low cost of the newsletter. The price of the newsletter subscription is linked with reader benefits, followed by a satisfaction guarantee. In the closing the writer requests action and makes it easy to take. A strategic postscript offers a final incentive: a free gift for prompt action. This letter typifies successful sales letters. It sounds conversational, it offers reader benefits, and it motivates action.

Online Sales Letters

As consumers become more comfortable with online shopping, they will be receiving more e-mail sales letters, such as that shown in Figure 7.6 (p. 177). Chapters.indigo.ca started its online bookselling several years ago and has seen business expand significantly. To promote its online business, Chapters wrote a short e-mail message to current customers announcing its Rewards Program benefits. After defining the central selling feature, the letter presents a low-key sales pitch for Chapters' expanded product offerings.

This message contains some important lessons for writers of online sales messages.

✓ Quick Check

Consumers can expect to receive more online sales letters as e-business grows.

- **Be selective.** Send messages only to targeted, preselected customers. E-mail users detest "spam" (unsolicited sales and other messages). However, receivers are surprisingly receptive to offers specifically for them. Remember that today's customer is somebody—not anybody.
- **Make the recipient feel special.** Notice that the Chapters message begins by placing the receiver in a group of customers who "will never pay full price again." Although this message may have been seen by thousands of customers, they felt that they could become part of a special group of customers.
- **Keep the message short and conversational.** The Chapters message contains only a few short paragraphs. Because on-screen text is taxing to read, be brief. Also make the message sound like casual conversation.
- **Focus on one or two central selling points.** In the Chapters sales message, the only real pitch is how easy it is to save at Chapters.
- **Provide means for being removed from mailing list.** It's polite and good business to include a statement that tells receivers how to be removed from the sender's mailing database.
- **Project sincerity.** Sending a simple, low-key message and encouraging feedback help establish a tone of sincerity in the message.

FIGURE 7.5 Successful Sales Letter

WORKPLACE EQUITY INSTITUTE, INC.

533 Winfield Road
Squamish, BC V1L 2H4

February 13, 2007

Mr. C. D. Avery, President
Avery Enterprises, Inc.
2043 Frasier Street
Kelowna, BC V5L 2E2

Dear Mr. Avery:

Gains attention with startling statement — If you had told me a couple of years ago that any time I hired, fired, or appraised an employee I could be facing review from the Human Rights Commission, I'd have said you were crazy.

Builds interest with emotional appeals — Just last October, though, I read about an employee who claimed that he had been fired because he had complained that his company had not kept its promises to him. He filed a complaint with the Commission and was later awarded either reinstatement or a year's severance pay for wrongful dismissal! You're probably as alarmed as I am about how difficult it is in today's world to ensure that your company practises fair treatment for all its employees. Issues like discrimination, wrongful dismissal, sexual harassment, and employee testing are becoming more and more common. Employees are taking action to ensure their rights are protected. Now more than ever employers need to know and protect the rights of everyone in their workplaces.

As a business owner, you may be aware of what constitutes fair treatment. But what about all the managers in your company who aren't as knowledgeable? How can you train them to avoid stumbling accidentally into improper—or even worse, illegal—behaviour?

Reduces resistance by creating desire and associating price with reader benefit — The best way to prepare your managers is with our easy-to-read newsletter called the MANAGER'S UPDATE. Twice a month, this four-page letter delivers valuable advice to the managers you pick. They will learn to focus on positive behaviours and avoid those "red flag" promises, practices, and actions that lead to claims of unfair treatment. And with legal fees starting at $200 and $300 an hour, you know how costly it is to defend against any claim. That's where MANAGER'S UPDATE can save you thousands of dollars—and at a cost of less than 85 cents an issue.

Makes it easy to respond — To start your subscription immediately, just sign the enclosed reservation form. Fill in the number of copies you want, and return the form in the postage-paid envelope. I'll take care of the rest.

Sincerely,

Paul Cerilli

Paul Cerilli, President

PC:rjt

Motivates action with free gift — P.S. Respond within ten days and we'll rush you at no charge THE EMPLOYER'S OBLIGATION, a special reference book selling for $39.95 in bookstores.

FIGURE 7.6 Online Sales Message

Chapters Is Now Open

File Edit View Insert Format Tools Actions Help

Reply | Reply to All | Forward

From: Chapters.indigo.ca
Sent: Fri, 1 Oct 2000 02:45:22 - 0700 (PDT)
To: <jtillotson@liberty.org>
Cc:
Subject: Chapters Is Now Open

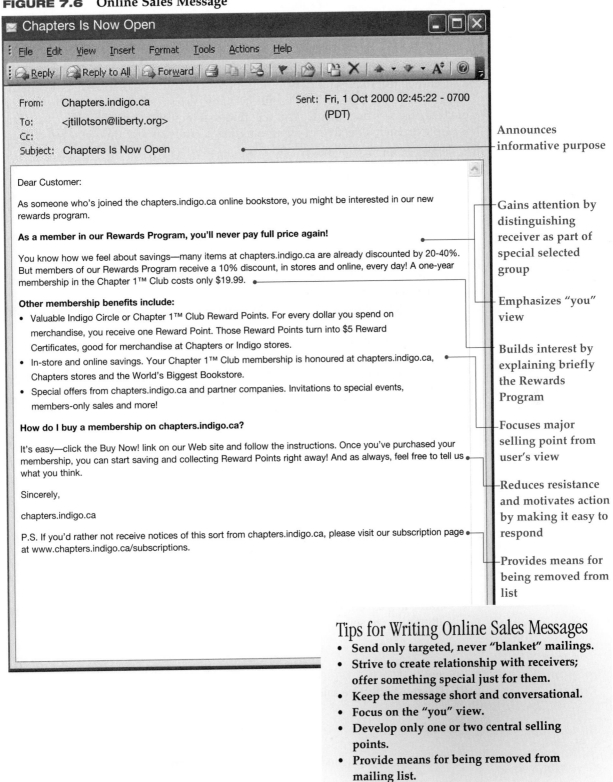

Dear Customer:

As someone who's joined the chapters.indigo.ca online bookstore, you might be interested in our new rewards program.

As a member in our Rewards Program, you'll never pay full price again!

You know how we feel about savings—many items at chapters.indigo.ca are already discounted by 20-40%. But members of our Rewards Program receive a 10% discount, in stores and online, every day! A one-year membership in the Chapter 1™ Club costs only $19.99.

Other membership benefits include:

- Valuable Indigo Circle or Chapter 1™ Club Reward Points. For every dollar you spend on merchandise, you receive one Reward Point. Those Reward Points turn into $5 Reward Certificates, good for merchandise at Chapters or Indigo stores.
- In-store and online savings. Your Chapter 1™ Club membership is honoured at chapters.indigo.ca, Chapters stores and the World's Biggest Bookstore.
- Special offers from chapters.indigo.ca and partner companies. Invitations to special events, members-only sales and more!

How do I buy a membership on chapters.indigo.ca?

It's easy—click the Buy Now! link on our Web site and follow the instructions. Once you've purchased your membership, you can start saving and collecting Reward Points right away! And as always, feel free to tell us what you think.

Sincerely,

chapters.indigo.ca

P.S. If you'd rather not receive notices of this sort from chapters.indigo.ca, please visit our subscription page at www.chapters.indigo.ca/subscriptions.

Announces informative purpose
Gains attention by distinguishing receiver as part of special selected group
Emphasizes "you" view
Builds interest by explaining briefly the Rewards Program
Focuses major selling point from user's view
Reduces resistance and motivates action by making it easy to respond
Provides means for being removed from list

Tips for Writing Online Sales Messages

- **Send only targeted, never "blanket" mailings.**
- **Strive to create relationship with receivers; offer something special just for them.**
- **Keep the message short and conversational.**
- **Focus on the "you" view.**
- **Develop only one or two central selling points.**
- **Provide means for being removed from mailing list.**
- **Make it easy to respond.**
- **Convey a tone of sincerity.**

Summing Up and Looking Forward

The ability to persuade is a powerful and versatile communication tool. In this chapter you learned to apply the indirect strategy in writing claim letters, making favour requests, writing persuasive suggestions, and writing sales letters. You also learned techniques for developing successful online sales messages. The techniques suggested here will be useful in many other contexts beyond the writing of these business documents. You will find that logical organization of arguments is also extremely effective in expressing ideas orally or any time you must overcome resistance to change.

Not all business messages are strictly persuasive. Occasionally, you must deny requests and deliver bad news. In the next chapter you will learn to use the indirect strategy in conveying negative news.

Critical Thinking

1. Why is the ability to persuade a significant trait in both business and personal relations?
2. The organization of a successful persuasive claim centres on the reasons and the closing. Why?
3. Should favour requests be written directly or indirectly? Discuss.
4. Why do individuals resist change?
5. Some individuals will never write a sales letter. Why is it nevertheless important for them to learn the techniques for doing so?

Chapter Review

6. In the indirect strategy, what should precede the main idea?

7. List at least four examples of persuasive favour requests.

8. Name at least eight items a salesperson should know about a product before attempting to sell it.

9. The most effective sales letters are sent to what kind of audience?

10. What is an unsolicited sales letter? Give an example.

11. What is a solicited sales letter? Give an example.

12. List at least five ways to gain a reader's attention in the opening of a sales letter.

13. In selling a product, when are rational appeals most effective?

14. Name six writing techniques that stimulate desire for a product.

15. How are online sales letters different from and similar to hard-copy sales letters?

Writing Improvement Exercises

7.1 Strategies. For each of the following situations, check the appropriate writing strategy.

	Direct Strategy	Indirect Strategy
16. An appeal for a contribution to Children's World, a charity	_____	_____
17. An announcement that in the future all dental, extended health, and life insurance benefits for employees will be reduced	_____	_____
18. A request to another company for verification of employment regarding a job applicant	_____	_____
19. A letter to a painting contractor demanding payment for replacing ceramic floor tiles damaged by sloppy painters	_____	_____
20. A request for information about an oak desk and computer workstation	_____	_____
21. A letter to a grocery store asking for permission to display posters advertising a school fundraising car wash	_____	_____
22. A request for a refund of the cost of a computer program that does not perform the functions its advertising claimed it would	_____	_____
23. A request for a refund of the cost of a hair dryer that stopped working after a month's use (the hair dryer carries a one-year warranty)	_____	_____
24. An invitation to a prominent author to speak before a student gathering	_____	_____
25. A memo to employees describing the schedule and selections of a new mobile catering service	_____	_____

Activities and Cases

7.2 Persuasive Claim: Exchanging Copiers. Analyze the following poorly written persuasive claim and list at least five major weaknesses. Outline an appropriate writing plan for a persuasive claim. After class discussion, your instructor may ask you to rewrite this message, rectifying its weaknesses. Address your letter to International Copy Services, 1506 Fourth Street S.W., Calgary, AB T7L 2E3. Assume that you are writing on your company's letterhead. Use your word processing software's professional letter template.

Gentlemen:

Three months ago we purchased four of your Regal Model SP-270F photocopiers, and we've had nothing but trouble ever since.

Our salesperson, Jason Woo, assured us that the SP-270F could easily handle our volume of 3000 copies a day. This seemed strange since the sales brochure said that the SP-270F was meant for 500 copies a day. But we believed Mr. Woo. Big mistake! Our four SP-270F copiers are down constantly; we can't go on like this. Because they're still under warranty, they eventually get repaired. But we're losing considerable business in downtime.

Your Mr. Woo has been less than helpful, so I telephoned the district manager, Heidi Berger. I suggested that we trade in our SP-270F copiers (which we got for $2500 each) for two S-55 models (at $13,500 each). However, Ms. Berger said she would have to charge 50 percent depreciation on our SP-270F copiers. What a ripoff! I think that 20 percent depreciation is more reasonable since we've had the machines only three months. Ms. Berger said she would get back to me, and I haven't heard from her since.

I'm writing to your headquarters because I have no faith in either Mr. Woo or Ms. Berger, and I need action on these machines. If you understood anything about business, you would see what a sweet deal I'm offering you. I'm willing to stick with your company and purchase a more expensive model—but I can't take such a loss on the SP-270F copiers. The SP-270F copiers are relatively new; you should be able to sell them with no trouble. And think of all the money you'll save by not having your repair technicians making constant trips to service our SP-270F copiers! Please let me hear from you immediately.

1. List at least five faults.

2. Outline a writing plan for a persuasive request.
   Opening:

   Body:

   Closing:

7.3 Favour Request: Inviting a Speaker. Analyze the following poorly written invitation. List its weaknesses and outline a writing strategy. If your instructor directs, revise it.

Dear Dr. Schulz:

Because you're a local Nanaimo author, we thought it might not be too much trouble for you to speak at our Canadian Association of Independent Management banquet May 5.

Some of us business students here at Glenbow Valley College admired your book *Beyond Race and Gender*, which appeared last spring and became such a hit across the country. One of our instructors said you were now the country's management guru. What exactly did you mean when you said that Canada is the "Mulligan stew" of the Americas?

Because we have no funds for honoraria, we have to rely on local speakers. Dr. Lester Pierfont and Deputy Mayor Shirley Slye were speakers in the past. Our banquets usually begin at 6:30 with a social hour, followed by dinner at 7:30 and the speaker from 8:30 until 9:00 or 9:15. We can arrange transportation for you and your wife if you need it.

We realize that you must be very busy, but we hope you'll agree. Please let our advisor, Duncan Rankin, have the favour of an early response.

---

1. List at least five weaknesses.

2. Outline a writing plan for a favour request.
   Opening:

   Body:

   Closing:

7.4 Persuasive Suggestion: Asking for Tuition Reimbursement. Analyze the poorly written e-mail below. List its weaknesses. If your instructor directs, revise it.

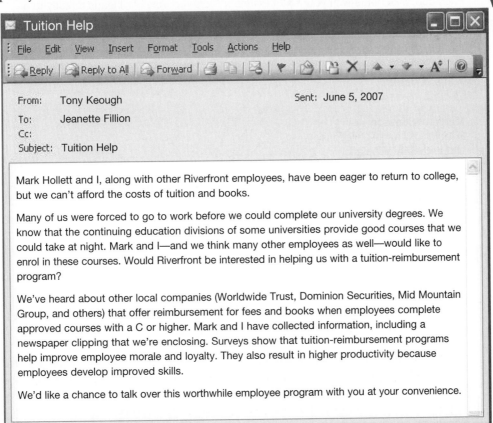

Mark Hollett and I, along with other Riverfront employees, have been eager to return to college, but we can't afford the costs of tuition and books.

Many of us were forced to go to work before we could complete our university degrees. We know that the continuing education divisions of some universities provide good courses that we could take at night. Mark and I—and we think many other employees as well—would like to enrol in these courses. Would Riverfront be interested in helping us with a tuition-reimbursement program?

We've heard about other local companies (Worldwide Trust, Dominion Securities, Mid Mountain Group, and others) that offer reimbursement for fees and books when employees complete approved courses with a C or higher. Mark and I have collected information, including a newspaper clipping that we're enclosing. Surveys show that tuition-reimbursement programs help improve employee morale and loyalty. They also result in higher productivity because employees develop improved skills.

We'd like a chance to talk over this worthwhile employee program with you at your convenience.

1. List at least five weaknesses in this e-mail.

2. Outline a writing plan for this e-mail.
   Opening:

   Body:

   Closing:

7.5 Sales Letter: Analyzing the Pitch. Read the following sales letter and analyze its effectiveness by answering the questions listed after the letter.

Dear Friend of University of Prince Edward Island,

You are part of a special group of alumni—doctors, lawyers, bankers, managers, professors—who have a wide variety of credit cards available to them. For this reason I am inviting you to choose the superior benefits of the UPEI *Platinum Preferred* Visa credit card.

The UPEI Alumni Association has planned, in association with Atlantic Bank, a superior credit card with excellent benefits, personalized customer care, and best of all, no annual fee.

Each purchase made with your UPEI *Platinum Preferred* Visa card leads directly to a contribution to the UPEI Alumni Association. This extra benefit costs nothing, but allows the Association to continue its vital work on campus and in the community.

Yours sincerely,

Margaret Simpson
Director of Alumni Relations
UPEI Alumni Association

a. What technique captures the reader's attention in the opening? Is it effective?
b. What are the central selling points?
c. Does the letter use rational, emotional, or a combination of appeals? Explain.
d. What technique builds interest in the product? Are benefits obvious?
e. How is price handled?
f. Does the letter anticipate reader resistance and offer counterarguments?
g. What action is the reader to take? How is the action made easy?

Your Task. Revise the above letter, adding any improvements you think necessary based on your answers to the above questions.

7.6 Persuasive Claim: Excessive Legal Fees. You are the business manager for McConnell's, a producer of gourmet ice cream. McConnell's has 12 ice cream shops in the Toronto area and a reputation for excellent ice cream. Your firm was approached by an independent ice cream vendor who wanted to use McConnell's name and recipes for ice cream to be distributed through grocery stores and drugstores. As business manager you worked with a law firm, Peretine, Valcon, and Associates, to draw up contracts regarding the use of McConnell's name and quality standards for the product.

When you received the bill from Louis Peretine, you couldn't believe it. The bill itemized 38 hours of attorney preparation, at $300 per hour, and 55 hours of paralegal assistance, at $75 per hour. The bill also showed $415 for telephone calls, which might be accurate because Mr. Peretine had to converse with McConnell's owners, who were living in Ireland at the time. However, you doubt that an experienced attorney would require 38 hours to draw up the contracts in question.

Perhaps some error was made in calculating the total hours. Moreover, you have checked with other businesses and found that excellent legal advice can be obtained for $200 per hour. McConnell's would like to continue using the services of Peretine, Valcon, and Associates for future legal business. Such future business is unlikely if an adjustment is not made on this bill.

Your Task. Write a persuasive request to Louis Peretine, Legal Counsel, Peretine, Valcon, and Associates, 2690 Whyte Avenue, Toronto, ON M2N 2E6.

7.7 Persuasive Favour/Action Request: Dining Gratuity Guidelines. As a server in the Tearoom Grill, you have occasionally arrived to clean a table only to find that the customer has left no tip. You know your service is excellent, but some customers just don't get it. They seem to think that tips are optional, a sign of appreciation. For servers, however, tips are 80 percent of their income. In a recent newspaper article, you learned that some restaurants—like the new Catch 22 House in Toronto—automatically add a 15 percent tip to the bill. In Calgary the Hoopla restaurant prints "gratuity guidelines" on cheques, showing customers what a 15 or 20 percent tip would be. You also know that American Express recently developed a gratuity calculation feature on its terminals. This means that diners don't even have to do the math!

Team

Your Task. Your fellow servers have asked you, because you are studying business communication, to write a serious letter to Doug Li, general manager of Tearoom Grill (3210 Hastings Street, Vancouver, BC V1N 3E5), persuading him to adopt mandatory tipping guidelines. Talk with fellow servers (classmates) to develop logical persuasive arguments.

7.8 Persuasive Favour Request: Inviting a Winner. As program chair of the Women in Business Association, a national group of businesswomen, you must persuade Joann R. Schulz to be the speaker at your annual conference April 14 in Toronto. Ms. Schulz was recently named Small Business Person of the Year by the Canadian Association of Independent Business.

After her 44-year-old husband died of a heart attack, Ms. Schulz threw herself into their fledgling company and eventually transformed it from a small research company into an international manufacturer of devices for treatment of eye problems. Under her leadership, her Edmonton company grew from 3 to 75 employees in six years. It now sells more than $5 million worth of artificial lenses in 22 countries.

Although you can offer Ms. Schulz only $1000, you have heard that she is eager to encourage female entrepreneurs. You feel she might be receptive to your invitation.

Your Task. Write a letter inviting Ms. Joann R. Schulz, President, NBR Industries, 345 Selkirk Ave., Edmonton, AB T6K 4E2, to speak to your group.

7.9 Persuasive Favour Request: Helping Out a Worthy Charity. You have been a supporter of the World Partnership Walk since you were 17 years old. Five years later, you have graduated from college and are working as the office manager for a small Ottawa-based law firm, Fraser, Ahmet, and Grandpre. Last year, you were able to persuade the three partners in the firm to become local corporate sponsors for the Ottawa World Partnership Walk. This year, you'd like to be more ambitious and recruit other local law firms to make a corporate donation. This year's walk happens at a busy time: soon after the annual Terry Fox Run and just before the annual AIDS Walk Ottawa. Still, you believe the World Partnership Walk is worthy of support by area law firms.

Your Task. Write a letter that you will personalize and send to 15 small- and medium-sized Ottawa-area law firms requesting they become corporate sponsors for this year's World Partnership Walk.

Related Web site: For more information on the World Partnership Walk, go to <www.worldpartnershipwalk.com>.

7.10 Personal Persuasive Suggestion: We Need a Change. In your own work or organization experience, identify a problem for which you have a solution. Should a procedure be altered to improve performance? Would a new or different piece of equipment help you perform your work better? Could some tasks be scheduled more efficiently? Are employees being used most effectively? Could customers be better served by changing something? Do you want to work other hours or perform other tasks?

Your Task. Once you have identified a situation requiring persuasion, write a memo to your boss or organization head. Use actual names and facts. Employ the concepts and techniques in this chapter to help you convince your boss that your idea should prevail. Include concrete examples, anticipate objections, emphasize reader benefits, and end with a specific action to be taken.

7.11 Persuasive E-Mail: Overusing Overnight Shipments. As office manager of Cambridge Software, write a memo persuading technicians, engineers, programmers, and other employees to reduce the number of overnight or second-day mail shipments. Your Federal Express and other shipping bills have been higher than expected, and you feel that staff members are overusing these services.

Encourage employees to send messages by e-mail. Sending an e-mail costs almost nothing, whether it's sent locally or halfway around the world. Attaching documents—whether as Word files or as PDF documents—is replacing faxing and couriering in today's business world. Obviously, there's a huge difference between the "almost nothing" cost of an e-mail and potentially hundreds of dollars for overnight courier service. If employees have to send a package, they should, whenever possible, obtain the courier service account number of the recipient and use it for charging the shipment.

Your Task. Ask employees to decide whether receivers are really going to mind receiving an e-mail document they have to read on screen or print out. You'd like to reduce overnight delivery services voluntarily by 50 percent over the next two months. Unless a sizeable reduction occurs, there may be significant consequences (e.g., suspension of courier privileges). Address your e-mail to all employees.

Web

7.12 Persuasive Letter or E-Mail: Persuading Your Member of Parliament. Assume you are upset about an issue of national importance, and you want your MP to know your position. Choose an issue about which you feel strongly: student loans, pension reform, human rights in other countries, environmental protection, the federal debt, employment insurance, taxation of common-law couples, the federal deficit, or some other area regulated by the federal government. Then write to your MP explaining your views.

For best results, consider these tips: (1) Use the proper form of address, such as *The Honourable John Smith, Dear Minister Smith* if you are writing to a cabinet minister, and *The Honourable Joan Doe, Dear Ms. Doe* if you are writing to an MP. (See <www.pch.gc.ca/progs/cpsc-ccsp/pe/address1_e.cfm> for a full discussion of correct forms of address.) (2) Identify yourself as a member of his or her riding.

(3) Immediately state your position (*I urge you to support/oppose … because*). (4) Present facts and illustrations and how they affect you personally. If legislation were enacted, how would you or your organization be better off or worse off? Avoid generalities. (5) Offer to provide further information. (6) Keep the letter polite, constructive, and brief.

Your Task. Obtain your MP's address. Use a search term such as "Canadian government." Enclosing your search term in quotation marks ensures that the words will be searched as a unit. Decide whether you should write an e-mail or a letter. Remember that although e-mail messages are fast, they don't carry as much influence as personal letters.

7.13 Sales Letter: Fitness at the Local Brewery. Health research shows that 33 percent of Canadians between age 20 and 64 are overweight.[4] Long-term health risks could be reduced if overweight employees shed their excess weight.

As a sales representative for Fitness Associates, you think your fitness equipment and programs could be instrumental in helping people lose weight. With regular exercise at an on-site fitness centre, employees lose weight and improve overall health. As employee health improves, absenteeism is reduced and overall productivity increases. And employees love working out before or after work. They make the routine part of their work day, and they often have work buddies who share their fitness regimen.

Though many companies resist spending money to save money, fitness centres need not be large or expensive to be effective. Studies show that moderately sized centres coupled with motivational and training programs yield the greatest success. For just $30,000, Fitness Associates will provide exercise equipment including stationary bikes, weight machines, and treadmills. Their fitness experts will design a fitness room, set up the fitness equipment, and design appropriate programs. Best of all, the one-time cost is usually offset by cost savings within one year of centre installation. For additional fees FA can also provide fitness consultants for employee fitness assessments. FA specialists will also train employees on proper use of equipment, and they will clean and manage the facility—for an extra charge, of course.

Your Task. Write a sales letter to Ms. Kathleen Stewart, Human Resources VP, Good Times Brewing Company, 3939 Brewery Row, Moose Jaw, SK S6H 0V9. Assume you are writing on company letterhead. Ask for an appointment to meet with her. Send her a brochure detailing the products and services that Fitness Associates provides. As an incentive, offer a free fitness assessment for all employees if Good Times Brewing installs a fitness facility by December 1.

7.14 Sales Letter: Persuading an Old Friend to Switch to ACCuracy Plus. You are the owner of Software Solutions, a Prince George, B.C.–based software consultancy. Recently, at a major industry trade show in Chicago, you were introduced to a new accounting software package, ACCuracy Plus. Quickly realizing its merits, you signed a deal with the American manufacturer to become the exclusive sales agent for the software in Canada, west of Ontario. Now that you own the right to sell the software, you have to make some sales. One day, while brainstorming possible clients, you remember your old friend from college, Tim Thom. While reading the newspaper last year you found out that Tim Thom has been promoted to VP Operations for Health & Co, a Victoria-based national retail chain selling vitamins, supplements, and natural foods. Even though you haven't seen or spoken to Tim in over eight years, you used to be good friends, and you believe a persuasive sales letter about your new software will not go unanswered. The question is, should you make a strong pitch for a sale, or should you just pitch for a get-together over lunch?

Your Task. Write a persuasive sales letter to Tim Thom, where you try to interest him in switching from his current accounting software to ACCuracy Plus.

Related Web sites: To build interest in ACCuracy Plus, browse the Internet for the features of its competitors like AccPac <www.accpac.com> and Microsoft's Great Plains <www.microsoft.com/BusinessSolutions/GreatPlains/default.aspx>. Be careful not to plagiarize when you write your letter.

Grammar/Mechanics Review—7

The following sentences contain errors in grammar, punctuation, capitalization, number style, usage, and spelling. Below each sentence write a corrected version.

1. Not one of the job candidates who we interviewed last week have written a thank-you message.

2. You would of laughed if you could of saw Carlos and I fixing the bosses printer.

3. Either the Marketing Director or the Sales Manager have to approve our departments budget for the next fiscal year.

4. Looking into the mirror of his new toyota prius Glenn slipped on his ray-ban sunglasses, and thought that he looked very cool.

5. Most wifes are listed as beneficiarys on insurance policys of their husbands'.

6. The CEO hisself is willing to support whomever we nominate as our represenative.

7. Our salesperson told Jacqueline and I that a wide range of services are available if we sign up.

8. Somebody on the boys team left their shoes on the bus.

9. $600 are more than I can afford to pay for rent although I do like that 3 bed-room apartment.

10. Flying over the rain forests of indonesia the trees formed a menacing, green carpet.

11. 4 candidates submitted applications, however only one had the neccessary skills.

12. Our Manager cautioned Samuel and I not to take the CEOs angry remarks personal.

13. Every employee who completes the course satisfactory, are entitled to have their fees reimbursed.

14. The following benefits are available to cardholders; travel planning, free checking account and low monthly interest.

15. Tornado warnings has been posted for the residence of: windsor barrie and sudbury.

Grammar/Mechanics Challenge—7

Document for Revision

The following memo has faults in grammar, punctuation, spelling, number form, wordiness, and negative words. Use standard proofreading marks (see Appendix B) to correct the errors. When you finish, your instructor can show you the revised version of this memo.

Memo

To: Sara W. Morrisseau, Vice-President
From: Jackson Pardell, Market Research
CC:
Date: August 5, 2006
Re: ANALYSIS OF GULPIT XL

Here is a summery of the research of Clemence Willis' and myself. Regarding the reduced sugar sports drink being introduced by our No. 1 compititor, GulpIT.

In just under a years time GulpIT developed this new drink, it combines together a mixture of 50 percent sugar and 50 percent artificial sweetener. Apparently GulpIT plans to spend over $8 million to introduce the drink, and to assess consumers reactions to it. It will be tested on the shelfs of convience stores grocerys and other mass merchants in five citys in the Atlantic provinces.

The companys spokesperson said, "The 'X' stands for excelent taste, and the 'L' stands for less sugar." Aimed at young adult's who don't like the taste of sweetener but who want to control calories. The new sports drink is a hybrid sugar and diet drink. Our studys show that simular drinks tryed in this country in the 1980's were unsucessful. On the other hand a 50 calorie low sugar sports drink introduced in Europe two year ago was well received, similarly in Japan a 40 calorie soda is now marketed sucessfully by a cola manufactuerer.

However our research in regard to trends and our analysis of GulpIT XL fails to indicate that this countrys consumers will be interested in a midcalorie sports drink. Yet the Toronto Stock Exchanges response to GulpITs announcement of it's new drink was not unfavourable.

In view of the foregoing the writer and his colleague are of the opinion that we should take a wait and see attitude. Toward the introduction of our own low sugar sports drink.

Eight Steps to Resolving Workplace Conflicts

"No part of life is conflict free. We don't always agree with people around us—our families, friends, neighbours or the people we work with every day." Although all workplaces suffer from conflict from time to time, some people think that workplace conflict is escalating.[5]

Several factors may be tied to increasing problems at work. One factor is our diverse workforce. Sharing ideas that stem from a variety of backgrounds, experiences, and personalities may lead to better problem solving, but it can also lead to conflict. Another factor related to increased conflict is the trend toward participatory management. In the past only bosses had to resolve problems, but now more employees are making decisions and facing conflict. This is particularly true of teams. Working together harmoniously involves a great deal of give and take, and conflict may result if some people feel that they are being taken advantage of. Finally, a significant source of workplace problems is increasing levels of stress. Statistics Canada reports that "the highest proportion of working Canadians—more than one-third (34%)—cited too many demands or hours as the most common source of stress in the workplace." Other sources of workplace stress include "poor interpersonal relations" and "risk of accident and injury."[6]

When problems do arise in the workplace, it's important for everyone to recognize that conflict is a normal occurrence and that it won't disappear if ignored. Conflict must be confronted and resolved. Effective conflict resolution requires good listening skills, flexibility, and a willingness to change. Individuals must be willing to truly listen and seek to understand rather than immediately challenge the adversary. In many workplace conflicts, involving a third party to act as a mediator is necessary.

Although problems vary greatly, the following steps offer a good basic process for resolving conflicts.[7]

1. **Be proactive.** Arrange a time when conflicting parties are willing to have a conversation in a nonthreatening environment.
2. **Listen to all sides.** Encourage each individual to describe the situation from his or her perspective.
3. **Diagnose before responding.** To promote empathic communication, follow this rule. No one may respond without first accurately summarizing the other person's previous remarks.
4. **Problem solve by focusing on interests.** Brainstorm together to develop multiple options for meeting the interests of each of the conflicting parties. Try to see each other as allies, rather than opponents, in solving the problem.
5. **Negotiate a solution.** Ensure that both parties are agreeable to the chosen solution.
6. **Communicate the solution formally.** It is important to formalize the agreement on paper or in some other way.
7. **Implement the solution and plan follow-up communication.** Meet again on an agreed-upon date to ensure satisfactory resolution of the conflict. The deadline makes it more likely that both parties will follow through on their part of the deal.
8. **Live the solution.** Act on the solution in the workplace.

Career Application

As leader of your work team, you were recently confronted by an angry team member. Julie, a story editor on your film production team, is upset because, for the third time in as many weeks, she was forced to give up part of her weekend for work. This time it was for a black-tie affair that everyone in the office tried to avoid. Julie is particularly angry with Yannick, who should have represented the team at this awards dinner. But he uttered the magic word: family. "Yannick says he has plans with his family, and it's like he gets to do anything," Julie complains to you. "I don't resent him or his devotion to his family. But I do resent it when my team constantly expects me to give up my personal time because I don't have kids. That's my choice, and I don't think I should be punished for it."[8]

Your Task

Using the principles outlined above, work out a conflict resolution plan for Julie and Yannick. Your instructor may wish to divide your class into three-person teams to role-play Julie, Yannick, and the team leader. Add any details to make a realistic scenario.

- What are the first steps in resolving this conflict?
- What arguments might each side present?
- What alternatives might be offered?
- What do you think is the best solution?
- How could it be implemented with the least friction?

Negative Messages

Despite the fact that we sometimes have to send negative messages at work, it is imperative to turn the situation around and focus on lessons learned and experience gained. Just think, if not for bad news, good news would not be as good![1]

Maria Duncan, *director, Production Finance, Alliance-Atlantis Communications Inc.*

LEARNING OBJECTIVES

1. Describe a plan for resolving business problems.
2. List the four components of an indirect bad-news message.
3. Learn various strategies for writing indirect negative messages.
4. Distinguish between the direct and the indirect pattern for business messages.
5. Apply the indirect pattern in refusing requests, refusing claims, and announcing bad news to customers and employees.
6. Identify situations in which the direct pattern is appropriate for breaking bad news.
7. Explain when the indirect strategy may be unethical.

Strategies for Breaking Bad News

✓ Quick Check

If your message delivers bad news, consider using the indirect strategy.

Letters, e-mails, and memos that carry negative news can have a significant impact on a company's success. As Maria Duncan suggests, the correct way to go about writing a bad-news message is to think positively. Because bad news disappoints, irritates, and sometimes angers the receiver, such messages must be written in a way that explains the bad news but retains goodwill at the same time.

The direct strategy, which you learned to apply in earlier chapters, presents the main idea first, even when it's bad news. The direct pattern appeals to efficiency-oriented writers who don't want to waste time with efforts to soften the effects of bad news.[2] Many business writers, however, prefer to use the indirect pattern in delivering negative messages. The indirect pattern is especially appealing to relationship-oriented writers. They care about how a message will affect its receiver.

Although the major focus of this chapter will be on developing the indirect pattern, you'll first learn the procedure that many business professionals follow in resolving business problems. It may surprise you. Then you'll study models of messages that use the indirect pattern to refuse requests, refuse claims, and announce bad news to customers and employees. Finally, you'll learn to identify instances in which the direct pattern may be preferable in announcing bad news.

Resolving Business Problems

In all businesses, things occasionally go wrong. Goods are not delivered, a product fails to perform as expected, service is poor, clients are incorrectly invoiced, or customers are misunderstood. All businesses offering products or services must sometimes deal with troublesome situations that cause unhappiness to customers and to employees. Whenever possible, these problems should be dealt with immediately and personally. One study found that a majority of business professionals resolve problems in the following manner:

1. Call the individual involved.
2. Describe the problem and apologize.
3. Explain why the problem occurred, what you are doing to resolve it, and how you will prevent it from happening again.
4. Follow up with a letter that documents the phone call and promotes goodwill.[3]

Dealing with problems immediately is very important in resolving conflict and retaining goodwill. Written correspondence is generally too slow for problems that demand immediate attention. But written messages are important (1) when personal contact is impossible, (2) to establish a record of the incident, (3) to formally confirm follow-up procedures, and (4) to promote good relations.

A bad-news follow-up letter is shown in Figure 8.1 (p. 194). Consultant Robert Buch found himself in the embarrassing position of explaining why he had given out the name of his client to a salesperson. The client, Data.com, Inc., had hired his firm, Buch Consulting Services, to help find an appropriate service for outsourcing its payroll functions. Without realizing it, Robert had mentioned to a potential vendor (Payroll Services, Inc.) that his client was considering hiring an outside service to handle its payroll. An overeager salesperson from Payroll Services immediately called on Data.com, thus angering the client. The client had hired the consultant to avoid this very kind of intrusion. Data.com did not want to be hounded by vendors selling their payroll services.

When he learned of the problem, the first thing consultant Robert Buch did was call his client to explain and apologize. But he also followed up with the letter shown in Figure 8.1. The letter not only confirms the telephone conversation but also adds the right touch of formality. It sends the nonverbal message that the matter is being taken seriously and that it is important enough to warrant a written letter.

Using the Indirect Pattern to Prepare the Reader

When sending a bad-news message that will upset or irritate the receiver, many business communicators use the indirect pattern. Revealing bad news indirectly shows sensitivity to your reader. Whereas good news can be announced quickly, bad news generally should be revealed gradually. By preparing the reader, you soften the impact. A blunt announcement of disappointing news might cause the receiver to stop reading and toss the message aside.

The indirect pattern enables you to keep the reader's attention until you have been able to explain the reasons for the bad news. The most important part of a

FIGURE 8.1 Bad-News Follow-Up Message

Buch Consulting Services

3091 Geddes Road, Suite 404
Vancouver, BC V5S 1E4

Voice: 604.499.2341
Web: www.buchconsulting.com

October 23, 2006

Ms. Noelle Vanier
Vice President, Human Resources
Data.com, Inc.
4205 Evergreen Avenue
Victoria, BC V1L 2W4

Dear Noelle:

Opens with agreement and apology →

You have every right to expect complete confidentiality in your transactions with an independent consultant. As I explained in yesterday's telephone call, I am very distressed that you were called by a salesperson from Payroll Services, Inc. This should not have happened, and I apologize to you again for inadvertently mentioning your company's name in a conversation with a potential vendor, Payroll Services, Inc.

Explains what caused problem and how it was resolved →

All clients of Buch Consulting are assured that their dealings with our firm are held in the strictest confidence. Because your company's payroll needs are so individual and because you have so many contract workers, I was forced to explain how your employees differed from those of other companies. The name of your company, however, should never have been mentioned. I can assure you that it will not happen again. I have informed Payroll Services that it had no authorization to call you directly and its actions have forced me to reconsider using its services for my future clients.

Promises to prevent recurrence →

A number of other payroll services offer excellent programs. I'm sure we can find the perfect partner to enable you to outsource your payroll responsibilities, thus allowing your company to focus its financial and human resources on its core business. I look forward to our next appointment when you may choose from a number of excellent payroll outsourcing firms.

Closes with forward look →

Sincerely,

Robert Buch

Robert Buch
Senior Consultant

Tips for Resolving Problems and Following Up

- **Whenever possible, call or see the individual involved. Don't e-mail instead.**
- **Describe the problem and apologize.**
- **Explain why the problem occurred.**
- **Explain what you are doing to resolve it.**
- **Explain how it will not happen again.**
- **Follow up with a letter that documents the personal message.**
- **Look forward to positive future relations.**

bad-news letter is the explanation, which you'll learn about shortly. The indirect plan consists of four main parts:

- Buffer opening
- Reasons given first in the body
- Bad news following in the body
- Pleasant closing

Buffering the Opening

A buffer is a device that reduces shock or pain. To buffer the pain of bad news, begin your letter with a neutral but meaningful statement that makes the reader continue reading. The buffer should be relevant and concise. Although it should avoid revealing the bad news immediately, it should not convey a false impression that good news follows. It should provide a natural transition to the explanation that follows. The individual situation, of course, will help determine what you should put in the buffer. Here are some possibilities for opening bad-news messages.

Quick Check

A buffer opens a bad news letter with a neutral, concise, relevant, and upbeat statement.

- **Best news.** Start with the part of the message that represents the best news. For example, in a memo that announces a new service along with a cutback in mailroom hours, you might write *To ensure that your correspondence goes out with the last pickup, we're starting a new messenger pickup service at 2:30 p.m. daily beginning June 1.*

Quick Check

A good buffer may include the best news, a compliment, appreciation, facts regarding the problem, a statement indicating understanding, or an apology.

- **Compliment.** Praise the receiver's accomplishments, organization, or efforts, but do so with honesty and sincerity. For instance, in a letter declining an invitation to speak, you could write *I admire The United Way for its fundraising projects in our community. I am honoured that you asked me to speak Friday, November 5.*
- **Appreciation.** Convey thanks to the reader for doing business, for sending something, for showing confidence in your organization, for expressing feelings, or simply for providing feedback. In a letter responding to a complaint about poor service, you might say *Thank you for telling us about your experience at our hotel and for giving us a chance to look into the situation.* Avoid thanking the reader, however, for something you are about to refuse.
- **Agreement.** Make a relevant statement with which both reader and receiver can agree. A letter that rejects a loan application might read *We both realize how much your business has been affected by the U.S. ban on Canadian beef in the past few years.*
- **Facts.** Provide objective information that introduces the bad news. For example, in a memo announcing cutbacks in the hours of the employees' cafeteria, you might say *During the past five years the number of employees eating breakfast in our cafeteria has dropped from 32 percent to 12 percent.*
- **Understanding.** Show that you care about the reader. In announcing a product defect, the writer can still manage to express concern for the customer: *We know you expect superior performance from all the products you purchase from OfficeCity. That's why we're writing personally about the Excell printer cartridges you recently ordered.*
- **Apology.** A study of letters responding to customer complaints revealed that 67 percent carried an apology of some sort.[4] If you do apologize, do it early, briefly, and sincerely. For example, a manufacturer of ice cream might respond to a customer's complaint with *We're genuinely sorry that you were disappointed with the price of the ice cream you recently purchased from one of our vendors. Your opinion is important to us, and we appreciate your giving us the opportunity to look into the problem you describe.*

Using the Indirect Pattern to Prepare the Reader

Presenting the Reasons

Quick Check

Bad-news messages should explain reasons before stating the negative news.

The most important part of a bad-news message is the section that explains why a negative decision is necessary. Without sound reasons for denying a request or refusing a claim, a letter will fail, no matter how cleverly it is organized or written. As part of your planning before writing, you analyzed the problem and decided to refuse a request for specific reasons. Before disclosing the bad news, try to explain those reasons. Providing an explanation reduces feelings of ill will and improves the chances that the reader will accept the bad news.

✔ Quick Check

Readers accept bad news more readily if they see that someone benefits.

- **Being cautious in explaining.** If the reasons are not confidential or legally questionable, you can be specific: *Growers supplied us with a limited number of patio roses, and our demand this year was twice that of last year.* In refusing a speaking engagement, tell why the date is impossible: *On January 17 we have a board of directors meeting that I must attend.*

- **Citing reader benefits.** Readers are more open to bad news if in some way, even indirectly, it may help them. Readers also accept bad news better if they recognize that someone or something else benefits, such as other workers or the environment: *Although we would like to consider your application, we prefer to fill managerial positions from within.* Avoid trying to show reader benefits, though, if they appear insincere: *To improve our service to you, we're increasing our brokerage fees.*

- **Explaining company policy.** Readers resent blanket policy statements prohibiting something: *Company policy prevents us from making cash refunds* or *Proposals may be accepted from local companies only* or *Company policy requires us to promote from within.* Instead of hiding behind company policy, gently explain why the policy makes sense: *We prefer to promote from within because it rewards the loyalty of our employees. In addition, we've found that people familiar with our organization make the quickest contribution to our team effort.* By offering explanations, you demonstrate that you care about your readers and are treating them as important individuals.

- **Choosing positive words.** Because the words you use can affect a reader's response, choose carefully. Remember that the objective of the indirect pattern is to hold the reader's attention until you've had a chance to explain the reasons justifying the bad news. To keep the reader in a receptive mood, avoid expressions that might cause the reader to tune out. Be sensitive to negative words such as *claim, error, failure, fault, impossible, mistaken, misunderstand, never, regret, unwilling, unfortunately,* and *violate.*

- **Showing that the matter was treated seriously and fairly.** In explaining reasons, demonstrate to the reader that you take the matter seriously, have investigated carefully, and are making an unbiased decision. Customers are more accepting of disappointing news when they feel that their requests have been heard and that they have been treated fairly. Avoid deflecting responsibility, known as passing the buck, or blaming others within your organization. Such unprofessional behaviour makes the reader lose faith in you and your company.

Cushioning the Bad News

Although you can't prevent the disappointment that bad news brings, you can reduce the pain somewhat by breaking the news sensitively. Be especially considerate when the reader will suffer personally from the bad news. A number of thoughtful techniques can lessen the impact.

- **Positioning the bad news.** Instead of spotlighting it, enclose the bad news between other sentences, perhaps among your reasons. Try not to let the refusal begin or end a paragraph—the reader's eye will linger on these high-visibility spots. Another technique that reduces shock is putting a painful idea in a subordinate clause: *Although another candidate was hired, we appreciate your interest in our organization and wish you every success in your job search.* Subordinate clauses often begin with words such as *although, as, because, if,* and *since.*

- **Using the passive voice.** Passive-voice verbs enable you to describe an action without connecting the action to a specific person. Whereas the active voice focuses attention on a person (*We don't give cash refunds*), the passive voice highlights the action (*Cash refunds are not given because …*). Use the passive voice for the bad news. In some instances you can combine passive-voice verbs and a subordinate clause: *Although ice cream vendors cannot be required to lower their prices, we are happy to pass along your comments for their consideration.*

- **Accentuating the positive.** As you learned earlier, messages are far more effective when you describe what you can do instead of what you can't do. Rather than *We will no longer accept requests for product changes after June 1*, try a more positive appeal: *We are accepting requests for product changes until June 1.*

- **Implying the refusal.** It's sometimes possible to avoid a direct statement of refusal. Often, your reasons and explanations leave no doubt that a request has been denied. Explicit refusals may be unnecessary and at times cruel. In this refusal to contribute to a charity, for example, the writer never actually says no: *Because we will soon be moving into new offices, all our funds are earmarked for moving and furnishings. We hope that next year we'll be able to support your worthwhile charity.* This implied refusal is effective even though the bad news is not stated. The danger of an implied refusal, of course, is that it can be so subtle that the reader misses it. Be certain that you make the bad news clear, thus preventing the need for further correspondence.

- **Suggesting a compromise or an alternative.** A refusal is not so harsh—for the sender or the receiver—if a suitable compromise, substitute, or alternative is available. In denying permission to a class to visit a research facility, for instance, this writer softens the bad news by proposing an alternative: *Although class tours of the entire research facility are not given due to safety and security reasons, we do offer tours of parts of the facility during our open house in the fall.*

You can further reduce the impact of the bad news by refusing to dwell on it. Present it briefly (or imply it), and move on to your closing.

Closing Pleasantly

After explaining the bad news sensitively, close the message with a pleasant statement that promotes goodwill. The closing should be personalized and may include a forward look, an alternative, good wishes, special offers, resale information, or an off-the-subject remark.

- **Forward look.** Anticipate future relations or business. A letter that refuses a contract proposal might read: *Thank you for your bid. We look forward to working with your talented staff when future projects demand your special expertise.*
- **Alternative.** If an alternative exists, end your letter with follow-through advice. For example, in a letter rejecting a customer's demand for replacement of landscaping plants, you might say, *We will be happy to give you a free inspection and consultation. Please call 746-8112 to arrange a date for a visit.*
- **Good wishes.** A letter rejecting a job candidate might read: *We appreciate your interest in our company. Good luck in your search to find the perfect match between your skills and job requirements.*
- **Special offers.** When customers complain—primarily about food products or small consumer items—companies often send coupons, samples, or gifts to restore confidence and to promote future business. In response to a customer's complaint about a frozen dinner, you could write *Thank you for your loyalty and*

Quick Check

Techniques for cushioning bad news include positioning it strategically, using the passive voice, emphasizing the positive, implying the refusal, and suggesting alternatives or compromises.

Quick Check

Closings to bad-news messages might include a forward look, an alternative, good wishes, special offers, and resale or sales promotional information.

for sharing in our efforts to make Green Valley frozen entrees the best they can be. We appreciate your input so much that we'd like to buy you dinner. We've enclosed a coupon to cover the cost of your next entree.

- **Resale or sales promotion.** When the bad news is not devastating or personal, references to resale information or promotion may be appropriate: *The laptops you ordered are unusually popular because they have more plug-ins for peripheral devices than any other laptop in their price range. To help you locate additional accessories for these computers, we invite you to visit our Web site at < … > where our on-line catalogue provides a huge selection of peripheral devices such as stereo speakers, printers, personal digital assistants, and digital pagers.*

Avoid endings that sound superficial, insincere, inappropriate, or self-serving. Don't invite further correspondence (*If you have any questions, do not hesitate …*), and don't rehash the bad news.

Refusing Requests

Most of us prefer to be let down gently when we're being refused something we want. That's why the indirect pattern works well when you must turn down requests for favours, money, information, action, and so forth. The following writing plan is appropriate when you must deny a routine request or claim.

 Writing Plan for Refusing Requests or Claims

- **Buffer.** Start with a neutral statement on which both reader and writer can agree, such as a compliment, appreciation, a quick review of the facts, or an apology.
- **Transition.** Include a key idea or word that acts as a transition to the reasons.
- **Reasons.** Present valid reasons for the refusal, avoiding words that create a negative tone. Include resale or sales promotion material if appropriate.
- **Bad news.** Soften the blow by de-emphasizing the bad news, using the passive voice, accentuating the positive, or implying a refusal.
- **Alternative.** Suggest a compromise, alternative, or substitute if possible.
- **Closing.** Renew good feelings with a positive statement. Avoid referring to the bad news, and look forward to continued business.

Two versions of a request refusal are shown in Figure 8.2. A magazine writer requested salary information for an article, but this information could not be released. The ineffective version begins with needless information that could be implied. The second paragraph creates a harsh tone with such negative words as *sorry*, *must refuse*, *violate*, and *liable*. Since the refusal precedes the explanation, the reader probably will not be in a receptive frame of mind to accept the reasons for refusing. Notice, too, that the bad news is emphasized by its placement in a short sentence at the beginning of a paragraph. It stands out and adds more weight to the rejection already felt by the reader.

Moreover, the refusal explanation is overly graphic, containing references to possible litigation. The tone at this point is threatening and unduly harsh. Then, suddenly, the author throws in a self-serving comment about the high salary and commissions of his salespeople. Instead of offering constructive alternatives, the ineffective version reveals only tiny bits of the desired data. Finally, the closing sounds too insincere and doesn't build goodwill.

FIGURE 8.2 Refusing a Request

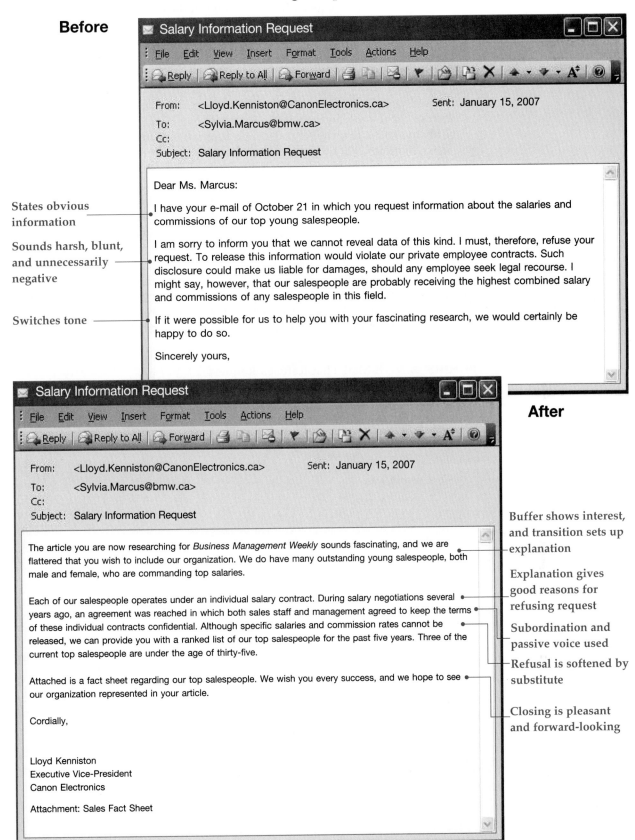

Before

States obvious information

Sounds harsh, blunt, and unnecessarily negative

Switches tone

☒ Salary Information Request

File Edit View Insert Format Tools Actions Help

Reply | Reply to All | Forward

From: <Lloyd.Kenniston@CanonElectronics.ca>   Sent: January 15, 2007
To: <Sylvia.Marcus@bmw.ca>
Cc:
Subject: Salary Information Request

Dear Ms. Marcus:

I have your e-mail of October 21 in which you request information about the salaries and commissions of our top young salespeople.

I am sorry to inform you that we cannot reveal data of this kind. I must, therefore, refuse your request. To release this information would violate our private employee contracts. Such disclosure could make us liable for damages, should any employee seek legal recourse. I might say, however, that our salespeople are probably receiving the highest combined salary and commissions of any salespeople in this field.

If it were possible for us to help you with your fascinating research, we would certainly be happy to do so.

Sincerely yours,

After

☒ Salary Information Request

File Edit View Insert Format Tools Actions Help

Reply | Reply to All | Forward

From: <Lloyd.Kenniston@CanonElectronics.ca>   Sent: January 15, 2007
To: <Sylvia.Marcus@bmw.ca>
Cc:
Subject: Salary Information Request

The article you are now researching for *Business Management Weekly* sounds fascinating, and we are flattered that you wish to include our organization. We do have many outstanding young salespeople, both male and female, who are commanding top salaries.

Each of our salespeople operates under an individual salary contract. During salary negotiations several years ago, an agreement was reached in which both sales staff and management agreed to keep the terms of these individual contracts confidential. Although specific salaries and commission rates cannot be released, we can provide you with a ranked list of our top salespeople for the past five years. Three of the current top salespeople are under the age of thirty-five.

Attached is a fact sheet regarding our top salespeople. We wish you every success, and we hope to see our organization represented in your article.

Cordially,

Lloyd Kenniston
Executive Vice-President
Canon Electronics

Attachment: Sales Fact Sheet

Buffer shows interest, and transition sets up explanation

Explanation gives good reasons for refusing request

Subordination and passive voice used

Refusal is softened by substitute

Closing is pleasant and forward-looking

In the more effective version of this refusal, the opening reflects the writer's genuine interest in the request. But it does not indicate compliance. The second sentence acts as a transition by introducing the words *salespeople* and *salaries*, repeated in the following paragraph. Reasons for refusing this request are objectively presented in an explanation that precedes the refusal. Notice that the refusal (*Although specific salaries and commission rates cannot be released*) is a subordinate clause in a long sentence in the middle of a paragraph. To further soften the blow, the letter offers an alternative. The cordial closing refers to the alternative, avoids mention of the refusal, and looks to the future.

It's always easier to write refusals when alternatives can be offered to soften the bad news. But often no alternatives are possible. The refusal shown in Figure 8.3 involves a delicate situation in which a manager has been asked by his superiors to violate a contract. Several of the engineers for whom he works have privately asked him to make copies of a licensed software program for them. They apparently want this program for their personal computers. Making copies is forbidden by the terms of the software licensing agreement, and the manager refuses to do this. Rather than saying no to each engineer who asks him, he sends all affected staff the e-mail shown in Figure 8.3.

The opening tactfully avoids suggesting that any engineer has actually asked to copy the software program. These professionals may prefer not to have their private requests made known. A transition takes the reader to the logical reasons against copying. Notice that the tone is objective, neither preaching nor con-

FIGURE 8.3 E-Mail That Refuses Request

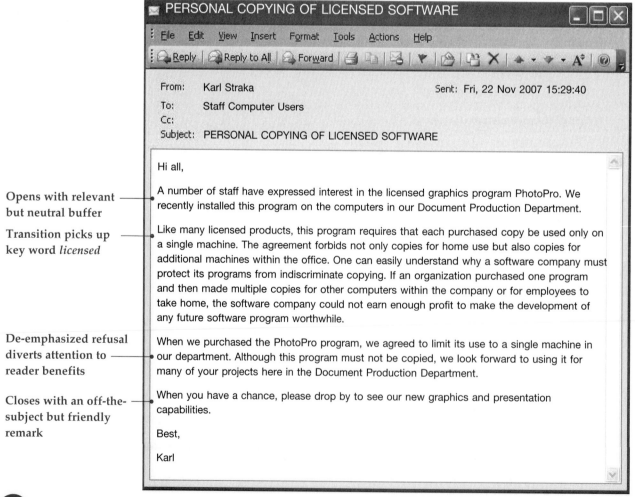

Opens with relevant but neutral buffer

Transition picks up key word *licensed*

De-emphasized refusal diverts attention to reader benefits

Closes with an off-the-subject but friendly remark

demning. The refusal is softened by being linked with a positive statement (*Although this program must not be copied, we look forward to using it for many of your projects here …*). To divert attention from the refusal, the memo ends with a friendly, off-the-subject remark.

Refusing Claims

All businesses offering products or services will receive occasional customer claims for adjustments. Claims may also arise from employees. Most of these claims are valid, and the customer or employee receives a positive response. Even unwarranted claims are sometimes granted because businesses genuinely desire to create a good public image and to maintain friendly relations with employees.

> **✓ Quick Check**
>
> Although most customer claims are granted, occasionally some must be refused.

Some claims, however, cannot be approved because the customer or employee is mistaken, misinformed, unreasonable, or possibly even dishonest. Letters responding to these claims deliver bad news. And the indirect strategy breaks bad news with the least pain. It also allows the sender to explain why the claim must be refused before the reader realizes the bad news and begins resisting.

In the letter shown in Figure 8.4 (p. 202), the writer denies a customer's claim for the difference between the price the customer paid for speakers and the price she saw advertised locally (which would have resulted in a cash refund of $151). While Premier Sound Sales does match any advertised lower price, the price-matching policy applies only to exact models. This claim must be rejected because the advertisement the customer submitted shows a different, older speaker model.

The letter to Wanda Vandermark opens with a buffer that agrees with a statement in the customer's letter. It repeats the key idea of product confidence as a transition to the second paragraph. Next comes an explanation of the price-matching policy. The writer does not assume that the customer is trying to pull a fast one. Nor does the writer suggest that the customer is a dummy who didn't read or understand the price-matching policy.

> **✓ Quick Check**
>
> When refusing customer claims, explain objectively and do not assume that the customer is foolish or dishonest.

The safest path is a neutral explanation of the policy along with precise distinctions between the customer's speakers and the older ones. The writer also gets a chance to resell the customer's speakers and demonstrate what a quality product they are. By the end of the third paragraph, it's evident to the reader that her claim is unjustified.

Notice how most of the components in an effective claim refusal are woven together in this letter: buffer, transition, explanation, and pleasant closing. The only missing part is an alternative, which was impossible in this situation.

Announcing Bad News to Customers and Employees

In addition to resolving claims, organizations occasionally must announce bad news to customers or to their own employees. Bad news to customers might involve rate increases, reduced service, changed procedures, new locations, or technical problems.

Bad news within organizations might involve declining profits, lost contracts, public relations controversies, and changes in policy.

> **✓ Quick Check**
>
> The choice of a direct or indirect strategy depends on the expected reaction of the receiver.

Whether you use a direct or an indirect pattern in delivering that news depends primarily on the anticipated reaction of the receiver. When the bad news affects customers or employees personally—such as reduction in available overtime hours, change in shift premium, or relocation plans—you can generally lessen its impact and promote better relations by explaining reasons before revealing the bad news.

FIGURE 8.4 Refusing a Claim

Premier Sound Sales

5920 Jasper Boulevard
Edmonton, Alberta T2C 2A6
Telephone: (780) 499-2341

Fax: (780) 499-5904
Web: www.premiersound.ca
E-mail: premier1@flash.ca

May 24, 2007

Ms. Wanda Vandermark
4205 54th Avenue S.E.
Calgary, Alberta T3L 2W4

Dear Ms. Vandermark:

You're absolutely right! We do take pride in selling the finest products at rock-bottom prices. The X Flex speakers you purchased last month are premiere concert hall speakers. They're the only ones we present in our catalogue because they're the best.

> Begins by agreeing with receiver

We have such confidence in our products and prices that we offer the price-matching policy you mention in your letter of May 20. That policy guarantees a refund of the price difference if you see one of your purchases offered at a lower price for 30 days after your purchase. To qualify for that refund, customers are asked to send us an advertisement or verifiable proof of the product price and model. As our catalogue states, this price-matching policy applies only to the same models.

> Explains price-matching policy

Our X Flex AM-5 II speakers sell for $749. You sent us a local advertisement showing a price of $598 for X Flex speakers. This advertisement, however, described an earlier version, the X Flex AM-4 model. The AM-5 speakers you received have a wider dynamic range and smoother frequency response than the AM-4 model. Naturally, the improved model you purchased costs a little more than the older AM-4 model advertised by your local dealer. Your speakers have a new three-chamber bass module that virtually eliminates harmonic distortion. The AM-5 speakers are also 20 percent more compact than the AM-4 model.

> Without actually saying no, shows why claim can't be honoured

You bought the finest compact speakers on the market, Ms. Vandermark. If you haven't installed them yet, you may be interested in ceiling mounts, shown in the enclosed catalogue on page 48. We value your business and invite your continued comparison shopping.

> Renews good feelings by building confidence in wisdom of purchase

Sincerely yours,

Melanie Tang

Melanie Tang
Customer Care Specialist

Enclosure

Writing Plan for Announcing Bad News to Customers and Employees

- **Buffer.** Open with a compliment, appreciation, facts, or good news with a neutral statement on which the reader and the writer can agree.
- **Transition.** Include a key idea or word that leads from the opening to the reasons.
- **Reasons.** Explain the logic behind the bad news; use positive words and try to show reader benefits if possible.
- **Bad news.** Position the bad news so that it does not stand out. Consider implying the bad news.
- **Alternative.** Suggest a compromise, alternative, or substitute if possible.
- **Closing.** Look forward positively. Provide information about an alternative, if appropriate.

In many businesses today employee extended health care plans are increasing in cost. Midland Enterprises had to announce a substantial increase to its employees. Figure 8.5 (p. 204) shows two versions of its bad-news message. The first version opens directly with the bad news. No explanation is given for why employee monthly deductions are rising. Although Midland has been absorbing the increasing costs in the past and has not charged employees, it takes no credit for this. Instead, the tone of the memo is defensive and unsatisfying to receivers.

The improved version of this bad-news memo, shown at the bottom of Figure 8.5, uses the indirect pattern. Notice that it opens with a relevant, upbeat buffer regarding extended health care benefits—but says nothing about increasing monthly costs. For a smooth transition, the second paragraph begins with a key idea from the opening (comprehensive package). The reasons section discusses rising costs with explanations and figures. The bad news (*you will be paying $109 a month*) is clearly presented but embedded within the paragraph.

Throughout, the writer strives to show the fairness of the company's position. The ending, which does not refer to the bad news, emphasizes how much the company is paying and what a wise investment it is. Notice that the entire memo demonstrates a kinder, gentler approach than that shown in the first draft. Of prime importance in breaking bad news to employees is providing clear, convincing reasons that explain the decision.

Quick Check

In announcing bad news to employees, consider starting with a neutral statement or something positive.

When to Use the Direct Pattern

Many bad-news letters are best organized indirectly, beginning with a buffer and reasons. The direct pattern, with the bad news first followed by the reasons and a pleasant closing, may be more effective, though, in situations such as the following:

- **When the bad news is not damaging.** If the bad news is insignificant (such as a small increase in cost) and doesn't personally affect the receiver, then the direct strategy certainly makes sense.
- **When the receiver may overlook the bad news.** With the crush of e-mails and other communications today, many readers skim messages, looking only at the opening. If they don't find substantive material, they may discard the message. Rate increases, changes in service, new policy requirements—these critical messages may require boldness to ensure attention.
- **When organization policy suggests directness.** Some companies expect all internal messages and announcements—even bad news—to be straightforward and presented without frills.
- **When the receiver prefers directness.** Busy managers may prefer directness. Such shorter messages enable the reader to get in the proper frame of mind immediately. If you suspect that the reader prefers that the facts be presented immediately, use the direct pattern.
- **When firmness is necessary.** Messages that must demonstrate determination and strength should not use delaying techniques. For example, the last in a series of collection letters that seek payment of overdue accounts may require a direct opener.

Quick Check

The direct pattern is appropriate when the bad news is not damaging, when the receiver might overlook the bad news, when the organization expects directness, when the receiver prefers directness, or when firmness is necessary.

Figure 8.6 (p. 205) shows an example of a typical direct bad-news message.

FIGURE 8.5 Memo That Announces Bad News to Employees

Before

MEMO TO: Staff

Beginning January 1 the monthly deduction from your paycheque for extended • — Hits readers with bad
health benefits will be increased to $109 (up from $42 last year). news without any
preparation

Every year extended benefits costs go up. Although we considered dropping • — Does not explain why
other benefits, Midland decided that the best plan was to keep the present costs are rising
comprehensive package. Unfortunately, we can't do that unless we pass along
some of the extra cost to you. Last year the company was forced to absorb — Fails to take credit for
the total increase in extended health premiums. However, such a plan this absorbing previous
year is inadvisable. • increases

We did everything possible to avoid the sharp increase in costs to you this • — Sounds defensive;
year. A rate schedule describing the increases in payments for your family and fails to give reasons
dependents is enclosed.

After

DATE: November 6, 2007

TO: Fellow Employees

FROM: Eduardo Martinez, President *EM*

SUBJECT: MAINTAINING QUALITY BENEFITS PACKAGE

Begins with positive   Extended health benefits programs have always been an important part of our
buffer   • commitment to employees here at Midland, Inc. We're proud that our total
benefits package continues to rank among the best in our industry.

Such a comprehensive package does not come without cost. In the last
decade extended health premiums have risen over 50 percent among compa-
Explains why costs   • nies belonging to our group insurance plan. Other insurance plans have been
are rising   even harder hit. We're told that several factors fuel the cost spiral: greater
number of services offered such as therapeutic massage and acupuncture,
increased average age of program users, and increased underwriting of drug
purchases for program members.

Just two years ago our monthly extended health benefits cost for each
employee was $415. It rose to $469 last year. We were able to absorb that
Reveals bad news   jump without increasing your contribution. But this year's hike to $539 forces
clearly but embeds it —   • us to ask you to share the increase. To maintain your current extended health
in paragraph   benefits, you will be paying $109 a month. The enclosed rate schedule de-
scribes the cost breakdown for families and dependents.

Ends positively by —   • Midland continues to pay the major portion of the extended health benefit
stressing the   program ($430 each month). We think it's a wise investment.
company's major
share of the costs   Enclosure

FIGURE 8.6   Direct Bad-News Message

December 2006

Dear Valued Bell Customers,

As of January 1, 2007, basic telephone service rates will be rising by 1.5 percent.

This change is taking place as a result of a recent CRTC decision, as well as for competitive reasons within the industry.

We appreciate your continued loyalty.

Toula Vassopoulos

Toula Vassopoulos
Customer Service Manager

Collection Letters

One of the most important processes in business is the collection process. Collection is the steps a company takes to ensure that its unpaid invoices are paid. The first phase in the collection process is usually the sending of a short reminder letter or e-mail that lets the client or customer know that his or her invoice is outstanding. Best practices stipulate that a copy of the outstanding invoice should be attached to this short reminder message, in case the client has misplaced the original.

An understanding of how to write a direct negative message becomes useful in the second step in the collection process. If the client or customer with the outstanding invoice does not reply in a timely manner to the short reminder message, it is time to write a direct bad-news message demanding payment. Figure 8.7 (p. 206) shows a typical example of such a letter.

The main objective of a bad-news collection letter is to receive payment, but at the same time to make sure that the goodwill of the client or customer is retained. According to CreditGuru.com, a website that offers advice on the collection process, the main features of a well-written collection letter are a reminder of the dates of the invoice, a reminder of the total amount outstanding, a request for immediate payment or payment by a specified date, a request for the payment to be sent by the quickest means (e.g., courier), and finally, a sense of urgency coupled with a unapologetic and a non-threatening tone.[5]

Ethics and the Indirect Pattern

You may worry that the indirect pattern is unethical or manipulative because the writer deliberately delays the main idea. But consider the alternative. Breaking bad news bluntly can cause pain and hard feelings. By delaying bad news, you soften the blow somewhat, as well as ensure that your reasoning will be read while the

The indirect strategy is unethical only if the writer intends to deceive the reader.

✓ *Quick Check*

FIGURE 8.7 Collection Letter

FRASER, AHMET, AND GRANDPRE

3017–66 Avenue Northwest, Suite 222
Edmonton, AB T6H 1Y2

August 14, 2007

Tom Przybylski
Unity Ltd.
9 Givins Dr., Unit 5
Edmonton, AB T2A 4X3

Dear Mr. Przybylski:

Re: Invoice No. 443-2006

Outstanding Amount Due: $19,567.87

You are indebted to the firm of Fraser, Ahmet, and Grandpre in the amount of $19,567.87, for services rendered and for which you were invoiced on March 30, 2007. A copy of the outstanding invoiced is enclosed for your reference, as is a copy of a reminder letter sent to you on July 2, 2007.

Unless we receive a certified cheque or money order, payable to Fraser, Ahmet, and Grandpre, in the amount of $19,567.87, or unless satisfactory payment arrangements are made within seven (7) business days, we are left no choice but to pursue collection of the amount owing. We are not prepared to continue carrying your accounts receivable and we will take all necessary steps for the recovery of this amount from you.

We do not wish to proceed in this fashion and would appreciate your cooperation instead. We look forward to hearing from you on or before August 21, 2007.

Yours sincerely,

Pat McAfee

Pat McAfee
Office Manager/Collections Clerk

---

receiver is still receptive. Your motives are not to deceive the reader or to hide the news. Rather, your goal is to be a compassionate, yet effective communicator.

The key to ethical communication lies in the motives of the sender. Unethical communicators intend to deceive. For example, Victoria's Secret, the clothing and lingerie chain, once offered free $10 gift certificates. However, when customers tried to cash the certificates, they found that they were required to make a minimum purchase of $50 worth of merchandise.[6] For this misleading, deceptive, and unethical offer, the chain paid a $100,000 fine. Although the indirect strategy provides a setting in which to announce bad news, it should not be used to avoid or misrepresent the truth.

Summing Up and Looking Forward

When faced with delivering bad news, you have a choice. You can announce it immediately, or you can delay it by presenting a buffer and reasons first. Many business communicators prefer the indirect strategy because it tends to preserve goodwill. In some instances, however, the direct strategy is effective in delivering bad news.

In this chapter you learned to write follow-up bad-news messages as well as to apply the indirect strategy in refusing requests, denying claims, and delivering bad news to employees. This same strategy is appropriate when you make persuasive requests or when you try to sell something. Now that you have completed your instruction in writing business e-mails, letters, and memos, you're ready to learn about writing longer business documents like proposals and reports. Chapter 9 introduces informal reports and Chapter 10 discusses proposals and formal reports.

Critical Thinking

1. A survey of business professionals revealed that most respondents reported that every effort should be made to resolve business problems in person.[7] Why is this logical? Why is this problematic?
2. Does bad news travel faster and farther than good news? Why? What implications would this have for companies responding to unhappy customers?
3. Consider times when you have been aware that others have used the indirect pattern in writing or speaking to you. How did you react?
4. Why is the "reasons" section of a bad-news message so important?
5. Some people feel that all employee news, good or bad, should be announced directly. Do you agree or disagree? Why?

Chapter Review

6. List the four steps that many business professionals follow in resolving business problems.

7. List the four main parts of the indirect pattern for revealing bad news.

8. What is a buffer?

9. List seven possibilities for opening bad-news messages.

10. List at least five words that might affect readers negatively.

11. How can the passive voice be used effectively in bad-news messages? Provide an original example.

12. What is the danger in implying a refusal?

13. List five techniques for closing a bad-news message.

14. What determines whether you announce bad news to customers or employees directly or indirectly?

15. List five instances when bad news should be announced directly.

Writing Improvement Exercises

8.1 Subordinate Clauses. You can soften the effect of bad news by placing it in a subordinate clause that begins with *although, since,* or *because.* The emphasis in a sentence is on the independent clause. Instead of saying *We cannot serve you on a credit basis,* try *Since we cannot serve you on a credit basis, we invite you to take advantage of our cash discounts and sale prices.*

Revise the following refusals so that the bad news appears in a subordinate clause.

16. We no longer print a complete catalogue. However, we now offer all our catalogue choices at our Web site, which is always up to date.

17. We hope to have our plant remodelling completed by June. We cannot schedule tours of the bottling plant until after we finish remodelling.

18. Northern Air cannot accept responsibility for expenses incurred indirectly from flight delays. However, we do recognize that this delay inconvenienced you.

8.2 Passive-Voice Verbs. Passive-voice verbs may be preferable in breaking bad news because they enable you to emphasize actions rather than personalities. Compare these two refusals:

Example: *Active voice:* I cannot authorize you to take three weeks of vacation in July.
Example: *Passive voice:* Three weeks of vacation in July cannot be authorized.

Revise the following refusals so that they use passive-voice instead of active-voice verbs.

19. We cannot refund cash for the items you purchased on credit.

20. I have already filled my schedule on the date you wish me to speak.

21. We do not examine patients until we have verified their health care number.

8.3 Implied Refusals. Bad news can be de-emphasized by implying a refusal instead of stating it directly. Compare these refusals:

Example: *Direct refusal:* We cannot send you a price list nor can we sell our lawn mowers directly to customers. We sell only through dealers, and your dealer is HomeCo, Inc.
Example: *Implied refusal:* Our lawn mowers are sold only through dealers, and your dealer is HomeCo, Inc.

Revise the following refusals so that the bad news is implied.

22. We cannot give cash refunds for returned merchandise. Our policy enables us to give only store credit and only for merchandise that is returned in its original packaging and that is resalable.

23. I find it impossible to contribute to the fundraising campaign this year. At present all the funds of my organization are needed to lease new equipment and offices for our new branch in Richmond. I hope to be able to support this fund in the future.

24. We cannot ship our fresh fruit baskets C.O.D. Your order was not accompanied by payment, so we are not shipping it. We have it ready, though, and will rush it to its destination as soon as you call us with your credit card number.

Activities and Cases

8.4 Follow-up Apology: Naming Rights-for-Computer Sales Agreement Goes Sour. As the director of partnerships for Inspire Canada, the largest retailer of computers in the country, you signed an agreement four months ago in July with Macdonald College, a community college in Picton, Ontario. The agreement stipulated that in exchange for the naming rights to the college's new academic building (now known as the Inspire Canada Information Centre), your company would provide computer hardware, software, and printers at a deep discount to the college for a five-year period. But now you have a difficult situation on your hands.

Over the past two months, the president of the college has been calling you almost weekly to complain about the problematic rollout of the agreement between Inspire Canada and the college. "Your company's name is on our building, and the media have painted you as a great corporate responsibility success story, but you haven't kept your half of the agreement," is a typical message you've received from the president. She has told you that your computer equipment has been shipped late in 90 percent of orders, causing severe problems for students and professors in September. Also, printers have malfunctioned in 85 percent of the labs on campus, causing widespread late submission of assignments. In response, you recently called the president and told her that Inspire is "doing everything it can to improve shipping procedures." You also promised to look into the printer problem.

Discuss the following options in resolving this business problem.

1. Following a telephone call to this unhappy customer, what should you do next?
   a. Leave it. A telephone call is enough. You did what you could to explain the problem, and words will not solve the problem anyway.
   b. Wait to see whether this customer calls again. After all, the next move is up to her. Respond only after repeated complaints.
   c. Send a short e-mail message repeating your apology and explanation.
   d. Immediately send a letter that apologizes, explains, and shows how seriously you have taken the problem and the customer's complaint.
2. You decide to write a follow-up letter. To open this letter, you should begin with a(n)
   a. Neutral statement such as *This letter is in response to your telephone complaint.*
   b. Defensive statement that protects you from legal liability such as *As I mentioned on the telephone, you are the only customer who has complained about shipping problems.*
   c. Apologetic statement that shows you understand and take responsibility for the problem.
   d. Off-the-subject remark such as *We're happy to hear that the college has increased its enrollment this fall.*
3. In the body of the follow-up letter, you should
   a. Explain why the problem occurred.
   b. Describe what you are doing to resolve the problem.
   c. Promise that you will do everything possible to prevent the problem from happening again.
   d. All of the above
4. In the closing of this letter, you should
   a. Avoid apologizing because it may increase your legal liabilities.
   b. Show appreciation for the customer's patience and patronage.
   c. Explain that company policy prohibits you from revealing the exact nature of the shipping and printer problems.
   d. Provide an action deadline.

Your Task. After circling your choices and discussing them in your class, write a follow-up letter to Dr. Marianne Porter, President, Macdonald College, 35 Regent St., Picton, ON K0K 3BC. In your letter, be proactive about solutions, but consider also that Dr. Porter has implied she may leak the story to the local and national media and/or seek the advice of the college's lawyer.

8.5 Request Refusal: Lease Payments Cannot Be Applied to Purchase. Analyze the following letter. List its weaknesses, and then revise it.

Dear Mr. Cervello:

Unfortunately, we cannot permit you to apply the lease payments you've been making for the past ten months toward the purchase of your Sako 600 copier.

Company policy does not allow such conversion. Have you ever wondered why we can offer such low leasing and purchase prices? Converting lease payments to purchases would mean overall higher prices for our customers. Obviously, we couldn't stay in business long if we agreed to proposals such as yours.

You've had the Sako 600 copier for ten months now, Mr. Cervello, and you say that you like its versatility and reliability. Perhaps we could interest you in another Sako model, such as the Sako 400 series. It may be closer to your price range. Do give us a call.

Sincerely,

---

1. List at least five faults in this letter.

2. Outline a plan for writing a refusal to a request.

Your Task. Revise this refusal. Send your letter to Mr. Walter Cervello, Vice-President of Operations at Copiers Plus, 508 W. Inverary Road, Kingston, ON K2G 1V8. You might mention that many customers are pleased with the Sako copiers, including the Sako 400 series that has nearly as many features as the Sako 600 series. You'd like to demonstrate the Sako 400. Supply any additional information.

8.6 Bad News to Customers: Retailers Unable to Deliver.[8] Who wouldn't want a new $770 digital MP3 player for $89.99? At the FutureShop Web site many delighted shoppers scrambled to order the bargain. Before FutureShop officials could correct the mistake, 340 of the mistakenly priced products were ordered online, representing a total of $230,000 off the original price tag.

FutureShop spared little time in correcting the problem and owning up to the mistake. The company said it would honour any single purchases but would reject bulk orders. The store immediately sent a message to the soon-to-be-disappointed bulk shoppers. The subject line made it clear a *Big Mistake!* had been made and the body of the message began with *We wish we could offer amazing deals like this every day. The price mistake on our new digital MP3 player probably went right by you, but rather than charge you such a large difference, I'm writing to alert you that this item has been removed from your recent order.*

As an assistant in the communication department at FutureShop, you saw the message that was sent to customers and tactfully suggested that the bad news might have been broken differently. Your boss says, "Okay, give it your best shot."

Your Task. Analyze the part of FutureShop's bad-news message given above. Using the principles suggested in this chapter, write an improved version. In the end, FutureShop decided to allow bulk order customers who ordered the player at $89.99 to reorder it for 20 percent less than the retail price, depending on the number ordered. Customers were directed to a special Web site to reorder (make up an address). Remember that FutureShop customers are youthful and hip. Keep your message upbeat.

Team

8.7 Request Refusal: Adieu to Cadillacs in Paris. "As I'm sure you've noticed, Cadillac has been on a bit of a roll lately with the worldwide launch of the all-new Seville and the much-awaited launch of the Escalade," begins the GM invitation letter. This letter has been sent to many of the top automotive journalists in the country inviting them to join GM's executives on a five-day all-expenses-paid press trip to Paris. Such excursions are not unusual. Big Three automakers routinely sponsor reporters' trips to ensure favourable local coverage from the big auto shows in Paris, Frankfurt, Geneva, and Tokyo.

GM particularly wants reporters at the Paris show. This is the show where it hopes to position Cadillac as a global luxury car manufacturer. The invitation letter, mailed in July, promises a "sneak peak at Cadillac's first major concept vehicle in nearly 10 years." But GM has only 20 spots available for the trip, and journalists have to request one of the spots. Suddenly, in late July, GM finds itself in the midst of an expensive strike. "All at once, what had seemed like a good idea is starting to look fiscally irresponsible," says J. Christopher Preuss, Cadillac spokesperson. Although exact figures are not available, some estimates are that the Paris trip could easily cost $12,000 per reporter. That's a large bill for a company facing a prolonged, damaging strike.

Your Task. As part of a group of interns working in the communications division of GM, you and your team have been asked to draft a letter to the journalists who signed up for the trip. Announce that GM must back out. About the best thing they can expect now is an invitation to the gala unveiling and champagne reception GM will sponsor in January at the annual Detroit auto show. At that time GM will brief reporters about Cadillac's "new vision" and unveil the eye-popping Escalade. Mr. Preuss is embarrassed about cancelling the Paris trip, but he feels GM must do what is financially prudent. Prepare a draft of the letter for the signature of J. Christopher Preuss. Address the first letter to Rodney M. Olafson, *Chronicle-Herald*, 185 Haggerty Road, Thunder Bay, ON P7E 5P6.

8.8 Request Refusal: The End of Free Credit Reports. You are part of the customer service team at Experian, the largest supplier of consumer and business credit information in the world. Experian took over TRW Information Systems & Services back in 1996. Experian currently employs more than 11,000 people in North America, the United Kingdom, Continental Europe, Africa, and Asia Pacific. As a service to consumers, Experian at one time provided complimentary credit reports. However, it now offers them only in certain locations and to certain groups of people.

Experian's Web site explains its new policy in its FAQs (frequently asked questions). Your supervisor says to you, "I guess not everyone is able to learn about our new policy by going to our Web site because we still receive a lot of phone requests for free reports. I'm unhappy with a letter we've been using to respond to these requests. I want you to compose a draft of a new form letter that we can send to people who inquire. You should look at our Web site to see who gets free reports and in what locations."

Because you are fairly new to Experian, you ask your boss what prompted the change in policy. She explains, "It was a good idea, but it got out of hand. So-called 'credit repair' companies would refer their clients to us for free credit reports, and then they advised their clients to dispute every item on the report. We had to change our policy. But you can read more about it at our Web site."

Your Task. You resolve to study the Experian Web site closely. Your task is to write a letter refusing the requests of people who want free credit reports. But you must also explain the reasons for the change in policy, as well as its exceptions. Decide whether you should tell consumers how to order a copy and how to pay for it. Although your letter will be used repeatedly for such requests, address your draft to Ms. Cherise Benoit, 250 Rue Bruce, Montreal, QC H2X 1E1. Sign it with your boss's name, Elisabeth Bourke.

8.9 Bad News for Customers: These Funds Are Worth Holding On To. You are a financial planner in Hamilton, Ontario, with over 200 clients. Since you began your practice as a financial planner, you have been a strong believer in BMC's mutual funds, which are heavily invested in the financial services sector. Over the past few years, though, these funds have been underperforming dismally. For example, in 2004, when the S&P/TSX Index was 14.5 percent, BMC funds were averaging 1 percent; in 2005 when the Index was at 5 percent, BMC funds averaged –5.5 percent; and in 2006 when the Index was at 3.4 percent, BMC funds averaged –6.4 percent. BMC funds have been criticized in major newspapers of late, and you have had at least five clients per week for the past few months calling to sell their funds. You believe BMC funds are still a good value because the financial services sector will rebound soon. Also, with Canadian demographic trends pointing to a large retired population in the next decade, you believe BMC funds are a smart investment.

Your Task. Write a letter to your clients in which you discuss the recent bad news about BMC funds, but at the same time, in which you attempt to put this bad news into a wider context.

Related Web site: For general information on Canadian mutual fund performance, go to <www.morningstar.ca>.

8.10 Claim Refusal: Wilted Landscaping. As Flora Powell, owner of Town & Country Landscaping, you must refuse the following request. Paul and Judy Alexander have asked that you replace the landscaping in the home they recently purchased in Canmore. You had landscaped that home nearly a year ago for the former owner, Mrs. Hunter, installing a sod lawn and many shrubs, trees, and flowers. It looked beautiful when you finished, but six months later, Mrs. Hunter sold the property and moved to Calgary. Four months elapsed before the new owners moved in. After four months of neglect and a hot, dry summer, the newly installed landscaping suffered.

You guarantee all your work and normally would replace any plants that do not survive. Under these circumstances, however, you do not feel justified in making any refund because your guarantee necessarily presumes proper maintenance on the part of the property owner. Moreover, your guarantee is made only to the individual who contracted with you—not to subsequent owners. You would like to retain the goodwill of the new owners, since this is an affluent neighbourhood and you hope to attract additional work here. On the other hand, you can't afford to replace the materials invested in this job. You believe that the lawn could probably be rejuvenated with deep watering and fertilizer.

Your Task. Write to Mr. and Mrs. Paul and Judy Alexander, 3318 Clearview Drive, Canmore, AB T2N 3E4, refusing their claim. You would be happy to inspect the property and offer suggestions to the Alexanders. In reality, you wonder whether the Alexanders might not have a claim against the former owner or the escrow agency for failing to maintain the property. Clearly, however, the claim is not against you.

Critical Thinking **8.11 Refusing a Claim: Evicting a Noisy Neighbour.** As Robert Hsu, you must deny the request of Arman Aryai, one of the tenants in your three-storey office building. Mr. Aryai, a CA, demands that you immediately evict a neighbouring tenant who plays loud music throughout the day, interfering with Mr. Aryai's conversations with clients and with his concentration. The noisy tenant, Bryant Haperot, seems to operate an entertainment booking agency and spends long hours in his office.

You know you can't evict Mr. Haperot immediately because of his lease. More-over, you hesitate to do anything drastic because paying tenants are hard to find. You called your lawyer, and he said that the first thing you should do is talk to the noisy tenant or write him a letter asking him to tone it down. If this doesn't work within 30 days, you could begin the eviction process.

Your Task. Decide on a course of action. Because Mr. Aryai doesn't seem to answer his telephone, you must write him a letter. You need a permanent record of this decision anyway. Write to Arman Aryai, CA, Suite 203, Pico Building, 1405 Bower Boulevard, Vancouver, BC V6L 1Y3. Deny his request, but tell him how you plan to resolve the problem.

8.12 Customer Bad News: Olympus Refuses Customer's Request to Repeat World Trip. Olympus Customer Service Manager Charlie Smith can't believe what he reads in a letter from Brian P. Coyle. This 27-year-old Ottawa resident actually wants Olympus to foot the bill for a repeat round-the-world trip because his Stylus Epic camera malfunctioned and he lost 12 rolls of film!

As soon as Smith saw the letter and the returned camera, he knew what was wrong. Of the two million Stylus Epic cameras made last year, 20,000 malfunctioned. A supplier squirted too much oil in the shutter mechanism, and the whole lot was recalled. In fact, Olympus spent almost $1 million to remove these cameras from store shelves. Olympus also contacted all customers who could be reached. In addition to the giant recall, the company quickly redesigned the cameras so that they would work even if they had excess oil. But somehow Coyle was not notified of the recall. When Smith checked the warranty files, he learned that this customer had not returned his warranty. Had the customer done so, he would have been notified in August, well before his trip.

Although customer service manager Smith is sorry for the mishap, he thinks that a request for $20,000 to replace "lost memories" is preposterous. Olympus has never assumed any responsibility beyond replacing a camera or film. This customer, however, seems to have suffered more than a routine loss of snapshots. Therefore, Smith decides to sweeten the deal by offering to throw in a digital camera valued at $600, more than double the cost of the Stylus Epic. One of the advantages of a digital camera is that it contains an LCD panel that enables the photographer to view stored images immediately. No chance of losing memories with this digital camera!

Your Task. As the assistant to Customer Service Manager Smith, you must write a letter that refuses the demand for $20,000 but retains the customer's goodwill. Tell this customer what you will do, and be sure to explain how Olympus reacted immediately when it discovered the Stylus Epic defect. Write a sensitive refusal to Brian P. Coyle, 594 Swindon Way, Ottawa, ON K1P 5V5.

8.13 Employee Bad News: Strikeout for Expanded Office Teams. Assume you are Walter Cervello, vice-president of operations at Copiers Plus, 508 W. Inverary Road, Kingston, ON K2G 1V8. Recently several of your employees requested that their spouses or friends be allowed to participate in Copiers Plus's intramural sports teams. Although the teams play only once a week during the season, these employees claim that they can't afford more time away from friends and family. Over 100 employees currently participate in the eight coed volleyball and softball teams, which are open to company employees only. The teams were designed to improve employee friendships and to give employees a regular occasion to have fun together.

If nonemployees were to participate, you're afraid that employee interaction would be limited. And while some team members might have fun if spouses or friends were included, you're not so sure all employees would enjoy it. You're not interested in turning intramural sports into "date night." Furthermore, the company would have to create additional teams if many nonemployees joined, and you don't want the administrative or equipment costs of more teams. Adding teams would also require changes to team rosters and game schedules, which could be a problem for some employees. You do understand the need for social time with friends and families, but guests are welcome as spectators at all intramural games. Besides, the company already sponsors a family holiday party and an annual company picnic.

Your Task. Write an e-mail or hard-copy memo to the staff denying the request of several employees to include nonemployees on Copiers Plus's intramural sports teams.

8.14 Employee Bad News: Refusing Holiday Season Event. In the past your office has always sponsored a holiday season party at a nice restaurant. As your company has undergone considerable downsizing and budget cuts during the past year, you know that no money is available for holiday entertaining.

Your Task. As executive vice-president, send an e-mail to Dina Gillian, office manager. Dina asked permission to make restaurant reservations for this year's holiday party. Refuse Dina, but offer some alternatives. How about a potluck dinner?

8.15 Customer Bad News: Image Consultant Plays Bad Guy. As the owner of Polished Pro Image Consultants, you hate the part of your job that requires you every so often to write collection letters. Your work is all about making people look good, so when they don't pay their bills, it's difficult for you to get in touch with them—it's as if nothing you taught them sunk in. Still, as a small business owner, you cannot afford a collections clerk, and you dread the cost of hiring a third-party collection agency to take care of your outstanding accounts. Recently, you provided extensive consulting services to David M. Fryer, a local businessperson who will be running in the next election to be the local member of Parliament. You billed Mr. Fryer for 18 hours at $100 per hour for in-person consulting, plus another 10 hours at $50 per hour for telephone consulting. In total, your invoice dated May 14, 2006, amounted to $2,300 plus GST. A reminder e-mail you sent to Mr. Fryer on June 30 went unanswered, and you've decided now that August has arrived, it's time to act. The only thing holding you back is that Mr. Fryer is prominent in your community, and while you definitely want your invoice paid, you're not sure you want to get on his bad side.

Your Task. Write a collection letter to Mr. David M. Fryer, President, Hexago Plastics, 230 Queen St., St. John, NB E3K 4N6

The following sentences contain errors in grammar, punctuation, capitalization, number style, usage, and spelling. Below each sentence write a corrected version.

1. The first province by province report describing Canada's tobacco use and tobacco control laws were recently released.

2. The report which was compiled by statistics canada showed adult smoking rates that varied from 5% of the population in alberta, to twelve percent in quebec.

3. As expected quebecs pattern of deaths related to smoking was nearly twice that of albertas.

4. Hailed by anti-tobacco groups as proof of the need for more stricter National regulations the report was dismissed by the tobacco industry as "old news".

5. Statistics canada said that the comparisons might stimulate changes in some provinces, but that the report was not part of any particular policy drive.

6. "Children are particularly vulnerable to second-hand smoke because they breathe faster than adults inhale more air proportionate to their body mass and their lungs are still growing and developing reported ugnat et al in the Canadian journal of public health.

7. Most likely to attract attention, are data related to smoking among High School students.

8. The 8 provinces with the lowest cigarette taxs has a higher than average number of smokers.

9. The provinces of newfoundland and british columbia have the highest provincial tobacco taxes at $22 a pack rank in the middle on percentage of smokers.

10. The québec-based "ACTI-Menu" health programs non smoking campaign encourages smokers who want to quit to pair up with a non smoking partner. Both partners sign a pledge with the smoker agreeing not to smoke for the period of march 1st to april 12th.

11. Walker Merryman a spokesperson for the tobacco institute said "This report is more rehash than research, it is not terribly useful for understanding why kids smoke".

12. Anti-tobacco supporters are urging government to support a proposal to severely restrict: advertising marketing and distribution of tobacco products.

13. The province of quebec however faces the biggest problem, nearly twenty-four percent of it's students who were daily smokers 15 to 19 years of age, reported smoking within the month in which they were surveyed.

14. In 2004 7% of young people aged 10 to 19 were beginning to smoke.

15. The governments tobacco education and information officer explained that its hard to restrict smoking when the provinces economy is linked so close to gaming which is linked to tobacco.

Grammar/Mechanics Challenge—8

Document for Revision

The following e-mail has faults in grammar, punctuation, spelling, number form, and negative words. Use standard proofreading marks (see Appendix B) to correct the errors. When you finish, your instructor can show you the revised version of this message.

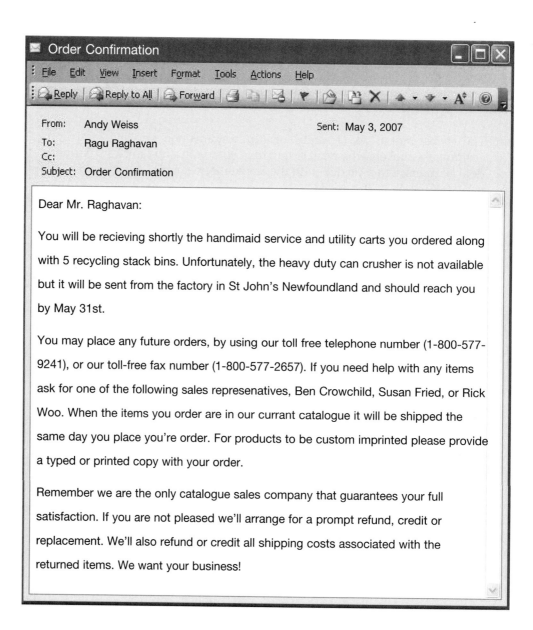

Order Confirmation

From: Andy Weiss   Sent: May 3, 2007
To: Ragu Raghavan
Cc:
Subject: Order Confirmation

Dear Mr. Raghavan:

You will be recieving shortly the handimaid service and utility carts you ordered along with 5 recycling stack bins. Unfortunately, the heavy duty can crusher is not available but it will be sent from the factory in St John's Newfoundland and should reach you by May 31st.

You may place any future orders, by using our toll free telephone number (1-800-577-9241), or our toll-free fax number (1-800-577-2657). If you need help with any items ask for one of the following sales represenatives, Ben Crowchild, Susan Fried, or Rick Woo. When the items you order are in our currant catalogue it will be shipped the same day you place you're order. For products to be custom imprinted please provide a typed or printed copy with your order.

Remember we are the only catalogue sales company that guarantees your full satisfaction. If you are not pleased we'll arrange for a prompt refund, credit or replacement. We'll also refund or credit all shipping costs associated with the returned items. We want your business!

Etiquette 101: A Quick Course in Business Social Skills

Etiquette, civility, and sensitivity may seem out of place in today's fast-moving and fiercely competitive global economy. But lately we're seeing signs that etiquette is returning to fashion in the world of commerce and industry. More and more employers are recognizing that good manners are good for business.

Schools offering management programs often now include a short course in manners. And companies are conducting manners seminars for trainee and veteran managers. Why is politeness regaining legitimacy as a leadership tool? Primarily because courtesy works. Good manners convey a positive image of an organization. People like to do business with people who show respect and treat others with civility.

Etiquette is more about attitude than about formal rules of behaviour. That attitude is a desire to make others feel comfortable. You don't have to become an etiquette nut, but you might need to polish your social competencies a little to be an effective businessperson today. Here are some time-honoured classic tips for communicators.[9]

- Smile and greet coworkers in passing.
- Return phone calls and e-mail messages promptly.
- Share recognition for joint projects.
- Use titles for higher-ranking coworkers; avoid the use of first names unless you are asked to be less formal.
- Be on time for meetings, and don't leave early.
- Pay attention during meetings. Save portable audio machines, knitting, or "busy work" for breaks or after work. Refrain from doodling.
- Contribute your fair share for office treats, gifts, or housekeeping duties.
- Pay attention to people's names so that you can remember them.
- Don't discuss sensitive topics (such as sex, religion, and politics) with people you don't know.
- Respect other people's space.
- Show interest in other people. Look at them; make eye contact. Ask questions. Laugh at others' jokes.
- Don't use social/business occasions to lobby for a raise, bonus, promotion, and so forth.
- Keep your hands to yourself. Some people don't like to be touched.
- Hold doors for men or women entering with you.
- Remember that "please" and "thank you" are always appropriate.

Career Application

You're part of a team of interns that is ending a two-month assignment at a large local firm. With graduation just around the corner, everyone has been looking for permanent jobs. One team member announces that he has been invited for a job interview that includes dinner. He wants to make a good impression, but he confides that he has had very few opportunities to eat at fine restaurants and he's feeling uneasy. He asks for advice.

Your Task

- What general tips of etiquette can you give regarding such things as appropriate dress, arriving at the restaurant, conversation, body language, napkins, and being introduced to people?
- What specific tips can you give regarding the use of silverware, what to order, when to begin eating, and how to eat?
- What kind of etiquette exists regarding technological gadgets like PDAs, cell phones, and digital pagers at a formal dinner meeting?
- What should the guest do to express appreciation after a dinner meeting?
- List your suggestions and bring them to class to discuss in teams.
- Script and then perform a dinner meeting situation where your team member doesn't make a good impression. Ask your classmates to count the number of etiquette mistakes made in the skit.

Related Web site: Visit <www.executiveplanet.com> for a list of entertaining and dining guidelines. Check out some of the recommendations for other countries while you are there. You can also read Amy Zunk's "How Rude!: PDA and Cellphone Etiquette in the New Millenium" at <www.geek.com/pdageek/features/cybermanners>.

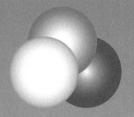

Reporting
Data

Informal Reports

As a project manager, I find that progress reports are excellent tools to keep clients up to speed. These reports detail the project's progression and provide valuable insight into whether the objectives are being met and if any fine-tuning is required in the assignment of resources and responsibilities.[1]

Heather Jack, *project manager, Bell Canada*

LEARNING OBJECTIVES

1. Define a report project and gather data.
2. Organize report data using effective headings.
3. Identify six kinds of informal reports and four report formats.
4. Present data objectively to gain credibility.
5. Write information and progress reports.
6. Write justification, recommendation, and feasibility reports.
7. Write summary reports and meeting minutes.

✔ Quick Check

Informal reports are relatively short (under ten pages) and are usually written in memo or letter format.

Good report writers, as Heather Jack implies, are good at simplifying facts so that anyone can understand them. Collecting information and organizing it clearly and simply into meaningful reports are skills that all successful businesspeople today require. In this age of information, reports play a significant role in helping decision makers solve problems. You can learn to write good reports by examining basic techniques and by analyzing appropriate models.

Because of their abundance and diversity, business reports are difficult to define. They may range from informal e-mail trip reports to formal 200-page financial forecasts. Reports may be presented orally in front of a group using PowerPoint, while many reports appear as e-mails, memos, and letters. Still others consist primarily of numerical data, such as tax reports or profit-and-loss statements. Although reports vary in length, content, format, organization, and level of formality, they all have one common purpose: they are systematic attempts to answer business questions and solve business problems. In this chapter we'll concentrate on informal reports. These reports tend to be short (under ten pages); use e-mail, memo, or letter format; and are personal in tone.

Functions of Reports

Most reports can be classified into two functional categories: information reports and analytical reports.

Information Reports

Reports that present data without analysis or recommendations are primarily informational. Although writers collect and organize facts, they are not expected to analyze the facts for readers. A trip report describing an employee's visit to a conference, for example, simply presents information. Other reports that present information without analysis involve routine operations, compliance with regulations, and company policies and procedures.

Analytical Reports

Reports that provide analysis and conclusions as well as data are analytical. If requested, writers also supply recommendations. Analysis is the process of breaking down a problem into its parts in order to understand it better and solve it (for example, each time you write an outline, as shown in Figure 3.2 on page 53, you are analyzing a problem). Analytical reports attempt to persuade readers to act or change their opinions. For example, a recommendation report that compares several potential locations for an employee fitness club might recommend one site, but not until after it has analyzed and discussed the alternatives. This analysis should persuade readers to accept the writer's choice.

Report Formats and Organization

How should a report look? The following four formats are frequently used.

- **Letter format** is appropriate for informal reports prepared by one organization for another. These reports are much like letters except that they are more carefully organized, using headings and lists where appropriate.
- **E-mail and Memo format** is common for informal reports written for circulation within an organization. These internal reports follow the conventions of e-mails and memos that you learned in Chapter 5—with the addition of headings.
- **Manuscript format** is used for longer, more complicated and more formal reports. Printed on plain paper, with a cover, title page, executive summary, and table of contents, these reports carefully follow a pattern that is described in detail in Chapter 10. A sophisticated use of major headings (first level), subheadings (second level) and sub-subheadings (third level) characterizes this format.
- **Prepared forms or templates** are useful in reporting routine activities such as accident reports or merchandise inventories. Standardized headings on these forms save time for the writer; forms also make similar information easy to locate.

✓ Quick Check

Informal reports may appear in four formats: letter, e-mail and memo, or manuscript form, or on prepared forms.

Today's reports and other business documents are far more sophisticated than typewritten documents of the past. Using a computer, you know how easy it is to make your documents look as if they were professionally printed. In fact, many business reports such as corporate annual reports are not typed; they are designed. As a report writer, you have a wide selection of fonts and formats from which to choose, plus a number of word processing capabilities to fashion attractive documents. Figure 9.1 (p. 224) offers suggestions to help you use these capabilities wisely.

FIGURE 9.1   Ten Tips for Designing Better Documents

Desktop publishing packages, word processing programs, and laser printers now make it possible for you to turn out professional-looking documents. The temptation, though, is to overdo it by incorporating too many features in one document. Here are ten tips for applying good sense and good design principles in "publishing" your documents:

- **Analyze your audience.** Avoid overly flashy type, colours, and borders for conservative business documents. Also consider whether your readers will be reading painstakingly or merely browsing. Lists and headings help those readers who are in a hurry.
- **Choose an appropriate type size.** For most business memos, letters, and reports, the body text should be 10 to 12 points tall (a point is 1/72 of an inch). Larger type looks amateurish, and smaller type is hard to read.
- **Use a consistent type font.** Although your software may provide a variety of fonts, stay with a single family of type within one document. The most popular fonts are Times New Roman, Arial, and Helvetica. For emphasis and contrast, you may vary the font size and weight with **bold**, *italic*, ***bold italic***, and other selections.
- **Don't justify right margins.** Textbooks, novels, newspapers, magazines, and other long works are usually set with justified (even) right margins. However, for shorter works ragged-right margins are recommended because such margins add white space and help readers locate the beginnings of new lines. Slower readers find ragged-right copy more legible.
- **Separate paragraphs and sentences appropriately.** The first line of a paragraph should be indented or preceded by a blank line. To separate sentences, typists have traditionally left two spaces. This spacing is still acceptable for most business documents. If you are preparing a newsletter or brochure, however, you may wish to adopt printer's standards, leaving one space after end punctuation.
- **Design readable headlines.** Use upper- and lower-case letters for the most readable headlines. All caps is generally discouraged because solid blocks of

capital letters interfere with recognition of word patterns. To further improve readability, select a sans serif typeface (one without cross strokes or embellishment), such as Helvetica or Arial.
- **Strive for an attractive page layout.** In designing title pages or visual aids, provide for a balance between print and white space. Also consider placing the focal point (something that draws the reader's eye) at the optical centre of a page—about three lines above the actual centre. Moreover, remember that the average reader scans a page from left to right and top to bottom in a Z pattern. Plan your visuals accordingly.
- **Use graphics and clip art with restraint.** Images created with spreadsheet or graphics programs can be imported into documents. Original drawings, photographs, and clip art can also be scanned or cut and pasted into documents. Use such images, however, only when they are well drawn, relevant, purposeful, and appropriately sized.
- **Avoid amateurish results.** Many beginning writers, eager to display every graphic device a program offers, produce busy, cluttered documents. Too many typefaces, ruled lines, images, and oversized headlines will overwhelm readers. Strive for simple, clean, and forceful effects.
- **Become comfortable with templates.** As mentioned in earlier chapters, word processing software has sophisticated templates that can be used by business writers. Also, most companies have their own report templates they will want you to follow. Because not all of us can be gifted designers, a report template such as Microsoft Word's "Elegant Report" can save a lot of time and produce professional-looking results. Templates are not magic, though. It takes time to learn how to make them work for you. Spend some time working with one of the report templates on your word processing software. Decide whether it makes more sense for you to use a template, to follow the examples in this book, or to make one up on your own. Your instructor may make the decision for you.

When it comes to the organization of your informal report, you have two choices. Like correspondence discussed earlier in this book, reports may be organized directly or indirectly. The choice rests on the content of your report and the expectations of your audience.

- The **direct pattern** is the most common organizational pattern for business reports. In an informational business report such as a trip report, the report opens with a short introduction, followed by the facts, and finally a summary.

Figure 9.2 shows such a direct-pattern information report. Notice that because it is an e-mail, the writer has dispensed with headings for her three sections. Many businesspeople prefer the direct pattern because it gives them the results of the report immediately. An analytical report may also be organized directly, especially when readers are supportive and familiar with the topic. In an analytical business report such as a recommendation report, the report opens with a short introduction, followed by the conclusions and recommendations, then the facts and findings, and finally the analysis and discussion. Figure 9.6, later in the chapter, shows a direct-pattern analytical report.

- The **indirect pattern** is also used when writing business reports. Information reports are never indirect, but analytical reports may be. The difference between direct and indirect analytical reports is simply the placement of the conclusions and recommendations. In an indirect-pattern report, the introduction comes first, followed by the facts and findings, the analysis and discussion, and only then by the conclusions and recommendations. This pattern is helpful when readers are unfamiliar with the problem. It's also useful when readers must be persuaded or when they may be disappointed, skeptical, or hostile

FIGURE 9.2 Information Report—E-Mail Format

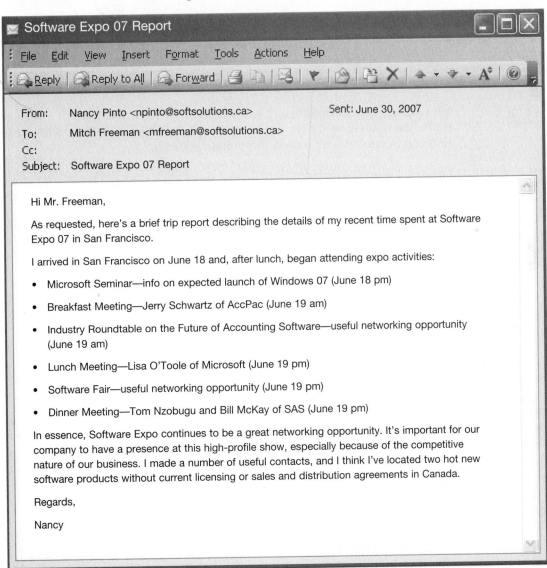

Report Formats and Organization

FIGURE 9.3 **Audience Analysis and Report Organization**

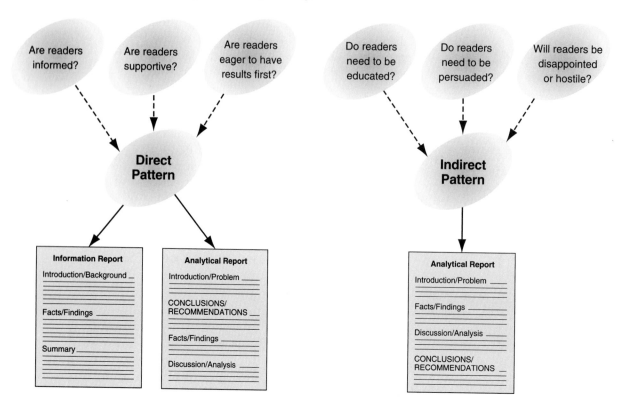

toward the report's findings. A side benefit of the indirect pattern is that it reads like a novel or movie, building "suspense" toward a climax, which is resolved in the conclusions and recommendations.

Figure 9.3 summarizes the questions you should ask yourself about your audience before writing your report, as well as your choices for structuring your informal business report.

Guidelines for Writing Informal Reports

Your natural tendency in preparing a report may be to sit down and begin writing immediately. If you follow this urge, however, you will very likely have to rewrite or even start again. Reports take planning, beginning with defining the project and gathering data. The following guidelines will help you plan your project.

Defining the Project

Begin a report by drafting a statement of purpose. Explain why you are writing the report.

Begin the process of report writing by defining your project. This definition should include a statement of purpose. Ask yourself: Am I writing this report to inform, to analyze, to solve a problem, or to persuade? The answer to this question should be a clear, accurate statement identifying your purpose. In informal reports the statement of purpose may be only one sentence; that sentence usually becomes part of the introduction. Notice how the following introductory statement describes the purpose of the report:

> This report presents information regarding professional development activities coordinated and supervised by the Human Resources Department between the first of the year and the present.

After writing a statement of purpose, analyze who will read your report. If your report is intended for your immediate supervisors and they are supportive of your project, you need not include extensive details, historical development, definition of terms, or persuasion. Other readers, however, may require background information and persuasive strategies.

The expected audience for your report influences your writing style, research method, vocabulary, areas of emphasis, and communication strategy. Remember, too, that your audience may consist of more than one set of readers. Reports are often distributed to secondary readers who may need more details than the primary reader.

Gathering Data

A good report is based on solid, accurate, verifiable facts. Typical sources of factual information for informal reports include (1) company records; (2) observation; (3) surveys, questionnaires, and inventories; (4) interviews; and (5) research.

Company Records. Many business-related reports begin with an analysis of company records and files. From these records you can observe past performance and methods used to solve previous problems. You can collect pertinent facts that will help determine a course of action.

Observation. Another logical source of data for many problems lies in personal observation and experience. For example, if you were writing a report on the need for additional computer equipment, you might observe how much the current equipment is being used and for what purpose.

Surveys, Questionnaires, and Inventories. Primary data from groups of people can be collected most efficiently and economically by using surveys, questionnaires, and inventories. For example, if you were part of a committee investigating the success of a campus recycling program, you might begin by using a questionnaire to survey use of the program by students and faculty. You might also do some informal telephoning to see if departments on campus know about the program and are using it.

Interviews. Talking with individuals directly concerned with the problem produces excellent primary information. Interviews also allow for one-on-one communication, thus giving you an opportunity to explain your questions and ideas in eliciting the most accurate information.

Electronic and Other Research. In doing secondary research information for reports, you would probably be interested in finding examples from other organizations that shed light on the problem identified in your report. You might also check out your competitors to see what they are currently doing and what they have done in the past. An extensive source of current and historical information is available electronically through online library databases and other online resources. From a home, office, or library computer you can obtain access to vast amounts of information provided by governments, newspapers, magazines, and companies from all over the world. For informal reports the most usable data will probably be found in periodicals and online resources. Chapter 10 contains more detailed suggestions about online research.

Developing an Appropriate Writing Style

Like other business messages, reports can range from informal to formal, depending on their purpose, audience, and setting. Research reports from consultants to their

Guidelines for Writing Informal Reports

FIGURE 9.4 Report-Writing Styles

	Informal Writing Style	Formal Writing Style
Use for ...	Short, routine reports	Theses
	Reports for familiar audiences	Research studies
	Noncontroversial reports	Controversial or complex reports
	Most reports for company insiders	(especially to outsiders)
Effect is ...	Feeling of warmth, personal	Impression of objectivity,
	involvement, closeness	accuracy, professionalism, fairness
		Distance created between writer and reader
Characteristics are ...	Use of first-person pronouns (I, we, me, my, us, our)	Absence of first-person pronouns; use of third-person (the researcher, the writer)
	Use of contractions (can't, don't)	Absence of contractions (cannot, do not)
	Emphasis on active-voice verbs (I conducted the study)	Use of passive-voice verbs (the study was conducted)
	Shorter sentences; familiar words	Complex sentences; long words
	Occasional use of humour, metaphors	Absence of humour and figures of speech
	Occasional use of colourful speech	Reduced use of coloruful adjectives and adverbs
	Acceptance of author's opinions and ideas	Elimination of "editorializing" (author's opinions, perceptions)

clients tend to be rather formal. Such reports must project an impression of objectivity, authority, and impartiality. But a report to your boss describing a trip to a conference (as in Figure 9.2) would probably have informal elements. You can see the differences between formal and informal styles in Figure 9.4.

In this chapter we are most concerned with an informal writing style. Your informal reports will probably be written for familiar audiences and involve noncontroversial topics. You may use first-person pronouns (I, we, me, my, us, our) and contractions (I'm, we'll). You'll emphasize active-voice verbs and strive for shorter sentences using familiar words.

Using Headings Effectively

Headings are helpful to both the report reader and the writer. For the reader they serve as an outline of the text, highlighting major ideas and categories. They also act as guides for locating facts and pointing the way through the text. Moreover, headings provide resting points for the mind and for the eye, breaking up large chunks of text into manageable and inviting segments. For the writer, headings force organization of the data into meaningful blocks.

You may choose functional or talking headings. Functional headings (such as *Introduction, Discussion of Findings,* and *Summary*) help the writer outline a report; they are used in the progress report shown in Figure 9.5 (p. 232). But talking headings (such as *Students Perplexed by Shortage of Parking* or *Short-Term Parking Solutions*) provide more information to the reader. Many of the examples in this chapter use functional headings for the purpose of instruction. To provide even greater clarity, you can make headings both functional and descriptive, such as *Recommendations: Shuttle and New Structures.* Whether your headings are talking or functional, keep them brief and clear. Here are general tips on displaying headings effectively:

✓ **Quick Check**

Functional headings show the outline of a report; talking headings provide more information.

- **Consistency.** The cardinal rule of headings is that they should be consistent. In other words, don't use informational headings in three of four cases and a talking heading in the fourth case. Or, don't use bolded headings for 80 percent of your report and underlined headings for the other 20 percent.
- **Strive for parallel construction.** Use balanced expressions such as *Visible Costs* and *Invisible Costs* rather than *Visible Costs* and *Costs That Don't Show*.
- **Use only short first- and second-level headings.** Many short business reports contain only one or two levels of headings. For such reports use first-level headings (centred, bolded) and/or second-level headings (flush left, bolded).
- **Capitalize and underline carefully.** Most writers use all capital letters (without underlines) for main titles, such as the report, chapter, and unit titles. For first- and second-level headings, they capitalize only the first letter of main words. For additional emphasis, they use a bold font.
- **Keep headings short but clear.** Try to make your headings brief (no more than eight words) but understandable. Experiment with headings that concisely tell who, what, when, where, and why.
- **Don't enclose headings in quotation marks.** Quotation marks are appropriate only for marking quoted words or words used in a special sense, such as slang. They are unnecessary in headings.
- **Don't use headings as antecedents for pronouns such as** *this, that, these,* **and** *those.* For example, when the heading reads *Laser Printers,* don't begin the next sentence with *These are often used with desktop publishing software.*

Being Objective

Reports are convincing only when the facts are believable and the writer is credible. You can build credibility in a number of ways:

- **Present both sides of an issue.** Even if you favour one possibility, discuss both sides and show through logical reasoning why your position is superior. Remain impartial, letting the facts prove your point.
- **Separate fact from opinion.** Suppose a supervisor wrote *Our department works harder and gets less credit than any other department in the company.* This opinion is difficult to prove, and it damages the credibility of the writer. A more convincing statement might be *Our productivity has increased 6 percent over the past year, and I'm proud of the extra effort my employees are making.* After you've made a claim or presented an important statement in a report, ask yourself: Is this a verifiable fact? If the answer is no, rephrase your statement to make it sound more reasonable.
- **Be sensitive and moderate in your choice of language.** Don't exaggerate. Instead of saying *most people think …* , it might be more accurate to say *some people think …* . Obviously, avoid using labels and slanted expressions. Calling someone an *idiot,* a *techie,* or an *elitist* demonstrates bias. If readers suspect that a writer is prejudiced, they may discount the entire argument.
- **Cite sources.** Tell your readers where the information came from by using lead-ins to your quotations and paraphrases, and by citing your sources. If you don't do so, you are probably guilty of plagiarism, which is discussed in more detail in Chapter 10. For example, in a report that reads *In a recent Vancouver Province article, Blake Spence, Director of Transportation, argues that the Sky Train must be expanded to cope with the influx of tourists expected during the 2010 Olympics. (A17),* "Blake Spence … argues that" is the lead-in, and "(A17)" is the page reference. Together these two elements are a citation.

 Quick Check

Reports are more believable if the author is impartial, separates fact from opinion, uses moderate language, and cites sources.

Six Kinds of Informal Reports

You are about to examine six categories of informal reports frequently written in business. In many instances the boundaries of the categories overlap; distinctions are not always clear-cut. Individual situations, goals, and needs may make one report take on some characteristics of a report in another category. Still, these general categories, presented here in a brief overview, are helpful to beginning writers. The reports will be illustrated and discussed in more detail below.

Quick Check

Reports that provide data are informational; reports that draw conclusions and make recommendations are analytical.

- **Information reports.** Reports that collect and organize information are informative or investigative. They may record routine activities such as daily, weekly, and monthly reports of sales or profits. They may investigate options, performance, or equipment. Although they provide information, they do not analyze that information.
- **Progress reports.** Progress reports monitor the headway of unusual or nonroutine activities. For example, progress reports would keep management informed about a committee's preparations for a trade show 14 months from now. Such reports usually answer three questions: (1) Is the project on schedule? (2) Are corrective measures needed? (3) What activities are next?
- **Justification/Recommendation reports.** Recommendation and justification reports are similar to information reports in that they present information. However, they offer analysis in addition to data. They attempt to solve problems by evaluating options and offering recommendations. Usually these reports revolve around a significant company decision.
- **Feasibility reports.** When a company or organization must decide whether to proceed with a plan of action based on a previously accepted recommendation, it may require a feasibility report that establishes how possible the plan is. For example, a company has decided to redesign its Web site, but how feasible is it to have the redesign accomplished in six months' time? A feasibility report would examine the practicality of implementing the recommendation or proposal.
- **Summary Reports.** A summary condenses the primary ideas, conclusions, and recommendations of a longer report or publication. Employees may be asked to write summaries of technical or research reports. Students may be asked to write summaries of periodical articles or books to sharpen their writing skills.
- **Minutes of meetings.** A final type of informal report is "the minutes" of a meeting. This is a record of the proceedings and action points of a meeting. Although informal business meetings today take place without minutes being recorded, many companies, organizations, clubs, committees, and boards still require minutes to be recorded. The person delegated to take notes at a meeting usually turns them into the minutes, distributes them to the participants after the meeting, asks for revisions, and then files the report. You'll find more information on meetings in Chapter 11.

Information Reports

Writers of information reports provide information without drawing conclusions or making recommendations. Some information reports are highly standardized, such as police reports, hospital admittance reports, monthly sales reports, or statistical reports on government program use. Many of these are fill-in reports using prepared forms or templates for recurring data and situations. Other information reports are more personalized, as illustrated in Figure 9.2 on page 225. They often include these sections:

Introduction

The introduction to an information report may be called *Introduction* or *Background*. In this section do the following: (1) explain why you are writing, (2) describe what methods and sources were used to gather information and why they are credible, (3) provide any special background information that may be necessary, (4) give the purpose of the report, if known, and (5) offer a preview of your findings. You'll notice in Figure 9.2 that not all five of these criteria are met, nor is a heading included, because it is a short informal information report. However, if you were writing an information report for a client in letter format, you would use the heading "Introduction" and try to fit in all five criteria.

Findings

The findings section of a report may also be called *Observations*, *Facts*, *Results*, or *Discussion*. Important points to consider in this section are organization and display. Consider one of these methods of organization: (1) chronological, (2) alphabetical, (3) topical, or (4) most to least important. You'll notice that in Figure 9.2, the writer uses a chronological method of organization.

To display the findings effectively, number paragraphs, underline or boldface key words, or use other graphic highlighting methods such as bullets. Be sure that words used as headings are parallel in structure. If the findings require elaboration, either include this discussion with each segment of the findings or place it in a separate section entitled *Discussion*.

Summary

A summary section is optional. If it is included, use it to summarize your findings objectively and impartially.

The information report shown in Figure 9.2 summarizes the facts laid out in bullet format by looking for commonalities (networking opportunities) and putting these facts into perspective (all Expo events led to exposure for Nancy's company). In addition, the significance of the facts is explained (Nancy may have found some new products for her company to sell in Canada).

Notice how easy this information report is to read. Short paragraphs, ample use of graphic highlighting, white space, and concise writing all contribute to improved readability.

Progress Reports

Progress reports describe the headway of unusual or nonroutine projects. Most progress reports include these four parts:

- The purpose and nature of the project
- A complete summary of the work already completed
- A thorough description of work currently in progress, including personnel, methods, and obstacles, as well as attempts to remedy obstacles
- A forecast of future activities in relation to the scheduled completion date, including recommendations and requests

In Figure 9.5 (p. 232) Maria Robinson explains the construction of a realty company branch office. She begins with a statement summarizing the construction progress in relation to the expected completion date. She then updates the reader with a brief recap of past progress. She emphasizes the present status of construction and concludes by describing the next steps to be taken.

FIGURE 9.5 Progress Report

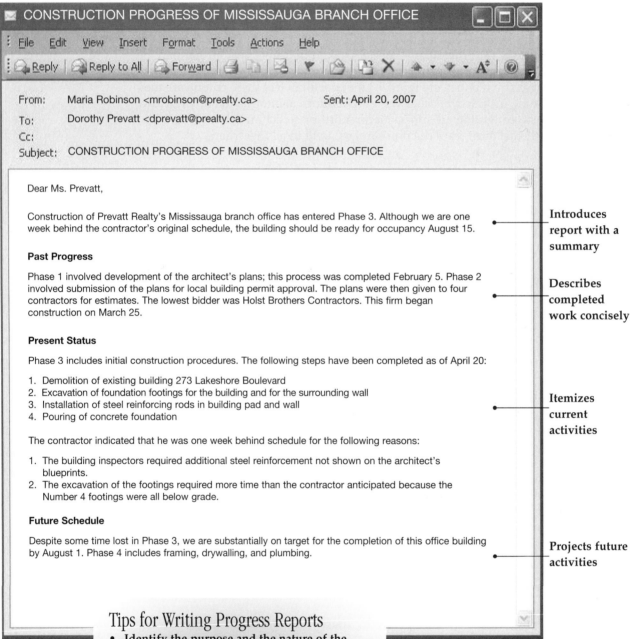

CONSTRUCTION PROGRESS OF MISSISSAUGA BRANCH OFFICE

File   Edit   View   Insert   Format   Tools   Actions   Help

Reply | Reply to All | Forward

From: Maria Robinson <mrobinson@prealty.ca>   Sent: April 20, 2007
To: Dorothy Prevatt <dprevatt@prealty.ca>
Cc:
Subject: CONSTRUCTION PROGRESS OF MISSISSAUGA BRANCH OFFICE

Dear Ms. Prevatt,

Construction of Prevatt Realty's Mississauga branch office has entered Phase 3. Although we are one week behind the contractor's original schedule, the building should be ready for occupancy August 15.
— Introduces report with a summary

Past Progress

Phase 1 involved development of the architect's plans; this process was completed February 5. Phase 2 involved submission of the plans for local building permit approval. The plans were then given to four contractors for estimates. The lowest bidder was Holst Brothers Contractors. This firm began construction on March 25.
— Describes completed work concisely

Present Status

Phase 3 includes initial construction procedures. The following steps have been completed as of April 20:

1. Demolition of existing building 273 Lakeshore Boulevard
2. Excavation of foundation footings for the building and for the surrounding wall
3. Installation of steel reinforcing rods in building pad and wall
4. Pouring of concrete foundation
— Itemizes current activities

The contractor indicated that he was one week behind schedule for the following reasons:

1. The building inspectors required additional steel reinforcement not shown on the architect's blueprints.
2. The excavation of the footings required more time than the contractor anticipated because the Number 4 footings were all below grade.

Future Schedule

Despite some time lost in Phase 3, we are substantially on target for the completion of this office building by August 1. Phase 4 includes framing, drywalling, and plumbing.
— Projects future activities

Tips for Writing Progress Reports
- Identify the purpose and the nature of the project immediately.
- Supply background information only if the reader must be educated.
- Describe the work completed.
- Discuss the work in progress, including personnel, activities, methods, and locations.
- Identify problems and possible remedies.
- Consider future activities.
- Close by giving the expected date of completion.

Some business communicators use progress reports to do more than merely report progress. These reports can also be used to offer ideas and suggest possibilities. Let's say you are reporting on the progress of redesigning the company Web site. You might suggest a different way to handle customer responses. Instead of making an official recommendation, which might be rejected, you can lay the foundation for a change within your progress report. Progress reports can also be used to build the image of a dedicated, conscientious employee.

Justification/Recommendation Reports

Both managers and employees must occasionally write reports that justify or recommend something, such as buying equipment, changing a procedure, hiring an employee, consolidating departments, or investing funds. Large organizations sometimes prescribe how these reports should be organized; they use forms with conventional headings. At other times, such reports are not standardized. For example, an employee takes it upon himself to write a report suggesting improvements in telephone customer service because he feels strongly enough about it. When you are free to select an organizational plan yourself, however, let your audience and topic determine your choice of direct or indirect structure.

Quick Check

Justification/recommendation reports analyze a problem, discuss options, and present a recommendation, solution, or action to be taken.

For nonsensitive topics and recommendations that will be agreeable to readers, you can organize directly according to the following sequence:

- In the introduction identify the problem or need briefly.
- Announce the recommendation, solution, or action concisely and with action verbs.
- Discuss pros, cons, and costs. Explain more fully the benefits of the recommendation or steps to be taken to solve the problem.
- Conclude with a summary specifying the recommendation and action to be taken.

Justin Brown applied the preceding process in writing the recommendation report shown in Figure 9.6 (p. 234). Justin is operations manager in charge of a fleet of trucks for a large parcel delivery company in Richmond, BC. When he heard about a new Goodyear smart tire with an electronic chip, Justin thought his company should give the new tire a try. His recommendation report begins with a short introduction to the problem followed by his two recommendations. Then he explains the product and how it would benefit his company. He concludes by highlighting his recommendation and specifying the action to be taken.

Feasibility Reports

Feasibility reports examine the practicality and advisability of following a course of action. They answer this question: Will this plan or proposal work? Feasibility reports are typically internal reports written to advise on matters such as consolidating departments, offering a wellness program to employees, or hiring an outside firm to handle a company's accounting or computing operations. These reports may also be written by consultants called in to investigate a problem. The focus in these reports is on the decision: stopping or proceeding with the proposal. Since your role is not to persuade the reader to accept the decision, you'll want to present the decision immediately. In writing feasibility reports, consider this plan:

Quick Check

Feasibility reports analyze whether a proposal or plan will work.

- Announce your decision immediately.
- Describe the background and problem necessitating the proposal.

Feasibility Reports

FIGURE 9.6   Justification/Recommendation Report—Memo Format

Applies memo format for short informal internal report

Interoffice Memo

Pacific Trucking, Inc.

DATE: July 19, 2006
TO: Bill Montgomery, Vice President
FROM: Justin Brown, Operations Manager   *JB*
SUBJECT: Pilot Testing Smart Tires

Next to fuel, truck tires are our biggest operating cost. Last year we spent $211,000 replacing and retreading tires for 495 trucks. This year the costs will be greater because prices have jumped at least 12 percent and because we've increased our fleet to 550 trucks. Truck tires are an additional burden since they require labour-intensive paperwork to track their warranties, wear, and retread histories. To reduce our long-term costs and to improve our tire tracking system, I recommend that we do the following:

Introduces problem briefly

Presents recommendations immediately

- Purchase 24 Goodyear smart tires.
- Begin a one-year pilot test on four trucks.

How Smart Tires Work

Smart tires have an embedded computer chip that monitors wear, performance, and durability. The chip also creates an electronic fingerprint for positive identification of a tire. By passing a hand-held sensor next to the tire, we can learn where and when a tire was made (for warranty and other information), how much tread it had originally, and its serial number.

Justifies recommendation by explaining product and benefits

How Smart Tires Could Benefit Us

Although smart tires are initially more expensive than other tires, they could help us improve our operations and save us money in four ways:

1. **Retreads.** Goodyear believes that the wear data is so accurate that we should be able to retread every tire three times, instead of our current two times. If that's true, in one year we could save at least $27,000 in new tire costs.
2. **Safety.** Accurate and accessible wear data should reduce the danger of blowouts and flat tires. Last year, drivers reported six blowouts.
3. **Record keeping and maintenance.** Smart tires could reduce our maintenance costs considerably. Currently, we use an electric branding iron to mark serial numbers on new tires. Our biggest headache is manually reading those serial numbers, decoding them, and maintaining records to meet safety regulations. Reading such data electronically could save us thousands of dollars in labour.
4. **Theft protection.** The chip can be used to monitor each tire as it leaves or enters the warehouse or yard, thus discouraging theft.

Enumerates items for maximum impact and readability

Explains recommendation in more detail

Summary and Action

Specifically, I recommend that you do the following:
- Authorize the special purchase of 24 Goodyear smart tires at $450 each, plus one electronic sensor at $1,200.
- Approve a one-year pilot test in our Lower Mainland territory that equips four trucks with smart tires and tracks their performance.

Specifies action to be taken

Tips for Memo Reports

- Use memo format for most short (ten or fewer pages) informal reports within an organization.
- Leave side margins of 1 to 1 ¼ inches.
- Sign your initials on the FROM line.
- Use an informal, conversational style.
- For a receptive audience, put recommendations first.
- For an unreceptive audience, put recommendations last.

- Discuss the benefits of the proposal.
- Describe any problems that may result.
- Calculate the costs associated with the proposal, if appropriate.
- Show the time frame necessary for implementation of the proposal.

Elizabeth Webb, customer service manager for a large insurance company in London, Ontario, wrote the feasibility report shown in Figure 9.7. Because her

FIGURE 9.7 Feasibility Report—E-mail Format

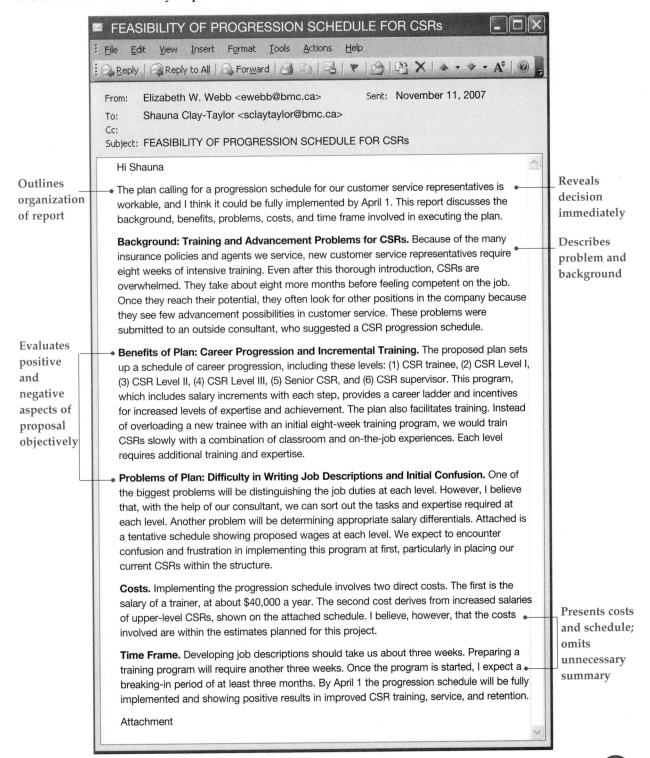

Outlines organization of report

Evaluates positive and negative aspects of proposal objectively

Reveals decision immediately

Describes problem and background

Presents costs and schedule; omits unnecessary summary

FEASIBILITY OF PROGRESSION SCHEDULE FOR CSRs

File Edit View Insert Format Tools Actions Help

Reply | Reply to All | Forward

From: Elizabeth W. Webb <ewebb@bmc.ca>   Sent: November 11, 2007
To: Shauna Clay-Taylor <sclaytaylor@bmc.ca>
Cc:
Subject: FEASIBILITY OF PROGRESSION SCHEDULE FOR CSRs

Hi Shauna

The plan calling for a progression schedule for our customer service representatives is workable, and I think it could be fully implemented by April 1. This report discusses the background, benefits, problems, costs, and time frame involved in executing the plan.

Background: Training and Advancement Problems for CSRs. Because of the many insurance policies and agents we service, new customer service representatives require eight weeks of intensive training. Even after this thorough introduction, CSRs are overwhelmed. They take about eight more months before feeling competent on the job. Once they reach their potential, they often look for other positions in the company because they see few advancement possibilities in customer service. These problems were submitted to an outside consultant, who suggested a CSR progression schedule.

Benefits of Plan: Career Progression and Incremental Training. The proposed plan sets up a schedule of career progression, including these levels: (1) CSR trainee, (2) CSR Level I, (3) CSR Level II, (4) CSR Level III, (5) Senior CSR, and (6) CSR supervisor. This program, which includes salary increments with each step, provides a career ladder and incentives for increased levels of expertise and achievement. The plan also facilitates training. Instead of overloading a new trainee with an initial eight-week training program, we would train CSRs slowly with a combination of classroom and on-the-job experiences. Each level requires additional training and expertise.

Problems of Plan: Difficulty in Writing Job Descriptions and Initial Confusion. One of the biggest problems will be distinguishing the job duties at each level. However, I believe that, with the help of our consultant, we can sort out the tasks and expertise required at each level. Another problem will be determining appropriate salary differentials. Attached is a tentative schedule showing proposed wages at each level. We expect to encounter confusion and frustration in implementing this program at first, particularly in placing our current CSRs within the structure.

Costs. Implementing the progression schedule involves two direct costs. The first is the salary of a trainer, at about $40,000 a year. The second cost derives from increased salaries of upper-level CSRs, shown on the attached schedule. I believe, however, that the costs involved are within the estimates planned for this project.

Time Frame. Developing job descriptions should take us about three weeks. Preparing a training program will require another three weeks. Once the program is started, I expect a breaking-in period of at least three months. By April 1 the progression schedule will be fully implemented and showing positive results in improved CSR training, service, and retention.

Attachment

company had been losing customer service reps (CSRs) after they were trained, she talked with the vice-president about the problem. He didn't want her to take time away from her job to investigate what other companies were doing to retain their CSRs. Instead, he suggested that they hire a consultant to investigate what other companies were doing to keep their CSRs. The vice-president then wanted to know whether the consultant's plan was feasible. Although Elizabeth's report is only one page long, it provides all the necessary information: background, benefits, problems, costs, and time frame.

Summary Reports

 Quick Check

A summary condenses the primary ideas, conclusions, and recommendations of a longer publication.

In today's knowledge economy, information is what drives organizations. Information is important because without it, business decisions cannot be made. Because there is a huge amount of information available today on any given topic (e.g., the millions of pages of Web material), people who make decisions don't always have the time to read and review all the information on a particular problem, issue, or topic. Therefore, decision makers need the essential elements of an issue or problem presented in a short, logical, easy-to-understand format that helps them quickly grasp what's vital.

Any time you take what someone else has written or said and reduce it to a concise, accurate, and faithful version of the original—in your own words—you are summarizing. A well-written summary report does three things: (1) it provides all the important points from the original without introducing new material; (2) it has a clear structure that often reflects the structure of the original material; and (3) it is independent of the original, meaning the reader of the summary can glean all essential information in the original without having to refer to it.

The ability to summarize well is a valuable skill for a number of reasons. Businesspeople are under pressure today to make decisions based on more information than ever before. Someone who can summarize that information into its key parts is way ahead of someone who cannot. Second, summarizing is a key communication task in many businesses today. For example, a financial advisor must be able to summarize reports on mutual funds and stocks so that her client can understand what's truly important. Third, the ability to summarize makes you a better writer. As you learn to pick apart the structure of articles, reports, and essays written by professional writers such as journalists, for example, you can introduce their tricks of the trade into your own writing. Finally, as part of writing the more complex reports discussed in Chapter 10, you will have to write executive summaries of your own work. Why not learn how to do this by summarizing other peoples' writing first?

There are four steps to writing an effective summary:

- **Read the material carefully for understanding.** Ideally, you will read the original three times. The first time you read to understand the topic. The second time you read with a pen, pencil, or highlighter in hand and you underline the main points (usually no more than three in an article-length piece). Finally, you should read again and underline or flag connections, patterns such as lists, contradictions, and similarities. These are often the sites of main points.
- **Lay out the structure of your summary.** This step is easy to accomplish. You simply write the main points you've underlined in the first step in a list. For example, the person summarizing the *Toronto Star* article in Figure 9.8 has identified three main points (MP), three contradictions (C), and two patterns (P). To lay out the structure of his summary, he would simply write:
  1. The federal government's retail debt program is costly, unsustainable, and should be phased out.

FIGURE 9.8 **Article for Summary**

Report queries value of Canada Savings Bonds

Ellen Roseman

Just before the Labour Day weekend, the federal government released a disturbing assessment of the Canada Savings Bond program.

Three-and-a-half million Canadians own the savings bonds, first offered in 1946. They are seen as secure and easily cashable.

But, according to consulting firm Cap Gemini Ernst & Young, the federal government's retail debt program is costly, unsustainable and should be phased out.

Finance Minister Ralph Goodale responded by saying he wouldn't make any changes at this time. The 2004-2005 sales campaign would go on as planned next month.

But I guarantee you'll think twice about the program's value if you read the Cap Gemini report.

You'll find it on the Internet at the finance department's website, www.fin.gc.ca. Make sure you search for the 164-page appendices, which I found far more interesting than the summarized 36-page final report.

Cap Gemini finished its work on Jan. 31, but the release was delayed until after the June 28 federal election.

"This certainly cuts into Paul Martin's image as a deficit fighter in the 1990s," says freedom-of-information activist Ken Rubin, who pushed for the report's publication (and is challenging the parts that were omitted).

Let's start with the Canada Investment and Savings Agency, set up in 1995 as a special operating agency within the finance department.

Its mandate was to reverse the declining trend in the holding of federal securities by individual investors.

At the time, the CSB campaign had $3.5 billion in gross sales. Today, sales are still stuck in the range of $2.8 billion to $3.5 billion a year.

The relaunch did not reverse the declining trend. And the addition of new products, such as the less cashable Canada Premium Bond designed for registered plans, simply cannibalized sales of regular savings bonds.

"The $2.2 billion drop in sales from 1998-1999 to 1999-2000 has not been recovered," Cap Gemini said.

"Management was not successful in meeting its targets, demonstrating an inability to predict the sales. The targets were lowered from 2000 onward, indicating that the program is no longer aiming to grow or even retain the stock."

Why are sales falling? You can name a few reasons without having to think too hard:

★ Lower interest rates. Recent savings bonds yielded 1.25 per cent in the first year, while the premium bonds yielded 2 per cent in the first year — less than what you could earn with a premium savings account.

★ Aggressive competition from banks. They currently pay 3.25 per cent on a five-year guaranteed investment certificate, compared with 2.79 per cent on an escalating-rate premium bond held for five years. And bank customers can get a bonus of a quarter to half a per cent above the posted GIC rate if they haggle.

★ More choices for investors, who are buying Government of Canada bonds through mutual funds or directly from investment dealers. These provide higher returns, though prices fluctuate.

When former finance minister and now Prime Minister Paul Martin set up the agency, the federal debt was high and rising and interest rates had moved sharply higher.

Today, with seven budget surpluses in a row, the government has less need to sustain a broad investor base.

"There is an insurance value in keeping this channel open," the finance department said in a release this month.

But consider the following when analyzing the costs and benefits of Canada Savings Bonds.

First damning argument: Marketing is expensive. The Canada Investment and Savings Agency's costs fell by only 1 per cent from 1997-1998 to 2002-2003. What was saved on media advertising was offset by higher commissions and bonuses paid to the sales force.

Second damning argument: Savings bonds sold through employers are used as savings accounts. This means high transaction costs, as investors redeem often and in small amounts. Sales and redemptions were equal in 2003, cancelling out the value of this distribution channel.

Third damning argument: There's little accountability to taxpayers. The agency's operations were not reviewed after five years, as dictated by its charter document. And the chief executive has kept her job for eight years, despite declining sales and market share.

I asked Goodale's office about the review of the retail debt program. It hasn't started yet, I was told yesterday, despite the fact the report has been in hand since the beginning of the year.

Exactly how much money is being lost on the marketing of Canada Savings Bonds? Even Cap Gemini couldn't figure that one out.

"The business plans and financial statements do not provide stakeholders with sufficient information to understand the objectives, performance or overall subsidy provided by government," the report concluded. Read it and weep.

2. There are three reasons why sales of Canada Savings Bonds are falling: lower interest rates, aggressive competition from banks, and more choices for investors.
3. The Canada Savings Bonds program is costly because marketing is expensive, the transaction costs are high, and there's little accountability to taxpayers.

- **Write a first draft.** In this step, you take your list from the step before (which uses the original author's exact language in many parts) and convert it into your own words. Our summary writer might write something like this:

> As requested, I've researched current opinion on the value of Canada Savings Bonds.
>
> The most useful article I found was by Ellen Roseman of the *Toronto Star*. In her article, "Report queries value of Canada Savings Bonds" (Sept. 15, 2004), Roseman makes one main point and supports her point with two types of evidence.
>
> - Roseman's main point is that the CSB program is too expensive, does not pay for itself, and should be eliminated. She bases her argument on an analysis of a report published by the consulting firm Cap Gemini Ernst & Young on January 31, which is now available on the Ministry of Finance's Web site.
>
> - The first argument Roseman uses to support her main point is that sales of CSBs have been falling steadily. This decline in sales is due to low interest rates, strong competition from the banking sector, and a wide choice of competing products for consumers.
>
> - The second argument Roseman makes to support her main point is that costs are up at the same time as sales are down. She attributes these costs to three main factors: the high cost of marketing the bonds, the high cost of transactions, and a lack of accountability on the part of the people who run the program and whose expenses appear to be out of control.
>
> I appreciated the opportunity to provide this summary. If there's anything else you need, please let me know.
>
> Sincerely,
>
> Brent Bingley

- **Proofread and revise.** The final step of writing a summary, like any written document, is to proofread for grammar, spelling, punctuation, and style mistakes and to rewrite where necessary. In the example above, the summary writer found a number of mistakes in his draft. He judged the phrase the *topic of current opinion on* to be wordy and rewrote it as *current opinion on*. He likewise found the word *called* to be wordy and deleted it. There are three instances where he should have written a number as a word instead of in numerical format. He also found a parallelism problem and changed *it should* to *should*. The phrase *ministry of finance* was spelled incorrectly, without capitals. Finally, two subject–verb agreement errors resulted in a change in verb tense to *have* from *has* and from *is* to *are*.

A final proofread and revised version of this descriptive summary report appears in Figure 9.9.

Minutes of Meetings

Quick Check

Meeting minutes record summaries of old business, new business, announcements, and reports as well as the precise wording of motions.

Minutes provide a summary of the proceedings of meetings. Formal, traditional minutes, illustrated in Figure 9.10 (p. 240), are written for large groups and legislative bodies. If you are the secretary of a meeting, you'll want to write minutes that do the following:

- Provide the name of the group, as well as the date, time, and place of the meeting.

FIGURE 9.9 **Summary Report—E-Mail Format**

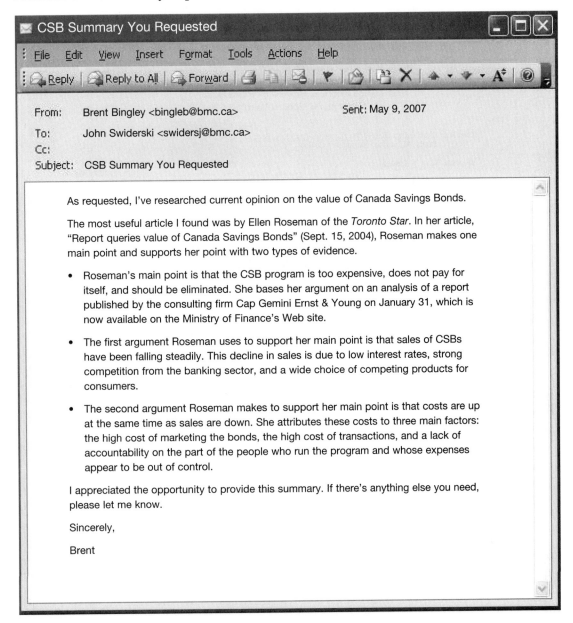

- Identify the names of attendees and absentees, if appropriate.
- Describe the disposition of previous minutes.
- Record old business, new business, announcements, and reports.
- Include the precise wording of motions; record the vote and action taken.
- Conclude with the name and signature of the person recording the minutes.

Notice in Figure 9.10 that secretary Carol Allen tries to summarize discussions rather than capture every comment. However, when a motion is made, she records it verbatim. She also shows in parentheses the name of the individual making the motion and the person who seconded it. By using all capital letters for "MOTION" and "PASSED," she makes these important items stand out for easy reference.

Informal minutes are usually shorter and easier to read than formal minutes. They may be formatted with three categories: summaries of topics discussed, decisions reached, and action items (showing the action item, the person responsible, and the due date).

FIGURE 9.10 Minutes of Meeting—Report Format

Shows attendees and absentees

Summarizes discussion; does not record every word

Summarizes new business and announcements

International Association of Administrative Professionals

Western Canada Division
Planning Committee Meeting
Conference Room B, Brunswick Plaza Hotel
November 4, 2007, 10 a.m.

Present: Carol Allen, Kim Jobe, LeeAnn Johnson, Barbara Leonard, Lee Schultz, Doris Williamson, Margaret Zappa

Absent: Ellen Williams

The meeting was called to order by Chair Kim Jobe at 10:05 a.m. Minutes from the July 11 meeting were read and approved.

Old Business

LeeAnn Johnson and Barbara Leonard reviewed the information distributed at the last meeting about hotels being considered for the Banff conference. LeeAnn said that the Fairmont Banff Springs has ample conference rooms and remodelled interiors. Barbara reported that the Mount Royal Hotel also has excellent banquet facilities, adequate meeting facilities, and rooms at $112 per night.
MOTION: To recommend that IAAP hold its International Convention at the Mount Royal Hotel, July 21–24, 2008. (Allen/Leonard). PASSED 6–1.

Reports

Lee Schultz reported on convention exhibits and her desire to involve more companies and products. Discussion followed regarding how this might be accomplished.
MOTION: That IAAP office staff develop a list of possible convention exhibitors. The list should be submitted at the next meeting. (Leonard/Schultz). PASSED 7–0.

New Business

The chair announced three possible themes for the convention, all of which focused on technology and the changing role of administrative assistants. Doris Williamson suggested the following possible title: "Vision Without Boundaries." Carol Allen suggested a communication theme. Several other possibilities were discussed. The chair appointed a subcommittee of Doris and Margaret to bring to the next committee meeting two or three concrete theme ideas.

Margaret Zappa thought that IAAP should be doing more to help members stay ahead in the changing workplace. She suggested workshops to polish skills in spreadsheet, database, presentations, and scheduling software.
MOTION: To recommend to IAAP that it investigate offering fee-based technology workshops at the national and regional conventions. (Zappa/Schultz). PASSED 5–2.

The meeting was adjourned at 11:50 by Kim Jobe.

Respectfully submitted,

Carol Allen

Carol Allen, Secretary

Describes disposition of previous minutes

Highlights motions, showing name of person making motion and person seconding it

Shows name and signature of person recording minutes

Summing Up and Looking Forward

This chapter presented six types of informal business reports: information reports, progress reports, justification/recommendation reports, feasibility reports, summaries, and minutes of meetings. Information reports generally provide data only. But justification/recommendation reports as well as feasibility reports and sometimes summary reports are more analytical in that they also evaluate the information, draw conclusions, and make recommendations. This chapter also discussed four formats for reports. Letter format is used for reports sent outside an organization; memo format is used for internal reports. More formal reports are formatted on plain paper with a manuscript design, while routine reports may be formatted on prepared forms. The chapter presented numerous model documents illustrating the many kinds of reports and their formats. Readers were also given tips for designing reports with desktop publishing programs to enhance their appearance.

All of the examples in this chapter are considered relatively informal. Longer, more formal reports are necessary for major investigations and research. These reports and proposals, along with suggestions for research methods, are presented in Chapter 10.

Critical Thinking

1. How do business reports differ from business letters?
2. Of the reports presented in this chapter, classify those that require indirect development versus those that require direct development.
3. How are the reports that you write for your courses similar to those presented here? How are they different?
4. Compare and contrast justification/recommendation and feasibility reports.

Chapter Review

5. List six kinds of informal reports. Be prepared to describe each.

6. List four formats suitable for reports. Be prepared to discuss each.

7. From the lists you made in Questions 5 and 6, select a report category and appropriate format for each of the following situations.
   a. Your supervisor asks you to read a long technical report and write a report that condenses the important points.

   b. You want to tell management about an idea you have for improving a procedure that you think will increase productivity.

   c. You just attended a meeting at which you were the only person taking notes. The person who ran the meeting sends you an e-mail asking if you could remind him of the important decisions that were made.

   d. As Engineering Department office manager, you have been asked to describe your highly regarded computer system for another department.

   e. As a police officer, you are writing a report of an arrest.

   f. At a mail-order catalogue company, your boss asks you to investigate ways to reduce the time that customers are kept waiting for service representatives to take their telephone orders. She wants your report to examine the problem and offer solutions.

8. If you were about to write the following reports, where would you gather information? Be prepared to discuss the specifics of each choice.
   a. You are a student representative on a curriculum committee. You are asked to study the course requirements in your major and make recommendations.

   b. As department manager, you must write job descriptions for several new positions you wish to establish in your department.

   c. You are proposing to management the replacement of a copier in your department.

   d. You must document the progress of a 12-month advertising campaign to alter the image of a clothing manufacturer's jeans.

9. What three questions do progress reports typically address?

10. What is the purpose of a meeting minutes report?

11. Information reports generally contain what three parts?

12. An article summary that your employer asks you to write should include what items?

13. What is the main difference between a descriptive summary and an evaluative summary?

Writing Improvement Exercises

14. **Practise summarizing.** Summarize the magazine article on page 243 in a 150-word e-mail to your business partner.
15. **Practise summarizing.** Summarize the newspaper article on page 244 in a 150-word e-mail to your boss.
16. **Practise summarizing/Role play.** Choose a newspaper or magazine article related to business and summarize it. Look ahead to Figure 12.3 on page 331 and turn your article summary into an oral presentation outline. Give your summary as a short presentation to your class, as if they were your work colleagues at a weekly staff meeting.

Patients rewarded

by Greg Fjetland, November 22, 2004

After her 13-year-old daughter Jessica was diagnosed with a rare brain tumour, Marlene Petersen of Kelowna, B.C., felt almost overwhelmed by the demands on her time. New to the province, with four other children at home and as many as six medical appointments for Jessica on just one day, "You can imagine how stressful the situation was," says Petersen. Fortunately, she was able to make use of a new health service launched in October.

 NavaHealth, a for-profit, privately owned company, leads B.C. residents through the labyrinthine health-care system by providing support and patient advocacy. With NavaHealth's president Elisabeth Riley helping her to understand Jessica's treatment, Petersen found coping with her daughter's illness far less overwhelming. "There's so much information coming at you, you can't remember it all," says Petersen. "You have questions that you forget to ask. And your emotions get in the way."

NavaHealth is the brainchild of Riley, currently dean of the School of Health Sciences at the British Columbia Institute of Technology. Riley began the planning for NavaHealth after she was laid off in the summer of 2002 from her position as president and CEO of the Children's & Women's Health Centre of B.C. in Vancouver. She realized from her long experience in the health sector that a service gap was widening. "The medical system is increasingly complex," says Riley. "It's not the fault of the system; it's just that medicine is so complex. We had only a doctor and a nurse in the system 50 years ago, and now look at how many health professionals and alternatives there are."

So Riley laid the groundwork for her new enterprise, including hiring IT professionals to create a database for health information and hiring registered nurses as "health navigators." With 10 navigators now working throughout British Columbia, NavaHealth provides services in person, by phone and e-mail. Navigators not only will accompany clients to appointments—the doctors are informed first—but can point out a wide range of appropriate services, including directing the client to community support services such as grief counselling, or private services such as contractors to adapt a home for handicap needs.

Riley is the sole owner of NavaHealth. She charges $100 an hour for the services of a navigator, which she splits with the RN. After an initial free consultation, payment is on a fee-for-service basis. Riley says she funded the launch of NavaHealth entirely out of her pocket. She watches her budget carefully: when a reporter calls her long distance on her cellphone, she calls him back on her land line to reduce the charges.

Helping patients comprehend their medical options is a large market, but where Riley might really strike gold is in targeting her services at what she calls the Sandwich Generation: those adults with both aging parents and children at home to care for. It's a market strongly supported by the demographics of the mid-life baby boomers who live in one part of the country while their parents live elsewhere. "Anyone who has had to balance the demands of caring for an aging parent along with demands from their work and their own family, knows how challenging that can be," Riley says.

While the British Columbia Medical Association doesn't have an official position on patients hiring paid consultants to accompany them to the doctor's office, BCMA president Dr. Jack Burak admits to some concerns. First, it's not a service that all patients can afford equally, and secondly, a patient with a paid advocate may expect a longer appointment with a doctor who has only limited time available. "I don't know how you meld those two concerns," Burak says.

Riley says the market will decide. Since opening her doors, she's received inquiries for her service from across the country and she estimates NavaHealth will break even within six months. Riley intends to expand her service nationwide with head offices in every province within five years. Now that's a healthy ambition.

TORONTO STAR

Boom in housing for executives on move

TONY WONG

BUSINESS REPORTER, May 25, 2005

David Morton has had just about every kind of request from executives moving to Toronto on short-term assignments and looking for housing. For a Fortune 500 company executive with a substantial monthly budget of $40,000, Morton was able to find a mansion in Rosedale, considered one of Toronto's best neighbourhoods.

The client's main requests were that the backyard be big enough for his children and their dog, and that the home be recently renovated.

While living in Rosedale isn't the typical request, Morton, the owner of MAC Furnished Rentals Inc., can place you in furnished accommodation for a short-term stay in Toronto from $3,000 a month all the way up to the $40,000 range and beyond.

"They could be moving for a new posting, to fill a short-term position, to look after a maternity leave—the reasons vary," said Morton, who has more than 100 units in Ottawa, Toronto and Sudbury.

According to a Royal LePage Relocation Services study released yesterday, the corporate-housing market in Canada was a $230 million business in 2004.

The most expensive city to relocate to was Vancouver, where it cost an average of $2,950 a month for furnished accommodation, or about $98 per night. Toronto was in close second place at $2,935, followed by Fort McMurray at $2,905.

Toronto has the largest supply of units, but Calgary, with less than a quarter of the population, comes in a close second because of the highly mobile oil and gas industry.

Royal LePage places Fort McMurray, with a population of just 56,000, in third place, but calls it the "corporate-housing capital of Canada," with the lowest vacancy rate driven by the boom in oil-sands production.

In Fort McMurray, the average stay is 90 days, compared with 47 in Toronto and 58 in Vancouver.

"The amount of corporate activity out of (Fort McMurray) is staggering," said Robert Peterman, director of assignment solutions for Royal LePage. "You're talking about one of the biggest oil-production areas in the world, and most of it is coming from that area."

Peterman said the corporate-housing market has grown significantly over the past several years, thanks to an improving economy.

Morton said his company, which started five years ago, has grown about 20 per cent annually.

While the Toronto area has experienced a surge of growth over the past several years, some of that was curtailed last year. Some smaller players left the business due to competition from rising vacancy rates caused by heavy condominium development and a downturn caused by the increase in the Canadian dollar, boosting prices for foreign filmmakers and other visitors, said Royal LePage.

While the market is generally made up of small, independent operators, the returns are now attractive enough to garner the attention of bigger chains, said Peterman.

"The corporate-housing market in Canada is extremely fragmented," Royal LePage said in its report. "Local suppliers range from independent investors with a single furnished suite to large full-suite hotels. Amenities, services and quality vary enormously."

In Toronto, several developers are looking at specially built suite lodges specifically for the corporate, long-term-stay market.

"If you look a few years back, most of the big firms had their own furnished apartments they could move their executives to," said Morton.

With corporate downsizing in the 1990s, the furnished apartments were sold, leaving a vacuum in the market that was filled by operators such as Morton.

Peterman said companies generally use furnished apartments over hotels as a "lifestyle choice" rather than a cost-saving issue, although it is generally cheaper to use corporate accommodations rather than place employees in hotel rooms.

"Some people do prefer living out of hotels. But if you are moving somewhere for three months, you generally would probably prefer to live in a bigger unit with a full kitchen and more of a home-like atmosphere," said Peterman.

It's also something of a misconception to think that placing an employee on temporary assignment rather than relocating him or her entirely is always more cost effective, Peterman said: "You've got to pay for accommodations, and then there are the bi-weekly trips back home, so this can add up pretty quickly."

Activities and Cases

Team **9.1 Evaluating Headings and Titles.** Identify the following report headings and titles as "talking" or "functional/descriptive." Discuss the usefulness and effectiveness of each.

a. Problem

b. Need for Tightening Computer ID System

c. Annual Budget

d. How Direct Mail Can Deliver Profits for Your Business

e. Case History: Rotunda Palace Hotel Focuses on Improving Service to Customers

f. Solving Our Networking Problems with an Extranet

g. Comparing Copier Volume, Ease of Use, and Speed

h. Alternatives

9.2 Information Report: The Less Glamorous Side of Being an Entrepreneur. You and two friends have decided to open a consulting business in Kitchener/Waterloo. You're all recent college business grads, and rather than work for a large corporation, you'd like to strike out on your own. The area you'd like to concentrate on is branding for not-for-profit organizations and educational institutions. Your three friends have already staked out the glamorous side of things, including business development, which leaves you with the "nuts and bolts." The company has been registered, but none of its banking issues have been dealt with. Your partners ask you to send them an e-mail about which bank has "the best deal" as well as "any other stuff you can find out."

Your Task. Write an e-mail information report to your three friends/partners investigating opening up a business account at two financial institutions. Do some more research into what it takes to start a small business and include this information in your report.

Related Web site: The government of Ontario maintains an excellent site on starting a small business in that province at <www.ontariocanada.com/ontcan/en/starting/st_small_bus/st_small-bus-intro.jsp>.

9.3 Information Report: Canadian Tech Company Expands into Asia. You work in business development for Hydrogenics, a Missisisauga, Ontario-based producer of clean energy products. Hydrogenics already has an office in Tokyo, but it feels it needs to expand its Asian operations. Your boss has asked you to investigate the partnership opportunities available for investors in Korea and China. He gives you a tight deadline of one week, and asks for the report to be sent to him via e-mail with any attachments you think are important.

Web

Your Task. Investigate the mechanics of opening an office and/or investing in Korea and China. Report your findings in an e-mail to Bob Khan, your boss.

Related Web sites: Important background information can be found at <www.hydrogenics.com>, <www.investkorea.org>, and <www.china.com.cn/market/72614.htm>.

Critical Thinking

9.4 Progress Report: Making Headway Toward Your Educational Goal. You made an agreement with your parents (or spouse, relative, or partner) that you would submit a progress report at this time describing headway toward your educational goal (employment, certificate, diploma, degree).

Your Task. In memo format write a progress report that fulfills your promise to describe your progress toward your educational goals. Address your progress report to your parents, spouse, relative, or partner. In your memo (1) describe your goal; (2) summarize the work you have completed thus far; (3) discuss thoroughly the work currently in progress, including your successes and anticipated obstacles; and (4) forecast your future activities in relation to your scheduled completion date.

9.5 Progress Report: Designing a Template for HR. You are the assistant to the Director of Human Resources at BASF's automotive paints plant in Windsor, Ontario. At a recent meeting of the management board, it was decided that the employee review process required an overhaul. Instead of once-yearly meetings with their immediate superior to "discuss any issues," the company has decided to institute a more accountable process in which all employees (including managers) must write a yearly progress report.

Your Task. Develop a template report for your boss, Sue Swinton, Director of HR, that can be filled out by all BASF Canada Windsor employees once a year. Keep in mind that employees are generally unenthusiastic about the employee review process. In other words, your template must be easy to fill out and logical.

Related Web sites: BASF Canada Windsor's site is <www.basf.com/basf-canada/abtslwin_overview_e.shtm>. You may also want to research best practices in performance management and the employee review process.

9.6 Recommendation Report: What Is It About Advertising? You are the CEO of a mid-size Vancouver-based advertising agency named Slam! Your company is in the enviable position of having secured the advertising contract for the 2010 Vancouver/Whistler Olympics. The problem is, you can't seem to keep your employees around long enough to ensure continuity within projects. It seems as though the advertising business is a revolving door: new college and university grads are eager to work for you, then six months later once you've trained them, they leave for more lucrative jobs at other agencies. You're too busy to figure out a solution or policy; in fact you're so busy you haven't got around to hiring a human resources manager. Instead you ask your research manager to write you a report on some possible solutions.

Your Task. As the research manager at Slam!, research and write a short e-mail recommendation report for your boss outlining some possible solutions to the "revolving door" problem. Your boss is well known as a spendthrift, so you'll have to be careful about how your phrase any expensive solutions…

Related Web site: Canada News Wire Group's recent story on this issue can be accessed at: <www.newswire.ca/en/releases/archive/March2005/09/c2364.html> but you should also do other research on the topic of employee retention. Be careful not to plagiarize from your sources when completing this report.

9.7 Recommendation Report: Expanding the Company Library. Despite the interest in online publications, managers and employees at your company still like to browse through magazines in the company library. Bonnie Finley, the company librarian, wants to add business periodicals to the library subscription list and has requested help from various company divisions.

Critical Thinking

Your Task. You've been asked to recommend four periodicals in your particular specialty (accounting, marketing, management, financial services, or human resorces). Visit your library and select four periodicals to recommend. Write a memo report to Ms. Finley describing the particular readership, usual contents, and scope of each periodical. To judge each adequately, you should examine several issues. Explain why you think each periodical should be ordered and who would read it. Convince the librarian that your choices would be beneficial to your department.

9.8 Justification Report: Evaluating Your Curriculum. You have been serving as a student member of a college curriculum advisory committee. The committee is expected to examine the course requirements for a degree, diploma, or certificate in your area.

Team

Your Task. In teams of three to five, decide whether the requirements are realistic and practical. What improvements can your team suggest? Interview other students, faculty members, and employers for their suggestions. Prepare a justification report in letter or memo format to send to the dean of your college proposing your suggestions. You anticipate that the head of your faculty or department may need to be persuaded to make any changes. Consider delaying your recommendations until after you have developed a foundation of explanation and reasons.

9.9 Justification Report: Purchasing New Equipment. In your work or your training, identify equipment that needs to be purchased or replaced (computer, printer, modem, DVD, copier, digital camera, etc.). Gather information about two different models or brands.

Your Task. Write a justification report comparing the two items. Establish a context by describing the need for the equipment. Discuss the present situation, emphasizing the current deficiencies. Describe the advantages of acquiring the new equipment.

9.10 Feasibility Report: CEO Not Convinced by Assistant's Recommendations. The CEO of Slam! from Case 9.6 above is not convinced. He received his research manager's recommendation report, which was well written and persuasive, but he doesn't yet believe that the recommendations she made (e.g., increasing pay, benefits, and vacation time) are practical or warranted. Still, her recommendation report was persuasive enough that the CEO has decided to spend money on a consultant's services. He wants a feasibility report written on the practicality of his research manager's suggestions.

Your Task. As the performance management consultant hired by Slam!'s CEO, write a short feasibility report, in letter format, to your client. Keep in mind that Slam! has roughly 35 employees working on the creative side of advertising, but it also has 15 employees working in account management and finance who are likely to be suspicious if their creative colleagues are "showered with gifts." Are there nonmonetary compromise solutions that would make the CEO's attempts to retain employees feasible and effective?

9.11 Summary Report: Condensing an Article About E-Mail Privacy. Your boss is worried because the company has no formal e-mail policy. Should employees be allowed to use e-mail for personal messages? May management monitor the messages of employees? She asks you to research this topic (or another topic on which you and your instructor agree).

Your Task. Using library databases, find a good newspaper, magazine, or other periodical article (around 1000 words). In a one- to two-page document, summarize the major points of the article. Also evaluate its strengths and weaknesses. Attach this summary document to an e-mail that you send to your boss, Justine Toller, Division Manager.

9.12 Summary Report: What Are They Saving About Us? As the Director of Foreign Operations for Beijing-based China Mining Corp., you have to be a savvy communicator. One the one hand, your domestic market is in desperate need of more sources of minerals and metals to feed a rapidly expanding industrial base. On the other hand, domestic supply of many metals and minerals is just about used up and you are forced to search for sources in other parts of the world. The problem—and this is where your savvy communicating comes in—is convincing the rest of the world that investment by China is okay. In particular, you've heard rumours that some Canadians are not happy about the prospect of their natural resources being controlled by foreign companies. You're just about to travel to Canada for some important meetings with government and mining industry leaders, but before you do, you want solid information on what Canadians are thinking and saying.

Your Task. As Director Huang's Canadian office manager in Calgary, you are asked via e-mail to quickly summarize "a few articles" that provide a picture of what Canadian opinion is today on foreign control of natural resources. After researching newspaper, magazine, and other periodical articles, reply to Mr. Huang with a short descriptive summary report.

9.13 Minutes: Recording the Proceedings of a Meeting. Ask your instructor to let you know when the next all-faculty or division or departmental meeting is taking place on your campus. Or, ask your student association or student council representative to let you know when the next association or council meeting is taking place. Or, next time you're at work or at your co-op job, ask your boss to let you sit in on a meeting. Volunteer to act as note-taker or secretary to this meeting.

Your Task. Record the proceedings of the meeting you attend in an informal meeting minutes report. Focus on reports presented, motions/action items, votes, and decisions reached.

9.14 Role Play: Everyone's Taking Minutes. Next time you have a group or team meeting related to one of your school assignments, videotape or audiotape one of your group or team meetings. Then, turn that meeting into a scripted skit. Perform the skit in front of your class.

Your Task. As an audience member, watch the skit discussed above. Assume you are the note-taker at the meeting. Create a minutes report for the meeting you just watched. Are there any elements of a meeting the group/team missed (e.g., motions, action statements, etc.)?

9.15 Longer Report: Solving a Problem. Choose a business or organization with which you are familiar and identify a problem such as poor quality, indifferent service, absenteeism at organization meetings, uninspired cafeteria food, outdated office equipment, unresponsive management, lack of communication, underappreciated employees, wasteful procedures, or a similar problem.

Your Task. Describe the problem in detail. Assume you are to report to management (or to the leadership of an organization) about the nature and scope of the problem. Decide which kind of report to prepare (information, recommendation, justification), and choose the format. How would you gather data to lend authority to your conclusions and recommendations? Determine the exact topic and report length after consultation with your instructor.

Grammar/Mechanics Review—9

The following sentences contain errors in grammar, punctuation, capitalization, number style, usage, and spelling. Pay special attention to eliminating expletives (there is, there are). Below each sentence write a corrected version.

Example: There were 2 employees who volunteered to head the united way campaign.
Revision: Two employees volunteered to head the United Way campaign.

1. There are three Vice-Presidents who report directly to the company President.

2. Although the meeting was first scheduled for May 2nd its been rescheduled for May 10th.

3. As a matter of fact there are figures that suggest that a medium size dog costs exactly six thousand four hundred dollars to raise for eleven years.

4. There were exhibitors at the Trade Show, who came from as far as australia and japan, to promote there products.

5. If there have been many customers who are complaining we must revamp delivery schedules.

6. Would you please remove the charge of 78 dollars from my July statement?

7. "Large companies," says Tate Steinke director of transportation at big rigs freight "are looking for ways to shrink shipping costs.

8. There were 25 Zoomout Cameras awarded as prizes at the end of the year awards' ceremony.

9. Because there are so many ontarians and quebeckers who flock to florida the price of rental units rises in the winter.

10. After travelling north on highway 101 exit at pritchard valley road, and follow the signs to birds hill estates.

11. In canada sixty-eight percent of the land is wilderness, however in africa only twenty-eight percent is wilderness.

12. On december 21st did we pay forty-two dollars a share to acquire 1/4th of the stocks in genetics, inc.

13. By eliminating 1 olive from each salad served in the first class section transway airlines saved forty thousand dollars.

14. There are many foreign language software programs that we stock including: russian, chinese, japanese, and dutch programs.

15. There is no canadian football league team that plays it's home games in a domed stadium that have ever won a grey cup.

Grammar/Mechanics Challenge—9

Document for Revision

The following progress report has faults in grammar, punctuation, spelling, number form, wordiness, and word use. Use standard proofreading marks (see Appendix B) to correct the errors. When you finish, your instructor can show you the revised version of this report.

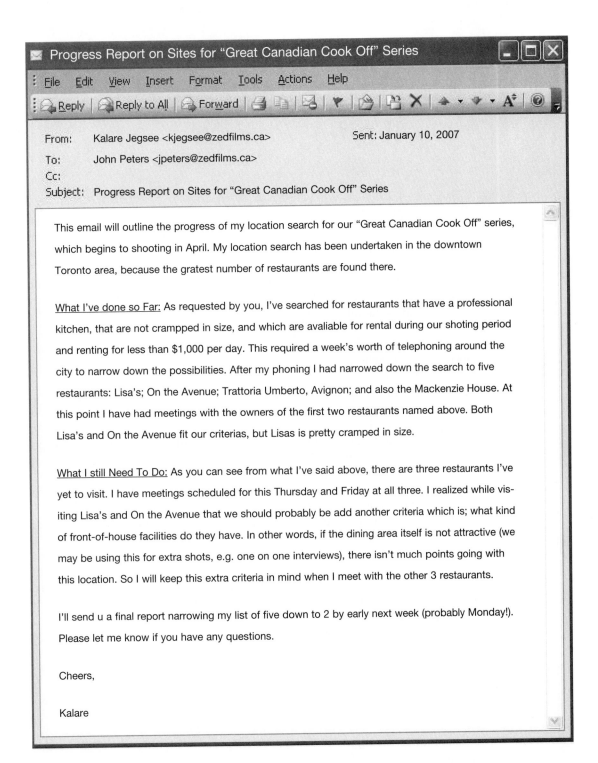

Progress Report on Sites for "Great Canadian Cook Off" Series

File   Edit   View   Insert   Format   Tools   Actions   Help

Reply | Reply to All | Forward

From: Kalare Jegsee <kjegsee@zedfilms.ca>   Sent: January 10, 2007

To: John Peters <jpeters@zedfilms.ca>

Cc:

Subject: Progress Report on Sites for "Great Canadian Cook Off" Series

This email will outline the progress of my location search for our "Great Canadian Cook Off" series, which begins to shooting in April. My location search has been undertaken in the downtown Toronto area, because the gratest number of restaurants are found there.

<u>What I've done so Far:</u> As requested by you, I've searched for restaurants that have a professional kitchen, that are not crampped in size, and which are avaliable for rental during our shoting period and renting for less than $1,000 per day. This required a week's worth of telephoning around the city to narrow down the possibilities. After my phoning I had narrowed down the search to five restaurants: Lisa's; On the Avenue; Trattoria Umberto, Avignon; and also the Mackenzie House. At this point I have had meetings with the owners of the first two restaurants named above. Both Lisa's and On the Avenue fit our criterias, but Lisas is pretty cramped in size.

<u>What I still Need To Do:</u> As you can see from what I've said above, there are three restaurants I've yet to visit. I have meetings scheduled for this Thursday and Friday at all three. I realized while visiting Lisa's and On the Avenue that we should probably be add another criteria which is; what kind of front-of-house facilities do they have. In other words, if the dining area itself is not attractive (we may be using this for extra shots, e.g. one on one interviews), there isn't much points going with this location. So I will keep this extra criteria in mind when I meet with the other 3 restaurants.

I'll send u a final report narrowing my list of five down to 2 by early next week (probably Monday!). Please let me know if you have any questions.

Cheers,

Kalare

Laying the Groundwork for Team Writing Projects

Chances are that you can look forward to some kind of team writing in your future career. You may collaborate voluntarily (seeking advice and differing perspectives) or involuntarily (through necessity or by assignment). Working with other people can be frustrating, particularly when some team members don't produce or when conflict breaks out. Team projects, though, can be harmonious and productive when members establish ground rules at the outset and adhere to guidelines such as the following.

Preparing to Work Together. Before you discuss the project, talk about how your group will function.

- Limit the size of your team, if possible, to three or four members. Larger groups have more difficulties. An odd number is usually preferable so that ties in voting are avoided.
- Name a meeting leader (to plan and conduct meetings), a recorder (to keep a record of group decisions), and an evaluator (to determine if the group is on target and meeting its goals).
- Decide whether your team will be governed by consensus (everyone must agree, no voting) or by majority rule.
- Compare schedules of team members, and set up the best meeting times. Plan to meet often. Avoid other responsibilities during meetings.
- Discuss the value of conflict. By bringing conflict into the open and encouraging confrontation, your team can prevent personal resentment and group dysfunction. Confrontation can actually create better final documents by promoting new ideas and avoiding the tendency for group members to agree to things they normally wouldn't just to avoid conflict.
- Discuss how you will deal with members who are not producing at a level acceptable to others in the group.

Planning the Document. Once you've established ground rules, you're ready to discuss the project and resulting document. Be sure to keep a record of the decisions your team makes.

- Establish the document's specific purpose and identify the main issues involved.
- Decide on the final form of the document. What parts will it have?
- Discuss the audience(s) for the document and what appeal would help it achieve its purpose.
- Develop a work plan. Assign jobs. Set deadlines.
- Decide how the final document will be written: individuals working separately on assigned portions, one person writing the first draft, the entire group writing the complete document together, or some other method.

Collecting Information. The following suggestions help teams gather accurate information:

- Brainstorm for ideas as a group.
- Decide who will be responsible for gathering what information.
- Establish deadlines for collecting information.
- Discuss ways to ensure the accuracy of the information collected.

Organizing, Writing, and Revising. As the project progresses, your team may wish to modify some of its earlier decisions.

- Review the proposed organization of your final document, and adjust it if necessary.
- Write the first draft. If separate team members are writing segments then collecting them by e-mail, they should confirm that their e-mails have reached the receiver.
- Meet to discuss and revise the draft(s).
- If individuals are working on separate parts, appoint one person (probably the best writer) to coordinate all the parts, striving for consistent style and format.

Editing and Evaluating. Before the document is submitted, complete these steps:

- Give one person responsibility for finding and correcting grammatical and mechanical errors.
- Meet as a group to evaluate the final document. Does it fulfill its purpose and meet the needs of the audience?

Career Application

Select a report topic from this chapter or Chapter 10. Assume that you must prepare the report as a team project. If you are working on a long report, your instructor may ask you to prepare individual progress reports as you develop your topic.

Your Task

- Form teams of three to five members.
- Prepare to work together by using the suggestions provided here.
- Plan your report by establishing its purpose, identifying the main issues, developing a work plan, and assigning tasks.
- Collect information, organize the data, and write the first draft.
- Decide how the document will be revised, edited, and evaluated.

Your instructor may assign grades not only on the final report but also on your team effectiveness and your individual contribution, as determined by fellow team members.

10 Proposals and Formal Reports

A research supplier report needs to clearly and concisely articulate insights and implications from the study, and no report is complete without actionable recommendations. I am particularly impressed if the writer demonstrates a good knowledge and understanding of the confectionery category and our business in particular. The quality of the final report is very important. It reflects on me personally, as I am the person managing the study. The report's quality will strongly influence my decision about whether to hire the same research company for future studies.[1]

Len Willschick, manager, Consumer and Market Intelligence, Wrigley Canada

LEARNING OBJECTIVES

1. Identify and explain the parts of informal and formal proposals.
2. Describe the preparatory steps for writing a formal report.
3. Collect data from secondary sources, including print and electronic sources.
4. Understand how to use the Web and online databases to locate reliable data and the consequences of plagiarism.
5. Discuss how to generate primary data from surveys, interviews, observation, and experimentation.
6. Understand the need for accurate documentation of data and the consequences of plagiarism.
7. Describe how to organize report data, create an outline, and write effective titles.
8. Illustrate data using tables, charts, and graphs.
9. Sequence 13 parts of a formal report.

✓ **Quick Check**

Proposals are persuasive offers to solve problems, provide services, or sell equipment.

P roposals are persuasive offers to solve problems, provide services, or sell equipment or other products. Let's say that the City of Fredericton wants to upgrade the computers and software in its human resources department. If it knows exactly what it wants, it would prepare a request for proposal (RFP) specifying its requirements. It then publicizes the RFP, and companies interested in bidding on the job submit proposals. RFPs are traditionally publicized in newspapers, but increasingly on special Web sites, such as <www.merx.com>, which is the best-known Canadian site.

Both large and small companies, organizations, and agencies are increasingly likely to use RFPs to solicit competitive bids on their projects. This enables them to compare "apples to apples." That is, they can compare the prices different companies would charge for completing the same project. RFPs also work for companies in situations where needs are not clear. An RFP can be issued stating broad expectations and goals within which bidding companies offer innovative solutions and price quotes. In most cases, a proposal also acts as a legal statement of work from which a contract for services is developed.

Many companies earn a sizable portion of their income from sales resulting from proposals. It's important to realize that not all proposals are solicited, in other words published in the newspaper or on Web sites. Unsolicited proposals are also important business documents. For example, if I'm a consultant who specializes in coaching and team-building skills, I can send an unsolicited proposal to a large organization like a bank, offering my services.

Whether they are solicited or unsolicited, the ability to write effective proposals is especially important today. In writing proposals, the most important thing to remember is that they are sales presentations. They must be persuasive, not merely mechanical descriptions of what you can do. You may recall from Chapter 7 that effective persuasive sales messages build interest by emphasizing benefits for the reader, reduce resistance by detailing your expertise and accomplishments, and motivate action by making it easy for the reader to understand and respond.

Quick Check

Both large and small companies today often use requests for proposals (RFPs) to solicit competitive bids on projects.

Informal Proposals

Proposals may be informal or formal; they differ primarily in length and format. Informal proposals are often presented in letter format. Sometimes called letter proposals, they contain six principal parts: introduction, background, proposal, staffing, budget, and authorization. The informal letter proposal shown in Figure 10.1 (p. 256) illustrates all six parts of a letter proposal. This proposal is addressed to a Calgary dentist who wants to improve patient satisfaction.

Quick Check

Informal proposals may contain an introduction, background information, the proposal, staffing requirements, a budget, and an authorization request.

Introduction

Most proposals begin by explaining briefly the reasons for the proposal and by highlighting the writer's qualifications. To make your introduction more persuasive, use persuasive techniques to gain the reader's attention. One proposal expert suggests these possibilities:

- Hint at extraordinary results with details to be revealed shortly.
- Promise low costs or speedy results.
- Mention a remarkable resource (well-known authority, new computer program, well-trained staff) available exclusively to you.
- Identify a serious problem (worry item) and promise a solution, to be explained later.
- Specify a key issue or benefit that you feel is the heart of the proposal.[2]

Quick Check

Effective proposal openers capture interest by promising extraordinary results or resources or by identifying key benefits, issues, or outcomes.

For example, Dana Swensen, in the introduction of the proposal shown in Figure 10.1, focused on a key benefit. In this proposal to conduct a patient satisfaction survey, Dana thought that the client, Dr. Larocque, would be most interested in specific recommendations for improving service to her patients. But Dana didn't hit on this benefit until after the first draft had been written. Indeed, it's often a good idea to put off writing the introduction to a proposal until after you have completed

FIGURE 10.1 Informal Proposal

SWENSEN RESEARCH ASSOCIATES

One Providence Plaza
Calgary, Alberta T1A 4E5
(403) 628-3011
www.sra.ca

May 15, 2007

Dr. Marie Larocque
1789 Clarkston Avenue
Calgary, AB T1L 5G4

Dear Dr. Larocque:

Helping you improve your practice is of the highest priority to us at Swensen Research Associates. We are pleased to submit the following proposal outlining our plan to help you more effectively meet your patients' needs by analyzing their views about your practice.

Background and Goals

We understand that you have been incorporating a total quality management system in your practice. Although you have every reason to believe your patients are pleased with the service you provide, you would like to give them an opportunity to discuss what they like and possibly don't like about your service. Based on our conversations, we understand that you would like the patient surveys to allow you to do the following:

- Determine the level of their satisfaction with you and your staff
- Elicit suggestions for improvement
- Learn more about how your patients discovered you
- Compare your "preferred" and "standard" patients

Proposed Plan

To help you achieve your goals, Swensen Research proposes the following plan:

Survey. A short but thorough questionnaire will probe the data you desire. This questionnaire will measure your patients' reactions to such elements as courtesy, professionalism, accuracy of billing, friendliness, and waiting time. After you approve it, the questionnaire will be sent to a carefully selected sample of 300 patients whom you have separated into groupings of "preferred" and "standard."

Analysis. Survey data will be analyzed by demographic segments, such as patient type, age, and gender. Our experienced team of experts, using state-of-the-art computer programs and advanced statistical measures, will study the (1) degree of patient satisfaction, (2) reasons for satisfaction or dissatisfaction, and (3) relationship between your "preferred" and "standard" patients. Moreover, our team will give you specific suggestions for making patient visits more pleasant.

Report. You will receive a final report with the key findings. The report will include tables summarizing all responses categorized by "preferred" and "standard" clients. Our staff will also draw conclusions based on these findings.

Marginal annotations:

Introduction grabs attention with "hook" that focuses on key benefit

Discusses circumstances leading to proposal and identifies four goals of survey

Plan is divided into logical segments for easy reading and interest building

---

other parts. For longer proposals the introduction also describes the scope and limitations of the project, as well as outlining the organization of the material to come.

2 Background, Problem, Purpose

The background section identifies the problem and discusses the goals or purposes of the project. The background is also the place to go over some recent history. In other words, briefly summarize what circumstances have led to your writing of the proposal. For example, in Figure 10.1, the "history" of the situation

FIGURE 10.1 Continued

Dr. Marie Larocque   Page 2   May 15, 2007

Schedule. With your approval, the following schedule has been arranged for your patient satisfaction survey:

Questionnaire development and mailing	June 1–16
Deadline for returning questionnaire	June 24
Data tabulation and processing	June 24–26
Completion of final report	July 1

Uses past-tense verbs to show that work has already started on the project

Our Team

Swensen Research Associates is a nationally recognized, experienced research consulting firm specializing in survey investigation. I have assigned your customer satisfaction survey to Dr. Kelly Miller, our director of research. Dr. Miller was trained at Queen's University and has successfully supervised our research program for the past nine years. Before joining SRA, she was a marketing analyst with Procter & Gamble Company.

Assisting Dr. Miller will be a team headed by Jacob Malau, our vice-president for operations. Mr. Malau earned a bachelor's degree in computer science and a master's degree in marketing from the University of Calgary. Within our organization he supervises our computer-aided telephone interviewing (CAT) system and manages our 30-person professional interviewing staff.

Staffing section builds credibility and reduces resistance by describing outstanding staff and facilities

Our Cost

	Estimated Hours	Rate	Total
Professional and administrative time			
Questionnaire development	3	$150/hr.	$ 450.00
Data processing and tabulation	16	50/hr.	800.00
Analysis of findings	15	150/hr.	2,250.00
Preparation of final report	5	150/hr.	750.00
Mailing costs			390.00
GST			324.80
Total cost			$4,964.80

Budget section itemizes costs carefully because a proposal is a contract offer

Authorization

Patient satisfaction is vital to the success of your practice. Our professionally designed and administered client survey will help you determine how best to meet the needs of your patients, thereby assuring the success of your practice. Specific results from your survey can be ready for you by July 1. Please sign the enclosed duplicate copy of this letter and return it to us with a retainer of $2,320 so that we may begin developing your survey immediately. The rates in this offer are in effect only until September 1. Thank you for giving us this chance to help you better serve your patients.

Authorization section summarizes benefits, makes response easy, and provides deadline

Sincerely,

Dana H. Swensen

Dana H. Swensen, President

DHS:pm
Enclosure

is alluded to in the sentence *We understand that you have been incorporating a total quality management system in your practice.*

In a proposal, your aim is to convince the reader that you understand the problem completely. Thus, if you are responding to an RFP, this means repeating its language. For example, if the RFP asks for the *design of a maintenance program for high-speed mail-sorting equipment*, you would use the same language in explaining the purpose of your proposal. This section might include segments entitled *Basic Requirements*, *Most Critical Tasks*, and *Most Important Secondary Problems.*

3) Plan, Schedule

In the plan section itself, you should discuss your proposal for solving the problem. In some proposals this is tricky because you want to disclose enough of your plan to secure the contract without giving away so much information that your services aren't needed. Without specifics, though, your proposal has little chance, so you must decide how much to reveal. Explain what you propose to do and how it will benefit the reader. Remember, too, that a proposal is a sales presentation. Sell your methods, product, and "deliverables"—items that will be left with the client. In this section some writers specify how the project will be managed, how its progress will be audited, and what milestones along the way will indicate the project is progressing as planned. Most writers also include a schedule of activities or a timetable showing when events take place.

4) Staffing

The staffing section of a proposal describes the credentials and expertise of the project leaders and the company as a whole. A well-written staffing section describes the capabilities of the whole company. Although the example in Figure 10.1 does not do so, staffing sections often list other high-profile jobs that have been undertaken by the company, as a way of building interest and reducing resistance. For example, before she mentioned Dr. Miller and Dr. Malau, Dana Swensen could have said, *Among our well-known clients are Husky Energy and the Calgary Board of Education.*

It may also identify the size and qualifications of the support staff, along with other resources such as computer facilities and special programs for analyzing statistics. In longer proposals, résumés of key people may be provided. The staffing or personnel section is a good place to endorse and promote your staff.

5) Budget

A central item in most proposals is the budget, a list of project costs. You need to prepare this section carefully because it represents a contract; you can't raise the price later—even if your costs increase. You can—and should—protect yourself with a deadline for acceptance. In the budget section some writers itemize hours and costs; others present a total sum only. A proposal to install a complex computer system might, for example, contain a detailed line-by-line budget. In the proposal shown in Figure 10.1, Dana Swensen felt that she needed to justify the budget for her firm's patient satisfaction survey, so she itemized the costs. But the budget included for a proposal to conduct a one-day seminar to improve employee

Reprinted by permission of Sidney Harris.

communication skills might be a lump sum only. Your analysis of the project will help you decide what kind of budget to prepare.

6) Authorization

Informal proposals often close with a request for approval or authorization. In addition, the closing should remind the reader of key benefits and motivate action. It might also include a deadline date beyond which the offer is invalid. At some companies, such as Hewlett-Packard, authorization to proceed is not part of the proposal. Instead, it is usually discussed after the customer has received the proposal. In this way the customer and the sales account manager are able to negotiate terms before a formal agreement is drawn.

Formal Proposals

Formal proposals differ from informal proposals not in style but in size and format. Formal proposals respond to big projects and may range from 5 to 200 or more pages. To facilitate comprehension and reference, they are organized into many parts. In addition to the six basic parts just described, formal proposals contain some or all of the following additional parts: copy of the RFP, letter of transmittal, abstract and/or executive summary, title page, table of contents, figures, and appendix.

Well-written proposals win contracts and business for companies and individuals. In fact, many companies, especially those that are run on a consulting model, depend entirely on proposals to generate their income. Companies such as Microsoft, Hewlett-Packard, and IBM employ staffs of people that do nothing but prepare proposals to compete for new business. For more information about industry standards and resources, visit the Web site of the Association of Proposal Management Professionals <www.apmp.org>.

Quick Check

Formal proposals respond to big projects and may contain 200 or more pages.

Preparing to Write Formal Reports

Formal reports, whether they offer only information or whether they also analyze that information and make recommendations, typically have three characteristics: formal tone, traditional structure, and considerable length. Formal research reports in business serve a very important function. They provide management with vital data for decision making. In this section we will consider the entire process of writing a formal report: preparing to write; researching, generating, documenting, organizing, and illustrating data; and presenting the final report.

Like proposals and informal reports, formal reports begin with a definition of the project. Probably the most difficult part of this definition is limiting the scope of the report. Every project has limitations. Decide at the outset what constraints influence the range of your project and how you will achieve your purpose. How much time do you have for completing your report? How much space will you be allowed for reporting on your topic? How accessible are the data you need? How thorough should your research be?

If you are writing about low morale among employees who work shifts, for example, how many of your 475 employees should you interview? Should you limit your research to company-related morale factors, or should you consider external factors over which the company has no control? In investigating variable-rate mortgages, should you focus on a particular group, such as first-time homeowners in a specific area, or should you consider all mortgage holders? The first

Quick Check

The primary differences between formal and informal reports are tone, structure, and length.

Quick Check

The planning of every report begins with a statement of purpose explaining the goal, significance, and limitations of the report.

Preparing to Write Formal Reports

step in writing a report, then, is determining the precise boundaries of the topic.

Once you have defined the project and limited its scope, write a statement of purpose. The statement of purpose should describe the goal, scope, significance, and limitations of the report. Notice how the following statement includes all four criteria:

> The purpose of this report is to explore employment possibilities for entry-level para-legal workers in the city of St. John's. It will consider typical salaries, skills required, opportunities, and working conditions. This research is significant because of the increasing number of job openings in the health records field. This report will not consider health care sector secretarial employment, which represents a different employment focus.

Outlines and Headings

Most writers agree that the clearest way to organize a report is to predetermine its main sections in an outline. Although the outline is not part of the final report, it is a valuable tool of the writer. It reveals at a glance the overall organization of the report. As you learned in Chapter 3, outlining involves dividing a topic into major sections and supporting those with details. Figure 10.2 shows an abbreviated outline of a report about forms of business ownership. Rarely is a real outline so perfectly balanced; some sections are usually longer than others. Remember, though, not to put a single topic under a major component. If you have only one subpoint, integrate it with the main item above it or reorganize. Use details, illustrations, and evidence to support subpoints.

The main points used to outline a report often become the main headings of the written report. In Chapter 9 you studied tips for writing talking and functional headings. Formatting those headings depends on what level they represent. Major headings, as you can see in Figure 10.3, are centred and typed in bold. Second-level headings start at the left margin, and third-level headings are indented and become part of a paragraph.

FIGURE 10.2 Outline Format

FORMS OF BUSINESS OWNERSHIP

I. Sole proprietorship (*first main topic*)
   A. Advantages of sole proprietorship (*first subdivision of Topic I*)
      1. Minimal capital requirements (*first subdivision of Topic A*)
      2. Control by owner (*second subdivision of Topic A*)
   B. Disadvantages of sole proprietorship (*second subdivision of Topic I*)
      1. Unlimited liability (*first subdivision of Topic B*)
      2. Limited management talent (*second subdivision of Topic B*)
II. Partnership (*second main topic*)
   A. Advantages of partnership (*first subdivision of Topic II*)
      1. Access of capital (*first subdivision of Topic A*)
      2. Management talent (*second subdivision of Topic A*)
      3. Ease of formation (*third subdivision of Topic A*)
   B. Disadvantages of partnership (*second subdivision of Topic II*)
      1. Unlimited liability (*first subdivision of Topic B*)
      2. Personality conflicts (*second subdivision of Topic B*)

FIGURE 10.3 Levels of Headings in Reports

2-inch top margin

REPORT, CHAPTER, AND PART TITLES
2 blank lines

The title of a report, chapter heading, or major part (such as CONTENTS or NOTES) should be centred in all caps. If the title requires more than one line, arrange it in an inverted triangle with the longest lines at the top. Begin the text a triple space (two blank lines) below the title, as shown here.

2 blank lines

First-Level Subheading
1 blank line

Headings indicating the first level of division are centred and bolded. Capitalize the first letter of each main word. Whether a report is single-spaced or double-spaced, most typists triple-space (leaving two blank lines) before and double-space (leaving one blank line) after a first-level subheading.

1 blank line

Every level of heading should be followed by some text. For example, we could not jump from "First-Level Subheading," shown above, to "Second-Level Subheading," shown below, without some discussion between.

Good writers strive to develop coherency and fluency by ending most sections with a lead-in that introduces the next section. The lead-in consists of a sentence or two announcing the next topic.

2 blank lines

Second-Level Subheading
1 blank line

Headings that divide topics introduced by first-level subheadings are bolded and begin at the left margin. Use a triple space before and a double space after a second-level subheading. If a report has only one level of heading, use either first- or second-level subheading style.

Always be sure to divide topics into two or more subheadings. If you have only one subheading, eliminate it and absorb the discussion under the previous major heading. Try to make all headings within a level grammatically equal. For example, all second-level headings might use verb forms (*Preparing*, *Organizing*, and *Composing*) or noun forms (*Preparation*, *Organization*, and *Composition*).

1 blank line

Third-level subheading. Because it is part of the paragraph that follows, a third-level subheading is also called a "paragraph subheading." Capitalize only the first word and proper nouns in the subheading. Bold the subheading and end it with a period. Begin typing the paragraph text immediately following the period, as shown here. Double-space before a paragraph subheading.

Places major headings in the centre; capitalizes initial letters of main words

Starts at left margin

Makes heading part of paragraph

Researching Secondary Data

One of the most important steps in the process of writing a report is research. Because a report is only as good as its data, you'll want to spend considerable time collecting data before you begin writing.

Data fall into two broad categories, primary and secondary. Primary data result from firsthand experience and observation. Secondary data come from reading what others have experienced and observed. One of the best-known organizations

Quick Check

Primary data come from firsthand experience and observation; secondary data, from reading.

that researches primary data is Consumers Union <www.consumerreports.org>, a nonprofit organization headquartered in Yonkers, New York. After testing all manner of consumer goods in its National Testing and Research Center—everything from cars to computers to fitness equipment—Consumers Union publishes its results in its best-selling magazine, *Consumer Reports*. Once published, the primary data generated in the Yonkers lab becomes secondary data. Now anyone—a student, a parent, or a newspaper reporter—can use the data. Secondary data are easier and less expensive to develop than primary data, which might involve interviewing large groups or sending out questionnaires.

You're going to learn first about secondary data because that's where nearly every research project should begin. Often, something has already been written about your topic. Reviewing secondary sources can save time and effort and help you avoid costly primary research to develop data that already exists. Most secondary material is available either in print or in online databases located in your school or company library.

Print Resources

Although we're seeing a steady movement away from print to electronic data, much information is available only in print.

If you are an infrequent library user, begin your research by talking with a reference librarian about your project. These librarians won't do your research for you, but they will steer you in the right direction. And they are very accommodating. Many libraries help you understand their computer, cataloguing, and retrieval systems by providing brochures, handouts, and workshops.

Books. Although sometimes outdated, books provide excellent historical, in-depth data on subjects. For example, if you are investigating best practices in Web site design, you will find numerous books with valuable information in your nearest library. Books are located through online catalogues that can be accessed in the library, on any campus computer, or from home with an Internet connection and valid password. Most library catalogues today enable you to learn not only whether a book is in the library but also whether it is currently available.

Periodicals. Magazines, pamphlets, and journals are called periodicals because of their recurrent or periodic publication. Journals, by the way, are compilations of scholarly articles. Articles in journals and other periodicals will be extremely useful to you because they are concise, limited in scope, and current, and can supplement information in books. For example, if you want to understand the latest trends and research in the business communication field, you would browse through recent volumes of the *Journal of Business Communication*.

Online Databases

As a writer of business reports today, you will probably use one or several online databases for your secondary research. Many writers turn to them first because they are fast, easy to use, and available online. By using these online resources you can look for the secondary data you require without ever leaving your office or home.

These databases provide both bibliographic (titles of documents and brief abstracts) and full-text documents. Most researchers prefer full-text documents. The strength of databases lies in the fact that they are current and field specific. For example, if you go to the George Brown College Library Web site <llc.georgebrown .ca/llc>, you will find a section called "eResources" and a link for "Databases by Subject." Clicking on this link brings you to a list of subjects. If you then click on "Business," a list of 17 databases appears. These business databases contain articles

Quick Check

Most researchers today begin by looking in online databases.

Quick Check

Review information online through research databases that are accessible by computer and searchable.

Quick Check

Although researchers are increasingly turning to electronic data, much data is available only in print.

Quick Check

Books provide historical, in-depth data; periodicals provide limited but current coverage.

from magazines, newspapers, and academic journals. They also contain material from newsletters, reports, company profiles, government statistical data, and other sources. Your own library will have similar resources. Libraries pay for these databases partly through your tuition fees or your tax dollars. If you do not have access to an institution's databases, there are free services you can access including the Virtual Reference Library at <www.virtualreferencelibrary.ca>.

Learning how to use an online database takes some practice. We suggest you go to your favourite library Web site and experiment with online databases. Choose a topic like *trends in business communication* and see what you come up with. Try to find one current article from a newspaper, a magazine, and a journal. Do you get better results when you use the basic or the advanced search function? Do you get better results by separating the topic into parts, for example, *trends* and *business* and *communication,* or by typing the whole phrase in at once? If you're having trouble, you can always sign up for a free guided seminar at your library, or ask a librarian for help next time you're at the library.

3 The Web

The best-known area of the Internet is the World Wide Web. The Web includes an enormous collection of resources useful to your research including those of major worldwide magazines, newspapers, libraries, and other research resource providers. Web pages provide resources in multiple formats including text, sound, and video files. Another valuable feature of Web pages is the way they are linked together. Beginning a search at one site can lead to linking with many other relevant sites that add valuable information you may not have considered as part of your research plan. Active links are often underlined words and phrases or text appearing in a different colour from the surrounding text. Links can also be icons or small images. The linking of millions of Web pages places a vast resource at your fingertips.

 Quick Check
The World Wide Web is a collection of individual pages offering information and links.

Web Opportunities and Challenges. To a business researcher, the Web offers a wide range of organizational information such as product facts, public relations material, mission statements, staff directories, press releases, current company news, government information, selected article reprints, collaborative scientific project reports, and employment information. While the Web can be a great resource to anyone needing facts quickly and inexpensively, it can also be very unreliable. Both the quality of the information and the technical access to Web sites can be unpredictable. In the Communication Workshop at the end of this chapter you'll learn more about sorting the legitimate sites from the hoaxes.

In addition to being unpredictable, the Web can be a frustrating and time-consuming place to locate information. This is because the Web is not primarily a research tool but a commercial tool. Try typing *trends in business communication* into your favourite search engine. What do you find? Chances are that mixed in with the few interesting and useful articles, a majority of the sites are trying to sell you a service or a product. The constantly changing contents of the Web and its lack of organization make it more problematic for research than using online databases.

Search Tools. Finding what you are looking for on the Web is like searching for a library book without using the catalogue. Fortunately, a number of search engines—such as Google <www.google.ca>, AltaVista Canada <www.altavista.ca>, and Canoe <www.canoe.ca>—are available. These search engines look up words in their indexes, but they don't survey everything. Because of the vastness of the Web, at any given time many pages have not been indexed. Nevertheless, they usually turn up more information than you want.

Like everything else about the Web, search engines are constantly evolving as developers change their features to attract more users. Always keep in mind that

 Quick Check
Search engines such as Google, AltaVista, and Canoe help you locate specific Web sites and information.

the search engines you use are commercial vehicles, and as such are prone to a bias in favour of commercial enterprises. Balance your use of the Web by using the more research-friendly (and bias-free) online library databases.

Internet Search Tips and Techniques. As one Web veteran put it, "the Web's 15 terabytes of data is more than ever like an iceberg—largely underwater."[3] Much of the best information on the Web is hard to find because of the way search engines work. They use Boolean logic (they separate words with *and*, *or*, and *not*) and a variety of punctuation marks such as commas and quotation marks. For you to make the most of the Web you will have to become familiar with the requirements of the search engines you use most. Here are a few tips to make you an intelligent Internet researcher:

- **Use two or three search engines.** Different Internet search engines turn up different results. One expert wisely observed: "Every search engine will give you good results some of the time. Every search engine will give you surprisingly bad results some of the time. No search engine will give you good results all of the time."[4]
- **Understand case sensitivity.** Generally use lowercase for your searches, unless you are searching for a term that is typically written in upper- and lowercase, such as a person's name.
- **Understand Boolean searching.** When searching for a group of words, such as *cost benefit analysis*, most search tools will also retrieve documents having only *cost* or *benefit* or *analysis* in them, which is not helpful to you as a researcher. To successfully research this phrase, enclose it in quotations as you type it into the engine: *cost benefit analysis.* Similarly, if you're interested in trends in business communication, use Boolean commands like *and* to make for a better search. For example, typing in *"trends and communication"* will achieve better results than typing *trends communication.* For a quick tutorial on Boolean searching, visit <llc.georgebrown.ca/llc/documents/boolean.html>.
- **Be specific.** Commonly used words make poor search keywords. For example, instead of *keeping employees*, use *employee retention.*
- **Omit articles and prepositions.** These are known as "stop words," and they do not add value to a search. Instead of *request for proposal*, use *proposal request.*
- **Use wild cards.** Most search engines support the use of *wild cards* in their search boxes—symbols, often asterisks, that can stand for *any* letter or series of letters of the alphabet. For example, in AltaVista the search term *bas** would find documents containing the words *bass*, *baste*, and *bassoon.*
- **Know your search tool.** When connecting to a search service for the first time, always read the description of its service, including its FAQs (frequently asked questions), Help, and How to Search sections.
- **Bookmark the best.** To keep better track of your favourite Internet sites, save them on your browser as bookmarks.
- **Be persistent.** If a search produces no results, check your spelling. Try synonyms and variations on words. Try to be less specific in your search term. If your search produces too many results, try to be more specific. Think of words that uniquely identify what you're looking for. And use as many relevant keywords as possible.

Generating Primary Data

Although you'll begin a business report by probing for secondary data, you'll probably need primary data to give a complete picture. Business reports that solve specific current problems typically rely on primary, firsthand data. If, for example, management wants to discover the cause of increased employee turnover in its Toronto office, it must investigate conditions in Toronto by collecting recent information. Providing answers to business problems often means generating primary data through surveys, interviews, observation, or experimentation.

Surveys

Surveys collect data from groups of people. When companies develop new products, for example, they often survey consumers to learn their needs. The advantages of surveys are that they gather data economically and efficiently. Mailed surveys reach big groups nearby or at great distances. Moreover, people responding to mailed surveys have time to consider their answers, thus improving the accuracy of the data.

Mailed surveys, of course, have disadvantages. Most of us rank them with junk mail, so response rates may be no higher than 10 percent. Furthermore, those who do respond may not represent an accurate sample of the overall population, thus invalidating generalizations from the group. Let's say, for example, that an insurance company sends out a survey questionnaire asking about provisions in a new policy. If only older people respond, the survey data cannot be used to generalize what people in other age groups might think. A final problem with surveys has to do with truthfulness. Some respondents exaggerate their incomes or distort other facts, thus causing the results to be unreliable. Nevertheless, surveys are still considered the best way to generate data for business and student reports.

Interviews

Some of the best report information, particularly on topics about which little has been written, comes from individuals. These individuals are usually experts or veterans in their fields. Consider both in-house and outside experts for business reports. Tapping these sources will call for in-person, e-mail, or telephone interviews. To elicit the most useful data, try these techniques:

- **Locate an expert.** Ask managers and individuals working in an area whom they consider to be most knowledgeable. Check membership lists of professional organizations, and consult articles about the topic or related topics. Most people enjoy being experts or at least recommending them. You could also post an inquiry to an Internet newsgroup. Choose your newsgroups carefully, though, to avoid being flooded with unwanted correspondence.
- **Prepare for the interview.** Learn about the individual you're interviewing as well as the background and terminology of the topic. Let's say you're interviewing a corporate communication expert about producing an in-house newsletter. You ought to be familiar with terms such as *font* and software such as PhotoShop, QuarkXpress, and Adobe Illustrator. In addition, be prepared by making a list of questions that pinpoint your areas of interest in the topic. Ask the interviewee if you may record the talk.
- **Make your questions objective and friendly.** Don't get into a debating match with the interviewee. And remember that you're there to listen, not to talk! Use open-ended, rather than yes-or-no, questions to draw experts out.
- **Watch the time.** Tell interviewees in advance how much time you expect to need for the interview. Don't overstay your appointment.
- **End graciously.** Conclude the interview with a general question, such as *Is there anything you'd like to add?* Express your appreciation, and ask permission to telephone or e-mail later if you need to verify points.

✔ *Quick Check*

Surveys yield efficient and economical primary data for reports.

✔ *Quick Check*

Although mailed surveys may suffer low response rates, they are still useful in generating primary data.

✔ *Quick Check*

Interviews with experts produce useful report data, especially when little has been written about a topic.

Observation and Experimentation

Quick Check

Some of the best report data come from firsthand observation and investigation.

Some kinds of primary data can be obtained only through firsthand observation and investigation. How long does a typical caller wait before a customer service representative answers the call? How is a new piece of equipment operated? Are complaints of sexual harassment being taken seriously? Observation produces rich data, but that information is especially prone to charges of subjectivity. One can interpret an observation in many ways. Thus, to make observations more objective, try to quantify them. For example, record customer telephone wait time for 60-minute periods at different times throughout a week. Or compare the number of sexual harassment complaints made with the number of investigations undertaken and resulting actions.

Experimentation produces data suggesting causes and effects. Informal experimentation might be as simple as a pre-test and post-test in a college course. Did students expand their knowledge as a result of the course? More formal experimentation is undertaken by scientists and professional researchers who control variables to test their effects. Assume, for example, that Mordens Candy Manufacturing Company in Winnipeg wants to test the hypothesis (which is a tentative assumption) that chocolate lifts people out of the doldrums. An experiment testing the hypothesis would separate depressed individuals into two groups: those who ate chocolate (the experimental group) and those who did not (the control group). What effect did chocolate have? Such experiments are not done haphazardly, however. Valid experiments require sophisticated research designs and careful attention to matching the experimental and control groups.

Documenting Data and Plagiarism

One of the most common complaints of college and university professors and employers is that their students and employees don't understand the importance of documentation. Documentation is the act of showing where your information came from, whether in a business report or in an academic essay. Young people who have grown up with the Internet sometimes find it hard to understand that *all* information, whether it comes from a book, a magazine, a newspaper, a pamphlet or brochure, a Web site, or a blog, is the property of someone else. If you use it and don't say that you've used it, you're stealing.

Put yourself in the shoes of a journalist. She makes her living by writing for a magazine. If you take a phrase or a sentence or a paragraph from what she's written and place it in your report without acknowledging that fact, you're infringing on the journalist's rights—you're stealing from her. Not documenting sources is dishonest, ethically problematic, and illegal. The crime is called plagiarism, and all colleges and universities have strict policies against it, including penalties such as a zero grade on the plagiarized assignment. If your instructor has not already discussed your institution's policy, you should ask him or her to do so.

Plagiarism is the act of not documenting your sources, of taking another person's ideas or published words and not acknowledging that fact. Any time you quote directly, paraphrase, or summarize information from a source, you must document it. Documentation in a business report serves three purposes:

- **Strengthens your argument.** Including good data from reputable sources will convince readers of your credibility and the logic of your reasoning.

- **Protects you.** Acknowledging your sources keeps you honest. It's unethical and illegal to use others' ideas without proper documentation.
- **Instructs the reader.** Citing references enables readers to pursue a topic further and make use of the information themselves.

Documentation is achieved through citations. A citation is the method used to show from where the idea or phrase or sentence was borrowed. The original reason behind citations (before plagiarism became a big problem) was to allow anyone reading your work to find your sources should he or she wish to do additional research. If someone says to you, "But you didn't cite it!" he or she means you didn't include a proper citation.

To use an example from the last chapter, in a report that reads *In a recent Vancouver Province article, Blake Spence, Director of Transportation, argues that the Sky Train must be expanded to cope with the influx of tourists expected during the 2010 Olympics (A17)*, the citation is the combination of the lead-in, *Blake Spence… argues*, and the page reference, *(A17)*. The basic elements of any citation are the author's name and the page number. There will be times when you don't have these two pieces of information. For more information on such cases, as well as the two main citation methods—footnote/endnote (or Chicago style) and parenthetic (or APA and MLA style)—please read Appendix C. Also study Figure 10.15 to see how sources are documented there.

Citing Electronic Sources. Standards for researchers using electronic sources are still evolving. When citing electronic media, you should hold the same goals as for print sources. That is, you want to give credit to the authors and to allow others to locate the same or updated information easily. However, since electronic sources are less stable than books or magazines, citation experts recommend more information be provided when citing electronic sources than when citing print sources. Since electronic sources can be changed easily, multiple publication dates may need to be included as well as the date on which the source was used. All citation experts suggest similar information be cited for an electronic source including the author's name (when available), document title, Web page or online database title, access date, and Web address. See Appendix C for more detailed information and examples of citing electronic sources.

Illustrating Data

Tables, charts, graphs, illustrations, and other visual aids can play an important role in clarifying, summarizing, and emphasizing information. Numerical data become meaningful, complex ideas are simplified, and visual interest is provided by the appropriate use of graphics. Here are general tips for making the most effective use of visual aids:

✔ Quick Check

Effective graphics clarify numerical data and simplify complex ideas.

- Clearly identify the contents of the visual aid with meaningful titles and labels (e.g., *Figure 1*).
- Refer the reader to the visual aid by discussing it in the text and mentioning its location and figure number (e.g., *as Figure 1 below shows...*).
- Locate the visual aid close to its reference in the text.
- Strive for vertical placement of visual aids. Readers are disoriented by horizontal pages in reports.
- Give credit to the source if appropriate (e.g., *Source: Statistics Canada*).

Tables

Probably the most frequently used visual aid in reports is the table. A table presents quantitative information in a systematic order of columns and rows. Here are tips for designing good tables, one of which is illustrated in Figure 10.4:

- Provide clear heads for the rows and columns.
- Identify the units in which figures are given (percentages, dollars, units per worker-hour, and so forth) in the table title, in the column or row head, with the first item in a column, or in a note at the bottom.
- Arrange items in a logical order (alphabetical, chronological, geographical, highest to lowest) depending on what you need to emphasize.
- Use *N/A* (not available) for missing data.
- Make long tables easier to read by shading alternate lines or by leaving a blank line after groups of five.

Bar Charts

Although they lack the precision of tables, bar charts enable you to make emphatic visual comparisons. Bar charts can be used to compare related items, illustrate changes in data over time, and show segments as part of a whole. Figures 10.5 through 10.8 show vertical, horizontal, grouped, and segmented bar charts that highlight income for an entertainment company called MPM. Note how the varied bar charts present information in different ways.

Many suggestions for tables also hold true for bar charts. Here are a few additional tips:

- Keep the length of each bar and segment proportional.
- Include a total figure in the middle of a bar or at its end if the figure helps the reader and does not clutter the chart.
- Start dollar or percentage amounts at zero.
- Avoid showing too much information, thus producing clutter and confusion.

Line Charts

The major advantage of line charts is that they show changes over time, thus indicating trends. Figures 10.9 through 10.11 show line charts that reflect revenue trends for the major divisions of MPM. Notice that line charts do not provide precise data. Instead, they give an overview or impression of the data. Experienced report writers use tables to list exact data; they use line charts or bar charts to spotlight important points or trends.

FIGURE 10.4   Table Summarizing Precise Data

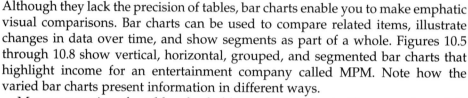

Figure 1
DYNAMO PRODUCTS
Number of Computers Sold, 2006

Region	1st Qtr.	2nd Qtr.	3rd Qtr.	4th Qtr.	Yearly Totals
Atlantic	13,302	15,003	15,550	16,210	60,065
Central	12,678	11,836	10,689	14,136	49,339
Prairie	10,345	11,934	10,899	12,763	45,941
Pacific	9,345	8,921	9,565	10,256	38,087
Total	45,670	47,694	46,703	53,365	193,432

FIGURE 10.5   Vertical Bar Chart

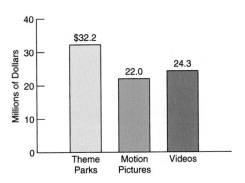

Figure 1

2006 MPM INCOME BY DIVISION

Source: *Industry Profiles* (New York: DataPro, 2006), p. 225.

FIGURE 10.6   Horizontal Bar Chart

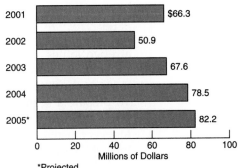

Figure 2

TOTAL MPM INCOME, 2001 TO 2005

*Projected.
Source: *Industry Profiles.*

FIGURE 10.7   Grouped Bar Chart

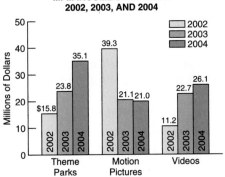

Figure 3

**MPM INCOME BY DIVISION
2002, 2003, AND 2004**

Source: *Industry Profiles.*

FIGURE 10.8   Segmented 100% Bar Chart

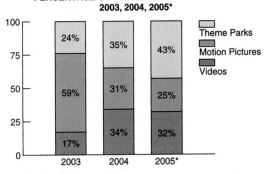

Figure 4

**PERCENTAGE OF TOTAL INCOME BY DIVISION
2003, 2004, 2005***

*Projected.
Source: *Industry Profiles.*

FIGURE 10.9   Simple Line Chart

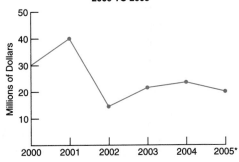

Figure 5

**MOTION PICTURE REVENUES
2000 TO 2005**

*Projected.
Source: *Industry Profiles.*

FIGURE 10.10   Multiple Line Chart

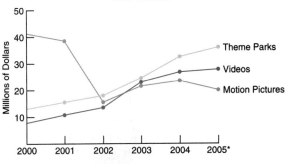

Figure 6

**COMPARISON OF DIVISION REVENUES
2000 TO 2005**

*Projected.
Source: *Industry Profiles.*

Illustrating Data

Simple line charts (Figure 10.9) show just one variable. Multiple line charts combine several variables (Figure 10.10). Segmented line charts (Figure 10.11), also called surface charts, illustrate how the components of a whole change over time.

Here are tips for preparing line charts:

- Begin with a grid divided into squares.
- Arrange the time component (usually years) horizontally across the bottom; arrange values for the other variable vertically.
- Draw small dots at the intersections to indicate each value at a given year.
- Connect the dots and add colour if desired.
- To prepare a segmented (surface) chart, plot the first value (say *video income*) across the bottom; add the next item (say *motion picture income*) to the first figures for every increment; for the third item (say *theme park income*) add its value to the total of the first two items. The top line indicates the total of the three values.

Pie Charts

✔ Quick Check

Pie charts are most useful in showing the proportion of parts to a whole.

Pie, or circle, charts help readers visualize a whole and the proportion of its components, or wedges. Pie charts, though less flexible than bar or line charts, are useful in showing percentages, as Figure 10.12 illustrates. For the most effective pie charts, follow these suggestions:

- Begin at the 12 o'clock position, drawing the largest wedge first. (Computer software programs don't always observe this advice, but if you're drawing your own charts, you can.)
- Include, if possible, the actual percentage or absolute value for each wedge.
- Use four to eight segments for best results; if necessary, group small portions into one wedge called "Other."
- Distinguish wedges with colour, shading, or cross-hatching.
- Keep all labels horizontal.

Flow Charts

✔ Quick Check

Flow charts use standard symbols to illustrate a process or procedure.

Procedures are simplified and clarified by diagramming them in a flow chart, as shown in Figure 10.13. Whether you need to describe the procedure for handling a customer's purchase order or outline steps in solving a problem, flow charts help the reader visualize the process. Traditional flow charts use the following symbols:

FIGURE 10.11 Segmented Line (Surface) Chart

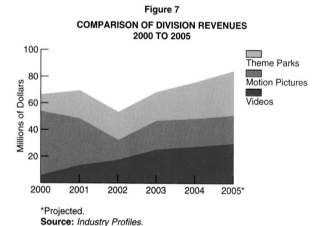

FIGURE 10.12 Pie Chart

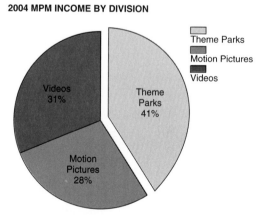

FIGURE 10.13 Flow Chart

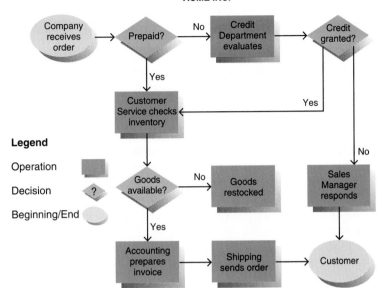

FLOW OF CUSTOMER ORDER THROUGH
ACME INC.

- Ovals to designate the beginning and end of a process
- Diamonds to denote decision points
- Rectangles to represent major activities or steps.

Organization Charts

Many large organizations are so complex that they need charts to show the chain of command, from the boss down to managers and employees. The chart in Figure 10.14 defines the hierarchy of authority from the board of directors to individual managers.

FIGURE 10.14 Organization Chart

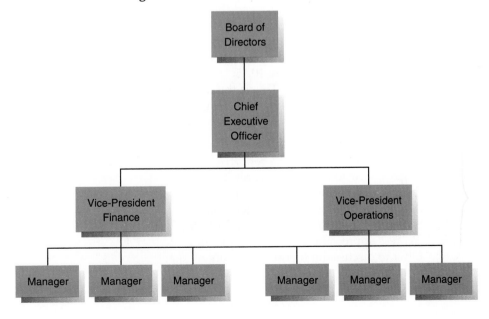

Using Your Computer to Produce Charts

Designing effective bar charts, pie charts, figures, and other graphics is easy with today's software. Spreadsheet programs such as Excel as well as presentation graphics programs such as Microsoft PowerPoint allow even nontechnical people to design quality graphics. These graphics can be printed directly on paper for written reports or used for transparency masters and slides for oral presentations. The benefits of preparing visual aids on a computer are near-professional quality, shorter preparation time, and substantial cost savings. To prepare computer graphics, follow these steps:

- Assemble your data, usually in table form (such as that in Figure 10.4, p. 268).
- Choose a chart type, such as a pie chart, grouped bar chart, vertical bar chart, horizontal bar chart, organization chart, or some other graphic.
- To make a pie chart, key in the data or select the data from an existing file.
- Add a title for the chart as well as any necessary labels.
- To make a bar or line chart, indicate the horizontal and vertical axes (reference lines or beginning points).
- Verify the legend, which your program may generate automatically.
- Print the final chart on paper or import into another program.

Presenting the Final Report

Long reports are generally organized into three major divisions: (1) prefatory parts, (2) body, and (3) supplementary parts. Following is a description of the order and content of each part. Refer to the model formal report in Figure 10.15 (starting on p. 276) for illustrations of most of these parts.

⁓ Prefatory Parts

- **Title fly.** A single page with the title begins a formal report. In less formal reports, the title fly is omitted. Our model report does not include this optional part. Compose the title of your report carefully so that it shows immediately what the report covers and what it does not cover.
- **Title page.** In addition to the title, the title page shows the author, the individual or organization who authorized the report, the recipient of the report, and the date.
- **Letter or memo or e-mail of authorization.** If a letter or memo authorized the report, it may be included in the prefatory material. This optional part is omitted from the model in Figure 10.15.
- **Letter or memo of transmittal.** This is the first impression the reader receives of the report; it should be given serious consideration. Use the direct strategy and include some or all of the suggestions here:

  1. Deliver the report (*Here is the report you authorized*).
  2. Present an overview of the report.
  3. Suggest how to read or interpret it.
  4. Describe limitations, if they exist.
  5. Acknowledge those who assisted you.
  6. Suggest follow-up studies, if appropriate.
  7. Express appreciation for the assignment.
  8. Offer to discuss the report personally.

Quick Check

A letter or memo of transmittal presents an overview of the report, suggests how to read it, describes limitations, acknowledges assistance, and expresses appreciation.

- **Table of contents.** Identify the name and location of every part of the report except the title fly, title page, and table of contents itself. Use spaced periods (dot leaders) to join each part with its page number.
- **Executive summary or abstract.** A summary condensing the entire report is a timesaving device summarizing the purpose, findings, and conclusions.

—Body of Report

- **Introduction or background.** After the prefatory parts, begin the body of the report with an introduction that includes any or all of the following items:

  1. Explanation of how the report originated and why it was authorized
  2. Description of the problem that prompted the report and the specific research questions to be answered
  3. Purpose of the report
  4. Scope (boundaries) and limitations or restrictions of the research
  5. Sources and methods of collecting data
  6. Summary of findings, if the report is written deductively
  7. Preview of the major sections of the report to follow, thus providing coherence and transition for the reader

> ✓ **Quick Check**
>
> A letter or memo of transmittal presents an overview of the report, suggests how to read it, describes limitations, acknowledges assistance, and expresses appreciation.

- **Discussion of findings.** This is the main section of the report and contains numerous headings and subheadings. It is unnecessary to use the title *Discussion of Findings*; many business report writers prefer to begin immediately with the major headings into which the body of the report is divided. Present your findings objectively, avoiding the use of first-person pronouns (*I, we*). Include *Direct Approach* tables, charts, and graphs if necessary to illustrate findings. Analytic and scientific reports may include another section entitled *Implications of Findings*, in which the findings are analyzed and related to the problem. Less formal reports contain the author's analysis of the research findings within the *Discussion* section.

  The readability of a report is greatly enhanced by skillful organization of the facts presented. You have already studied numerous writing strategies or plans of organization for shorter documents. Here is a brief overview of possible plans for the organization of formal reports:

- **Deductive strategy.** The deductive strategy presents main ideas first. A formal report organized deductively would begin by describing the report's recommendations. For example, if you were studying five possible locations for a proposed shopping centre, you would begin with the recommendation of the best site and follow with a discussion of other sites. Use this strategy *Know the difference* when the reader is supportive and knowledgeable.

- **Inductive strategy.** Inductive reasoning presents facts and discussion first, followed by conclusions and recommendations. Since formal reports generally seek to educate the reader, this order of presentation is often most effective. Following this strategy, a study of possible locations for a shopping centre would begin with data regarding all proposed sites followed by analysis of the information and conclusions drawn from that analysis.

  Once you've decided which overall organization strategy, inductive or deductive, to use for your report, you'll need to decide how to present the data in your Discussion section. You have at least four choices:

- **Chronological sequence.** Information presented using a time frame is arranged chronologically. This plan is effective for presenting historical data or for describing a procedure. A report on the development of a multinational company, for example, would be chronological. A report explaining

> ✓ **Quick Check**
>
> The overall presentation of a topic may be inductive or deductive, while parts of the report may be chronological (such as the background) or topical (such as a discussion of findings).

how to obtain federal funding for a project might be organized chronologically. Often topics are arranged in a past-to-present or present-to-past sequence.

- **Geographical or spatial arrangement.** Information arranged geographically or spatially is organized by physical location. For instance, a report analyzing a company's national sales might be divided into sections representing different geographical areas such as the Atlantic region, central Canada, the Prairie region, and the Pacific region.
- **Topical or functional arrangement.** Some subjects lend themselves to arrangement by topic or function. A report analyzing changes in the management hierarchy of an organization might be arranged in this manner. First, the report would consider the duties of the CEO followed by the functions of the general manager, business manager, marketing manager, and so forth.
- **Component or criteria arrangement.** Many business reports compare two or more solutions to a problem. For example, a company deciding where to open its new call centre may have three cities on a short list. The Discussion section of a formal research report making a final recommendation could be organized either by component or by criteria. In this case, the components may be Ottawa, Moncton, and Charlottetown, and the criteria may be infrastructure costs, workforce education level, and municipal tax incentives.

In organizing your Discussion section, you may find that you combine some of the preceding plans. However it's done, you must break your topic into major divisions, usually three to six. These major divisions can then be partitioned into smaller subdivisions. To identify these divisions, you may use functional heads (such as *CEO Responsibilities, GM Responsibilities, BM Responsibilities*) or talking heads that explain the contents of the text (such as *A Day in the Life of the CEO of Acme Ltd.*). You may want to review the suggestions for writing effective headings in Chapter 9.

- **Summary, conclusions, recommendations.** If the report has been largely informational, it ends with a summary of the data presented. If the report analyzes research findings, then it ends with conclusions drawn from the analyses. An analytic report frequently poses research questions. The conclusion to such a report reviews the major findings and answers the research questions. If a report seeks to determine a course of action, it may end with conclusions and recommendations. Recommendations regarding a course of action may be placed in a separate section or incorporated with the conclusions.

Supplementary Parts of Report

✓ Quick Check

Endnotes, a bibliography, and appendixes may appear after the body of the report.

- **Footnotes or endnotes.** See Appendix C for details on how to document sources. In the footnote method the source notes appear at the foot of each page. In the endnote method they are displayed immediately after the text on a page called "Notes." The trend today is away from the footnote or endnote method and toward the parenthetic method, which works all citations directly into the text of the report.

- **Works Cited.** Most formal reports include a works cited page that lists all *Learn MLA* sources consulted in the report research. See Appendix C for more information.
- **Appendix.** The appendix contains any supplementary information needed to clarify the report. Charts and graphs illustrating significant data are generally part of the report proper. However, extra information that might be included in an appendix are such items as a sample questionnaire, a questionnaire cover letter, correspondence relating to the report, maps, other reports, and optional tables.

FIGURE 10.15 Model Formal Report

Title Page

Includes report title in all caps with longer line above shorter line

Highlights name of report recipient

Identifies report writer

Omits page number

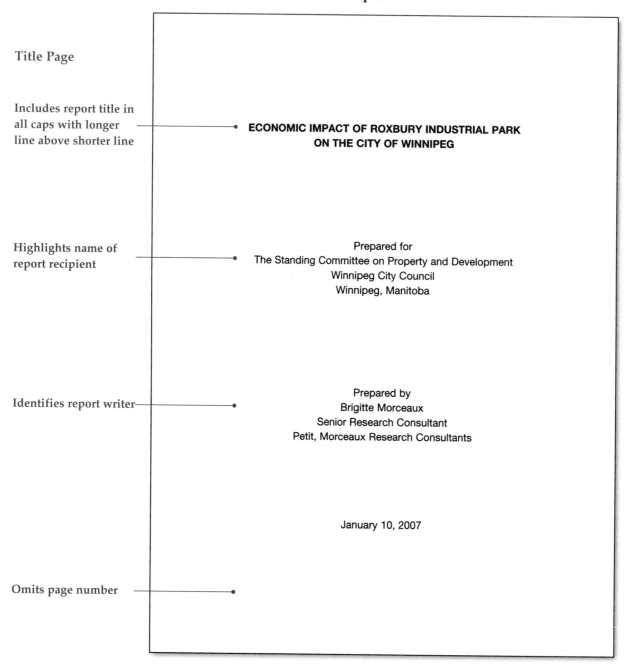

ECONOMIC IMPACT OF ROXBURY INDUSTRIAL PARK
ON THE CITY OF WINNIPEG

Prepared for
The Standing Committee on Property and Development
Winnipeg City Council
Winnipeg, Manitoba

Prepared by
Brigitte Morceaux
Senior Research Consultant
Petit, Morceaux Research Consultants

January 10, 2007

The title page is usually arranged in four evenly balanced areas. If the report is to be bound on the left, move the left margin and centre point .5 cm to the right. Notice that no page number appears on the title page, although it is counted as "page i." In designing the title page, be careful to avoid anything unprofessional—such as too many type fonts, italics, oversized print, and inappropriate graphics. Keep the title page simple and professional.

FIGURE 10.15 **(Continued)** Letter of Transmittal

PETIT, MORCEAUX INDUSTRIAL CONSULTANTS

588 Main Street
Winnipeg, Manitoba R2L 1E6

www.petitmorceaux.com
(204) 549-1101

January 12, 2007

Councillor Richard Moody
Chairperson
The Standing Committee on Property and Development
City of Winnipeg
Winnipeg, MB R2L 1E9

Dear Councillor Moody:

The attached report, requested by the Standing Policy Committee on Property and Development in a letter dated May 20, describes the economic impact of Roxbury Industrial Park on the city of Winnipeg. We believe you will find the results of this study useful in evaluating future development of industrial parks within the city limits.

Announces report and identifies authorization

This study was designed to examine economic impact in three areas:

(1) Current and projected tax and other revenues accruing to the city from Roxbury Industrial Park

(2) Current and projected employment generated by the park

(3) Indirect effects on local employment, income, and economic growth

Gives broad overview of report purposes

Primary research consisted of interviews with 15 Roxbury Industrial Park tenants and managers, in addition to a 2006 survey of over 5,000 RIP employees. Secondary research sources included the Annual Budget of the City of Winnipeg, other government publications, periodicals, books, and online resources. Results of this research, discussed more fully in this report, indicate that Roxbury Industrial Park exerts a significant beneficial influence on the Winnipeg metropolitan economy.

Describes primary and secondary research

I would be pleased to discuss this report and its conclusions with you at your request. My firm and I thank you for your confidence in selecting our company to prepare this comprehensive report.

Offers to discuss report; expresses appreciation

Sincerely,

Brigitte Morceaux

Brigitte Morceaux
Senior Research Consultant

BM:mef

Attachment

A letter or memo of transmittal announces the report topic and explains who authorized it. It describes the project briefly and previews the conclusions, if the reader is supportive. Such messages generally close by expressing appreciation for the assignment, suggesting follow-up actions, acknowledging the help of others, or offering to answer questions. The margins for the transmittal should be the same as for the report, about 3 cm on all sides.

FIGURE 10.15 **(Continued)** Table of Contents and List of Figures

Uses leaders to guide eye from heading to page number

Indents secondary headings to show levels of outline

Includes tables and figures in one list for simplified numbering

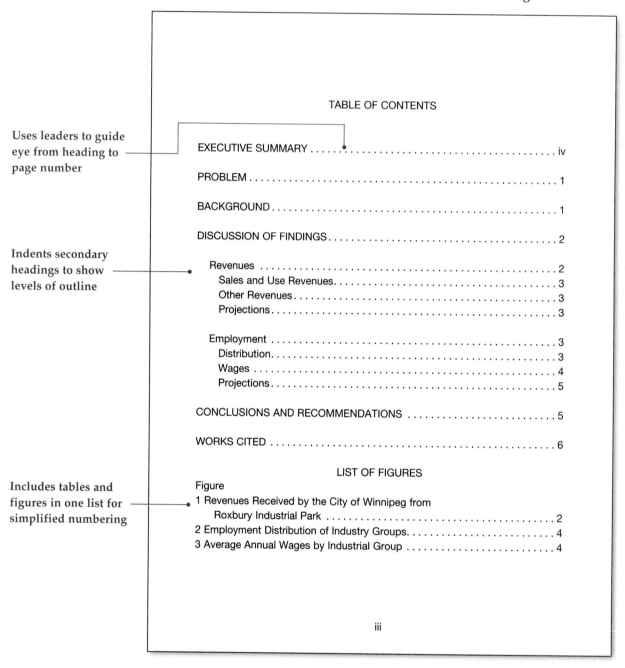

TABLE OF CONTENTS

LIST OF FIGURES

iii

Because the table of contents and the list of figures for this report are small, they are combined on one page. Notice that the titles of major report parts are in all caps, while other headings are a combination of upper- and lowercase letters. The style duplicates those within the report. Word processing programs enable you to generate a contents page automatically, including leaders and accurate page numbering—no matter how many times you revise.

FIGURE 10.15 (Continued) Executive Summary

EXECUTIVE SUMMARY

Winnipeg can benefit from the development of industrial parks like the Roxbury Industrial Park. Both direct and indirect economic benefits result, as shown by this in-depth study conducted by Petit, Morceaux Industrial Consultants. The study was authorized by the Standing Committee on Property and Development when Goldman-Lyon & Associates sought City Council's approval for the proposed construction of a G-L industrial park. The City Council requested evidence demonstrating that an existing development could actually benefit the city. — *Opens directly with major research findings*

Our conclusion that Winnipeg benefits from industrial parks is based on data supplied by a survey of 5,000 Roxbury Industrial Park employees, personal interviews with managers and tenants of RIP, City and Provincial documents, and professional literature. — *Identifies data sources*

Analysis of the data revealed benefits in three areas: — *Summarizes organization of report*

(1) Revenues. The City of Winnipeg earned nearly $1 million in tax and other revenues from the Roxbury Industrial Park in 2006. By 2010 this income is expected to reach $1.7 million (in constant 2006 dollars).

(2) Employment. In 2006 RIP businesses employed a total of 7,035 workers, who earned an average wage of $28,120. By 2010 RIP businesses are expected to employ directly nearly 15,000 employees who will earn salaries totalling over $450 million.

(3) Indirect benefits. Because of the multiplier effect, by 2010 Roxbury Industrial Park will directly and indirectly generate a total of 38,362 jobs in the Winnipeg area.

On the basis of these findings, it is recommended that development of additional industrial parks be encouraged to stimulate local economic growth. — *Condenses recommendations*

iv

An executive summary or abstract highlights report findings, conclusions, and recommendations. Its length depends on the report it summarizes. A 100-page report might require a ten-page summary. Shorter reports may contain one-page summaries, as shown here. Unlike letters of transmittal (which may contain personal pronouns and references to the writer), summaries are formal and impersonal. They use the same margins as the body of the report.

FIGURE 10.15 (Continued) Introduction

ECONOMIC IMPACT OF ROXBURY INDUSTRIAL PARK

PROBLEM

This study was designed to analyze the direct and indirect economic impact of Roxbury Industrial Park on the city of Winnipeg. Specifically, the study seeks answers to these questions:

(1) What current tax and other revenues result directly from this park? What tax and other revenues may be expected in the future?

(2) How many and what kind of jobs are directly attributable to the park? What is the employment picture for the future?

(3) What indirect effects has Roxbury Industrial Park had on local employment, incomes, and economic growth?

BACKGROUND

The Standing Committee on Property and Development commissioned this study of Roxbury Industrial Park at the request of Winnipeg City Council. Before authorizing the development of a proposed Goldman-Lyon industrial park, the City Council requested a study examining the economic effects of an existing park. Members of Council wanted to determine to what extent industrial parks benefit the local community, and they chose Roxbury Industrial Park as an example.

For those who are unfamiliar with it, Roxbury Industrial Park is a 40-hectare industrial park located in Winnipeg about 2.5 kilometres from the centre of the city. Most of the area lies within a specially designated area known as Redevelopment Project No. 2, which is part of the Winnipeg Capital Region Development Commission's planning area. Planning for the park began in 1988; construction started in 1990.

1

Lists three problem questions

Describes authorization for report and background of study

The introduction of a formal report contains the title printed 5 cm from the top edge. Titles for major parts of a report (such as *Problem, Background, Findings, and Conclusions*) are centred in all caps. First-level headings (such as *Employment* on page 3 of the report) are printed with bold upper- and lowercase letters. Second-level headings (such as *Distribution* on page 3) begin at the left side. See Figure 10.3 for an illustration of heading formats.

FIGURE 10.15 **(Continued)** Introduction and Discussion

The park now contains 14 building complexes with over 25,000 square metres of completed building space. The majority of the buildings are used for office, research and development, marketing and distribution, or manufacturing uses. Approximately 5 hectares of the original area are yet to be developed.

Data for this report came from a 2006 survey of over 5,000 Roxbury Industrial Park employees, interviews with 15 RIP tenants and managers, the Annual Budget of the City of Winnipeg, current books, articles, journals, and on-line resources. Projections for future revenues resulted from analysis of past trends and *Estimates of Revenues for Debt Service Coverage, Redevelopment Project Area 2* (Miller 78–79).

— Provides specifics for data sources

— MLA-style parenthetical citation

DISCUSSION OF FINDINGS

The results of this research indicate that major direct and indirect benefits have accrued to the City of Winnipeg and surrounding municipal areas as a result of the development of Roxbury Industrial Park. The research findings presented here fall into three categories: (a) revenues, (b) employment, and (c) indirect effects.

— Previews organization of report

Revenues

Roxbury Industrial Park contributes a variety of tax and other revenues to the city of Winnipeg. Figure 1 summarizes revenues.

— Uses topical arrangement

Figure 1

— Places figure close to textual reference

REVENUES RECEIVED BY THE CITY OF WINNIPEG
FROM ROXBURY INDUSTRIAL PARK

Current Revenues and Projections to 2010

	2006	2010
Property taxes	$604,140	$1,035,390
Revenues from licences	126,265	216,396
Business taxes	75,518	129,424
Provincial service receipts	53,768	92,134
Licences and permits	48,331	82,831
Other revenues	64,039	111,987
Total	$972,061	$1,668,162

Source: City of Winnipeg Chief Financial Officer, *2006 Annual Report*. Retrieved 16 Jan. 2006 <http://www.winnipeg.ca/interhom/departments/cfo/reports.stm>: 103.

2

Notice that this formal report is single-spaced. Many businesses prefer this space-saving format. However, some organizations prefer double-spacing, especially for preliminary drafts. If you single-space, do not indent paragraphs. If you double-space, do indent the paragraphs. Page numbers may be centred near the bottom of the page or placed near the upper right corner at the margin. Strive to leave comfortable top, bottom, and side margins. References follow the Modern Language Association (MLA) citation style. Notice that citations appear as references in the "Works Cited" section with a corresponding parenthetical reference to the author in the text of the report at the appropriate location.

FIGURE 10.15 **(Continued)** Discussion

Continues interpreting
figures in table

Sales and Use Revenues

As shown in Figure 1, the city's largest source of revenues from RIP is the property tax. Revenues from this source totalled $604,140 in 2006, according to the City of Winnipeg Standing Committee on Finance (Annual Report 103). Property taxes accounted for more than half of the park's total contribution to the City of $972,061.

Other Revenues

Other major sources of City revenues from RIP in 2006 include revenues from licences such as motor vehicle in lieu fees, trailer coach licences ($126,265), business taxes ($75,518), and provincial service receipts ($53,768).

Projections

Total City revenues from RIP will nearly double by 2010, producing an income of $1.7 million. This projection is based on an annual growth rate of 1.4 percent in constant 2006 dollars.

Employment

One of the most important factors to consider in the overall effect of an industrial park is employment. In Roxbury Industrial Park the distribution, number, and wages of people employed will change considerably in the next five years.

Sets stage for next
topics to be discussed

Distribution

A total of 7,035 employees currently work in various industry groups at Roxbury Industrial Park, as shown below in Figure 2. The largest number of workers (58 percent) is employed in manufacturing and assembly operations. In the next largest category, the computer and electronics industry employs 24 percent of the workers. Some overlap probably exists because electronics assembly could be included in either group. Employees also work in publishing (9 percent), warehousing and storage (5 percent), and other industries (4 percent).

Although the distribution of employees at Roxbury Industrial Park shows a wide range of employment categories, it must be noted that other industrial parks would likely generate an entirely different range of job categories.

3

Only the most important research findings are interpreted and discussed for readers. The depth of discussion depends on the intended length of the report, the goal of the writer, and the expectations of the reader. Because the writer wants this report to be formal in tone, she avoids *I* and *we* in all discussions.

FIGURE 10.15 (Continued) Discussion

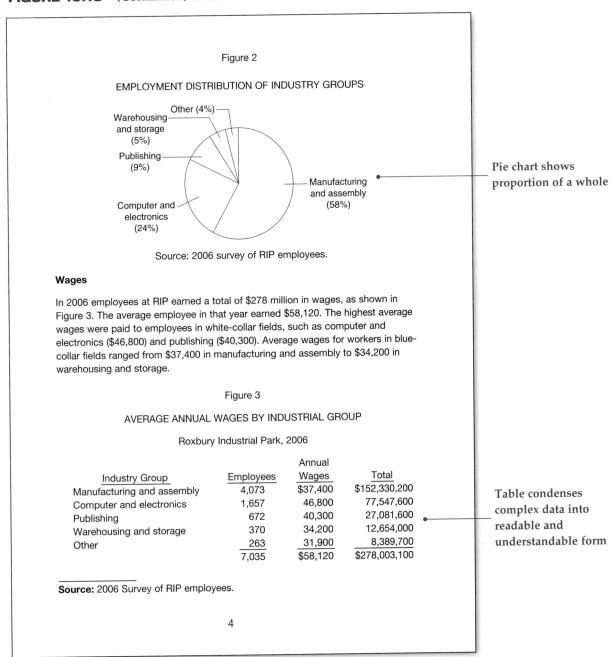

Figure 2

EMPLOYMENT DISTRIBUTION OF INDUSTRY GROUPS

Source: 2006 survey of RIP employees.

Pie chart shows proportion of a whole

Wages

In 2006 employees at RIP earned a total of $278 million in wages, as shown in Figure 3. The average employee in that year earned $58,120. The highest average wages were paid to employees in white-collar fields, such as computer and electronics ($46,800) and publishing ($40,300). Average wages for workers in blue-collar fields ranged from $37,400 in manufacturing and assembly to $34,200 in warehousing and storage.

Figure 3

AVERAGE ANNUAL WAGES BY INDUSTRIAL GROUP

Roxbury Industrial Park, 2006

Industry Group	Employees	Annual Wages	Total
Manufacturing and assembly	4,073	$37,400	$152,330,200
Computer and electronics	1,657	46,800	77,547,600
Publishing	672	40,300	27,081,600
Warehousing and storage	370	34,200	12,654,000
Other	263	31,900	8,389,700
	7,035	$58,120	$278,003,100

Table condenses complex data into readable and understandable form

Source: 2006 Survey of RIP employees.

4

If you use figures or tables, be sure to introduce them in the text (for example, *as shown below in Figure 3*). Although it's not always possible, try to place them close to the spot where they are first mentioned. To save space, you can print the title of a figure at its side. Because this report contains few tables and figures, the writer named them all "Figures" and numbered them consecutively.

FIGURE 10.15 (Continued) Discussion, Conclusions, and Recommendations

Clarifies information and explains what it means in relation to original research questions

Projections

By 2010 Roxbury Industrial Park is expected to more than double its number of employees, bringing the total to over 15,000 workers. The total payroll in 2007 will also more than double, producing over $450 million (using constant 2006 dollars) in salaries to RIP employees. These projections are based on an 8 percent growth rate, along with anticipated increased employment as the park reaches its capacity (Miller 78–79).

Future development in the park will influence employment and payrolls. As Ivan Novak, RIP project manager, stated in an interview, much of the remaining five hectares is planned for medium-rise office buildings, garden offices, and other structures for commercial, professional, and personal services (September 2006). Average wages for employees are expected to increase because of an anticipated shift to higher-paying white-collar jobs. Industrial parks often follow a similar pattern of evolution (Badri 38–45). Like many industrial parks, RIP evolved from a warehousing centre into a manufacturing complex.

Summarizes conclusions and recommendations

CONCLUSIONS AND RECOMMENDATIONS

Analysis of tax revenues, employment data, personal interviews, and professional literature leads to the following conclusions and recommendations about the economic impact of Roxbury Industrial Park on the City of Winnipeg:

1. Property tax and other revenues produced nearly $1 million in income to the city of Winnipeg in 2006. By 2010 revenues are expected to produce $1.7 million in city income.

2. RIP currently employs 7,035 employees, the majority of whom are working in manufacturing and assembly. The average employee in 2006 earned $38,120.

3. By 2010 RIP is expected to employ more than 15,000 workers producing a total payroll of over $450 million.

4. Employment trends indicate that by 2010 more RIP employees will be engaged in higher-paying white-collar positions.

On the basis of these findings, we recommend that the City Council of Winnipeg authorize the development of additional industrial parks to stimulate local economic growth.

5

After discussing and interpreting the research findings, the writer articulates what she considers the most important conclusions and recommendations. Longer, more complex reports may have separate sections for conclusions and resulting recommendations. In this report they are combined. Notice that it is unnecessary to start a new page for the conclusions.

FIGURE 10.15 (Continued) Works Cited

WORKS CITED

Badri, Mahmood A. "Infrastructure, Trends, and Economic Effects of Industrial
    Parks." *www.industryweek.com.* 1 Apr. 2000: 38–45. Retrieved 15 Dec. 2006.

City of Winnipeg Chief Financial Officer. *2006 Annual Report.* Retrieved 16 Jan. 2007
    <http://www.winnipeg.ca/interhom/departments/cfo/reports.stm>.

Miller, Arthur M. *Estimates of Revenues for Debt Service Coverage, Redevelop-
    ment Project Area No. 2.* Winnipeg, MB: Rincon Press, 2006.

Novak, Ivan M. E-mail interview. 30 Sept. 2006.

Arranges references in alphabetical order

Follows Modern Language Association documentation style

Summing Up and Looking Forward

Proposals are offers to solve problems, provide services, or sell equipment or goods. Both small and large businesses today write proposals to generate income. Informal proposals may be as short as two pages; formal proposals may be 200 pages or more. Regardless of the size, proposals contain standard parts that must be developed persuasively.

Formal reports present well-organized information systematically. The information may be collected from primary or secondary sources. All ideas borrowed from others must be documented. Good reports contain appropriate headings and illustrations.

Written reports are vital to decision makers. But oral reports can be equally important. In Chapters 11 and 12 you will learn how to organize and give oral presentations, as well as how to conduct meetings and communicate effectively on the telephone.

Critical Thinking

1. Why is the writing of proposals an important function in many businesses?
2. Discuss this statement, made by three well-known professional business writers: "Nothing you write will be completely new."[5]
3. Is information obtained on the Web as reliable as information obtained from journals, newspapers, and magazines? Explain.
4. Should all reports be written so that they follow the sequence of investigation—that is, description of the initial problem, analysis of issues, data collection, data analysis, and conclusions? Why or why not?
5. Distinguish between primary and secondary data. Which data are more likely to be useful in a business report?

6. What are the six principal parts of an informal proposal? Be prepared to explain each.

7. How are formal proposals different from informal proposals?

8. What is the first step in writing a formal report?

9. Do formal business reports generally rely more heavily on primary or secondary data?

10. List three sources of secondary information, and be prepared to discuss how valuable each might be in writing a formal report about updating your company's accounting procedures.

11. Define these terms: *browser, URL, search engine.*

12. List four levels of headings, and explain how they are different.

13. Pie charts are most helpful in showing what?

14. Line graphs are most effective in showing what?

15. List three reasons for documenting data in a business report.

16. List the parts of a formal report. Be prepared to discuss each.

17. Detecting and Eliminating Plagiarism. A student doing business research comes across the *Canadian Business* article reprinted in Chapter 9, page 243. She uses the article's second paragraph in a report. Below is an extract from her report. Identify where and why she has plagiarized and revise her report so that no plagiarism exists.

New Health Care Solutions

One of the most exciting business opportunities in the field of Health Care is the provision of private consulting services. For example, NavaHealth, a for-profit, privately owned company, leads B.C. residents through the labyrinthine health-care system by providing support and patient advocacy. The owner of this company has had to invest heavily, but she plans to make a profit in less than a year.

18. Detecting and Eliminating Plagiarism. A student doing business research comes across the *Toronto Star* article reprinted in Chapter 9, page 244. He uses the article's fifth paragraph in an essay. Below is an extract from his essay. Identify where and why he has plagiarized and revise his essay so that no plagiarism exists.

As mentioned earlier, one of the fringe benefits of a hot economy is the spin-off effects it creates. One of the spin-off effects of the hot Canadian economy, especially in places like Alberta, is the corporate housing market. A study released recently by Royal LePage Relocation Services states that this market was worth $230 million in Canada in 2004. Another spin-off of the hot economy is corporate travel, corporate retreats, and corporate entertaining, which I will discuss below.

Activities and Cases

10.1 Researching Secondary and Primary Data. In teams, discuss how you would collect information for each of the following report topics. Would your research be primary, secondary, or a combination of methods? What resources would be most useful—books, articles, the Web, interviewing?

a. The history of unions
b. Which public relations firm will best improve the image of a company so that its stock price increases
c. The cause of the high absenteeism in one department of a company
d. The latest Canadian Centre for Occupational Health and Safety (CCOHS) advice that might affect your small business
e. The traffic count at a possible location for a fast food restaurant
f. What the heads of three departments think about changing the official routine for developing each year's budget in your company
g. The costs and features of a new telephone/voice mail system for your company
h. How users are reacting to a new accounting software program recently released
i. How to meet international quality standards (ISO certification) so that you can sell your products in Europe

Team

10.2 Outlining. You work for a recruiting firm that helps businesses find candidates for jobs. Over the years, many clients have asked for suggestions on the best way to interview job candidates. Your supervisor asks you to write a short report on how to become a great interviewer. Here are some ideas you gathered from your own experience and that of other recruiters:

One of the most important qualities of a successful interview is efficient use of the interview time. Most businesspeople hate the hiring process because it interrupts their daily routine and throws off their schedules. But you have found that if you block out an afternoon or a whole day, you don't feel so frustrated. In addition, shutting out all interruptions and setting aside 45 minutes for each interview can also be helpful.

Interviewing is an inexact art because judging the talents and abilities of people is very subjective. To select the best candidate, you must begin with a list of all the job duties. Then you select the three duties with the highest priorities. Naturally, you would then ask questions to discover what candidate can perform those duties best.

Every interview should have objectives. What do you want to achieve? One of the most important goals is uncovering the experience that qualifies the candidate to do the job. Another important element is the correlation you see between the candidate and your company's values. A major final objective is selling the candidate on the opportunity with your company.

Your Task. Select the most important information and organize it into an outline such as that shown in Figure 10.2. You should have three main topics with three subdivisions under each. Assume that you would gather more information later. Add a title.

Team **10.3 Selecting Visual Aids.** In teams, identify the best visual aid (table, bar chart, line chart, pie chart, flow chart, organization chart) to illustrate the following data:

a. Instructions for workers telling them how to distinguish between worker accidents that must be reported to appropriate provincial agencies and those that need not be reported

b. Figures showing what proportion of every provincial tax dollar is spent on education, social services, health care, debt, and other expenses

c. Data showing the academic, administrative, and operation divisions of a college, from the president to department chairs and deans

d. Figures showing the operating profit of a company for the past five years

e. Figures comparing the sales of DVD players, flat-screen TVs, and personal computers for the past five years

f. Percentages showing the causes of forest fires (lightning, 73 percent; arson, 5 percent; campfires, 9 percent; and so on) in the Canadian Rockies

g. Figures comparing the cost of basic TV cable service in five areas of Canada for the past ten years (the boss wants to see exact figures)

10.4 Evaluating Visual Aids. From *Maclean's, Canadian Business, BusinessWeek The Economist*, or some other publication, locate one example each of a table, a pie chart, a line chart, a bar chart, and an organization chart. Bring copies of these visual aids to class. How effectively could the data have been expressed in words, without the graphics? Is the appropriate graphic form used? How is the graphic introduced in the text? Your instructor may ask you to submit a short e-mail recommendation report discussing how to improve visual aids.

10.5 Visual Aids in Annual Reports: How Do We Compare with the Best? You are the assistant to the director of investor relations at Canfinco, a large Canadian company. One of your important shareholders recently wrote a letter to the board of directors complaining about the quality of your annual reports, in particular the quality of the visual aids. Your boss, the director, is now worried about his job. He asks you to do some quick research on how to improve your company's annual report. You figure the best way to do this is to pick a few of Canada's top companies and comb through their annual reports, analyzing their use of visual aids. You choose Telus, Canadian Tire, and Loblaws for your research.

Your Task. Using the Web, find three recent annual reports published by Telus, Canadian Tire, and Loblaws. Read these reports and make notes as you go on the effectiveness of the visual aids and of graphics and layout in general. Critique the readability, clarity, and success in visualizing data of these reports. Are the aids introduced in the text? What similarities do you see among the three reports? E-mail your recommendation report to your boss.

Related Web site: Check out the Canadian Institute of Chartered Accountants (CICA) Web site describing the annual Corporate Reporting Awards it hands out for the best corporate annual reports in Canada. Of particular interest are the judging criteria and the examples of past winners: <www.cica.ca/index.cfm/ci_id/131/la_id/1.htm>.

10.6 Annotated Bibliography. Select a business topic or issue that interests you. Controversial or current topics will often work best for this type of exercise, because there will be a lot of information available. For example, the question of whether foreign companies should be allowed to buy Canadian natural resources companies is a current controversial question. In some parts of Canada, the question of whether mandatory retirement should be abolished is also a current topic. Imagine that you have been asked to write an essay, report, or article on the topic you've chosen. What will your next step be?

Your Task. Professional researchers begin the process of writing by compiling an annotated bibliography. This is a list of sources on the topic followed by an annotation, or brief summary. Using your library's online databases—*not* the Web— find five sources (two newspaper articles, two periodical articles, one other) that contain relevant information on your topic. Read each source and summarize it in 75 to 100 words. Compile an annotated bibliography in MLA style, with a citation of your source followed by a brief summary. Format the annotated bibliography as part of a memo you are sending to your instructor (e.g., "As you requested, below is my annotated bibliography on the topic of…").

10.7 Informal Proposal: Don't Give Up Your Day Job. As a struggling student, single parent, or budding entrepreneur, you decide to start your own part-time business (Web site design, word processing, or something similar). Select a company or professional in your city that might need your services. Assess your expertise and equipment. Check out the competition. What are competitors offering, and what do they charge?

Critical Thinking

Your Task. Prepare a letter proposal offering your services to a specific individual.

10.8 Informal Proposal: Student Views Consulting Inc. Imagine you are in your last semester of college or university. As part of your business program, there is a course you can take called "Consulting Business Simulation." This course allows students to simulate running a consulting business for a semester. You enroll in the course and on the first day of class the instructor says, "There's only one requirement in this course and it's worth 100 percent of your grade. You will design, conduct, and write a research proposal and project of your choice for this institution. You won't get paid for it, but you'll have gained a lot of experience that will look good on your résumé." You choose to work with two other students and you call yourselves Student Views Consulting Inc. You decide to tackle the problem of poor customer service at your institution.

Your Task. Write a proposal to the Director of Student Services at your college. Propose that your consulting firm carry out a detailed study on current student satisfaction at your institution, which you understand has been problematic lately. For example, there have been questions about how effectively telephone, e-mail, and in-person queries are being handled in various college departments and offices. Also, how the service level at your institution compares to that of competing institutions in the same area has been questioned. Describe the background of this problem and draft a schedule of the work to be done. Cost out this research realistically. When it comes to describing the prior work of Student Views Consulting Inc., make up a realistic list of prior work. Format this proposal as a letter to the Director of Student Services.

Critical Thinking

10.9 Formal Report: Readability of Insurance Policies. The 21st Century Insurance Company is concerned about the readability of its policies. Consumers are complaining they can't understand their insurance policies. As part of its quality assurance program, 21st Century hires you as a consultant to study its standard policy and make recommendations.

Examine a life, home, or extended health insurance policy that you or a friend or relative holds. Study the policy for jargon, confusing language, long sentences, and unclear antecedents. Evaluate its format, print size, paper and print quality, amount of white space, and use of headings. Does it have an index or glossary? Are difficult terms defined? How easy is it to find specifics, should a policyholder want to check something?

In addition to the data you collect from your own examination of the policy, 21st Century gives you the following data from a recent policyholder survey:

Response to statement: "I am able to read and understand the language and provisions of my policy."

Age Group	Strongly Agree	Agree	Undecided	Disagree	Strongly Disagree
18–34	2%	9%	34%	41%	14%
35–49	2	17	38	33	10
50–64	1	11	22	35	31
65+	1	2	17	47	33

Your Task. Prepare a report for Heather St. Amant, Vice-President, 21st Century Insurance Company, discussing your analysis, conclusions, and recommendations for improving its basic policy.

Related Web site: For background information on this topic go directly to the Task Force on the Future of the Canadian Financial Services Sector's report at <http://finservtaskforce.fin.gc.ca/research/pdf/RR8_V1b_e.pdf>.

10.10 Formal Report: Quick Service Restaurant Checkup. The national franchising headquarters for a quick service chain has received complaints about the service, quality, and cleanliness of one of its restaurants in your area. You have been sent to inspect and to report on what you see.

Your Task. Select a quick service restaurant in your area. Visit on two or more occasions. Make notes about how many customers were served, how quickly they received their food, and how courteously they were treated. Observe the number of employees and supervisors working. Note the cleanliness of observable parts of the restaurant. Inspect the washroom as well as the exterior and surrounding grounds. Sample the food. Your boss is a stickler for details; he has no use for general statements like *The washroom was not clean*. Be specific. Draw conclusions. Are the complaints justified? If improvements are necessary, make recommendations. Address your report to Lawrence C. Shymko, President.

10.11 Formal Report: Consumer Product Investigation. Study a consumer product that you might consider buying. Are you (or your family) interested in purchasing a DVD player, computer, digital camera, iPOD, microwave, car, van, camcorder, or some other product? Your investigation should include primary data collected from interviews with users, owners, salespersons, service technicians, and so forth. You'll also find rich resources on the Web and in sales brochures and pamphlets. Conduct secondary research by studying (and citing) magazine articles in such publications as *Consumer Reports*. Be sure to narrow your topic by setting boundaries to your search. For example, are you interested in an economy van with good mileage that will be driven 80 kilometres daily? Are you in the market for an economical auto-focus camera?

Your Task. In your report include an introduction that discusses why you selected this product and for whom it is intended (for example, a DVD player for a middle-class family who would use it primarily for watching rented DVDs). Perhaps provide some background data about the product gleaned from your reading. In the *Discussion* section you might discuss such topics as price, warranty, specific features, and service reputation. Draw conclusions from your data, and make a recommendation. Address the report to your instructor. Your instructor may ask your class to work in pairs on this project.

10.12 Formal Report: Communication Skills on the Job. Collect information regarding communication skills used by individuals in a particular career field (accounting, management, marketing, office administration, paralegal, and so forth). Interview three or more individuals in a specific occupation in that field. Determine how much and what kind of writing they do. Do they make oral presentations? Do they use PowerPoint? If so, what do they think of its effectiveness? How much time do they spend in telephone communication? How often do they use e-mail? For what? Do they have a PDA? Do they find themselves communicating more or less than in past years? Are they happy or unhappy about the amount of communicating they have to do? What recommendations do they have for training for this position?

Your Task. Write a report that discusses the findings from your interviews. What conclusions can you draw regarding communication skills in this field? What recommendations would you make for individuals entering this field? Your instructor may ask you to research the perception of businesspeople over the past ten years regarding the communication skills of employees. To gather such data, conduct library or online database research.

10.13 Informal Proposal: Setting Up a Web site. As a consultant, you have been asked to investigate the cost of setting up a Web site for Arni Arason, who owns a small wine distribution business in Stratford, Ontario, named Fruit of the Gods Inc. He hopes to begin with a simple, basic Web site, but he wants it to be user friendly, and he wants customers to be able to buy wine from the site with a credit card.

Web

Critical Thinking

Your Task. Use search engines on the Internet to locate information. Try "Web site development" as a search term. Visit several sites that offer to build Web sites. Focus on those that seem most professional. Look to see when the site was last updated. Read the promotional material and decide whether it is well written. Remember, anyone can post a Web site. Investigate the general characteristics of

Activities and Cases

a Web site, how to create and promote a site, and how to maintain a Web server. Mr. Arason wants a low-cost but high-quality site. Develop cost figures. Draw conclusions and make recommendations in a letter proposal to Mr. Arason.

Related Web site: The Ontario Imported Wine-Spirit Beer Association, which Arni Arason hopes to join soon, has background information about the wine distribution business: <www.oiwsba.com>.

10.14 Formal Report: Selecting a Location for a Satellite Campus. The college or university you attend has recently been experiencing unprecedented growth. Student enrollment has been up for five years in a row, research and donation money has been on the increase, and the number of international students applying for admission is also up. The board of directors has asked the director of development to look into the idea of planning a small satellite campus in an outlying area of the city. The question is, where to locate the satellite?

Your Task. Using your own college or university as the example for this report, research and write a formal report offering a recommendation about where to locate a satellite campus. What components (e.g., locations) will you choose to structure your report? What criteria would be important to the board of directors? Price of land? Proximity to public transportation? Proximity to other institutions? Proximity to large population base? Where will you find data on these criteria?

Grammar/Mechanics Review—10

The following sentences contain errors in grammar, punctuation, capitalization, number style, usage, and spelling. Below each sentence write a corrected version.

1. Each of our applicants are rated on the following factors; skills, experience, education, and people skills.

2. Although Bianca and him agreed to pay two months rent in advance the landlord refused to rent to them.

3. The nations airlines threatened to stop service on Monday at 5 p.m..

4. Our 3 top sales reps, Lucinda, Rafael, and Alasie—received cash bonus's of one thousand dollars each.

5. Did we send 2 copies of the proposal to SuperCom, Inc?

6. If you were me would you step into the managers shoes at this time.

7. Anji wondered whether all two hundred of our brochures would be delivered within the 2 week mailing period?

8. A complete glossary of terms, see page 200 are available to help readers' understand difficult terms.

9. In Globe and Mail you will find an article titled The Blossoming of Internet Chat, however we could not locate it online.

10. Mr Ferranto, Ms Toney, and Miss Cabot has each recieved a new computer.

11. (Direct quotation) The teacher said, A clear conscious is usually the sign of a bad memory.

12. Would you please send me this years rankings of all your stock funds?

13. A host of ethical issues surround business including economic justice, corporate morality and whistleblowing.

14. Greenshield Investments developed it's own code of ethics however its difficult to inforce such a code.

15. For those whom are interested the online version of Canadian News and World Reports university rankings are now available.

Grammar/Mechanics Challenge—10

Document for Revision

The following report executive summary has faults in grammar, punctuation, spelling, number form, wordiness, and word use. Use standard proofreading marks (see Appendix B) to correct the errors. When you finish, your instructor can show you the revised version of this summary.

EXECUTIVE SUMMARY

Problem

The Canadian salmon industry must expand it's markets abroad particularly in regard to Japan. Although consumption of salmon is decreasing in Canada they are increasing in Japan. The problem that is for the canadian salmon industry is developing apropriate marketing strategies to boost its current sale in Japanese markets.

Summary of Findings

This report analyzes the Japanese market which currently consumes six hundred thousand tons of salmon per year, and is growing rapidly. Much of this salmon is supplied by imports which at this point in time total about 35% of sales. Our findings indicate that not only will this expand, but the share of imports will continue to grow. The trend is alarming to Japanese salmon industry leaders, because this important market, close to a $billion a year, is increasingly subject to the influence of foreign imports. Declining catches by Japans own Salmon fleet as well as a sharp upward turn in food preference by affluent Japanese consumers, has contributed to this trend.

Recommendations

Based on our analisys we reccommend the following 5 marketing strategys for the Canadian Salmon industry.

1. Farm greater supplys of atlantic farmed salmon to export.

2. We should market our own value added products.

3. Sell fresh salmon direct to the Tokyo Central Wholesale market.

4. Sell to other Japanese markets also.

5. Direct sales should be made to Japanese Supermarket chains.

Web Evaluation: Hoax? Scholarly Research? Advocacy?

Most of us tend to think that any information turned up via a Web search engine has somehow been evaluated as part of a valid selection process.[6] Not true. The truth is that the Internet is rampant with unreliable sites that reside side by side with reputable sites. Anyone with a computer and an Internet connection can publish anything on the Web.

Unlike library-based research, information at many sites has not undergone the editing or scrutiny of scholarly publication procedures. The information we read in journals and most reputable magazines is reviewed, authenticated, and evaluated. That's why we have learned to trust these sources as valid and authoritative. But information on the Web is much less reliable. Some sites are obvious hoaxes. Others exist to distribute propaganda. Still others want to sell you something. To use the Web meaningfully, you must scrutinize what you find. Here are specific questions to ask as you examine a site:

- **Currency.** What is the date of the Web page? When was it last updated? Is some of the information obviously out of date? If the information is time sensitive and the site has not been updated recently, the site is probably not reliable.
- **Authority.** Who publishes or sponsors this Web page? What makes the presenter an authority? Is a contact address available for the presenter? Learn to be skeptical about data and assertions from individuals whose credentials are not verifiable.
- **Content.** Is the purpose of the page to entertain, inform, convince, or sell? Who is the intended audience, judging from content, tone, and style? Can you assess the overall value of the content compared with that of the other resources on this topic? Web presenters with a skewed point of view cannot be counted on for objective data.
- **Accuracy.** Do the facts that are presented seem reliable to you? Do you find errors in spelling, grammar, or usage? Do you see any evidence of bias? Are footnotes provided? If you find numerous errors and if facts are not referenced, you should be alert that the data may be questionable.

For more information on evaluating Web sites, check out the University of California at Berkeley's excellent Web site, <www.lib.berkeley.edu/TeachingLib/Guides/Internet/FindInfo.html#Outline>. Of particular interest is the "Evaluating Web Pages: Why and How" link.

Career Application

Your supervisor wants to see how good your Web assessment skills are. You've been asked to conduct research at three of the following sites:

www.edmunds.com

www.canada.com

www.buydehydratedwater.com

www.workplace.ca

Your Task

Answer the following questions:

- What evidence can you find to determine whether these sites represent hoaxes, personal opinion, or reliable information?
- Are the sources for factual information clearly listed so that they can be verified?
- Can you tell who publishes or sponsors the page?
- Are the organization's biases clearly stated?
- Is advertising clearly differentiated from informational content?
- Would you use these sites for scholarly research? Why or why not?

Developing Speaking Skills

11

CHAPTER

Communicating in Person, by Telephone, and in Meetings

Before meeting with clients, I gather as much information as possible. The more information, the better prepared I can be to meet their needs. Preparation is key for any meeting. It's important to meet face-to-face with my clients to get to know them on a personal level. In our meetings, we work together to establish client goals, plan for future needs, and monitor client progress.[1]

Orna Spira, *investment advisor, CIBC Wood Gundy*

LEARNING OBJECTIVES

1. Understand how to improve face-to-face workplace communication including using your voice as a communication tool.

2. Specify procedures for promoting positive workplace relations through conversation.

3. Review techniques for offering constructive criticism on the job, responding professionally to workplace criticism, and resolving workplace conflicts.

4. Identify ways to polish professional telephone skills, including traditional phones and cell phones.

5. List techniques for making the best use of voice mail.

6. Follow procedures for planning and participating in productive business and professional meetings.

✔ *Quick Check*

Strong oral communication skills can help you be hired and succeed on the job.

O ral communication skills consistently rank near the top of competencies valued by employers. Companies are looking for employees who can interact successfully with customers, work smoothly with coworkers, and provide meaningful feedback to managers. Expressing yourself well and communicating effectively with others are skills that are critical to job placement, workplace performance, career advancement, and organizational success.

Earlier in this book you studied the communication process, effective listening techniques, and nonverbal communication skills. Intervening chapters helped you develop good writing skills. The next two chapters will round out your communication expertise by focusing on oral communication skills. In your business or professional career, you will be judged not only by what you say but also by the way you say it. In this chapter we'll help you become a more successful speaker when you communicate in person, by telephone, and in meetings.

Because technology provides many alternate communication channels, you may think that face-to-face communication is no longer essential or even important in business and professional transactions. You've already learned that e-mail is now the preferred communication channel because it is faster, cheaper, and easier than telephone, mail, or fax. Yet, despite their popularity and acceptance, alternate communication technologies can't replace the richness or effectiveness of face-to-face communication.[2] Imagine that you want to tell your boss how you solved a problem. Would you settle for a one-dimensional phone call, a fax, or an e-mail when you could step into her office and explain in person?

Face-to-face conversation has many advantages. It allows you to be persuasive and expressive because you can use your voice and body language to make a point. You are less likely to be misunderstood because you can read feedback and make needed adjustments. In conflict resolution, you can reach a solution more efficiently and cooperate to create greater levels of mutual benefit when communicating face to face.[3] Moreover, people want to see each other to satisfy a deep human need for social interaction. For numerous reasons, communicating in person remains the most effective of all communication channels. In this chapter you'll explore helpful business and professional interpersonal speaking techniques, starting with viewing your voice as a communication tool.

✓ Quick Check

One-dimensional communication technologies cannot replace the richness or effectiveness of face-to-face communication.

Using Your Voice as a Communication Tool

It's been said that language provides the words, but your voice is the music that makes words meaningful.[4] You may believe that a beautiful or powerful voice is unattainable. After all, this is the voice you were born with, and it can't be changed. Actually, the voice is a flexible instrument. Actors hire coaches to help them eliminate or acquire accents or proper inflection for challenging roles. For example, two of Canada's leading theatre companies, the Stratford and Shaw festivals in Ontario, both have speech coaches on staff to teach actors various accents and voice techniques. Celebrities, business executives, and everyday people consult voice and speech therapists to help them shake bad habits or help them speak so that they can be understood and not sound less intelligent than they are. Rather than consult a high-paid specialist, you can pick up useful tips for using your voice most effectively by learning how to control such elements as pronunciation, tone, pitch, volume, rate, and emphasis.

✓ Quick Check

Like an actor, you can change your voice to make it a more powerful communication tool.

Pronunciation. Pronunciation involves saying words correctly and clearly with the accepted sounds and accented syllables. You'll be at a distinct advantage in your job if, through training and practice, you learn to pronounce words correctly. Some of the most common errors, shown in Figure 11.1 (p. 300), include adding or omitting vowels, omitting consonants, reversing sounds, and slurring sounds. In casual conversation with your friends, correct pronunciation is not a big deal. But on the job you want to sound intelligent, educated, and competent. If you mispronounce words or slur phrases together, you risk being misunderstood as well as giving a poor impression of yourself. How can you improve your pronunciation skills? The best way is to listen carefully to educated people, read aloud from well-written newspapers like *The Globe and Mail* and the *National Post*, look up words in the dictionary, and avoid errors such as those in Figure 11.1.

✓ Quick Check

Proper pronunciation means saying words correctly and clearly with the accepted sounds and accented syllables.

Tone. The tone of your voice sends a nonverbal message to listeners. It identifies your personality and your mood. Some voices sound enthusiastic and friendly, conveying the impression of an upbeat person who is happy to be with the listener. But voices can also sound controlling, patronizing, slow-witted, angry, or childish. This doesn't mean that the speaker necessarily has that attribute. It may

FIGURE 11.1   Pronunciation Errors to Avoid

Adding vowel sounds	*athlete* (NOT *ath-a-lete*)
	disastrous (NOT *disas-ter-ous*)
Omitting vowel sounds	*federal* (NOT *fed-ral*)
	ridiculous (NOT *ri-dic-lous*)
	generally (NOT *gen-rally*)
Substituting vowel sounds	*get* (NOT *git*)
	separate (NOT *sep-e-rate*)
Adding consonant sounds	*butter* (NOT *budder*)
	statistics (NOT *sta-stis-tics*)
	especially (NOT *ex-specially*)
Omitting consonant sounds	*library* (NOT *libery*)
	perhaps (NOT *praps*)
Confusing or distorting sounds	*ask* (NOT *aks*)
	hundred (NOT *hunderd*)
	accessory (NOT *assessory*)
Slurring sounds	*didn't you* (NOT *dint ya*)
	going to (NOT *gonna*)

mean that the speaker is merely carrying on a family tradition or pattern learned in childhood. To check your voice tone, record your voice and listen to it critically. Is it projecting a positive quality about you?

Pitch. Effective speakers use a relaxed, controlled, well-pitched voice to attract listeners to their message. Pitch refers to sound vibration frequency; that is, it indicates the highness or lowness of a sound. In Canada, speakers and listeners prefer a variety of pitch patterns. Voices are most attractive when they rise and fall in conversational tones. Flat, monotone voices are considered boring and ineffectual. In business, communicators strive for a moderately low voice, which is thought to be pleasing and professional.

Volume and Rate. Volume indicates the degree of loudness or the intensity of sound. Just as you adjust the volume on your radio or television, you should adjust the volume of your speaking to the occasion and your listeners. When speaking face to face, you generally know whether you are speaking too loudly or softly by looking at your listeners. Are they straining to hear you? To judge what volume to use, listen carefully to the other person's voice. Use it as a guide for adjusting your voice. Rate refers to the pace of your speech. If you speak too slowly, listeners are bored and their attention wanders. If you speak too quickly, listeners can't understand you. Most people normally talk at about 125 words a minute. If you're the kind of speaker who speeds up when talking in front of a group of people, monitor the nonverbal signs of your listeners and adjust your rate as needed.

Emphasis. By emphasizing or stressing certain words, you can change the meaning you are expressing. For example, read these sentences aloud, emphasizing the italicized words:

Matt said the hard drive failed again. (Matt knows what happened.)
Matt *said* the hard drive failed again. (But he may be wrong.)
Matt said the hard drive failed *again*? (Did he really say that?)

Quick Check

Speaking in a moderately low-pitched voice at about 125 words a minute makes you sound pleasing and professional.

As you can see, emphasis affects the meaning of the words and the thought expressed. To make your message interesting and natural, use emphasis appropriately. You can raise your volume to sound authoritative and raise your pitch to sound disbelieving. Lowering your volume and pitch makes you sound professional or reasonable.

Some speakers today are prone to "uptalk." This is a habit of using a rising inflection at the end of a sentence resulting in a singsong pattern that makes statements sound like questions. Once used exclusively by teenagers, uptalk is increasingly found in the workplace, with negative results. When statements sound like questions, speakers seem weak and tentative. Their messages lack conviction and authority. On the job, managers afflicted by uptalk may have difficulty convincing staff members to follow directions because their voice inflection implies that other valid options are available. If you want to sound confident and competent, avoid uptalk.

Promoting Positive Workplace Relations Through Conversation

In the workplace, conversations may involve giving and taking instructions, providing feedback, exchanging ideas on products and services, participating in performance appraisals, or engaging in small talk about such things as families and sports. Face-to-face conversation helps people work together harmoniously and feel that they are part of the larger organization. There are several guidelines, starting with using correct names and titles, that promote positive workplace conversations.

Use Correct Names and Titles. Although the world seems increasingly informal, it's still wise to use titles and last names when addressing professional adults (*Mrs. Smith, Mr. Rivera*). In some organizations senior staff members will speak to junior employees on a first-name basis, but the reverse may not be encouraged. Probably the safest plan is to ask your superiors how they want to be addressed. Customers and others outside the organization should always be addressed by title and last name.

When you meet strangers, do you have trouble remembering their names? You can improve your memory considerably if you associate the person with an object, place, colour, animal, job, adjective, or some other memory hook. For example,

"I had to spend the money I budgeted for your raise on a therapist after listening to your endless complaining."

© Ted Goff (www.tedgoff.com)

computer pro Kevin, Miami Kim, silver-haired Mr. Lee, bull-dog Chris, bookkeeper Lynn, traveller Ms. Janis. The person's name will also be more deeply imbedded in your memory if you use it immediately after being introduced, in subsequent conversation, and when you part.

Choose Appropriate Topics. In some workplace activities, such as social gatherings or interviews, you will be expected to engage in small talk. Be sure to stay away from controversial topics with someone you don't know very well. Avoid politics, religion, or current event items that can start heated arguments until you know the person better. To initiate appropriate conversations, read newspapers and listen to radio and TV shows discussing current events. Make a mental note of items that you can use in conversation, taking care to remember where you saw or heard the news items so that you can report accurately and authoritatively. Try not to be defensive or annoyed if others present information that upsets you.

Avoid Negative Remarks. Workplace conversations are not the place to complain about your colleagues, your friends, the organization, or your job. No one enjoys listening to whiners. And your criticism of others may come back to haunt you. A snipe at your boss or a complaint about a fellow worker may reach him or her, sometimes embellished or distorted with meanings you did not intend. Be circumspect in all negative judgments. Remember, some people love to repeat statements that will stir up trouble or set off internal workplace wars. It's best not to give them the ammunition.

Listen to Learn. In conversations with colleagues, subordinates, and customers, train yourself to expect to learn something from what you are hearing. Being attentive is not only instructive but also courteous. Beyond displaying good manners, you'll probably find that your conversation partner has information that you don't have. Being receptive and listening with an open mind means not interrupting or prejudging. Let's say you very much want to be able to work at home for part of your workweek. You try to explain your ideas to your boss, but he cuts you off shortly after you start. He says, "It's out of the question; we need you here every day." Suppose instead he says, "I have strong reservations about your telecommuting, but maybe you'll change my mind"; and he settles in to listen to your presentation. Even if your boss decides against your request, you will feel that your ideas were heard and respected.

Give Sincere and Specific Praise. A wise person once said, "Man does not live by bread alone. He needs to be buttered up once in a while." Probably nothing promotes positive workplace relationships better than sincere and specific praise. Whether the compliments and appreciation are travelling upward to management, downward to workers, or horizontally to colleagues, everyone responds well to recognition. Organizations run more smoothly and morale is higher when people feel appreciated. In your workplace conversations, look for ways to recognize good work and good people. And try to be specific. Instead of "You did a good job in leading that meeting," try something more specific, such as "Your leadership skills certainly kept that meeting short, focused, and productive."

Offering Constructive Criticism on the Job

No one likes to receive criticism, and most of us don't like to give it either. But in the workplace cooperative endeavours demand feedback and evaluation. How are we doing on a project? What went well? What failed? How can we improve our efforts? Today's workplace often involves team projects. As a team member, you will be called on to judge the work of others. In addition to working on teams, you can also expect to become a supervisor or manager one day. As such, you will need to evaluate subordinates. Good employees seek good feedback from their

Quick Check

You will be most effective in workplace conversations if you use correct names and titles, choose appropriate topics, avoid negative and judgmental remarks, and give sincere and specific praise.

supervisors. They want and need timely, detailed observations about their work to reinforce what they do well and help them overcome weak spots. But making that feedback palatable and constructive is not always easy. Depending on your situation, you may find some or all of the following suggestions helpful when you must deliver constructive criticism:

- **Mentally outline your conversation.** Think carefully about what you want to accomplish and what you will say. Find the right words at the right time and in the right setting.
- **Generally, use face-to-face communication.** Most constructive criticism is better delivered in person rather than in e-mail messages or memos. Personal feedback offers an opportunity for the listener to ask questions and give explanations. Occasionally, however, complex situations may require a different strategy. You might prefer to write out your opinions and deliver them by telephone or in writing. A written document enables you to organize your thoughts, include all the details, and be sure of keeping your cool. Remember, though, that written documents create permanent records—for better or worse.
- **Focus on improvement.** Instead of attacking, use language that offers alternative behaviour. Use phrases such as "Next time, you could . . . ."
- **Offer to help.** Criticism is accepted more readily if you volunteer to help in eliminating or solving the problem.
- **Be specific.** Instead of a vague assertion such as "Your work is often late," be more specific: "The specs on the Riverside job were due Thursday at 5 p.m., and you didn't hand them in until Friday." Explain how the person's performance jeopardized the entire project.
- **Avoid broad generalizations.** Don't use words such as *should, never, always,* and other encompassing expressions as they may cause the listener to shut down and become defensive.
- **Discuss the behaviour, not the person.** Instead of "You seem to think you can come to work any time you want," focus on the behaviour: "Coming to work late means that we have to fill in with someone else until you arrive."
- **Use the word *we* rather than *you*.** "We need to meet project deadlines," is better than saying "You need to meet project deadlines." Emphasize organizational expectations rather than personal ones. Avoid sounding accusatory.
- **Encourage two-way communication.** Even if well-planned, criticism is still hard to deliver. It may surprise or hurt the feelings of the employee. Consider ending your message with, "It can be hard to hear this type of feedback. If you would like to share your thoughts, I'm listening."
- **Avoid anger, sarcasm, and a raised voice.** Criticism is rarely constructive when tempers flare. Plan in advance what you will say and deliver it in low, controlled, and sincere tones.
- **Keep it private.** Offer praise in public; offer criticism in private. "Setting an example" through public criticism is never a wise management policy.

Quick Check

Offering constructive criticism is easier if you plan what you will say, focus on improvement, offer to help, be specific, discuss the behaviour and not the person, speak privately face to face, and avoid anger.

Responding Professionally to Workplace Criticism

As much as we hate giving criticism, we dislike receiving it even more. Yet, the workplace requires that you not only provide it but also be able to accept it. When being criticized, you probably will feel that you are being attacked. You can't just sit back and relax. Your heart beats faster, your temperature shoots up, your face reddens, and you respond with the classic "fight or flight" syndrome. You feel that you want to instantly retaliate or escape from the attacker. But focusing on your feelings distracts you from hearing the content of what is being said, and it prevents you from responding professionally. Some or all of the following suggestions will guide you in reacting positively to criticism so that you can benefit from it:

Improving Face-to-Face Workplace Communication

Quick Check

When being criticized, you should listen, paraphrase, and clarify what is said; if you agree, apologize or explain what you will do differently.

- **Listen without interrupting.** Even though you might want to protest, make yourself hear the speaker out.
- **Determine the speaker's intent.** Unskilled communicators may throw "verbal bricks" with unintended negative-sounding expressions. If you think the intent is positive, focus on what is being said rather than reacting to poorly chosen words.
- **Acknowledge what you are hearing.** Respond with a pause, a nod, or a neutral statement such as "I understand you have a concern." This buys you time. Do not disagree, counterattack, or blame, which may escalate the situation and harden the speaker's position.
- **Paraphrase what was said.** In your own words restate objectively what you are hearing; for example, "So what you're saying is ..."
- **Ask for more information if necessary.** Clarify what is being said. Stay focused on the main idea rather than interjecting side issues.
- **Agree—if the comments are accurate.** If an apology is in order, give it. Explain what you plan to do differently. If the criticism is on target, the sooner you agree, the more likely you will engender respect from the other person.

Quick Check

If you feel you are being criticized unfairly, disagree respectfully and constructively; look for a middle position.

- **Disagree respectfully and constructively—if you feel the comments are unfair.** After hearing the criticism, you might say, "May I tell you my perspective?" Or you could try to solve the problem by saying, "How can we improve this situation in a way you believe we can both accept?" If the other person continues to criticize, say "I want to find a way to resolve your concern. When do you want to talk about it next?"
- **Look for a middle position.** Search for a middle position or a compromise. Be genial even if you don't like the person or the situation.

Resolving Workplace Conflicts

Conflict is a normal part of every workplace, but it is not always negative. When managed properly, conflict can improve decision making, clarify values, increase group cohesiveness, stimulate creativity, decrease tensions, and reduce dissatisfaction. Unresolved conflict, however, can destroy productivity and seriously reduce morale. You will be better prepared to resolve workplace conflict if you know the five most common response patterns as well as a six-step procedure for dealing with conflict.

Common Conflict Response Patterns. Imagine a time when you were very upset with a workplace colleague, boss, or a teammate. How did you respond? Experts who have studied conflict say that most of us deal with it in one of the following predictable patterns:

Quick Check

Although avoidance does not solve conflicts, it may be the best response for some situations, such as when the issue is trivial.

- **Avoidance/withdrawal.** Instead of trying to resolve the conflict, one person or the other simply withdraws. Avoidance of conflict generally results in a "lose–lose" situation because the problem festers and no attempt is made to understand the issues causing the conflict. On the other hand, avoidance may be the best response when the issue is trivial, when potential losses from an open conflict outweigh potential gains, or when insufficient time is available to work through the issue adequately.
- **Accommodation/smoothing.** When one person gives in quickly, the conflict is smoothed over and surface harmony results. This may be the best method when the issue is minor, when damage to the relationship would harm both parties, and when tempers are too hot for productive discussion.
- **Compromise.** In this pattern both people give up something of lesser importance to gain something more important. Compromise may be the best approach when both parties stand to gain, when a predetermined "ideal" solution is not required, and when time is short.

- **Competition/forcing.** This approach results in a contest in which one person comes out on top, leaving the other with a sense of failure. This method ends the conflict, but it may result in hurt feelings and potential future problems from the loser. This strategy is appropriate when a decision or action must be immediate and when the parties recognize the power relationship between themselves.
- **Collaboration/problem solving.** In this pattern both parties lay their cards on the table and attempt to reach consensus. This approach works when the involved people have common goals but they disagree over how to reach them. Conflict may arise from misunderstanding or a communication breakdown. Collaboration works best when all parties are trained in problem-solving techniques.[5]

Six-Step Procedure for Dealing with Conflict. Probably the best pattern for resolving conflicts entails collaboration and problem-solving procedures. But this method requires a certain amount of training. Fortunately, experts in the field of negotiation have developed a six-step pattern that you can try the next time you need to resolve a conflict:

1. **Listen.** To be sure you understand the problem, listen carefully. If the other person doesn't seem to be listening to you, you need to set the example and be the first to listen.
2. **Understand the other point of view.** Once you listen, it's much easier to understand the other's position. Show your understanding by asking questions and paraphrasing. This will also verify what you think the other person means.
3. **Show a concern for the relationship.** By focusing on the problem, not the person, you can build, maintain, and even improve relationships. Show an understanding of the other person's situation and needs. Show an overall willingness to come to an agreement.
4. **Look for common ground.** Identify your interests and help the other side to identify its interests. Learn what you have in common, and look for a solution to which both sides can agree.
5. **Invent new problem-solving options.** Spend time identifying the interests of both sides. Then brainstorm to invent new ways to solve the problem. Be open to new options.
6. **Reach an agreement based on what's fair.** Seek to determine a standard of fairness that is acceptable to both sides. Then weigh the possible solutions, and choose the best option.[6]

Polishing Your Professional Telephone and Voice Mail Skills

The telephone is the most universal—and, some would say, the most important—piece of equipment in offices today.[7] For many businesspeople, it is a primary contact with the outside world. Some observers predicted that e-mail and faxes would "kill off phone calls."[8] In fact, the amazing expansion of wireless communication has given the telephone a new and vigorous lease on life. Telephones are definitely here to stay. But many of us do not use them efficiently or effectively. In this chapter we'll focus on traditional telephone techniques as well as voice mail efficiency.

Making Productive Telephone Calls

Before making a telephone call, decide whether the intended call is necessary. Could you find the information yourself? If you wait a while, would the problem resolve itself? Perhaps your message could be delivered more efficiently by some other means. One U.S. company found that telephone interruptions consumed about 18 percent of staff members' workdays. Another study found that two-thirds of all calls were less important than the work they interrupted.[9] Alternatives to telephone calls include e-mail, memos, or calls to voice mail systems. If a telephone call must be made, consider using the following suggestions to make it fully productive.

- **Plan a mini-agenda.** Have you ever been embarrassed when you had to make a second telephone call because you forgot an important item the first time? Before placing a call, jot down notes regarding all the topics you need to discuss. Following an agenda guarantees not only a complete call but also a quick one. You'll be less likely to wander from the business at hand while rummaging through your mind trying to remember everything.
- **Use a three-point introduction.** When placing a call, immediately (1) name the person you are calling, (2) identify yourself and your affiliation, and (3) give a brief explanation of your reason for calling. For example: "May I speak to Larry Levin? This is Hillary Dahl of Acme Ltd., and I'm seeking information about a software program called Power Presentations." This kind of introduction enables the receiving individual to respond immediately without asking further questions.
- **Be brisk if you are rushed.** For business calls when your time is limited, avoid questions such as "How are you?" Instead, say, "Lisa, I knew you'd be the only one who could answer these two questions for me." Another efficient strategy is to set a "contract" with the caller: "Hi, Lisa, I have only ten minutes, but I really wanted to get back to you."
- **Be cheerful and accurate.** Let your voice show the same kind of animation that you radiate when you greet people in person. In your mind try to envision the individual answering the telephone. A smile can certainly affect the tone of your voice, so smile at that person. Moreover, be accurate about what you say. "Hang on a second; I'll be right back" rarely is true. Better to say, "It may take me two or three minutes to get that information. Would you prefer to hold or have me call you back?"
- **Bring it to a close.** The responsibility for ending a call lies with the caller. This is sometimes difficult to do if the other person rambles on. You may need to use suggestive closing language, such as "I've certainly enjoyed talking with you," "I've learned what I needed to know, and now I can proceed with my work," "Thanks for your help," or "I must go now, but may I call you again in the future if I need . . . ?"
- **Avoid telephone tag.** If you call someone who's not in, ask when it would be best for you to call again. State that you will call at a specific time—and do it. If you ask a person to call you, give a time when you can be reached—and then be sure you are in at that time.
- **Leave complete voice mail messages.** Remember that there's no rush when you leave a voice mail message. Always enunciate clearly. And be sure to provide a complete message, including your name, telephone number, and the time and date of your call. Explain your purpose so that the receiver can be ready with the required information when returning your call.

Receiving Productive Telephone Calls

With a little forethought you can make your telephone a productive, efficient work tool. Developing good telephone manners also reflects well on you and on your organization.

- **Identify yourself immediately.** In answering your telephone or someone else's, provide your name, title or affiliation, and, possibly, a greeting. For

Quick Check

You can make productive telephone calls by planning an agenda, identifying the purpose, being courteous and cheerful, and avoiding rambling.

example, "Larry Levin, Proteus Software. How may I help you?" Force yourself to speak clearly and slowly. Remember that the caller may be unfamiliar with what you are saying and fail to recognize slurred syllables.

- **Be responsive and helpful.** If you are in a support role, be sympathetic to callers' needs. Instead of "I don't know," try "That's a good question; let me investigate." Instead of "We can't do that," try "That's a tough one; let's see what we can do." Avoid "No" at the beginning of a sentence. It sounds especially abrasive and displeasing because it suggests total rejection.
- **Be cautious when answering calls for others.** Be courteous and helpful, but don't give out confidential information. Better to say, "She's away from her desk" or "He's out of the office" than to report a colleague's exact whereabouts.
- **Take messages carefully.** Few things are as frustrating as receiving a potentially important phone message that is illegible. Repeat the spelling of names and verify telephone numbers. Write messages legibly and record their time and date. Promise to give the messages to intended recipients, but don't guarantee return calls.
- **Explain what you're doing when transferring calls.** Give a reason for transferring, and identify the extension to which you are directing the call in case the caller is disconnected.

> ✓ **Quick Check**
> You can improve your telephone reception skills by identifying yourself, acting responsive, being helpful, and taking accurate messages.

Using Cell Phones for Business

Cell phones enable you to conduct business from virtually anywhere at any time. More than a plaything or a mere convenience, the cell phone has become an essential part of communication in many of today's workplaces. As with many new technologies, a set of rules or protocol on usage is still evolving for cell phones. How are they best used? When is it acceptable to take calls? Where should calls be made? Most of us have experienced thoughtless and rude cell phone behaviour. To avoid offending, smart business communicators practise cell phone etiquette, as outlined in Figure 11.2. In projecting a professional image, they are careful about location, time, and volume in relation to their cell phone calls.

> ✓ **Quick Check**
> Cell phones are important workplace communication tools, but they must be used without offending others.

FIGURE 11.2 **Practising Courteous and Responsible Cell Phone Use**

Business communicators find cell phones to be enormously convenient and real time-savers. But rude users have generated a backlash against inconsiderate callers. Here are specific suggestions for using cell phones safely and responsibly:

- **Be courteous to those around you.** Don't force those near you to hear your business. Apologize and make amends gracefully for occasional cell phone blunders.
- **Observe wireless-free quiet areas.** Don't allow your cell phone to ring in theatres, restaurants, museums, classrooms, important meetings, and similar places. Use the cell phone's silent/vibrating ring option. A majority of travellers prefer that cell phone conversations *not* be held on most forms of public transportation.
- **Speak in low, conversational tones.** Microphones on cell phones are quite sensitive, thus making it unnecessary to talk loudly. Avoid "cell yell."
- **Take only urgent calls.** Make full use of your cell phone's caller ID feature to screen incoming calls. Let voice mail take those calls that are not pressing.
- **Drive now, talk later.** Pull over if you must make a call. Talking while driving increases the chance of accidents fourfold, about the same as driving while intoxicated.

"Do you mind? I happen to be on the phone!"

Location. Use good judgment in placing or accepting cell phone calls. Some places are dangerous or inappropriate for cell phone use. Turn off your cell phone when entering a conference room, interview, theatre, place of worship, or any other place where it could be distracting or disruptive to others. Taking a call in a crowded room or bar makes it difficult to hear and reflects poorly on you as a professional. A bad connection also makes a bad impression. Static or dropped signals create frustration and miscommunication. Don't sacrifice professionalism for the sake of a garbled phone call. It's smarter to turn off your phone in an area where the signal is weak and when you are likely to have interference. Use voice mail and return the call when conditions are better.

Quick Check

Avoid taking cell phone calls when you are talking with someone else and avoid "cell yell."

Time. Often what you are doing is more important than whatever may come over the air waves to you on your phone. For example, when you are having an important discussion with a business partner, customer, or superior, it is rude to allow yourself to be interrupted by an incoming call. It's also poor manners to practise multitasking while on the phone. What's more, it's dangerous. Although you might be able to read and print out e-mail messages, deal with a customer at the counter, and talk on your cell phone simultaneously, it's impolite and risky. Lack of attention results in errors and a lack of respect. If a phone call is important enough to accept, then it's important enough to stop what you are doing and attend to the conversation.

Volume. Many people raise their voices when using their cell phones. "Cell yell" results, much to the annoyance of anyone nearby. Raising your voice is unnecessary since most phones have excellent microphones that can pick up even a whisper. If the connection is bad, louder volume will not improve the sound quality. As in face-to-face conversations, a low, modulated voice sounds professional and projects the proper image.

Making the Best Use of Voice Mail

Voice mail links a telephone system to a computer that digitizes and stores incoming messages. Some systems also provide functions such as automated attendant menus, allowing callers to reach any associated extension by pushing specific buttons on a touch-tone telephone. For example, a ski resort in British Columbia uses voice mail to answer routine questions that once were routed through an operator: *Welcome to Panorama. For information on accommodations, press 1; for snow conditions, press 2; for ski equipment rental, press 3,* and so forth.

Within some companies, voice mail accounts for 90 percent of all telephone messages.[10] Its popularity results from serving many functions, the most important of which is message storage. Because as many as half of all business calls require no discussion or feedback, the messaging capabilities of voice mail can mean huge savings for businesses. Incoming information is delivered without interrupting potential receivers and without all the niceties that most two-way conversations require. Stripped of superfluous chitchat, voice mail messages allow communicators to focus on essentials. Voice mail also eliminates telephone tag, inaccurate message taking, and time-zone barriers. Critics complain, nevertheless, that automated systems seem cold and impersonal and are sometimes confusing and irritating. In any event, here are some ways that you can make voice mail work more effectively for you.

✓ Quick Check

Voice mail eliminates telephone tag, inaccurate message taking, and time-zone barriers; it also allows communicators to focus on essentials.

- **Announce your voice mail.** If you rely principally on a voice mail message system, identify it on your business stationery and cards. Then, when people call, they will be ready to leave a message.
- **Prepare a warm and informative greeting.** Make your mechanical greeting sound warm and inviting, both in tone and content. Identify yourself and your organization so that callers know they have reached the right number. Thank the caller and briefly explain that you are unavailable. Invite the caller to leave a message or, if appropriate, call back. Here's a typical voice mail greeting: "Hi! This is Larry Levin of Proteus Software, and I appreciate your call. You've reached my voice mailbox because I'm either working with customers or talking on another line at the moment. Please leave your name, number, and reason for calling so that I can be prepared when I return your call." Give callers an idea of when you will be available, such as "I'll be back at 2:30" or "I'll be out of my office until Wednesday, May 20." If you screen your calls as a time-management technique, try this message: "I'm not near my phone right now, but I should be able to return calls after 3:30."
- **Test your message.** Call your number and assess your message. Does it sound inviting? Sincere? Understandable? Are you pleased with your tone? If not, says one consultant, have someone else, perhaps a professional, record a message for you.

Planning and Participating in Productive Business and Professional Meetings

As businesses become more team oriented and management becomes more participatory, people are attending more meetings than ever. One survey of managers found that they were devoting as many as two days a week to various gatherings.[11] Yet, meetings are almost universally disliked. Typical comments include "We have too many of them," "They don't accomplish anything," and "What a waste of time!" In spite of employee reluctance and despite terrific advances in communication and team technology, face-to-face meetings are not going to disappear. In discussing the future of meetings, Akio Morita, former chairman of Sony Corporation, said that he expects "face-to-face meetings will still be the number one form of communication in the twenty-first century."[12] So, get used to them. Meetings are here to stay. Our task, then, as business communicators, is to learn how to make them efficient, satisfying, and productive.

✓ Quick Check

Because you can expect to attend many workplace meetings, learn to make them efficient, satisfying, and productive.

Meetings, by the way, consist of three or more individuals who gather to pool information, solicit feedback, clarify policy, seek consensus, and solve problems. But meetings have another important purpose for you. They represent opportunities. Because they are a prime tool for developing staff, they are career-critical. According to one Canadian company's Web site, "It is ... true that careers (rightly or wrongly) have been made or broken through performance at meetings."[13] At meetings judgments are formed and careers are made. Therefore, instead of treating them as thieves of your valuable time, try to see them as golden opportunities to demonstrate your leadership, communication, and problem-solving skills. So that you can make the most of these opportunities, here are techniques for planning and conducting successful meetings.

Deciding Whether a Meeting Is Necessary

Call meetings only when necessary, and invite only key people.

No meeting should be called unless the topic is important, can't wait, and requires an exchange of ideas. If the flow of information is strictly one way and no immediate feedback will result, then don't schedule a meeting. For example, if people are merely being advised or informed, send an e-mail, memo, or letter. Leave a telephone or voice mail message, but don't call a costly meeting. Remember, the real expense of a meeting is the lost productivity of all the people attending. To decide whether the purpose of the meeting is valid, it's a good idea to consult the key people who will be attending. Ask them what outcomes are desired and how to achieve those goals. This consultation also sets a collaborative tone and encourages full participation.

Selecting Participants

Problem-solving meetings should involve five or fewer people.

The number of meeting participants is determined by the purpose of the meeting, as shown in Figure 11.3. If the meeting purpose is motivational, such as an employee awards ceremony for Bombardier, then the number of participants is unlimited. But to make decisions, according to studies at 3-M Corporation, the best number is five or fewer participants.[14] Ideally, those attending should be people who will make the decision and people with information necessary to make the decision. Also attending should be people who will be responsible for implementing the decision and representatives of groups who will benefit from the decision.

Distributing an Agenda

Before a meeting, pass out a meeting agenda showing topics to be discussed and other information.

At least two days in advance of a meeting, distribute an agenda of topics to be discussed. Also include any reports or materials that participants should read in advance. For continuing groups, you might also include a copy of the minutes of the previous meeting. To keep meetings productive, limit the number of agenda items. Remember, the narrower the focus, the greater the chances for success. A good agenda, as illustrated in Figure 11.4, covers the following information:

FIGURE 11.3 **Meeting Purpose and Number of Participants**

Purpose	Ideal Size
Intensive problem solving	5 or fewer
Problem identification	10 or fewer
Information reviews and presentations	30 or fewer
Motivational	Unlimited

FIGURE 11.4 Typical Meeting Agenda

AGENDA
Adventure Travel Canada
Staff Meeting
September 4, 2006
10 to 11 a.m.
Conference Room

		Person	Proposed Time
I.	Call to order; roll call		
II.	Approval of agenda		
III.	Approval of minutes from previous meeting		
IV.	Committee reports		
	A. Web site update	Kevin	5 minutes
	B. Tour packages	Lisa	10 minutes
V.	Old business		
	A. Equipment maintenance	John	5 minutes
	B. Client escrow accounts	Alicia	5 minutes
	C. Internal newsletter	Adrienne	5 minutes
VI.	New business		
	A. New accounts	Sarah	5 minutes
	B. Pricing policy for trips	Marcus	15 minutes
VII.	Announcements		
VIII.	Chair's summary, adjournment		

- Date and place of meeting
- Start time and end time
- Brief description of each topic, in order of priority, including the names of individuals who are responsible for performing some action
- Proposed allotment of time for each topic
- Any premeeting preparation expected of participants

Getting the Meeting Started

To avoid wasting time and irritating attendees, always start meetings on time—even if some participants are missing. Waiting for latecomers causes resentment and sets a bad precedent. For the same reasons, don't give a quick recap to anyone who arrives late. At the appointed time, open the meeting with a three- to five-minute introduction that includes the following:

✔ **Quick Check**

Start meetings on time and open with a brief introduction.

- Goal and length of the meeting
- Background of topics or problems
- Possible solutions and constraints
- Tentative agenda
- Ground rules to be followed

A typical set of ground rules might include arriving on time, communicating openly, being supportive, listening carefully, participating fully, confronting conflict frankly, and following the agenda. More formal groups follow parliamentary procedures based on Robert's Rules. For example, in a meeting run using Robert's Rules, there is a way to stop a person from talking too long. It's called "calling the question," which means ending the current discussion and voting on the previous question (or motion) right away. Before you can call the question, however, you have to be recognized by the chair of the meeting, move the "previous question," have your motion seconded, and receive a two-thirds majority vote in favour of calling the question. Most business meetings do not follow Robert's Rules, except perhaps at the highest levels (board meetings), because of the specialized knowledge required to run a meeting in this way.

In most typical business meetings, after establishing basic ground rules, the leader should ask whether participants agree thus far. Ideally, the next step is to assign one attendee to take minutes and one to act as a recorder. The recorder stands at a flipchart or whiteboard and lists the main ideas being discussed and agreements reached.

Moving the Meeting Along

After the preliminaries, the leader should say as little as possible. Like a talk show host, an effective leader makes "sure that each panel member gets some air time while no one member steals the show."[15] Remember that the purpose of a meeting is to exchange views, not to hear one person, even the leader, do all the talking. If the group has one member who monopolizes, the leader might say, "Thanks, for that perspective, Kurt, but please hold your next point while we hear how Ann would respond to that." This technique also encourages quieter participants to speak up.

To avoid allowing digressions to sidetrack the group, try generating a "parking lot" list. This is a list of important but divergent issues that should be discussed at a later time. Another way to handle digressions is to say, "Folks, we are getting off track here. Forgive me for pressing on, but I need to bring us back to the central issue of . . . ."[16] It's important to adhere to the agenda and the time schedule. Equally important, when the group seems to have reached a consensus, is to summarize the group's position and check to see whether everyone agrees.

Dealing with Conflict

Conflict is natural and even desirable in workplaces, but it can cause awkwardness and uneasiness. In meetings, conflict typically develops when people feel unheard or misunderstood. If two people are in conflict, the best approach is to encourage each to make a complete case while group members give their full attention. Let each one question the other. Then, the leader should summarize what was said, and the group should offer comments. The group may modify a recommendation or suggest alternatives before reaching consensus on a direction to follow.

Handling Dysfunctional Group Members

When individuals are performing in a dysfunctional role (such as blocking discussion, attacking other speakers, joking excessively, or withdrawing), they should be handled with care and tact. The following specific techniques can help a meeting leader control some group members and draw others out:

- **Lay down the rules in an opening statement.** Give a specific overall summary of topics, time allotment, and expected behaviour. Warn that speakers who digress will be interrupted.
- **Seat potentially dysfunctional members strategically.** Experts suggest seating a difficult group member immediately next to the leader. It's easier to bypass a person in this position. Make sure the person with dysfunctional behaviour is not seated in a power point, such as at the end of table or across from the leader.
- **Avoid direct eye contact.** Direct eye contact is a nonverbal signal that encourages talking. Thus, when asking a question of the group, look only at those whom you wish to answer.

- **Assign dysfunctional members specific tasks.** Ask a potentially disruptive person, for example, to be the group recorder.
- **Ask members to speak in a specific order.** Ordering comments creates an artificial, rigid climate and should be done only when absolutely necessary. But such a regimen ensures that everyone gets a chance to participate.
- **Interrupt monopolizers.** If a difficult member dominates a discussion, wait for a pause and then break in. Summarize briefly the previous comments or ask someone else for an opinion.
- **Encourage nontalkers.** Give only positive feedback to the comments of reticent members. Ask them direct questions about which you know they have information or opinions.
- **Give praise and encouragement** to those who seem to need it, including the distracters, the blockers, and the withdrawn.[17]

Ending with a Plan

End the meeting at the agreed time or earlier if possible. The leader should summarize what has been decided, who is going to do what, and by what time. It may be necessary to ask people to volunteer to take responsibility for completing action items agreed to in the meeting. No one should leave the meeting without a full understanding of what was accomplished. One effective technique that encourages full participation is "once around the table." Everyone is asked to summarize briefly his or her interpretation of what was decided and what happens next. Of course, this closure technique works best with smaller groups. The leader should conclude by asking the group to set a time for the next meeting. He or she should also assure the group that a report will follow and thank participants for attending.

Quick Check

End the meeting with a summary of accomplishments and a review of action items; follow up by reminding participants of their assigned tasks.

"That's all very nice, Jefferson, but do you have any other new business?"

Following Up Actively

If minutes were taken, they should be distributed within a couple of days after the meeting. An example of a formal minutes report is found in Figure 9.10 on page 240. Figure 11.5 shows an informal minutes report, which is the kind you'll see more often in the business world today. It is up to the leader to see that what was decided at the meeting is accomplished. The leader may need to call or e-mail people to remind them of their assignments and also to volunteer to help them if necessary.

FIGURE 11.5 Minutes of Meeting, Informal—Report Format

Grand Beach Homeowners' Association

Board of Directors Meeting
April 12, 2007

MINUTES

Directors Present: J. Weinstein, A. McGraw, J. Carlson, C. Stefanko,
A. Pettus

Directors Absent: B. Hookym

Summary of Topics Discussed

- Report from Architectural Review Committee. Copy attached.
- Landscaping of centre divider on P.T.H. 59. Three options considered: hiring private landscape designer, seeking volunteers from community, assigning association custodian to complete work.
- Collection of outstanding assessments. Discussion of delinquent accounts and possible actions. — *Summarizes discussion*
- Use of beach club by film companies. Pros: considerable income. Cons: damage to furnishings, loss of facility to homeowners.
- Nomination of directors to replace those with two-year appointments.

Decisions Reached

- Hire private landscaper to renovate and plant centre divider on P.T.H. 59.
- Attach liens to homes of members with delinquent assessments. — *Capsulizes decisions rather than showing motions and voting*
- Submit to general membership vote the question of renting the beach club to film companies.

Action Items

Item	Responsibility	Due Date
1. Landscaping bid	J. Carson	May 1
2. Attorney for liens	B. Hookym	April 20
3. Creation of nominating committee	A. Pettus	May 1

Highlights items for action

Summing Up and Looking Forward

In this chapter you studied how to improve face-to-face communication in the workplace. You can use your voice as a communication tool by focusing on pronunciation, tone, pitch, volume, rate, and emphasis. In workplace conversations, you should use correct names and titles, choose appropriate topics, avoid negative remarks, listen to learn, and be willing to offer sincere and specific praise. You studied how to give and take constructive criticism on the job. You also learned about five common response patterns as well as a six-step plan for resolving interpersonal workplace conflicts. The chapter also presented techniques for polishing your professional telephone and voice mail skills, including making and receiving productive telephone calls. Finally, you learned how to plan and participate in productive business and professional meetings.

This chapter focused on developing speaking skills in face-to-face workplace communication. The next chapter covers an additional facet of oral communication, that of giving presentations. Learning to speak before groups is important to your career success because you will probably be expected to do so occasionally. You'll learn helpful techniques and practise applying them so that you can control stage fright in making polished presentations.

Critical Thinking

1. Is face-to-face communication always preferable to one-dimensional channels of communication such as e-mail and fax? Why or why not?
2. In what ways can conflict be a positive force in the workplace?
3. Commentators often predict that new communications media will destroy old ones. Do you think e-mail, PDAs, and instant messaging will kill off phone calls? Why or why not?
4. Why do so many people hate voice mail when it is an efficient system for recording messages?
5. How can business meetings help you advance your career?

Chapter Review

6. Name five elements that you control in using your voice as a communication tool.

7. What topics should be avoided in workplace conversations?

8. List six techniques that you consider most important when delivering constructive criticism.

9. If you are criticized at work, what are eight ways that you can respond professionally?

Chapter Review

10. What are five common responses to workplace conflicts? Which response do you think is most constructive?

11. What is a three-point introduction for a telephone call?

12. Name five ways in which callers can practise courteous and responsible cell phone use.

13. When should a business meeting be held?

14. What is an agenda and what should it include?

15. List eight tactics that a meeting leader can use in dealing with dysfunctional participants.

Writing Improvement Exercises

16. Constructive Criticism. You work for a large company that is organized in work teams. Your work team, in the company's marketing department, meets weekly for a quick half-hour meeting to review the week's activities and projects. The meetings are run by the team leader, Mandy Miller. The team leader is a position of extra responsibility with a higher salary than that of other marketing staffers. For the past three months, Mandy has been regularly missing or showing up late for meetings. No one has said anything but you. You had a conversation with Mandy in the cafeteria three weeks ago in which you relayed your concerns to her in as positive a way as possible. Mandy has again started to miss meetings. You feel it's appropriate to send an e-mail to the director of the marketing department, letting him know what's been happening, that you've talked to Mandy, and that things haven't improved.

17. Meeting Agenda. It's now two months after you've sent your e-mail to the director of marketing. In the meantime, Mandy Miller has been relieved of her extra responsibility as team leader. To your great surprise, your boss has asked you to be the new team leader. You are preparing for your first meeting and you decide to do something Mandy rarely did, which is to e-mail a meeting agenda to your colleagues. Besides discussing the changeover from Mandy to yourself at the meeting, activities to be discussed include the final proofreading of an important catalogue that is going to the printer on Friday and a conference call with your colleagues in the Vancouver office on the roll-out of 2010 Olympics merchandise. You are well liked by your colleagues, and you want to manage this meeting so that it doesn't look like you're "taking over" the department.

18. Meeting Minutes. Because the weekly marketing team meetings happen so frequently, you're not sure whether it's important to send out formal meeting minutes. Instead, you decide to send out a weekly "Meeting Recap" e-mail after each meeting. At this morning's meeting—your first as team leader—things went well. Mandy made a point of congratulating you on your new position (without sarcasm). You appointed Tom Mavrogianis to be in charge of the catalogue proof-read (deadline Thursday afternoon) and Mandy Miller to be in charge of running Friday's conference with the Vancouver office. Mandy mentioned she needed the specs on the 2010 Olympic toques and caps before the meeting, and you promised to get them to her. Also, an unexpected item of business came up at the meeting when Tom reminded you that it was time to start planning the annual department retreat. Besides Tom, Mandy, and you, Bill Brockton was at the meeting, while Nahla Karim was absent.

Activities and Cases

11.1 Pronunciation. You can improve your effectiveness and credibility as a speaker if you pronounce words correctly.

Team

Your Task. In teams or in class discussion, study the following list of words. What vowel do you think is frequently omitted or mispronounced? How can you be sure of the correct pronunciation? How can you improve your own pronunciation of these words?

accurate	manufacturer
burglar	original
company	popular
disastrous	positive
eleven	responsible
entrance	separately
excellent	singular
family	terrible
federal	usually
history	variable
liability	veteran

11.2 Voice Quality. Recording your voice gives you a chance to learn how your voice sounds to others and provides an opportunity for you to improve its effectiveness. Don't be surprised if you fail to recognize your own voice.

Your Task. Record yourself reading a newspaper or magazine article.

a. If you think your voice sounds a bit high, practise speaking slightly lower.
b. If your voice is low or expressionless, practise speaking slightly louder and with more inflection.
c. Ask a colleague, teacher, or friend to provide feedback on your pronunciation, pitch, volume, rate, and professional tone.

11.3 Role Play: Delivering and Responding to Criticism. Develop your skills in handling criticism by joining with a partner to role-play critical messages you might deliver and receive on the job.

Your Task. Designate one person "A" and the other "B." A describes the kinds of critical messages she or he is likely to receive on the job and identifies who might deliver them. In Scenario 1, B takes the role of the critic and delivers the criticism in an unskilled manner. A responds using techniques described in this chapter. In Scenario 2, B again is the critic but delivers the criticism using techniques described in this chapter. A responds again. Then A and B reverse roles and repeat Scenarios 1 and 2.

Team

11.4 Role Play: Discussing Workplace Criticism. In the workplace, criticism is often delivered thoughtlessly.

Your Task. In teams of two or three, describe a time when you were criticized by an untrained superior or colleague. What made the criticism painful? What goal do you think the critic had in mind? How did you feel? How did you respond? Considering techniques discussed in this chapter, how could the critic have improved his or her delivery? How does the delivery technique affect the way a receiver responds to criticism? Script the situation you've just discussed and present it to the rest of the class in a before and after scenario.

11.5 Responding to Workplace Conflicts. Experts say that we generally respond to conflict in one of the following patterns: avoidance/withdrawal, accommodation/smoothing, compromise, competition/forcing, or collaboration/problem solving.

Your Task. For each of the following conflict situations, name an appropriate response pattern(s) and be prepared to explain your choice.

a. A company policy manual is posted and updated at an internal Web page. Employees must sign that they have read and understand the manual. A conflict arises when one manager insists that employees should sign electronically. Another manager thinks that a paper form should be signed by employees so that better records may be kept. What conflict response pattern is most appropriate?

b. Jeff and Mark work together but frequently disagree. Today they disagree on what computer disks to purchase for an order that must be submitted immediately. Jeff insists on buying Brand X computer disks. Mark knows that Brand X is made by a company that markets an identical disk at a slightly lower price. However, Mark doesn't have stock numbers for the cheaper disks at his fingertips. How should Mark respond?

c. A manager and his assistant plan to attend a conference together at a resort location. Six weeks before the conference, the company announces a cutback and limits conference support to only one person. The assistant, who has developed a presentation specifically for the conference, feels that he should be the one to attend. Travel arrangements must be made immediately. What conflict response pattern will most likely result?

d. Two vice-presidents disagree on a company e-mail policy. One wants to ban personal e-mail totally. The other thinks that an outright ban is impossible to implement. He is more concerned with limiting Internet misuse, including visits to online game, porn, and shopping sites. The vice-presidents agree that they need an e-mail policy, but they disagree on what to allow and what to prohibit. What conflict response pattern is appropriate?

e. Customer service rep Jackie comes to work one morning and finds Alexa sitting at Workstation 2. Although the customer service reps have no special workstation assigned to them, Jackie has the longest seniority and has always assumed that Workstation 2 was hers. Other workstations were available, but the supervisor told Alexa to use Workstation 2 that morning because she didn't know that Jackie would be coming in. When Jackie arrives and sees "her" workstation occupied, she becomes angry and demands that Alexa vacate the station. What conflict response pattern might be most appropriate for Alexa and the supervisor?

11.6 Rules for Wireless Phone Use in Sales. As one of the managers of Wrigley Canada, a gum and confectionery company, you are alarmed at a newspaper article you just read. A stockbroker for BMO Nesbitt Burns was making cold calls on his personal phone while driving. His car hit and killed a motorcyclist. The brokerage firm was sued and accused of contributing to an accident by encouraging employees to use cellular telephones while driving. To avoid the risk of paying huge damages awarded by an emotional jury, the brokerage firm offered the victim's family a $500,000 settlement.

Team

Your Task. Individually or in teams write an e-mail to Wrigley sales reps outlining company suggestions (or should they be rules?) for safe wireless phone use in cars. Check library databases for articles that discuss cell phone use in cars. Look for additional safety ideas. In your message to sales reps, try to suggest receiver benefits. How is safe cell phone use beneficial to the sales rep?

11.7 Role Play: Improving Telephone Skills. Acting out the roles of telephone caller and receiver is an effective technique for improving skills. To give you such practice, your instructor will divide the class into pairs.

Your Task. Read each scenario and rehearse your role silently. Then improvise the role with your partner. After improvising a couple of times, script one of the situations and present it to the rest of the class.

PARTNER 1

a. You are the personnel manager of Datatronics, Inc. Call Elizabeth Franklin, office manager at Computers Plus. Inquire about a job applicant, Chelsea Chavez, who listed Ms. Franklin as a reference.

PARTNER 2

You are the receptionist for Computers Plus. The caller asks for Elizabeth Franklin, who is home sick today. You don't know when she will be able to return. Answer the call appropriately.

PARTNER 1

b. Call Ms. Franklin again the following day to inquire about the same job applicant, Chelsea Chavez. Ms. Franklin answers today, but she talks on and on, describing the applicant in great detail. Tactfully close the conversation.

PARTNER 2

You are now Ms. Franklin, office manager. Describe Chelsea Chavez, an imaginary employee. Think of someone with whom you've worked. Include many details, such as her ability to work with others, her appearance, her skills at computing, her schooling, her ambition, and so forth.

c. You are now the receptionist for Tom Wing, of Wing Imports. Answer a call for Mr. Wing, who is working in another office, at ext. 134, where he will accept calls.

You are now an administrative assistant for lawyer Michael Murphy. Call Tom Wing to verify a meeting date Mr. Murphy has with Mr. Wing. Use your own name in identifying yourself.

d. You are now Tom Wing, owner of Wing Imports. Call your lawyer, Michael Murphy, about a legal problem. Leave a brief, incomplete message.

You are now the receptionist for lawyer Michael Murphy. Mr. Murphy is skiing in Tremblant and will return in two days, but he doesn't want his clients to know where he is. Take a message.

e. Call Mr. Murphy again. Leave a message that will prevent telephone tag.

Take a message again.

11.8 Role Play: Investigating Oral Communication in Your Field. Despite the popularity of communications technologies such as PDAs, e-mail, and instant messaging that require people to write, oral communication still plays an important role in the lives of most people working in business.

Your Task. Working in teams of three or four, interview three individuals in your professional field. How is oral communication important in this profession? What are some typical oral communication tasks in a given day, week, or month? As a percentage, how much time is spent communicating orally versus in writing? Besides person-to-person discussions, telephone conversations, and meetings, can this individual name other types of oral communication used at work? Does the need for oral skills change as one advances? What suggestions can this individual make to newcomers to the field for developing proficient oral communication skills? Once you've completed your interviews, script a ten-minute panel discussion between an interviewer and two or three experts on oral communication. Perform the skit in front of the class and discuss it afterward.

11.9 Analyzing a Meeting. You've learned a number of techniques in this chapter for planning and participating in meetings. Here's your chance to put your knowledge to work.

Your Task. Attend a structured meeting of a college, social, business, or other organization. Compare the manner in which the meeting is conducted with the suggestions presented in this chapter. Why did the meeting succeed or fail? Prepare a brief recommendation report for your instructor or be ready to discuss your findings in class.

11.10 Planning a Meeting. In many ways, a typical college or university class or lecture is like a meeting. A number of participants come together to share information and sometimes to solve problems. With the permission of your instructor, plan the next meeting of your class as a business meeting.

Your Task. Ask your instructor for his or her lesson plan for the next class. Based on the lesson plan, in a small team write an agenda for next week's meeting. Distribute this agenda to the rest of your classmates via e-mail at least one day before the meeting. So that your instructor is not the only person talking during the meeting, divide his or her lesson plan into chunks that can be "delivered" by other meeting participants. Assuming that not everyone in the class can have an active role at the meeting, but that everyone does need some sort of responsibility, what will be the responsibility of these "passive" participants? Will you need any visual aids for your meeting? If so, who will be in charge of them?

11.11 Running a Meeting. The best way to learn to run a meeting is to actually do it.

Your Task. Using the agenda your team wrote in Activity 11.10, run part of your next class as a meeting. Many decisions will have to be made. Who will chair the meeting? (It does not necessarily have to be your instructor—in fact it may be better if it's not.) What will the chair say to get the meeting started? What reports will be given at the meeting? How will you generate discussion at this meeting, considering that it's a mock meeting and the participants are your classmates, many of whom may be nontalkers? What will you do if the meeting gets off track? You may want to "plant" one of your team members as a disruptive meeting participant. Does the chair know how to deal with this disruptive person? Consider changing the normal seating arrangement of your class to more closely approximate a meeting. Who will take notes at this meeting? How will the meeting end and who will be in charge of following up?

Grammar/Mechanics Review—11

The following sentences contain errors in grammar, punctuation, capitalization, number style, usage, and spelling. Below each sentence write a corrected version.

1. The five top food service franchisors in the country are the following, mcdonald's, subway sandwiches & salads, burger king, 7-eleven, and tim hartons.

2. Fairlee Wells Corporation which is based in thunder bay ontario and it's german partner has developed a commercial-size cooker to make french fries that taste greasy but are not.

3. Although the time and temperature is set by the user the cooker adjusts itself automatically.

4. The President and Chief Executive of Fairlee Wells said, "this machine is programmed to learn.

5. We rented the 8205 sq. metre building in winnipegs exchange district to many small space tenants.

6. As a manager the most important task is planning.

7. Proper tools and modern equipment makes business's run smooth.

8. Looking back through history, no Prime Minister raises deeper philosophical issues than sir John A. Macdonald.

9. Last Fall, the Kejimkujik National Park based bicycle manufacturer TiCycle installed a network to link 5 PC's in it's factory and retail store.

10. Drove by a series of decisive actions Rogers Wireless membership grew by nearly two and a half million.

11. At the Delta residence inn in Edmonton alberta a 1 bedroom suite costs about one hundred and thirty dollars a night.

12. One of the most popular amenities offerred by top tier extended stay hotels are the free Buffet breakfast.

13. Just between you and I do you prefer a backpacking trip to the rockies or river rafting down the snake river.

14. We had less than fifteen items but others in the grocery store line were over the limit.

15. The President, Ceo, and 3 Managers will tour our facilitys in nova scotia and newfoundland.

Grammar/Mechanics Challenge—11

Document for Revision

The following report showing meeting minutes has faults in grammar, punctuation, spelling, number form, wordiness, and word use. Use standard proofreading marks (see Appendix B) to correct the errors. When you finish, your instructor can show you the revised version of this summary.

Canadian Federation of Small Business
Policy Board Committee
February 4, 2007

Present: Debra Chinnapongse, Tweet Jackson, Irene Kishita, Barry Knaggs, Kevin Poepoe, and Ralph Mason

Absent: Alex Watanabe

The meeting was call to order by Chair Kevin Poepo at 9:02 a.m. in the morning. Minutes from the January 6th meeting was read and approve.

Old Business

Debra Chinnapongse discussed the cost of the annual awards luncheon. That honours outstanding members. The ticket price ticket does not cover all the expenses incured. Major expenses include: awards and complementary lunches for the judges, VIP guests and volunteers. CFSB can not continue to make up the difference between income from tickets and costs for the luncheon. Ms. Chinnapongse reported that it had come to her attention that other associations relied on members contributions for their awards' programs.

MOTION: To send a Letter to board members asking for there contributions to support the annual awards luncheon. (Chinapongse/Kishita). PASSED 6-0.

Reports

Barry Knaggs reported that the media relations committee sponsored a get acquainted meeting in November. More than eighty people from various agencys attended.

The Outreach Committee reports that they have been asked to assist the Partnership for Small Business, an Ottawa-based organization in establishing a speakers bureau of Canadian small business owners. It would be available to speak at schools and colleges about small business and employment.

New Business

The chair announced a Planning Meeting to be held in March regarding revising the agri-business plan. In other New Business Ralph Mason reported that the staff had purchased fifty tickets for members, and our committees to attend the Zig Ziglar seminar in the month of March.

Next Meeting

The next meeting of the Policy Boare Committee will be held in early Aprl at the Lord Elgin hotel, Ottawa. At that time the meeting will conclude with a tour of the seaway Networks inc. offices in Kanata.

The meeting adjourned at 10:25 am by Keven Poepoe.

Respectfully submitted,

_____

Grammar/Mechanics Challenge—11

How to Deal With Difficult People at Work

Difficult people in the workplace challenge your patience and your communication skills. In your work life and in your personal life, you are often confronted by people who are negative, manipulative, uncooperative, or just plain difficult. Although everyone is irritable or indecisive at times, some people are so difficult that they require us to react with special coping skills. In his well-known book *Coping With Difficult People*, psychologist and management consultant Robert M. Bramson provides helpful advice in dealing with a number of personality types.

Bullies try to overwhelm with intimidation, arrogance, righteous indignation, and outright anger. To cope, try the following:

- Give them time to run down; maintain eye contact.
- Don't worry about being polite; state your opinions forcefully.
- Don't argue or be sarcastic; be ready to be friendly.

Snipers hide behind cover. They attack by teasing and making not-too-subtle digs. To cope, try the following:

- "Smoke" them out; refuse to be attacked indirectly. Ask questions such as, "What did you mean by your remark?" "Sounds as if you are ridiculing me. Are you?"
- Ask the group to confirm or deny the sniper's criticism. "Anyone else see it that way?" Get other points of view.
- Acknowledge the underlying problem and try to find a feasible solution.

Exploders blow up in frustrated rage; they have an adult tantrum. To cope, try the following:

- Give them time to cool off and regain control on their own.
- If they don't stop, break into the tirade by saying, "Stop!"
- Show that you take them seriously.
- Find a way to take a breather and get some privacy with them.

Complainers find fault with everything. Some complaints are made directly; others are made indirectly to third parties. To cope, try the following:

- Listen attentively, even if you feel guilty or impatient.
- Acknowledge what they are saying and paraphrase to see whether you understand.
- Don't agree or apologize, even if you feel you should.
- Avoid the accusation–defence–reaccusation pattern.
- Try to solve the problem by (a) asking specific informational questions, (b) assigning fact-finding tasks, or (c) asking for the complaint in writing.
- If all else fails, ask the complainer, "How do you want this discussion to end?"

Indecisive stallers are unable to make decisions. Their stalling makes them difficult to work with. To cope, try the following:

- Encourage stallers to tell you about conflicts or reservations that prevent the decision. Listen for clues.
- Help stallers solve their problems by (a) acknowledging past problems nondefensively, (b) examining the facts, and (c) proposing alternative solutions in priority order.
- Give support after a decision has been made.

Career Application

In most workplaces you can expect to meet one or more truly difficult people. To provide practice in dealing with such people, develop a coping plan.

Your Task

In a memo to yourself, write responses to the following:

1. Describe in detail the behaviour of a person whom you find to be difficult.
2. Analyze and describe your understanding of that behaviour.
3. Review your past interactions with this person. Did you get along better with this person before?
4. Decide what coping behaviour would be appropriate.
5. Acknowledge what might need to change in yourself to best carry out the most promising coping behaviour.
6. Prepare an action plan explaining what you will do and by what date.

Giving Oral Presentations

Giving presentations is a skill that can be learned. While it's not rocket science it also isn't the same as an informal conversation with friends. Identify your audience and the key messages you want them to remember. Put yourself in their chairs. Tell real-life stories to make the presentation come alive and illustrate your points. Make eye contact with the audience, not with your notes or slides. Prepare and rehearse. Prepare and rehearse again. Be yourself and remember that everyone is nervous about standing up and speaking in public.[1]

Lee Jacobson, *brand producer and communications consultant, Lee Jacobson Consultants*

LEARNING OBJECTIVES

1. Discuss two important first steps in preparing effective oral presentations.

2. Explain the major elements in organizing the content of a presentation, including the introduction, body, and conclusion.

3. Identify techniques for gaining audience rapport, including using effective imagery, providing verbal signposts, and sending appropriate nonverbal messages.

4. Discuss designing and using effective visual aids, handouts, and computer presentation materials.

5. Specify delivery techniques for use before, during, and after a presentation.

Organizations today are increasingly interested in hiring people with good presentation skills. Why? The business world is changing. Technical skills aren't enough to guarantee success. You also need to be able to communicate ideas effectively in presentations to customers, vendors, members of your team, and management. Your presentations will probably be made to inform, influence, or motivate action. And the opportunities to make these presentations are increasing, even for nonmanagement employees.[2] Powerful speaking skills draw attention to you and advance your career. But reading a textbook is not enough to help you develop solid speaking skills. You also need coaching and chances to practise your skills. In this book you will learn the fundamentals, and in your course you will be able to try out your skills and develop confidence.

In getting ready for an oral presentation, you may feel a great deal of anxiety. For many people fear of speaking before a group is almost as great as the fear of pain. We get butterflies in our stomachs just thinking about it. When you feel those butterflies, though, speech coach Dianne Booher advises getting them in formation and visualizing the swarm as a powerful push propelling you to a peak performance.[3] For any presentation, you can reduce your fears and lay the foundation for a professional performance by focusing on five areas: preparation, organization, audience rapport, visual aids, and delivery.

Deciding What You Want to Accomplish

The most important part of your preparation is deciding your purpose. Do you want to sell a group insurance policy to a prospective client? Do you want to persuade management to increase the marketing budget? Do you want to inform customer service reps of three important ways to prevent miscommunication? Whether your goal is to persuade or to inform, you must have a clear idea of where you are going. At the end of your presentation, what do you want your listeners to remember or do?

Quick Check

Preparing for an oral presentation means identifying your purpose and knowing the audience.

Eric Evans, a loan officer at TD Canada Trust, faced such questions as he planned a talk for a class in small business management. (You can see the outline for his talk in Figure 12.3, p. 331.) Eric's former business professor had asked him to return to campus and give the class advice about borrowing money from banks in order to start new businesses. Because Eric knew so much about this topic, he found it difficult to extract a specific purpose statement for his presentation. After much thought he narrowed his purpose to this: *To inform potential entrepreneurs about three important factors that loan officers consider before granting start-up loans to launch small businesses.* His entire presentation focused on ensuring that the class members understood and remembered three principal ideas.

Understanding Your Audience

A second key element in preparation is analyzing your audience, anticipating its reactions, and making appropriate adaptations. Understanding four basic audience types, summarized in Figure 12.1 (p. 328), helps you decide how to organize your presentation. A friendly audience, for example, will respond to humour and personal experiences. A neutral audience requires an even, controlled delivery style. The talk would probably be filled with facts, statistics, and expert opinions. An uninterested audience that is forced to attend requires a brief presentation. Such an audience might respond best to humour, cartoons, colourful visuals, and startling statistics. A hostile audience demands a calm, controlled delivery style with objective data and expert opinion.

Quick Check

Audience analysis issues include size, age, gender, experience, attitude, and expectations.

Other elements, such as age, education, experience, and size of audience will affect your style and message content. Analyze the following questions to help you determine your organizational pattern, delivery style, and supporting material.

- How will this topic appeal to this audience?
- How can I relate this information to their needs?
- How can I earn respect so that they accept my message?
- What would be most effective in making my point? Facts? Statistics? Personal experiences? Expert opinion? Humour? Cartoons? Graphic illustrations? Demonstrations? Case histories? Analogies?
- What measures must I take to ensure that this audience remembers my main points?

FIGURE 12.1 Succeeding With Four Audience Types

Audience Members	Organizational Pattern	Delivery Style	Supporting Material
Friendly They like you and your topic	Use any pattern; try something new; involve the audience	Be warm, pleasant, open; use lots of eye contact, smiles	Include humour, personal examples and experiences
Neutral They are calm, rational; their minds are made up but they think they are objective	Present both sides of issue; use pro–con or problem–solution patterns; save time for audience questions	Be controlled; do nothing showy; use confident, small gestures	Use facts, statistics, expert opinion, comparison and contrast; avoid humour, personal stories, and flashy visuals
Uninterested They have short attention spans; they may be there against their will	Be brief, no more than three points; avoid topical and pro–con patterns that seem lengthy to audience	Be dynamic and entertaining; move around, use large gestures	Use humour, cartoons, colourful visuals, powerful quotations, startling statistics
	Avoid darkening the room, standing motionless, passing out handouts, using boring visuals, or expecting audience to participate		
Hostile They want to take charge or to ridicule speaker; defensive, emotional	Use noncontroversial pattern such as topical, chronological, or geographical	Be calm, controlled; speak evenly and slowly	Include objective data and expert opinion; avoid anecdotes and humour
	Avoid question-and-answer period, if possible; otherwise, use a moderator or accept only written questions		

Organizing Content for a Powerful Impact

 Quick Check

Good organization and intentional repetition help your audience understand and retain what you say.

Once you have determined your purpose and analyzed the audience, you're ready to collect information and organize it logically. Good organization and conscious repetition are the two most powerful keys to audience comprehension and retention. In fact, many speech experts recommend the following admittedly repetitious, but effective, plan:

Step 1: Tell them what you're going to say.
Step 2: Say it.
Step 3: Tell them what you've just said.

In other words, repeat your main points in the introduction, body, and conclusion of your presentation. Although it sounds boring, this strategy works surprisingly well. Let's examine how to construct the three parts of an effective presentation.

Capturing Attention in the Introduction

How many times have you heard a speaker begin with, *It's a pleasure to be here.* Or, *I'm honoured to be asked to speak.* Boring openings such as these get speakers off to

"Please don't make me use
another water balloon to
keep your attention."

© Ted Goff (www.tedgoff.com)

a dull start. Avoid such banalities by striving to accomplish three goals in the introduction to your presentation:

- Capture listeners' attention and get them involved.
- Identify yourself and establish your credibility.
- Preview your main points.

If you're able to appeal to listeners and involve them in your presentation right from the start, you're more likely to hold their attention until the finish. Consider some of the same techniques that you used to open sales letters: a question, a startling fact, a joke, a story, or a quotation. Some speakers achieve involvement by opening with a question or command that requires audience members to raise their hands or stand up. You'll find additional techniques for gaining and keeping audience attention in Figure 12.2 on page 330.

To establish your credibility, you need to describe your position, knowledge, or experience—whatever qualifies you to speak. Try also to connect with your audience. Listeners are particularly drawn to speakers who reveal something of themselves and identify with them. A consultant addressing office workers might reminisce about how he started as a temporary worker; a CEO might tell a funny story in which the joke is on herself.

After capturing attention and establishing yourself, you'll want to preview the main points of your topic, perhaps with a visual aid. You may wish to put off actually writing your introduction until after you have organized the rest of the presentation and crystallized your principal ideas.

Take a look at Eric Evans's introduction, shown in Figure 12.3 (p. 331), to see how he integrated all the elements necessary for a good opening.

Organizing the Body

The biggest problem with most oral presentations is a failure to focus on a few principal ideas. Thus, the body of your short presentation (20 or fewer minutes) should include a limited number of main points, say, two to four. Develop each main point with adequate, but not excessive, explanation and details. Too many details can obscure the main message, so keep your presentation simple and logical. Remember, listeners have no pages to leaf back through should they become confused.

✓ Quick Check
Attention-grabbing openers include questions, startling facts, jokes, anecdotes, and quotations.

✓ Quick Check
The best oral presentations focus on a few key ideas.

FIGURE 12.2 Nine Winning Techniques for Gaining and Keeping Audience Attention

Experienced speakers know how to capture the attention of an audience and how to maintain that attention during a presentation. You can give your presentations a boost by trying these nine proven techniques.

- **A promise.** Begin with a promise that keeps the audience expectant. For example, *By the end of this presentation I will have shown you how you can increase your sales by 50 percent!*
- **Drama.** Open by telling an emotionally moving story or by describing a serious problem that involves the audience. Throughout your talk include other dramatic elements, such as a long pause after a key statement. Change your vocal tone or pitch. Professionals use high-intensity emotions such as anger, joy, sadness, and excitement.
- **Eye contact.** As you begin, command attention by surveying the entire audience to take in all listeners. Take two to five seconds to make eye contact with as many people as possible.
- **Movement.** Leave the lectern area whenever possible. Walk around the conference table or between the aisles of your audience. Try to move toward your audience, especially at the beginning and end of your talk.
- **Questions.** Keep listeners active and involved with rhetorical questions. Ask for a show of hands to get each listener thinking. The response will also give you a quick gauge of audience attention.
- **Demonstrations.** Include a member of the audience in a demonstration. For example, *I'm going to show you exactly how to implement our four-step customer courtesy process, but I need a volunteer from the audience to help me.*
- **Samples/gimmicks.** If you're promoting a product, consider using items to toss out to the audience or to award as prizes to volunteer participants. You can also pass around product samples or promotional literature. Be careful, though, to maintain control.
- **Visuals.** Give your audience something to look at besides yourself. Use a variety of visual aids in a single session. Also consider writing the concerns expressed by your audience on a flipchart or on the board as you go along.
- **Self-interest.** Review your entire presentation to ensure that it meets the critical *What's-in-it-for-me* audience test. Remember that people are most interested in things that benefit them.

When Eric Evans began planning his presentation, he realized immediately that he could talk for hours on his topic. He also knew that listeners are not good at separating major and minor points. Thus, instead of submerging his listeners in a sea of information, he sorted out a few principal ideas. In the mortgage business, loan officers generally ask the following three questions of each applicant for a small business loan: (1) Are you ready to "hit the ground running" in starting your business? (2) Have you done your homework? and (3) Have you made realistic projections of potential sales, cash flow, and equity investment? These questions would become his main points, but Eric wanted to streamline them further so that his audience would be sure to remember them. He capsulized the questions in three words: *experience, preparation,* and *projection.* As you can see in Figure 12.3, Eric prepared a sentence outline showing these three main ideas. Each is supported by examples and explanations.

How to organize and sequence main ideas may not be immediately obvious when you begin working on a presentation. In Chapter 10 you studied a number

Chapter 12 Giving Oral Presentations

FIGURE 12.3 Oral Presentation Outline

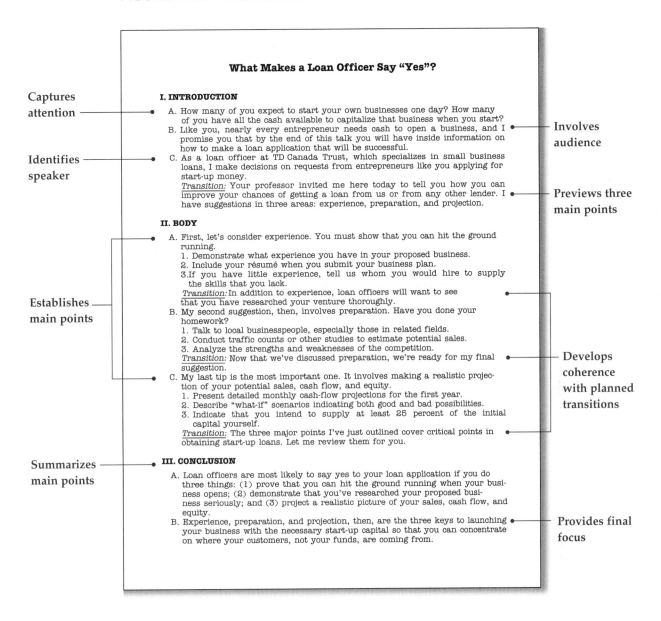

What Makes a Loan Officer Say "Yes"?

Captures attention —

Identifies speaker —

I. INTRODUCTION

A. How many of you expect to start your own businesses one day? How many of you have all the cash available to capitalize that business when you start?
B. Like you, nearly every entrepreneur needs cash to open a business, and I promise you that by the end of this talk you will have inside information on how to make a loan application that will be successful.
C. As a loan officer at TD Canada Trust, which specializes in small business loans, I make decisions on requests from entrepreneurs like you applying for start-up money.
   Transition: Your professor invited me here today to tell you how you can improve your chances of getting a loan from us or from any other lender. I have suggestions in three areas: experience, preparation, and projection.

— Involves audience

— Previews three main points

Establishes main points —

II. BODY

A. First, let's consider experience. You must show that you can hit the ground running.
   1. Demonstrate what experience you have in your proposed business.
   2. Include your résumé when you submit your business plan.
   3. If you have little experience, tell us whom you would hire to supply the skills that you lack.
   Transition: In addition to experience, loan officers will want to see that you have researched your venture thoroughly.
B. My second suggestion, then, involves preparation. Have you done your homework?
   1. Talk to local businesspeople, especially those in related fields.
   2. Conduct traffic counts or other studies to estimate potential sales.
   3. Analyze the strengths and weaknesses of the competition.
   Transition: Now that we've discussed preparation, we're ready for my final suggestion.
C. My last tip is the most important one. It involves making a realistic projection of your potential sales, cash flow, and equity.
   1. Present detailed monthly cash-flow projections for the first year.
   2. Describe "what-if" scenarios indicating both good and bad possibilities.
   3. Indicate that you intend to supply at least 25 percent of the initial capital yourself.
   Transition: The three major points I've just outlined cover critical points in obtaining start-up loans. Let me review them for you.

— Develops coherence with planned transitions

Summarizes main points —

III. CONCLUSION

A. Loan officers are most likely to say yes to your loan application if you do three things: (1) prove that you can hit the ground running when your business opens; (2) demonstrate that you've researched your proposed business seriously; and (3) project a realistic picture of your sales, cash flow, and equity.
B. Experience, preparation, and projection, then, are the three keys to launching your business with the necessary start-up capital so that you can concentrate on where your customers, not your funds, are coming from.

— Provides final focus

of patterns for organizing written reports. Those patterns—reviewed, amplified, and illustrated here—are equally appropriate for oral presentations.

- **Chronology.** Example: A presentation describing the history of a problem, organized from the first sign of trouble to the present.
- **Geography/space.** Example: A presentation about the changing diversity of the workforce, organized by regions in the country (East Coast, West Coast, and so forth).
- **Topic/function/conventional grouping.** Example: A report discussing mishandled airline baggage, organized by names of airlines.
- **Comparison/contrast (pro/con).** Example: A report comparing organic farming methods with those of modern industrial farming.
- **Journalism pattern.** Example: A report describing how identity thieves can ruin your good name. Organized by *who, what, when, where, why,* and *how.*
- **Value/size.** Example: A report describing fluctuations in housing costs, organized by prices of homes.

Quick Check

Organize your report by time, geography, function, importance, or some other method that is logical to the receiver.

Organizing Content for a Powerful Impact

- **Importance.** Example: A report describing five reasons that a company should move its headquarters to a specific city, organized from the most important reason to the least important.
- **Problem/solution.** Example: A company faces a problem such as declining sales. A solution such as reducing the staff is offered.
- **Simple/complex.** Example: A report explaining genetic modification of plants, organized from simple seed production to complex gene introduction.
- **Best case/worst case.** Example: A report analyzing whether two companies should merge, organized by the best-case result (improved market share, profitability, good employee morale) opposed to the worse-case result (devalued stock, lost market share, poor employee morale).

In the presentation shown in Figure 12.3, Eric arranged the main points by importance, placing the most important point last where it had maximum effect. When organizing any presentation, prepare a little more material than you think you will actually need. Savvy speakers always have something useful in reserve (such as an extra handout, transparency, or idea)—just in case they finish early.

Summarizing in the Conclusion

Nervous speakers often rush to wrap up their presentations because they can't wait to flee the stage. But listeners will remember the conclusion more than any part of a speech. That's why you should spend some time to make it most effective. Strive to achieve two goals:

✓ Quick Check

Effective conclusions summarize main points and allow the speaker to exit gracefully.

- Summarize the main themes of the presentation.
- Include a statement that allows you to leave the podium gracefully.

Some speakers end limply with comments such as "I guess that's about all I have to say." This leaves bewildered audience members wondering whether they should continue listening. Skilled speakers alert the audience that they are finishing. They use phrases such as, *In conclusion, As I end this presentation,* or *It's time for me to stop.* Then they proceed immediately to the conclusion. Audiences become justly irritated with a speaker who announces the conclusion but then digresses with one more story or talks on for ten more minutes.

A straightforward summary should review major points and focus on what you want the listeners to do, think, or remember. You might say, *In bringing my presentation to a close, I will restate my major purpose. . . .* Or, *In summary, my major purpose has been to . . .; in support of my purpose, I have presented three major points. They are (a) . . . , (b) . . . , and (c). . . .* Notice how Eric Evans, in the conclusion shown in Figure 12.3, summarized his three main points and provided a final focus to listeners.

If you are promoting a recommendation, you might end as follows: *In conclusion, I recommend that we retain Matrixx Marketing to conduct a telemarketing campaign beginning September 1 at a cost of X dollars. To complete this recommendation, I suggest that we (a) finance this campaign from our operations budget, (b) develop a persuasive message describing our new product, and (c) name Lisa Beck to oversee the project.*

In your conclusion you might want to use an anecdote, an inspiring quotation, or a statement that ties in the attention-capturing opener and offers a new insight. Whatever you choose, be sure to include a closing thought that indicates you are finished. For example, *This concludes my presentation. After investigating many marketing firms, we are convinced that Matrixx is the best for our purposes. Your authorization of my recommendations will mark the beginning of a very successful campaign for our new product. Thank you.*

How the Best Speakers Build Audience Rapport

Good speakers are adept at building audience rapport. They form a bond with the audience; they entertain as well as inform. How do they do it? Based on observations of successful and unsuccessful speakers, we learn that the good ones use a number of verbal and nonverbal techniques to connect with the audience. Some of their helpful techniques include providing effective imagery, supplying verbal signposts, and using body language strategically.

Effective Imagery

You'll lose your audience quickly if your talk is filled with abstractions, generalities, and dry facts. To enliven your presentation and enhance comprehension, try using some of these techniques:

- **Analogies.** A comparison of similar traits between dissimilar things can be effective in explaining and drawing connections. For example, *Product development is similar to the process of conceiving, carrying, and delivering a baby.* Or, *Downsizing and restructuring are similar to an overweight person undergoing a regimen of dieting, habit changing, and exercise.*

Quick Check

Use analogies, metaphors, similes, personal anecdotes, personalized statistics, and worst- and best-case scenarios instead of dry facts.

- **Metaphors.** A comparison between otherwise dissimilar things without using the words *like* or *as* results in a metaphor. For example, *Our competitor's CEO is a snake when it comes to negotiating* or *My desk is a garbage dump.*
- **Similes.** A comparison that includes the words *like* or *as* is a simile. For example, *Building a business team is like building a sports team—you want people not only with the right abilities, but also with the willingness to work together.* Or, *She's as happy as someone who just won the lottery.*
- **Personal anecdotes.** Nothing connects you faster or better with your audience than a good personal story. In a talk about e-mail techniques, you could reveal your own blunders that became painful learning experiences. In a talk to potential investors, the founder of a new ethnic magazine might tell a story about growing up without enough positive ethnic role models.
- **Personalized statistics.** Although often misused, statistics stay with people—particularly when they relate directly to the audience. A speaker discussing job searching might say, *Look around the room. Only three out of five graduates will find a job immediately after graduation.* If possible, simplify and personalize facts. For example, *The sales of Creemore Springs Brewery totalled 5 million cases last year. That means a full case of Creemore was consumed by every man, woman, and child in the Greater Toronto area.*
- **Worst- and best-case scenarios.** Hearing the worst that could happen can be effective in driving home a point. For example, *If we do nothing about our computer backup system now, it's just a matter of time before the entire system crashes and we lose all of our customer contact information. Can you imagine starting from scratch in building all of your customer files again? However, if we fix the system now, we can expand our customer files and actually increase sales at the same time.*
- **Examples.** If all else fails, remember that an audience likes to hear specifics. If you're giving a presentation on office etiquette, for example, instead of just saying, *Rudeness in the workplace is a growing problem,* it's always better to say something like *Rudeness in the workplace is a growing problem. For example, we've heard from some of our clients that our customer service representatives could improve their tone of voice.*

How the Best Speakers Build Audience Rapport

Verbal Signposts

Speakers must remember that listeners, unlike readers of a report, cannot control the rate of presentation or flip back through pages to review main points. As a result, listeners get lost easily. Knowledgeable speakers help the audience recognize the organization and main points in an oral message with verbal signposts. They keep listeners on track by including helpful previews, summaries, and transitions, such as these:

- **Previewing**
  The next segment of my talk presents three reasons for . . . .
  Let's now consider the causes of . . . .

- **Switching directions**
  Thus far we've talked solely about . . . ; now let's move to . . . .
  I've argued that . . . and . . . , but an alternate view holds that . . . .

- **Summarizing**
  Let me review with you the major problems I've just discussed . . . .
  You see, then, that the most significant factors are . . . .

You can further improve any oral presentation by including appropriate transitional expressions such as *first, second, next, then, therefore, moreover, on the other hand, on the contrary,* and *in conclusion*. These expressions lend emphasis and tell listeners where you are headed. Notice in Eric Evans' outline, in Figure 12.3, the specific transitional elements are designed to help listeners recognize each new principal point.

Nonverbal Messages

Although what you say is most important, the nonverbal messages you send can also have a potent effect on how well your message is received. How you look, how you move, and how you speak can make or break your presentation. The following suggestions focus on nonverbal tips to ensure that your verbal message is well received.

- **Look terrific.** Like it or not, you will be judged by your appearance. For everything but small in-house presentations, be sure you dress professionally. The rule of thumb is that you should dress at least as well as the best-dressed person in the company.
- **Animate your body.** Be enthusiastic and let your body show it. Emphasize ideas to enhance points about size, number, and direction. Use a variety of gestures, but try not to consciously plan them in advance.
- **Punctuate your words.** You can keep your audience interested by varying your tone, volume, pitch, and pace. Use pauses before and after important points. Allow the audience to take in your ideas.
- **Get out from behind the podium.** Avoid being planted behind the podium. Movement makes you look natural and comfortable. You might pick a few places in the room to walk to. Even if you must stay close to your visual aids, make a point of leaving them occasionally so that the audience can see your whole body.
- **Vary your facial expression.** Begin with a smile, but change your expressions to correspond with the thoughts you are voicing. You can shake your head to show disagreement, roll your eyes to show disdain, look heavenward for guidance, or wrinkle your brow to show concern or dismay. To see how speakers convey meaning without words, mute the sound on your TV and watch the facial expressions of any well-known talk show host.

Planning Visual Aids, Handouts, and Computer Presentations

Before you give a business presentation, consider this wise Chinese proverb: "Tell me, I forget. Show me, I remember. Involve me, I understand." Your goals as a speaker are to make listeners understand, remember, and act on your ideas. To get them interested and involved, include effective visual aids. Some experts say that we acquire 85 percent of all our knowledge visually. Therefore, an oral presentation that incorporates visual aids is far more likely to be understood and retained than one lacking visual enhancement.

Good visual aids have many purposes. They emphasize and clarify main points, thus improving comprehension and retention. They increase audience interest, and they make the presenter appear more professional, better prepared, and more persuasive. Furthermore, research shows that the use of visual aids actually shortens meetings.[4] Visual aids are particularly helpful for inexperienced speakers because the audience concentrates on the aid rather than on the speaker. Good visuals also serve to jog the memory of a speaker, thus improving self-confidence, poise, and delivery.

> ✓ **Quick Check**
>
> Visual aids clarify points, improve comprehension, and aid retention.

Types of Visual Aids

Fortunately for today's speakers, many forms of visual media are available to enhance a presentation. Figure 12.4 (p. 336) describes a number of visual aids and compares their degree of formality, and other considerations. Three of the most popular visuals are overhead projectors, handouts, and computer visuals.

Overhead Projectors. Student and professional speakers alike rely on the overhead projector and document camera for many reasons. Most meeting areas are equipped with projectors and screens. Moreover, acetate transparencies for the overhead are cheap, easily prepared on a computer or copier, and simple to use. Similarly, projecting a page from a book or a newspaper article with a document camera is effective. And, because rooms need not be darkened, a speaker using transparencies or a document camera can maintain eye contact with the audience. A word of caution, though: stand to the side of the projector so that you don't obstruct the audience's view.

Handouts. You can enhance and complement your presentations by distributing pictures, outlines, brochures, articles, charts, summaries, or other supplements. Speakers who use computer presentation programs often prepare a set of their slides along with notes to hand out to viewers with mixed results. Often, the audience doesn't pay attention to the speaker but noisily flips through the printed-out pages of the computer presentation. Timing the distribution of any handout, though, is tricky. If given out during a presentation, your handouts tend to distract the audience, causing you to lose control. Thus, it's probably best to discuss most handouts during the presentation but delay distributing them until after you finish.

Computer Visuals. With today's excellent software programs—such as Power-Point, Harvard Graphics Advanced Presentation, Freelance Graphics, and Corel Presentations—you can create dynamic, colourful presentations with your computer. The output from these programs is generally shown on a monitor or a screen. With a little expertise and advanced equipment, you can create a multi-media presentation that includes stereo sound, video clips, and hyperlinks, as described in the following discussion of electronic presentations.

FIGURE 12.4 Presentation Enhancers

Medium	Audience Size	Formality Level	Advantages and Disadvantages
Computer slides	2–200	Formal or informal	Presentation software programs are easy to use and cheap and produce professional results. They should not, however, replace or distract from the speaker's message. Darkened room can put audience to sleep.
Overhead projector/ document camera	2–200	Formal or informal	Transparencies produce neat, legible visuals that are cheap and easy to make. Speaker keeps contact with audience. Transparencies and/or magnifying an existing document may, however, look low tech.
Flipchart	2–200	Informal	Easels and charts are readily available and portable. Useful for working discussions and informational presentations. Speaker can prepare display in advance or on the spot.
Write-and-wipe board	2–200	Informal	Porcelain-on-steel surface replaces messy chalkboard. Speaker can wipe clean with cloth. Useful for working discussions.
Video monitor	2–100	Formal or informal	A VCR or DVD display features motion and sound. Videos, and DVDs, however, require skill, time, and equipment to prepare.
Props	2–200	Formal or informal	Product samples, prototypes, symbols, or gimmicks can produce vivid images that audiences remember.
Handouts	Unlimited	Formal or informal	Audience appreciates take-home items such as outlines, tables, charts, reports, brochures, or summaries. Handouts, however, can divert attention from speaker.

Designing an Impressive Computer Presentation

Quick Check

Computer-aided presentations are economical, flexible, professional, and easy to prepare.

The content of most presentations today hasn't changed, but the medium certainly has. At meetings and conferences many speakers now use computer programs, such as PowerPoint, to present, defend, and sell their ideas most effectively. PowerPoint is a software program that facilitates design of text and graphics on slides that can be displayed on a laptop computer or projected to a screen. PowerPoint slides can also be sent out as an e-mail attachment, distributed via web download, or printed as a booklet. The latest gadgets even enable you to plan your PowerPoint presentation on a PDA.[5] Many business speakers use PowerPoint because it helps them organize their thoughts, is relatively inexpensive, and produces flashy high-tech visuals. Used skillfully, PowerPoint can make an impressive, professional presentation.

Yet, PowerPoint has its critics. PowerPoint, say its detractors, is turning the nation's businesspeople into a "mindless gaggle of bullet-pointed morons."[6]

✔ *Quick Check*

Critics say that PowerPoint is too regimented and produces "bullet-pointed morons."

Behind the inflated rhetoric is a fair bit of wisdom. Writing in *Canadian Business* magazine, Andrew Wahl paints an all too familiar picture: "We've all been there, sitting in some dark, airless space, straining to keep our eyes open during a presentation that drones on and on. A screen glows with a seemingly endless series of slides and charts, bullet points and words streaking and spinning round. But it's all in vain. Befuddled by the barrage of information, you fail to glean anything of use. The presentation ends, the lights come up, and you stumble away in a haze, thirsty for comprehension."[7] Wahl goes on to describe a number of problems with relying too heavily on PowerPoint, but without a doubt the greatest two are the curse of too many words on slides, which leads to audience exhaustion and divided attention, and the curse of the presenter who merely reads his or her slides, often turned away from the audience.

The ease with which most of us use PowerPoint has led to a false sense of security. We seem to have forgotten that to be effective, presenters using PowerPoint must first be effective presenters, period. Effective presenters do not overwhelm an audience by assuming it will be happy to read multiple slides with multiple lines or paragraphs of text, nor do they rely so heavily on a screen image that no one is paying attention to or listening to them. In other words, smart business presenters have to keep the attention of their audience by deploying the skills discussed above and in Chapter 11. They cannot assume that simply because they have a well-designed PowerPoint presentation, their actual *presentation* will go well. Of course, learning how to use templates, working with colour, building bullet points, and add multimedia effects are valuable skills, and the rest of this section examines best practices in using computer presentation software.

Using Templates to Your Advantage

To begin your training in using an electronic presentation program, you'll want to examine its templates. These professionally designed formats combine harmonious colours, borders, and fonts for pleasing visual effects. One of the biggest problems in corporate presentations is inconsistency. Presentations include a hodgepodge collection of informal slides with different fonts and clashing colours. Templates avoid this problem by showing what fonts should be used for different level headings.

Templates also provide guidance in laying out each slide, as shown in Figure 12.5 (p. 338). You can select a layout for a title page, a bulleted list, a bar chart, a double-column list, an organization chart, and so on. To present a unified and distinctive image, some companies develop a customized template with their logo and a predefined colour scheme. As one expert says, "This prevents salespeople from creating horrid colour combinations on their own."[8] But templates are helpful only if you use them when you first begin preparing your presentation. Applying a template when you are nearly finished involves a lot of rekeying and rewriting.

A final piece of advice about presentation templates is that you should resist the temptation toward tackiness. Some novice businesspeople and students assume that because a template with a palm tree and cactus exists, and because they think it looks good, that it will look professional. It won't. Remember that visual professionalism means simplicity, not cuteness or busyness.

Working With Colour

You don't need training in colour theory to create presentation images that impress your audience rather than confuse them. You can use the colour schemes from the design templates that come with your presentation program, as shown in Figure 12.6 (p. 339), or you can alter them. Generally, it's best to use a colour palette of five

✔ *Quick Check*

Background and text colours depend on the lightness of the room.

FIGURE 12.5 Selecting a Slide Layout in Microsoft PowerPoint

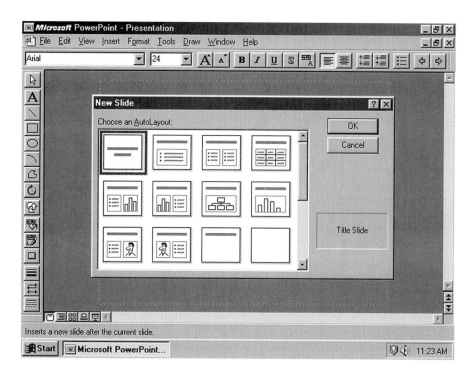

or fewer colours for an entire presentation. Use warm colours—reds, oranges, and yellows—to highlight important elements. Use the same colour for like elements. For example, all slide titles should be the same colour. The colour for backgrounds and text depends on where the presentation will be given. Use light text on a dark background for presentations in darkened rooms. Use dark text on a light background for computer presentations in lighted rooms and for projecting transparencies.

When many people are working together to prepare a slide presentation, be sure that they all choose colours that are in PowerPoint's colour scheme menu. When other colours are used, making changes becomes a tedious exercise in individual slide-editing.[9]

Building Bullet Points

✓ Quick Check

Bullet points should be short phrases that are parallel.

When you prepare your slides, translate the major headings in your presentation outline into titles for slides. Then build bullet points using short phrases. In Chapter 5 you learned to improve readability by using graphic highlighting techniques, including bullets, numbers, and headings. In preparing a PowerPoint presentation, you will use those same techniques.

Let's say, for example, that Matt wants to persuade the boss of his small company to install a voice mail system. His boss is resisting because he says that voice mail will cost too much. Matt wants to emphasize benefits that result in increased productivity. Here is a portion of the text he wrote:

Text of Presentation

Because voice mail allows callers to deliver detailed information to office personnel with just one telephone call, telephone tag can be eliminated. In addition, some research has found that up to 75 percent of all business calls do not reach the desired party. Whatever the actual number, people do tend to make far fewer callbacks when they have a voice mailbox in which their callers can leave messages. Although voice mail can't match the timeliness of a live telephone call, it's the next best thing for getting the word out when time is of the essence. Finally, voice mail

FIGURE 12.6 Choosing a Colour Scheme in Microsoft PowerPoint

Tips for Choosing the Best Colours in Visuals

- **Develop a colour palette of five or fewer colours.**
- **Use the same colour for similar elements.**
- **Use dark text on a light background for presentations in bright rooms.**
- **Use light text on a dark background for presentations in darkened rooms.**
- **Use dark text on a light background for transparencies.**
- **Beware of light text on light backgrounds and dark text on dark backgrounds.**

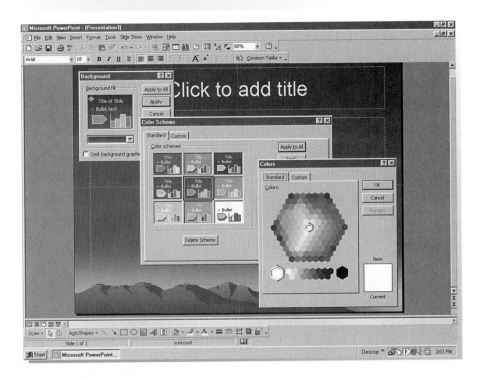

PowerPoint software provides a selection of designed templates, but you can also develop your own colour scheme.

frees callers from the prospect of being placed on hold indefinitely when the person they want is temporarily unavailable. Callers can immediately leave a voice message, bypassing the hold interval altogether.

To convert the preceding text into bullet points, Matt started with a title and then listed the main ideas that related to that title. He made sure all the items were parallel. Matt went through many revisions before creating the following bulleted list. Notice that the heading promotes reader benefits. Notice also that the bullet points are concise. They should be key words or phrases, not complete sentences, because the most effective presentations use visuals as signposts along the way. It's up to Matt to speak to each bulleted point, to engage his audience.

Text Converted to Bullet Points
Voice Mail Can Make Your Calls More Efficient
- Eliminates telephone tag
- Reduces callbacks
- Improves timely communication
- Shortens "hold" times

Quick Check

Text can be converted to bullet points by experimenting with key phrases that are concise and balanced grammatically.

Designing an Impressive Computer Presentation

One of the best features of electronic presentation programs is the "build" capability. You can focus the viewer's attention on each specific item as you add bullet points line by line. The bulleted items may "fly" in from the left, right, top, or bottom. They can also build or dissolve from the centre. As you add each new bullet point, leave the previous ones on the slide but show them in lightened text. In building bulleted points or in moving from one slide to the next, you can use slide transition elements, such as "wipe-outs," glitter, ripple, liquid, and vortex effects. But don't overdo it. Experts suggest choosing one transition effect and applying it consistently.[10]

FIGURE 12.7   **Preparing a PowerPoint Presentation**

Tips for Preparing and Using Slides

- **Keep all visuals simple; spotlight major points only.**
- **Use the same font size and style for similar headings.**
- **No more than seven words on a line, and four total lines, plus a title**
- **Be sure that everyone in the audience can see the slides.**
- **Show a slide, allow the audience to read it, then paraphrase it. Do NOT read from a slide.**
- **Rehearse by practising talking to the audience, not to the slides.**

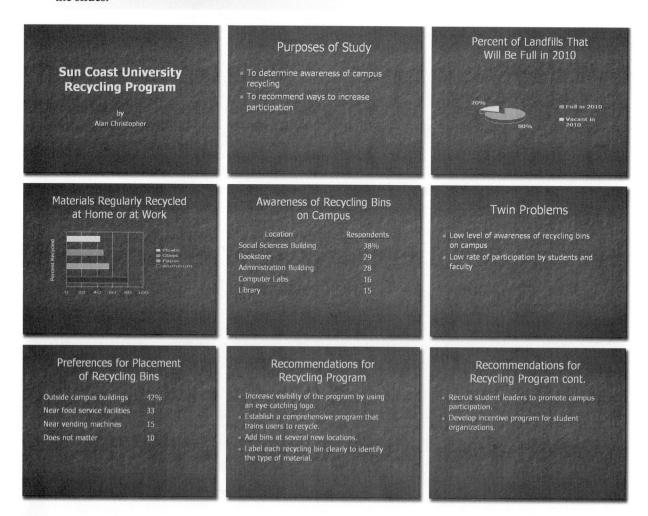

For the most effective presentations, each slide should include no more than seven words in a line. Furthermore, no slide should have more than four lines, plus a title. An effective PowerPoint presentation is found in Figure 12.7. Remember that presentation slides summarize; they don't tell the whole story. That's the job of the presenter.

Adding Multimedia and Other Effects

Many presentation programs also provide libraries of multimedia features to enhance your content. These include sound, animation, and video elements. For example, you could use sound effects to "reward" correct answers from your audience. Similarly, video clips—when used judiciously—can add excitement and depth to a presentation. You might use video to capture attention in a stimulating introduction, to show the benefits of a product in use, or to bring the personality of a distant expert or satisfied customer right into the meeting room.

Another way to enliven a presentation is with photographic images, which are now easy to obtain electronically thanks to the prevalence of low-cost scanners and digital cameras. Most programs are also capable of generating hyperlinks ("hot" spots on the screen) that allow you to jump instantly to relevant data or multimedia content.

Producing Speaker's Notes and Handouts

Most computer presentation programs offer a variety of presentation options. In addition to printouts of your slides, you can make speaker's notes, as shown in Figure 12.8. These are wonderful aids for practising your talk; they remind you of the supporting comments for the abbreviated material in your slides. Many programs allow you to print miniature versions of your slides with numerous slides to a page, if you wish. These miniatures are handy if you want to preview your talk to a sponsoring organization or if you wish to supply the audience with a summary of your presentation.

FIGURE 12.8 **Speaker's Notes for a Computer Presentation**

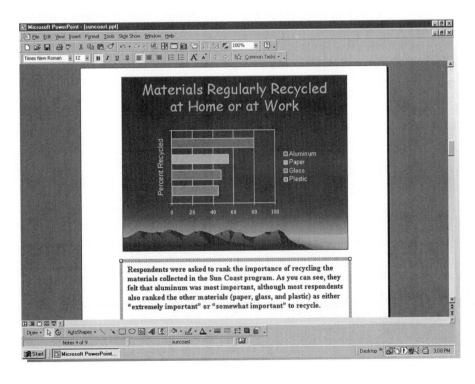

Speaker's notes enable you to print discussion items beneath each slide, thus providing handy review material for practice.

Developing Web-Based Presentations and Electronic Handouts

Because of many technological improvements, you can now give a talk without even travelling off-site. In other words, you can put your slides "on the road." Web presentations with slides, narration, and speaker control are emerging as a less costly alternative to videoconferencing, which can be expensive. For example, you could initiate a meeting via a conference call, narrate using a telephone, and have participants see your slides from the browsers on their computers. If you prefer, you could skip the narration and provide a prerecorded presentation. Web-based presentations have many applications, including providing access to updated training or sales data whenever needed.[11] Larry Magid, computer expert and noted speaker, suggests still another way that speakers can use the Web. He recommends posting your slides on the Web even if you are giving a face-to-face presentation. Attendees appreciate these *electronic handouts* because they don't have to carry them home.[12]

Avoiding Being Upstaged by Your Slides

Although computer presentations are great aids, they cannot replace you. In developing a presentation, don't expect your slides to carry the show.

Your goal is to avoid letting PowerPoint "steal your thunder." Here are suggestions for keeping control in your slide presentation:

- Use your slides primarily to summarize important points. For each slide have one or more paragraphs of narration to present to your audience.
- Remember that your responsibility is to *add value* to the information you present. Explain the analyses leading up to the major points and what each point means.
- Look at the audience, not the screen.
- Leave the lights as bright as you can. Make sure the audience can see your face and eyes.
- Darken the screen while you discuss points, tell a story, give an example, or involve the audience.
- Maintain a connection with the audience by using a laser pointer to highlight slide items to discuss.
- Don't rely totally on PowerPoint. Help the audience visualize your points by using other techniques. Drawing a diagram on a white board or flip chart can be more engaging than showing slide after slide of static drawings. Showing real objects is a welcome relief from slides.
- Remember that your slides merely supply a framework for your presentation. Your audience came to see and hear you.[13]

Polishing Your Delivery and Following Up

Once you've organized your presentation and prepared visuals, you're ready to practise delivering it. Here are suggestions for selecting a delivery method, along with specific techniques to use before, during, and after your presentation.

Delivery Method

Inexperienced speakers often feel that they must memorize an entire presentation to be effective. Unless you're a professional performer, however, you will sound wooden and unnatural. Moreover, forgetting your place can be embarrassing Therefore, memorizing an entire oral presentation is not recommended. However, memorizing significant parts—the introduction, the conclusion, and perhaps a meaningful quotation—can be dramatic and impressive.

If memorizing won't work, is reading your presentation the best plan? Definitely not. Reading to an audience is boring and ineffective. Because reading suggests that you don't know your topic well, the audience loses confidence in your expertise. Reading also prevents you from maintaining eye contact. You can't see audience reactions; consequently, you can't benefit from feedback.

Neither the memorizing nor the reading method creates convincing presentations. The best plan, by far, is a "notes" method. Plan your presentation carefully and talk from note cards or an outline containing key sentences and major ideas. By preparing and then practising with your notes, you can talk to your audience in a conversational manner. Your notes should be neither entire paragraphs nor single words. Instead, they should contain a complete sentence or two to introduce each major idea. Below the topic sentence(s), outline subpoints and illustrations. Note cards will keep you on track and prompt your memory, but only if you have rehearsed the presentation thoroughly.

Quick Check
The best method for delivering your presentation is speaking from carefully prepared note cards.

Delivery Techniques

Nearly everyone experiences some degree of stage fright when speaking before a group. "If you hear someone say he or she isn't nervous before a speech, you're talking either to a liar or a very boring speaker," says corporate speech consultant Dianna Booher.[14] In other words, you can capitalize on the adrenaline that is coursing through your body by converting it to excitement and enthusiasm for your performance. But you can't just walk in and "wing it." People who don't prepare suffer the most anxiety and give the worst performances. You can learn to make effective oral presentations by focusing on four areas: preparation, organization, visual aids, and delivery.

Being afraid is quite natural and results from actual physiological changes occurring in your body. Faced with a frightening situation, your body responds with the fight-or-flight response, discussed more fully in Figure 12.9 on page 344. You can learn to control and reduce stage fright, as well as to incorporate techniques for effective speaking, by using the following strategies and techniques before, during, and after your presentation.

Quick Check
Stage fright is both natural and controllable.

"In this seminar we'll discuss a simple technique for overcoming your fear of speaking in public."

© Ted Goff (www.tedgoff.com)

Polishing Your Delivery and Following Up

FIGURE 12.9 Conquer Stage Fright With These Techniques

Ever get nervous before giving a speech? Everyone does. And it's not all in your head, either. When you face something threatening or challenging, your body reacts with what psychologists call the fight-or-flight response. This response provides your body with increased energy to deal with threatening situations. It also creates those sensations—dry mouth, sweaty hands, increased heartbeat, and stomach butterflies—that we associate with stage fright. The fight-or-flight response arouses your body for action—in this case, giving a speech.

Since everyone feels some form of apprehension before speaking, it's impossible to eliminate the physiological symptoms altogether. But you can help reduce their effects with the following techniques:

- **Breathe deeply.** Use deep breathing to ease your fight-or-flight symptoms. Inhale to a count of ten, hold this breath to a count of ten, and exhale to a count of ten. Concentrate on your counting and your breathing; both activities reduce your stress.

- **Convert your fear.** Don't view your sweaty palms and dry mouth as evidence of fear. Interpret them as symptoms of exuberance, excitement, and enthusiasm to share your ideas.
- **Know your topic.** Feel confident about your topic. Select a topic that you know well and that is relevant to your audience.
- **Use positive self-talk.** Remind yourself that you know your topic and are prepared. Tell yourself that the audience is on your side—because it is.
- **Shift the spotlight to your visuals.** At least some of the time the audience will be focusing on your slides, transparencies, handouts, or whatever you have prepared—and not on you.
- **Ignore any stumbles.** Don't apologize or confess your nervousness. If you keep going, the audience will forget any mistakes quickly.
- **Feel proud when you finish.** You'll be surprised at how good you feel when you finish. Take pride in what you've accomplished, and your audience will reward you with applause and congratulations. And, of course, your body will call off the fight-or-flight response and return to normal.

Before Your Presentation

Thorough preparation, extensive rehearsal, and stress-reduction techniques can lessen stage fright.

- **Prepare thoroughly.** One of the most effective strategies for reducing stage fright is knowing your subject thoroughly. Research your topic diligently and prepare a careful sentence outline. Those who try to "wing it" usually suffer the worst butterflies—and make the worst presentations.
- **Rehearse repeatedly.** When you rehearse, practise your entire presentation, not just the first half. Place your outline sentences on separate cards. You may also wish to include transitional sentences to help you move to the next topic. Use these cards as you practise, and include your visual aids in your rehearsal. Rehearse alone or before friends and family. Also try rehearsing on audio- or videotape so that you can evaluate your effectiveness.
- **Time yourself.** Most audiences tend to get restless during longer talks. Thus, try to complete your presentation in no more than 20 minutes. Set a timer during your rehearsal to measure your speaking time.
- **Request a lectern.** Every beginning speaker needs the security of a high desk or lectern from which to deliver a presentation. It serves as a note holder and a convenient place to rest wandering hands and arms.
- **Check the room.** Before you talk, make sure that a lectern has been provided. If you are using sound equipment or a projector, be certain they are operational. Check electrical outlets and the position of the viewing screen. Ensure that the seating arrangement is appropriate to your needs.
- **Greet members of the audience.** Try to make contact with a few members of the audience when you enter the room, while you are waiting to be introduced, or when you walk to the podium. Your body language should convey friendliness, confidence, and enjoyment.
- **Practise stress reduction.** If you feel tension and fear while you are waiting your turn to speak, use stress-reduction techniques, such as deep breathing. Additional techniques to help you conquer stage fright are presented in Figure 12.9.

During Your Presentation

- **Begin with a pause.** When you first approach the audience, take a moment to adjust your notes and make yourself comfortable. Establish your control of the situation.
- **Present your first sentence from memory.** By memorizing your opening, you can immediately establish rapport with the audience through eye contact. You'll also sound confident and knowledgeable.
- **Maintain eye contact.** If the size of the audience overwhelms you, pick out two individuals on the right and two on the left. Talk directly to these people.
- **Control your voice and vocabulary.** This means speaking in moderated tones but loudly enough to be heard. Eliminate verbal static, such as *ah, er, you know,* and *um.* Silence is preferable to meaningless fillers when you are thinking of your next idea.
- **Put the brakes on.** Many novice speakers talk too rapidly, displaying their nervousness and making it difficult for audience members to understand their ideas. Slow down and listen to what you are saying.
- **Move naturally.** You can use the lectern to hold your notes so that you are free to move about casually and naturally. Avoid fidgeting with your notes, your clothing, or items in your pockets. Learn to use your body to express a point.
- **Use visual aids effectively.** Discuss and interpret each visual aid for the audience. Move aside as you describe it so that it can be seen fully. Use a pointer if necessary.
- **Avoid digressions.** Stick to your outline and notes. Don't suddenly include clever little anecdotes or digressions that occur to you on the spot. If it's not part of your rehearsed material, leave it out so that you can finish on time. Remember, too, that your audience may not be as enthralled with your topic as you are.
- **Summarize your main points.** Conclude your presentation by reiterating your main points or by emphasizing what you want the audience to think or do. Once you have announced your conclusion, proceed to it directly.

Quick Check

Eye contact, a moderate tone of voice, and natural movements enhance a presentation.

After Your Presentation

- **Distribute handouts.** If you prepared handouts with data the audience will need, pass them out when you finish.
- **Encourage questions.** If the situation permits a question-and-answer period, announce it at the beginning of your presentation. Then, when you finish, ask for questions. Set a time limit for questions and answers.
- **Repeat questions.** Although the speaker may hear the question, audience members often do not. Begin each answer with a repetition of the question. This also gives you thinking time. Then, direct your answer to the entire audience.
- **Reinforce your main points.** You can use your answers to restate your primary ideas ("I'm glad you brought that up because it gives me a chance to elaborate on . . ."). In answering questions, avoid becoming defensive or debating the questioner.
- **Keep control.** Don't allow one individual to take over. Keep the entire audience involved.
- **Avoid *Yes, but* answers.** The word *but* immediately cancels any preceding message. Try replacing it with *and.* For example, *Yes, X has been tried. And Y works even better because . . . .*
- **End with a summary and appreciation.** To signal the end of the session before you take the last question, say something like *We have time for just one more question.* As you answer the last question, try to work it into a summary of your main points. Then, express appreciation to the audience for the opportunity to talk with them.

Quick Check

The time to answer questions, distribute handouts, and reiterate main points is after a presentation.

This chapter presented techniques for giving effective oral presentations. Good presentations begin with analysis of your purpose and your audience. Organizing the content involves preparing an effective introduction, body, and closing. The introduction should capture the listener's attention, identify the speaker, establish credibility, and preview the main points. The body should discuss two to four main points, with appropriate explanations, details, and verbal signposts to guide listeners. The conclusion should review the main points, provide a final focus, and allow the speaker to leave the podium gracefully. You can improve audience rapport by using effective imagery including examples, analogies, metaphors, similes, personal anecdotes, statistics, and worst/best-case scenarios. In illustrating a presentation, use simple, easily understood visual aids to emphasize and clarify main points. If you employ PowerPoint, you can enhance the presentation by using templates, layout designs, and bullet points.

In delivering your presentation, outline the main points on note cards and rehearse repeatedly. During the presentation consider beginning with a pause and presenting your first sentence from memory. Make eye contact, control your voice, speak and move naturally, and avoid digressions. After your talk distribute handouts and answer questions. End gracefully and express appreciation.

The final two chapters of this book focus on your ultimate goal—getting a job or advancing in your career. You'll learn how to write a persuasive résumé and how to succeed in an employment interview.

Critical Thinking

1. Why is it necessary to repeat key points in an oral presentation?
2. How can a speaker make the most effective use of visual aids?
3. If PowerPoint is so effective, why are people speaking out against using it in presentations?
4. How can speakers prevent electronic presentation software from stealing their thunder?
5. What techniques are most effective for reducing stage fright?

Chapter Review

6. The planning of an oral presentation should begin with serious thinking about what two factors?

7. Name three goals to be achieved in the introduction of an oral presentation.

8. What should the conclusion to an oral presentation include?

9. Name three ways for a speaker to use verbal signposts in a presentation. Illustrate each.

10. List seven techniques for creating effective imagery in a presentation. Be prepared to discuss each.

11. List ten ways that an oral presentation may be organized.

12. Name specific advantages and disadvantages of computer presentation software.

13. Why is a PowerPoint slide with less text preferable to one with more text?

14. What delivery method is most effective for speakers?

Writing Improvement Exercises

15. PowerPoint Practice. Using the summary you wrote in Chapter 9, Exercise 14 (page 242), develop two electronic presentations to go along with this summary. In the first presentation, make the mistake of having too many words on your slides. In the second presentation, correct this mistake. Give both presentations to your class and see if students can identify the problematic presentation, and tell you why it's problematic.

16. PowerPoint Practice. Using the summary you wrote in Chapter 9, Exercise 15 (page 242), develop two electronic presentations to go along with this summary. In the first presentation, make the mistake of having too busy or tacky a design to your slides. In the second presentation, correct this mistake. Give both presentations to your class see if students can identify the problematic presentation, and tell you why it's problematic.

17. PowerPoint Practice. Using the summary you wrote in Chapter 9, Exercise 16 (page 242), develop an electronic presentation to go along with this summary. Present you presentation twice, once making the mistake of reading from the screen or slides and a second time correcting this mistake. See if students can identify the problematic presentation, and tell you why it's problematic.

12.1 Preparing an Oral Presentation. You work for a mid-size financial services firm with 15 financial advisors on staff. When you started in the job two years ago, you were sharing a computer with another advisor. Then a year ago the company decided to invest in laptop computers. All 15 advisors received a laptop for their own use. Recently, there have been grumblings around the office that the firm is not keeping up with the reality of communication technology today. In essence, a number of your colleagues want company-issued PDAs. It doesn't matter to them if it's a BlackBerry, a Palm Pilot, or a Treo, they just want a PDA.

Your Task. As the newest member on staff, and a trusted friend of the firm's manager, you are asked to research the topic of PDAs versus traditional personal computers or laptops and report at the next firm staff meeting. What are the advantages and disadvantages of this new technology? Should the firm make the investment in PDAs so soon after buying everyone a new laptop? Is a PDA necessary for a financial advisor? Your boss hasn't projected a bias one way or the other, but knowing him as well as you do, you're pretty sure he's not keen on the idea of spending more money. Present your findings and recommendations to your colleagues.

12.2 The Pros and Cons of PowerPoint. One of the reasons your boss in Activity 12.1 purchased new laptops last year was to improve the professionalism of the firm. In other words, he wanted each advisor to have a laptop in front of him or her during all client meetings. In his opinion, having a laptop open and on when a client walks into a meeting room is much more effective than simply having a pile of paper sitting on the table. To this end, he made sure the laptops were loaded with the most recent version of Microsoft Office, including Power-Point. Now that you are to give a presentation to the rest of the staff on the pros and cons of PDAs, you figure you better use PowerPoint.

Your Task. Devise two different presentations that answer the problem in Activity 12.1. One of the presentations will use PowerPoint, as described in this chapter. The other presentation will not use PowerPoint, but instead other visual aids or no aids at all. Deliver both presentations in front of the same group. Ask the group to rate both of the presentations using the same agreed-upon criteria. Do not intentionally make one presentation less effective than the other. Afterward, discuss the scores each presentation achieved.

12.3 Preparing, Rehearsing, and Critiquing an Oral Presentation. Just as the chapters in this book on business writing stress the importance of a revision stage, so too oral communication must be revised if it is to be effective. In other words, until you are a seasoned veteran, you should get into the habit of rehearsing your oral presentations. Likewise, you should get into the habit of offering constructive criticism to your peers and colleagues when they solicit it, and of accepting the same criticism when it is offered to you.

Your Task. In groups of four or five, select an issue with business ramifications that interests you. For example, people have strongly held views on the issue of whether or not Canada should allow privatized health care. Investigate your chosen issue in a couple of newspaper or magazine articles found through library online databases, and prepare an oral presentation based on your research. Rehearse the complete oral presentation in front your group. Your audience members will politely raise their hand and interrupt your presentation each time they believe there needs to be improvement (e.g., your voice trails off, you mispronounce a word, you fidget nervously, your body language is sending the wrong signal, you've lost your train of thought, etc.). Accept their constructive criticism and keep rehearsing. Appoint someone to be note taker each time a presentation is being rehearsed, so that at the end each of you has a list of "notes"—much like a theatre director would give to actors during rehearsal—that you can use to improve future presentations. Are there any common elements among the group members' notes?

12.4 Investigating Oral Presentations in Your Field. One of the best sources of career information is someone in your field.

Your Task. Interview one or two individuals in your professional field. How are oral presentations important in this profession? Does the frequency of oral presentations change as one advances? What suggestions can these people make to newcomers to the field for developing proficient oral presentation skills? What are the most common reasons for giving oral presentations in this profession? Discuss your findings with your class.

12.5 Outlining an Oral Presentation. For many people the hardest part of preparing an oral presentation is developing the outline.

Your Task. Select an oral presentation topic from the list in Activity 12.8 (p. 350) or suggest an original topic. Prepare an outline for your presentation using the following format.

Title _____

Purpose _____

	I. INTRODUCTION
Gain attention of audience	A.
Involve audience	B.
Establish credibility	C.
Preview main points	D.
Transition	
	II. BODY
Main point	A.
Illustrate, clarify, contrast	1.
	2.
	3.
Transition	
Main point	B.
Illustrate, clarify, contrast	1.
	2.
	3.
Transition	
Main point	C.
Illustrate, clarify, contrast	1.
	2.
	3.
Transition	
	III. CONCLUSION
Summarize main points	A.
Provide final focus	B.
Encourage questions	C.

12.6 Discovering New Presentation Tips

Your Task. Using your library's online databases, perform a subject search for *business presentations*. Read at least three articles that provide suggestions for giving business presentations. If possible, print the most relevant findings. Select at least eight good tips or techniques that you did *not* learn from this chapter. Your instructor may ask you to bring them to class for discussion or to submit a short e-mail or memo report outlining your tips.

12.7 Researching Job-Application Information

Your Task. Using your library's online databases, perform a subject search for one of the following topics. Find as many articles as you can. Then organize and present a five- to ten-minute informative talk to your class.

a. Do recruiters prefer one- or two-page résumés?
b. How do applicant tracking systems work?
c. How are inflated résumés detected and what are the consequences?
d. What's new in writing cover letters in job applications?
e. What is online résumé fraud?
f. What are some new rules for résumés?

12.8 Choosing a Topic for an Oral Presentation

Your Task. Select a topic from the list below. Prepare a five- to ten-minute oral presentation. Consider yourself an expert who has been called in to explain some aspect of the topic before a group of interested people. Since your time is limited, prepare a concise yet forceful presentation with effective visual aids.

a. What is the career outlook in a field of your choice?
b. How has the Internet changed job searching?
c. What are the advantages and disadvantages of instant messaging as a method of workplace communication?
d. How do employees use online services?
e. What is telecommuting, and for what kind of workers is it an appropriate work alternative?
f. How much choice should parents have in selecting schools for their young children (parochial, private, and public)?
g. What travel location would you recommend for college students at Christmas (or another holiday or in summer)?
h. What is the economic outlook for a given product (such as domestic cars, laptop computers, digital cameras, fitness equipment, or a product of your choice)?
i. How can your organization or institution improve its image?
j. Why should people invest in a company or scheme of your choice?
k. What brand and model of computer and printer represent the best buy for college students today?
l. What franchise would offer the best investment opportunity for an entrepreneur in your area?
m. How should a job candidate dress for an interview?
n. What should a guide to proper cell phone use include?
o. Are internships worth the effort?
p. How is an administrative assistant different from a secretary?
q. Where should your organization hold its next convention?

r. What is your opinion of the statement "Advertising steals our time, defaces the landscape, and degrades the dignity of public institutions"?[15]

s. How can businesspeople reduce the amount of e-mail spam they receive?

t. What is the outlook for real estate (commercial or residential) investment in your area?

u. What are the pros and cons of videoconferencing for [name an organization]?

v. Are today's communication technologies (e-mail, instant messaging, text messaging, PDAs, etc.) making us more productive or just more stressed out?

w. What kinds of gifts are appropriate for businesses to give clients and customers during the holiday season?

x. How are businesses and conservationists working together to protect the world's dwindling tropical forests?

y. Should employees be able to use computers in a work environment for anything other than work-related business?

Grammar/Mechanics Challenge—12

Document for Revision

The following executive summary of a report has faults in grammar, punctuation, spelling, number form, wordiness, and word use. Use standard proofreading marks (see Appendix B) to correct the errors. When you finish, your instructor can show you the revised version of this abstract.

EXECUTIVE SUMMARY

Purpose of Report

The purposes of this report is (1) To determine the Sun coast university campus communitys awareness of the campus recycling program and (2) To recommend ways to increase participation. Sun Coasts recycling program was intended to respond to the increasing problem of waste disposal, to fulfil it's social responsibility as an educational institution, and to meet the demands of legislation that made it a requirement for individuals and organizations to recycle.

A Survey was conducted in an effort to learn about the campus communities recycling habits and to make an assessment of the participation in the recycling program that is current. 220 individuals responded to the Survey but twenty-seven Surveys could not be used. Since Sun coast universitys recycling program include only aluminum, glass, paper and plastic at this point in time these were the only materials considered in this Study.

Recycling at Sun coast

Most Survey respondants recognized the importance of recycling, they stated that they do recycle aluminum, glass, paper and plastic on a regular basis either at home or at work. However most respondants displayed a low-level of awareness, and use of the on campus program. Many of the respondants was unfamilar with the location of the bins around campus; and therefore had not participated in the Recycling Program. Other responses indicated that the bins were not located in convenent locations.

Reccommendations for increasing recycling participation

Recommendations for increasing participation in the Program include the following;

1. relocating the recycling bins for greater visability

2. development of incentive programs to gain the participation of on campus groups

3. training student volunteers to give on campus presentations that give an explanation of the need for recycling, and the benefits of using the Recycling Program

4. we should increase Advertising in regard to the Program

Chapter 12 Giving Oral Presentations

The Worst Deadly Sin in a Presentation

Audiences appreciate speakers with polished delivery techniques, but they are usually relatively forgiving when mistakes occur. One thing they don't suffer gladly, though, is unethical behaviour. Executives in a comprehensive research survey agreed that the "worst deadly sin" a speaker can commit in a presentation is demonstrating a lack of integrity.

What kinds of unethical behaviour do audiences reject? They distrust speakers who misrepresent, exaggerate, and lie. They also dislike cover-ups and evasiveness. The following situations clearly signal trouble for speakers because of the unethical actions involved:

- A sales rep, instead of promoting his company's products, suggests that his competitor's business is mismanaged, is losing customers, or offers seriously flawed products.
- A manager distorts a new employee insurance plan, underemphasizing its deficiencies and overemphasizing its strengths.
- A sales rep fabricates an answer to a tough question instead of admitting ignorance.
- A financial planner tries to prove her point by highlighting an irrelevant statistic.

Career Application

The largest brokerage firm in the United States, Merrill Lynch, recently suffered a major blow to its credibility and paid a $100 million settlement. Why? Its analysts privately called particular Internet stocks "crap" or "dogs," while publicly recommending them in presentations to customers.

Your Task

In small groups or with the entire class, discuss what might motivate a speaker to commit "the worst deadly sin." When have you heard presentations in which you doubted the integrity of the speaker? What unethical presentation techniques have you seen on television? What happens when a speaker loses credibility?

Communicating
for
Employment

13

The Job Search, Résumés, and Cover Letters

CHAPTER

Gone are the days when you could do a job search by showing up at an organization with your résumé. In today's competitive environment, where security and technology "guard the entrance" to the hiring manager's door, your cover letter and résumé are the key to getting the interview. You have one fleeting moment to let the reader know what you have to offer. The wrong format or spelling and grammatical errors can quickly put you out of the running.[1]

Christine Shreves, *human resources consultant, George Brown College*

LEARNING OBJECTIVES

1. Prepare for employment by identifying your interests, evaluating your assets, recognizing the changing nature of jobs, choosing a career path, and studying traditional and electronic job search techniques.

2. Compare and contrast chronological, functional, and combination résumés.

3. Organize and format the parts of a résumé to produce a persuasive product.

4. Identify techniques that prepare a résumé for computer scanning, faxing, and e-mailing.

5. Write a persuasive cover letter to accompany your résumé.

Whether you are applying for your first permanent position, competing for promotion, or changing careers, you'll be more successful if you understand employment strategies and how to promote yourself with a winning résumé. This chapter provides up-to-date advice in preparing for employment, searching the job market, writing a persuasive résumé, and developing an effective cover letter.

Preparing for Employment

Quick Check

Finding a satisfying career means learning about oneself, the job market, and the employment process.

You may think that the first step in finding a job is writing a résumé, but the job search process actually begins long before you are ready to prepare your résumé. Regardless of the kind of employment you seek, you must invest time and effort getting ready. You can't hope to find the position of your dreams without (1) knowing yourself, (2) knowing the job market, and (3) knowing the employment process.

In addition to searching for career information and choosing a specific job objective, you should be studying the job market and becoming aware of the substantial changes in the nature of work. You'll also want to understand how to use the latest Internet resources in your job search. When you have finished all this preparation, you're ready to design a persuasive résumé and job application letter. These documents should be appropriate for small businesses as well as for larger organizations that may be using résumé-scanning programs. Following these steps, summarized in Figure 13.1 and described in this chapter, gives you a master plan for landing a job you really want.

Identifying Your Interests

The employment process begins with introspection. This means looking inside yourself to analyze what you like and dislike so that you can make good employment choices. Career counsellors charge large sums for helping individuals learn about themselves. You can do the same kind of self-examination—without spending any money. For guidance in choosing a field that eventually proves to be satisfying, answer the following questions. If you have already chosen a field, think carefully about how your answers relate to that choice.

- Do I enjoy working with people, data, or things?
- How important is it to be my own boss?
- How important are salary, benefits, and job stability?
- How important are working conditions, colleagues, and job stimulation?
- Would I rather work for a large or small company?
- Must I work in a specific city, geographical area, or climate?
- Am I looking for security, travel opportunities, money, power, or prestige?
- How would I describe the perfect job, boss, and coworkers?

Quick Check

Analyzing your likes and dislikes helps you make wise employment decisions.

Quick Check

Answering specific questions can help you choose a career.

FIGURE 13.1 The Employment Search

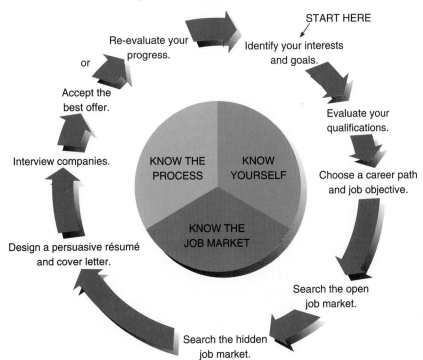

Preparing for Employment

Evaluating Your Qualifications

Quick Check

Assessing your skills and experience prepares you to write a persuasive résumé.

In addition to your interests, assess your qualifications. Employers today want to know what assets you have to offer them. Your responses to the following questions will target your thinking as well as prepare a foundation for your résumé. Remember that employers seek more than empty assurances; they will want proof of your qualifications.

- What computer skills can I offer? (What specific software programs can I name?)
- What other skills have I acquired in school, on the job, or through activities? How can I demonstrate these skills?
- Do I work well with people? What proof can I offer? (Consider extracurricular activities, clubs, and jobs.)
- Am I a leader, self-starter, or manager? What evidence can I offer?
- Do I speak, write, or understand another language?
- Do I learn quickly? Am I creative? How can I demonstrate these characteristics?
- Do I communicate well in speech and in writing? How can I verify these talents?

Recognizing the Changing Nature of Jobs

Quick Check

Downsizing and flatter organizations have resulted in people feeling less secure in their jobs.

As you learned in Chapter 1, the nature of the workplace is changing. One of the most significant changes involves the concept of the "job." Following the downsizing in many organizations in the early 1990s and the movement toward flattened organizations throughout the rest of the decade, fewer people are employed in permanent positions. Many employees are feeling less job security, although they are doing more work.

In their research paper entitled "The Changing Workplace: Challenges for Public Policy," Betcherman and Chaykowski describe the three key ways in which work is being transformed. In Canada, "non-standard" work, including temporary and short-term work, contract work, and self-employed work, is increasing as is the amount of time people work in a week and the amount of work done outside traditional working hours.[2] At the same time, Canadian corporations are increasing their commitment to flexible work arrangements and employee empowerment.[3]

Quick Check

"Jobs" are becoming more flexible and less permanent.

People are increasingly working for themselves or smaller companies, or they are becoming consultants or specialists who work on tasks or projects under arrangements too fluid to be called "jobs." And because new technologies can spring up overnight making today's skills obsolete, employers are less willing to hire people into jobs with narrow descriptions.

What do these changes mean for you? For one thing, you should no longer think in terms of a lifelong career with a single company. In fact, you can't even expect reasonably permanent employment for work well done. This social contract between employer and employee is no longer a given. And predictable career paths within companies have largely disappeared. "The work world has shifted substantially and new attitudes, skills, and knowledge are required to succeed in your working life. As a result, 'career self-management' is emerging as a way not only of surviving, but also of thriving in this new economy."[4] In the new workplace you can expect to work for multiple employers on flexible job assignments associated with teams and projects.

Because of this changing nature of work, you can never become complacent about your position or job skills. Be prepared for constant retraining and updating of your skills. People who learn quickly and adapt to change are valued individuals who will always be in demand especially in a climate of surging change.

Choosing a Career Path

Today's job market is vastly different from that of a decade or two ago. As a result of job trends and personal choices, the average Canadian can expect to change careers at least three times and change jobs at least seven times in a lifetime. Some of you probably have not yet settled on your first career choice; others are embarking on a second or perhaps third career. Although you may be changing jobs in the future, you still need to train for a specific career area now. In choosing an area, you'll make the best decisions when you can match your interests and qualifications with the requirements and rewards in specific careers. But where can you find career information? Here are some suggestions:

- **Visit your school career or counselling centre.** Most have literature, inventories, software programs, and Internet connections that allow you to investigate such fields as accounting, finance, office technology, information systems, hotel management, and so forth.
- **Search the Internet.** Many job search sites on the Web offer career planning information and resources. For example, Workopolis Campus.com helps you link to various career search resources in its "Resource Centre" link.
- **Use your library.** Many print and online resources are especially helpful. Consult the latest edition of the *Index of Occupational Titles*, the U.S. government's *Occupational Outlook Handbook* <www.bls.gov/oco>, and "Jobs, Workers, Training, and Careers" at the Government of Canada's Web site <www.jobsetc.ca> for information about career duties, qualifications, salaries, and employment trends.
- **Take a summer job, internship, or part-time position in your field.** Nothing is better than trying out a career by actually working in it or in a similar area. Many companies offer internships and temporary jobs to begin training students and to develop relationships with them. These relationships sometimes blossom into permanent positions.
- **Interview someone in your chosen field.** People are usually flattered when asked to describe their careers. Inquire about needed skills, required courses, financial and other rewards, benefits, working conditions, future trends, and entry requirements.
- **Monitor the classified ads.** Early in your education career, begin monitoring want ads and Web sites of companies in your career area. Check job availability, qualifications sought, duties, and salary range. Don't wait until you're about to graduate to see how the job market looks.
- **Join professional organizations in your field.** Frequently, these organizations offer student membership status and reduced rates. You'll get inside information on issues, career news, and possible jobs.

Using Traditional Job Search Techniques

Finding the perfect job requires an early start and a determined effort. Whether you use traditional or online job search techniques, you should be prepared to launch an aggressive campaign. And you can't start too early. Students are told early on that a degree or diploma alone doesn't guarantee a good job. They are cautioned that final grades make a difference to employers. And they are advised of the importance of experience and networking. Here are some traditional steps that job candidates take:

- **Study classified ads in local and national newspapers.** Be aware, though, that classified ads are only one small source of jobs. Nearly two-thirds, representing the "hidden" job market, are unadvertised.

✓ Quick Check

People can expect to have eight to ten jobs in three or more different careers in a lifetime.

✓ Quick Check

Career information can be obtained at school career centres and libraries, from the Internet, in classified ads, and from professional organizations.

✓ Quick Check

Summer and part-time jobs and internships are good opportunities to learn about different careers.

✓ Quick Check

A traditional job search campaign might include checking classified ads and announcements in professional publications, contacting companies, and developing a network of contacts.

- **Check announcements in publications of professional organizations.** If you do not have a student membership, ask your professors to share current copies of professional journals, newsletters, and so on. Your college library is another good source.
- **Contact companies in which you're interested, even if you know of no current opening. Write an unsolicited letter and include your résumé.** Follow up with a telephone call. Check the company's Web site for employment possibilities and procedures.
- **Sign up for school interviews with visiting company representatives.** Campus recruiters may open your eyes to exciting jobs and locations.
- **Ask for advice from your instructors.** They often have contacts and ideas for expanding your job search.
- **Develop your own network of contacts.** Networking still accounts for most of the jobs found by candidates. Therefore, plan to spend a considerable portion of your job search time developing a personal network. The Communication Workshop at the end of this chapter gives you step-by-step instructions for traditional networking as well as some ideas for online networking.

Using Electronic Job Search Techniques

Just as the Internet has changed the way the world works, it's also changing the nature of the job search. Increasing numbers of employers are listing their job openings at special Web sites that are similar to newspaper classified ads as shown in Figure 13.2. Companies are also listing job openings at their own Web sites, providing a more direct connection to employment opportunities.

- **Canada's Job Bank**, a Human Resources Development Canada site, <jb-ge.hrdc-drhc.gc.ca/Intro_En.asp> lists more than 46,000 jobs across the country with up to 2,000 new jobs posted every day. The service is free.

FIGURE 13.2   **Results from Online Job Search**

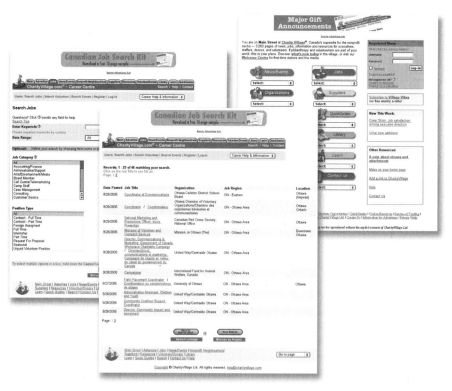

Chapter 13 The Job Search, Résumés, and Cover Letters

- **JobsEtc.ca**, a Government of Canada–hosted Web site at <www.jobsetc.ca>, offers a wealth of information including the top 15 job Web sites in Canada.
- **Charityvillage.com** is a Web site at <www.charityvillage.com> that advertises jobs in the nonprofit sector. Often overlooked by students and graduates, this site offers a wealth of opportunities in traditional business areas such as accounting, finance, customer service, and marketing, all in the nonprofit sector.
- **Workopolis.ca** is Canada's biggest job site. Use Workopolis to register and save your résumé online, build and save job searches, and track job opportunities. You can also research a company, interact with career advisors, and read employment-related newspaper articles.
- **Monster.ca** offers access to information on Canadian and international jobs. It enables company searches, arranges chat sessions on helpful topics for job seekers, and posts pages of targeted career advice.

Perhaps even better are the job openings listed at company Web sites. Check out your favourite companies to see what positions are open. Use your favourite search engine to search a company's Web site. Some companies even have online résumé forms that encourage job candidates to submit their qualifications immediately.

Hundreds of job sites now flood the Internet, and increasing numbers of companies offer online recruiting. In spite of these opportunities, landing a job is still much easier if you have personal contacts in a career area.

The Persuasive Résumé

After reviewing traditional and online employment market and job lead resources, you'll focus on writing a persuasive résumé. Such a résumé does more than merely list your qualifications. It packages your assets into a convincing advertisement that sells you for a specific job. The goal of a persuasive résumé is winning an interview. Even if you are not in the job market at this moment, preparing a résumé now has advantages. Having a current résumé makes you look well organized and professional should an unexpected employment opportunity arise. Moreover, preparing a résumé early can help you recognize weak areas and give you time to bolster your credentials.

Choosing a Résumé Style

Your qualifications and career goal will help you choose from among three résumé styles: chronological, functional, and combination.

Chronological. Most popular with recruiters is the chronological résumé, shown in Figure 13.3 (p. 362). It lists work history job by job, starting with the most recent position. Recruiters favour the chronological format because such résumés quickly reveal a candidate's experience and education record. The chronological style works well for candidates who have experience in their field of employment and for those who show steady career growth. But for many students and others who lack extensive experience, the functional résumé format may be preferable.

✓ Quick Check

Chronological résumés focus on past employment; functional résumés focus on skills.

Functional. The functional résumé, shown in Figure 13.4 (p. 363), focuses attention on a candidate's skills rather than on past employment. Like a chronological résumé, the functional résumé begins with the candidate's name, address, telephone number, job objective, and education. Instead of listing jobs, though, the functional résumé groups skills and accomplishments in special categories, such as *Supervisory and Management Skills* or *Retailing and Marketing Experience*. This résumé style highlights accomplishments and can de-emphasize a negative

FIGURE 13.3 Chronological Résumé

SIMONE AYOTTE
1148 Gurnett Drive
Hamilton, ON L9C 7K1

Phone: (905) 814-9322   E-mail: sayotte@hotmail.com

OBJECTIVE   Position with financial services organization installing accounting software and
providing user support, where computer experience and proven communication
and interpersonal skills can be used to improve operations.

EXPERIENCE   **Accounting software consultant**, Financial Specialists, Hamilton, Ontario
June 2005 to present
● Design and install accounting systems for businesses such as 21st Century
  Real Estate, Cargo Insurance, Aurora Lumber Company, and others
● Provide ongoing technical support and consultation for regular clients
● Help write proposals, such as recent one that won $250,000 contract

Office manager (part-time), Post Premiums, Toronto, Ontario
June 2000 to May 2005
● Conceived and implemented improved order processing and filing system
● Managed computerized accounting system; trained new employees to use it
● Worked with team to develop local area network

Bookkeeper (part-time), Sunset Avionics, Hamilton, Ontario
August 1998 to May 2000
● Kept books for small airplane rental and repair service
● Performed all bookkeeping functions including quarterly internal audit

EDUCATION   **Mohawk College**, Hamilton, Ontario
Working toward a diploma in accounting: 25 out of 40 credits completed

Humber College, Toronto, Ontario
Certificate in bookkeeping, 2000
GPA 3.6/4.0

Computer Associates training seminars, summer and fall 2005
Certificates of completion
Seminars in consulting ethics, marketing, and ACCPAC accounting software

SPECIAL SKILLS   ● Proficient in MS Office Applications, PageMaker, and Lotus
● Skilled in ACCPAC Plus, MAS90, and Solomon IV accounting software
● Trained in technical writing, including proposals and documentation
● Experienced in office administration and management
● Fluent in French

HONOURS AND   Dean's list, three semesters
ACTIVITIES   Member, Academic Affairs Advisory Committee, Mohawk College, 2004–2005

Includes detailed objective in response to advertisement

Uses present-tense verbs for current job

Shows job title in bold for readability

Chronological format arranges jobs and education by dates

White space around headings creates open look

Highlights technical, management, and communication skills

Simone Ayotte uses a chronological résumé to highlight her work experience, most of which is related directly to the position she seeks. Although she is a recent graduate, she has accumulated experience in two part-time jobs and one full-time job. If she had wished to emphasize her special skills (which is not a bad idea considering her heavy computer expertise), she could have placed the special skills section just after her objective.

FIGURE 13.4 Functional Résumé

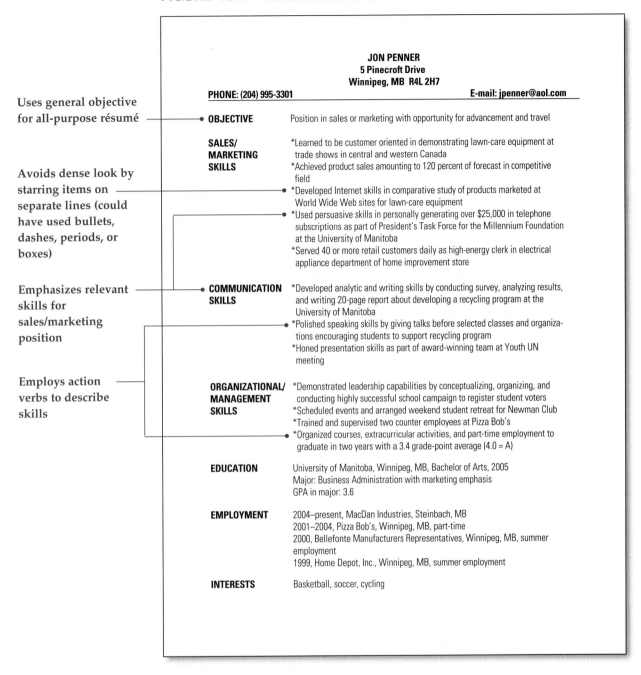

Uses general objective for all-purpose résumé

Avoids dense look by starring items on separate lines (could have used bullets, dashes, periods, or boxes)

Emphasizes relevant skills for sales/marketing position

Employs action verbs to describe skills

JON PENNER
5 Pinecroft Drive
Winnipeg, MB R4L 2H7
PHONE: (204) 995-3301   E-mail: jpenner@aol.com

OBJECTIVE   Position in sales or marketing with opportunity for advancement and travel

SALES/
MARKETING
SKILLS
*Learned to be customer oriented in demonstrating lawn-care equipment at trade shows in central and western Canada
*Achieved product sales amounting to 120 percent of forecast in competitive field
*Developed Internet skills in comparative study of products marketed at World Wide Web sites for lawn-care equipment
*Used persuasive skills in personally generating over $25,000 in telephone subscriptions as part of President's Task Force for the Millennium Foundation at the University of Manitoba
*Served 40 or more retail customers daily as high-energy clerk in electrical appliance department of home improvement store

COMMUNICATION
SKILLS
*Developed analytic and writing skills by conducting survey, analyzing results, and writing 20-page report about developing a recycling program at the University of Manitoba
*Polished speaking skills by giving talks before selected classes and organizations encouraging students to support recycling program
*Honed presentation skills as part of award-winning team at Youth UN meeting

ORGANIZATIONAL/
MANAGEMENT
SKILLS
*Demonstrated leadership capabilities by conceptualizing, organizing, and conducting highly successful school campaign to register student voters
*Scheduled events and arranged weekend student retreat for Newman Club
*Trained and supervised two counter employees at Pizza Bob's
*Organized courses, extracurricular activities, and part-time employment to graduate in two years with a 3.4 grade-point average (4.0 = A)

EDUCATION   University of Manitoba, Winnipeg, MB, Bachelor of Arts, 2005
Major: Business Administration with marketing emphasis
GPA in major: 3.6

EMPLOYMENT   2004–present, MacDan Industries, Steinbach, MB
2001–2004, Pizza Bob's, Winnipeg, MB, part-time
2000, Bellefonte Manufacturers Representatives, Winnipeg, MB, summer employment
1999, Home Depot, Inc., Winnipeg, MB, summer employment

INTERESTS   Basketball, soccer, cycling

Jon Penner, a recent graduate, chose this functional format to de-emphasize his limited work experience and emphasize his potential in sales and marketing. Within each of the three major categories, he lists specific achievements, all of which are introduced by action verbs. He has also included a number of keywords that could be helpful if his résumé is scanned. He included an employment section to satisfy recruiters.

employment history. People who have changed jobs frequently or who have gaps in their employment records may prefer the functional résumé. Recent graduates with little employment experience often find the functional résumé useful.

Functional résumés are also called skill résumés. Although the functional résumé of Jon Penner shown in Figure 13.4 concentrates on skills, it does include a short employment section because recruiters expect it. Notice that Jon breaks his skills into three categories. An alternative—and easier—method is to make one large list, perhaps with a title such as *Areas of Accomplishment, Summary of Qualifications*, or *Areas of Expertise and Ability*.

Combination. The combination résumé style, shown in Figure 13.5, draws on the best features of the chronological and functional résumés. This style emphasizes a candidate's capabilities while also including a complete job history. The combination résumé is a good choice for recent graduates because it enables them to profile what they can do for a prospective employer. If the writer has a specific job in mind, the items should be targeted to that job description.

Arranging the Parts

Quick Check

Résumés should be arranged with the most important qualifications first.

Although résumés have standard parts, their arrangement and content should be strategically planned. The most persuasive résumés emphasize skills and achievements aimed at a particular job or company. They show a candidate's most important qualifications first, and they de-emphasize any weaknesses. To avoid a cluttered look, you must arrange the parts of your résumé with no more than six headings. No two résumés are ever exactly alike, but most writers consider the following parts.

Main Heading. Your résumé should always begin with your name, address, telephone number, and e-mail address. If possible, include a telephone number where messages may be left for you. Prospective employers tend to call the next applicant when no one answers. Adding your e-mail address makes contacting you more convenient. Avoid showing both permanent and temporary addresses; some specialists say that dual addresses immediately identify about-to-graduate college students. Keep the main heading as uncluttered and simple as possible. And don't include the word *résumé*; it's like putting the word *letter* above correspondence.

Quick Check

Include a career objective for a specific, targeted position; omit an objective on a general résumé.

Career Objective. Opinion is divided on the effect of including a career objective on a résumé. Recruiters think such statements indicate that a candidate has made a commitment to a career. Moreover, career objectives make recruiters' lives easier by quickly classifying the résumé. But such declarations can also disqualify a candidate if the stated objective doesn't match a company's job description. As one expert warns, "vague, general résumés often get lost among the crowd. It is important to tailor objectives to highlight specific industry experience."[5]

You have four choices regarding career objectives:

1. Include a career objective only when applying for a specific, targeted position. For example, the following responds to an advertised position: *Objective: To work in the health care industry as a human resources trainee with exposure to recruiting, training, and benefits administration.*
2. Omit a career objective, especially if you are preparing an all-purpose résumé.
3. Include a general statement, such as *Objective: Challenging position in urban planning* or *Job Goal: Position in sales/marketing.*
4. Omit an objective on the résumé but include it in the cover letter, where it can be tailored to a specific position.

FIGURE 13.5 Combination Résumé

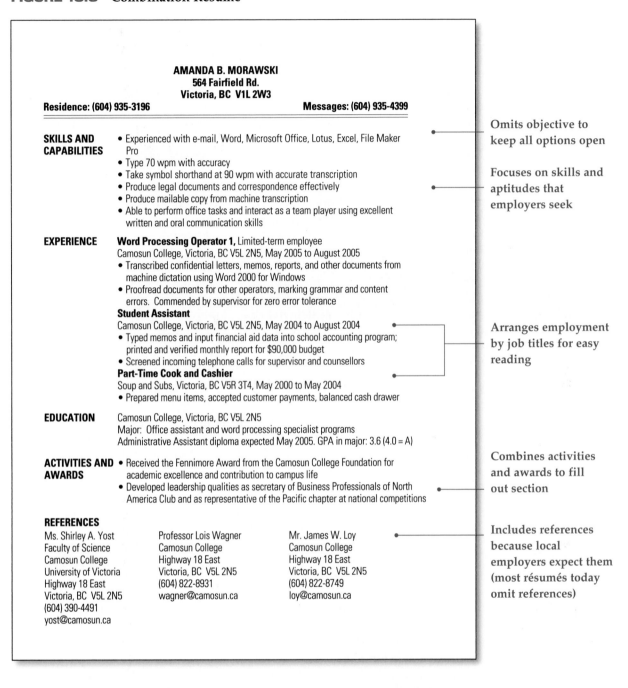

AMANDA B. MORAWSKI
564 Fairfield Rd.
Victoria, BC V1L 2W3

Residence: (604) 935-3196   Messages: (604) 935-4399

SKILLS AND CAPABILITIES
- Experienced with e-mail, Word, Microsoft Office, Lotus, Excel, File Maker Pro
- Type 70 wpm with accuracy
- Take symbol shorthand at 90 wpm with accurate transcription
- Produce legal documents and correspondence effectively
- Produce mailable copy from machine transcription
- Able to perform office tasks and interact as a team player using excellent written and oral communication skills

Omits objective to keep all options open

Focuses on skills and aptitudes that employers seek

EXPERIENCE
Word Processing Operator 1, Limited-term employee
Camosun College, Victoria, BC V5L 2N5, May 2005 to August 2005
- Transcribed confidential letters, memos, reports, and other documents from machine dictation using Word 2000 for Windows
- Proofread documents for other operators, marking grammar and content errors. Commended by supervisor for zero error tolerance

Student Assistant
Camosun College, Victoria, BC V5L 2N5, May 2004 to August 2004
- Typed memos and input financial aid data into school accounting program; printed and verified monthly report for $90,000 budget
- Screened incoming telephone calls for supervisor and counsellors

Part-Time Cook and Cashier
Soup and Subs, Victoria, BC V5R 3T4, May 2000 to May 2004
- Prepared menu items, accepted customer payments, balanced cash drawer

Arranges employment by job titles for easy reading

EDUCATION
Camosun College, Victoria, BC V5L 2N5
Major: Office assistant and word processing specialist programs
Administrative Assistant diploma expected May 2005. GPA in major: 3.6 (4.0 = A)

ACTIVITIES AND AWARDS
- Received the Fennimore Award from the Camosun College Foundation for academic excellence and contribution to campus life
- Developed leadership qualities as secretary of Business Professionals of North America Club and as representative of the Pacific chapter at national competitions

Combines activities and awards to fill out section

REFERENCES

Ms. Shirley A. Yost	Professor Lois Wagner	Mr. James W. Loy
Faculty of Science	Camosun College	Camosun College
Camosun College	Highway 18 East	Highway 18 East
University of Victoria	Victoria, BC V5L 2N5	Victoria, BC V5L 2N5
Highway 18 East	(604) 822-8931	(604) 822-8749
Victoria, BC V5L 2N5	wagner@camosun.ca	loy@camosun.ca
(604) 390-4491		
yost@camosun.ca		

Includes references because local employers expect them (most résumés today omit references)

Because Amanda Morawski wanted to highlight her skills and capabilities along with her experience, she combined the best features of functional and traditional résumés. This résumé style is becoming increasingly popular. Although it's not standard practice, Susan included references because employers in her area expect them.

Note: For more résumé models, see Figures 13.10–13.13.

FIGURE 13.6   Action Verbs for Persuasive Résumés

Management Skills	Communication Skills	Research Skills	Technical Skills	Teaching Skills
administered	addressed	clarified	assembled	adapted
analyzed	arbitrated	collected	built	advised
consolidated	arranged	critiqued	calculated	clarified
coordinated	collaborated	diagnosed	computed	coached
delegated	composed	evaluated	designed	communi-cated
developed	convinced	examined	devised	coordinated
directed	developed	extracted	engineered	developed
evaluated	drafted	identified	executed	enabled
improved*	edited	inspected	fabricated	encouraged
increased	explained	interpreted	maintained	evaluated
organized	formulated	interviewed	operated	explained
oversaw	interpreted	investigated	overhauled	facilitated
planned	negotiated	organized	programmed	guided
prioritized	persuaded	summarized	remodelled	informed
recommended	promoted	surveyed	repaired	instructed
scheduled	publicized	systematized	solved	persuaded
strengthened	recruited		upgraded	set goals
supervised	translated			trained
	wrote			

*The underlined words are especially good for pointing out accomplishments.

Some consultants warn against using the term *entry-level* in your objective, as it emphasizes lack of experience. Many aggressive job applicants today prepare individual résumés that are targeted for each company or position sought. Thanks to word processing, the task is easy.

Education. The next component on your résumé is your education—if it is more noteworthy than your work experience. In this section you should include the name and location of schools, dates of attendance, major fields of study, and degrees, diplomas, and certificates received. Your grade point average and/or class ranking are important to prospective employers. One way to enhance your GPA is to calculate it in your major courses only (for example, *3.6/4.0 in major*).

A list of completed courses makes dull reading: refer to courses only if you can relate them to the position sought. When relevant, include certificates earned, seminars attended, and workshops completed. Because employers are interested in your degree of self-sufficiency, you might want to indicate the percentage of your education for which you paid. If your education is incomplete, include such statements as *B.A. degree expected June 2006* or *80 units completed in 120-unit program*. Entitle this section *Education*, *Academic Preparation*, or *Professional Training*.

Work Experience or Employment History. Anyone seeking a job today must recognize the value of experience. When asked what advice she had for people with little experience, résumé expert Yana Parker replied, "Get some!"[6] She suggests internships, part-time jobs, or even volunteer work in your career area.

If your work experience is significant and relevant to the position sought, this information should appear before education. List your most recent employment first and work backward, including only those jobs that you think will help you win the targeted position. A job application form may demand a full employment history, but your résumé may be selective. (Be aware, though, that time gaps in your employment history will probably be questioned in the interview.) For each position show the following:

Quick Check

The work experience section of a résumé should list specifics and quantify achievements.

FIGURE 13.6 Continued

Financial Skills	Creative Skills	Helping Skills	Clerical or Detail Skills	More Verbs for Accomplishments
administered	acted	assessed	approved	achieved
advised	conceptualized	assisted	catalogued	expanded
allocated	created	clarified	classified	improved
analyzed	customized	coached	collected	pioneered
appraised	designed	counselled	compiled	reduced (losses)
audited	developed	demonstrated	generated	resolved (problems)
balanced	directed	diagnosed	inspected	restored
budgeted	established	educated	monitored	spearheaded
calculated	founded	expedited	operated	transformed
computed	illustrated	facilitated	organized	
developed	initiated	familiarized	prepared	
forecasted	instituted	guided	processed	
managed	introduced	motivated	purchased	
marketed	invented	referred	recorded	
planned	originated	represented	screened	
projected	performed		specified	
researched	planned		systematized	
	revitalized		tabulated	

Source: Adapted from Yana Parker, *The Damn Good Résumé Guide* (Berkeley, CA: Ten Speed Press). Reprinted with permission.

- Employer's name, city, and province
- Dates of employment, including month and year
- Most important job title
- Significant duties, activities, accomplishments, and promotions

Describe your employment achievements concisely but concretely. Avoid generalities such as *Worked with customers*. Be more specific, with statements such as *Served 40 or more retail customers a day; Successfully resolved problems about custom stationery orders;* or *Acted as intermediary among customers, printers, and suppliers*. If possible, quantify your accomplishments, such as *Conducted study of equipment needs of 100 small businesses in Edmonton; Personally generated orders for sales of $90,000 annually; Keyboarded all the production models for a 250-page employee procedures manual;* or *Assisted editor in layout, design, and news writing for 12 issues of division newsletter*.

In addition to technical skills, employers seek individuals with communication, management, and interpersonal capabilities. This means you'll want to select work experiences and achievements that illustrate your initiative, dependability, responsibility, resourcefulness, and leadership. Employers also want people who can work in teams. Thus, include statements such as *Collaborated with interdepartmental task force in developing 10-page handbook for temporary workers* and *Headed student government team that conducted most successful voter registration in school history*.

Statements describing your work experience become forceful and persuasive by using action verbs, such as those listed in Figure 13.6 and illustrated in Figure 13.7 (p. 368).

Capabilities and Skills. Recruiters want to know specifically what you can do for their companies. Therefore, list your special skills, such as *Proficient in preparing correspondence and reports using MS Word*. Include your ability to use computer programs, office equipment, other languages, or sign language. Describe proficiencies you have acquired through training and experience, such as *Trained in computer accounting, including general ledger, accounts receivable,*

✓ *Quick Check*

Emphasize the skills and aptitudes that recommend you for a specific position.

FIGURE 13.7 Using Action Verbs to Strengthen Your Résumé

Identified weaknesses in internship program and researched five alternative programs.

Reduced delivery delays by an average of three days per order.

Streamlined filing system reducing 400-item backlog to 0.

Organized holiday awards program for 1200 attendees and 140 awardees.

Created a 12-point checklist for managers to use when requesting temporary workers.

Designed five posters announcing new employee suggestion program.

Calculated shipping charges for overseas deliveries and recommended most economical rates.

Managed 24-station computer network linking data and employees in three departments.

Distributed and **explained** voter registration forms to over 500 prospective student voters.

Praised by top management for enthusiastic teamwork and achievement.

Secured national recognition from Parks Canada for tree project.

accounts payable, and payroll. Use expressions such as *competent in, skilled in, proficient with, experienced in,* and *ability to;* for example, *Competent in typing, editing, and/or proofreading reports, tables, letters, memos, manuscripts, and business forms.*

You'll also want to highlight exceptional aptitudes, such as working well under stress and learning computer programs quickly. If possible, provide details and evidence that back up your assertions; for example, *learned image manipulation using Photoshop in 40 hours with little instruction.* Search for examples of your writing, speaking, management, organizational, and interpersonal skills—particularly those talents that are relevant to your targeted job.

For recent graduates, this section can be used to give recruiters evidence of your potential. Instead of *Capabilities,* the section might be called *Skills and Abilities.*

Awards, honours, and activities are appropriate for résumés; most personal information is not.

Awards, Honours, and Activities. If you have three or more awards or honours, highlight them by listing them under a separate heading. If not, put them with activities. Include awards, scholarships (financial and other), fellowships, honours, recognition, commendations, and certificates. Be sure to identify items clearly. Your reader may be unfamiliar, for example, with fraternities or sororities, honoraries, and awards; explain what they mean. Instead of saying *Recipient of Star award,* give more details: *Recipient of Star award, given by Red River College to outstanding graduates who combine academic excellence and extracurricular achievement.*

It's also appropriate to include school, community, and professional activities. Employers are interested in evidence that you are a well-rounded person. This section provides an opportunity to demonstrate leadership and interpersonal skills. Strive to use action statements. For example, instead of saying *Treasurer of business club,* explain more fully: *Collected dues, kept financial records, and paid bills while serving as treasurer of 35-member business management club.*

Personal Information. Today's résumés omit personal information, such as birth date and marital status. Such information doesn't relate to genuine occupational qualifications, and employers and recruiters are legally barred from asking for such information. Some job seekers do, however, include hobbies or interests (such as skiing or photography) that might grab the recruiter's attention or serve as conversation starters. You should also indicate your willingness to travel or to relocate, since many companies will be interested.

References. Listing references on a résumé is favoured by some recruiters and opposed by others. Such a list takes up valuable space. Moreover, it is not normally instrumental in securing an interview—few companies check references before the interview. Instead, they prefer that a candidate bring to the interview a list of individuals willing to discuss her or his qualifications. If you do list them, use parallel form. For example, if you show a title for one person (*Professor, Dr., Mrs.*), show titles for all. Include mailing addresses, e-mail addresses, and telephone numbers with area codes.

Whether or not you include references on your résumé, you should have their names available when you begin your job search. Ask three to five instructors or previous employers whether they are willing to answer inquiries regarding your qualifications for employment. Be sure, however, to provide them with an opportunity to refuse. No reference is better than a negative one. Do not include personal or character references, such as friends or neighbours, because recruiters rarely consult them. Companies are more interested in the opinions of objective individuals.

Quick Check

References are unnecessary for the résumé, but they should be available for the interview.

Making Your Résumé Computer-Friendly

Thus far our résumé advice has been aimed at human readers. However, the first reader of your résumé may well be a computer. Some companies now use computer programs to reduce hiring costs and make résumé information more accessible. The process of résumé scanning is shown in Figure 13.8 (p. 370).

Before you send your résumé, you should learn whether the recipient uses scanning software. One way to find out is to call any company where you plan to apply and ask if it scans résumés electronically. If you can't get a clear answer and you have even the slightest suspicion that your résumé might be read electronically, you'd be smart to prepare a plain, scannable version.

A scannable résumé must sacrifice many of the graphic possibilities that savvy writers employ. Computers aren't impressed by graphics; they prefer résumés that are free of graphics and fancy fonts. To make a computer-friendly résumé, you'll want to apply the following suggestions about its physical appearance.

Quick Check

Use of scanners requires job candidates to prepare computer-friendly résumés.

- **Avoid unusual typefaces, underlining, and italics.** Moreover, don't use boxing, shading, or other graphics to highlight text. These features don't scan well. Most applicant-tracking programs, however, can accurately read bold print, solid bullets, and asterisks.
- **Use 10-to-14-point type.** Because touching letters or unusual fonts are likely to be misread, it's safest to use a large, well-known font, such as 12-point Times New Roman or Helvetica. This may mean that your résumé will require two pages. After printing, inspect your résumé to see if any letters touch— especially in your name.
- **Use smooth white paper, black ink, and quality printing.** Avoid coloured and textured papers as well as dot-matrix printing.
- **Be sure that your name is the first line on the page.** Don't use fancy layouts, which may confuse a scanner.
- **Provide white space.** To ensure separation of words and categories, leave plenty of white space. For example, instead of using parentheses to enclose a telephone area code, insert blank spaces, such as 613 555-1212. Leave blank lines around headings.
- **Avoid double columns.** When listing job duties, skills, computer programs, and so forth, don't tabulate items into two- or three-column lists. Scanners read across and may convert tables into a disarray.

Quick Check

Computer-friendly résumés are free of graphics and fancy fonts.

FIGURE 13.8 What a Résumé-Scanning Program Does

Reads résumé with scanner

Identifies job categories and ranks applicants

Generates letters of rejection or interview offers

Stores information or actual résumé image for future searches

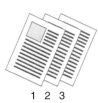

OFFER

1 2 3

- **Don't fold or staple your résumé.** Send it in a large envelope so that you can avoid folds. Words that appear on folds may not be scanned correctly. Avoid staples, because the indentions left after they are removed may cause pages to stick.
- **Use abbreviations carefully.** Minimize unfamiliar abbreviations, but maximize easily recognized abbreviations—especially those within your field, such as CAD or COBRA or CGA. When in doubt spell out. Computers are less addled by whole words.
- **Include your entire address and telephone number.** Be sure your résumé contains your e-mail address, as well as your street address, telephone numbers with area codes, and fax number, if available.
- **Be prepared to provide your résumé in Plain Text format.** This format offers electronic documents as text only and is immediately readable by all computer programs. It eliminates italics, bold, underlining, and unusual keyboard characters but allows you to e-mail your résumé in a format that you know will work for all computers.

Emphasizing Keywords

Quick Check

Keywords are nouns that describe specific candidate traits or job requirements.

Quick Check

A computer-friendly résumé may contain a keyword summary filled with words (usually nouns) that describe the job or candidate.

In addition to paying attention to the physical appearance of your résumé, you must also be concerned with keywords. Keywords are usually nouns that describe what an employer wants. Suppose a manager at Canadian Tire wants to hire an administrative assistant with special proficiencies. That manager might submit the following keywords to the Canadian Tire applicant-tracking system: *Administrative Assistant, Computer Skills, MS Office, Self-Starter, Report Writing, Proofreading, Communication Skills.* The system would then search through all the résumés on file to see which ones best match the requirements.

The Royal Bank of Canada receives hundreds of résumés every year. They suggest using a keyword summary to assist recruiters who use keyword matching techniques when searching résumé databases. This list of keyword descriptors immediately follows your name and address on your résumé.[7] A keyword summary, as illustrated in Figure 13.13 (p. 375), should contain your targeted job title and alternative labels, as well as previous job titles, skills, software programs, and selected jargon known in your field. It concentrates on nouns rather than on verbs or adjectives.

To construct your summary, go through your core résumé and mark all relevant nouns. Also try to imagine what eight to ten words an employer might use to describe the job you want. Then select the 25 best words for your summary.

Because interpersonal traits are often requested by employers, consult Figure 13.9. You may entitle your list *Keyword Summary*, *Keyword Profile*, or *Keyword Index*. Here's an example of a possible keyword summary for a junior accountant:

Keyword Summary
Accountant: Public. Junior. Staff. PricewaterhouseCoopers. Administration. AJ Hawkins—Accounting. Payables. Receivables. Payroll Experience. Quarterly Reports. Unemployment Reports. Communication Skills. Computer Skills. Excel. MS Office. PCs. Mainframes. Internet. Web. Networks. J. D. Edwards Software. Ability to learn software. Accurate. Dean's List. Award of Merit. Team player. Willing to travel. Relocate.

After an introductory keyword summary, your résumé should contain the standard parts discussed in this chapter. Remember that the keyword section merely helps ensure that your résumé will be selected for inspection. Then human eyes take over. Therefore, you'll want to observe the other writing tips you've learned to make your résumé attractive and forceful. Figures 13.10 through 13.12 (pp. 372–374) show additional examples of chronological and combination résumés. Notice that the scannable résumé in Figure 13.13 is not drastically different from the others. It does, however, include a keyword summary.

Risking Your Future with an Inflated Résumé

A résumé is expected to showcase a candidate's strengths and minimize weaknesses. For this reason, recruiters expect a certain degree of self-promotion. But some résumé writers step over the line that separates honest self-marketing from deceptive half-truths and flat-out lies. Distorting facts on a résumé is unethical; lying is illegal. And either practice can destroy a career.

Although recruiters can't check everything, most will verify previous employment and education before hiring candidates. Over half will require official transcripts. InfoCheck, a Canadian résumé verification service, indicates that they do about 800 background checks a month for their corporate customers. InfoCheck has uncovered some pretty dramatic stories of résumé fraud but none perhaps more dramatic than the following: "A candidate had used someone else's identity

✓ Quick Check

Deception on a résumé, even if discovered much later, can result in firing.

FIGURE 13.9   Interpersonal Keywords Most Requested by Employers Using Résumé-Scanning Software*

Ability to delegate	Creative	Leadership	Self-accountable
Ability to implement	Customer-oriented	Multitasking	Self-managing
Ability to plan	Detail-minded	Open communication	Setting priorities
Ability to train	Ethical	Open-minded	Supportive
Accurate	Flexible	Oral communication	Takes initiative
Adaptable	Follow instructions	Organizational skills	Team building
Aggressive worker	Follow through	Persuasive	Team player
Analytical ability	Follow up	Problem solving	Tenacious
Assertive	High energy	Public speaking	Willing to travel
Communication skills	Industrious	Results-oriented	
Competitive	Innovative	Safety-conscious	

*Reported by Resumix, a leading producer of résumé-scanning software.
Source: Joyce Lain Kennedy and Thomas J. Morrow, *Electronic Résumé Revolution* (New York: John Wiley & Sons), 70. Reprinted by permission of John Wiley & Sons, Inc.

FIGURE 13.10 Enhanced Résumé

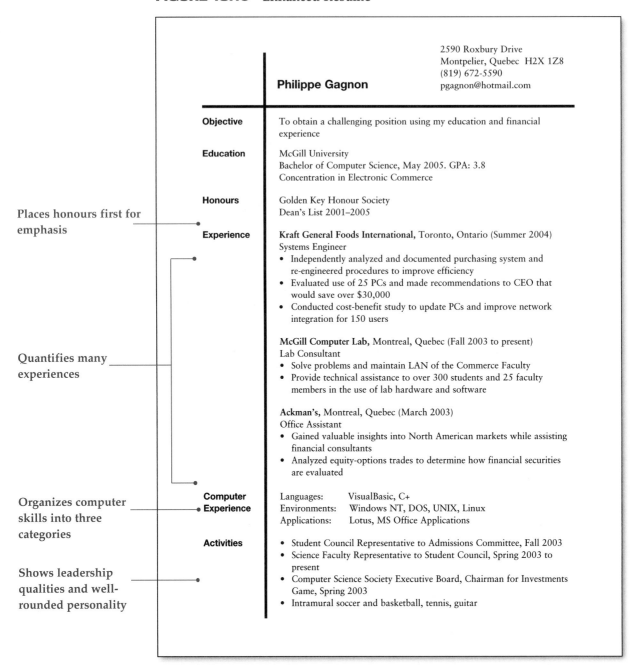

Philippe Gagnon

2590 Roxbury Drive
Montpelier, Quebec H2X 1Z8
(819) 672-5590
pgagnon@hotmail.com

Objective

To obtain a challenging position using my education and financial experience

Education

McGill University
Bachelor of Computer Science, May 2005. GPA: 3.8
Concentration in Electronic Commerce

Honours

Golden Key Honour Society
Dean's List 2001–2005

Places honours first for emphasis

Experience

Kraft General Foods International, Toronto, Ontario (Summer 2004)
Systems Engineer
- Independently analyzed and documented purchasing system and re-engineered procedures to improve efficiency
- Evaluated use of 25 PCs and made recommendations to CEO that would save over $30,000
- Conducted cost-benefit study to update PCs and improve network integration for 150 users

McGill Computer Lab, Montreal, Quebec (Fall 2003 to present)
Lab Consultant
- Solve problems and maintain LAN of the Commerce Faculty
- Provide technical assistance to over 300 students and 25 faculty members in the use of lab hardware and software

Ackman's, Montreal, Quebec (March 2003)
Office Assistant
- Gained valuable insights into North American markets while assisting financial consultants
- Analyzed equity-options trades to determine how financial securities are evaluated

Quantifies many experiences

Computer Experience

Languages: VisualBasic, C+
Environments: Windows NT, DOS, UNIX, Linux
Applications: Lotus, MS Office Applications

Organizes computer skills into three categories

Activities

- Student Council Representative to Admissions Committee, Fall 2003
- Science Faculty Representative to Student Council, Spring 2003 to present
- Computer Science Society Executive Board, Chairman for Investments Game, Spring 2003
- Intramural soccer and basketball, tennis, guitar

Shows leadership qualities and well-rounded personality

Although Philippe Gagnon had little paid work experience off campus, his résumé looks impressive because of his relevant summer, campus, and intern experiences. He describes specific achievements related to finance, his career goal. This version of his résumé is enhanced with desktop publishing features because he knows it will not be scanned.

FIGURE 13.11   Combination Résumé

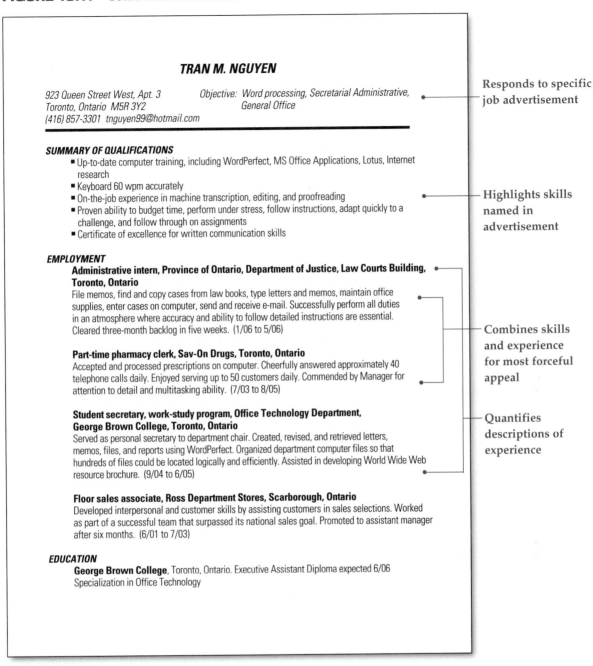

TRAN M. NGUYEN

923 Queen Street West, Apt. 3
Toronto, Ontario M5R 3Y2
(416) 857-3301 tnguyen99@hotmail.com

Objective: Word processing, Secretarial Administrative,
General Office

Responds to specific job advertisement

SUMMARY OF QUALIFICATIONS
- Up-to-date computer training, including WordPerfect, MS Office Applications, Lotus, Internet research
- Keyboard 60 wpm accurately
- On-the-job experience in machine transcription, editing, and proofreading
- Proven ability to budget time, perform under stress, follow instructions, adapt quickly to a challenge, and follow through on assignments
- Certificate of excellence for written communication skills

Highlights skills named in advertisement

EMPLOYMENT

Administrative intern, Province of Ontario, Department of Justice, Law Courts Building, Toronto, Ontario
File memos, find and copy cases from law books, type letters and memos, maintain office supplies, enter cases on computer, send and receive e-mail. Successfully perform all duties in an atmosphere where accuracy and ability to follow detailed instructions are essential. Cleared three-month backlog in five weeks. (1/06 to 5/06)

Part-time pharmacy clerk, Sav-On Drugs, Toronto, Ontario
Accepted and processed prescriptions on computer. Cheerfully answered approximately 40 telephone calls daily. Enjoyed serving up to 50 customers daily. Commended by Manager for attention to detail and multitasking ability. (7/03 to 8/05)

Combines skills and experience for most forceful appeal

Student secretary, work-study program, Office Technology Department, George Brown College, Toronto, Ontario
Served as personal secretary to department chair. Created, revised, and retrieved letters, memos, files, and reports using WordPerfect. Organized department computer files so that hundreds of files could be located logically and efficiently. Assisted in developing World Wide Web resource brochure. (9/04 to 6/05)

Quantifies descriptions of experience

Floor sales associate, Ross Department Stores, Scarborough, Ontario
Developed interpersonal and customer skills by assisting customers in sales selections. Worked as part of a successful team that surpassed its national sales goal. Promoted to assistant manager after six months. (6/01 to 7/03)

EDUCATION
George Brown College, Toronto, Ontario. Executive Assistant Diploma expected 6/06
Specialization in Office Technology

Tran Nguyen's résumé is submitted in response to an advertisement specifying skills for a staff accountant. The combination format allows him to highlight the skills his education and limited experience have provided. To make the résumé look professional, he uses the italic, bold, and scalable-font features of his word processing program.

FIGURE 13.12 Chronological Résumé

Fiona Savate

1438 Mountain Drive
Vancouver, BC V1L 2E9

(604) 877 9613
fsavate@freemail.com

Objective: Senior Financial Management

Professional History and Achievements

November 2002 to May 2006 Controller
WinPak Plastics, Inc. Vancouver, BC (maker of plastic containers)
- Directed all facets of accounting and cash management for 160-employee, $100-million business
- Supervised inventory and production data processing operations and tax compliance
- Created cost accounting by product and pricing based on gross margin
- Increased line of credit with 12 major suppliers

September 2000 to October 2002 Controller
Burgess, Inc. Vancouver, BC (manufacturer of industrial batteries)
- Managed all accounting, cash, payroll, credit, and collection operations for 75-employee business
- Implemented a new system for cost accounting, inventory control, and accounts payable, resulting in a $100,000 annual savings in computer operations
- Reduced staff from 10 persons to 5 with no loss in productivity
- Successfully reduced inventory levels from $1.1 million to $600,000
- Helped develop new cash management system that significantly increased cash flow

August 1997 to June 2000 Treasurer/Controller
Cedar Builders, Vancouver, BC (manufacturer of log houses)
- Supervised accounts receivable/payable cash management, payroll, and insurance
- Directed monthly and year-end closings, banking relations, and product costing
- Refinanced company with long-term loan, ensuring continued operational stability
- Successfully lowered company's insurance premiums by 7 percent

February 1994 to June 1997 General Bookkeeper/Accountant (part-time)
Flo-Form Inc. Vancouver, BC (manufacturer of countertops)
- Completed monthly and year-end closing of ledgers for $2 million business
- Audited freight bills, acted as interdepartmental liaison, prepared financial reports

Additional Information

Education:
Bachelor of Applied Business Administration in Accounting and Information Technology completed through distance education at Southern Alberta Institute of Technology (SAIT) December 2001

Diploma in Business Accounting, Camosun College, Victoria, BC, received June 1998

Certification: CGA designation received December 2001

Personal: Will travel and/or relocate

Explains nature of employer's business because it is not immediately recognizable

Emphasizes steady employment history by listing dates first

Describes and quantifies specific achievements

Uses action verbs but includes many nouns for possible computer scanning

De-emphasizes education because work history is more important for mature candidates

---

Because Fiona Savate has many years of experience and seeks high-level employment, she focuses on her experience. Notice how she includes specific achievements and quantifies them whenever possible.

FIGURE 13.13   Computer-Friendly Résumé

CARA MAFFIC
3340 Bay Drive
Regina, SK S2R 3L3
306 742-4490

KEYWORDS

Operations Department. Operations Officer. Bookkeeping. Accounting. Payables.
Receivables. Management. Customer Service. Communication. Organizational Skills.
Computer Skills. Spreadsheets. Internet. BBA.

OBJECTIVE

Position in operations department of bank, including operations officer, or customer
service representative.

EXPERIENCE

National Bank, Regina, SK S1L 2W3
July 2005 to present
Customer Service Representative
- Cheerfully greet customers, make deposits and withdrawals, accurately enter on
  computer. Balance up to $10,000 in cash with computer log daily within 15-minute
  time period.
- Solve customer problems and answer questions patiently. Issue cashier's
  cheques, savings bonds, and traveller's cheques. Commended for accuracy and ability
  to work under pressure.

Ames Aviation Maintenance Company, Regina, SK S3S 2L4
June 2002 to June 2005
Bookkeeper
- Managed all bookkeeping functions including accounts payable, accounts receivable,
  payroll, and tax reports for small business.

EDUCATION

University of Saskatchewan, Regina SK
Completing Bachelor of Business Administration

STRENGTHS

Computer: Accounting software, banking CRT experience, MS Office Applications,
                  Internet searching. Learn new programs quickly.

Interpersonal: Persuasive, communicative, open-minded. Selected to represent our
                  branch on company Diversity Committee. Able to set priorities and
                  follow through. Maintain 3.2 GPA while working nearly full-time to pay
                  for university.

Professional: Two years' customer service representative experience. Certificate of
                  Merit, presented by National Bank to outstanding new employees.

Annotations:

- Places name alone at top of résumé where scanner expects to find it
- Includes job title desired, alternative titles, skills, and other words that might match job description
- Surrounds headings with white space for accurate scanning
- Prevents inaccurate scanning by using type font in which letters do not touch
- Uses synonyms for some data (BBA in keyword section and Bachelor of Business Administration here) to protect against possible scanning confusion
- Mentions some interpersonal traits known to be most requested by employers

Cara Maffic prepared this résumé free of graphics and fancy formatting so that it
would scan well if read by a computer. Notice that she begins with a keyword
summary that contains job titles, skills, traits, and other descriptive words. She hopes
that some of these keywords will match those submitted by an employer. To improve
accurate scanning, she avoids italics, vertical and horizontal lines, and double
columns.

when he applied to be a school principal. The candidate said he had 15 years' teaching experience and the right degree. He actually had five prior convictions, including fraud and impersonation. The person named in the résumé had passed away some time before."[8]

No job seeker wants to be in the unhappy position of explaining résumé errors or defending misrepresentation. Avoiding the following common problems can keep you off the hot seat:

- **Inflated education, grades, or honours.** Some job candidates claim diplomas, certificates, or degrees from colleges or universities when in fact they merely attended classes. Others increase their grade point averages or claim fictitious honours. Any such dishonest reporting is grounds for dismissal when discovered.
- **Enhanced job titles.** Wanting to elevate their status, some applicants misrepresent their titles. For example, one technician called himself a "programmer" when he had actually programmed only one project for his boss. A mail clerk who assumed added responsibilities conferred upon herself the title of "supervisor." Even when the description seems accurate, it's unethical to list any title not officially granted.
- **Puffed-up accomplishments.** Some job seekers inflate their employment experience or achievements. One clerk, eager to make her photocopying duties sound more important, said that she assisted the vice-president in communicating and distributing employee directives. A graduate who spent the better part of six months watching rented DVDs described the activity as "independent film study." The latter statement may have helped win an interview, but it cost him the job. In addition to avoiding puffery, guard against taking sole credit for achievements that required many people. When recruiters suspect dubious claims on résumés, they may ask specific—and potentially embarrassing—questions during their interviews.
- **Altered employment dates.** Some candidates extend the dates of employment to hide unimpressive jobs or to cover up periods of unemployment and illness. Let's say that several years ago Catriona was unemployed for fourteen months between working for Company A and being hired by Company B. To make her employment history look better, she adds seven months to her tenure with Company A and seven months to Company B. Now her employment history has no gaps, but her résumé is dishonest and represents a potential trap for her.

Applying the Final Touches

Quick Check

In addition to being well written, a résumé must be carefully formatted and meticulously proofread.

Because your résumé may be the most important document you will ever write, you should expect to revise it many times. With so much information in concentrated form and with so much riding on its outcome, your résumé demands careful polishing, proofreading, and critiquing.

As you revise, be certain to verify all the facts, particularly those involving your previous employment and education. Don't be caught in a mistake, or worse, distortion of previous jobs and dates of employment.

As you continue revising, look for other ways to improve your résumé. For example, consider consolidating headings. By condensing your information into as few headings as possible, you'll produce a clean, professional-looking document. Study other résumés for valuable formatting ideas. Ask yourself what graphic highlighting techniques you can use to improve readability: capitalization, underlining, indenting, and bulleting. Experiment with headings and styles to achieve a pleasing, easy-to-read message. Moreover, look for ways to eliminate wordiness. For example, instead of *Supervised two employees who worked at the counter*, try *Supervised two counter employees*. Review Chapter 4 for more tips on writing concisely.

Above all, make your résumé look professional. Avoid anything humorous or attempts to be witty, such as a help-wanted poster with your name or picture inside. Eliminate the personal pronoun *I*. The abbreviated, objective style of a résumé precludes the use of personal pronouns. Use white, off-white, or buff-coloured heavy bond paper (24-pound) and a quality laser printer.

After revising, proofread, proofread, and proofread again: for spelling and mechanics, for content, and for format. Then, have a knowledgeable friend or relative proofread it again. This is one document that must be perfect.

By now you may be thinking that you'd like to hire someone to write your résumé. Don't. First, you know yourself better than anyone else could know you. Second, you'll end up with either a generic or a one-time résumé. A generic résumé in today's highly competitive job market will lose out to a targeted résumé nine times out of ten. Equally useless is a one-time résumé aimed at a single job. What if you don't get that job? Because you will need to revise your résumé many times as you seek a variety of jobs, be prepared to write (and rewrite) it yourself.

A final word about résumé-writing services. Some tend to produce eye-catching, elaborate documents with lofty language, fancy borders, and fuzzy thinking. Here's an example of empty writing: "Seeking a position that will utilize academic achievements and hands-on experience while providing for career-development opportunities." Save your money and buy elegant interview clothing instead.

✓ **Quick Check**

Because résumés must be perfect, they should be proofread many times.

Faxing or E-Mailing Your Résumé

In this hurried world, employers increasingly want information immediately. If you are asked to fax or e-mail your résumé, take a second look at it. The key to success is *space*. Without it, letters and characters blur. Underlines blend with the words above, and bold print may look blurred. How can you improve your chances of making a good impression when you must fax or e-mail your résumé?

If you are faxing your printed résumé, select a font with adequate space between each character. Thinner fonts—such as Times, Garamond, Arial, Courier, and Bookman—are clearer than thicker ones. Use a 12-point or larger font, and avoid underlines, which may look broken or choppy when faxed. To be safe, get a transmission report to ensure that all pages were transmitted satisfactorily. Finally, follow up with your polished, printed résumé.

If you are e-mailing your résumé, you should prepare a Plain Text version. It will eliminate bold, italics, underlining, tabulated indentions, and unusual characters. To prevent lines from wrapping at awkward spots, keep your line length to 65 characters or less. You can, of course, transmit a fully formatted, attractive résumé if you send it as an attachment and your receiver is using a compatible e-mail program. To avoid disappointment, attach one fully formatted résumé, one Plain Text résumé, and one cut-and-pasted résumé in the body of your e-mail.

Nearly everyone writes a résumé by adapting a model, such as those in Figures 13.3–13.5 and 13.10–13.13. The chronological résumé for Fiona Savate shown in Figure 13.12 is typical of candidates with considerable working experience. Although she describes four positions that span a 14-year period, she manages to fit her résumé on one page. However, two-page résumés are justified for people with long work histories.

✓ **Quick Check**

Résumés to be faxed should have ample space between letters, be printed in 12-point or larger font, and avoid underlines.

✓ **Quick Check**

Résumés that are sent by e-mail transmit best as Plain Text files without tabs or underlines, and without italic, bold, or unusual characters.

The Persuasive Cover Letter

To accompany your résumé, you'll need a persuasive cover letter. The cover letter has three purposes: (1) introducing the résumé, (2) highlighting ways your strengths will benefit the reader, and (3) obtaining an interview. In many ways your cover letter is a sales letter; it sells your talents and tries to beat the competition. It

✓ **Quick Check**

Cover letters introduce résumés, relate writer strengths to reader benefits, and seek an interview.

will, accordingly, include many of the techniques you learned for sales presentations in Chapter 7.

Human resource professionals disagree on how long to make cover letters. Many prefer short letters with no more than four paragraphs; instead of concentrating on the letter, these readers focus on the résumé. Others desire longer letters that supply more information, thus giving them a better opportunity to evaluate a candidate's qualifications and gauge his or her personality. They argue that hiring and training new employees is expensive and time consuming; extra data can guide them in making the best choice the first time. Use your judgment; if you feel, for example, that you need space to explain in more detail what you can do for a prospective employer, do so.

Regardless of its length, a cover letter should have three primary parts: (1) an opening that gets attention, (2) a body that builds interest and reduces resistance, and (3) a closing that motivates action.

Gaining Attention in the Opening

Quick Check

The opening in a cover letter gets attention by addressing the receiver by name.

The first step in gaining the interest of your reader is addressing that individual by name. Rather than sending your letter to the "Personnel Manager" or "Human Resources Department," try to identify the name of the appropriate individual. Make it a rule to call the organization for the correct spelling and the complete address. This personal touch distinguishes your letter and demonstrates your serious interest.

How you open your cover letter depends largely on whether your résumé is for a position that is solicited or unsolicited. If an employment position has been announced and applicants are being solicited, you can use a direct approach. If you do not know whether a position is open and you are prospecting for a job, use an indirect approach. Whether direct or indirect, the opening should attract the attention of the reader. Strive for openings that are more imaginative than *Please consider this letter an application for the position of …* or *I would like to apply for … .*

Quick Check

Openings for solicited jobs refer to the source of the information, the job title, and qualifications for the position.

Openings for Solicited Jobs. Here are some of the best techniques to open a letter of application for a job that has been announced:

- **Refer to the name of an employee in the company.** Remember that employers always hope to hire known quantities rather than complete strangers:

  Mitchell Sims, a member of your Customer Service Department, told me that DataTech is seeking an experienced customer service representative. The attached summary of my qualifications demonstrates my preparation for this position.

  At the suggestion of Ms. Claudette Guertin of your Human Resources Department, I submit my qualifications for the position of personnel assistant.

- **Refer to the source of your information precisely.** If you are answering an advertisement, include the exact position advertised and the name and date of the publication. For large organizations it's also wise to mention the section of the newspaper where the ad appeared:

  Your advertisement in the Careers section of the June 1 *Vancouver Sun* for a junior accountant (competition 06-003) greatly appeals to me. With my accounting training and computer experience, I believe I could serve DataTech well.

  The September 10 issue of the *National Post* reports that you are seeking a mature, organized, and reliable administrative assistant (competition 06-A54) with excellent communication skills.

Susan Butler, placement director at Carleton University, told me that DataTech has an opening for a technical writer with knowledge of Web design and graphics.

- **Refer to the job title and describe how your qualifications fit the requirements.** Human resources directors are looking for a match between an applicant's credentials and the job needs:

  Will an honours graduate with a degree in recreation studies and two years of part-time experience organizing social activities for a retirement community qualify for your position of activity director?

  Because of my specialized training in computerized accounting at Simon Fraser University, I feel confident that I have the qualifications you described in your advertisement for an accountant trainee.

Openings for Unsolicited Jobs. If you are unsure whether a position actually exists, you may wish to use a more persuasive opening. Since your goal is to convince this person to read on, try one of the following techniques:

- **Demonstrate interest in and knowledge of the reader's business.** Show the human resources director that you have done your research and that this organization is more than a mere name to you:

  Since the Canadian Automobile Association is organizing a new information management team for its recently established group insurance division, could you use the services of a well-trained information systems graduate who seeks to become a professional underwriter?

- **Show how your special talents and background will benefit the company.** Human resources directors need to be convinced that you can do something for them:

  Could your rapidly expanding publications division use the services of an editorial assistant who offers exceptional language skills, an honours degree from Brandon University, and two years' experience in producing a school literary publication?

In applying for an advertised job, Mabel Lam wrote the solicited cover letter shown in Figure 13.14 (p. 380). Notice that her opening identifies the position and the newspaper completely so that the reader knows exactly what advertisement Mabel refers to. Using features on her word processing program, Mabel designed her own letterhead that uses her name and looks like professionally printed letterhead paper.

More challenging are unsolicited letters of application, such as Jon Penner's shown in Figure 13.15 (p. 381). Because he hopes to discover or create a job, his opening must grab the reader's attention immediately. To do that, he capitalizes on company information appearing in the newspaper. Jon purposely kept his application letter short and to the point because he anticipated that a busy executive would be unwilling to read a long, detailed letter. Jon's unsolicited letter "prospects" for a job. Some job candidates feel that such letters may be even more productive than efforts to secure advertised jobs, since "prospecting" candidates face less competition. Notice that Jon's letter uses a standard return address consisting of his street, city, and the date.

FIGURE 13.14 Solicited Cover Letter

Mabel Lam

1770 Hawthorne Place, Red Deer AB T4R 3L2

May 23, 2007

Mr. William A. Caldwell
Director, Human Resources
Del Rio Enterprises
Calgary, AB T2A 3L4

Dear Mr. Caldwell:

Your advertisement for an assistant product manager, appearing May 22 in Section C of the *National Post*, immediately caught my attention because my education and training closely parallel your needs.

Your ad states that the job includes "assisting in the coordination of a wide range of marketing programs as well as analyzing sales results and tracking marketing budgets." A recent internship at Ventana Corporation introduced me to similar tasks. Assisting the marketing manager enabled me to analyze the promotion, budget, and overall sales success of two products Ventana was evaluating. My ten-page report examined the nature of the current market, the products' life cycles, and their sales/profit return. In addition to this research, I helped formulate a product merchandising plan and answered consumers' questions at a local trade show.

Intensive course work in marketing and management, as well as proficiency in computer spreadsheets and databases, has given me the kind of marketing and computer training that Del Rio would expect in a product manager. Moreover, my recent retail sales experience and participation in school organizations have helped me develop the kind of customer service and interpersonal skills necessary for an effective product manager.

After you have examined the enclosed résumé for details of my qualifications, I would be happy to answer questions. Please call me to arrange an interview at your convenience so that we may discuss how my marketing experience, computer training, and interpersonal skills could contribute to Del Rio Enterprises.

Sincerely,

Mabel Lam

Mabel Lam

Enclosure

Uses personally designed letterhead

Addresses proper person by name and title

Gains attention by identifying job and exact page where ad appeared

Builds interest by relating writer's experiences to job

Builds interest by discussing schooling

Builds interest by discussing experience

Refers reader to résumé

Motivates action by asking for interview and repeating main qualifications

Building Interest in the Body

Quick Check

The body of a cover letter should build interest, reduce resistance, and discuss relevant personal traits.

Once you have captured the attention of the reader, you can use the body of the letter to build interest and reduce resistance. Keep in mind that your résumé emphasizes what you have done; your cover letter stresses what you can do for the employer.

Your first goal is to relate your remarks to a specific position. If you are responding to an advertisement, you'll want to explain how your preparation and experience fill the stated requirements. If you are prospecting for a job, you may

FIGURE 13.15 Unsolicited Cover Letter

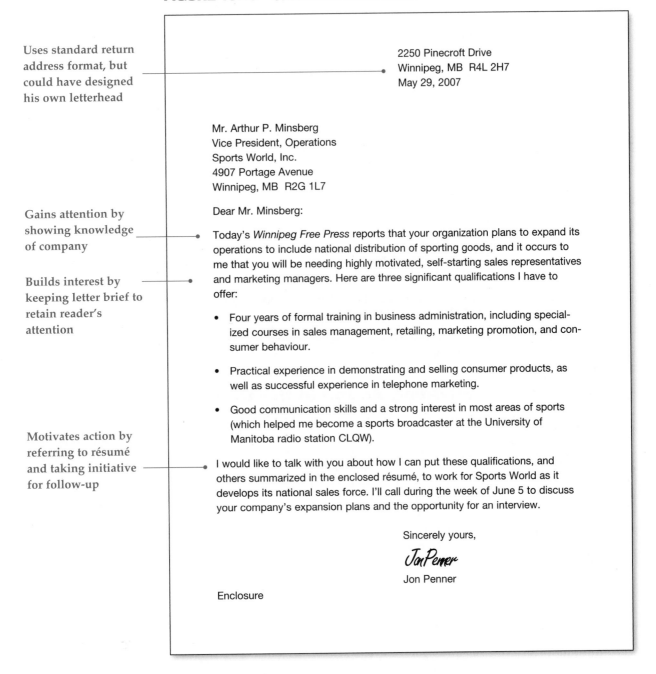

Uses standard return address format, but could have designed his own letterhead

2250 Pinecroft Drive
Winnipeg, MB R4L 2H7
May 29, 2007

Mr. Arthur P. Minsberg
Vice President, Operations
Sports World, Inc.
4907 Portage Avenue
Winnipeg, MB R2G 1L7

Dear Mr. Minsberg:

Gains attention by showing knowledge of company

Today's *Winnipeg Free Press* reports that your organization plans to expand its operations to include national distribution of sporting goods, and it occurs to me that you will be needing highly motivated, self-starting sales representatives and marketing managers. Here are three significant qualifications I have to offer:

Builds interest by keeping letter brief to retain reader's attention

- Four years of formal training in business administration, including specialized courses in sales management, retailing, marketing promotion, and consumer behaviour.

- Practical experience in demonstrating and selling consumer products, as well as successful experience in telephone marketing.

- Good communication skills and a strong interest in most areas of sports (which helped me become a sports broadcaster at the University of Manitoba radio station CLQW).

Motivates action by referring to résumé and taking initiative for follow-up

I would like to talk with you about how I can put these qualifications, and others summarized in the enclosed résumé, to work for Sports World as it develops its national sales force. I'll call during the week of June 5 to discuss your company's expansion plans and the opportunity for an interview.

Sincerely yours,

Jon Penner

Enclosure

not know the exact requirements. Your employment research and knowledge of your field, however, should give you a reasonably good idea of what is expected for this position.

It's also important to emphasize reader benefits. In other words, you should describe your strong points in relation to the needs of the employer. In one employment survey many human resources professionals expressed the same view: "I want you to tell me what you can do for my organization. This is much more important to me than telling me what courses you took in college or what 'duties' you performed on your previous jobs."[9] Instead of *I have completed courses in business communication, report writing, and technical writing,* try this:

✓ **Quick Check**

Spotlighting reader benefits means matching one's personal strengths to an employer's needs.

Courses in business communication, report writing, and technical writing have helped me develop the research and writing skills required of your technical writers.

Choose your strongest qualifications and show how they fit the targeted job. And remember, students with little experience are better off spotlighting their education and its practical applications, as these candidates did:

> Because you seek an architect's apprentice with proven ability, I submit a drawing of mine that won second place in the Algonquin College drafting contest last year.

> Successfully transcribing over 100 letters and memos in my college transcription class gave me experience in converting the spoken word into the written word, an exacting communication skill demanded of your legal assistants.

In the body of your letter, you'll also want to discuss relevant personal traits. Employers are looking for candidates who, among other things, are team players, take responsibility, show initiative, and learn easily. Finally, in this section or the next, you should refer the reader to your résumé. Do so directly or as part of another statement, as shown here:

> Please refer to the attached résumé for additional information regarding my education, experience, and references.

> As you will notice from my résumé, I will graduate in June with a bachelor's degree in business administration.

Motivating Action in the Closing

Quick Check

The closing of a cover letter should include a request for an interview.

After presenting your case, you should conclude with a spur to action. This is where you ask for an interview. If you live in a distant city, you may request an employment application or an opportunity to be interviewed by the organization's nearest representative. However, never ask for the job. To do so would be presumptuous and naive. In requesting an interview, suggest reader benefits or review your strongest points. Sound sincere and appreciative. Remember to make it easy for the reader to agree by supplying your telephone number and the best times to call you. And keep in mind that some human resources directors prefer that you take the initiative to call them. Here are possible endings:

> I hope this brief description of my qualifications and the additional information on my résumé indicate to you my genuine desire to put my skills in accounting to work for you. Please call me at (416) 488-2291 before 10 a.m. or after 3 p.m. to arrange an interview.

> To add to your staff an industrious, well-trained word processing specialist with proven communication skills, call me at (604) 492-1433 to arrange an interview. I can meet with you at any time convenient to your schedule.

> Next week, after you have examined the attached résumé, I will call you to discuss the possibility of arranging an interview.

Avoiding "I" Dominance

As you revise your application letter, notice how many sentences begin with *I*. Although it's impossible to talk about yourself without using *I*, you can reduce the number of sentences beginning with this pronoun by using two techniques. First, place *I* in the middle of sentences instead of dominating the opening. Instead of *I was the top salesperson in my department*, try *While working in X department, I did Y*

Chapter 13 The Job Search, Résumés, and Cover Letters

and Z and among 15 coworkers, I received top ratings from my managers. Incorporating *I* into the middle of sentences considerably reduces its domination.

Another technique for avoiding "I" dominance involves making activities and outcomes, and not yourself, the subjects of sentences. For example, rather than *I took classes in business communication and computer applications,* say *Classes in business communication and computer applications prepared me to … .* Instead of *I enjoyed helping customers,* say *Helping customers taught me to be patient under stress.*

Final Tips

Like the résumé, your cover letter must look professional and suggest quality. This means using a traditional letter style, such as block or modified block. Also, be sure to print it on the same bond paper as your résumé. More and more writers today are designing their own letterhead paper, or they adapt one of the templates available with their word processing programs. Be sure to use restraint, though, so that your letterhead looks truly professional, such as that shown in Figure 13.14. Finally, proofread your application letter several times; then, have a friend read it for content and mechanics.

Quick Check

A cover letter should look professional and suggest quality.

Summing Up and Looking Forward

In today's competitive job market, an employment search begins with identifying your interests, evaluating your qualifications, and choosing a career path. Finding the perfect job will mean a concentrated effort devoted to checking classified advertisements, networking, and studying online job possibilities. In applying for jobs, you'll want to submit a persuasive résumé that sells your skills and experience. Whether you choose a chronological, functional, or combination résumé style, you should tailor your assets to fit the position sought. If you think your résumé might be scanned, emphasize keywords and keep the format simple. A persuasive cover letter should introduce your résumé and describe how your skills and experiences match those required.

Now, if your résumé and cover letter have been successful, you'll proceed to the employment interview, one of life's most stressful experiences. The last chapter in this book provides helpful suggestions for successful interviewing and follow-up communication.

Critical Thinking

1. How has the concept of the job changed, and how will it affect your employment search?
2. How is a résumé different from a company employment application?
3. Some job candidates think that applying for unsolicited jobs can be more fruitful than applying for advertised openings. Discuss the advantages and disadvantages of letters that "prospect" for jobs.
4. *Ethical Issue:* At work, fellow employee Karl lets it slip that he did not complete the degree he claims on his résumé. You have never liked Karl, but he does satisfactory work. You are both competing for the same promotion. You are considering writing an anonymous note to the boss telling him to verify Karl's degree. Use the tools in the Ethics Workshop on page 72 to decide whether this is an ethical action.
5. A cover letter is a persuasive letter, but do you really want to reduce a potential employer's resistance? Why might this be dangerous?

6. List at least five questions that you should ask yourself to identify your employment interests.

7. List five or more sources of career information.

8. How are most jobs likely to be found? Through the classified ads? Employment agencies? Networking? Explain.

9. What is the goal of your résumé?

10. Describe a chronological résumé and discuss its advantages.

11. Describe a functional résumé and discuss its advantages.

12. What are the disadvantages of a functional résumé?

13. When does it make sense to include a career objective on your résumé?

14. In a chronological résumé, what information should you include for the jobs you list?

15. In addition to technical skills, what traits and characteristics do employers seek?

16. List some suggestions for making a résumé easily scannable by a computer.

17. What are keywords and why are they important in résumé scanning? Give examples.

18. If you are e-mailing your résumé, why is it wise to send a text-only version?

19. What are the three purposes of a cover letter?

20. How can you make it easy for a recruiter to reach you?

Writing Improvement Exercises

21. Cover Letter Opening. James Nickson has just graduated from college with a three-year diploma in accounting. With the help of his college's career centre, James has begun applying for full-time employment. Below is the opening of one of James's cover letters. Analyze the letter, identify any problems, and rewrite this section of the letter following the guidelines in this chapter.

To whom it may concern,

It was a stroke of luck to find the job advertisement in the local newspaper last week for your company. I've always wanted to work for a company like yours, and this job opening may now give me the opportunity! My name is Jim Nickson and I just graduated in Accounting at a local college.

22. Cover Letter Body. Below is the body of James Nickson's cover letter. Analyze the letter, identify any problems, and rewrite this section of the letter following the guidelines in this chapter.

As you can see from my enclosed résumé, I am a strong student, and I am also a good team player. I think these skills would be useful to me in your company. For example, I took a course in Auditing in which I received the highest GPA in the program. Finally, I have worked as a bookkeeper for the past two summers.

23. Cover Letter Closing. The closing of James Nickson's cover letter is found below. Analyze the letter, identify any problems, and rewrite this section of the letter following the guidelines in this chapter.

In closing, permit me to be blunt and say that there's nothing I'd like more than the opportunity to work for your company. I know I would be an asset to your organization. I look forward to hearing from you at your earliest convenience.

Best,

Jim Nickson

Activities and Cases

13.1 Interests and Qualifications Inventory. It's often surprising what kind of information you can find out about your fellow classmates in a classroom setting. Imagine you are conducting a study for your college's co-op office or student association about future aspirations of students. The co-op office or student association wants to know the future career interests of the college's students as well as their current qualifications.

Your Task. Choose three people in your class (preferably classmates you don't know very well) and interview them. Ask them the questions listed on page 357 under "Identifying Your Interests" and then the questions on page 358 under "Evaluating Your Qualifications." Develop a profile of each of your interviewees, and e-mail this profile to your instructor. Your instructor may choose to share the "inventory" with you in a later class. How might you use this inventory for future networking purposes?

13.2 Evaluating Your Qualifications. Prepare four worksheets that inventory your own qualifications in the areas of employment, education, capabilities and skills, and honours and activities. Use active verbs when appropriate.

a. *Employment.* Begin with your most recent job or internship. For each position list the following information: employer; job title; dates of employment; and three to five duties, activities, or accomplishments. Emphasize activities related to your job goal. Strive to quantify your achievements.

b. *Education.* List degrees, certificates, diplomas, and training accomplishments. Include courses, seminars, or skills that are relevant to your job goal. Calculate your grade point average in your major.

c. *Capabilities and skills.* List all capabilities and skills that recommend you for the job you seek. Use words such as *skilled, competent, trained, experienced,* and *ability to.* Also list five or more qualities or interpersonal skills necessary for a successful individual in your chosen field. Write action statements demonstrating that you possess some of these qualities. Empty assurances aren't good enough; try to show evidence (*Developed teamwork skills by working with a committee of eight to produce a ...*).

d. *Awards, honours, and activities.* Explain any awards so that the reader will understand them. List school, community, and professional activities that suggest you are a well-rounded individual or possess traits relevant to your target job.

13.3 Choosing a Career Path. Visit your school library, local library, or employment centre. Select an appropriate resource such as Human Resource Development Canada's National Occupational Classification <www23 .hrdc-drhc.gc.ca/2001/e/generic/welcome.shtml> to find a description for a position for which you could apply in two to five years. Photocopy or print the pages from the resource you chose that describe employment in the area in which you are interested. If your instructor directs, attach these copies to the cover letter you will write in Activity 13.9. Were you able to find the job that interests you? If not, where else can you find information on this job?

13.4 Searching the Job Market. Clip a job advertisement from the classified section of a newspaper or print one from a career site on the Web. Select an ad describing the kind of employment you are seeking now or plan to seek when you graduate. Save this advertisement to attach to the résumé you will write in Activity 13.8.

13.5 Posting a Résumé on the Web. Research at least three online employment sites where you could post your résumé. In an e-mail to your instructor, imagine you are providing text for the updating of your college's career centre Web site. Describe the procedure involved in posting résumés on these three sites in a clear set of steps, and list the advantages and disadvantages of each site.

Web

13.6 Draft Document: Résumé. Analyze the following résumé. Discuss its strengths and weaknesses. Your instructor may ask you to revise sections of this résumé before showing you an improved version.

Winona Skudra
5349 Main Street
Saskatoon, SK S2N 0B4
Phone: (d) (306) 834-4583 (n) (306) 594-2985

Seeking to be hired at Meadow Products as an intern in Accounting

SKILLS: Accounting, Internet, Windows 98, Excel, PowerPoint, Freelance Graphics

EDUCATION

Now working on B.Comm. in Business Administration. Major, Management and Accounting; GPA is 3.5. Expect to graduate in June, 2007.

EXPERIENCE:

Assistant Accountant, 2000 to present. March and McLennan, Inc., Bookkeeping/Tax Service, Saskatoon. I keep accounting records for several small businesses accurately. I prepare 150 to 200 individual income tax returns each year. For Hill and Hill Trucking I maintain accurate and up-to-date A/R records. And I prepare payroll records for 16 employees at three firms.

Peterson Controls Inc., Saskatoon. Data Processing Internship, 2004 to present. I design and maintain spreadsheets and also process weekly and monthly information for production uptime and downtime. I prepare graphs to illustrate uptime and downtime data.

Saskatoon Curling Club. Accounts Payable Internship, 2003 to 2004. Took care of accounts payable including filing system for the club. Responsible for processing monthly adjusting entries for general ledger. Worked closely with treasurer to give the Board budget/disbursement figures regularly.

Activities and Cases

Saskatoon High School, Saskatoon. I marketed the VITA program to students and organized volunteers and supplies. Official title: Coordinator of Volunteer Income Tax Assistance Project.

COMMUNITY SERVICE: March of Dimes Drive, Central High School; All Souls Lutheran Church, coordinator for Children's Choir

---

13.7 Draft Document: Cover Letter. Analyze each section of the following cover letter written by an accounting major about to graduate.

Dear Human Resources Director:

Please consider this letter as an application for the position of staff accountant that I saw advertised in the *Saskatoon Star Phoenix*. Although I have had no paid work experience in this field, accounting has been my major in college and I'm sure I could be an asset to your company.

For four years I have studied accounting, and I am fully trained for full-charge bookkeeping as well as electronic accounting. I have completed 36 credits of college accounting and courses in business law, economics, statistics, finance, management, and marketing. In addition to my course work, during the tax season I have been a student volunteer for VITA. This is a project to help individuals in the community prepare their income tax returns, and I learned a lot from this experience. I have also received some experience in office work and working with figures when I was employed as an office assistant for Copy Quick, Inc.

I am a competent and responsible person who gets along pretty well with others. I have been a member of some college and social organizations and have even held elective office.

I feel that I have a strong foundation in accounting as a result of my course work and my experience. Along with my personal qualities and my desire to succeed, I hope that you will agree that I qualify for the position of staff accountant with your company.

Sincerely,

13.8 Résumé. Using the data you developed in Activity 13.2, write your résumé. Aim it at a full-time job, part-time position, or internship. Attach a job listing for a specific position (from Activity 13.4). Revise your résumé until it is perfect.

13.9 Cover Letter. Write an application letter introducing your résumé from Activity 13.8. Revise your application letter until it is perfect.

13.10 Unsolicited Cover Letter. As you read in this chapter, job applications are not always solicited. As part of your college education, you have no doubt come into contact with periodicals related to your field. For example, you may have read articles in *Canadian Business, Report on Business, HR Reporter, Marketing,* or any number of other magazines. In these magazines, you've come across the names of various business people, either because they were featured in an article, or else because they were quoted as experts.

Your Task. Using your college or local library, read through an issue of a business-related periodical or your local newspaper's business section. Look for a businessperson who is mentioned, quoted, or featured in that periodical. Write that person an unsolicited cover letter asking for an entry-level position or internship either for the summer or upon graduation. Make sure to revise this letter sufficiently, and hand it in to your instructor for comments before actually mailing it.

Grammar/Mechanics Review—13

The following sentences contain errors in grammar, punctuation, capitalization, number style, usage, and spelling. Below each sentence write a corrected version.

1. Please send the softwear to myself or whomever submited the order.

2. All committe members except Tracy and he knew the assignment, and were prepared with there reports when they were do.

3. Was any of the managers absent on the Monday following the 4 day weekend.

4. The Governments crash-worthiness standards all call for the use of two and a half metre 79 kilo dummys.

5. The makers of Saturn however decided to use dummys ranging from nineteen kilo children to 59 kilo females to burly 112 kilo males.

6. The president made an off the record comment but members of the board soon heard it repeated.

7. We retained only a 4 year old printer, however it will be inspected year-by-year.

8. Before five p.m. we must return all 3 computers to our 7th Avenue office.

9. Canada post announced on July 1st that it would increase rates by 4.5%.

10. The three Cs of credit is the following, character, capacity, and capitol.

11. Porter Kohl said that his Father gave him the following advice on making speeches—"Be sincere, be breif; and be seated.

12. Some trucks acceded the 2000 kilogram weight limit, others were under it.

13. Each of the quickly-printed computer books have been priced to sell at ten dollars and ninety-five cents.

14. If you will send the shipment to Elizabeth or I; it's contents will be inspected throughly.

15. The itinerary for Luke and he included 3 countrys holland france and germany.

Grammar/Mechanics Challenge—13

Document for Revision

The following résumé (shortened for this exercise) has faults in grammar, punctuation, spelling, number form, verb form, wordiness, and word use. Use standard proofreading marks (see Appendix B) to correct the errors. When you finish, your instructor can show you the revised version of this résumé.

MEGAN A. Kozlov

245 Topsail Street

St. John's, Newfoundland A1B 3Z4

EDUCATION

Memorial University, St. John's, Newfoundland. Bachelor of Arts Degree expected in June 2006. Major English.

EXPERIENCE:

- Administrative Assistant. Host Systems, St. John's. 2003 too pressent. Responsible for entering data on Macintosh computer. I had to insure accuracy and completness of data that was to be entered. Another duty was maintaining a clean and well-organized office. I also served as Office Courier.

- Lechter's Housewares. Outlook Newfoundland. 2nd Asst. Mgr I managed store in absence of mgr. and asst. mgr. I open and close registers. Ballanced daily reciepts. Ordered some mds. I also had to supervise 2 employes, earning rabid promotion.

- Clerk typist. Sunshine Travel Outlook. 2000–2001. (part time) Entered travel information on IBM PC. Did personalized followup letters to customer inquirys. Was responsible for phones. I also handled all errands as courier.

STRENGTHS

Microsoft Office Applications, transcription, poofreading.

Can type 50 words/per/minute.

I am a fast learner, and very accurate.

Word-perfect, Excell, InterNet

How to Use Traditional and Online Networking to Explore the Hidden Job Market

Not all jobs are advertised in classified ads or listed in job databases. The "hidden" job market, according to some estimates, accounts for as much as two-thirds of all positions available. Companies don't always announce openings publicly because it's time consuming to interview all the applicants, many of whom are not qualified. But the real reason that companies resist announcing a job is that they dislike hiring "strangers." One recruiter says that when she needs to hire, she first looks around among her friends and acquaintances. If she can't find anyone suitable, she then turns to advertising.[10] It's clear that many employers are more comfortable hiring a person they know.

The key to finding a good job, then, is converting yourself from a "stranger" into a known quantity. One way to become a known quantity is by networking. You can use either traditional methods or online resources.

Traditional Networking

- *Step 1: Develop a list.* Make a list of anyone who would be willing to talk with you about finding a job. List your friends, relatives, former employers, former coworkers, classmates from grade school and high school, college friends, members of your religious group, people in social and athletic clubs, present and former teachers, neighbours, and friends of your parents.
- *Step 2: Make contacts.* Call the people on your list or, even better, try to meet with them in person. To set up a meeting, say "Hi, Aunt Martha! I'm looking for a job and I wonder if you could help me out. When could I come over to talk about it?" During your visit be friendly, well organized, polite, and interested in what your contact has to say. Provide a copy of your résumé, and try to keep the conversation centred on your job search area. Your goal is to get two or more referrals. In pinpointing your request, ask two questions. "Do you know of anyone who might have an opening for a person with my skills?" If not, "Do you know of anyone else who might know of someone who would?"
- *Step 3: Follow up on your referrals.* Call the people whose names are on your referral list. You might say something like, "Hello. I'm Carlos Ramos, a friend of Connie Cole. She suggested that I call and ask you for help. I'm looking for a position as a marketing trainee, and she thought you might be willing to see me and give me a few ideas." Don't ask for a job. During your referral interview ask how the individual got started in this line of work, what he or she likes best (or least) about the work, what career paths exist in the field, and what problems must be overcome by a newcomer. Most important, ask how a person with your background and skills might get started in the field. Send an informal thank-you note to anyone who helps you in your job search, and stay in touch with the most promising contacts. Ask whether you may call every three weeks or so during your job search.

Online Networking

As with traditional networking, the goal is to make connections with people who are advanced in their fields. Ask for their advice about finding a job. Most people like talking about themselves, and asking them about their experiences is an excellent way to begin an online correspondence that might lead to "electronic mentoring" or a letter of recommendation from an expert in the field. "Hanging out" at an online forum, discussion group, or newsgroup where industry professionals can be found is also a great way to keep tabs on the latest business trends and potential job leads.

- *Web-Based Discussion Groups, Forums, and Boards.* An especially good discussion group resource for beginners is Yahoo! Groups (http://groups.yahoo .com). You may choose from groups ranging from Business & Finance to Romance & Relationships and on to Science. If you click the "Business & Finance" listing, you will see listings for more specialized groups. Click "Employment and Work," and you will find career groups including construction, customer service, secretaries, court reporting, interior design, and so on.
- *Mailing Lists and Newsgroups.* The most relevant Internet discussions can be found on mailing lists. You can subscribe to an e-mail newsletter or discussion group at Topica (http://lists.topica.com). To post and read newsgroup (Usenet) messages, try the Google Web site (http://www.google.ca) and click "Groups."

Career Application

Everyone who goes out on the job market needs to develop his or her own network. Assume you are ready to change jobs or look for a permanent position. Begin developing your personal network.

Your Task

- Conduct at least one referral interview and report on it to your class.
- Join one professional mailing list. Ask your instructor to recommend an appropriate mailing list for your field.
- Take notes on discussions at your mailing list and report your reactions and findings to your class.

14

Employment Interviews and Follow-Up Messages

CHAPTER

Nothing delights interviewers more than candidates who have done their homework. They want to know that a candidate has done a little research on the company or industry ... and understands the challenges it is facing. As a bonus, the most heartwarming candidates have actually given a little thought to the job they are applying for.[1]

Michael Stern, *president, Michael Stern Associates Inc., an executive search firm headquartered in Toronto*

LEARNING OBJECTIVES

1. Distinguish between screening interviews and hiring/placement interviews.
2. Identify information resources in investigating target employers.
3. Explain how to prepare for employment interviews.
4. Recognize how to control nonverbal messages and how to fight interview fears.
5. Be prepared to answer favourite interview questions and know how to close an interview.
6. Itemize topics and behaviours to avoid in interviews.
7. Write follow-up letters and other employment messages.

Job interviews, for most of us, are intimidating; no one enjoys being judged and, possibly, rejected. Should you expect to be nervous about an upcoming job interview? Of course. Everyone is uneasy about being scrutinized and questioned. But think of how much more nervous you would be if you had no idea what to expect in the interview and if you were unprepared.

This chapter presents different kinds of interviews and shows you how to prepare for them. You'll learn how to gather information about an employer, as well as how to reduce nervousness, control body language, and fight fear during an interview. You'll pick up tips for responding to recruiters' favourite questions and learn how to cope with illegal questions and salary matters. Moreover, you'll receive pointers on significant questions you can ask during an interview. Finally, you'll learn what you should do as a successful follow-up to an interview.

Yes, you can expect to be nervous. But you can also expect to succeed in an interview when you know what's coming and when you prepare thoroughly. Remember, it's often the degree of preparation that determines who gets the job.

Job applicants generally face two kinds of interviews: screening interviews and hiring/placement interviews. You must succeed in the first to proceed to the second.

Screening Interviews

Screening interviews screen candidates to eliminate those who fail to meet minimum requirements. Initial screening is often done by telephone or by computer.

A telephone screening interview may be as short as five minutes. But don't treat it casually. It's not just another telephone call. If you don't perform well during the telephone interview, it may be your last interview with that organization. While the following suggestions are meant for screening interviews, keep them in mind if you must participate in a hiring interview over the telephone. Here's how you can be prepared for a telephone interview:

- Keep a list near the telephone of positions for which you have applied.
- Have your résumé, references, a calendar, and a notepad handy.
- If caught off guard, ask if you can call back in a few minutes. Organize your materials and yourself.
- Sell your qualifications, and, above all, sound enthusiastic.

Several Canadian career coaches suggest it is important to politely and directly offer the facts the interviewer seeks, and refrain from volunteering additional information such as salary expectations. Save this kind of information for the probing questions that will occur in first and second interviews. The screening interview is used to "weed out" candidates, so they will never reach the next step.[2]

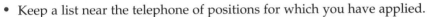
✓ **Quick Check**
Screening interviews are intended to eliminate those who fail to meet minimum requirements.

Hiring/Placement Interviews

The most promising candidates selected from screening interviews will be invited to hiring/placement interviews. Although these interviews are the real thing, in many ways they are like a game. Trained interviewers try to uncover any negative information that will eliminate a candidate. The candidate tries to minimize faults and emphasize strengths to avoid being eliminated. Like most games, the more practice you get, the better you perform because you know what to expect. Hiring/placement interviews are conducted in depth and may take many forms.

✓ **Quick Check**
In hiring/placement interviews, recruiters try to uncover negative information while candidates try to minimize faults and emphasize strengths.

- **One-on-one interviews** are most common. You can expect to sit down with a company representative or two and talk about the job and your qualifications. If the representative is the hiring manager, questions will be specific and job related. If the representative is from the human resources department, the questions will probably be more general.
- **Sequential and group interviews** are common with companies that rule by consensus. You may face many interviewers in sequence, all of whom you must listen to carefully and respond to positively. Many group interviews are conducted by teams. With team interviews, begin to think in terms of "we" instead of "I." Individual achievement is less important in group interviews than how you contributed to a team effort. Strive to stay focused, summarize important points, and ask good questions.
- **Stress interviews** are meant to test your reactions. If asked rapid-fire questions from many directions, take the time to slow things down. For example, *I would be happy to answer your question, Ms. X, but allow me to finish responding to Mr. Z.*

If greeted with silence, another stress technique, you might say *Would you like me to begin the interview? Let me tell you about myself.* Or ask a question such as *Can you give me more information about the position?* The best way to handle stress questions is to remain calm and give carefully considered answers.

Investigating the Target

One of the most important steps in being successful at the interview game is gathering information about a prospective employer. In learning about a company, you may uncover information that convinces you that this is not the company for you. It's always better to learn about negatives early in the process. More likely, though, the information you collect will help you tailor your application and interview responses to the organization's needs. Recruiters are impressed by candidates who have done their homework.

Digging for Company Information

✔ Quick Check

Researching an organization enlightens candidates and impresses recruiters.

For Canadian companies that are publicly held, you can generally learn a great deal from annual reports and financial disclosure reports available at <www.sedar.com>. Company information is also available from *Dun and Bradstreet Canada* <www.dnb.ca>, and Canadian Business Resource <www.cbr.ca>. One of the best things a job-seeker can do is to get into the habit of reading the newspaper regularly. The best place to go for current information on Canadian companies is the business section of the two national newspapers, the *National Post* and *The Globe and Mail.* Your local city or town newspaper will occasionally profile local businesses. Finally, large and small companies alike also maintain their own Web sites, bursting with helpful information. Another way to learn about an organization is to call the receptionist or the interviewer directly. Ask what you can read to prepare for the interview. Here are some specifics to research:

✔ Quick Check

Study company leaders, organizational strategies, finances, products, customers, competition, and advertising.

- Find out all you can about company leaders. Their goals, ambitions, and values are often adopted by the entire organization—including your interviewer.
- Investigate the business philosophy of the leaders, such as their priorities, strategies, and managerial approaches. Are you a good match with your target employer? If so, be sure to let the employer know that there is a correlation between its needs and your qualifications.
- Learn about the company's accomplishments and setbacks. This information should help you determine where you might make your best contribution.
- Study the company's finances. Are they so shaky that a takeover is imminent? If so, look elsewhere. Try to get your hands on an annual report. Many larger companies now post them on their Web sites.
- Examine the company's products and customers. What excites you about this company?
- Check out the competition. What are its products, strengths, and weaknesses?
- Analyze the company's advertising, including sales and marketing brochures. One candidate, a marketing major, spent a great deal of time poring over brochures from an aerospace contractor. During his initial interview, he shocked and impressed the recruiter with his knowledge of the company's guidance systems. The candidate had, in fact, relieved the interviewer of his least-favourite task—explaining the company's complicated technology.

Learning about Smaller Companies

For smaller companies and those that are not publicly owned, you'll probably have to dig a little deeper. You might start with the local library. Ask the reference librarian to help you locate information. Newspapers might contain stories or press releases with news of an organization. Visit the Better Business Bureau or Chamber of Commerce to discover whether the company has had any difficulties with other companies or consumers. Also, find out what kinds of contributions has the company made to the local community. Try your local Canada Business Service Centre for company information and annual reports.

Talking with company employees is always a good idea, if you can manage it. They are probably the best source of inside information. Try to be introduced to someone who is currently employed—but not working in the immediate area where you wish to be hired. Be sure to seek out someone who is discreet.

You know how flattered you feel when an employer knows about you and your background. That feeling works both ways. Employers are pleased when job candidates take an interest in them. Be ready to put in plenty of effort in investigating a target employer because this effort really pays off at interview time.

Quick Check

The best source of inside information is company employees.

Preparing and Practising

After you have learned about the target organization, study the job description. It not only helps you write a focused résumé but also enables you to match your education, experience, and interests with the employer's position. Finding out the duties and responsibilities of the position will help you practise your best response strategies.

One of the best ways to prepare involves itemizing your (1) most strategic skills, (2) greatest areas of knowledge, (3) strongest personality traits, and (4) key accomplishments. Write this information down and practise relating these strengths to the kinds of questions frequently asked in interviews. Here are some specific tips for preparation:

Quick Check

Practise success stories that emphasize your most strategic skills, areas of knowledge, strongest personality traits, and key accomplishments.

- Practise, practise, practise. Recite answers to typical interview questions in a mirror, with a friend, while driving in your car, or in spare moments. Keep practising until you have the best responses down pat.
- Consider videotaping or tape-recording a practice session to see and hear how you really come across. Do you look and sound enthusiastic?
- Expect to explain problem areas on your résumé. For example, if you have little or no experience, you might emphasize your recent training and up-to-date skills. If you have gaps in your résumé, be prepared to answer questions about them positively and truthfully.
- Try to build interviewing experience with less important jobs first. You will become more confident and better able to sell your strengths with repeated interviewing exposure. Think of it as a game that requires practice.

Sending Positive Nonverbal Messages

What comes out of your mouth and what's written on your résumé are not the only messages an interviewer receives about you. Nonverbal messages also create powerful impressions. Here are suggestions that will help you send the right nonverbal messages during interviews:

Quick Check

Send positive nonverbal messages by arriving on time, being courteous, dressing professionally, greeting the interviewer confidently, controlling your body movements, making eye contact, and smiling.

- Arrive on time or a little early. If necessary, find the location on a trial run a few days before the interview so that you know where to park, how much time the drive takes, and what office to find.
- Be courteous and congenial to everyone. Remember that you are being judged not only by the interviewer but by the receptionist and anyone else who sees you before and after the interview. They will notice how you sit, what you read, and how you look.

- Introduce yourself to the receptionist and wait to be invited to sit.
- Dress professionally. Even if some employees in the organization dress casually, you should look qualified, competent, and successful. One young applicant complained to his girlfriend about having to wear a suit for an interview when everyone at the company dressed casually. She replied, "You don't get to wear the uniform, though, until you make the team!"
- Greet the interviewer confidently. Extend your hand, look him or her directly in the eye, and say, "I'm pleased to meet you, Mr. X. I am Z." In this culture a firm, not crushing, handshake sends a nonverbal message of poise and assurance.
- Wait for the interviewer to offer you a chair. Make small talk with upbeat comments, such as "This is a beautiful headquarters. How many employees work here?" Don't immediately begin rummaging in your briefcase for your résumé. Being at ease and unrushed suggest that you are self-confident.
- Control your body movements. Keep your hands, arms, and elbows to yourself. Don't lean on a desk. Sit erect, leaning forward slightly. Keep your feet on the floor.
- Make eye contact frequently but don't get into a staring contest. A direct eye gaze, at least in Canada, suggests interest and trustworthiness.
- Smile enough to convey a positive attitude. Have a friend give you honest feedback on whether you generally smile too much or not enough.
- Sound enthusiastic and interested—but sincere.

Fighting Fear

Quick Check

Fight fear by practising, preparing 110 percent, breathing deeply, and knowing that you are in charge for part of the interview.

Expect to be nervous. It's natural. Other than public speaking, employment interviews are the most dreaded events in many people's working lives. One of the best ways to overcome fear is to know what happens in a typical interview. Figure 14.1 describes how a recruiter usually structures an interview. You can further reduce your fears by following these suggestions:

- Practise interviewing as much as you can—especially with real companies. The more times you experience the interview situation, the less nervous you will be.
- Prepare 110 percent! Know how you will answer the most frequently asked questions. Be ready with success stories. Rehearse your closing statement. One of the best ways to reduce butterflies is to know that you have done all you can to be ready for the interview.
- Take deep breaths, particularly if you feel anxious while waiting for the interviewer. Deep breathing makes you concentrate on something other than the interview and also provides much-needed oxygen.
- Remember that the interviewer isn't the only one who is gleaning information. You have come to learn about the job and the company. In fact, during some parts of the interview, you will be in charge. This should give you courage.

Answering Questions

Quick Check

How you answer questions can be as important as the answers themselves.

The way you answer questions can be almost as important as what you say. Use the interviewer's name and title from time to time when you answer: *Ms. Lyon, I would be pleased to tell you about ... .* People like to hear their own names. But be sure you are pronouncing the name correctly.

Occasionally it may be necessary to refocus and clarify vague questions. Some interviewers are inexperienced and ill at ease in the role. You may even have to ask your own question to understand what was asked: *By ... do you mean ...?*

Consider closing some of your responses with *Does that answer your question?* or *Would you like me to elaborate on any particular experience?*

Chapter 14 Employment Interviews and Follow-Up Messages

FIGURE 14.1 **Steps in an Employment Interview from a Recruiter's Perspective**

Step 1	**Step 2**	**Step 3**
Before interview, review candidate's résumé.	Check career objective. Look for skills; note items to pursue.	Greet candidate. Introduce self. Make candidate feel comfortable.

Step 4	**Step 5**	**Step 6**
Describe open position. Confirm candidate's interest in position.	Give brief overview of organization.	Using résumé, probe for evidence of relevant skills and traits.

Step 7	**Step 8**	**Step 9**
Solicit questions from candidate.	Close interview by promoting organization and explaining next step.	Fill out evaluation form.

Always aim your answers at the key characteristics interviewers seek: expertise and competence, motivation, interpersonal skills, decision-making skills, enthusiasm for the job, and a pleasing personality. And remember to stay focused on your strengths. Don't reveal weaknesses, even if you think they make you look human. You won't be hired for your weaknesses, only for your strengths.

Use proper English and enunciate clearly. Remember, you will definitely be judged by how well you communicate. Avoid slurred words such as *gonna* and *y'know*, as well as slangy expressions such as *yeah*, *like*, and *whatever*. Also eliminate verbal static (*ah, and, uhm*). As you practise for the interview, a good idea is to record answers to expected interview questions. Is your speech filled with verbal static?

You can't expect to be perfect in an employment interview. No one is. But you can increase your chances of success by avoiding certain topics and behaviours such as those described in Figure 14.2 on page 400.

Quick Check

Stay focused on the skills and traits that employers seek; don't reveal weaknesses.

All-Time Favourite Questions with Selected Answers

Employment interviews are all about questions. And most of the questions are not new. You can actually anticipate 90 to 95 percent of all questions that will be asked before you ever walk into an interview room.[3]

The following questions represent all-time favourites asked of recent graduates and other job seekers. You'll find get-acquainted questions, experience and accomplishment questions, future-oriented questions, squirm questions, and money questions. To get you thinking about how to respond, we've provided an answer or discussion for the first question in each group. As you read the remaining questions in each group, think about how you could respond most effectively.

Quick Check

You can anticipate 90 to 95 percent of all questions you will be asked in an interview.

FIGURE 14.2 Interview Actions to Avoid

1. Don't ask for the job. It's naive, undignified, and unprofessional. Wait to see how the interview develops.

2. Don't be negative about your previous employer, supervisors, or colleagues. The tendency is for interviewers to wonder if you would speak about their companies similarly.

3. Don't be a threat to the interviewer. Avoid suggesting directly or indirectly that your goal is to become head honcho, a path that might include the interviewer's job.

4. Don't be late or too early for your appointment. Arrive five minutes before you are scheduled.

5. Don't discuss controversial subjects, and don't use profanity.

6. Don't emphasize salary or benefits. If the interview goes well and these subjects have not been addressed, you may mention them toward the end of the interview.

7. Don't be negative about yourself or others. Never dwell on your liabilities.

8. Don't interrupt. Not only is it impolite but it also prevents you from hearing a complete question or remark.

9. Don't accept an offer until you have completed all your interviews.

Questions to Get Acquainted

After opening introductions, recruiters generally try to start the interviewing questioning period with personal questions that put the candidate at ease. They are also striving to gain a picture of the candidate to see if he or she will fit into the organization's culture.

Quick Check

Prepare for get-acquainted questions by practising a short formula response.

1. Tell me about yourself.

Experts agree that you must keep this answer short (one to two minutes tops) but on target. Try practising this formula: "My name is _____. I have completed _____ degree with a major in _____. Recently I worked for _____ as a _____. Before that I worked for _____ as a _____. My strengths are _____ (interpersonal) and _____ (technical)." Try rehearsing your response in 30-second segments devoted to your education, your work experience, and your qualities/skills. Some candidates end with "Now that I've told you about myself, can you tell me a little more about the position?"

2. What was your area of specialization in college/university, and why did you choose it?
3. If you had it to do over again, would you choose the same major? Why?
4. Tell me about your college/university (or your major) and why you chose it.
5. Do you prefer to work by yourself or with others? Why?
6. What are your key strengths?

7. What are some things you do in your spare time? Hobbies? Sports?
8. How did you happen to apply for this job?
9. What particular qualifications do you have for this job?
10. Do you consider yourself a team player? Describe your style as a team player.

Questions about Your Experience and Accomplishments

After questions about your background and education, the interview generally becomes more specific with questions about your experience and accomplishments.

1. Why should we hire you when we have applicants with more experience or better credentials?

In answering this question, remember that employers often hire people who present themselves well instead of others with better credentials. Emphasize your personal strengths that could be an advantage with this employer. Are you a hard worker? How can you demonstrate it? Have you had recent training? Some people have had more years of experience but actually have less knowledge because they have done the same thing over and over. Stress your experience using the latest methods and equipment. Be sure to mention your computer training and use of the Internet and Web. Emphasize that you are open to new ideas and learn quickly.

2. Tell me about your part-time jobs, internships, or other experience.
3. What were your major accomplishments in each of your past jobs?
4. Why did you change jobs?
5. What was a typical work day like?
6. What job functions did you enjoy most? Least? Why?
7. Who was the toughest boss you ever worked for and why?
8. What were your major achievements in college/university?
9. Tell me about a difficult situation in a previous work situation and how you dealt with it.

Quick Check

Employers will hire a candidate with less experience and fewer accomplishments if he or she can demonstrate the skills required.

Questions about the Future

Questions that look into the future tend to stump some candidates, especially those who have not prepared adequately. Some of these questions give you a chance to discuss your personal future goals, while others require you to think on your feet and explain how you would respond in hypothetical situations.

1. Where do you expect to be five years from now?

It's a sure sign of failure to respond that you'd like to have the interviewer's job. Instead, show an interest in the current job and in making a contribution to the organization. Talk about the levels of responsibility you'd like to achieve. One employment counsellor suggests showing ambition but not committing to a specific job title. Suggest that you will have learned enough to have progressed to a position where you will continue to grow.

Quick Check

When asked about the future, show ambition and interest in succeeding with this company.

2. If you get this position, what would you do to be sure you fit in?
3. If your supervisor gave you an assignment and then left town for two weeks, what would you do?
4. This is a large (or small) organization. Do you think you'd like that environment?

5. If you were aware that a coworker was falsifying data, what would you do?
6. If your supervisor was dissatisfied with your work and you thought it was acceptable, how would you resolve the conflict?
7. Do you plan to continue your education?

Questions to Make You Squirm

The following questions may make you uncomfortable, but the important thing to remember is to answer truthfully without dwelling on your weaknesses. As quickly as possible, convert any negative response into a discussion of your strengths.

1. What are your key weaknesses?

It's amazing how many candidates knock themselves out of the competition by answering this question poorly. Actually, you have many choices. You can present a strength as a weakness (*Some people complain that I'm a workaholic or too attentive to details*). You can mention a corrected weakness (*I found that I really needed to learn about the Internet, so I took a course*). You could cite an unrelated skill (*I really need to brush up on my French*). You can cite a learning objective (*One of my long-term goals is to learn more about international management. Does your company have any plans to expand overseas?*). Another possibility is to reaffirm your qualifications (*I have no weaknesses that affect my ability to do this job*).

2. If you could change one thing about your personality, what would it be and why?
3. What would your former boss say about you?
4. What do you want the most from your job? Money? Security? Power?
5. How did you prepare for this interview?
6. Do you feel you achieved the best grade point average of which you were capable in your education?
7. Relate an incident in which you faced an ethical dilemma. How did you react? How did you feel?
8. If your supervisor told you to do something a certain way, and you knew that way was dead wrong, what would you do?

"Apart from being a CEO and a job bagging bagels, what other work experience do you have?"

© Ted Goff. www.tedgoff.com

Questions about Money

Although money is a very important consideration, don't let it enter the interview process too soon. Some interviewers forget to mention money at all, while others ask what you think you are worth. Here are some typical money questions.

1. How much money are you looking for?

One way to handle salary questions is to ask politely to defer the discussion until it's clear that a job will be offered to you. (*I'm sure when the time comes, we'll be able to work out a fair compensation package. Right now, I'd rather focus on whether we have a match*). Another possible response is to reply candidly that you can't know what to ask until you know more about the position and the company. If you continue to be pressed for a dollar figure, give a salary range. Be sure to do research before the interview so that you know what similar jobs are paying. For example, check the full-time earnings estimates published at Job Futures <www.jobfutures.ca>.

2. How much are you currently earning?
3. How did you finance your education?
4. How much money do you expect to earn at age _____?

For more tips on how to negotiate a salary, see the Communication Workshop at the end of this chapter.

✓ Quick Check

Defer a discussion of salary until later in the interview when you know more about the job and whether it will be offered.

Questions for You to Ask

At some point in the interview, you will be asked if you have any questions. Your questions should not only help you gain information but also impress the interviewer with your thoughtfulness and interest in the position. Remember that the interview is an opportunity for you to see how you would fit with the company as well. You must be happy with the prospect of working for this organization. You want a position for which your skills and personality are matched. Use this opportunity to find out whether this job is right for you.

✓ Quick Check

Your questions should impress the interviewer but also draw out valuable information about the job.

1. What will my duties be (if not already discussed)?
2. Tell me what it's like working here in terms of the people, management practices, work loads, expected performance, and rewards.
3. Why is this position open? Did the person who held it previously leave?
4. What training programs are available from this organization? What specific training will be given for this position?
5. What are the possibilities for promotion from this position?
6. Who would be my immediate supervisor?
7. What is the organizational structure, and where does this position fit in?
8. Is travel required in this position?
9. How is job performance evaluated?
10. Assuming my work is excellent, where do you see me in five years?
11. How long do employees generally stay with this organization?
12. What are the major challenges for a person in this position?
13. What can I do to make myself more employable to you?
14. What is the salary for this position?
15. When will I hear from you regarding further action on my application?

Fielding Illegal Questions

Because human rights legislation protects job applicants from discrimination, interviewers may not ask questions such as those in the following list. Nevertheless, you may face an inexperienced or unscrupulous interviewer who does ask

✓ Quick Check

You may respond to an illegal question by asking tactfully how it relates to the responsibilities of the position.

some of these questions. How should you react? If you find the question harmless and if you want the job, go ahead and answer. If you think that answering would damage your chance to be hired, try to deflect the question tactfully with a response such as, *Could you tell me how my marital status relates to the responsibilities of this position?* Or you could use the opportunity to further emphasize your strengths. An older worker responding to a question about age might mention experience, fitness, knowledge, maturity, stability, or extensive business contacts. You might also wish to reconsider working for an organization that sanctions such procedures.

Here are some questions that you may or may not want to answer:

1. Are you married, divorced, separated, single, or living common-law?
2. Is your spouse subject to transfer in his/her job? Tell me about your spouse's job.
3. What is your corrected vision? (But it is legal to ask about quality of vision if visual acuity is directly related to safety or some other factor of the job.)
4. Do you have any disabilities? Do you drink or take drugs? Have you ever received psychiatric care or been hospitalized for emotional problems? Have you ever received workers' compensation? (But it is legal to ask if you have any condition that could affect your ability to do the job or if you have any condition that should be considered during selection.)
5. Have you ever been arrested? Have you ever been convicted of a crime? Do you have a criminal record? (But if bonding is a requirement of the job, it is legal to ask if you are eligible.)
6. How old are you? What is your date of birth? Can I see your birth certificate? (But it is legal to ask *Are you eligible to work under Canadian laws pertaining to age restrictions?*)
7. In what other countries do you have a current address? (But it is legal to ask *What is your current address, and how long have you lived there?*)
8. What is your maiden name? (But it is legal to ask *What is your full name?*)
9. What is your religion? How often do you attend religious services? Would you work on a specific religious holiday? Can you provide a reference from a clergyperson or religious leader?
10. Do you have children? What are your child care arrangements? (But it is legal to ask *Can you work the required hours?* and *Are you available for overtime?*)
11. Where were you born? Were you born in Canada? Can you provide proof of citizenship? (But it is legal to ask *Are you legally entitled to work in Canada?*)
12. Were you involved in military service in another country? (But it is legal to ask about Canadian military service.)
13. What is your first language? Where did you receive your language training? (But it is legal to ask if you understand, read, write, and/or speak the language(s) required for the job.)
14. How much do you weigh? How tall are you?
15. What is your sexual orientation?
16. Are you under medical care? Who is your family doctor? Are you receiving therapy or counselling? (But it is legal to make offers of employment conditional on successful completion of a medical exam that is relevant to that job.)

Closing the Interview

After the recruiter tells you about the organization and after you have asked your questions, the interviewer will signal the end of the interview, usually by standing up or by expressing appreciation that you came. If not addressed earlier, you should at this time find out what action will follow. Too many candidates leave the interview without knowing their status or when they will hear from the recruiter.

You may learn that your résumé will be distributed to several departments for review. If this is the case, be sure to ask when you will be contacted. When you are ready to leave, briefly review your strengths for the position and thank the interviewer for telling you about the organization and for considering you for the position. Ask if you may leave an additional copy of your résumé or your list of references. If the recruiter says nothing about notifying you, ask, "When can I expect to hear from you?" You can follow this by saying, "If I don't hear from you by then, may I call you?"

After leaving the interview, make notes of what was said in case you are called back for a second interview. Also, note your strengths and weaknesses so that you can work to improve in future interviews. Be sure to alert your references (whom you prepared in advance with a copy of your résumé, highlighted with sales points). Finally, write a thank-you letter, which will be discussed shortly.

If you don't hear from the recruiter within five days (or at the specified time), call him or her. Practise saying something like, "I'm wondering what else I can do to convince you that I'm the right person for this job."

✓ **Quick Check**
End the interview by thanking the interviewer, reviewing your strengths for this position, and asking what action will follow.

Follow-Up Letters and Other Employment Documents

Although the résumé and cover letter are your major tasks, other important letters and documents are often required during the employment process. You may need to make requests or write follow-up letters. Because each of these tasks reveals something about you and your communication skills, you'll want to put your best foot forward. These documents often subtly influence company officials to extend an interview or offer a job.

Reference Request

Most employers expect job candidates at some point to submit names of individuals who are willing to discuss the candidates' qualifications. Before you list anyone as a reference, however, be sure to ask permission. Try to do this in person. Ask an instructor, for example, if he or she would be willing and has the time to act as your reference. If you detect any sign of reluctance, don't force the issue. Your goal is to find willing individuals who think well of you.

What your references need most is information about you. What should they stress to prospective employers? Let's say you're applying for a specific job that requires a letter of recommendation. Professor Degen has already agreed to be a reference for you. To get the best letter of recommendation from Professor Degen, help her out. Write a letter telling her about the position, its requirements, and the recommendation deadline. Include a copy of your résumé. You might remind her of a positive experience with you (*You said my report was well organized*) that she could use in the recommendation. Remember that references need evidence to support generalizations. Give them appropriate ammunition, as the student has done in the following request:

Dear Professor Degen:

Recently I applied for the position of administrative assistant in the Human Resources Department of Host International. Because you kindly agreed to help me, I am now asking you to write a letter of recommendation to Host.

✓ *Quick Check*
Identify the target position and company. Tell immediately why you are writing.

The position calls for good organizational, interpersonal, and writing skills, as well as computer experience. To help you review my skills and training, I enclose my résumé. As you may recall, I earned an A in your business communication class, and you commended my long report for its clarity and organization.

Please send your letter before July 1 in the enclosed stamped, addressed envelope. I'm grateful for your support, and I promise to let you know the results of my job search.

Application or Résumé Follow-Up

If your letter or application generates no response within a reasonable time, you may decide to send a short follow-up e-mail letter such as the following. Doing so (1) jogs the memory of the human resources officer, (2) demonstrates your serious interest, and (3) allows you to emphasize your qualifications or to add new information.

Dear Ms. Stritz:

Please know I am still interested in becoming an administrative support specialist with Data Tech Inc.

Since I submitted an application in May, I have completed my schooling and have been employed as a summer replacement for office workers in several downtown offices. This experience has honed my word processing and communication skills. It has also introduced me to a wide range of office procedures.

Please keep my application in your active file and let me know when I may put my formal training, technical skills, and practical experience to work for you.

Interview Follow-Up

After a job interview you should always send a brief e-mail of thanks whether that interview occurs in person or on the telephone. This courtesy sets you apart from other applicants (many of whom may not bother). Your letter also reminds the interviewer of your visit as well as suggesting your good manners and genuine enthusiasm for the job.

Follow-up e-mails are most effective if sent immediately after the interview. In your e-mail refer to the date of the interview, the exact job title for which you were interviewed, specific topics discussed, and whether the interview was on the telephone or in person. Avoid worn-out phrases, such as *Thank you for taking the time to interview me*. Be careful, too, about overusing *I*, especially to begin sentences. Most important, show that you really want the job and that you are qualified for it. Notice how the following letter conveys enthusiasm and confidence:

Dear Ms. Singh:

Talking with you Thursday, May 23, about the graphic designer position was both informative and interesting.

Thanks for describing the position in such detail. Your current project designing the annual report in four colours on a Macintosh sounds fascinating as well as quite challenging.

Now that I've learned in greater detail the specific tasks of your graphic designers, I'm more than ever convinced that my computer and creative skills can make a genuine contribution to your graphic productions. My training in design and layout using Photoshop ensures that I could be immediately productive on your staff.

You will find me an enthusiastic and hard-working member of any team effort. I'm eager to join the graphics staff at your St. John headquarters, and I look forward to hearing from you soon.

This e-mail example can also be modified to work as a follow up to a telephone interview. By replacing *Talking with you* with *Our telephone conversation of*, the e-mail becomes an effective response to a telephone interview.

Rejection Follow-Up

If you didn't get the job and you think it was perfect for you, don't give up. Employment consultant Patricia Windelspecht advises, "You should always respond to a rejection letter.... I've had four clients get jobs that way." In a rejection follow-up e-mail, it's okay to admit you're disappointed. Be sure to add, however, that you're still interested and will contact them again in a month in case a job opens up. Then follow through for a couple of months—but don't overdo it. "There's a fine line between being professional and persistent and being a pest," adds consultant Windelspecht.[4] Here's an example of an effective rejection follow-up e-mail:

> Dear Mr. Crowston:
>
> Although I'm disappointed that someone else was selected for your accounting position, I appreciate your promptness and courtesy in notifying me.
>
> Because I firmly believe that I have the technical and interpersonal skills needed to work in your fast-paced environment, I hope you will keep my résumé in your active file. My desire to become a productive member of your staff remains strong.
>
> I enjoyed our interview, and I especially appreciate the time you and Mr. Kuzina spent describing your company's expansion into international markets. To enhance my qualifications, I've enrolled in a course in International Accounting at Sheridan College.
>
> Should you have an opening for which I am qualified, you may reach me at (905) 719-3901. In the meantime, I will call you in a month to discuss employment possibilities.

Application Form

Some organizations require job candidates to fill out job application forms instead of submitting résumés. This practice permits them to gather and store standardized data about each applicant. Here are some tips for filling out such forms:

- Carry a card summarizing the vital statistics not included on your résumé. If you are asked to fill out an application form in an employer's office, you will need a handy reference to the following data: social insurance number, graduation dates, and beginning and ending dates of all employment; salary history; full names, titles, and present work addresses of former supervisors; and full names, occupational titles, occupational addresses, and telephone numbers of persons who have agreed to serve as references.
- Look over all the questions before starting. Fill out the form neatly, printing if your handwriting is poor.
- Answer all questions. Write *Not applicable* if appropriate.
- Be prepared for a salary question. Unless you know what comparable employees are earning in the company, the best strategy is to suggest a salary range or to write *Negotiable* or *Open*.
- Ask if you may submit your résumé in addition to the application form.

Quick Check

Personalize your e-mail by mentioning topics discussed in the interview.

Quick Check

Subordinate your disappointment to your appreciation at being notified promptly and courteously.

Quick Check

Emphasize your continuing interest. Express confidence in meeting the job requirements.

Quick Check

Refer to specifics of your interview. If possible, explain how you are improving your skills.

Whether you face a screening interview or a hiring/placement interview, you must be well prepared. You can increase your chances of success and reduce your stress considerably by knowing how interviews are typically conducted and by investigating the target company thoroughly. Practise answering typical questions, including legal and illegal ones. Consider recording or videotaping a mock interview so that you can check your body language and improve your answering techniques.

Close the interview by thanking the interviewer, reviewing your main strengths for the position, and asking what the next step is. Follow up with a thank-you letter and a call back, if appropriate.

You have now completed 14 chapters of rigorous instruction aimed at developing your skills so that you can be a successful business communicator. Remember that this book represents a starting point. For instance, this book has not offered specific suggestions for how to communicate using a PDA device such as a BlackBerry. Your employer may however expect you to be able to adapt what you learned about writing e-mails in Chapter 5 to writing with a PDA. Your skills as a business communicator will continue to grow on the job as you apply the principles you have learned and expand your expertise.

Critical Thinking

1. Is it normal to be nervous about an employment interview, and what can be done to overcome this fear?
2. What can you do to improve the first impression you make at an interview?
3. In employment interviews, do you think that behavioural questions (such as *Tell me about a business problem you have had and how you solved it*) are more effective than traditional questions (such as *Tell me what you are good at and why*)?
4. Why is it important to avoid discussing salary early in an interview?
5. Why should a job candidate write a thank-you e-mail after an interview?

Chapter Review

6. If you have sent out your résumé to many companies, what information should you keep near your telephone and why?

7. Your first interview is with a small local company. What kind of information should you seek about this company and where could you expect to find it?

8. Name at least two ways in which you can practise for the interview and receive feedback on your performance.

9. Name at least six interviewing behaviours you can exhibit that send positive nonverbal messages.

10. What is your greatest fear of what you might do or what might happen to you during an employment interview? How can you overcome your fears?

11. Should you be candid with an interviewer when asked about your weaknesses?

12. How can you clarify vague questions from recruiters?

13. How should you respond if you are asked why a company should hire you when it has applicants with more experience or better credentials?

14. How should you respond to questions you believe to be illegal?

15. List the various kinds of follow-up letters.

Writing Improvement Exercises

16. Scripting Answers to Typical Interview Questions. You've probably already been through a number of job interviews in your life, but they may not have been formal like the interviews you will go through when you start applying for post-college jobs. Script a one- to two-minute answer to the following interview question, and memorize it. Do not use the template on page 400. Then practise speaking the answer in a natural voice so that it doesn't look like you've memorized it.

Question: Tell me about yourself and your previous work experience.

17. Scripting Answers to Typical Interview Questions. Script a one- to two-minute answer to the following typical interview question, and memorize it. Then practise speaking the answer in a natural voice so that it doesn't look like you've memorized it.

Question: Tell me about a time in a previous job when you faced a difficulty or a criticism or a problem and how you dealt with it.

Follow-Up Question: What would you do differently if this problem happened again?

18. Scripting Answers to Typical Interview Questions. Script a one- to two-minute answer to the following typical interview question, and memorize it. Then practise speaking the answer in a natural voice so that it doesn't look like you've memorized it.

Question: Tell me about a former boss or coworker whom you admire a lot and why you admire him or her.

Now that you've memorized these three answers, practise interviewing a partner. As you ask each other questions, surprise each other by slightly modifying the questions so they're not exactly as printed above. This modification will force you to improvise on the spot, a valuable interviewing skill.

Activities and Cases

Web

14.1 Researching an Organization. Select an organization where you would like to be employed. Assume you've been selected for an interview. Using resources described in this chapter, locate information about the organization's leaders and their business philosophy. Find out about the organization's accomplishments, setbacks, finances, products, customers, competition, and advertising. Prepare a summary report documenting your findings.

14.2 Building Interview Skills. Successful interviews require diligent preparation and repeated practice. To be best prepared, you need to know what skills are required for your targeted position. In addition to computer and communication skills, employers generally want to know whether a candidate works well with a team, accepts responsibility, solves problems, is efficient, meets deadlines, shows leadership, saves time and money, and is a hard worker.

Your Task. Consider a position for which you are eligible now or one for which you will be eligible when you complete your education. Identify the skills and traits necessary for this position. If you prepared a résumé in Chapter 13, be sure that it addresses these targeted areas. Now prepare interview worksheets listing at least ten technical and other skills or traits you think a recruiter will want to discuss in an interview for your targeted position.

14.3 Preparing Success Stories. You can best showcase your talents if you are ready with your own success stories that show how you have developed the skills or traits required for your targeted position.

Your Task. Using the worksheets you prepared in Activity 14.2, prepare success stories that highlight the required skills or traits. Select three to five stories to develop into answers to potential interview questions. For example, here's a typical question: "How does your background relate to the position we have open?" A possible response: "As you know, I have just completed an intensive training program in _____. In addition, I have over three years of part-time work experience in a variety of business settings. In one position I was selected to manage a small business in the absence of the owner. I developed responsibility and customer-service skills in filling orders efficiently, resolving shipping problems, and monitoring key accounts. I also inventoried and organized products worth over $200,000. When the owner returned from a vacation to Florida, I was commended for increasing sales and was given a bonus in recognition of her gratitude." People relate to and remember stories. Try to shape your answers into memorable stories.

14.4 Polishing Answers to Interview Questions. Practice makes perfect in interviewing. The more often you rehearse responses to typical interview questions, the closer you are to getting the job.

Your Task. Select three questions from each of the five question categories discussed in this chapter (pp. 400–403). Write your answers to each set of questions. Try to incorporate skills and traits required for the targeted position. Polish these answers and your delivery technique by practising in front of a mirror or a video or audio recorder.

14.5 Knowing What to Ask. When it is your turn to ask questions during the interview process, be ready.

Your Task. Decide on three to five questions that you would like to ask during an interview. Write these questions out and practise asking them so that you sound confident and sincere.

14.6 Role Play: Practising Answering Interview Questions. One of the best ways to understand interview dynamics and to develop confidence is to role-play the parts of interviewer and candidate.

Team

Your Task. Choose a partner from your class. Make a list of five interview questions from those presented in this chapter. In team sessions you and your partner will role-play an actual interview. One acts as interviewer, the other as the candidate. Prior to the interview, the candidate tells the interviewer what job and company he/she is applying to. For the interview, the interviewer and candidate should dress appropriately and sit in chairs facing each other. The interviewer greets the candidate and makes him/her comfortable. The candidate gives the interviewer a copy of his/her résumé. The interviewer asks three (or more depending on your instructor's time schedule) questions from the candidate's list. The interviewer may also ask follow-up questions if appropriate. When finished, the interviewer ends the meeting graciously. After one interview, reverse roles and repeat.

14.7 Video-recording an Interview. Seeing how you look during an interview can help you improve your body language and presentation style. Your instructor may act as interviewer, or an outside businessperson may be asked to conduct mock interviews in your classroom.

Your Task. Engage a student or campus specialist to video-record each interview. Review your performance and critique it looking for ways to improve. Your instructor may ask class members to offer comments and suggestions on individual interviews.

14.8 Handling Difficult Interview Questions. Although some questions are not appropriate in job interviews, many interviewers will ask them anyway—whether intentionally or unknowingly. Being prepared is important.

Your Task. How would you respond in the following scenario? Let's assume you are being interviewed at one of the top companies on your list of potential employers. The interviewing committee consists of a human resources manager and the supervising manager of the department where you would work. At various times during the interview the supervising manager has asked questions that made you feel uncomfortable. For example, he asked if you were married. You know this question is illegal, but you saw no harm in answering it. But then he asked how old you were. Since you started college early and graduated in two years, you are worried that you may not be considered mature enough for this position. But you have most of the other qualifications required and you are convinced you could succeed on the job. How should you answer this question?

14.9 Saying Thanks for the Interview. You've just completed an exciting employment interview, and you want the interviewer to remember you.

Your Task. Write a follow-up thank-you e-mail to Ronald T. Ranson, Human Resources Development, Electronic Data Sources, 132 Maplegrove Plaza, Montreal, QC H1L 2W4 (or a company of your choice).

14.10 Refusing to Take No for an Answer. After an excellent interview with Electronic Data Sources (or a company of your choice), you're depressed to learn that it hired someone else. But you really want to work for the company.

Your Task. Write a follow-up e-mail to Ronald T. Ranson, Human Resources Development, Electronic Data Sources, 132 Maplegrove Plaza, Montreal, QC H1L 2W4 (or a company of your choice). Indicate that you are disappointed but still interested.

Web

14.11 Answering Difficult Questions in a Virtual Interview. The Monster.ca site offers an entertaining online practice interview with questions ranging from easy to challenging. Even an experienced interviewee is unlikely to get all of these questions right the first time.

Your Task. Visit the Monster.ca site, sign up for a free account, click on "Practice your interviewing," and answer the virtual interview questions. Be prepared to discuss the advice for handling questions about salaries and your weaknesses. Do you agree with Monster's suggestions?

Related Web site: <www.monster.ca>.

Web

14.12 Searching for Advice. You can find wonderful, free, and sometimes entertaining information about job search strategies, career tips, and interview advice on the Web.

Your Task. Use a search engine or visit a site such as Workopolis.ca to locate links to job search and résumé sites. From any Web site featuring interview information, make a list of at least five good interview pointers—ones that were not covered in this chapter. Send an e-mail message to your instructor describing your findings.

Related Web site: <www.workopolis.ca.>

Grammar/Mechanics Review—14

The following sentences contain errors in grammar, punctuation, capitalization, number style, usage, and spelling. Below each sentence write a corrected version.

1. City officials begged the two companys board of directors not to dessert they're locations, and not to abandon local employees.

2. One store listed its Seiko Watch at eighty dollars; while its competitor listed the same watch at seventy-five dollars.

3. Here are a group of participating manufactures who you may wish to contact regarding there Web cites.

4. If we are to remain friends this personal information must be kept strictly between you and I.

5. As soon as the merger is complete we will inform the entire staff, until then its business as usual.

6. Smart organizations can boost profit's allmost one hundred percent by retaining just five percent more of there customers.

7. Many companies sell better at home then abroad; because they lack over-seas experience.

8. The quality of the e-mails, letters, memos and reports in this organization need to be improved.

9. The additional premium you were charged which amounted to fifty-five collars and 40 cents was issued because of you're recent accident.

10. The entire team of thirty-five managers were willing to procede with the proposal for asian expansion.

11. Several copys of the sales' report was sent to the CEO and I immediatley after we requested it.

12. Stored on open shelfs in room 17 is a group of office supplys and at least 7 boxes of stationary.

13. Darren Highsmith who was recently appointed Sales Manager submitted 6 different suggestions for increasing sales.

14. China the worlds fastest growing country will be snapping up personal computers at a thirty percent rate by 2010.

15. Congratulations, your finished!

Document for Revision

The following interview thank-you e-mail has faults in grammar, punctuation, spelling, wordiness, and word use. Use standard proofreading marks (see Appendix B) to correct the errors. When you finish, your instructor can show you the revised version of this e-mail.

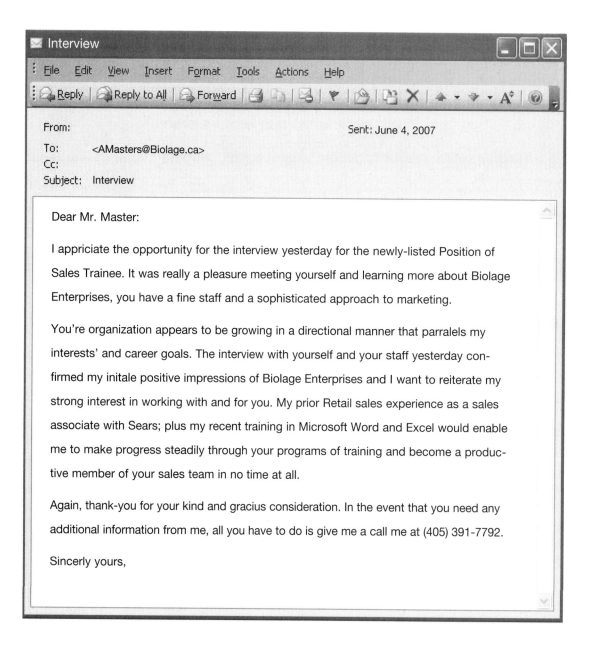

Interview

File Edit View Insert Format Tools Actions Help

Reply | Reply to All | Forward

From: Sent: June 4, 2007
To: <AMasters@Biolage.ca>
Cc:
Subject: Interview

Dear Mr. Master:

I appriciate the opportunity for the interview yesterday for the newly-listed Position of Sales Trainee. It was really a pleasure meeting yourself and learning more about Biolage Enterprises, you have a fine staff and a sophisticated approach to marketing.

You're organization appears to be growing in a directional manner that parralels my interests' and career goals. The interview with yourself and your staff yesterday confirmed my initale positive impressions of Biolage Enterprises and I want to reiterate my strong interest in working with and for you. My prior Retail sales experience as a sales associate with Sears; plus my recent training in Microsoft Word and Excel would enable me to make progress steadily through your programs of training and become a productive member of your sales team in no time at all.

Again, thank-you for your kind and gracius consideration. In the event that you need any additional information from me, all you have to do is give me a call me at (405) 391-7792.

Sincerly yours,

Let's Talk Money: Negotiating a Salary

When to talk about salary causes many job applicants concern. Some advisors recommend bringing the issue up immediately; others suggest avoiding the topic entirely. What happens if the company asks for salary expectations in the job advertisement? The best plan is to be prepared to discuss salary when required but not to force the issue. The important thing to remember is that almost all salaries are negotiable. The following suggestions come from Michael Sheckter, MBA, operator of the Marketing Advisory, consultant in the marketing community and frequent contributor to Workopolis.ca.[5]

Suggestion No. 1: Talk money only when requested.

If the interested company asks for salary expectations in the job advertisement, then put it in the cover letter—if not, try to hold off as long as possible. Your goal is to avoid discussing salary until you know that the interviewing company is interested. If salary comes up and you are not sure whether the job is being offered to you, it's time for you to be blunt. Here are some things you could say:

Are you making me a job offer?

What salary range do you pay for positions with similar requirements?

I'm very interested in the position, and my salary would be negotiable.

Tell me what you have in mind for the salary range.

Suggestion No. 2: Know the salary range for similar jobs in similar organizations but be aware of an amount that would motivate you.

Remember though that if you provide an amount that is too high you will price yourself out of the market. If the amount is too low you might be sorry. Everyone wants to make money but salary by itself should not be a reason to take or reject a job. The important thing here is to think in terms of a wide range. Let's say you are hoping to start at between $30,000 and $40,000. To an interviewer, you might say, *I was looking for a salary in the low to the high thirties.*

Suggestion No. 3: Start by considering what you are making now.

Remember to be realistic. You probably have some idea of what the interviewing company is willing to pay for this position. You definitely know what you are getting paid in your current job. Try to find a reasonable compromise between the two and think about a salary that would motivate and reward. Keep in mind that it can be useful to suggest a range that is slightly higher than what you expect. That way you'll have some room to negotiate should it be required.

Suggestion No. 4: Consider a salary offer before reacting.

Why would anyone refuse a job offer before it's made? It happens all the time. Let's say you were hoping for a salary of $27,000. The interviewer tells you that the salary scheduled for this job is $24,000. You respond, *Oh, that's out of the question!* Before being offered the job, you have, in effect, refused it.

Suggestion No. 5: Trust that a fair and reasonable salary will be offered.

Generally, companies can't afford to offer salaries that are too low. If they do, they will lose people too easily to other opportunities that pay fairly. Be ready to bargain if offered a low starting salary.

Many salaries are negotiable. Companies are often willing to pay more for someone who interviews well and fits their culture. If the company seems right to you and you are pleased with the sound of the open position but you have been offered a low salary, say *That is somewhat lower than I had hoped but this position does sound exciting. If I were to consider this, what sorts of things could I do to quickly become more valuable to this organization?*

Another possibility is to ask for more time to think about the low offer. Tell the interviewer that this is an important decision, and you need some time to consider the offer. The next day you can call and say *I am flattered by your offer but I cannot accept because the salary is lower than I would like. Perhaps you could reconsider your offer or keep me in mind for future openings.*

Suggestion No. 6: Know your "walk away" number.

Be serious about your salary expectations, and ask yourself what you really want to get—would you be willing to walk away from a job that didn't pay your expected amount?

A good benchmark is to know your "walk away" number. Pick the number you would like to have, make it realistic and reasonable—maybe they will meet it, maybe they will make a counteroffer.

Career Application

You've just passed the screening interview and have been asked to come in for a personal interview with the human resources representative and the hiring manager of a company where you are very eager to work. Although you are delighted with the company, you have promised yourself that you will not accept any position that pays less than $30,000 to start.

Your Task

- In teams of two, role-play the position of interviewer and interviewee.
- *Interviewer:* Set the interview scene. Discuss preliminaries, and then offer a salary of $29,000.
- *Interviewee:* Respond to preliminary questions and then to the salary offer of $29,000.
- Reverse roles so that the interviewee becomes the interviewer. Repeat the scenario.

A

Reference Guide to Document Formats

Business documents carry two kinds of messages. Verbal messages are conveyed by the words chosen to express the writer's ideas. Nonverbal messages are conveyed by the appearance of a document. If you compare an assortment of letters from various organizations, you will notice immediately that some look more attractive and more professional than others. The nonverbal message of the professional-looking documents suggests that they were sent by people who are careful, informed, intelligent, and successful. Understandably, you're more likely to take seriously documents that use attractive stationery and professional formatting techniques.

Over the years certain practices and conventions have arisen regarding the appearance and formatting of business documents. Although these conventions offer some choices (such as letter and punctuation styles), most business letters follow standardized formats. To ensure that your documents carry favourable nonverbal messages about you and your organization, you'll want to give special attention to the appearance and formatting of your letters, envelopes, e-mails memos, and fax cover sheets.

Appearance

To ensure that a message is read and valued, you need to give it a professional appearance. Two important elements in achieving a professional appearance are stationery and placement of the message on the page.

Stationery. Most organizations use high-quality stationery for business documents. This stationery is printed on paper with good weight and cotton-fibre content.

Paper is measured by weight and may range from 9 pounds (thin onionskin paper) to 32 pounds (thick card and cover stock). Most office stationery is in the 16-to-24-pound range. Lighter 16-pound paper is generally sufficient for internal documents. Heavier 20-to-24-pound paper is used for printed letterhead stationery.

Paper is also judged by its cotton-fibre content. Cotton fibre makes paper stronger, softer in texture, and less likely to yellow. Good-quality stationery contains 25 percent or more cotton fibre.

Spacing after Punctuation. In the past, typists left two spaces after end punctuation (periods, question marks, and so forth). This practice was necessary, it was thought, because typewriters did not have proportional spacing and sentences were easier to read if two spaces separated them. Fortunately, today's word processors make available the same fonts used by professional typesetters.

The question of how many spaces to leave after concluding punctuation is one of the most frequently asked questions at the Modern Language Association site <www.mla.org>. MLA experts point out that most publications today have the same spacing after a punctuation mark as between words on the same line. Influenced by the look of typeset publications (e.g., this book), many writers now leave only one space after end punctuation. As a practical matter, however, it is not wrong to use two spaces.

Letter Placement. The easiest way to place letters on the page is to use the defaults of your word processing program. The defaults are usually set for side margins of 2.5 cm. Many companies today find these margins acceptable.

If you want to adjust your margins to better balance shorter letters, use the following chart:

Words in Body of Letter	Side Margins	Blank Lines After Date
Under 200	4 to 5 cm	4 to 10
Over 200	2.5 cm	2 to 3

Experts say that a "ragged right" margin is easier to read than a justified (even) margin. You might want to turn off the justification feature of your word processing program if it automatically justifies the right margin.

Letter Parts

Professional-looking business letters are arranged in a conventional sequence with standard parts. Following is a discussion of how to use these letter parts properly. Figure A.1 illustrates the parts in a block-style letter. (See Chapter 6 for additional discussion of letters and their parts.)

Letterhead. Most business organizations use 8½-by-11-inch paper printed with a letterhead displaying their official name, street address, Web site address, e-mail address, and telephone and fax numbers. The letterhead may also include a logo and an advertising tag-line such as *Ebank: A new way to bank.*

Dateline. On letterhead paper you should place the date two blank lines below the last line of the letterhead or 5 cm from the top edge of the paper (line 13). On plain paper place the date immediately below your return address. Since the date goes on line 13, start the return address an appropriate number of lines above it. The most common dateline format is as follows: *June 9, 2006.* Don't use *th* (or *rd*) when the date is written this way. For European or military correspondence, use the following dateline format: *9 June 2006.* Notice that no commas are used.

Addressee and Delivery Notations. Delivery notations such as *FAX TRANSMISSION, FEDERAL EXPRESS, MESSENGER DELIVERY, CONFIDENTIAL,* or *CERTIFIED MAIL* are typed in all capital letters two blank lines above the inside address.

Inside Address. Type the inside address—that is, the address of the organization or person receiving the letter—single-spaced, starting at the left margin. The number of lines between the dateline and the inside address depends on the size of the letter body, the type size (point or pitch size), and the length of the typing lines. Generally, two to ten lines are appropriate.

Be careful to duplicate the exact wording and spelling of the recipient's name and address on your documents. Usually, you can copy this information from the letterhead of the correspondence you are answering. If, for example, you are responding to *Jackson & Perkins Company,* don't address your letter to *Jackson and Perkins Corp.*

Letter Parts

FIGURE A.1 Block and Modified Block Letter Styles

Letterhead ————

peerless **graphics**

8 9 3 D i l l i n g h a m B o u l e v a r d S t o n y P l a i n , A B

Phone (403) 667-8880   Fax (403) 667-8830   www.peergraph.com

↓ line 13, or 2 blank lines below letterhead

Dateline ————

September 13, 2007

↓ 2 to 10 blank lines

Inside address ————

Mr. T. M. Wilson, President
Visual Concept Enterprises
1256 Lumsden Avenue
Nordegg, AB T0M 3T0

↓ 1 blank line

Salutation ————

Dear Mr. Wilson

↓ 1 blank line

Subject line ————

SUBJECT: BLOCK LETTER STYLE

↓ 1 blank line

This letter illustrates block letter style, about which you asked. All typed lines begin at the left margin. The date is usually placed 5 cm from the top edge of the paper or two lines below the last line of the letterhead, whichever position is lower.

Body ————

This letter also shows open punctuation. No colon follows the salutation, and no comma follows the complimentary close. Although this punctuation style is efficient, we find that most of our customers prefer to include punctuation after the salutation and the complimentary close.

If a subject line is included, it appears two lines below the salutation. The word SUBJECT is optional. Most readers will recognize a statement in this position as the subject without an identifying label. The complimentary close appears two lines below the end of the last paragraph.

↓ 1 blank line

Sincerely

Mark H. Wong

↓ 3 to 4 blank lines

Complimentary close
and signature block

Mark H. Wong
Graphics Designer

↓ 1 blank line

Modified block style,
mixed punctuation

MHW:pil

In block-style letters, as shown above, all lines begin at the left margin. In modified block-style letters, as shown at the left, the date is centred or aligned with the complimentary close and signature block, which start at the centre. The date may also be backspaced from the right margin. Paragraphs may be blocked or indented. Mixed punctuation includes a colon after the salutation and a comma after the complimentary close. Open punctuation, shown above, omits the colon following the salutation and omits the comma following the complimentary closing.

Always be sure to include a courtesy title such as *Mr., Ms., Mrs., Dr.,* or *Professor* before a person's name in the inside address—for both the letter and the envelope. Although many women in business today favour *Ms.,* you'll want to use whatever title the addressee prefers.

Remember that the inside address is not included for readers (who already know who and where they are). It's there to help writers accurately file a copy of the message.

In general, avoid abbreviations (such as *Ave.* or *Co.*) unless they appear in the printed letterhead of the document being answered.

Attention Line. An attention line allows you to send your message officially to an organization but to direct it to a specific individual, officer, or department. However, if you know an individual's complete name, it's always better to use it as the first line of the inside address and avoid an attention line. Here are two common formats for attention lines:

MultiMedia Enterprises
931 Calkins Road
Toronto, ON M3W 1E6

ATTENTION MARKETING DIRECTOR

MultiMedia Enterprises
Attention: Marketing Director
931 Calkins Road
Toronto, ON M3W 1E6

Attention lines may be typed in all caps or with upper- and lowercase letters. The colon following *Attention* is optional. Notice that an attention line may be placed two lines below the address block or printed as the second line of the inside address. You'll want to use the latter format if you're composing on a word processor because the address block may be copied to the envelope and the attention line will not interfere with the last-line placement of the postal code. (Mail can be sorted more easily if the postal code appears in the last line of a typed address.)

Whenever possible, use a person's name as the first line of an address instead of putting that name in an attention line. Some writers use an attention line because they fear that letters addressed to individuals at companies may be considered private. They worry that if the addressee is no longer with the company, the letter may be forwarded or not opened. Actually, unless a letter is marked "Personal" or "Confidential," it will very likely be opened as business mail.

Salutation. Place the letter greeting, or salutation, two lines below the last line of the inside address or the attention line (if used). If the letter is addressed to an individual, use that person's courtesy title and last name (*Dear Mr. Lanham*). Even if you are on a first-name basis (*Dear Leslie*), be sure to add a colon (not a comma or a semicolon) after the salutation, unless you are using open punctuation. Do not use an individual's full name in the salutation (not *Dear Mr. Leslie Lanham*) unless you are unsure of gender (*Dear Leslie Lanham*).

For letters with attention lines or those addressed to organizations, the selection of an appropriate salutation has become more difficult. Formerly, *Gentlemen* was used generically for all organizations. With increasing numbers of women in business management today, however, *Gentlemen* is outdated. Because no universally acceptable salutation has emerged as yet, you'll probably be safest with *Ladies and Gentlemen* or *Gentlemen and Ladies.*

One way to avoid the salutation dilemma is to address a document to a specific person. Another alternative is to use the simplified letter style, which conveniently omits the salutation (and the complimentary close).

Subject and Reference Lines. Although experts suggest placing the subject line one blank line below the salutation, many businesses actually place it above the salutation. Use whatever style your organization prefers. Reference lines often show policy or file numbers; they generally appear two lines above the salutation.

Body. Most business letters and memorandums are single-spaced, with double line spacing between paragraphs. Very short messages may be double-spaced with indented paragraphs.

Complimentary Close. Typed two lines below the last line of the letter, the complimentary close may be formal (*Very truly yours*) or informal (*Sincerely* or *Respectfully*). The simplified letter style omits a complimentary close.

Signature Block. In most letter styles the writer's typed name and optional identification appear three to four blank lines below the complimentary close. The combination of name, title, and organization information should be arranged to achieve a balanced look. The name and title may appear on the same line or on separate lines, depending on the length of each. Use commas to separate categories within the same line, but not to conclude a line.

Sincerely,

Jeremy M. Wood

Jeremy M. Wood, Manager
Technical Sales and Services

Respectfully,

Casandra Baker-Murillo

Casandra Baker-Murillo
Executive Vice-President

Courtesy titles (*Mr., Ms., Mrs.,* or *Miss*) should be used before names that are not readily distinguishable as male or female. They should also be used before names containing only initials and international names. The title is usually placed in parentheses, but it may appear without them.

Yours truly,

Ms. K.C. Tripton

(Ms.) K. C. Tripton
Project Manager

Sincerely,

Mr. Leslie Hill

(Mr.) Leslie Hill
Public Policy Department

Some organizations include their names in the signature block. In such cases the organization name appears in all caps two lines below the complimentary close, as shown here.

Sincerely,
LITTON COMPUTER SERVICES

Ms. Shelina A. Simpson

Ms. Shelina A. Simpson
Executive Assistant

Reference Initials. If used, the initials of the typist and writer are typed two lines below the writer's name and title. Generally, the writer's initials are capitalized and the typist's are lowercased, but this format varies.

Enclosure Notation. When an enclosure or attachment accompanies a document, a notation to that effect appears two lines below the reference initials. This notation reminds the typist to insert the enclosure in the envelope, and it reminds the recipient to look for the enclosure or attachment. The notation may be spelled out (*Enclosure*, *Attachment*), or it may be abbreviated (*Enc.*, *Att.*). It may indicate the number of enclosures or attachments, and it may also identify a specific enclosure (*Enclosure: Form 1099*).

Copy Notation. If you make copies of correspondence for other individuals, you may use *cc* to indicate carbon copy, *pc* to indicate photocopy, or merely *c* for any kind of copy. A colon following the initial(s) is optional.

Second-Page Heading. When a letter extends beyond one page, use plain paper of the same quality and colour as the first page. Identify the second and succeeding pages with a heading consisting of the name of the addressee, the page number, and the date. Use either of the following two formats:

Ms. Rachel Ruiz   2   May 3, 2007

Ms. Rachel Ruiz
Page 2
May 3, 2007

Both headings appear on line 7 followed by two blank lines to separate them from the continuing text. Avoid using a second page if you have only one line or the complimentary close and signature block to fill that page.

Plain-Paper Return Address. If you prepare a personal or business letter on plain paper, place your address immediately above the date. Do not include your name; you will type (and sign) your name at the end of your letter. If your return address contains two lines, begin typing it on line 11 so that the date appears on line 13. Avoid abbreviations except for a two-letter province/territory abbreviation.

580 East Leffels Street
Dartmouth, NS B6R 2F3
December 14, 2007

Ms. Ellen Siemens
Retail Credit Department
Union National Bank
1220 Dunsfield Boulevard
Halifax, NS B4L 2E2

Dear Ms. Siemens:

For letters prepared in the block style, type the return address at the left margin. For modified block-style letters, start the return address at the centre to align with the complimentary close.

Letter Styles

Business letters are generally prepared in one of three formats. The most popular is the block style, but the simplified style has much to recommend it.

Block Style. In the block style, shown in Figure A.1, all lines begin at the left margin. This style is a favourite because it is easy to format.

Modified Block Style. The modified block style differs from block style in that the date and closing lines appear in the centre, as shown at the bottom of Figure A.1. The date may be (1) centred, (2) begun at the centre of the page (to align with the closing lines), or (3) backspaced from the right margin. The signature block—including the complimentary close, writer's name and title, or organization identification—begins at the centre. The first line of each paragraph may begin at the left margin or may be indented five or ten spaces. All other lines begin at the left margin.

Simplified Style. Introduced by the Administrative Management Society a number of years ago, the simplified letter style, shown in Figure A.2, requires little formatting. Like the block style, all lines begin at the left margin. A subject line appears in all caps two blank lines below the inside address and two blank lines above the first paragraph. The salutation and complimentary close are omitted. The signer's name and identification appear in all caps four blank lines below the last paragraph. This letter style is efficient and avoids the problem of appropriate salutations and courtesy titles.

Punctuation Styles

Two punctuation styles are commonly used for letters. *Open* punctuation, shown with the block-style letter in Figure A.1, contains no punctuation after the salutation or complimentary close. *Mixed* punctuation, shown with the modified block style letter in Figure A.1, requires a colon after the salutation and a comma after the complimentary close. Many business organizations prefer mixed punctuation, even in a block style letter.

If you choose mixed punctuation, be sure to use a colon—not a comma or semicolon—after the salutation. Even when the salutation is a first name, the colon is appropriate.

Envelopes

An envelope should be of the same quality and colour of stationery as the letter it carries. Because the envelope introduces your message and makes the first impression, you need to be especially careful in addressing it. Moreover, how you fold the letter is important.

Return Address. The return address is usually printed in the upper left corner of an envelope, as shown in Figure A.3 (p. 426). In large companies some form of identification (the writer's initials, name, or location) may be typed or handwritten above the company name and return address. This identification helps return the letter to the sender in case of nondelivery.

On an envelope without a printed return address, single-space the return address in the upper left corner. Beginning on line 3 on the fourth space (approximately 12 mm or ½ inch) from the left edge, type the writer's name, title, company, and mailing address.

Mailing Address. On legal-sized No. 10 envelopes (10.5 cm by 24 cm), begin the address on line 13 about 11.5 cm from the left edge, as shown in Figure A.3. For small envelopes (7.5 cm by 15 cm), begin typing on line 12 about 6.2 cm from the left edge.

FIGURE A.2 Simplified Letter Style

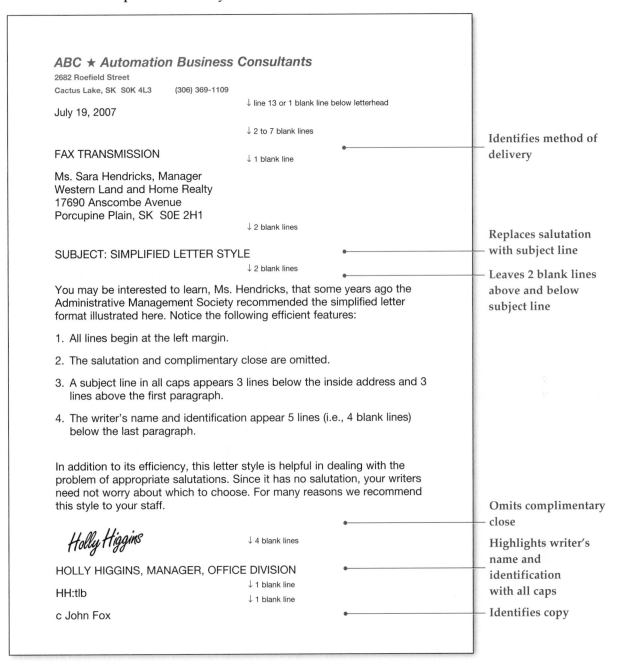

ABC ★ Automation Business Consultants
2682 Roefield Street
Cactus Lake, SK S0K 4L3   (306) 369-1109

↓ line 13 or 1 blank line below letterhead

July 19, 2007

↓ 2 to 7 blank lines

FAX TRANSMISSION   ↓ 1 blank line   ● ─── Identifies method of delivery

Ms. Sara Hendricks, Manager
Western Land and Home Realty
17690 Anscombe Avenue
Porcupine Plain, SK S0E 2H1

↓ 2 blank lines

SUBJECT: SIMPLIFIED LETTER STYLE   ● ─── Replaces salutation with subject line
↓ 2 blank lines   ● ─── Leaves 2 blank lines above and below subject line

You may be interested to learn, Ms. Hendricks, that some years ago the Administrative Management Society recommended the simplified letter format illustrated here. Notice the following efficient features:

1. All lines begin at the left margin.

2. The salutation and complimentary close are omitted.

3. A subject line in all caps appears 3 lines below the inside address and 3 lines above the first paragraph.

4. The writer's name and identification appear 5 lines (i.e., 4 blank lines) below the last paragraph.

In addition to its efficiency, this letter style is helpful in dealing with the problem of appropriate salutations. Since it has no salutation, your writers need not worry about which to choose. For many reasons we recommend this style to your staff.

Holly Higgins   ↓ 4 blank lines   ● ─── Omits complimentary close

HOLLY HIGGINS, MANAGER, OFFICE DIVISION   ● ─── Highlights writer's name and identification with all caps
↓ 1 blank line
HH:tlb
↓ 1 blank line

c John Fox   ● ─── Identifies copy

Canada Post recommends that addresses be typed in all caps without any punctuation. This Postal Service style, shown in the small envelope in Figure A.3, was originally developed to facilitate scanning by optical character readers. Today's OCRs, however, are so sophisticated that they scan upper- and lowercase letters easily. Many companies today prefer to use the same format for the envelope as for the inside address. If the same format is used, writers can take advantage of word processing programs to "copy" the inside address to the envelope, thus saving keystrokes and reducing errors. Having the same format on both the inside address and the envelope also looks more professional and consistent. For these reasons you may choose to use the familiar upper- and lowercase combination format. But you will want to check with your organization to learn its preference.

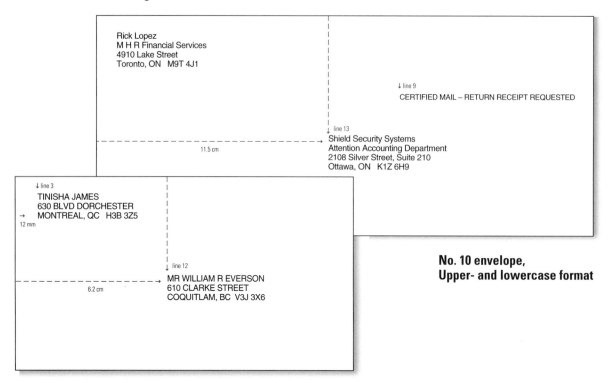

Rick Lopez
M H R Financial Services
4910 Lake Street
Toronto, ON   M9T 4J1

↓ line 9
CERTIFIED MAIL – RETURN RECEIPT REQUESTED

↓ line 13
Shield Security Systems
Attention Accounting Department
2108 Silver Street, Suite 210
Ottawa, ON   K1Z 6H9

11.5 cm

**No. 10 envelope,
Upper- and lowercase format**

↓ line 3
TINISHA JAMES
630 BLVD DORCHESTER
→   MONTREAL, QC   H3B 3Z5
12 mm

↓ line 12
→ MR WILLIAM R EVERSON
610 CLARKE STREET
COQUITLAM, BC V3J 3X6
6.2 cm

No. 6 ¾ envelope, uppercase format

In addressing your envelopes for delivery in North America, use the two-letter province, territory, and state abbreviations shown in Figure A.4. Notice that these abbreviations are in capital letters without periods.

Folding. The way a letter is folded and inserted into an envelope sends additional nonverbal messages about a writer's professionalism and carefulness. Most businesspeople follow the procedures shown here, which produce the least number of creases to distract readers.

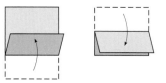

For large No. 10 envelopes, begin with the letter face up. Fold slightly less than one third of the sheet toward the top, as shown in the following diagram. Then fold down the top third to within 6 to 7 mm of the bottom fold. Insert the letter into the envelope with the last fold toward the bottom of the envelope.

For small No. 8 envelopes, begin by folding the bottom up to within 6 to 7 mm of the top edge. Then fold the right third over to the left. Fold the left third to within 6 to 7 mm of the last fold. Insert the last fold into the envelope first.

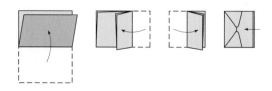

FIGURE A.4 Abbreviations of Provinces, Territories, and States

Province or Territory	Two-Letter Abbreviation	Province	Two-Letter Abbreviation
Alberta	AB	Nova Scotia	NS
British Columbia	BC	Nunavut	NU
Manitoba	MB	Ontario	ON
New Brunswick	NB	Prince Edward Island	PE
Newfoundland and		Quebec	QC
Labrador	NL	Saskatchewan	SK
Northwest Territories	NT	Yukon Territory	YT

State or Territory	Two-Letter Abbreviation	State or Territory	Two-Letter Abbreviation
Alabama	AL	Missouri	MO
Alaska	AK	Montana	MT
Amercian Samoa	AS	Nebraska	NE
Arizona	AZ	Nevada	NV
Arkansas	AR	New Hampshire	NH
California	CA	New Jersey	NJ
Colorado	CO	New Mexico	NM
Connecticut	CT	New York	NY
Delaware	DE	North Carolina	NC
District of Columbia	DC	North Dakota	ND
Florida	FL	North Mariana Islands	MP
Georgia	GA	Ohio	OH
Guam	GU	Oklahoma	OK
Hawaii	HI	Oregon	OR
Idaho	ID	Palau	PW
Illinois	IL	Pennsylvania	PA
Indiana	IN	Puerto Rico	PR
Iowa	IA	Rhode Island	RI
Kansas	KS	South Carolina	SC
Kentucky	KY	South Dakota	SD
Louisiana	LA	Tennessee	TN
Maine	ME	Texas	TX
Marshall Islands	MH	Utah	UT
Maryland	MD	Vermont	VT
Massachusetts	MA	Virgin Islands	VI
Michigan	MI	Virginia	VA
Micronesia	FM	Washington	WA
Minnesota	MN	West Virginia	WV
Minor Outlying Islands	UM	Wisconsin	WI
Mississippi	MS	Wyoming	WY

E-Mail Messages

Because e-mail is an evolving communication medium, formatting and usage are still fluid. The following suggestions, illustrated in Figure A.5 (p. 428) and also in Figure 5.2 on page 101, may guide you in setting up the parts of an e-mail message. Always check, however, with your organization so that you can observe its practices.

To Line. Include the receiver's e-mail address after *To*. If the receiver's address is recorded in your address book, you just have to click on it. Be sure to enter all addresses carefully since one mistyped letter prevents delivery.

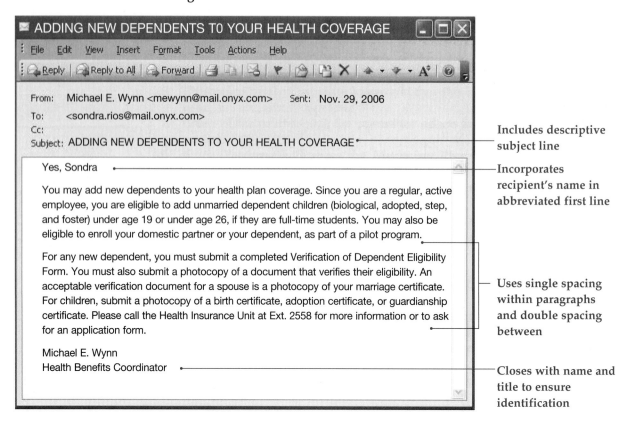

From **Line.** Most e-mail programs automatically include your name and e-mail address after *From*.

Cc and Bcc. Insert the e-mail address of anyone who is to receive a copy of the message. *Cc* stands for carbon copy or courtesy copy. Don't be tempted, though, to send needless copies just because it's so easy. *Bcc* stands for *blind carbon copy*. Some writers use *bcc* to send a copy of the message without the addressee's knowledge. Writers also use the *bcc* line for mailing lists. When a message is being sent to a number of people and their e-mail addresses should not be revealed, the *bcc* line works well to conceal the names and addresses of all receivers.

Subject. Identify the subject of the e-mail message with a brief but descriptive summary of the topic. Be sure to include enough information to be clear and compelling. Capitalize the initial letters of principal words, or capitalize the entire line if space permits.

Salutation. Include a brief greeting, if you like. Some writers use a salutation such as *Dear Selina* followed by a comma or a colon. Others are more informal with *Hi, Selina!*, or *Good morning* or *Greetings*. Some writers simulate a salutation by including the name of the receiver in an abbreviated first line, as shown in Figure A.5. Others writers treat an e-mail message like a memo and skip the salutation entirely.

Message. Cover just one topic in your message, and try to keep your total message under one screen in length. Single-space and be sure to use both upper- and lowercase letters. Double-space between paragraphs, and use graphic high-lighting (bullets, numbering) whenever you are listing three or more items.

Closing. Conclude an external message, with *Cheers* or *Best wishes*, followed by your name. If the recipient is unlikely to know you, it's not a bad idea to include your title and organization. Many e-mail users include a signature file with identi-fying information embellished with keyboard art. Use restraint, however, because signature files take up precious space. Writers of e-mail messages sent within orga-nizations may omit a closing and even skip their names at the ends of messages because receivers recognize them from identification in the opening lines.

Attachment. Use the attachment window or button to select the file name of any file you wish to send with your e-mail message. You can also attach a Web page to your message.

Memos

As discussed in Chapter 5, memos deliver messages within organizations. Many offices use computer memo templates imprinted with the organization name and logo and, optionally, the department or division names, as shown in Figure A.6. Although the design and arrangement of memos vary, they usually include the basic elements of *TO, FROM, DATE,* and *SUBJECT*. Large organizations may include other identifying headings, such as *FILE NUMBER, FLOOR, EXTENSION, LOCATION,* and *DISTRIBUTION*.

If no computer template is available, memos may be typed on company letter-head or on plain paper, as shown in Figure A.7 (p. 430). On a full sheet of paper, start on line 13; on a half sheet, start on line 7. Double-space and type in all caps the guide words: *TO:, FROM:, DATE:, SUBJECT:*. Align all the fill-in information two spaces after the longest guide word (SUBJECT:). Leave three lines after the

FIGURE A.6 Printed Memo Forms

BANK OF MONTREAL
Mortgage Department

BMO ▲

Interoffice
Memorandum

DATE:

TO:

FROM:

SUBJECT:

PYRAMID INDUSTRIES
Internal Memorandum

TO: DATE:

FROM: FILE:

SUBJECT:

FIGURE A.7 Memo on Plain Paper

↓ line 10
MEMO

→
3 cm

DATE: February 3, 2007

TO: Dawn Stewart, Manager
Sales and Marketing *JM*

FROM: Jay Murray, Vice-President
Operations

SUBJECT: TELEPHONE SERVICE REQUEST FORMS

↓ 2 blank lines

To speed telephone installation and improve service within the Bremerton facility, we are starting a new application procedure.

Service request forms will be available at various locations within the three buildings. When you require telephone service, obtain a request form at one of the locations that is convenient for you. Fill in the pertinent facts, obtain approval from your division head, and send the form to Brent White. Request forms are available at the following locations:

last line of the heading and begin typing the body of the memo. Like business letters, memos are single-spaced.

Memos are generally formatted with side margins of 3.5 cm (1¼ inches), or they may conform to the printed memo form. For more information about memos, see Chapter 5.

Fax Cover Sheet

Documents transmitted by fax are usually introduced by a cover sheet, such as that shown in Figure A.8. As with memos, the format varies considerably. Important items to include are (1) the name and fax number of the receiver, (2) the name and fax number of the sender, (3) the number of pages being sent, and (4) the name, telephone number, and e-mail address of the person to notify in case of unsatisfactory transmission.

When the document being transmitted requires little explanation, you may prefer to attach an adhesive note (such as a Post-it™ fax transmittal form) instead of a full cover sheet. These notes carry essentially the same information as shown in our printed fax cover sheet. They are perfectly acceptable in most business organizations and can save considerable paper and transmission costs.

FAX TRANSMISSION

DATE: _____

TO: _____   **FAX NUMBER:** _____
_____
_____

FROM: _____   **FAX NUMBER:** _____
_____
_____

NUMBER OF PAGES TRANSMITTED INCLUDING THIS COVER SHEET: ___

MESSAGE:

If any part of this fax transmission is missing or not clearly received, please contact:

NAME: _____

PHONE: _____

E-MAIL: _____

B Proofreading Marks

PROOFREADING MARK	DRAFT COPY	FINAL COPY
Align horizontally	TO: Rick Munoz	TO: Rick Munoz
Align vertically	166.32 / 132.45	166.32 / 132.45
Capitalize	Coca-cola	Coca-Cola
	runs on ms-dos	runs on MS-DOS
Close up space	meeting at 3 p. m.	meeting at 3 p.m.
Centre	Recommendations	Recommendations
Delete	in my final judgement	in my judgment
Insert apostrophe	our companys product	our company's product
Insert comma	you will of course	you will, of course,
Insert semicolon	value therefore, we feel	value; therefore, we feel
Insert hyphen	tax free income	tax-free income
Insert period	Ms Holly Hines	Ms. Holly Hines
Insert quotation mark	shareholders receive a bonus	shareholders receive a "bonus"
Insert space	wordprocessing program	word processing program
Lowercase (remove capitals)	the Vice-President	the vice-president
Move to left	HUMAN RESOURCES	Human Resources
Move to right	I. Labour costs	I. Labour costs
Spell out	A. Findings of study	A. Findings of study
	aimed at 2 depts	aimed at two departments
Start new paragraph	Keep the screen height at eye level.	Keep the screen height at eye level.
Stet (don't delete)	officials talked openly	officials talked openly
Transpose	accounts recievable	accounts receivable
Use boldface	Conclusions	**Conclusions**
Use italics	The Perfect Résumé	*The Perfect Résumé*
Start new line	Globex, 23 Acorn Lane	Globex / 23 Acorn Lane
Run lines together	Invoice No. / 122059	Invoice No. 122059

Documentation Formats

Careful writers work hard to document properly any data appearing in reports or messages for many reasons. Citing sources strengthens a writer's argument, as you learned in Chapter 10. Acknowledging sources also shields writers from charges of plagiarism. Moreover, good references help readers pursue further research. Fortunately, word processing programs have taken much of the pain out of documenting data, particularly for footnotes and endnotes.

Source and Content Notes

Before we discuss specific documentation formats, you should know the difference between source notes and content notes. Source notes identify quotations, paraphrased passages, and author references. They lead readers to the sources of cited information, and they must follow a consistent format. Content notes, on the other hand, enable writers to add comments, explain information not directly related to the text, or refer readers to other sections of a report.

Two Documentation Methods for Source Notes

For years researchers have struggled to develop the perfect documentation system—one that is efficient for the writer and crystal-clear to the reader. Most of these systems can be grouped into two methods: the footnote/endnote method and the parenthetic method.

Footnote/Endnote Method. Writers using footnotes or endnotes insert a small superscript (raised) figure into the text close to the place where a reference is mentioned. This number leads the reader to a footnote at the bottom of the page or to an endnote at the end of the report. Footnotes or endnotes contain a complete description of the source document. In this book we have used the endnote method. We chose this style because it least disrupts the text. Most of the individual citation formats in this book follow the traditional style suggested in *The Chicago Manual of Style*, 15th ed. (Chicago: The University of Chicago Press, 2002). Here are some of the most frequently used endnotes, styled in accordance with the *Chicago Manual*. They are numbered here with full-sized numbers; your word processor, however, may show endnotes with superscript figures. Either form is acceptable.

Book, One Author
1. Sara White, *Profiting in the Knowledge Age: A Canadian Guide to the Future* (Toronto: McKnight Publishing, 2001), 25.

Book, Many Authors
2. Manny Colver, Dan Smith, and Jeremy Devport, *Careers in the 21st Century* (Scarborough, ON: ITP Nelson, 2000), 356–358.

Academic Journal Article

3. John Drovich, "Peace in the Middle East," *Canadian Journal of International Studies* 19, no. 5 (2001): 23–45.

Monthly Magazine Article

4. Bill Safer, "Future Leadership," *Canadian Management*, April 2002, 45.

Newspaper Article

5. Trisha Khan, "Beyond 2000: Working in the Next Century," *Winnipeg Free Press*, August 22, 2001, B3.

Government Publication

6. Human Resources Development Canada, *How to Find a Job* (Ottawa: Supply and Services Canada, 2000), 30.

Online Services

7. Loblaw Companies Ltd., *Great Stores Start With…: 2004 Annual Report*, http://www.loblaw.com/en/inv_ar.html#, p. 14 (accessed May 23, 2005).

Interview

8. Geoffrey H. Wilson (senior vice-president, Investor Relations and Public Affairs, Loblaw Companies Ltd.), personal interview, May 25, 2005.

In referring to a previously mentioned footnote, cite the page number along with the author's last name or a shortened form of the title if no author is given. The Latin forms *ibid.*, *op. cit.*, and *et al.* are rarely seen in business reports today. A portion of a business report using the endnote method for source citation is found in Figure C.1.

Parenthetic Method. Many writers of scholarly works prefer to use a parenthetic style to cite references. In this method a reference to the author appears in parentheses close to the place where it is mentioned in the text. Some parenthetic styles show the author's last name and date of publication (for example, *Cook 2000*), while others show the author's last name and page cited (for example, *Cook 24*). One of the most well-known parenthetic systems is the Modern Language Association (MLA) format. The long report shown in Figure 10.15 illustrates this format. To provide guidance in preparing your academic and business papers, we'll focus on the MLA format.

Which Method for Business? Students frequently ask, "But what documentation system is most used in business?" Actually no one method dominates. Many businesses have developed their own hybrid systems. These companies generally supply guidelines illustrating their in-house style to employees. Before starting any research project on the job, you'll want to inquire about your organization's preferred documentation style. You can also look in your company's files for examples of previous reports.

MLA Style—Modern Language Association

The MLA citation style uses parenthetic author references in the text. These in-text citations guide the reader to a bibliography called "Works Cited." Following are selected characteristics of the MLA style. For more information, consult Joseph Gibaldi, *MLA Handbook for Writers of Research Papers*, 6th ed. (New York: The Modern Language Association of America, 2003).

These changes are introducing challenges to companies operating both in Canada and abroad. Obviously, all of these employees need specific business and technology skills, but they also need to be aware of, and be sensitive to, the cultures in which they are living and working.[1] The Bank of Montreal has targeted several of these areas in which to enhance services. Chinese-Canadian business has increased 400 percent in the last five years.[2]

Women are increasing their role as both customer and worker. By the year 2003 women are expected to compose 47 percent of the labour force in Canada, as compared with 27 percent in 1961.[3] However, women hold only about 6 percent of the top management positions in organizations in the industrialized world.[4]

Companies that focus on diversity are improving their bottom line. Recently, Federal Express was named in *The Financial Post* as one the 100 best companies to work for in Canada. Canadian Pacific Forest Products received recognition for ensuring that selection committees had diverse membership, for their development of antiharassment policies, and for other diversity initiatives.[5]

Notes

1. Brenda Lynn, "Diversity in the Workplace: Why We Should Care," *CMA Management Accounting Magazine* 70, no. 5 (June 2000): 9–12.

2. Richard Sommer, "Firms Gain Competitive Strength from Diversity (Says Report by Conference Board of Canada)," *Financial Post,* 9 May 2001, 31.

3. British Columbia, Ministry of Education, Skills and Training, *The Impact of Demographic Change* (Victoria: Ministry of Education, Skills, and Training, 2002), 35.

4. R. J. Burke and C. A. McKeen, "Do Women at the Top Make a Difference? Gender Proportions and the Experiences of Managerial and Professional Women," *Human Relations* 49, no. 8 (2002): 1093–1104.

5. British Columbia, 36.

In-Text Citations

Within the text the author's last name and relevant page reference appear in parentheses, such as "(Chartrand 310)." In-text citations should be placed close to the reference they cite. Notice that no separating comma appears. If the author's name is mentioned in the text, cite only the page number in parentheses. If you don't know the author's name (e.g., when quoting from a Web site or blog), use the title of the Web site section or blog entry you took the information from in your in-text citation. Your goal is to avoid interrupting the flow of your writing. Thus, you should strive to place the parenthetical reference where a pause would naturally occur, but as near as possible to the material documented. Note the following examples:

Author's Name in Text

Peters also notes that stress could be a contributing factor in the health problems reported thus far (135).

Author's Name Unknown

One Web site goes so far as to claim that new communication technologies such as BlackBerrys and multi-purpose cell phones will soon make in-person conversations "a thing of the past" ("Talking Not Cool").

Author's Name in Reference

The study was first published in 1958 (Peters 127–135).

Authors' Names in Text

Others, like Bergstrom and Voorhees (243–251), support a competing theory.

Authors' Names in Reference

Others support a competing theory (e.g., Bergstrom and Voorhees 243–251).

When citing films, television programs, or electronic references, MLA style recommends that you include in the text, rather than in a parenthetical reference, the name of the person or organization that begins the corresponding entry in the works-cited list.

Electronic Source with Author

William J. Kennedy's <u>Bits and Bites</u> discusses new computer technologies in the context of the digital telecommunications revolution. (In the "Works Cited" list, the reader would find a complete reference under the author's name.)

Electronic Source Without Author

More companies today are using data mining to unlock hidden value in their data. The data mining program "TargetSource," described at the Tener Solutions Group Web site, helps organizations predict consumer behaviour. (In the "Works Cited" list, the reader would find a complete reference under "Tener Solutions Group," the organization that owns the Web site.)

Works Cited

In-text citations lead the reader to complete bibliographical citations in the "Works Cited." This alphabetical listing may contain all works consulted or only those mentioned in the text. Check with your instructor or editor to learn what method is preferred. Below are selected guidelines summarizing important elements of the MLA format for "Works Cited," as shown in Figure C.2.

- **Hanging indented style.** Indent the second and succeeding line for each item. Single-space within entries and double-space between.
- **Book and Web site titles.** Underline the titles of books and use "headline style" for capitalization. This means that the initial letters of all main words are capitalized:

Lewe, Glenda, & Carol D. MacLeod. <u>Step into the World of Workplace Learning: A Collection of Authentic Workplace Materials</u>. Scarborough, ON: Nelson Thomson Learning, 2001.

"ACE Aviation to take minority stake in merged U.S. airline." <u>CBC.ca</u>. 2005. Retrieved 23 May 2005 <www.cbc.ca/story/business/national/2005/05/19/merger-050519.html>.

- **Magazine titles.** For the titles of magazine articles, include the date of publication but omit volume and issue numbers:

Lee, Mary M. "Investing in International Relationships." <u>Business Monthly</u> 18 Feb. 2000.

FIGURE C.2 Model MLA Bibliography of Sample References

Works Cited

Air Canada. <u>2004 Annual Report.</u> Retrieved 26 May 2005 <http://www.
    aircanada.com/en/about/investor/index.html#reports>.
— Online annual report

Beresford, Marcia. "The Shift in Profit." <u>Maclean's</u> 24 Oct. 2001: 25–26.
— Magazine article

British Columbia Ministry of Education, Skills and Training, <u>The Impact of
    Demographic Change</u>. Victoria: Ministry of Education, Skills and Training,
    2002.
— Government publication

"Clementine@work." <u>SPSS Web Site.</u> Retrieved 7 Sept. 2005. <http://www.
    spss.com/customer/clem_stories/>.
— Company Web site, no author

"Globalization Often Means That the Fast Track Leads Overseas." <u>The Globe
    and Mail</u>, 16 June 2002: A10.
— Newspaper article, no author

Jahl, Andrew. "PowerPoint of No Return." <u>Canadian Business</u>. 24 Nov. 2003:
    14–15. CBCA Current Affairs. George Brown College Library. Retrieved 27
    May 2005.
— Online research database magazine article, where "CBCA Current Affairs" is the research database

Lancaster, Hal. "When Taking a Tip from a Job Network, Proceed with Caution."
    <u>The Wall Street Journal</u>, 7 Feb. 2002: B1.
— Newspaper article, one author

Mark, John. "Feds Provide Summary of New Privacy Legislation for Internet Users."
    5 June 2002 <u>globe and mail.com</u>. Retrieved 9 June 2005 <http://www.
    globeandmail.com/servlet.story/RTGAM.20020605.privacy/National>.
— Online newspaper article

"Message Treatment." <u>Communication, Culture and Media Studies</u> Web site.
    Retrieved 23 May 2005 <www.cultsock.ndirect.co.uk/MUHome/cshtml/>.
— Web site, no author

Murdry, Henry. "Consumers Still Driving the Economy." <u>Marketing News Online</u>,
    31 Aug. 2001. Retrieved 1 Sept. 2005 <http://www.
    canadianmarketingmagazine.ca/consumers.story>.
— Online magazine article

Pinnacle Security Services. <u>What Employers Should Know About Employees</u>,
    2nd ed. Toronto: Pinnacle Information Centre, 2002.
— Brochure

Rivers, John. Personal interview. 16 May 2005.
— Interview

Rosen, Richard, and Ethel Montgomery. <u>How to Make a Buck and Still Be a
    Decent Human Being</u>. New York: HarperCollins, 1998.
— Book, two authors

Weathers, Nicholas. "Key Trends in Systems Development." <u>Journal of Informa-
    tion Management</u> 3.2 (2000): 5–20.
— Journal article with volume and issue numbers

- **Journal articles.** For journal articles follow the same format as for magazine articles except include the volume number, issue number (if needed), and the year of publication inside parentheses:

    Green, Deidre. "A Textbook Case for Online Searching," <u>CMAJ: Canadian Medical
        Association Journal</u> 164:7 (2001). ["164:7" indicates volume 164, issue 7.]

- **Italics and underscoring.** MLA style recommends underscoring book, magazine, and journal titles because underscores are easier to read than italics. Italics, however, are preferred in many organizations. Check with your instructor or organization for the preferred style.

Electronic References

The objective in citing sources, whether print publications or electronic publications, is to provide enough information that your reader can locate your sources. In addition to the information provided for all print sources (e.g., author's name if available, title, date of publication, etc.), a citation for an electronic source requires at least two other kinds of information. First, you must provide the date when you accessed the source. Second, you must provide the source's electronic address between angle brackets (e.g., <www.cbc.ca>). The electronic address (or URL) is the final part of an electronic source citation.

Although MLA style does not suggest including the word "Retrieved" before the access date, we include it to distinguish the retrieval date from the publication date. Figure C.2 illustrates the electronic and other formats for many different kinds of references. The MLA also posts some helpful guidelines for documenting electronic sources at its Web site <www.mla.org>; follow the prompts to "Documenting Sources from the World Wide Web."

The MLA makes the following recommendations for citing electronic sources:

- Give the same information for electronic sources as you would if you were citing a print publication (e.g., author name, title, page number).
- Give all relevant dates. Because electronic sources can change or move, cite the date the document was produced (if available) as well as the date you accessed the information. Do not use any punctuation to separate the date you received the information and the URL. If the electronic publication is or was available in print form (that is, as a book or in a journal), include the original print publication date before the other dates.
- Include the electronic address or universal resource locator (URL) where you found your information. Provide entire URLs in angle brackets (<, >), being sure to break lines only after a slash, dot, or hyphen. Never add a hyphen to mark a break in the address.
- Download and print any citation information for future reference.

Article in an Online Journal

Chrisman, Laura, and Laurence Phillips. "Postcolonial Studies and the British Academy." <u>Jouvert</u> 3:3. (1999). Retrieved 10 June 2001 <http://social.chass.ncsu.edu/jouvert/v3i3/chrisph/htm>.

Brown, Ronnie R. "Photographs That Should Have Been Taken." <u>Room of One's Own</u> 18:2 (Summer 1995). Retrieved 26 May 2002 <http://www.islandnet.com/Room/enter/poetry/photos.htm>.

Article in an Online Newspaper or on a Newswire

These sites change very frequently—in some cases daily—so it is a good idea to download or record URL and citation information immediately.

Scarth, Deborah. "Many Top University Students Use Tutors to Keep an Edge." <u>Globe and Mail Online</u>. 4 June 2000. Retrieved 5 Oct. 2000 <http://www.globeandmail.com/dailyglobe2/150/learning/Many-top-university-students-use-tutors-to-keep-an-edge+.shtm>.

"Canada's Unemployment Rate Dips." <u>CBC News Online</u>. 4 June 2000. Retrieved 5 Aug. 2000 <http://www.cbcnews.cbc.ca/cgi-bin/templates/view.cgi?/news/1999/06/04/unemploy990604>.

Article in an Online Magazine

Caragata, Warren. "Guide to Y2K." <u>Maclean's Online</u>. 19 Apr. 2000. Retrieved 5 June 2000 <http://www.macleans.ca/pub-doc/1999/04/19/Cover/4998.html>.

Professional or Personal Web Site

List the publication information in the following order: the name of the creator of the site, the title of the site (underlined), a description (for example, *Home page*, neither underlined nor italicized nor enclosed in quotation marks), the date you accessed the information, and the electronic address. If some of this information is unavailable, cite whatever is available.

> Canadiantire.ca. Investor Relations page. Retrieved 28 May 2005 <www.
> canadiantire.ca>.

> Ellison, Sara. Sara's Home Page. Sarah's Astronomy Stuff. Retrieved 29 July 2005
> <http://orca.phys.uvic.ca/~sara/>.

Online Book

Many books are now available electronically, either independently or as part of a scholarly project. Follow the general recommendations for citing books in print, but include the additional information as required for electronic citations.

If it is available, give the name of the author first; if not, give the name of the editor, translator, or compiler, followed by a period and then the appropriate abbreviation (*ed.*, *trans.*, or *comp.*). Next give the title of the work (underlined), the name of the editor, translator, or compiler (if relevant), the publication information, the date you accessed the information, and the address. The publication information will vary depending on whether the text has been previously published in print form. If it has not been previously published, give the date it was published electronically and the name of any associated organization or university. If it has been previously published in print form, include, if available, the city of publication, the name of the publisher and the year of publication, followed by the date of electronic publication, and the name of any associated organization or university. In either case, complete your citation with the date you accessed the information and the electronic address.

> Montgomery, Lucy Maud. Anne of Green Gables. 1908. Retrieved 30 May 2001
> <http://www.literature.org/authors/montgomery-lucy-maud/anne-of-green-
> gables/>.

> Dewey, John. Democracy and Education. London: Macmillan, 1916. 22 Nov. 1995.
> Retrieved 5 June 2001 <http://www.ilt.columbia.edu/academic/texts/dewey/
> d_e/contents.html>.

Scholarly Project or Information Services

Information on a wide variety of topics is available through scholarly projects or in information services. If you are using information taken from these sources, cite the title of the project or information service first (underlined), followed by the name of the editor (if available), any relevant and available electronic publication information (for example, version number, date of electronic publication or most recent update, and name of any sponsoring institution or organization), the date you accessed the information, and the network address.

> The Orlando Project: An Integrated History of Women's Writing in the British Isles.
> 1998. Department of English, University of Alberta. 1998. Retrieved 25 April
> 2000 <http://www.ualberta.ca/ORLANDO/>.

> "South Yorkshire." Encyclopedia Britannica Online. 26 May 2001 <http://members.
> eb.com/bol/topic?eu=70678&sctn=1>.

Other Electronic Sources. The citations for other electronic sources will follow the recommendations for print versions with some additional required information.

Be sure to include the type of document you are citing (for example, transcript, online posting, or e-mail) between the date of publication and the date you accessed the information. End your citation with the date you accessed the information and the network address.

Television/Radio

Mansbridge, Peter. "Sears Saga." The National. CBC-TV. 4 June 2001. Transcript. 5 June 2001 <http://www.tv.cbc.ca/national/trans/current.html>.

E-Mail Communication

Pen Canada. "Your Inquiries to PEN." E-mail to author. 3 July 2005.

Online Posting

Murley, Susan. "Technical Writing." Online posting. 2 May 2000. MLA Grad List. 3 May 2000 <e-grad@nwe.ufl.edu>.

Material from an Online Research Database

Online services such as ProQuest and LexisNexis provide a variety of databases that your college library will have. Give the name of the service before the date you accessed the information. Indicate the method by which you retrieved the information. For example, if you used a keyword search, write "keyword" (neither in quotation marks nor underlined) at the end of your citation, followed by a colon and the keyword you used to find your information.

Golden, Anne. "Do Our Foreign Investment Laws Still Have Legs?" The Globe and Mail. 1 Dec. 2004: A23. CBCA Current Affairs. Retrieved 2 March 2005. Keyword: Noranda and Minmetals.

APA Style—American Psychological Association

Popular in the social and physical sciences, the American Psychological Association (APA) documentation style uses parenthetic citations. That is, each author reference is shown in parentheses when cited in the text. Below are selected features of the APA style. For more information see the *Publication Manual of the American Psychological Association,* 5th Edition (Washington, DC: American Psychological Association, 2001).

In-Text Citation

In-text citations consist of the author's last name, year of publication, and pertinent page number(s). These items appear in parentheses usually at the end of a clause or end of a sentence in which material is cited. This parenthetic citation, as shown in the following illustration, directs readers to a reference list at the end of the report where complete bibliographic information is recorded.

The strategy of chicken king Don Tyson was to expand aggressively into other "center-of-the-plate" proteins, such as pork, fish, and turkey (Berss, 2000, p. 64).

Bibliography

All reference sources are alphabetized in a bibliography entitled "References." Below are selected guidelines summarizing important elements of the APA bibliographic format:

- Include authors' names with the last name first followed by initials, such as **Smith, M. A.** First and middle names are not used.
- Show the date of publication in parentheses, such as **Smith, M. A. (2001)**.
- Italicize the titles of books and use "sentence-style" (sometimes called *down style*) capitalization. This means that only the first word of a title, proper nouns, or the first word after an internal colon is capitalized. Book titles are followed by the place of publication and publisher's name, such as **Smith, M. A. (2001).** *Communication for managers.* **Elmsford, NY: Pergamon Press.**
- Type the titles of magazine and journal articles without italics or quotation marks. Use sentence-style capitalization for article titles. However, italicize the names of magazines and journals and capitalize the initial letters of all important words. Also italicize the volume number, such as **Cheung, H. K., & Burn, J. M. (1994). Distributing global information systems resources in multinational companies—a contingency model.** *Journal of Global Information Management,* **2(3), 14–27.** ["2(3), 14–27" indicates volume 2, issue 3, pages 14–27.]
- Space only once following periods and colons.
- Do not include personal communications (such as interviews, telephone conversations, e-mail, and messages from nonarchived discussion groups and online forums) in the reference list, since they are not retrievable.

Electronic References

When print information is available, APA suggests placing it first followed by online information. For example, a newspaper article: **Schellhardt, T. D. (1999, March 4). In a factory schedule, where does religion fit in?** *The Wall Street Journal,* **pp. B1, B12. Retrieved March 5, 1999, from http://interactive.wsj.com** For additional discussion and examples, visit the APA Web site <**www.apastyle.org/elecref.html**>.

Figure C.3, on the next page, shows the format of an APA Reference List.

FIGURE C.3 Model APA Bibliography Sample References

References

Online annual report
Air Canada. (2004). *2004 annual report*. Retrieved May 26, 2005, from http://www .aircanada.com/en/about/investor/index.html#reports

Magazine article
Berss, M. (2000, October 24). Protein man. *Forbes, 154,* 64–66.

Newspaper article, no author
Globalization often means that the fast track leads overseas. (1999, June 16). *The Financial Post,* p. A10.

Online research database magazine article
Jahl, A. (2003, November 24). PowerPoint of no return. *Canadian Business*, 14–15. Retrieved May 27, 2005, from CBCA Current Affairs, George Brown College Library.

Newspaper article, one author
Lancaster, H. (1998, February 7). When taking a tip from a job network, proceed with caution. *The Wall Street Journal,* p. B1.

Online newspaper article
Markoff, J. (1999, June 5). Voluntary rules proposed to help ensure privacy for Internet users. *The New York Times*. Retrieved June 9, 2005, from http://www.nytimes .com/library/cyber/week/y05dat.html

Online magazine article
Murphy, H. L. (1998, August 31). Saturn's orbit still high with consumers. *Marketing News Online*. Retrieved September 1, 2004, from http://www.ama.org/pubs/ mn/0818n1.htm

Brochure
Pinkerton Investigation Services. (1998). *The employer's guide to investigation services* (3rd ed.) [Brochure]. Atlanta, GA: Pinkerton Information Center.

Book, two authors
Rose, R. C., & Garrett, E. M. (1998). *How to make a buck and still be a decent human being*. New York: HarperCollins.

Government publication
Statistics Canada. (1995). *A portrait of persons with disabilities: Target groups project*. Ottawa, ON: Department of Industry, Science and Technology.

Web site, no author
Transmission models—criticism. (2005). *Communication, Culture and Media Studies*. Retrieved 23 May 2005 from http://www.cultshock.ndirect.co.uk/MUHome/cshtml/

Journal article with volume and issue numbers
Wetherbee, J. C., Vitalari, N. P., & Milner, A. (1998). Key trends in systems development in Europe and North America. *Journal of Global Information Management, 3*(2), 5–20.

Grammar/Mechanics Handbook

Because many students need a review of basic grammar and mechanics, we provide a number of resources below. The Grammar/Mechanics Handbook, which offers you a rapid systematic review, consists of four parts:

- **Grammar/Mechanics Diagnostic Test.** This 65-point Grammar/Mechanics Diagnostic Test helps you assess your strengths and weaknesses in eight areas of grammar and mechanics.
- **Grammar/Mechanics Profile.** The G/M Profile enables you to pinpoint specific areas in which you need remedial instruction or review.
- **Grammar Review with Checkup and Editing Exercises.** A concise set of guidelines reviews basic principles of grammar, punctuation, capitalization, and number style. The review also provides checkup and quiz exercises that help you interact with the principles of grammar and test your comprehension. The guidelines not only provide a study guide for review but also serve as a reference manual throughout the writing course. The grammar review can be used for classroom-centred instruction or for self-guided learning.
- **Confusing Words and Frequently Misspelled Words.** A selected list of confusing words, along with a list of 160 frequently misspelled words, completes the Grammar/Mechanics Handbook.

The first step in your systematic review of grammar and mechanics involves completing a diagnostic test.

Grammar/Mechanics Diagnostic Test

Name _____

This diagnostic test is intended to reveal your strengths and weaknesses in using the following:

plural nouns	adjectives	punctuation
possessive nouns	adverbs	capitalization style
pronouns	prepositions	number style
verbs	conjunctions	

The test is organized into sections corresponding to these categories. In sections A–H, each sentence is either correct or has one error related to the category under which it is listed. If a sentence is correct, write C. If it has an error, underline the error and write the correct form in the space provided. Use ink to record your answers. When you finish, check your answers with your instructor and fill out the Grammar/Mechanics Profile at the end of the test.

A. Plural Nouns

branches _____

Example: The newspaper named editors in chief for both branchs.

_____

_____

_____

_____

_____

1. Three of the lawyers representing the defendants were from citys in other provinces.
2. Four students discussed the pros and cons of attending colleges or universities.
3. Since the 1990s, most companys have begun to send bills of lading with shipments.
4. Neither the Johnsons nor the Morris's knew about the changes in beneficiaries.
5. The manager asked all secretaries to work on the next four Saturday's.

B. Possessive Nouns

_____

_____

_____

_____

_____

6. We sincerely hope that the jurys judgment reflects the stories of all the witnesses.
7. In a little over two months time, the analysts had finished three reports for the president.
8. Mr. Franklins staff is responsible for all accounts receivable contracted by customers purchasing electronics parts.
9. At the next shareholders meeting, we will discuss benefits for employees and dividends for shareholders.
10. Three months ago several employees in the sales department complained of Mrs. Kwons smoking.

C. Pronouns

me _____

Example: Whom did you ask to replace Tom and I?

_____

_____

_____

_____

_____

11. My manager and myself were willing to send the copies to whoever needed them.
12. Some of the work for Mr. Gagne and I had to be reassigned to Mark and him.
13. Although it's motor was damaged, the car started for the mechanic and me.
14. Just between you and me, only you and I know that she will be transferred.
15. My friend and I applied for employment at Reynolds, Inc., because of their excellent employee benefits.

D. Verb Agreement

has _____

Example: The list of arrangements have to be approved by Tim and her.

_____

_____

_____

_____

16. The keyboard, printer, and monitor costs less than I expected.
17. A description of the property, together with several other legal documents, were submitted by my lawyer.
18. There was only two enclosures and the letter in the envelope.
19. Neither the manager nor the employees in the office think the solution is fair.
20. Because of the holiday, our committee prefer to delay its action.

E. Verb Mood, Voice, and Tense

_____

_____

_____

_____

21. If I was able to fill your order immediately, I certainly would.
22. To operate the machine, first open the CD caddy and then you insert the CD.
23. If I could chose any city, I would select Vancouver.
24. Those papers have laid on his desk for more than two weeks.

Grammar/Mechanics Handbook

25. The auditors have went over these accounts carefully, and they have found ——————————
no discrepancies.

F. Adjectives and Adverbs

26. Until we have a more clearer picture of the entire episode, we shall proceed ——————————
cautiously.
27. For about a week their newly repaired copier worked just beautiful. ——————————
28. The recently elected prime minister benefited from his coast to coast campaign. ——————————
29. Mr. Snyder only has two days before he must complete the end-of-the-year ——————————
report.
30. The architects submitted there drawings in a last-minute attempt to beat the ——————————
deadline.

G. Prepositions and Conjunctions

31. Can you tell me where the meeting is scheduled at? ——————————
32. It seems like we have been taking this test forever. ——————————
33. Our investigation shows that the distribution department is more efficient ——————————
then the sales department.
34. My courses this semester are totally different than last semester's. ——————————
35. Do you know where this shipment is going to? ——————————

H. Commas

For each of the following sentences, insert any necessary commas. Count the
number of commas that you added. Write that number in the space provided. All
punctuation must be correct to receive credit for the sentence. If a sentence
requires no punctuation, write C.

Example: However, because of developments in theory and computer applications ∧   <u>2</u>——————————
management is becoming more of a science.

36. For example management determines how orders assignments and respon- ——————————
sibilities are delegated to employees.
37. Your order Mrs. Tahan will be sent from Toronto Ontario on July 10. ——————————
38. When you need service on any of your pieces of equipment we will be happy ——————————
to help you Mr. Hamel.
39. Kevin Long who is the project manager at Techdata suggested that I call you. ——————————
40. You have purchased from us often and your payments in the past have ——————————
always been prompt.

I. Commas and Semicolons 1

Add commas and semicolons to the following sentences. In the space provided,
write the number of punctuation marks that you added.

41. The salesperson turned in her report however she did not indicate what time ——————————
period it covered.
42. Some interest payments may be tax deductible dividend payments are not. ——————————
43. We are opening a branch office in Kelowna and hope to be able to serve all ——————————
your needs from that office by the middle of January.
44. As suggested by the committee we must first secure adequate funding then ——————————
we may consider expansion.
45. When you begin to conduct research for a report consider the many library ——————————
sources available namely books periodicals government publications and
databases.

J. Commas and Semicolons 2

_____ 46. After our office manager had the printer repaired it jammed again within the first week although we treated it carefully.

_____ 47. Our experienced courteous staff has been trained to anticipate your every need.

_____ 48. In view of the new law that went into effect April 1 our current liability insurance must be increased however we cannot immediately afford it.

_____ 49. As stipulated in our contract your agency will supervise our graphic arts and purchase our media time.

_____ 50. As you know Mrs. Laurendeau we aim for long-term business relationships not quick profits.

K. Other Punctuation

Each of the following sentences may require dashes, colons, question marks, quotation marks, periods, and underscores, as well as commas and semicolons. Add the appropriate punctuation to each sentence. Then, in the space provided, write the total number of marks that you added.

3 _____ **Example:** Price service and reliability these are our prime considerations.

_____ 51. The following members of the department volunteered to help on Saturday Kim Carlos Dan and Sylvia.

_____ 52. Mr. Danner, Miss Reed, and Mrs. Rossi usually arrived at the office by 8 30 a. m.

_____ 53. Three of our top managers Tim, Marcy, and Asad received cash bonuses.

_____ 54. Did the vice-president really say "All employees may take Friday off

_____ 55. We are trying to locate an edition of _Maclean's_ that carried an article entitled E-Mail Beats Office Politics

L. Capitalization

For each of the following sentences, circle any letter that should be capitalized. In the space provided, write the number of circles that you marked.

3 _____ **Example:** Vice-president daniels devised a procedure for expediting purchase orders from area 4 warehouses.

_____ 56. although english was his first language, he also spoke spanish and could read french.

_____ 57. on a trip to the east coast, uncle henry visited the bay of fundy.

_____ 58. karen enrolled in classes in history, german, and sociology.

_____ 59. the business manager and the vice-president each received a new macintosh computer.

_____ 60. jane lee, the president of kendrick, inc., will speak to our conference in the spring.

M. Number Style

Decide whether the numbers in the following sentences should be written as words or as figures. Each sentence either is correct or has one error. If it is correct, write C. If it has an error, underline it and write the correct form in the space provided.

five _____ **Example:** The bank had 5 branches in three suburbs.

_____ 61. More than 2,000,000 people have visited the Parliament Buildings in the past five years.

Grammar/Mechanics Handbook

62. Of the 35 letters sent out, only three were returned.
63. We set aside forty dollars for petty cash, but by December 1 our fund was depleted.
64. The meeting is scheduled for May 5th at 3 p.m.
65. In the past 20 years, nearly 15 percent of the population changed residences at least once.

Grammar/Mechanics Profile

In the spaces at the right, place a check mark to indicate the number of correct answers you had in each category of the Grammar/Mechanics Diagnostic Test.

		Number Correct*				
		5	4	3	2	1
1–5	Plural Nouns	____	____	____	____	____
6–10	Possessive Nouns	____	____	____	____	____
11–15	Pronouns	____	____	____	____	____
16–20	Verb Agreement	____	____	____	____	____
21–25	Verb Mood, Voice, and Tense	____	____	____	____	____
26–30	Adjectives and Adverbs	____	____	____	____	____
31–35	Prepositions and Conjunctions	____	____	____	____	____
36–40	Commas	____	____	____	____	____
41–45	Commas and Semicolons 1	____	____	____	____	____
46–50	Commas and Semicolons 2	____	____	____	____	____
51–55	Other Punctuation	____	____	____	____	____
56–60	Capitalization	____	____	____	____	____
61–65	Number Style	____	____	____	____	____

Note: 5 = have excellent skills; 4 = need light review; 3 = need careful review; 2 = need to study rules; 1 = need serious study and follow-up reinforcement.

Grammar Review

Parts of Speech (1.01)

1.01 Functions. English has eight parts of speech. Knowing the functions of the parts of speech helps writers better understand how words are used and how sentences are formed.

a. *Nouns.* Name persons, places, things, qualities, concepts, and activities (for example, *Kevin, Montreal, computer, joy, work, banking*).
b. *Pronouns.* Substitute for nouns (for example, *he, she, it, they*).
c. *Verbs.* Show the action of a subject or join the subject to words that describe it (for example, *walk, heard, is, was jumping*).
d. *Adjectives.* Describe or limit nouns and pronouns and often answer the questions what kind? how many? and which one? (for example, *fast sale, ten items, good manager*).
e. *Adverbs.* Describe or limit verbs, adjectives, or other adverbs and frequently answer the questions when? how? where? or to what extent? (for example, *tomorrow, rapidly, here, very*).
f. *Prepositions.* Join nouns or pronouns to other words in sentences (for example, *desk **in** the office, ticket **for** me, letter **to** you*).

g. **Conjunctions.** Connect words or groups of words (for example, *you **and** I, Marc **or** Nikola*).

h. **Interjections.** Express strong feelings (for example, *Wow! Oh!*).

Nouns (1.02–1.06)

Nouns name persons, places, things, qualities, concepts, and activities. Nouns may be classified into a number of categories.

1.02 Concrete and Abstract. Concrete nouns name specific objects that can be seen, heard, felt, tasted, or smelled. Examples of concrete nouns are *telephone, dollar, IBM,* and *grape.* Abstract nouns name generalized ideas such as qualities or concepts that are not easily pictured. *Emotion, power,* and *tension* are typical examples of abstract nouns.

Business writing is most effective when concrete words predominate. It's clearer to write *We need 16-pound bond paper* than to write *We need office supplies.* Chapter 4 provides practice in developing skill in the use of concrete words.

1.03 Proper and Common. Proper nouns name specific persons, places, or things and are always capitalized (*Nortel, Minnedosa, Dinah*). All other nouns are common nouns and begin with lowercase letters (*company, city, student*). Rules for capitalization are presented in Sections 3.01–3.16.

1.04 Singular and Plural. Singular nouns name one item; plural nouns name more than one. From a practical view, writers seldom have difficulty with singular nouns. They may need help, however, with the formation and spelling of plural nouns.

1.05 Guidelines for Forming Noun Plurals

a. Add *s* to most nouns (*chair, chairs; mortgage, mortgages; Monday, Mondays*).

b. Add *es* to nouns ending in *s, x, z, ch,* or *sh* (*bench, benches; boss, bosses; box, boxes; Schultz, Schultzes*).

c. Change the spelling in irregular noun plurals (*man, men; foot, feet; mouse, mice; child, children*).

d. Add *s* to nouns that end in *y* when *y* is preceded by a vowel (*jockey, jockeys; valley, valleys; journey, journeys*).

e. Drop the *y* and add *ies* to nouns ending in *y* when *y* is preceded by a consonant (*company, companies; city, cities; secretary, secretaries*).

f. Add *s* to the principal word in most compound expressions (*editors in chief, fathers-in-law, bills of lading, runners-up*).

g. Add *s* to most numerals, letters of the alphabet, words referred to as words, degrees, and abbreviations (*5s, 1990s, Bs, ands, CAs, yrs.*). Note that metric abbreviations take neither a period nor an *s* to make them plural.

h. Add *'s* only to clarify letters of the alphabet that might be misread, such as *A's, I's, M's,* and *U's* and *i's, p's,* and *q's.* An expression like *c.o.d.s* requires no apostrophe because it would not easily be misread.

1.06 Collective Nouns. Nouns such as *staff, faculty, committee, group,* and *herd* refer to a collection of people, animals, or objects. Collective nouns may be considered singular or plural depending upon their action. See Section 1.10i for a discussion of collective nouns and their agreement with verbs.

Review Exercise A—Nouns

In the space provided for each item, write *a* or *b* to complete the following statements accurately. When you finish, compare your responses with those provided.

Answers are provided for odd-numbered items. Your instructor has the remaining answers. For each item on which you need review, consult the numbered principle shown in parentheses.

1. Nearly all (a) editor in chiefs, (b) editors in chief demand observance of standard punctuation.
2. Several (a) jockeys, (b) jockies worked on the case together.
3. Please write to the (a) Davis's, (b) Davises about the missing contract.
4. The industrial complex has space for nine additional (a) companys, (b) companies.
5. That accounting firm employs two (a) secretaries, (b) secretarys for five CGAs.
6. Four of the wooden (a) benches, (b) benchs must be repaired.
7. The home was constructed with numerous (a) chimneys, (b) chimnies.
8. Tours of the production facility are made only on (a) Tuesdays, (b) Tuesday's.
9. We asked the (a) Jones's, (b) Joneses to contribute to the fundraising drive.
10. Both my (a) sister-in-laws, (b) sisters-in-law agreed to the settlement.
11. The stock market is experiencing abnormal (a) ups and downs, (b) up's and down's.
12. Three (a) mouses, (b) mice were seen near the garbage cans.
13. This office is unusually quiet on (a) Sundays, (b) Sunday's.
14. Several news (a) dispatchs, (b) dispatches were released during the strike.
15. Two major (a) countries, (b) countrys will participate in trade negotiations.
16. Some young children have difficulty writing their (a) bs and ds, (b) b's and d's.
17. The (a) board of directors, (b) boards of directors of all the major companies participated in the surveys.
18. In their letter the (a) Metzes, (b) Metzs said they intended to purchase the property.
19. In shipping we are careful to include all (a) bill of sales, (b) bills of sale.
20. Over the holidays many (a) turkies, (b) turkeys were consumed.

---

1. b (1.05f) 3. b (1.05b) 5. a (1.05e) 7. a (1.05d) 9. b (1.05b) 11. a (1.05g) 13. a (1.05a) 15. a (1.05e) 17. b (1.05f) 19. b (1.05f) (Only odd-numbered answers are provided. Consult your instructor for the others.)

Grammar/Mechanics Checkup—1

Nouns

Review Sections 1.01–1.06 above. Then study each of the following statements. Underline any mistakes and write a correction in the space provided. Record the appropriate Handbook section and letter that illustrates the principle involved. If a sentence is correct, write C. When you finish, compare your responses with those provided on page 505. If your answers differ, carefully study again the principles shown in parentheses.

Example: Two surveys revealed that many companys will move to the new industrial park.   <u>companies</u>   (1.05e)

1. Several attornies worked on the three cases simultaneously.   _____
2. Counter business is higher on Saturday's, but telephone business is greater on Sundays.   _____
3. Some of the citys in Kevin's report offer excellent opportunities.   _____

4. Frozen chickens and turkies are kept in the company's lockers.
5. All secretaries were asked to check supplies and other inventorys.
6. Only the Nashs and the Lopezes brought their entire families.
7. In the 1980s profits grew rapidly; in the 1990's investments lagged.
8. Both editor in chiefs instituted strict proofreading policies.
9. Luxury residential complexs are part of the architect's plan.
10. Trustees in three municipalitys are likely to approve increased school taxes.
11. The instructor was surprised to find three Jennifer's in one class.
12. Andre sent descriptions of two valleys in France to us via the Internet.
13. How many copies of the statements showing your assets and liabilitys did you make?
14. My monitor makes it difficult to distinguish between o's and a's.
15. Both runner-ups complained about the winner's behaviour.

Pronouns (1.07–1.09)

Pronouns substitute for nouns. They are classified by case.

1.07 Case. Pronouns function in three cases, as shown in the following chart.

Nominative Case	Objective Case	Possessive Case
(used for subjects of verbs and subject complements)	(used for objects of prepositions and objects of verbs)	(used to show possession)
I	me	my, mine
we	us	our, ours
you	you	your, yours
he	him	his
she	her	her, hers
it	it	its
they	them	their, theirs
who, whoever	whom, whomever	whose

1.08 Guidelines for Selecting Pronoun Case

a. Pronouns that serve as subjects of verbs must be in the nominative case:

He and I (not *Him and me*) decided to apply for the jobs.

b. Pronouns that follow linking verbs (such as *am, is, are, was, were, be, being, been*) and rename the words to which they refer must be in the nominative case.

It must have been she (not *her*) who placed the order. (The nominative-case pronoun *she* follows the linking verb *been* and renames *It*.)

If it was he (not *him*) who called, I have his number. (The nominative-case pronoun *he* follows the linking verb *was* and renames *It*.)

c. Pronouns that serve as objects of verbs or objects of prepositions must be in the objective case:

Mr. Laporte asked them to complete the proposal. (The pronoun *them* is the object of the verb *asked*.)

All computer printouts are sent to him. (The pronoun *him* is the object of the preposition *to*.)

Just between you and me, profits are falling. (The pronoun *me* is one of the objects of the preposition *between*.)

d. Pronouns that show ownership must be in the possessive case. Possessive pronouns (such as *hers, yours, ours, theirs,* and *its*) require no apostrophes:

   We found my diskette, but yours (not *your's*) may be lost.

   All parts of the machine, including its (not *it's*) motor, were examined.

   The house and its (not *it's*) contents will be auctioned.

   Don't confuse possessive pronouns and contractions. Contractions are shortened forms of subject-verb phrases (such as *it's* for *it is, there's* for *there is,* and *they're* for *they are*).

e. When a pronoun appears in combination with a noun or another pronoun, ignore the extra noun or pronoun and its conjunction. In this way pronoun case becomes more obvious:

   The manager promoted Jasper and me (not *I*). (Ignore *Jasper and.*)

f. In statements of comparison, mentally finish the comparative by adding the implied missing words:

   Next year I hope to earn as much as she. (The verb *earns* is implied here: *as much as she earns.*)

g. Pronouns must be in the same case as the words they replace or rename. When pronouns are used with appositives, ignore the appositive:

   A new contract was signed by us (not *we*) employees. (Temporarily ignore the appositive *employees* in selecting the pronoun.)

   We (not *us*) citizens have formed our own organization. (Temporarily ignore the appositive *citizens* in selecting the pronoun.)

h. Pronouns ending in *self* should be used only when they refer to previously mentioned nouns or pronouns:

   The CEO herself answered the telephone.

   Robert and I (not *myself*) are in charge of the campaign.

i. Use objective-case pronouns as objects of the prepositions *between, but, like,* and *except*:

   Everyone but John and him (not *he*) qualified for the bonus.

   Employees like Miss Gallucci and her (not *she*) are hard to replace.

j. Use *who* or *whoever* for nominative-case constructions and *whom* or *whomever* for objective-case constructions. In making the correct choice, it's sometimes helpful to substitute *he* for *who* or *whoever* and *him* for *whom* or *whomever*:

   For whom was this book ordered? (*This book was ordered for him/whom?*)

   Who did you say would drop by? (*Who/he ... would drop by?*)

   Deliver the package to whoever opens the door. (In this sentence the clause *whoever opens the door* functions as the object of the preposition *to*. Within the clause itself *whoever* is the subject of the verb *opens*. Again, substitution of *he* might be helpful: *He/Whoever opens the door.*)

1.09 Guidelines for Making Pronouns Agree with Their Antecedents. Pronouns must agree with the words to which they refer (their antecedents) in gender and in number.

Grammar Review

a. Use masculine pronouns to refer to masculine antecedents, feminine pronouns to refer to feminine antecedents, and neutral pronouns to refer to antecedents without gender:

The woman opened her office door. (Feminine gender applies.)

A man sat at his desk. (Masculine gender applies.)

This computer and its programs fit our needs. (Neutral gender applies.)

b. Use singular pronouns to refer to singular antecedents:

Common-gender pronouns (such as *him* or *his*) traditionally have been used when the gender of the antecedent is unknown. Business writers construct sentences to avoid the need for common-gender pronouns. Study these examples for alternatives to the use of common-gender pronouns:*

Each student must submit a report on Monday.

All students must submit their reports on Monday.

Each student must submit his or her report on Monday. (This alternative is least acceptable, since it is wordy and calls attention to itself.)

c. Use singular pronouns to refer to singular indefinite subjects and plural pronouns for plural indefinite subjects. Words such as *anyone, something,* and *anybody* are considered indefinite because they refer to no specific person or *object*. Some indefinite pronouns are always singular; others are always plural.

Always Singular

anybody	everyone	somebody
anyone	everything	someone
anything	neither	
each	nobody	
either	no one	

Always Plural

both
few
many
several

Somebody in the group of touring women left her (not *their*) purse in the museum.

Either of the companies has the right to exercise its (not *their*) option to sell shares.

d. Use singular pronouns to refer to collective nouns and organization names:

The engineering staff is moving its (not *their*) facilities on Friday. (The singular pronoun *its* agrees with the collective noun *staff* because the members of staff function as a single unit.)

Jones, Cohen, & James, Inc., has (not *have*) cancelled its (not *their*) contract with us. (The singular pronoun *its* agrees with *Jones, Cohen, & James, Inc.,* because the members of the organization are operating as a single unit.)

e. Use a plural pronoun to refer to two antecedents joined by *and,* whether the antecedents are singular or plural:

Our company president and our vice-president will be submitting their expenses shortly.

f. Ignore intervening phrases—introduced by expressions such as *together with, as well as,* and *in addition to*—that separate a pronoun from its antecedent:

*See Chapter 2 for additional discussion of common-gender pronouns and inclusive language.

One of our managers, along with several salespeople, is planning his retirement. (If you wish to emphasize both subjects equally, join them with *and*: *One of our managers and several salespeople are planning their retirements.*)

g. When antecedents are joined by *or* or *nor*, make the pronoun agree with the antecedent closest to it.

Neither Jackie nor Kim wanted her (not *their*) desk moved.

Review Exercise B—Pronouns

In the space provided for each item, write *a*, *b*, or *c* to complete the statement accurately. When you finish, compare your responses with those provided. For each item on which you need review, consult the numbered principle shown in parentheses.

1. Mr. Behrens and (a) I, (b) myself will be visiting sales personnel in the New Brunswick district next week. _____
2. Joel promised that he would call; was it (a) him, (b) he who left the message? _____
3. Much preparation for the seminar was made by Mrs. Willmar and (a) I, (b) me before the brochures were sent out. _____
4. The Employee Benefits Committee can be justly proud of (a) its, (b) their achievements. _____
5. A number of inquiries were addressed to Jonelle and (a) I, (b) me, (c) myself. _____
6. (a) Who, (b) Whom did you say the letter was addressed to? _____
7. When you visit Mutual Trust, inquire about (a) its, (b) their certificates. _____
8. Copies of all reports are to be reviewed by Mr. Khan and (a) I, (b) me, (c) myself. _____
9. Apparently one of the female applicants forgot to sign (a) her, (b) their application. _____
10. Both the printer and (a) it's, (b) its cover are missing. _____
11. I've never known any man who could work as fast as (a) him, (b) he. _____
12. Just between you and (a) I, (b) me, the share price will fall by afternoon. _____
13. Give the supplies to (a) whoever, (b) whomever ordered them. _____
14. (a) Us, (b) We employees have been given an unusual voice in choosing benefits. _____
15. On her return from Mexico, Mrs. Lamas, along with many other passengers, had to open (a) her, (b) their luggage for inspection. _____
16. Either Jason or Raymond will have (a) his, (b) their work reviewed next week. _____
17. Any woman who becomes a charter member of this organization will be able to have (a) her, (b) their name inscribed on a commemorative plaque. _____
18. We are certain that (a) our's, (b) ours is the smallest wristwatch available. _____
19. Everyone has completed the reports except Danica and (a) he, (b) him. _____
20. Lack of work disturbs Mr. Jin as much as (a) I, (b) me. _____

1. a (1.08h) 3. b (1.08c) 5. b (1.08c, 1.08e) 7. a (1.09d) 9. a (1.09b) 11. b (1.08f) 13. a (1.08j) 15. a (1.09f) 17. a (1.09b) 19. b (1.08i)

Grammar/Mechanics Checkup—2

Pronouns

Review Sections 1.07–1.09 above. Then study each of the following statements. In the space provided, write the word that completes the statement correctly and the number of the Handbook principle illustrated. When you finish, compare your responses with those provided on page 505 again. If your responses differ, carefully study again the principles in parentheses.

__its__ (1.09d)   **Example:**   The Recreation and Benefits Committee will be submitting (its, their) report soon.

_____   1. I was expecting the manager to call. Was it (he, him) who left the message?

_____   2. Every one of the members of the men's soccer team had to move (his car, their cars) before the game could begin.

_____   3. A serious disagreement between management and (he, him) caused his resignation.

_____   4. Does anyone in the office know for (who, whom) this stationery was ordered?

_____   5. It looks as if (her's, hers) is the only report that cites electronic sources.

_____   6. Ms. Simmons asked my colleague and (I, me, myself) to help her complete the work.

_____   7. My friend and (I, me, myself) were also asked to work on Saturday.

_____   8. Both printers were sent for repairs, but (yours, your's) will be returned shortly.

_____   9. Give the budget figures to (whoever, whomever) asked for them.

_____   10. Everyone except the broker and (I, me, myself) claimed a share of the commission.

_____   11. No one knows that problem better than (he, him, himself).

_____   12. Investment brochures and information were sent to (we, us) shareholders.

_____   13. If any one of the tourists has lost (their, her) scarf, she should see the driver.

_____   14. Neither the glamour nor the excitement of the position had lost (its, it's, their) appeal.

_____   15. Any new subscriber may cancel (their, his or her) subscription within the first month.

Cumulative Editing Quiz 1

Use proofreading marks (see Appendix B) to correct errors in the following sentences. All errors must be corrected to receive credit for the sentence. Check with your instructor for the answers.

Example: Nicholas and ~~him~~ *he* made all ~~there~~ *their* money in the 1990's.

1. Just between you and I, whom do you think would make the best manager?

2. Either Sari or me is responsible for correcting all errors in news dispatchs.

3. Several attornies asked that there cases be postponed.

4. One of the secretarys warned Sharif and I to get the name of whomever answered the phone.

5. The committee sent there decision to the president and I last week.

6. Who should Angela or me call to verify the three bill of sales received today?

7. Several of we employees complained that it's keyboard made the new computer difficult to use.

8. All the CEO's agreed that the low interest rates of the early 2000's could not continue.

9. Every customer has a right to expect there inquirys to be treated courteously.

10. You may send you're contribution to Eric or myself or to whomever is listed as your representative.

Verbs (1.10–1.15)

Verbs show the action of a subject or join the subject to words that describe it.

1.10 Guidelines for Agreement with Subjects. One of the most troublesome areas in English is subject-verb agreement. Consider the following guidelines for making verbs agree with subjects.

a. A singular subject requires a singular verb:

The stock market opens at 10 a.m. (The singular verb *opens* agrees with the singular subject *market*.)

He doesn't (not *don't*) work on Saturday.

b. A plural subject requires a plural verb:

On the packing slip several items seem (not *seems*) to be missing.

c. A verb agrees with its subject regardless of prepositional phrases that may intervene:

This list of management objectives is extensive. (The singular verb *is* agrees with the singular subject *list*.)

Every one of the letters shows (not *show*) proper form.

d. A verb agrees with its subject regardless of intervening phrases introduced by *as well as, in addition to, such as, including, together with*, and similar expressions:

An important memo, together with several letters, was misplaced. (The singular verb *was* agrees with the singular subject *memo*.)

The president as well as several other top-level executives approves of our proposal. (The singular verb *approves* agrees with the subject *president*.)

e. A verb agrees with its subject regardless of the location of the subject:

Here is one of the letters about which you asked. (The verb *is* agrees with its subject *one*, even though it precedes *one*. The adverb *here* cannot function as a subject.)

There are many problems yet to be resolved. (The verb *are* agrees with the subject *problems*. The adverb *there* cannot function as a subject.)

In the next office are several printers. (In this inverted sentence the verb *are* must agree with the subject *printers*.)

f. Subjects joined by *and* require a plural verb:

Analyzing the reader and organizing a strategy are the first steps in letter writing. (The plural verb *are* agrees with the two subjects, *analyzing* and *organizing*.)

The tone and the wording of the letter were persuasive. (The plural verb *were* agrees with the two subjects, *tone* and *wording*.)

g. Subjects joined by *or* or *nor* may require singular or plural verbs. Make the verb agree with the closer subject:

Neither the memos nor the report is ready. (The singular verb *is* agrees with *report*, the closer of the two subjects.)

Grammar Review

h. The following indefinite pronouns are singular and require singular verbs: *anyone, anybody, anything, each, either, every, everyone, everybody, everything, many a, neither, nobody, nothing, someone, somebody,* and *something*:

Either of the alternatives that you present is acceptable. (The verb *is* agrees with the singular subject *either*.)

i. Collective nouns may take singular or plural verbs, depending on whether the members of the group are operating as a unit or individually:

Our management team is united in its goal.

The faculty are sharply divided on the tuition issue. (Although acceptable, this sentence sounds better recast: *The faculty members are sharply divided on the tuition issue*.)

j. Organization names and titles of publications, although they may appear to be plural, are singular and require singular verbs.

Deme, Sokolov, and Horne, Inc., has (not *have*) hired a marketing consultant.

Thousands of Investment Tips is (not *are*) again on the best-seller list.

1.11 Voice. Voice is that property of verbs that shows whether the subject of the verb acts or is acted upon. Active-voice verbs direct action from the subject toward the object of the verb. Passive-voice verbs direct action toward the subject.

Active voice: Our employees write excellent letters.
Passive voice: Excellent letters are written by our employees.

Business writing that emphasizes active-voice verbs is generally preferred because it is specific and forceful. However, passive-voice constructions can help a writer be tactful. Strategies for effective use of active- and passive-voice verbs are presented in Chapter 3.

1.12 Mood. Three verb moods express the attitude or thought of the speaker or writer toward a subject: (1) the **indicative** mood expresses a fact; (2) the **imperative** mood expresses a command; and (3) the **subjunctive** mood expresses a doubt, a conjecture, or a suggestion.

Indicative: I am looking for a job.
Imperative: Begin your job search with the want ads.
Subjunctive: I wish I were working.

Only the subjunctive mood creates problems for most speakers and writers. The most common use of subjunctive mood occurs in clauses including *if* or *wish*. In such clauses substitute the subjunctive verb *were* for the indicative verb *was*:

If he were (not *was*) in my position, he would understand.
Mr. Dworski acts as if he were (not *was*) the boss.
I wish I were (not *was*) able to ship your order.

The subjunctive mood may be used to maintain goodwill while conveying negative information. The sentence *I wish I were able to ship your order* sounds more pleasing to a customer than *I cannot ship your order*, although, for all practical purposes, the two sentences convey the same negative message.

1.13 Tense. Verbs show the time of an action by their tense. Speakers and writers can use six tenses to show the time of sentence action; for example:

Grammar/Mechanics Handbook

Present tense:	I work; he works.
Past tense:	I worked; she worked.
Future tense:	I will work; he will work.
Present perfect tense:	I have worked; he has worked.
Past perfect tense:	I had worked; she had worked.
Future perfect tense:	I will have worked; he will have worked.

1.14 Guidelines for Verb Tense

a. Use present tense for statements that, although they may be introduced by past-tense verbs, continue to be true:

What did you say his name is? (Use the present tense *is* if his name has not changed.)

b. Avoid unnecessary shifts in verb tenses:

The manager saw (not *sees*) a great deal of work yet to be completed and remained to do it herself.

Although unnecessary shifts in verb tense are to be avoided, not all the verbs within one sentence have to be in the same tense; for example:

She said (past tense) that she likes (present tense) to work late.

1.15 Irregular Verbs. Irregular verbs cause difficulty for some writers and speakers. Unlike regular verbs, irregular verbs do not form the past tense and past participle by adding *-ed* to the present form. Here is a partial list of selected troublesome irregular verbs. Consult a dictionary if you are in doubt about a verb form.

Troublesome Irregular Verbs

Present	Past	Past Participle *(always use helping verbs)*
begin	began	begun
break	broke	broken
choose	chose	chosen
come	came	come
drink	drank	drunk
go	went	gone
lay (to place)	laid	laid
lie (to rest)	lay	lain
ring	rang	rung
see	saw	seen
write	wrote	written

a. *Use only past-tense verbs to express past tense.* Notice that no helping verbs are used to indicate simple past tense:

The auditors went (not *have went*) over our books carefully.

He came (not *come*) to see us yesterday.

b. *Use past participle forms for actions completed before the present time.* Notice that past participle forms require helping verbs:

Steve had gone (not *went*) before we called. (The past participle *gone* is used with the helping verb *had*.)

Grammar Review

c. *Avoid inconsistent shifts in subject, voice, and mood.* Pay particular attention to this problem area, for undesirable shifts are often characteristic of student writing.

Inconsistent: When Mrs. Moscovitch read the report, the error was found. (The first clause is in the active voice; the second, passive.)

Improved: When Mrs. Moscovitch read the report, she found the error. (Both clauses are in the active voice.)

Inconsistent: The clerk should first conduct an inventory. Then supplies should be requisitioned. (The first sentence is in the active voice; the second, passive.)

Improved: The clerk should first conduct an inventory. Then he or she should requisition supplies. (Both sentences are in the active voice.)

Inconsistent: All workers must wear security badges, and you must also sign a daily time card. (This sentence contains an inconsistent shift in subject from *all workers* in first clause to *you* in second clause.)

Improved: All workers must wear security badges, and they must also sign a daily time card.

Inconsistent: Begin the transaction by opening an account; then you enter the customer's name. (This sentence contains an inconsistent shift from the imperative mood in first clause to the indicative mood in second clause.)

Improved: Begin the transaction by opening an account; then enter the customer's name. (Both clauses are now in the indicative mood.)

Review Exercise C—Verbs

In the space provided for each item, write *a* or *b* to complete the statement accurately. When you finish, compare your responses with those provided. For each item on which you need review, consult the numbered principle shown in parentheses.

1. A list of payroll deductions for our employees (a) was, (b) were sent to the personnel manager.
2. There (a) is, (b) are a customer service engineer and two salespeople waiting to see you.
3. Increased computer use and more complex automated systems (a) is, (b) are found in business today.
4. Crews, Meliotes, and Bauve, Inc., (a) has, (b) have opened an office in St. John's.
5. Yesterday Mrs. Phillips (a) choose, (b) chose a new office on the second floor.
6. The man who called said that his name (a) is, (b) was Johnson.
7. Office Computing and Networks (a) is, (b) are beginning a campaign to increase readership.
8. Either of the flight times (a) appears, (b) appear to fit my proposed itinerary.
9. If you had (a) saw, (b) seen the rough draft, you would better appreciate the final copy.
10. Across from our office (a) is, (b) are the parking structure and the information office.
11. Although we have (a) began, (b) begun to replace outmoded equipment, the pace is slow.
12. Specific training as well as ample experience (a) is, (b) are important for that position.
13. Inflation and increased job opportunities (a) is, (b) are resulting in increased numbers of working women.
14. Neither the organizing nor the staffing of the program (a) has been, (b) have been completed.

15. If I (a) was, (b) were you, I would ask for a raise. _____
16. If you had (a) wrote, (b) written last week, we could have sent a brochure. _____
17. The hydraulic equipment that you ordered (a) is, (b) are packed and will be shipped Friday. _____
18. One of the reasons that sales have declined in recent years (a) is, (b) are lack of effective advertising. _____
19. Either of the proposed laws (a) is, (b) are going to affect our business negatively. _____
20. Bankruptcy statutes (a) requires, (b) require that a failed company pay its debts to secured creditors first. _____

1. a (1.10c) 3. b (1.10f) 5. b (1.15a) 7. a (1.10j) 9. b (1.15b) 11. b (1.15b) 13. b (1.10f) 15. b (1.12) 17. a (1.10a) 19. a (1.10h)

Review Exercise D—Verbs

In the following sentence pairs, choose the one that illustrates consistency in use of subject, voice, and mood. Write *a* or *b* in the space provided. When you finish, compare your responses with those provided. For each item on which you need review, consult the numbered principle shown in parentheses.

1. (a) You need more than a knowledge of equipment; one also must be able to interact well with people. _____
   (b) You need more than a knowledge of equipment; you also must be able to interact well with people.
2. (a) Maurice and Jon were eager to continue, but Bob wanted to quit. _____
   (b) Maurice and Jon were eager to continue, but Bob wants to quit.
3. (a) The salesperson should consult the price list; then you can give an accurate quote to a customer. _____
   (b) The salesperson should consult the price list; then he or she can give an accurate quote to a customer.
4. (a) Read all the instructions first; then you install the printer program. _____
   (b) Read all the instructions first, and then install the printer program.
5. (a) She was an enthusiastic manager who always had a smile for everyone. _____
   (b) She was an enthusiastic manager who always has a smile for everyone.

1. b (1.15c) 3. b (1.15c) 5. a (1.14b)

Grammar/Mechanics Checkup—3

Verbs

Review Sections 1.10–1.15 above. Then study each of the following statements. Underline any verbs that are used incorrectly. In the space provided, write the correct form (or *C* if correct) and the number of the Handbook principle illustrated. When you finish, compare your responses with those provided on page 505. If your responses differ, carefully study again the principles in parentheses.

Example: Our inventory of raw materials <u>were</u> presented as collateral for a short-term loan. was_____ (1.10c)

1. Located across town is a research institute and our product-testing facility. _____
2. Can you tell me whether a current list with all customers' names and addresses have been sent to marketing? _____

3. The credit union, along with 20 other large national banks, offer a variety of savings plans.

4. Neither the plans that this bank offers nor the service just rendered by the teller are impressive.

5. Locating a bank and selecting a savings/chequing plan often require considerable research and study.

6. The budget analyst wants to know whether the Equipment Committee are ready to recommend a printer.

7. Either of the printers that the committee selects is acceptable to the budget analyst.

8. If Mr. Tutchone had chose the Maximizer Plus savings plan, his money would have earned maximum interest.

9. Although the applications have laid there for two weeks, they may still be submitted.

10. Nadia acts as if she was the manager.

11. One of the reasons that our Nunavut sales branches have been so costly are the high cost of living.

In the space provided, write the letter of the sentence that illustrates consistency in subject, voice, and mood.

12. (a) If you will read the instructions, the answer can be found.
    (b) If you will read the instructions, you will find the answer.

13. (a) All employees must fill out application forms; only then will you be insured.
    (b) All employees must fill out application forms; only then will they be insured.

14. (a) First, take an inventory of equipment; then, order supplies.
    (b) First, take an inventory of equipment; then, supplies must be ordered.

15. (a) Select a savings plan that suits your needs; deposits may be made immediately.
    (b) Select a savings plan that suits your needs; begin making deposits immediately.

Cumulative Editing Quiz 2

Use proofreading marks (see Appendix B) to correct errors in the following sentences. All errors must be corrected to receive credit for the sentence. Check with your instructor for the answers.

1. Assets and liabilitys is what my partner and myself must investigate.

2. If I was you, I would ask whomever is in charge for their opinion.

3. The faculty agree that it's first concern is educating students.

4. The book and it's cover was printed in Japan.

5. Waiting to see you is a sales representative and a job applicant who you told to drop by.

6. Every employee could have picked up his ballot if he had went to the cafeteria.

7. Your choice of mutual funds and bonds are reduced by this plan and it's restrictions.

8. My uncle and her come to visit my parents and myself last night.

9. According to both editor in chiefs, the tone and wording of all our letters needs revision.

10. The Davis'es, about who the article was written, said they were unconcerned with the up's and down's of the stock market.

Adjectives and Adverbs (1.16–1.17)

Adjectives describe or limit nouns and pronouns. They often answer the questions what kind? how many? or which one? Adverbs describe or limit verbs, adjectives, or other adverbs. They often answer the questions when? how? where? or to what extent?

1.16 Forms. Most adjectives and adverbs have three forms, or degrees: **positive**, **comparative**, and **superlative**.

	Positive	Comparative	Superlative
Adjective:	clear	clearer	clearest
Adverb:	clearly	more clearly	most clearly

Some adjectives and adverbs have irregular forms:

	Positive	Comparative	Superlative
Adjective:	good	better	best
	bad	worse	worst
Adverb:	well	better	best

Adjectives and adverbs composed of two or more syllables are usually compared by the use of *more* and *most*; for example:

The Payroll Department is more efficient than the Shipping Department.

Payroll is the most efficient department in our organization.

1.17 Guidelines for Use

a. Use the comparative degree of the adjective or adverb to compare two persons or things; use the superlative degree to compare three or more:

Of the two letters, which is better (not *best*)?

Of all the plans, we like this one best (not *better*).

b. Do not create a double comparative or superlative by using -er with *more* or -est with *most*:

His explanation couldn't have been clearer (not *more clearer*).

c. A linking verb (*is, are, look, seem, feel, sound, appear,* and so forth) may introduce a word that describes the verb's subject. In this case be certain to use an adjective, not an adverb:

The characters on the monitor look bright (not *brightly*). (Use the adjective *bright* because it follows the linking verb *look* and modifies the noun *characters*. It answers the question *What kind of characters?*)

The company's letter made the customer feel bad (not *badly*). (The adjective *bad* follows the linking verb *feel* and describes the noun *customer*.)

d. Use adverbs, not adjectives, to describe or limit the action of verbs:

The business is running smoothly (not *smooth*). (Use the adverb *smoothly* to describe the action of the verb *is running*. *Smoothly* tells how the business is running.)

Grammar Review

Don't take his remark personally (not *personal*). (The adverb *personally* describes the action of the verb take.)

e. Two or more adjectives that are joined to create a compound modifier before a noun should be hyphenated:

The four-year-old child was tired.

Our agency is planning a coast-to-coast campaign.

Hyphenate a compound modifier following a noun only if your dictionary shows the hyphen(s):

Our speaker is very well-known. (Include the hyphen because most dictionaries do.)

The tired child was four years old. (Omit the hyphens because the expression follows the word it describes, *child*, and because dictionaries do not indicate hyphens.)

f. Keep adjectives and adverbs close to the words that they modify:

She asked for a cup of hot coffee (not a *hot cup of coffee*).

Patty had only two days of vacation left (not *Patty only had two days*).

Students may sit in the first five rows (not *in the five first rows*).

He has saved almost enough money for the trip (not *He has almost saved*).

g. Don't confuse the adverb *there* with the possessive pronoun *their* or the contraction *they're*:

Put the documents there. (The adverb *there* means "at that place or at that point.")

There are two reasons for the change. (The adverb *there* is used as filler preceding a linking verb.)

We already have their specifications. (The possessive pronoun *their* shows ownership.)

They're coming to inspect today. (The contraction *they're* is a shortened form of *they are*.)

Review Exercise E—Adjectives and Adverbs

In the space provided for each item, write *a*, *b*, or *c* to complete the statement accurately. If two sentences are shown, select (a) or (b) to indicate the one expressed more effectively. When you finish, compare your responses with those provided. For each item on which you need review, consult the numbered principle shown in parentheses.

1. After the interview, Kyoko looked (a) calm, (b) calmly.
2. If you had been more (a) careful, (b) carefuler, the box might not have broken.
3. Because a new manager was appointed, the advertising campaign is running very (a) smooth, (b) smoothly.
4. To avoid a (a) face to face, (b) face-to-face confrontation, she wrote a letter.
5. Bayani completed the employment test (a) satisfactorily, (b) satisfactory.
6. I felt (a) bad, (b) badly that he was not promoted.
7. Which is the (a) more, (b) most dependable of the two models?
8. Can you determine exactly what (a) there, (b) their, (c) they're company wants us to do?
9. Of all the copiers we tested, this one is the (a) easier, (b) easiest to operate.

10. (a) Mr. Aldron almost was ready to accept the offer.   _____
    (b) Mr. Aldron was almost ready to accept the offer.
11. (a) We only thought that it would take two hours for the test.   _____
    (b) We thought that it would take only two hours for the test.
12. (a) Please bring me a glass of cold water.   _____
    (b) Please bring me a cold glass of water.
13. (a) The committee decided to retain the last ten tickets.   _____
    (b) The committee decided to retain the ten last tickets.
14. New owners will receive a (a) 60-day, (b) 60 day trial period.   _____
15. The time passed (a) quicker, (b) more quickly than we expected.   _____
16. We offer a (a) money back, (b) money-back guarantee.   _____
17. Today the financial news is (a) worse, (b) worst than yesterday.   _____
18. Please don't take his comments (a) personal, (b) personally.   _____
19. You must check the document (a) page by page, (b) page-by-page.   _____
20. (a) We try to file only necessary paperwork.   _____
    (b) We only try to file necessary paperwork.

---

1. a (1.17c) 3. b (1.17d) 5. a (1.17d) 7. a (1.17a) 9. b (1.17a) 11. b (1.17f) 13. a (1.17f)
15. b (1.17d) 17. a (1.17a) 19. a (1.17e)

Grammar/Mechanics Checkup—4

Adjectives and Adverbs

Review Sections 1.16 and 1.17 above. Then study each of the following statements. Underline any inappropriate forms. In the space provided, write the correct form (or C if correct) and the number of the Handbook principle illustrated. You may need to consult your dictionary for current practice regarding some compound adjectives. When you finish, compare your responses with those provided on page 505. If your answers differ, carefully study again the principles in parentheses.

live-and-let-live
(1.17e)

Example: He was one of those individuals with a live and let live attitude.

1. Most of our long time customers have credit card accounts.   _____
2. Many subscribers considered the $50 per year charge to be a bargain.   _____
3. Other subscribers complained that $50 per year was exorbitant.   _____
4. The Internet supplied the answer so quick that we were all amazed.   _____
5. He only had $5 in his pocket.   _____
6. Some experts predict that double digit inflation may return.   _____
7. Jeremy found a once in a lifetime opportunity.   _____
8. Although the car was four years old, it was in good condition.   _____
9. Of the two colours, which is best for a Web background?   _____
10. Professor Candace Carbone is well known in her field.   _____
11. Channel 12 presents up to the minute news broadcasts.   _____
12. Lower tax brackets would lessen the after tax yield of some bonds.   _____
13. The conclusion drawn from the statistics couldn't have been more clearer.   _____
14. This new investment fund has a better than fifty fifty chance of outperforming the older fund. _____
15. If you feel badly about the transaction, contact your portfolio manager.   _____

Prepositions (1.18)

Prepositions are connecting words that join nouns or pronouns to other words in a sentence. The words *about, at, from, in,* and *to* are examples of prepositions.

1.18 Guidelines for Use

a. Include necessary prepositions:

What type of software do you need? (Not *What type software*.)

I graduated from high school two years ago. (Not *I graduated high school*.)

b. Omit unnecessary prepositions:

Where is the meeting? (Not *Where is the meeting at?*)

Both printers work well. (Not *Both of the printers*.)

Where are you going? (Not *Where are you going to?*)

c. Avoid the overuse of prepositional phrases:

Weak: We have received your application for credit at our branch in the Halifax area.
Improved: We have received your credit application at our Halifax office.

d. Repeat the preposition before the second of two related elements:

Applicants use the résumé effectively by summarizing their most important experiences and by relating their education to the jobs sought.

e. Include the second preposition when two prepositions modify a single object:

George's appreciation of and aptitude for computers led to a promising career.

Conjunctions (1.19)

Conjunctions connect words, phrases, and clauses. They act as signals, indicating when a thought is being added, contrasted, or altered. Coordinate conjunctions (such as *and, or, but*) and other words that act as connectors (such as *however, therefore, when, as*) tell the reader or listener in what direction a thought is heading. They're like road signs signalling what's ahead.

1.19 Guidelines for Use

a. Use coordinating conjunctions to connect only sentence elements that are parallel or balanced.

Weak: His report was correct and written in a concise manner.
Improved: His report was correct and concise.

Weak: Management has the capacity to increase fraud, or reduction can be achieved through the policies it adopts.
Improved: Management has the capacity to increase or reduce fraud through the policies it adopts.

b. Do not use the word *like* as a conjunction:

It seems as if (not *like*) this day will never end.

c. Avoid using *when* or *where* inappropriately. A common writing fault occurs in sentences with clauses introduced by *is when* and *is where*. Written English ordinarily requires a noun (or a group of words functioning as a noun) following the linking verb *is*. Instead of acting as conjunctions in these constructions, the words *where* and *when* function as adverbs, creating faulty grammatical equations (adverbs cannot complete equations set up by linking verbs). To avoid the problem, revise the sentence, eliminating *is when* or *is where*.

Weak: A bullish market is when prices are rising in the stock market.
Improved: A bullish market is created when prices are rising in the stock market.

Weak: A flowchart is when you make a diagram showing the step-by-step progression of a procedure.
Improved: A flowchart is a diagram showing the step-by-step progression of a procedure.

Weak: Word processing is where you use a computer and software to write.
Improved: Word processing involves the use of a computer and software to write.

A similar faulty construction occurs in the expression *I hate when*. English requires nouns, noun clauses, or pronouns to act as objects of verbs, not adverbs.

Weak: I hate when we're asked to work overtime.
Improved: I hate it when we're asked to work overtime.
Improved: I hate being asked to work overtime.

d. Don't confuse the adverb *then* with the conjunction *than*. *Then* means "at that time"; *than* indicates the second element in a comparison:

We would rather remodel than (not *then*) move.

First, the equipment is turned on; then (not *than*) the program is loaded.

Review Exercise F—Prepositions and Conjunctions

In the space provided for each item, write *a* or *b* to indicate the sentence that is expressed more effectively. When you finish, compare your responses with those provided. For each item on which you need review, consult the numbered principle shown in parentheses.

1. (a) Do you know where this shipment is being sent? _____
    (b) Do you know where this shipment is being sent to?
2. (a) She was not aware of nor interested in the company insurance plan. _____
    (b) She was not aware nor interested in the company insurance plan.
3. (a) Mr. Samuels graduated college last June. _____
    (b) Mr. Samuels graduated from college last June.
4. (a) "Flextime" is when employees arrive and depart at varying times. _____
    (b) "Flextime" is a method of scheduling worktime in which employees arrive and depart at varying times.
5. (a) Both employees enjoyed setting their own hours. _____
    (b) Both of the employees enjoyed setting their own hours.
6. (a) I hate when the tape sticks in my VCR. _____
    (b) I hate it when the tape sticks in my VCR.
7. (a) What style of typeface should we use? _____
    (b) What style typeface should we use?
8. (a) Business letters should be concise, correct, and written clearly. _____
    (b) Business letters should be concise, correct, and clear.
9. (a) Mediation in a labour dispute occurs when a neutral person helps union _____
    and management reach an agreement.

Grammar Review

(b) Mediation in a labour dispute is where a neutral person helps union and management reach an agreement.

_____ 10. (a) It looks as if the plant will open in early January.
(b) It looks like the plant will open in early January.

_____ 11. (a) We expect to finish up the work soon.
(b) We expect to finish the work soon.

_____ 12. (a) At the beginning of the program in the fall of the year at the central office, we experienced staffing difficulties.
(b) When the program began last fall, the central office experienced staffing difficulties.

_____ 13. (a) Your client may respond by letter or a telephone call may be made.
(b) Your client may respond by letter or by telephone.

_____ 14. (a) A résumé is when you make a written presentation of your education and experience for a prospective employer.
(b) A résumé is a written presentation of your education and experience for a prospective employer.

_____ 15. (a) Stacy exhibited both an awareness of and talent for developing innovations.
(b) Stacy exhibited both an awareness and talent for developing innovations.

_____ 16. (a) This course is harder then I expected.
(b) This course is harder than I expected.

_____ 17. (a) An ombudsman is an individual hired by management to investigate and resolve employee complaints.
(b) An ombudsman is when management hires an individual to investigate and resolve employee complaints.

_____ 18. (a) I'm uncertain where to take this document to.
(b) I'm uncertain where to take this document.

_____ 19. (a) By including accurate data and by writing clearly, you will produce effective memos.
(b) By including accurate data and writing clearly, you will produce effective memos.

_____ 20. (a) We need computer operators who can load software, monitor networks, and files must be duplicated.
(b) We need computer operators who can load software, monitor networks, and duplicate files.

---

1. a (1.18b) 3. b (1.18a) 5. a (1.18b) 7. a (1.18a) 9. a (1.19c) 11. b (1.18b) 13. b (1.19a) 15. a (1.18e) 17. a (1.19c) 19. a (1.18d)

Grammar/Mechanics Checkup—5

Prepositions and Conjunctions

Review Sections 1.18 and 1.19 above. Then study each of the following statements. Write *a* or *b* to indicate the sentence in which the idea is expressed more effectively. Also record the number of the Handbook principle illustrated. When you finish, compare your responses with those provided on page 505. If your answers differ, carefully study again the principles shown in parentheses.

b_____ **(1.18a)** **Example:** (a) Raoul will graduate college this spring.
(b) Raoul will graduate from college this spring.

_____ 1. (a) DataTech enjoyed greater profits this year then it expected.
(b) DataTech enjoyed greater profits this year than it expected.

2. (a) I hate it when we have to work overtime. _____
   (b) I hate when we have to work overtime.
3. (a) Dr. Simon has a great interest and appreciation for the study of robotics. _____
   (b) Dr. Simon has a great interest in and appreciation for the study of robotics.
4. (a) Gross profit is where you compute the difference between total sales and _____
   the cost of goods sold.
   (b) Gross profit is computed by finding the difference between total sales and the cost of goods sold.
5. (a) We advertise to increase the frequency of product use, to introduce com- _____
   plementary products, and to enhance our corporate image.
   (b) We advertise to have our products used more often, when we have com-
   plementary products to introduce, and we are interested in making our corporation look better to the public.
6. (a) What type printer do you prefer? _____
   (b) What type of printer do you prefer?
7. (a) Where are you going to? _____
   (b) Where are you going?
8. (a) The sale of our Halifax office last year should improve this year's profits. _____
   (b) The sale of our office in Halifax during last year should improve the profits for this year.
9. (a) Do you know where the meeting is at? _____
   (b) Do you know where the meeting is?
10. (a) The cooling-off rule is a provincial government rule that protects con- _____
    sumers from making unwise purchases at home.
    (b) The cooling-off rule is where the provincial government has made a rule that protects consumers from making unwise purchases at home.
11. (a) Meetings can be more meaningful if the agenda is stuck to, the time _____
    frame is followed, and if someone keeps follow-up notes.
    (b) Meetings can be more meaningful if you stick to the agenda, follow the time frame, and keep follow-up notes.
12. (a) They printed the newsletter on yellow paper like we asked them to do. _____
    (b) They printed the newsletter on yellow paper as we asked them to do.
13. (a) A code of ethics is a set of rules indicating appropriate standards of _____
    behaviour.
    (b) A code of ethics is where a set of rules indicates appropriate standards of behaviour.
14. (a) We need an individual with an understanding and serious interest in _____
    black-and-white photography.
    (b) We need an individual with an understanding of and serious interest in black-and-white photography.
15. (a) The most dangerous situation is when employees ignore the safety rules. _____
    (b) The most dangerous situation occurs when employees ignore the safety rules.

Cumulative Editing Quiz 3

Use proofreading marks (see Appendix B) to correct errors in the following sentences. All errors must be corrected to receive credit for the sentence. Check with
your instructor for the answers.

1. If Treena types faster then her, shouldn't Treena be hired?

2. We felt badly that Mark's home was not chose for the tour.

3. Neither the company nor the workers is pleased at how slow the talks seems
   to be progressing.

4. Just between you and I, it's better not to take his remarks personal.

5. After completing there floor by floor inventory, managers will deliver there reports to Mr. Quinn and I.

6. If the telephone was working, Jean and myself could have completed our calls.

7. Powerful software and new hardware allows us to send the newsletter to whomever is currently listed in our database.

8. The thirteen year old girl and her mother was given hot cups of tea after there ordeal.

9. We begun the work two years ago, but personnel and equipment has been especially difficult to obtain.

10. Today's weather is worst then yesterday.

Punctuation Review

Commas 1 (2.01-2.04)

2.01 Series. Commas are used to separate three or more equal elements (words, phrases, or short clauses) in a series. To ensure separation of the last two elements, careful writers always use a comma before the conjunction in a series:

Business letters usually contain a dateline, address, salutation, body, and closing. (This series contains words.)

The job of an ombudsman is to examine employee complaints, resolve disagreements between management and employees, and ensure fair treatment. (This series contains phrases).

Trainees complete basic keyboarding tasks, technicians revise complex documents, and editors proofread completed projects. (This series contains short clauses.)

2.02 Direct Address. Commas are used to set off the names of individuals being addressed:

Your inquiry, Mrs. Johnson, has been referred to me.

We genuinely hope that we may serve you, Mr. Lee.

2.03 Parenthetical Expressions. Skilled writers use parenthetical words, phrases, and clauses to guide the reader from one thought to the next. When these expressions interrupt the flow of a sentence and are unnecessary for its grammatical completeness, they should be set off with commas. Examples of commonly used parenthetical expressions follow:

all things considered	however	needless to say
as a matter of fact	in addition	nevertheless
as a result	incidentally	no doubt
as a rule	in fact	of course
at the same time	in my opinion	on the contrary
consequently	in the first place	on the other hand
for example	in the meantime	therefore
furthermore	moreover	under the circumstances

As a matter of fact, I wrote to you just yesterday. (Phrase used at the beginning of a sentence.)

We will, in the meantime, send you a replacement order. (Phrase used in the middle of a sentence.)

Your satisfaction is our first concern, needless to say. (Phrase used at the end of a sentence.)

Do not use commas if the expression is necessary for the completeness of the sentence:

Tamara had no doubt that she would finish the report. (Omit commas because the expression is necessary for the completeness of the sentence.)

2.04 Dates, Addresses, and Geographical Items. When dates, addresses, and geographical items contain more than one element, the second and succeeding elements are normally set off by commas.

a. Dates:

The conference was held February 2 at our home office. (No comma is needed for one element.)

The conference was held February 2, 2001, at our home office. (Two commas set off the second element.)

The conference was held Tuesday, February 2, 2001, at our home office. (Commas set off the second and third elements.)

In February 2001 the conference was held. (This alternate style omitting commas is acceptable if only the month and year are written.)

b. Addresses:

The letter addressed to Mr. Jim W. Ellman, 600 Novella St., Red Deer, AB T0B 2P3, should be sent today. (Commas are used between all elements except the province and postal code, which in this special instance are considered a single unit.)

c. Geographical items:

She moved from Windsor, Ontario, to Truro, Nova Scotia. (Commas set off the province—unless it appears at the end of the sentence, in which case only one comma is used.)

In separating cities from provinces or territories and days from years, many writers remember the initial comma but forget the final one, as in the examples that follow:

The package from Edmonton, Alberta{,} was lost.

We opened June 1, 1995{,} and have grown steadily since.

Review Exercise G—Commas 1

Insert necessary commas in the following sentences. In the space provided write the number of commas that you add. Write *C* if no commas are needed. When you finish, compare your responses with those provided. For each item on which you need review, consult the numbered principle shown in parentheses.

1. As a rule we do not provide complimentary tickets. _____
2. You may be certain Mr. Kirchoff that your policy will be issued immediately. _____
3. I have no doubt that your calculations are correct. _____

_____ 4. The safety hazard on the contrary can be greatly reduced if workers wear rubber gloves.

_____ 5. Every accredited TV newscaster radio broadcaster and newspaper reporter had access to the media room.

_____ 6. Deltech's main offices are located in Vancouver British Columbia and Regina Saskatchewan.

_____ 7. The employees who are eligible for promotions are Terry Evelyn Maneesh Rosanna and Yves.

_____ 8. During the warranty period of course you are protected from any parts or service charges.

_____ 9. Many of our customers include architects engineers lawyers and others who are interested in database management programs.

_____ 10. I wonder Ms. Stevens if you would send my letter of recommendation as soon as possible.

_____ 11. The new book explains how to choose appropriate legal protection for ideas trade secrets copyrights patents and restrictive covenants.

_____ 12. The factory is scheduled to be moved to 2250 North Main Street Belleville Ontario L4A 1T2 within two years.

_____ 13. You may however prefer to correspond directly with the manufacturer in Hong Kong.

_____ 14. Are there any alternatives in addition to those that we have already considered?

_____ 15. The rally has been scheduled for Monday January 12 in the football stadium.

_____ 16. A cheque for the full amount will be sent directly to your home Mr. Ivanic.

_____ 17. Goodstone Tire & Rubber for example recalled 400,000 steel-belted radial tires because some tires failed their rigorous tests.

_____ 18. Alex agreed to unlock the office open the mail and check all the equipment in my absence.

_____ 19. In the meantime thank you for whatever assistance you are able to furnish.

_____ 20. Research facilities were moved from Montreal Quebec to Fredericton New Brunswick.

---

1. rule, (2.03) 3. C (2.03) 5. newscaster, radio broadcaster, (2.01) 7. Terry, Evelyn, Vicki, Rosanna, (2.01) 9. architects, engineers, lawyers, (2.01) 11. ideas, trade secrets, copyrights, patents, (2.01) 13. may, however, (2.03) 15. Monday, January 12, (2.04a) 17. Rubber, for example, (2.03) 19. meantime, (2.03)

Grammar/Mechanics Checkup—6

Commas 1

Review Sections 2.01–2.04 above. Then study each of the following statements and insert necessary commas. In the space provided, write the number of commas that you add; write *0* if no commas are needed. Also record the number of the Handbook principle illustrated. When you finish, compare your responses with those on page 505. If your answers differ, carefully study again the principles shown in parentheses.

2_____ (2.01)   **Example:** In this class students learn to write clear and concise business letters⋏ memos⋏and reports.

_____ 1. We do not as a rule allow employees to take time off for dental appointments.

_____ 2. You may be sure Ms. Schwartz that your car will be ready by 4 p.m.

_____ 3. Anyone who is reliable conscientious and honest should be very successful.

4. A conference on sales motivation is scheduled for May 5 at the Plainsview Hotel beginning at 2 p.m. _____

5. As a matter of fact I just called your office this morning. _____

6. We are relocating our distribution centre from Calgary Alberta to La Morenie Quebec. _____

7. In the meantime please continue to send your orders to the regional office. _____

8. The last meeting recorded in the minutes was on February 4 2001 in Windsor. _____

9. Ms. Horne Mr. Hae Mrs. Andorra and Mr. Baker are our new representatives. _____

10. The package mailed to Ms. Leslie Holmes 3430 Larkspur Lane Regina Saskatchewan S5L 2E2 arrived three weeks after it was mailed. _____

11. The manager feels needless to say that the support of all employees is critical. _____

12. Eric was assigned three jobs: checking supplies replacing inventories and distributing delivered goods. _____

13. We will work diligently to retain your business Mr. Fuhai. _____

14. The vice-president feels however that all sales representatives need training. _____

15. The name selected for a product should be right for that product and should emphasize its major attributes.

Commas 2 (2.05–2.09)

2.05 Independent Clauses. An independent clause is a group of words that has a subject and a verb and that could stand as a complete sentence. When two such clauses are joined by *and, or, nor,* or *but,* use a comma before the conjunction:

We can ship your merchandise July 12, but we must have your payment first.

Net income before taxes is calculated, and this total is then combined with income from operations.

Notice that each independent clause in the preceding two examples could stand alone as a complete sentence. Do not use a comma unless each group of words is a complete thought (that is, has its own subject and verb).

Net income before taxes is calculated and is then combined with income from operations. (No comma is needed because no subject follows *and*.)

2.06 Dependent Clauses. Dependent clauses do not make sense by themselves; for their meaning they depend on independent clauses.

a. *Introductory clauses.* When a dependent clause precedes an independent clause, it is followed by a comma. Such clauses are often introduced by *when, if,* and *as*:

When your request came, we responded immediately.

As I mentioned earlier, Sandra James is the manager.

b. *Terminal clauses.* If a dependent clause falls at the end of a sentence, use a comma only if the dependent clause is an afterthought:

The meeting has been rescheduled for October 23, if this date meets with your approval. (Comma used because dependent clause is an afterthought.)

We responded immediately when we received your request. (No comma is needed.)

c. *Essential versus nonessential clauses.* If a dependent clause provides information that is unneeded for the grammatical completeness of a sentence, use commas to set it off. In determining whether such a clause is essential or

Punctuation Review

nonessential, ask yourself whether the reader needs the information contained in the clause to identify the word it explains:

Our district sales manager, who just returned from a trip to our Prairie region office, prepared this report. (This construction assumes that there is only one district sales manager. Since the sales manager is clearly identified, the dependent clause is not essential and requires commas.)

The salesperson who just returned from a trip to our Prairie region office prepared this report. (The dependent clause in this sentence is necessary to identify which salesperson prepared the report. Therefore, use no commas.)

The position of assistant sales manager, which we discussed with you last week, is still open. (Careful writers use *which* to introduce nonessential clauses. Commas are also necessary.)

The position that we discussed with you last week is still open. (Careful writers use *that* to introduce essential clauses. No commas are used.)

2.07 Phrases. A phrase is a group of related words that lacks both a subject and a verb. A phrase that precedes a main clause is followed by a comma only if the phrase contains a verb form or has five or more words:

Beginning November 1, Mutual Trust will offer two new combination chequing/savings plans. (A comma follows this introductory phrase because the phrase contains the verb form *Beginning*.)

To promote their plan, we will conduct an extensive direct mail advertising campaign. (A comma follows this introductory phrase because the phrase contains the verb form *To promote*.)

In a period of only one year, we were able to improve our market share by 30 percent. (A comma follows the introductory phrase—actually two prepositional phrases—because its total length exceeds five words.)

In 1999 our organization installed a multi-user system that could transfer programs easily. (No comma needed after the short introductory phrase.)

2.08 Two or More Adjectives. Use a comma to separate two or more adjectives that equally describe a noun. A good way to test the need for a comma is this: mentally insert the word *and* between the adjectives. If the resulting phrase sounds natural, a comma is used to show the omission of *and*:

We're looking for a versatile, bug-free operating system. (Use a comma to separate *versatile* and *bug-free* because they independently describe *operating system*. *And* has been omitted.)

Our experienced, courteous staff is ready to serve you. (Use a comma to separate *experienced* and *courteous* because they independently describe *staff*. *And* has been omitted.)

It was difficult to refuse the sincere young telephone caller. (No commas are needed between *sincere* and *young* because *and* has not been omitted.)

2.09 Appositives. Words that rename or explain preceding nouns or pronouns are called appositives. An appositive that provides information not essential to the identification of the word it describes should be set off by commas:

Rozmin Kamani, the project director for Sperling's, worked with our architect. (The appositive, *the project director for Sperling's*, adds nonessential information. Commas set it off.)

Review Exercise H—Commas 2

Insert only necessary commas in the following sentences. In the space provided, indicate the number of commas that you add for each sentence. If a sentence requires no commas, write C. When you finish, compare your responses with those provided. For each item on which you need review, consult the numbered principle shown in parentheses.

1. A corporation must be registered in the province in which it does business and it must operate within the laws of that province. _____

2. The manager made a point-by-point explanation of the distribution dilemma and then presented his plan to solve the problem. _____

3. If you will study the cost analysis you will see that our company offers the best system at the lowest price. _____

4. Molly Epperson who amassed the greatest number of sales points was awarded the bonus trip to Hawaii. _____

5. The salesperson who amasses the greatest number of sales points will be awarded the bonus trip to Hawaii. _____

6. To promote goodwill and to generate international trade we are opening offices in the Far East and in Europe. _____

7. On the basis of these findings I recommend that we retain Raine Jada as our counsel. _____

8. Mary Lam is a dedicated hard-working employee for our company. _____

9. The bright young student who worked for us last summer will be able to return this summer. _____

10. When you return the completed form we will be able to process your application. _____

11. We will be able to process your application when you return the completed form. _____

12. The employees who have been with us over ten years automatically receive additional insurance benefits. _____

13. Knowing that you wanted this merchandise immediately I took the liberty of sending it by Express Parcel Services. _____

14. The central processing unit requires no scheduled maintenance and has a self-test function for reliable performance. _____

15. International competition nearly ruined the Canadian shoe industry but the textile industry remains strong. _____

16. Joyce D'Agostino our newly promoted office manager has made a number of worthwhile suggestions. _____

17. For the benefit of employees recently hired we are offering a two-hour seminar regarding employee benefit programs. _____

18. Please bring your suggestions and those of Mr. Maisonneuve when you attend our meeting next month. _____

19. The meeting has been rescheduled for September 30 if this date meets with your approval. _____

20. Some of the problems that you outline in your recent memo could be rectified through more stringent purchasing procedures. _____

---

1. business, (2.05) 3. analysis, (2.06a) 5. C (2.06c) 7. findings, (2.07) 9. C (2.08) 11. C (2.06b) 13. immediately, (2.07) 15. industry, (2.05) 17. hired, (2.07) 19. September 30, (2.06b)

Commas 2

Review Sections 2.05–2.09 above. Then study each of the following statements and insert necessary commas. In the space provided write the number of commas that you add; write *0* if no commas are needed. Also record the number of the Handbook principle(s) illustrated. When you finish, compare your responses with those provided on page 505. If your answers differ, carefully study again the principles shown in parentheses.

1   **2.06a**   **Example:** When businesses encounter financial problems⌄they often reduce their administrative staffs.

1. As stated in the warranty this printer is guaranteed for one year.
2. Today's profits come from products currently on the market and tomorrow's profits come from products currently on the drawing boards.
3. Companies introduce new products in one part of the country and then watch how the product sells in that area.
4. One large automobile manufacturer which must remain nameless recognizes that buyer perception is behind the success of any new product.
5. The imaginative promising agency opened its offices April 22 in Cambridge.
6. The sales associate who earns the highest number of recognition points this year will be honoured with a bonus vacation trip.
7. Ian Sims our sales manager in the North Bay area will present the new sales campaign at the June meeting.
8. Our new product has many attributes that should make it appealing to buyers but it also has one significant drawback.
9. Although they have different technical characteristics and vary considerably in price and quality two or more of a firm's products may be perceived by shoppers as almost the same.
10. To motivate prospective buyers we are offering a cash rebate of $25.

Review of Commas 1 and 2

11. When you receive the application please fill it out and return it before Monday January 3.
12. On the other hand we are very interested in hiring hard-working conscientious individuals.
13. In March we expect to open a new branch in Bragg Creek which is an area of considerable growth.
14. As we discussed on the telephone the ceremony is scheduled for Thursday June 9 at 3 p.m.
15. Dr. Adams teaches the morning classes and Ms. Miori is responsible for evening sections.

Commas 3 (2.10–2.15)

2.10 Degrees and Abbreviations. Degrees following individuals' names are set off by commas. Abbreviations such as *Jr.* and *Sr.* are also set off by commas unless the individual referred to prefers to omit the commas:

Anne G. Turner, M.B.A., joined the firm.

Michael Migliano, Jr., and Michael Migliano, Sr., work as a team.

Anthony A. Gensler Jr. wrote the report. (The individual referred to prefers to omit commas.)

The abbreviations *Inc.* and *Ltd.* are set off by commas only if a company's legal name has a comma just before this kind of abbreviation. To determine a company's practice, consult its stationery or a directory listing:

Firestone and Blythe, Inc., is based in Canada. (Notice that two commas are used.)

Computers Inc. is extending its franchise system. (The company's legal name does not include a comma before *Inc.*)

2.11 Omitted Words. A comma is used to show the omission of words that are understood:

On Monday we received 15 applications; on Friday, only 3. (Comma shows the omission of *we received*.)

2.12 Contrasting Statements. Commas are used to set off contrasting or opposing expressions. These expressions are often introduced by such words as *not, never, but,* and *yet*:

The consultant recommended tape storage, not floppy-disk storage, for our operations.

Our budget for the year is reduced, yet adequate.

The greater the effort, the greater the reward.

If increased emphasis is desired, use dashes instead of commas, as in *Only the sum of $100—not $1000—was paid on this account.*

2.13 Clarity. Commas are used to separate words repeated for emphasis. Commas are also used to separate words that may be misread if not separated:

The building is a long, long way from completion.

Whatever is, is right.

No matter what, you know we support you.

2.14 Quotations and Appended Questions
  a. A comma is used to separate a short quotation from the rest of a sentence. If the quotation is divided into two parts, two commas are used:

    The manager asked, "Shouldn't the managers control the specialists?"

    "Not if the specialists," replied Xiang, "have unique information."

  b. A comma is used to separate a question appended (added) to a statement:

    You will confirm the shipment, won't you?

2.15 Comma Overuse. Do not use commas needlessly. For example, commas should not be inserted merely because you might drop your voice if you were speaking the sentence:

One of the reasons for expanding our operations in the Atlantic region is{,} that we anticipate increased sales in that area. (Do not insert a needless comma before a clause.)

Punctuation Review

I am looking for an article entitled{,} "State-of-the-Art Communications." (Do not insert a needless comma after the word *entitled*.)

A number of food and nonfood items are carried in convenience stores such as{,} 7-Eleven and Stop-N-Go. (Do not insert a needless comma after *such as*.)

We have{,} at this time{,} an adequate supply of parts. (Do not insert needless commas around prepositional phrases.)

Review Exercise I—Commas 3

Insert only necessary commas in the following sentences. Remove unnecessary commas with the delete sign (✐). In the space provided, indicate the number of commas inserted or deleted in each sentence. If a sentence requires no changes, write C. When you finish, compare your responses with those provided. For each item on which you need review, consult the numbered principle shown in parentheses.

1. We expected Charles Bedford not Krystina Rudko to conduct the audit.
2. Brian said "We simply must have a bigger budget to start this project."
3. "We simply must have" said Brian "a bigger budget to start this project."
4. In August customers opened at least 50 new accounts; in September, only about 20.
5. You returned the merchandise last month didn't you?
6. In short employees will now be expected to contribute more to their own retirement funds.
7. The better our advertising and recruiting the stronger our personnel pool will be.
8. Mrs. Delgado investigated selling her shares not her real estate to raise the necessary cash.
9. "On the contrary" said Ms. Mercer "we will continue our present marketing strategies."
10. Our company will expand into surprising new areas such as, women's apparel and fast foods.
11. What we need is more not fewer suggestions for improvement.
12. Randall Clark B. Comm. and Jonathon Georges M.B.A. joined the firm.
13. "Canada is now entering" said CEO Saunders "the Knowledge Age."
14. One of the reasons that we are inquiring about the publisher of the software is, that we are concerned about whether that publisher will be in the market five years from now.
15. The talk by D. A. Spindler Ph.D. was particularly difficult to follow because of his technical and abstract vocabulary.
16. The month before a similar disruption occurred in distribution.
17. We are very fortunate to have, at our disposal, the services of excellent professionals.
18. No matter what you can count on us for support.
19. Mary Sandoval was named legislative counsel; Jacy Freeman executive adviser.
20. The data you are seeking can be found in an article entitled, "The Fastest Growing Game in Computers."

1. Bedford, Rudko, (2.12) 3. have," said Brian, (2.14a) 5. month, (2.14b) 7. recruiting, (2.12) 9. contrary," Mercer, (2.14a) 11. more, not fewer, (2.12) 13. entering," Saunders, (2.14a) 15. Spindler, Ph.D., (2.10) 17. have at our disposal (2.15) 19. Freeman, (2.11)

Commas 3

Review Sections 2.10–2.15 above. Then study each of the following statements and insert necessary commas. In the space provided write the number of commas that you add; write *0* if no commas are needed. Also record the number of the Handbook principle(s) illustrated. When you finish, compare your responses with those provided on page 505. If your answers differ, carefully study the principles again shown in parentheses.

Example: It was Lucia Bosano,not Melinda Ho,who was given the Kirkland account.   <u>2</u>   (2.12)

1. "The choice of a good name" said President Etienne "cannot be overestimated." _____
2. Hanna H. Cox Ph.D. and Katherine Meridian M.B.A. were hired as consultants. _____
3. Their August 15 order was shipped on Monday wasn't it? _____
4. The Web is most useful in providing customer service such as on-line catalogue information and verification of shipping dates. _____
5. The bigger the investment the greater the profit. _____

Review Commas 1, 2, 3

6. As you requested your order for cartridges file folders and copy paper will be sent immediately. _____
7. We think however that you should re-examine your Web site and that you should consider redesigning its navigation system. _____
8. Within the next eight-week period we hope to hire Mina Vidal who is currently CEO of a small consulting firm. _____
9. Our convention will attract more participants if it is held in a resort location such as Collingwood the Laurentians or Banff. _____
10. If everyone who applied for the position were interviewed we would be overwhelmed. _____
11. In the past ten years we have employed over 30 well-qualified individuals many of whom have selected banking as their career. _____
12. Kimberly Johansson who spoke to our class last week is the author of a book entitled *Writing Winning Résumés.* _____
13. A recent study of productivity that was conducted by authoritative researchers revealed that Canadian workers are more productive than workers in Europe or Japan. _____
14. The report concluded that Canada's secret productivity weapon was not bigger companies more robots or even brainier managers. _____
15. As a matter of fact the report said that Canada's productivity resulted from the rigours of unprotected hands-off competition. _____

Cumulative Editing Quiz 4

Use proofreading marks (see Appendix B) to correct errors and omissions in the following sentences. All errors must be corrected to receive credit for the sentence. Check with your instructor for the answers.

1. Business documents must be written clear, to ensure that readers comprehend the message quick.

2. Needless to say the safety of our employees have always been most important to the president and I.

3. Agriculture Canada which provide disaster loans are setting up an office in Miami Manitoba.

4. Many entrepreneurs who want to expand there markets, have choosen to advertise heavy.

5. Our arbitration committee have unanimously agreed on a compromise package but management have been slow to respond.

6. Although the business was founded in the 1970's its real expansion took place in the 1990s.

7. According to the contract either the dealer or the distributor are responsible for repair of the product.

8. Next June, Lamont and Jones, Inc., are moving their headquarters to Calgary Alberta.

9. Our company is looking for intelligent, articulate, young, people who has a desire to grow with an expanding organization.

10. As you are aware each member of the jury were asked to avoid talking about the case.

Semicolons (2.16)

2.16 Independent Clauses, Series, Introductory Expressions

a. *Independent clauses with conjunctive adverbs.* Use a semicolon before a conjunctive adverb that separates two independent clauses. Some of the most common conjunctive adverbs are *therefore, consequently, however,* and *moreover*:

Business letters should sound conversational; therefore, familiar words and contractions are often used.

The bank closes its doors at 3 p.m.; however, the ABM is open 24 hours a day.

Notice that the word following a semicolon is not capitalized (unless, of course, that word is a proper noun).

b. *Independent clauses without conjunctive adverbs.* Use a semicolon to separate closely related independent clauses when no conjunctive adverb is used:

Some interest payments are tax deductible; dividend payments are not.

Ambient lighting fills the room; task lighting illuminates each workstation.

Use a semicolon in compound sentences, not in complex sentences:

After one week the paper feeder jammed; we tried different kinds of paper. (Use a semicolon in a compound sentence.)

After one week the paper feeder jammed, although we tried different kinds of paper. (Use a comma in a complex sentence. Do not use a semicolon after *jammed*.)

The semicolon is very effective for joining two closely related thoughts. Don't use it, however, unless the ideas are truly related.

c. *Independent clauses with other commas.* Normally, a comma precedes *and, or,* and *but* when those conjunctions join independent clauses. However, if either clause contains commas, change the comma preceding the conjunction to a semicolon to ensure correct reading:

If you arrive in time, you may be able to purchase a ticket; but ticket sales close promptly at 8 p.m.

Our primary concern is financing; and we have discovered, as you warned us, that money sources are quite scarce.

d. *Series with internal commas.* Use semicolons to separate items in a series when one or more of the items contains internal commas:

Delegates from Brandon, Manitoba; Lethbridge, Alberta; and North Bay, Ontario, attended the conference.

The speakers were Katrina Lang, manager, Riko Enterprises; Henry Holtz, vice-president, Trendex, Inc.; and Margaret Slater, personnel director, West Coast Productions.

e. *Introductory expressions.* Use a semicolon when an introductory expression such as *namely, for instance, that is,* or *for example* introduces a list following an independent clause:

Switching to computerized billing are several local companies; namely, Ryson Electronics, Miller Vending Services, and Blaque Advertising.

The author of a report should consider many sources; for example, books, periodicals, databases, and newspapers.

Colons (2.17–2.19)

2.17 Listed Items

a. *With colon.* Use a colon after a complete thought that introduces a formal list of items. A formal list is often preceded by such words and phrases as *these, thus, the following,* and *as follows.* A colon is also used when words and phrases like these are implied but not stated:

Additional costs in selling a house involve the following: title examination fee, title insurance costs, and closing fee. (Use a colon when a complete thought introduces a formal list.)

Collective bargaining focuses on several key issues: cost-of-living adjustments, fringe benefits, job security, and hours of work. (The introduction of the list is implied in the preceding clause.)

b. *Without colons.* Do not use a colon when the list immediately follows a *to be* verb or a preposition:

The employees who should receive the preliminary plan are James Sachi, Ramona Speers, and Rose Paquet. (No colon is used after the verb *are.*)

We expect to consider equipment for Accounting, Legal Services, and Payroll. (No colon is used after the preposition *for.*)

2.18 Quotations. Use a colon to introduce long one-sentence quotations and quotations of two or more sentences:

Our consultant said: "This system can support up to 32 users. It can be used for decision support, computer-aided design, and software development operations at the same time."

2.19 Salutations. Use a colon after the salutation of a business letter:

Gentlemen:

Dear Ms. Tsang:

Dear Odin:

Review Exercise J—Semicolons, Colons

In the following sentences, add semicolons, colons, and necessary commas. For each sentence indicate the number of punctuation marks that you add. If a sentence requires no punctuation, write C. When you finish, compare your responses with those provided. For each item on which you need review, consult the numbered principle shown in parentheses.

_____ 1. A strike in Montreal has delayed shipments of parts consequently our production has fallen behind schedule.

_____ 2. Our branch in Burnaby specializes in industrial real estate our branch in Island Lakes concentrates on residential real estate.

_____ 3. The sedan version of the automobile is available in these colours Olympic red metallic silver and Aztec gold.

_____ 4. If I can assist the new manager please call me however I will be gone from June 10 through June 15.

_____ 5. The individuals who should receive copies of this announcement are Jeff Doogan Alicia Green and Kim Wong.

_____ 6. We would hope of course to send personal letters to all prospective buyers but we have not yet decided just how to do this.

_____ 7. Many of our potential customers are in southern British Columbia therefore our promotional effort will be strongest in that area.

_____ 8. Since the first of the year we have received inquiries from one lawyer two accountants and one information systems analyst.

_____ 9. Three dates have been reserved for initial interviews January 15 February 1 and February 12.

_____ 10. Several staff members are near the top of their salary ranges and we must reclassify their jobs.

_____ 11. Several staff members are near the top of their salary ranges we must reclassify their jobs.

_____ 12. Several staff members are near the top of their salary ranges therefore we must reclassify their jobs.

_____ 13. If you open an account within two weeks you will receive a free cookbook moreover your first 500 cheques will be printed at no cost to you.

_____ 14. Monthly reports from the following departments are missing Legal Department Human Resources Department and Engineering Department.

_____ 15. Monthly reports are missing from the Legal Department Human Resources Department and Engineering Department.

_____ 16. Since you became director of that division sales have tripled therefore I am recommending you for a bonus.

_____ 17. The convention committee is considering Dartmouth Nova Scotia Moncton New Brunswick and Charlottetown Prince Edward Island.

_____ 18. Several large companies allow employees access to their personnel files namely Nortel Corel Corp. and Ford Canada.

_____ 19. Sylvie first asked about salary next she inquired about benefits.

_____ 20. Sylvie first asked about the salary and she next inquired about benefits.

1. parts; consequently, (2.16a) 3. colours: Olympic red, metallic silver, (2.01, 2.17a)
5. Doogan, Alicia Green, (2.01, 2.17b) 7. British Columbia; therefore, (2.16a)

9. interviews: January 15, February 1, (2.01, 2.17a) 11. ranges; (2.16b) 13. weeks, cookbook; moreover, (206a, 2.16a) 15. Department, Human Resources Department, (2.01, 2.17b) 17. Dartmouth, Nova Scotia; Moncton, New Brunswick; Charlottetown, (2.16d) 19. salary; (2.16b)

Grammar/Mechanics Checkup—9

Semicolons and Colons

Review Sections 2.16–2.19 above. Then study each of the following statements. Insert any necessary punctuation. Use the delete symbol to omit unnecessary punctuation. In the space provided indicate the number of changes you made and record the number of the Handbook principle(s) illustrated. (When you replace one punctuation mark with another, count it as one change.) If you make no changes, write *0*. This exercise concentrates on semicolon and colon use, but you will also be responsible for correct comma use. When you finish, compare your responses with those shown on page 505. If your responses differ, carefully study again the specific principles shown in parentheses.

Example: The job of Mr. Wellworth is to make sure that his company has enough cash to meet its obligations, moreover, he is responsible for locating credit when needed.   2 _____ (2.16a)

1. Short-term financing refers to a period of under one year long-term financing on the other hand refers to a period of ten years or more. _____

2. Cash resulting from product sales does not arrive until December therefore our cash flow becomes critical in October and November. _____

3. We must negotiate short-term financing during the following months September October and November. _____

4. Large corporations that offer huge amounts of trade credit are, automobile dealers, utility companys, oil companys, and computer hardware manufacturers. _____

5. Although some firms rarely, if ever, need to borrow short-term money many businesses find that they require significant credit to pay for current production and sales costs. _____

6. A grocery store probably requires no short-term credit, a greeting card manufacturer however typically would need considerable short-term credit. _____

7. We offer three basic types of credit loans promissory notes and floating lines of credit. _____

8. Speakers at the conference on credit include the following businesspeople Mary Ann Mahan financial manager Ritchie Industries Terry L. Buchanan comptroller International Bank and Edmée Cavalier operations Business Bank of Canada. _____

9. The prime interest rate is set by the Bank of Canada and this rate goes up or down as the cost of money to the bank itself fluctuates. _____

10. Most banks are in business to lend money to commercial customers for example retailers service companies manufacturers and construction firms. _____

11. Avionics, Inc. which is a small electronics firm with a solid credit rating recently applied for a loan but the Federal Business Development Bank refused the loan application because the risk was too great. _____

12. When Avionics, Inc., was refused by Federal Business Development Bank its financial managers submitted applications to the following Worldwide Investments, Dominion Securities, and Mid Mountain Group. _____

13. The cost of financing capital investments at the present time is very high therefore Avionics' managers may elect to postpone certain expansion projects. _____

14. If interest rates reach as high as 18 percent the cost of borrowing becomes prohibitive and many businesses are forced to reconsider or abandon projects that require financing.

15. Several investors decided to pool their resources then they could find attractive investments.

Apostrophes (2.20–2.22)

2.20 Basic Rule. The apostrophe is used to show ownership, origin, authorship, or measurement.

Ownership:	We are looking for Dmitri's keys.
Origin:	At the president's suggestion, we doubled the order.
Authorship:	The accountant's annual report was questioned.
Measurement:	In two years' time we expect to reach our goal.

a. *Ownership words not ending in* s. To place the apostrophe correctly, you must first determine whether the ownership word ends in an *s* sound. If it does not, add an apostrophe and an *s* to the ownership word. The following examples show ownership words that do not end in an *s* sound:

the employee's file	(the file of a single employee)
a member's address	(the address of a single member)
a year's time	(the time of a single year)
a month's notice	(notice of a single month)
the company's building	(the building of a single company)

b. *Ownership words ending in* s. If the ownership word does end in an *s* sound, usually add only an apostrophe:

several employees' files	(files of several employees)
ten members' addresses	(addresses of ten members)
five years' time	(time of five years)
several months' notice	(notice of several months)
many companies' buildings	(buildings of many companies)

A few singular nouns that end in *s* are pronounced with an extra syllable when they become possessive. To these words, add *'s*.

my boss's desk
the waitress's table
the actress's costume

Use no apostrophe if a noun is merely plural, not possessive:

All the sales representatives, as well as the secretaries and managers, had their names and telephone numbers listed in the directory.

2.21 Names. The writer may choose either traditional or popular style in making singular names that end in an *s* sound possessive. The traditional style uses the apostrophe plus an *s*, while the popular style uses just the apostrophe. Note that only with singular names ending in an *s* sound does this option exist.

Traditional style	**Popular style**
Russ's computer	Russ' computer
Mr. Jones's car	Mr. Jones' car
Mrs. Morris's desk	Mrs. Morris' desk
Ms. Horowitz's job	Ms. Horowitz' job

The possessive form of plural names is consistent: the *Joneses'* car, the *Horowitzes'* home, the *Morrises'* daughter.

2.22 Gerunds. Use *'s* to make a noun possessive when it precedes a gerund, a verb form used as a noun:

Mr. Smith's smoking prompted a new office policy. (Mr. Smith is possessive because it modifies the gerund *smoking*.)

It was Britta's careful proofreading that revealed the discrepancy.

Review Exercise K—Apostrophes

Insert necessary apostrophes in the following sentences. In the space provided for each sentence, indicate the number of apostrophes that you added. If none were added, write *C*. When you finish, compare your responses with those provided. For each item on which you need review, consult the numbered principle shown in parentheses.

1. Your account should have been credited with six months interest. _____
2. If you go to the third floor, you will find Mr. Londons office. _____
3. All the employees personnel folders must be updated. _____
4. In a little over a year's time, that firm was able to double its sales. _____
5. The Harrises daughter lived in Whitehorse for two years. _____
6. An inventors patent protects his or her patent for several years. _____
7. Both companies headquarters will be moved within the next six months. _____
8. That position requires at least two years experience. _____
9. Some of their assets could be liquidated; therefore, a few of the creditors were satisfied. _____
10. All secretaries workstations were equipped with terminals. _____
11. The package of electronics parts arrived safely despite two weeks delay. _____
12. Many nurses believe that nurses notes are not admissible evidence. _____
13. According to Mr. Cortez latest proposal, all employees would receive an additional holiday. _____
14. Many of our members names and addresses must be checked. _____
15. His supervisor frequently had to correct Jacks financial reports. _____
16. We believe that this firms service is much better than that firms. _____
17. Mr. Schur estimated that he spent a years profits in reorganizing his staff. _____
18. After paying six months rent, we were given a receipt. _____
19. The contract is not valid without Ms. Harris signature. _____
20. It was Mr. Smiths signing of the contract that made us happy. _____

---

1. months' (2.20b) 3. employees' (2.20b) 5. Harrises' (2.21) 7. companies' (2.20b) 9. C (2.20b) 11. weeks' (2.20b) 13. Cortez' [or Cortez's] (2.21) 15. Jack's (2.21) 17. year's (2.20a) 19. Harris' [or Harris's] (2.21)

Grammar/Mechanics Checkup—10

Possessives

Review Sections 2.20–2.22 above. Then study each of the following statements. Underline any inappropriate form. Write a correction in the space provided, and record the number of the Handbook principle(s) illustrated. If a sentence is correct, write *C*. When you finish, compare your responses with those on page 505. If your answers differ, carefully study again the principles shown in parentheses.

years' (2.20b) **Example:** In just two years time, the accountants and managers devised an entirely new system.

_____ 1. Two supervisors said that Mr. Ruskins work was excellent.
_____ 2. In less than a years time, the offices of both lawyers were moved.
_____ 3. None of the employees in our Electronics Department had taken more than two weeks vacation.
_____ 4. All the secretaries agreed that Ms. Lanhams suggestions were practical.
_____ 5. After you obtain your boss approval, send the application to Human Resources.
_____ 6. We tried to sit in our favourite server section, but all her tables were filled.
_____ 7. Despite Kaspar grumbling, his wife selected two bonds and three stocks for her investments.
_____ 8. The apartment owner requires two months rent in advance from all applicants.
_____ 9. Four companies buildings were damaged in the fire.
_____ 10. In one months time we hope to be able to complete all the address files.
_____ 11. One secretaries desk will have to be moved to make way for the computer.
_____ 12. Several sellers permits were issued for two years.
_____ 13. Marks salary was somewhat higher than David.
_____ 14. Latikas job in accounts receivable ends in two months.

Cumulative Editing Quiz 5

Use proofreading marks (see Appendix B) to correct errors and omissions in the following sentences. All errors must be corrected to receive credit for the sentence. Check with your instructor for the answers.

1. The three C's of credit are the following character capacity and capital.

2. We hope that we will not have to sell the property however that may be our only option.

3. As soon as the supervisor and her can check this weeks sales they will place an order.

4. Any of the auditors are authorized to proceed with an independent action however only the CEO can alter the councils directives.

5. Although reluctant technicians sometimes must demonstrate there computer software skills.

6. On April 6 1998 we opened an innovative fully-equipped employee computer centre.

7. A list of maintenance procedures and recommendations are in the owners manual.

8. The Morrises son lived in London Ontario however there daughter lived in Saint John New Brunswick.

9. Employment interviews were held in Winnipeg Manitoba Calgary Alberta and Victoria British Columbia.

10. Mr. Lees determination courage and sincerity could not be denied however his methods was often questioned.

Other Punctuation (2.23-2.29)

2.23 Periods

a. *Ends of sentences.* Use a period at the end of a statement, command, indirect question, or polite request. Although a polite request may have the same structure as a question, it ends with a period:

Corporate legal departments demand precise skills from their workforce. (End a statement with a period.)

Get the latest data by reading current periodicals. (End a command with a period.)

Mr. Rand wondered whether we had sent any follow-up literature. (End an indirect question with a period.)

Would you please re-examine my account and determine the current balance. (A polite request suggests an action rather than a verbal response.)

b. *Abbreviations and initials.* Use periods after initials and after many abbreviations.

R. M. Johnson	c.o.d.	Ms.
M.D.	a.m.	Mr.
Inc.	i.e.	Mrs.

Use just one period when an abbreviation falls at the end of a sentence:

Guests began arriving at 5:30 p.m.

2.24 Question Marks. Direct questions are followed by question marks:

Did you send your proposal to Datatronix, Inc.?

Statements with questions added are punctuated with question marks.

We have completed the proposal, haven't we?

2.25 Exclamation Points. Use an exclamation point after a word, phrase, or clause expressing strong emotion. In business writing, however, exclamation points should be used sparingly:

Incredible! The entire network is down.

2.26 Dashes. The dash (constructed at a keyboard by striking the hyphen key twice in succession) is a legitimate and effective mark of punctuation when used according to accepted conventions. As an emphatic punctuation mark, however, the dash loses effectiveness when overused.

a. *Parenthetical elements.* Within a sentence a parenthetical element is usually set off by commas. If, however, the parenthetical element itself contains internal commas, use dashes (or parentheses) to set it off:

Three top salespeople—Tom Judkins, Morgan Templeton, and Mary Yashimoto—received bonuses.

b. *Sentence interruptions.* Use a dash to show an interruption or abrupt change of thought:

News of the dramatic merger—no one believed it at first—shook the financial world.

Ship the materials Monday—no, we must have them sooner.

Sentences with abrupt changes of thought or with appended afterthoughts can usually be improved through rewriting.

c. ***Summarizing statements.*** Use a dash (not a colon) to separate an introductory list from a summarizing statement:

Sorting, merging, and computing—these are tasks that our data processing programs must perform.

2.27 Parentheses. One means of setting off nonessential sentence elements involves the use of parentheses. Nonessential sentence elements may be punctuated in one of three ways: (1) with commas, to make the lightest possible break in the normal flow of a sentence; (2) with dashes, to emphasize the enclosed material; and (3) with parentheses, to de-emphasize the enclosed material. Parentheses are frequently used to punctuate sentences with interpolated directions, explanations, questions, and references:

The cost analysis (which appears on page 8 of the report) indicates that the copy machine should be leased.

Units are lightweight (approximately 500 g) and come with a leather case and operating instructions.

The IBM laser printer (have you heard about it?) will be demonstrated for us next week.

A parenthetical sentence that is not embedded within another sentence should be capitalized and end-punctuated:

The Model 20 has stronger construction. (You may order a Model 20 brochure by circling 304 on the reader service card.)

2.28 Quotation Marks

a. ***Direct quotations.*** Use double quotation marks to enclose the exact words of a speaker or writer:

"Keep in mind," Mrs. Fontaine said, "that you'll have to justify the cost of automating our office."

The boss said that automation was inevitable. (No quotation marks are needed because the exact words are not quoted.)

b. ***Quotations within quotations.*** Use single quotation marks (apostrophes on the typewriter) to enclose quoted passages within quoted passages:

In her speech, Ms. Deckman remarked, "I believe it was the poet Robert Frost who said, 'All the fun's in how you say a thing.'"

c. ***Short expressions.*** Slang, words used in a special sense, and words following *stamped* or *marked* are often enclosed within quotation marks:

Rafael described the damaged shipment as "gross." (Quotation marks enclose slang.)

Students often have trouble spelling the word "separate." (Quotation marks enclose words used in a special sense.)

Jobs were divided into two categories: most stressful and least stressful. The jobs in the "most stressful" list involved high risk or responsibility. (Quotation marks enclose words used in a special sense.)

The envelope marked "Confidential" was put aside. (Quotation marks enclose words following *marked*.)

In the four preceding sentences, the words enclosed within quotation marks could instead be set in italics, if italics are available.

d. **Definitions**. Double quotation marks are used to enclose definitions. The word or expression being defined should be underscored or set in italics:

The term *penetration pricing* is defined as "the practice of introducing a product to the market at a low price."

e. **Titles**. Use double quotation marks to enclose titles of literary and artistic works, such as magazine and newspaper articles, chapters of books, movies, television shows, poems, lectures, and songs. Names of major publications—such as books, magazines, pamphlets, and newspapers—are set in italics (or underscored) or typed in capital letters.

Particularly helpful was the chapter in Smith's EFFECTIVE WRITING TECHNIQUES entitled "Right Brain, Write Well!"

John's article, "E-Mail Blunders," appeared in the *Toronto Star*; however, we could not locate it in a local library.

f. **Additional considerations**. Periods and commas are always placed inside closing quotation marks. Semicolons and colons, on the other hand, are always placed outside quotation marks:

Mrs. Levesque said, "I could not find the article entitled 'Cell Phone Etiquette.'"

The president asked for "absolute security": all written messages were to be destroyed.

Question marks and exclamation points may go inside or outside closing quotation marks, as determined by the form of the quotation:

Sales Manager Motega said, "Who placed the order?" (The quotation is a question.)

When did the sales manager say, "Who placed the order?" (Both the incorporating sentence and the quotation are questions.)

Did the sales manager say, "Narwinder placed the order"? (The incorporating sentence asks question; the quotation does not.)

"In the future," shouted Bob, "ask me first!" (The quotation is an exclamation.)

2.29 Brackets. Within quotations, square brackets are used by the quoting writer to enclose his or her own inserted remarks. Such remarks may be corrective, illustrative, or explanatory:

June Cardillo said, "CRTC [Canadian Radio-television and Telecommunications Commission] has been one of the most widely criticized agencies of the federal government."

Review Exercise L—Other Punctuation

Insert necessary punctuation in the following sentences. In the space provided for each item, indicate the number of punctuation marks that you added. Count sets of parentheses and dashes as two marks. Emphasis or de-emphasis will be indicated for some parenthetical elements. When you finish, compare your responses with those provided. For each item on which you need review, consult the numbered principle shown in parentheses.

1. Will you please stop payment on my Cheque No. 233
2. (Emphasize.) Your order of October 16 will be on its way you have my word by October 20.
3. Mr Sirakides, Mrs Sylvester, and Miss Sidhu have not yet responded
4. Wanda Penner asked if the order had been sent cod
5. Interviews have been scheduled for 3:15 pm, 4 pm, and 4:45 pm
6. (De-emphasize.) Three knowledgeable individuals the plant manager, the construction engineer, and the construction supervisor all expressed concern about soil settlement.
7. Fantastic The value of our shares just rose 10 points on the stock market exchange
8. The word de facto means existing in fact regardless of the legal situation.
9. (De-emphasize.) Although the appliance now comes in limited colours brown, beige, and ivory, we expect to see new colours available in the next production run.
10. Was it the manager who said "What can't be altered must be endured
11. The stock market went ballistic over the news of the takeover.
12. Because the envelope was marked Personal, we did not open it.
13. Price, service, and reliability these are our prime considerations in equipment selection.
14. The letter carrier said Would you believe that this package was marked Fragile
15. (Emphasize.) Three branch managers Kelly Cardinal, Stan Meyers, and Ivan Sergo will be promoted.
16. (De-emphasize.) The difference between portable and transportable computers see Figure 4 for weight comparisons may be considerable.
17. All the folders marked Current Files should be sent to Human Resources.
18. I am trying to find the edition of Canadian Business that carried an article entitled The Future Without Shock.
19. Martha Simon MD and Gail Nemire RN were hired by Healthnet, Inc
20. The computer salesperson said This innovative, state-of-the-art laptop sells for a fraction of the cost of big-name computers.

1. 233. (2.23a) 3. Mr. Ms. responded. (2.23a, 2.23b) 5. p.m. p.m. p.m. (2.23b) 7. Fantastic! exchange! (2.25) 9. (brown ivory) (2.27) 11. "ballistic" (2.28c) 13. reliability— (2.26c) 15. managers—Sergo—(2.26a) 17. "Current Files" (2.28c) 19. Simon, M.D., Nemire, R.N., Inc. (2.23b)

Grammar/Mechanics Checkup—11

Other Punctuation

Although this checkup concentrates on Sections 2.23–2.29 above, you may also refer to other punctuation principles. Insert any necessary punctuation. In the space provided, indicate the number of changes you make and record the number of the Handbook principle(s) illustrated. Count each mark separately; for example, a set of parentheses counts as 2. If you make no changes, write 0. When you finish, compare your responses with those provided on page 506. If your responses differ, carefully study again the specific principles shown in parentheses.

Example: (De-emphasize.) The consumption of cereal products is highest in certain provinces (Manitoba, Saskatchewan, Alberta, and Newfoundland), but this food trend is spreading to other parts of the country.

1. (Emphasize.) The convention planning committee has invited three managers Yu Wong, Frank Behr, and Yvette Sosa to make presentations. _____
2. Would you please Miss Fundy use your computer to recalculate these totals. _____
3. (De-emphasize.) A second set of demographic variables see Figure 13 on page 432 includes nationality, religion, and race. _____
4. Because the word recommendation is frequently misspelled we are adding it to our company style book. _____
5. Recruiting, hiring, and training these are three important functions of a human resources officer. _____
6. The office manager said, Who placed an order for two dozen printer cartridges _____
7. Have any of the research assistants been able to locate the article entitled How Tax Reform Will Affect You _____
8. (Emphasize.) The biggest oil-producing provinces Alberta, Newfoundland, and Ontario are experiencing significant tax cuts. _____
9. Have you sent invitations to Mr Kieran E Manning, Miss Kathy Tanguay, and Ms Petra Bonaventura? _____
10. Dr. Y. W. Yellin wrote the chapter entitled Trading on the Options Market that appeared in a book called Securities Markets. _____
11. James said, "I'll be right over" however he has not appeared yet. _____
12. In business the word liability may be defined as any legal obligation requiring payment in the future. _____
13. Because the work was scheduled to be completed June 10 we found it necessary to hire temporary workers to work June 8 and 9. _____
14. Did any c o d shipments arrive today _____
15. Hooray I have finished this checkup haven't I _____

Grammar/Mechanics Checkup—12

Punctuation Review

Review Sections 1.19 and 2.01–2.29. Study the groups of sentences below. In the space provided write the letter of the one that is correctly punctuated. When you finish, compare your responses with those on page 506. If your responses differ, carefully study again the principles in parentheses.

1. a. Our accounting team makes a point of analyzing your business operations, and getting to know what's working for you and what's not. _____
   b. We are dedicated to understanding your business needs over the long term, and taking an active role when it comes to creating solutions.
   c. We understand that you may be downsizing or moving into new markets, and we want to help you make a seamless transition.
2. a. If you are growing, or connecting to new markets, our team will help you accomplish your goals with minimal interruptions. _____
   b. When you look at our organization chart, you will find the customer at the top.
   c. Although we offer each customer a dedicated customer account team we also provide professional general services.
3. a. The competition is changing; therefore, we have to deliver our products and services more efficiently. _____

    b.   Although delivery systems are changing; the essence of banking remains the same.

    c.   Banks will continue to be available around the corner, and also with the click of a mouse.

_____   4. a.   One of the reasons we are decreasing the number of our ABMs, is that two thirds of the bank's customers depend on customer care representatives for transactions.

    b.   We are looking for an article entitled, "Online Banking."

    c.   Banks are at this time competing with nontraditional rivals that can provide extensive financial services.

_____   5. a.   We care deeply about the environment; but we also care about safety and good customer service.

    b.   The president worked with environmental concerns; the vice-president focused on customer support.

    c.   Our Web site increases our productivity, it also improves customer service.

_____   6. a.   Employees who will be receiving salary increases are: Terri, Mark, Rob, and Géza.

    b.   The following employees are eligible for bonuses: Robin, Olivia, Bill, and Jorge.

    c.   Our consulting firm is proud to offer Web services for: site design, market analysis, e-commerce, and hosting.

_____   7. a.   All secretaries' computers were equipped with Excel.

    b.   Both lawyers statements confused the judge.

    c.   Some members names and addresses must be rekeyed.

_____   8. a.   Our committee considered convention sites in Regina, Saskatchewan, Charlottetown, Prince Edward Island; and Banff, Alberta.

    b.   Alizar was from Humbolt, Saskatchewan; Josh was from The Pas, Manitoba, and Rachel was from Whitehorse, Yukon.

    c.   The following engineers were approved: J. W. Ellis, civil; Dr. Thomas Lu, structural; and W. R. Proudlove, mechanical.

_____   9. a.   The package from Albany, New York was never delivered.

    b.   We have scheduled an inspection tour on Tuesday, March 5, at 4 p.m.

    c.   Send the check to M. E. Williams, 320 Summit Ridge, Elizabethtown, Ontario K6T 1A9 before the last mail pickup.

_____   10. a.   The best plan of action in my opinion, is a straightforward approach.

    b.   Under the circumstances we could not have hoped for better results.

    c.   Our department will, in the meantime, reduce its services.

_____   11. a.   If you demand reliable, competent service, you should come to us.

    b.   We could not resist buying cookies from the enthusiastic, young Girl Guide.

    c.   Our highly trained technicians, with years of experience are always available to evaluate and improve your network environment.

_____   12. a.   We guarantee same-day, not next-day, service.

    b.   Our departmental budget requests are considerably reduced yet adequate.

    c.   The nominating committee selected Todd Shimoyama, not Suzette Chase as its representative.

_____   13. a.   Their wealthy uncle left $1 million to be distributed to Hayden, Carlotta, and Susanna.

    b.   Their wealthy uncle left $1 million to be distributed to Hayden, Carlotta and Susanna.

    c.   Our agency will maintain and upgrade your computers, printers, copiers and fax machines.

_____   14. a.   Beginning June 1, we will service many top vendors, including: Compaq, Hewlett Packard, IBM, Dell and Mita.

b. To promote our new business we are offering a 10 percent discount.

c. In a period of only one month, we gained 150 new customers.

15. a. We specialize in network design, however we also offer troubleshooting _____
and consulting.

b. We realize that downtime is not an option; therefore, you can count on us for reliable, competent service.

c. Our factory-trained and certified technicians perform repair at your location, or in our own repair depot for products under warranty and out of warranty.

Cumulative Editing Quiz 6

Use proofreading marks (see Appendix B) to correct errors and omissions in the following sentences. All errors must be corrected to receive credit for the sentence. Check with your instructor for the answers.

1. Although the envelope was marked Confidential the vice-presidents assistant thought it should be opened.

2. Would you please send my order c.o.d?

3. To be eligible for an apartment you must pay two months rent in advance.

4. We wanted to use Russ computer, but forgot to ask for permission.

5. Wasnt it Jeff Singh not Eileen Lee who requested a 14 day leave.

6. Miss. Judith L. Beam is the employee who the employees council elected as their representative.

7. The Leader Post our local newspaper featured an article entitled The Worlds Most Expensive Memo.

8. As soon as my manager or myself can verify Ricks totals we will call you, in the meantime you must continue to disburse funds.

9. Just inside the entrance, is the receptionists desk and a complete directory of all departments'.

10. Exports from small companys has increased thereby affecting this countrys trade balance positively.

Style and Usage

Capitalization (3.01–3.16)

Capitalization is used to distinguish important words. However, writers are not free to capitalize all words they consider important. Rules or guidelines governing capitalization style have been established through custom and use. Mastering these guidelines will make your writing more readable and more comprehensible.

3.01 Proper Nouns. Capitalize proper nouns, including the specific names of persons, places, schools, streets, parks, buildings, religions, holidays, months, agreements, programs, services, and so forth. Do not capitalize common nouns that make only general references.

Proper Nouns	Common Nouns
Michael DeNiro	a salesperson in electronics
Germany, Japan	major trading partners of Canada

George Brown College	a community college
Assiniboine Park	a park in the city
Phoenix Room, Delta Inn	a meeting room in the hotel
Catholicism, Buddhism	two religions
Canada Day, New Year's Day	two holidays
Priority Post	a special package delivery service
Lions Gate Bridge	a bridge
Consumer Protection Act	a law to protect consumers
Winnipeg Chamber of Commerce	a chamber of commerce
Digby Municipal Airport	a municipal airport

3.02 Proper Adjectives. Capitalize most adjectives that are derived from proper nouns:

Greek symbol	British thermal unit
Roman numeral	Norwegian ship
Xerox copy	Inuit land claims

Do not capitalize the few adjectives that, although originally derived from proper nouns, have become common adjectives through usage. Consult your dictionary when in doubt:

manila folder	diesel engine
india ink	french fries

3.03 Geographic Locations. Capitalize the names of specific places such as cities, states, mountains, valleys, lakes, rivers, oceans, and geographic regions:

Iqaluit	Lake Ontario
Rocky Mountains	Arctic Ocean
Cape Breton Island	James Bay
the East Coast	the Pacific Northwest

3.04 Organization Names. Capitalize the principal words in the names of all business, civic, educational, governmental, labour, military, philanthropic, political, professional, religious, and social organizations:

Inland Steel Company	Board of Directors, Teachers' Credit Union
*The Globe and Mail**	The Rainbow Society
Toronto Stock Exchange Commission	Securities and Exchange
United Way	Psychological Association of Manitoba
Child and Family Services	Mennonite Brethren Bible College

3.05 Academic Courses and Degrees. Capitalize particular academic degrees and course titles. Do not capitalize references to general academic degrees and subject areas:

Professor Bernadette Ordian, Ph.D., will teach Accounting 221 next fall.

Beth Snyder, who holds bachelor's and master's degrees, teaches marketing classes.

René enrolled in classes in history, business English, and management.

3.06 Personal and Business Titles

a. Capitalize personal and business titles when they precede names:

Vice-President Ames	Uncle Edward
Board Chairman Frazier	Councillor Hebert
Member of Parliament Ronald Fontaine	Sales Manager Klein
Professor McLean	Dr. Myra Rosner

*Capitalize *the* only when it is part of the official name of an organization, as printed on the organization's stationery.

b. Capitalize titles in addresses, salutations, and closing lines:

Mr. Juan deSanto
Director of Purchasing
Space Systems, Inc.
Richmond, BC V3L 4A6

Very truly yours,

Clara J. Smith
Supervisor, Marketing

c. Capitalize titles of high government rank or religious office, whether they precede a name, follow a name, or replace a name.

the Prime Minister of Canada
the Premier's office
the Lieutenant-Governor of
　British Columbia
J. W. Ross, Minister of Finance

Gaston Pelletier, Senator
the Speaker of the House of Commons
an audience with the Pope

d. Do not capitalize most common titles following names:

The speech was delivered by Wayne Hsu, president, Inter-Tel Canada.

Lois Herndon, chief executive officer, signed the order.

e. Do not capitalize common titles appearing alone:

Please speak to the supervisor or to the office manager.

Neither the president nor the vice-president was asked.

However, when the title of an official appears in that organization's minutes, bylaws, or other official document, it may be capitalized.

f. Do not capitalize titles when they are followed by appositives naming specific individuals:

We must consult our director of research, Ronald E. Weston, before responding.

g. Do not capitalize family titles used with possessive pronouns:

my mother　　　　our aunt　　　　your father　　　　his cousin

h. Capitalize titles of close relatives used without pronouns:

Both Mother and Father must sign the contract.

3.07 Numbered and Lettered Items. Capitalize nouns followed by numbers or letters (except in page, paragraph, line, and verse references):

Flight 34, Gate 12
Volume I, Part 3
Invoice No. 55489
Model A5673
Rural Route 10

Plan No. 2
Warehouse 33-A
Figure 8.3
Serial No. C22865404-2
page 6, line 5

3.08 Points of the Compass. Capitalize *north, south, east, west,* and their derivatives when they represent specific geographical regions. Do not capitalize the points of the compass when they are used in directions or in general references.

Specific Regions	**General References**
from the South	heading north on the highway
living in the North	west of the city
Easterners, Westerners	western Ontario, southern Saskatchewan
going to the Middle East	the northern part of Canada
from the East Coast	the east side of the street

3.09 Departments, Divisions, and Committees. Capitalize the names of departments, divisions, or committees within your own organization. Outside your organization capitalize only specific department, division, or committee names:

> The inquiry was addressed to the Legal Department in our Consumer Products Division.

> John was appointed to the Employee Benefits Committee.

> Send your résumé to their human resources division.

> A planning committee will be named shortly.

3.10 Governmental Terms. Do not capitalize the words *federal, government, nation,* or *province* unless they are part of a specific title:

> Unless federal support can be secured, the state project will be abandoned.

> The Provincial Employees' Pension Fund is looking for secure investments.

3.11 Product Names. Capitalize product names only when they refer to trademarked items. Except in advertising, common names following manufacturers' names are not capitalized:

Magic Marker	Apple computer
Kleenex tissues	Swingline stapler
Q-tips	3M diskettes
Levi 501 jeans	Sony dictation machine
DuPont Teflon	Canon camera

3.12 Literary Titles. Capitalize the principal words in the titles of books, magazines, newspapers, articles, movies, plays, songs, poems, and reports. Do not capitalize articles (*a, an, the*), short conjunctions (*and, but, or, nor*), and prepositions of fewer than five (some say four) letters (*in, to, by, for,* etc.) unless they begin or end the title:

> Jackson's *What Job Is for You*? (Capitalize book titles.)

> Gant's "Software for the Executive Suite" (Capitalize principal words in article titles.)

> "Performance Standards to Go By" (Capitalize article titles.)

> "The Improvement of Fuel Economy with Alternative Motors" (Capitalize report titles.)

3.13 Beginning Words. In addition to capitalizing the first word of a complete sentence, capitalize the first word in a quoted sentence, independent phrase, item in an enumerated list, and formal rule or principle following a colon:

> The business manager said, "All purchases must have requisitions." (Capitalize first word in a quoted sentence.)

> Yes, if you agree. (Capitalize an independent phrase.)

> Some of the duties of the position are as follows:

> 1. Editing and formatting Word files

> 2. Receiving and routing telephone calls

> 3. Verifying records, reports, and applications (Capitalize items in an enumerated list.)

> One rule has been established through the company: No smoking is allowed in open offices. (Capitalize a rule following a colon.)

3.14 Celestial Bodies. Capitalize the names of celestial bodies such as Mars, Saturn, and Neptune. Do not capitalize the terms *earth*, *sun*, or *moon* unless they appear in a context with other celestial bodies:

Where on earth did you find that manual typewriter?

Venus and Mars are the closest planets to Earth.

3.15 Ethnic References. Capitalize terms that refer to a particular culture, language, or race:

Oriental	Hebrew
Caucasian	Indian
Latino	Japanese
Persian	Judeo-Christian

3.16 Seasons. Do not capitalize seasons:

In the fall it appeared that winter and spring sales would increase.

Review Exercise M—Capitalization

In the following sentences correct any errors that you find in capitalization. Circle any lowercase letter that should be changed to a capital letter. Draw a slash (/) through a capital letter that you wish to change to a lowercase letter. In the space provided, indicate the total number of changes you have made in each sentence. If you make no changes, write *0*. When you finish, compare your responses with those provided. For each item on which you need review, consult the numbered principle shown in parentheses.

Example: Bill McAdams, currently Assistant Manager in our Personnel department, will be promoted to Manager of the Employee Services division.   5 _____

1. The pensions act, passed in 1949, established the present system of social security. _____
2. Our company will soon be moving its operations to the west coast. _____
3. Marilyn Hunter, m.b.a., received her bachelor's degree from McGill university in montreal. _____
4. The President of Datatronics, Inc., delivered a speech entitled "Taking off into the future." _____
5. Please ask your Aunt and your Uncle if they will come to the Lawyer's office at 5 p.m. _____
6. Your reservations are for flight 32 on air canada leaving from gate 14 at 2:35 p.m. _____
7. Once we establish an organizing committee, arrangements can be made to rent holmby hall. _____
8. Bob was enrolled in history, spanish, business communications, and physical education courses. _____
9. Either the President or the Vice-President of the company will make the decision about purchasing xerox copiers. _____
10. Rules for hiring and firing Employees are given on page 7, line 24, of the Contract. _____
11. Some individuals feel that canadian management does not have the sense of loyalty to their employees that japanese management has. _____
12. Where on Earth can we find better workers than Robots? _____
13. The minister of finance said, "we must encourage our domestic producers to compete internationally." _____

14. After crossing the lion's gate bridge, we drove to Southern British Columbia for our vacation.
15. All marketing representatives of our company will meet in the empire room of the red lion motor inn.
16. Richard Elkins, ph.d., has been named director of research for spaceage strategies, inc.
17. The special keyboard for the IBM Computer must contain greek symbols for Engineering equations.
18. After she received a master's degree in electrical engineering, Joanne Dudley was hired to work in our product development department.
19. In the Fall our organization will move its corporate headquarters to the franklin building in downtown vancouver.
20. Dean Amador has one cardinal rule: always be punctual.

1. Pensions Act (3.01) 3. M.B.A. University Montreal (3.01, 3.05) 5. aunt uncle lawyer's (3.06e, 3.06g) 7. Holmby Hall (3.01) 9. president vice-president Xerox (3.06e, 3.11) 11. Canadian Japanese (3.02) 13. We foreign (3.10, 3.13) 15. Empire Room Red Lion Motor Inn (3.01) 17. computer Greek engineering (3.01, 3.02, 3.11) 19. fall Franklin Building Vancouver (3.01, 3.03, 3.16)

Grammar/Mechanics Checkup—13

Capitalization

Review Sections 3.01–3.16 above. Then study each of the following statements. Circle any lowercase letter that should be capitalized. Draw a slash (/) through any capital letter that you wish to change to lowercase. Indicate in the space provided the number of changes you made in each sentence and record the number of the Handbook principle(s) illustrated. If you made no changes, write *0*. When you finish, compare your responses with those provided on page 506. If your responses differ, carefully study again the principles in parentheses.

4   (3.01, 3.06a)   **Example:** After consulting our /attorneys for /legal advice, Vice-/president Fontaine signed the /contract.

1. All canadian passengers from Flight 402 must pass through Customs Inspection at Gate 17 upon arrival at Pearson international airport.
2. Personal tax rates for japanese citizens are low by International standards; rates for japanese corporations are high, according to Iwao Nakatani, an Economics Professor at Osaka university.
3. In the end, Business passes on most of the burden to the Consumer: What looks like a tax on Business is really a tax on Consumption.
4. Abel enrolled in courses in History, Sociology, Spanish, and Computer Science.
5. Did you see the *Maclean's* article entitled "Careers in horticulture are nothing to sneeze at"?
6. Although I recommend Minex Printers sold under the brandname MPLazerJet, you may purchase any Printers you choose.
7. According to a Federal Government report, any development of Provincial waterways must receive an environmental assessment.
8. The deputy prime minister of canada said, "this country continues to encourage Foreign investment."
9. The Comptroller of Ramjet International reported to the President and the Board of Directors that canada revenue agency was beginning an investigation of their Company.

10. My Mother, who lives near Plum Coulee, reports that protection from the Sun's rays is particularly important when travelling to the South. _____

11. Our Managing Editor met with Leslie Hawkins, Manager of the Advertising Sales Department, to plan an Ad Campaign for our special issue. _____

12. Next week, Editor in Chief Mercredi plans an article detailing the astounding performance of the euro. _____

13. To reach Terrasee Vaudreuil park, which is located on an Island in the St. Lawrence river, tourists pass over the vanier bridge. _____

14. On page 6 of the catalogue you will see that the computer science department is offering a number of courses in programming. _____

15. Please consult figure 3.2 in chapter 5 for statistics Canada figures regarding non-english-speaking residents. _____

Cumulative Editing Quiz 7

Use proofreading marks (see Appendix B) to correct errors and omissions in the following sentences. All errors must be corrected to receive credit for the sentence. Check with your instructor for the answers.

1. The Manager thinks that you attending the three day seminar is a good idea, however we must find a replacement.

2. We heard that professor watson invited edward peters, president of micropro, inc. to speak to our business law class.

3. Carla Jones a new systems programmer in our accounting department will start monday.

4. After year's of downsizing and restructuring canada has now become one of the worlds most efficient manufacturers.

5. When our company specialized in asian imports our main office was on the west coast.

6. Company's like amway discovered that there unique door to door selling methods was very successful in japan.

7. If you had given your sony camera to she or I before you got on the roller coaster it might have stayed dry.

8. Tracy recently finished a bachelors degree in accounting, consequently she is submitting many résumé's to companys across the country.

9. The Lopezs moved from Edmonton Alberta to Vancouver British Columbia when mr lopez enrolled at the university of british columbia.

10. When we open our office in montreal we will need employees whom are fluent in english and french.

Number Style (4.01–4.13)

Usage and custom determine whether numbers are expressed in the form of figures (for example, *5*, *9*) or in the form of words (for example, *five*, *nine*). Numbers expressed as figures are shorter and more easily understood, yet numbers expressed as words are necessary in certain instances. The following guidelines are observed in expressing numbers in written sentences. Numbers that appear on business forms—such as invoices, monthly statements, and purchase orders—are always expressed as figures.

4.01 General Rules

a. The numbers one through ten are generally written as words. Numbers above ten are written as figures:

The bank had a total of nine branch offices in three suburbs.

All 58 employees received benefits in the three categories shown.

A shipment of 45,000 light bulbs was sent from two warehouses.

b. Numbers that begin sentences are written as words. If a number beginning a sentence involves more than two words, however, the sentence should be written so that the number does not fall at the beginning.

Fifteen different options were available in the annuity programs.

A total of 156 companies participated in the promotion (not *One hundred fifty-six companies participated in the promotion*).

4.02 Money. Sums of money $1 or greater are expressed as figures. If a sum is a whole dollar amount, omit the decimal and zeros (whether or not the amount appears in a sentence with additional fractional dollar amounts):

We budgeted $30 for blank CDs, but the actual cost was $37.96.

On the invoice were items for $6.10, $8, $33.95, and $75.

Sums less than $1 are written as figures that are followed by the word *cents*:

By shopping carefully, we can save 15 cents per blank CD.

4.03 Dates. In dates, numbers that appear after the name of the month are written as cardinal figures (*1, 2, 3,* etc.). Those that stand alone or appear before the name of a month are written as ordinal figures (*1st, 2nd, 3nd,** etc.):

The Personnel Practices Committee will meet May 7.

On the 5th day of February and again on the 25th, we placed orders.

In domestic business documents, dates generally take the following form: *January 4, 2001.* An alternative form, used primarily in military and foreign correspondence, begins with the day of the month and omits the comma: *4 January 2001.*

4.04 Clock Time. Figures are used when clock time is expressed with *a.m.* or *p.m.* Omit the colon and zeros in referring to whole hours. When exact clock time is expressed with the contraction *o'clock,* either figures or words may be used:

Mail deliveries are made at 11 a.m. and 3:30 p.m.

At four (or 4) o'clock employees begin to leave.

4.05 Addresses and Telephone Numbers

a. Except for the number one, house numbers are expressed in figures:

540 Elm Street	17802 Parliament Avenue
One Desmeurons Boulevard	2 Highland Street

---

*Some writers today are using the more efficient *2d* and *3d* instead of *2nd* and *3rd.*

b. Street names containing numbers ten or lower are written entirely as words. For street names involving numbers greater than ten, figures are used:

330 Third Street   3440 Seventh Avenue

6945 East 32 Avenue   4903 West 103 Street

If no compass direction (*North*, *South*, *East*, *West*) separates a house number from a street number, the street number is expressed in ordinal form (*-st*, *-d*, *-th*).

256 42d Street   1390 11th Avenue

c. Telephone numbers are expressed with figures. When used, the area code is placed in parentheses preceding the telephone number:

Please call us at (818) 347-0551 to place an order.

Mr. Sui asked you to call (619) 554-8923, Ext. 245, after 10 a.m.

4.06 Related Numbers. Numbers are related when they refer to similar items in a category within the same reference. All related numbers should be expressed as the largest number is expressed. Thus if the largest number is greater than ten, all the numbers should be expressed in figures:

Only 5 of the original 25 applicants completed the processing. (Related numbers require figures.)

The two plans affected 34 employees working in three sites. (Unrelated numbers use figures and words.)

Petro-Canada operated 86 rigs, of which 6 were rented. (Related numbers require figures.)

The company hired three accountants, one customer service representative, and nine sales representatives. (Related numbers under ten use words.)

4.07 Consecutive Numbers. When two numbers appear consecutively and both modify a following noun, generally express the first number in words and the second in figures. If, however, the first number cannot be expressed in one or two words, put it in figures also (*120 34-cent stamps*). Do not use commas to separate the figures.

Historians divided the era into four 25-year periods. (Use word form for the first number and figure form for the second.)

We ordered ten 30-page colour brochures. (Use word form for the first number and figure form for the second.)

Did the manager request 150 100-watt bulbs? (Use figure form for the first number since it would require more than two words.)

4.08 Periods of Time. Periods of time are generally expressed in word form. However, figures may be used to emphasize business concepts such as discount rates, interest rates, warranty periods, credit terms, loan or contract periods, and payment terms:

This business was incorporated over fifty years ago. (Use words for a period of time.)

Any purchaser may cancel a contract within 72 hours. (Use figures to explain a business concept.)

The warranty period is 5 years. (Use figures for a business concept.)

Cash discounts are given for payment within 30 days. (Use figures for a business concept.)

4.09 Ages. Ages are generally expressed in word form unless the age appears immediately after a name or is expressed in exact years and months:

At the age of twenty-one, Elizabeth inherited the business.

Wanda Unger, 37, was named acting president.

At the age of 4 years and 7 months, the child was adopted.

4.10 Round Numbers. Round numbers are approximations. They may be expressed in word or figure form, although figure form is shorter and easier to comprehend:

About 600 (or *six hundred*) stock options were sold.

It is estimated that 1000 (or *one thousand*) people will attend.

For ease of reading, round numbers in the millions or billions should be expressed with a combination of figures and words:

At least 1.5 million readers subscribe to the ten top magazines.

Deposits in money market accounts totalled more than $115 billion.

4.11 Weights and Measurements. Weights and measurements are expressed with figures:

The new deposit slip measures 5 by 15 cm.

Her new suitcase weighed only 1.2 kg.

Regina is 750 kilometres from Calgary.

4.12 Fractions. Simple fractions are expressed as words. Complex fractions may be written either as figures or as a combination of figures and words:

Over two thirds of the shareholders voted.

This microcomputer will execute the command in 1 millionth of a second. (Combination of words and numbers is easier to comprehend.)

She purchased a one-fifth share in the business.*

4.13 Percentages and Decimals. Percentages are expressed with figures that are followed by the word *percent*. The percent sign (%) is used only on business forms or in statistical presentations:

We had hoped for a 7 percent interest rate, but we received a loan at 8 percent.

Over 50 percent of the residents supported the plan.

Decimals are expressed with figures. If a decimal expression does not contain a whole number (an integer) and does not begin with a zero, a zero should be placed before the decimal point:

The actuarial charts show that 1.74 out of 1,000 people will die in any given year.

Inspector Norris found the setting to be .005 centimetres off. (Decimal begins with a zero and does not require a zero before the decimal point.)

*Fractions used as adjectives require hyphens.

Considerable savings will accrue if the unit production cost is reduced by 0.1 percent. (A zero is placed before a decimal that neither contains a whole number nor begins with a zero).

Quick Chart—Expression of Numbers

Use Words	Use Figures
Numbers ten and under	Numbers 11 and over
Numbers at beginning of sentence	Money
Periods of time	Dates
Ages	Addresses and telephone numbers
Fractions	Weights and measurements
	Percentages and decimals

Review Exercise N—Number Style

Circle *a* or *b* to indicate the preferred number style. Assume that these numbers appear in business correspondence. When you finish, compare your responses with those provided. For each item on which you need review, consult the numbered principle shown in parentheses.

1. (a) 2 alternatives   (b) two alternatives   _____
2. (a) Seventh Avenue   (b) 7th Avenue   _____
3. (a) sixty sales reps   (b) 60 sales reps   _____
4. (a) November ninth   (b) November 9   _____
5. (a) forty dollars   (b) $40   _____
6. (a) on the 23d of May   (b) on the twenty-third of May   _____
7. (a) at 2:00 p.m.   (b) at 2 p.m.   _____
8. (a) 4 two-hundred-page books   (b) four 200-page books   _____
9. (a) at least 15 years ago   (b) at least fifteen years ago   _____
10. (a) 1,000,000 viewers   (b) 1 million viewers   _____
11. (a) twelve cents   (b) 12 cents   _____
12. (a) a sixty-day warranty   (b) a 60-day warranty   _____
13. (a) ten percent interest rate   (b) 10 percent interest rate   _____
14. (a) 4/5 of the voters   (b) four fifths of the voters   _____
15. (a) the rug measures two by four metres   (b) the rug measures 2 by 4 metres   _____
16. (a) about five hundred people attended   (b) about 500 people attended   _____
17. (a) at eight o'clock   (b) at 8 o'clock   _____
18. (a) located at 1 Broadway Boulevard   (b) located at One Broadway Boulevard   _____
19. (a) three computers for twelve people   (b) three computers for 12 people   _____
20. (a) 4 out of every 100 licences   (b) four out of every 100 licences   _____

1. b (4.01a) 3. b (4.01a) 5. b (4.02) 7. b (4.04) 9. b (4.08) 11. b (4.02) 13. b (4.13) 15. b (4.11) 17. a or b (4.04) 19. b (4.06)

Grammar/Mechanics Checkup—14

Number Style

Review Sections 4.01–4.13 above. Then study each of the following pairs. Assume that these expressions appear in the context of letters, reports, or e-mails. Write *a* or *b* in the space provided to indicate the preferred number style and record the number of the Handbook principle illustrated. When you finish, compare your responses with those on page 506. If your responses differ, carefully study again the principles in parentheses.

a _____ (4.01a)   **Example:**   (a) six investments (b) 6 investments

_____   1. (a) sixteen credit cards   (b) 16 credit cards
_____   2. (a) Fifth Avenue   (b) 5th Avenue
_____   3. (a) 34 newspapers   (b) thirty-four newspapers
_____   4. (a) July eighth   (b) July 8
_____   5. (a) twenty dollars   (b) $20
_____   6. (a) on the 15th of June   (b) on the fifteenth of June
_____   7. (a) at 4:00 p.m.   (b) at 4 p.m.
_____   8. (a) 3 200-page reports   (b) three 200-page reports
_____   9. (a) over 18 years ago   (b) over eighteen years ago
_____   10. (a) 2,000,000 people   (b) 2 million people
_____   11. (a) fifteen cents   (b) 15 cents
_____   12. (a) a thirty-day warranty   (b) a 30-day warranty
_____   13. (a) 2/3 of the e-mails   (b) two thirds of the e-mails
_____   14. (a) two telephones for 15 employees   (b) 2 telephones for 15 employees
_____   15. (a) 6 of the 130 letters   (b) six of the 130 letters.

Cumulative Editing Quiz 8

Use proofreading marks (see Appendix B) to correct errors and omissions in the following sentences. All errors must be corrected to receive credit for the sentence. Check with your instructor for the answers.

1. The prime minister of Canada recommended a 30 day cooling off period in the united nations peace negotiations.

2. Please meet at my lawyers office at four p.m. on May 10th to sign our papers of incorporation.

3. A Retail Store at 405 7th avenue had sales of over one million dollars last year.

4. Every new employee must receive their permit to park in lot 5-A or there car will be towed.

5. Mr thompson left three million dollars to be divided among his 4 children rachel, timothy, rebecca and kevin.

6. Most companys can boost profits almost one hundred percent by retaining only 5% more of there current customers.

7. Although the bill for coffee and doughnuts were only three dollars and forty cents Pavel and myself had trouble paying it.

8. Only six of the 19 employees, who filled out survey forms, would have went to hawaii as their vacation choice.

9. Danielles report is more easier to read then david because her's was better organized and had good headings.

10. At mcdonald's we devoured 4 big macs 3 orders of french fries and 5 coca colas for lunch.

accede:	to agree or consent	*everyday:*	ordinary
exceed:	over a limit	*farther:*	a greater distance
accept:	to receive	*further:*	additional
except:	to exclude; (*prep.*) but	*formally:*	in a formal manner
advice:	suggestion, opinion	*formerly:*	in the past
advise:	to counsel or recommend	*hole:*	an opening
affect:	to influence	*whole:*	complete
effect:	(*n.*) outcome, result; (*v.*) to bring about, to create	*imply:*	to suggest indirectly
		infer:	to reach a conclusion
all ready:	prepared	*liable:*	legally responsible
already:	by this time	*libel:*	damaging written statement
all right:	satisfactory	*loose:*	not fastened
alright:	unacceptable variant spelling	*lose:*	to misplace
altar:	structure for worship	*miner:*	person working in a mine
alter:	to change	*minor:*	a lesser item; person under age
appraise:	to estimate	*patience:*	calm perseverance
apprise:	to inform	*patients:*	people receiving medical treatment
assure:	to promise		
ensure:	to make certain	*personal:*	private, individual
insure:	to protect from loss	*personnel:*	employees
capital:	(*n.*) city that is seat of government; wealth of an individual; (*adj.*) chief	*precede:*	to go before
		proceed:	to continue
		precedence:	priority
		precedents:	events used as an example
capitol:	building that houses state or national lawmakers	*principal:*	(*n.*) capital sum; school official; (*adj.*) chief
cereal:	breakfast food	*principle:*	rule of action
serial:	arranged in sequence	*stationary:*	immovable
cite:	to quote; to summon	*stationery:*	writing material
site:	location	*than:*	conjunction showing comparison
sight:	a view; to see	*then:*	adverb meaning "at that time"
complement:	that which completes		
compliment:	to praise or flatter	*their:*	possessive form of they
conscience:	regard for fairness		
conscious:	aware	*there:*	at that place or point
council:	governing body	*they're:*	contraction of they are
counsel:	to give advice; advice	*to:*	a preposition; the sign of the infinitive
desert:	arid land; to abandon		
dessert:	sweet food	*too:*	an adverb meaning "also" or "to an excessive extent"
device:	invention or mechanism		
devise:	to design or arrange		
disburse:	to pay out	*two:*	a number
disperse:	to scatter widely	*waiver:*	abandonment of a claim
elicit:	to draw out		
illicit:	unlawful	*waver:*	to shake or fluctuate
every day:	each single day		

160 Frequently Misspelled Words

absence	desirable	independent	prominent
accommodate	destroy	indispensable	qualify
achieve	development	interrupt	quantity
acknowledgment	disappoint	irrelevant	questionnaire
across	dissatisfied	itinerary	receipt
adequate	division	judgment	receive
advisable	efficient	knowledge	recognize
analyze	embarrass	legitimate	recommendation
annually	emphasis	library	referred
appointment	emphasize	licence	regarding
argument	employee	maintenance	remittance
automatically	envelope	manageable	representative
bankruptcy	equipped	manufacturer	restaurant
becoming	especially	mileage	schedule
beneficial	evidently	miscellaneous	secretary
budget	fiscal	mortgage	separate
business	exaggerate	necessary	similar
calendar	excellent	nevertheless	sincerely
cancelled	exempt	ninety	software
catalogue	existence	ninth	succeed
changeable	extraordinary	noticeable	sufficient
column	familiar	occasionally	supervisor
committee	fascinate	occurred	surprise
congratulate	feasible	offered	tenant
conscience	February	omission	therefore
conscious	foreign	omitted	thorough
consecutive	forty	opportunity	though
consensus	fourth	opposite	through
consistent	friend	ordinarily	truly
control	genuine	paid	undoubtedly
convenient	government	pamphlet	unnecessarily
correspondence	grammar	permanent	usable
courteous	grateful	permitted	usage
criticize	guarantee	pleasant	using
decision	harass	practical	usually
deductible	height	prevalent	valuable
defendant	hoping	privilege	volume
definitely	immediate	probably	weekday
dependent	incidentally	procedure	writing
describe	incredible	profited	yield

Key to Grammar/ Mechanics Checkups

Checkup 1
1. attorneys (1.05d) **2.** Saturdays (1.05a) **3.** cities (1.05e) **4.** turkeys (1.05d) **5.** inventories (1.05e) **6.** Nashes (1.05b) **7.** 1990s (1.05g) **8.** editors in chief (1.05f) **9.** complexes (1.05b) **10.** counties (1.05e) **11.** Jennifers (1.05a) **12.** C (1.05d) **13.** liabilities (1.05e) **14.** C (1.05h) **15.** runners-up (1.05f)

Checkup 2
1. he (1.08b) **2.** his car (1.09b) **3.** him (1.08c) **4.** whom (1.08j) **5.** hers (1.08d) **6.** me (1.08c) **7.** I (1.08a) **8.** yours (1.08d) **9.** whoever (1.08j) **10.** me (1.08i) **11.** he (1.08f) **12.** us (1.08g) **13.** her (1.09c) **14.** its (1.09g) **15.** his or her (1.09b)

Checkup 3
1. *are* for *is* (1.10e) **2.** *has* for *have* (1.10c) **3.** *offers* for *offer* (1.10d) **4.** *is* for *are* (1.10g) **5.** C (1.10f) **6.** *is* for *are* (1.10i) **7.** C (1.10h) **8.** chosen (1.15) **9.** *lain* for *laid* (1.15) **10.** *were* for *was* (1.12) **11.** *is* for *are* (1.10c) **12.** b (1.15c) **13.** b (1.15c) **14.** a (1.15c) **15.** b (1.15c)

Checkup 4
1. long-time (1.17e) **2.** $50-per-year (1.17e) **3.** C (1.17e) **4.** quickly (1.17d) **5.** had only (1.17f) **6.** double-digit (1.17e) **7.** once-in-a-lifetime (1.17e) **8.** C (1.17e) **9.** better (1.17a) **10.** well-known (1.17e) **11.** up-to-the-minute (1.17e) **12.** after-tax (1.17e) **13.** couldn't have been clearer (1.17b) **14.** fifty-fifty (1.17e) **15.** feel bad (1.17c)

Checkup 5
1. b (1.19d) **2.** a (1.19d) **3.** b (1.18e) **4.** b (1.19c) **5.** a (1.19a) **6.** b (1.18a) **7.** b (1.19d) **8.** a (1.18c) **9.** b (1.18b) **10.** a (1.19c) **11.** b (1.19a) **12.** b (1.19b) **13.** a (1.19c) **14.** b (1.18c) **15.** b (1.19c)

Checkup 6
1. (2) not, as a rule, (2.03) **2.** (2) sure, Mrs. Schwartz, (2.02) **3.** (2) reliable, conscientious, (2.01) **4.** (0) **5.** (1) fact, (2.03) **6.** (3) Calgary, Alberta, La Morenie, (2.04c) **7.** (1) meantime, (2.03) **8.** (2) February 4, 2001, (2.04a) **9.** (2) Ms. Horne, Mr. Hae, (2.01) **10.** (4) Holmes, Lane, Regina, Saskatchewan S5L 2E2, (2.04b) **11.** (2) feels, needless to say, (2.03) **12.** (2) supplies, replacing inventories, (2.01) **13.** (1) business, (2.02) **14.** (2) feels, however, (2.03) **15.** 0

Checkup 7
1. (1) warranty, (2.06a) **2.** (1) market, (2.05) **3.** (0) (2.05) **4.** (2) manufacturer, nameless, (2.06c) **5.** (1) imaginative, (2.08) **6.** (0) (2.06c) **7.** (2) Sims, area, (2.09) **8.** (1) buyers, (2.05) **9.** (1) quality, (2.06a) **10.** (1) buyers, (2.07) **11.** (2) application, Monday, (2.06a, 2.04a) **12.** (2) hand, hard-working, (2.03, 2.08) **13.** (1) Bragg Creek, (2.06c) **14.** (3) telephone, Thursday, June 9, (2.06a, 2.04a) **15.** (1) classes, (2.05)

Checkup 8
1. (2) name," Etienne, (2.14a) **2.** Cox, Ph.D., Meridian, M.B.A., (2.10) **3.** (1) Monday, (2.14b) **4.** (0) (2.15) **5.** (1) investment, (2.12) **6.** (3) requested, cartridges, folders, (2.06a, 2.01) **7.** (2) think, however, (2.03) **8.** (2) period, Vidal, (2.07, 2.06c) **9.** (2) Collingwood, Laurentians, (2.01, 2.15) **10.** (1) interviewed, (2.06a, 2.06c) **11.** (2) years, individuals, (2.07, 2.09) **12.** (2) Johansson, week, (2.05c, 2.15) **13.** (0) (2.06c) **14.** (2) companies, robots, (2.01) **15.** (2) act, unprotected, (2.03, 2.08)

Checkup 9
1. (3) one year; long-term financing, hand, (2.03, 2.16b) **2.** (2) December; therefore, (2.16a) **3.** (3) months: September, October, (2.01, 2.17a) **4.** (1) are [omit comma] (2.17b) **5.** (1) money, (2.06a, 2.16b) **6.** (3) short-term credit; manufacturer, however, (2.03, 2.16a) **7.** (3) credit: loans, promissory notes, (2.03, 2.16a) **8.** (8) business-people: Mary Ann Mahan, financial manager, Ritchie Industries; Buchanan, comptroller, Edmée Cavalier, operations, (2.16d, 2.17) **9.** (1) Canada, (2.05) **10.** (5) customers; for example, retailers, service companies, manufacturers, (2.16e) **11.** (2) Inc., rating, (2.06c, 2.16c) **12.** (2) Bank, applications to the following: (2.06a, 2.17a) **13.** (2) high; therefore, (2.16) **14.** (2) 18 percent, prohibitive; (2.06a, 2.16c) **15.** (1) resources; (2.16b)

Checkup 10
1. Mr. Ruskin's (2.20a, 2.21) **2.** year's (2.20a) **3.** weeks' (2.20b) **4.** Ms. Lanham's (2.21) **5.** boss's (2.20b) **6.** server's (2.20b) **7.** Kaspar's (2.22) **8.** months' (2.20b) **9.** companies' (2.20b) **10.** month's (2.20a) **11.** secretary's (2.20b) **12.** sellers' (2.20b) **13.** Mark's, David's (2.20a) **14.** Latika's (2.20a)

Checkup 11

1. (2) managers—Yu Sosa— (2.26a, 2.27) **2.** (3) please, Miss Fundy, totals? (2.20, 2.23a) **3.** (2) variables (see Figure 13 on page 432) (2.27) **4.** (3) "recommendation" misspelled, (2.06a, 2.28c) **5.** (1) training— (2.26c) **6.** (2) said, "Who cartridges?" (2.28f) **7.** (3) "How You"? (2.28e, 2.28f) **8.** (2) provinces—Alberta, Newfoundland, and Ontario— (2.26a) **9.** (4) Mr. Kieran E. Manning, Miss Kathy Tanguay, and Ms. Petra (2.23b, 2.24) **10.** (3) "Trading Market" <u>Securities Markets</u> (2.28e) **11.** (2) over"; however, (2.16, 2.28f) **12.** (3) <u>liability</u> defined as "any future." (2.28d) **13.** (1) June 10; (2.06) **14.** (4) c.o.d. today? (2.23b, 2.24) **15.** (3) Hooray! checkup, haven't I? (2.24, 2.25)

Checkup 12

1. c (2.05) **2.** b (2.06) **3.** a (2.16a) **4.** c (2.15) **5.** b (2.16b) **6.** b (2.17a) **7.** a (2.20) **8.** c (2.16d) **9.** b (2.04a) **10.** c (2.03) **11.** a (2.08) **12.** a (2.12) **13.** a (2.01) **14.** c (2.07) **15.** b (2.16)

Checkup 13

1. (5) Canadian customs inspection International Airport (3.01, 3.02, 3.07) **2.** (6) Japanese international Japanese economics professor University (3.01, 3.02, 3.04, 3.06d) **3.** (4) business consumer business consumption (3.01, 3.13) **4.** (4) history sociology computer science (3.05) **5.** (5) Horticulture Are Nothing Sneeze At (3.12) **6.** (2) diskettes diskettes (3.11) **7.** (3) federal government provincial (3.10) **8.** (3) Canada This foreign (3.01, 3.06c, 3.13) **9.** (8) comptroller president board directors Canada Revenue Agency company (3.01, 3.04, 3.06c) **10.** (2) mother sun's (3.03, 3.06g, 3.08, 3.14) **11.** (5) managing editor manager ad campaign (3.01, 3.06d, 3.06e, 3.09) **12.** (3) Austrian German Italian (3.02, 3.06a, 3.16) **13.** (4) Park island Vanier Bridge (3.01, 3.03) **14.** (3) Computer Science Department (3.05, 3.07, 3.09) **15.** (4) Figure Chapter Statistics English (3.02, 3.04, 3.07)

Checkup 14

1. b (4.01a) **2.** a (4.05b) **3.** a (4.01a) **4.** b (4.03) **5.** b (4.02) **6.** a (4.03) **7.** b (4.04) **8.** b (4.07) **9.** b (4.08) **10.** b (4.10) **11.** b (4.02) **12.** b (4.08) **13.** b (4.12) **14.** a (4.06) **15.** a (4.06)

Notes

Chapter 1

1. Rick Spence, "Seven Trends That Could Make or Break Your Business," *Profit* Magazine, May 2005, www.profitguide.com. Accessed April 26, 2005.

2. Backdraft Corporation, "History & Clients," www.backdraft.org/history.htm (accessed April 26, 2005).

3. Statistics Canada predicts that by 2017, visible minorities will in fact be the majority of the population in major centres like Toronto, Vancouver, and Montreal. See Statistics Canada, *The Daily*, March 22, 2005, www.statcan.ca/Daily/English/050322/d050322b.htm.

4. Anne Papmehl, "Remote Access," *CMA Management*, 75, no, 3 (May 2001): 11.

5. Desmond Beckstead and Tara Vinodrai, "Dimensions of Occupational Changes in Canada's Knowledge Economy, 1971–1996," The Canadian Economy in Transition Series, Catalogue no. 11-622-MIE—No. 004, Statistics Canada, 2003, www.statcan.ca/cgi-bin/downpub/listpub.cgi?catno=11-622-MIE2003004 (accessed April 26, 2005).

6. J. Burgoon, D. Coker, and R. Coker, "Communicative Explanations," *Human Communication Research* 12 (1986): 463–494.

7. Ray Birdwhistell, *Kinesics and Context* (Philadelphia: University of Pennsylvania Press, 1970).

8. E. T. Hall, *The Hidden Dimension* (Garden City, NY: Doubleday, 1966), 107–122.

9. Catherine Bell, "Prime Impressions Corporate Training," "Prime Impressions Telecoaching," www.prime-impressions.com (accessed April 26, 2005).

10. Anthony Wilson-Smith, "A Quiet Passion," *Maclean's*, July 1, 1995, 8–12.

11. Jon P. Alston and Theresa M. Morris. "Comparing Canadian and American Values: New Evidence from National Surveys," *Canadian Review of American Studies*, 26(3) (Autumn 1996), 301–315.

12. Seymour Martin Lipset, *Continental Divide: The Values and Institutions of the United States and Canada* (New York: Routledge, 1991).

13. Norman McGuinness and Nigel Campbell, "Selling Machinery to China: Chinese Perceptions of Strategies and Relationships," *Journal of International Business Studies* 22, no. 3 (1991): 187.

14. Statistics Canada, CANSIM, Matrices 6367 (estimates), 6900 (projections), www.statcan.ca/english/Pgdb/People/Population/demo23c.htm; and Matrix 3472, available www.statcan.ca/english/Pgdb/People/Labour/labor05.htm (accessed April 23, 2002).

15. Virginia Galt, "Western Union Remakes Canadian Image: Profits from Overseas Hiring, Staff Diversity," *The Globe and Mail*, November 23, 2004, B1.

16. Lee Gardenswartz and Anita Rowe, "Helping Managers Solve Cultural Conflicts," *Managing Diversity*, August 1996, www.jalmc.org/hlp-mgr.htm (accessed April 23, 2002).

17. Pete Engardio, "Hmm. Could Use a Little More Snake," *BusinessWeek*, March 15, 1993, 53.

Chapter 2

1. John DeGoey, personal interview, April 28, 2005.

2. Editorial Staff, "Canadian CEOs Are Big on Communication," *CMA Management*, 74, no. 9 (November 2000): 8.

3. Don Tapscott, "R U N2 It?" *Enroute* Magazine, October 2003, 35–36.

4. Kevin Marron, "Instant Messaging Comes of Age," *The Globe and Mail*, November 1, 2001, p. B30.

5. Earl N. Harbert, "Knowing Your Audience," in *The Handbook of Executive Communication*, ed. John L. Digaetani (Homewood, IL: Dow Jones/Irwin, 1986), 17.

6. James Adams, "Post Drops Columnist for Alleged Plagiarism," *The Globe and Mail*, November 6, 2004, A12.

Chapter 3

1. Shelly Chagnon, personal interview, April 28, 2005.

2. Nicholas Russell, "Russell's Rules for Good Writing," *Canadian Association of Newspaper Editors*, May 4, 1996; www.cane.ca/english/me_res_russell.htm (accessed May 2, 2001).

3. The UVic Writer's Guide, "The First Draft," *UVic English*, http://web.uvic.ca/wguide/Pages/EssayWritingFirstDraft.html (accessed May 2, 2001).

4. Maryann V. Piotrowski, *Effective Business Writing* (New York: Harper Perennial, 1996), 12.

Chapter 4

1. Stephanie Mikelbrencis, personal interview, May 24, 2005.

2. Chan Tran, "Signs of Status Even in E-Mail," *Workforce* 80, no. 6 (June 2001): 18.

Chapter 5

1. Peter Schneider, personal interview, May 1, 2005.

2. "Canadians Lead the World in Internet Use," *Canadian Press*, May 28, 2001.

3. Editors, "We've Got (Lots of) Mail," *School Library Journal* 46, no. 12 (December 2000): 44.

4. Statistics Canada, "Perspectives on Labour and Income," *Working with Computers* 13, no. 2 (Summer 2001).
5. Sinclair Stewart, "CIBC Turns up Heat as Fight with Genuity Hits Home," *The Globe and Mail*, February 17, 2005, B4.
6. Nova Scotia Human Rights Commission, "Rights on Religion or Creed," www.gov.ns.ca/humanrights/rights/religionorcreed.htm (accessed April 27, 2005).
7. Editors. "'Surfeillance' in the Workplace," *Worklife Report*, 12(4) (2000), 13.
8. Ibid.
9. Ibid.
10. Chris Wood and Brenda Branswell, "Do You Know Who's Watching You?" *Maclean's*, February 19, 2001.
11. Ibid.

Chapter 6

1. Reg Pirie, "The Lost Art of Business Letter Writing," *CanadaOne Magazine*, June 1999, www.canadaone.com/ezine/june99/letters.html (accessed April 29, 2005).
2. Judith Colbert, Helene Carty, and Paul Beam, "Practice: Assessing Financial Documents for Readability," Task Force on the Future of the Canadian Financial Services Sector, finservtaskforce.fin.gc.ca/research/pdf/RR8_V1b_e.pdf (accessed April 29, 2005).
3. Marcia Mascolini, "Another Look at Teaching the External Negative Message," *The Bulletin of the Association of Business Communication*, June 1994, 46.
4. Pamela Gilbert, "Two Words That Can Help a Business Thrive," *The Wall Street Journal*, December 30, 1996, A12.
5. Canadian Business for Social Responsibility, "Definition of Key Terms," *GoodCompany: Guidelines for Corporate Social Performance*, www.cbsr.bc.ca/files/GoodCompany-SummaryDocument.pdf (accessed May 1, 2005).

Chapter 7

1. Jose Ribau, personal interview, April 29, 2005.
2. Editors, Doing Business in Canada Web Site, Section 2.7, www.dbic.com/guide/tm2-7.html (accessed January 10, 2002).
3. Neil Morton, "Some Like It Cold," *Canadian Business*, September 1997, 99.
4. Canadian Fitness and Lifestyle Research Institute, "2002 Physical Activity Monitor," www.cflri.ca/cflri/pa/surveys/2002survey/2002survey.html (accessed November 3, 2005).
5. Government of Canada, Public Service Commission, Recourse Branch, "Workplace Conflict? Making the Right Choice," July 2000.
6. Statistics Canada, "Sources of Workplace Stress," *The Daily*, June 25, 2003, www.statcan.ca/Daily/English/030625/d030625c.htm (accessed April 21, 2005).

7. Bernard Morrow and Lauren M. Bernardi, "Resolving Workplace Disputes," *Canadian Manager*, 24, no. 1 (Spring 1999): 17.
8. Nora Wood, "Singled Out," *Incentive*, July 1998, 20–23.

Chapter 8

1. Maria Duncan, personal interview, April 28, 2005.
2. Mohan R. Limaye, "Further Conceptualization of Explanations in Negative Messages," *Business Communication Quarterly*, June 1997, 46.
3. Elizabeth M. Dorn, "Case Method Instruction in the Business Writing Classroom," *Business Communication Quarterly*, March 1999, 51–52.
4. Marcia Mascolini, "Another Look at Teaching the External Negative Message," *Bulletin of the Association for Business Communication*, June 1994, 47.
5. "Collection Letters," CreditGuru.com, www.creditguru.com/collection.htm (accessed April 30, 2005).
6. Michael Granberry, "Lingerie Chain Fined $100,000 for Gift Certificates," *Los Angeles Times*, November 14, 1992, D3.
7. Elizabeth M. Dorn, "Case Method Instruction," 51–52.
8. Tyler Hamilton, "Price Snafu Stings Web Retailer," *Toronto Star*, November 17, 2000, C01.
9. Based on Robert D. Ramsey, "Social Skills for Supervisors," *Supervision*, January 1997, 5–7; Marjorie Brody, "Test Your Manners I.Q.," *Successful Meetings*, September 1999, 145–146; Edith Helmich, "Business Etiquette for a Technological Age," www.hightechcareers.com/doc799/how-to799.html (accessed December 8, 1999).

Chapter 9

1. Heather Jack, personal interview, May 12, 2005.

Chapter 10

1. Len Willschick, personal interview, May 24, 2005.
2. Herman Holtz, *The Consultant's Guide to Proposal Writing* (New York: John Wiley, 1990), 188.
3. Joel Deane, "Study: Vast Stretches of the Web Not Indexed by Search Engines," *eWeek*, July 8, 1999, available at ZDNet Tech Update http://techupdate.zdnet.com/techupdate/stories/main/0,14179,1015425,00.html.
4. Susan Feldman, quoted in Annette Skov, "Internet Quality," *Database*, August/September 1998.
5. Gerald J. Alred, Walter E. Olin, and Charles T. Brusaw, *The Professional Writer* (New York: St. Martin's Press, 1992), 78.
6. M. Theodore Farries, II, Jeanne D. Maes, and Ulla K. Bunz, "References and Bibliography: Citing the Internet," *Journal of Applied Business Research*, Summer 1998, 33–36.

Chapter 11

1. Orna Spira, personal interview, May 27, 2005.
2. Shearlean Duke, "E-Mail: Essential in Media Relations, But No Replacement for Face-to-Face Communication," *Public Relations Quarterly* (Winter 2001): 19; Lisa M. Flaherty, Kevin J. Pearce, and Rebecca B. Rubin, "Internet and Face-to-Face Communication: Not Functional Alternatives," *Communication Quarterly* (Summer 1998): 250.
3. Aimee L. Drolet and Michael W. Morris, "Rapport in Conflict Resolution: Accounting for How Face-to-Face Contact Fosters Mutual Cooperation in Mixed-Motive Conflicts," *Journal of Experimental Social Psychology* (January 2000): 26.
4. Jean Miculka, *Speaking for Success* (Cincinnati: South-Western, 1999), 19.
5. Cheryl Hamilton with Cordell Parker, *Communicating for Success*, 6e (Belmont, CA: Wadsworth, 2001), 100–104.
6. Miculka, *Speaking*, 127.
7. "Fire Up Your Phone Skills," *Successful Meetings*, November 2000, 30.
8. Winston Fletcher, "How to Make Sure It's a Good Call," *Management Today*, February 2000, 34.
9. "Did You know That . . .," *Boardroom Reports*, August 15, 1992.
10. Elizabeth Guilday, "Voicemail Like a Pro," *Training & Development*, October 2000, 68.
11. Hal Lancaster, "Learning Some Ways to Make Meetings Slightly Less Awful," *The Wall Street Journal*, May 26, 1998, B1.
12. Tom McDonald, "Minimizing Meetings," *Successful Meetings*, June 1996, 24.
13. "I've Got to Go to Another ... Meeting." *Interventions: The EFAP Journal of CMR Canada*, November 2000. www.cmrcanada.ca/InterventionsNov2000.html (accessed May 25, 2005).
14. John C. Bruening, "There's Good News About Meetings," *Managing Office Technology*, July 1996, 24–25.
15. Kirsten Schabacker, "A Short, Snappy Guide to Meaningful Meetings," *Working Women*, June 1991, 73.
16. J. Keith Cook, "Try These Eight Guidelines for More Effective Meetings," *Communication Briefings* Bonus Item, April 1995, 8a. See also Morey Stettner, "How to Manage a Corporate Motormouth, *Investor's Business Daily*, October 8, 1998, A1.
17. Hamilton and Parker, *Communicating*, 311–312.

Chapter 12

1. Lee Jacobson, personal interview, May 25, 2005.
2. Jeff Olson, *The Agile Manager's Guide to Giving Great Presentations* (Bristol, VT: Velocity Printing, 1999), 8.
3. Dianna Booher, *Executive's Portfolio of Model Speeches for All Occasions* (Upper Saddle River, NJ: Prentice Hall, 1991), 260.
4. Wharton Applied Research Center, "A Study of the Effects of the Use of Overhead Transparencies on Business Meetings, Final Report" cited in "Short, Snappy Guide to Meaningful Presentations," *Working Woman*, June 1991, 73.
5. "On That Next Business Trip, Leave the Laptop Behind . . . And Do It All on Your PDA, New Mobile Software," *Internet Wire*, 18 June 2002, p1008169u4447. See also "PowerPoint Presentations From Your Pocket PC," *PC Magazine*, 9 April 2002, p. NA.
6. Tad Simons, "When Was the Last Time PowerPoint Made You Sing?" *Presentations*, July 2001, 6.
7. Andrew Wahl, "PowerPoint of No Return," *Canadian Business*, November 2003, www.canadianbusiness.com/article.jsp?content=20031124_56691_56691 (accessed May 11, 2005).
8. Jennifer Rotondo, "Customized PowerPoint Templates Make Life Easier," *Presentations*, July 2001, 25–26.
9. Jim Endicott, "It Always Pays to Have a Clean, Professional Package," *Presentations*, June 2002, 26–28.
10. Jim Endicott, "For Better Presentations, Avoid PowerPoint Pitfalls," *Presentations*, June 1998, 36–37.
11. Robert J. Boeri, "Fear of Flying? Or the Mail? Try the Web Conferencing Cure," *Emedia Magazine*, March 2002, 49.
12. Victoria Hall Smith, "Gigs by the Gigabyte," *Working Woman*, May 1998, 115.
13. Joan Lloyd, "Engage Your Audience @ Work," *Baltimore Business Journal*, December 14, 2001, 35.
14. Booher, *Executive's Portfolio*, 259.
15. Michael Jackson, quoted in "Garbage In, Garbage Out," *Consumer Reports*, December 1992, 755.

Chapter 13

1. Christine Shreves, personal interview, May 20, 2005.
2. Gordon Betcherman and Richard Chaykowski, "The Changing Workplace: Challenges for Public Policy R-96-13E," *Applied Research Branch, Strategic Policy, Human Resources Development Canada*, 1st Internet ed., 1998, 10; www.hrdc-drhc.gc.ca/arb/publications/research/abr-96-13e.shtml (accessed December 1, 2001).
3. Ibid., 11.
4. Alberta Learning Information Service, "8.0 Career Self-Management," *Alberta Work Search On-Line*, Government of Alberta, www.alis.gov.ab.ca/worksearch/topic.cfm?chapterid=73&chapter=8 (accessed December 1, 2001).
5. Marc Belaiche, "Tips on Improving Your Resume," *Canadian Manager* 23, no. 3 (Fall 1998): 17.
6. Interview by author, 21 January 1997.
7. "Consider Adding a Keyword Summary," *Royal Bank of Canada*, www.royalbank.com/fastforward/apply_res.html (accessed December 1, 2001).
8. Infocheck, "Six Ways to Catch Resume Lies," *emergit.com*; www.emergit.com/html/content_cur/profiles/08-27-2001_resume.jsp (accessed December 1, 2001).
9. Harriet M. Augustin, "The Written Job Search: A Comparison of the Traditional and a Nontraditional

Approach," *The Bulletin of the Association for Business Communication*, September 1991, 13.

10. Judith Schroer, "Seek a Job With a Little Help From Your Friends," *USA Today*, November 19, 1990, B1.

Chapter 14

1. Michael Stern, "Dear Sir: You Are An Oaf ... ," *Canadian Business*, April 1998, 38.

2. Candace Davies, "A Screening Interview Is Used to Disqualify Candidates," February 8, 2002, http://job-interview-questions.candocareer.com/screening.htm (accessed June 3, 2002).

3. Caryl Rae Krannich and Ronald L. Krannich, *Dynamite Answers to Interview Questions* (Manassas Park, VA: Impact Publications, 1994), 46.

4. Julia Lawlor, "Networking Opens More Doors to Jobs," *USA Today*, November 19, 1990, B7.

5. Michael Shekter, "How to State Your Salary Expectations," www.workopolis.ca (accessed September 21, 2001).

Index

Pronoun–antecedent agreement, 451–453
Pronoun case, 451
Pronouns, 62, 450–454
Pronunciation, 299
Proofreading, 74, 81–83, 96, 238
   marks, 432
Proper adjectives, 492
Proper nouns, 448, 491
Proposal, 30, 254–259
Provocative messages, 171
Publication Manual of the American Psychological Association, 440
Public space, 9
Public speaking. *See* Oral presentations
Punctuation, 81
   apostrophe, 482–483
   colon, 479
   comma, 468–478
   dash, 485–486
   exclamation point, 485
   parenthesis, 486
   period, 485
   question mark, 485
   quotation marks, 486–487
   semicolon, 478
Punctuation styles, 424
Purpose, 29

Question mark, 485
Questionnaires, 227
Quotation marks, 486–487
Quotations, 475, 479, 486–487
Quotations within quotations, 486

Rational appeals, 171, 175
Reader benefit, 172
Receiver (communication), 4
Recommendation, letters of/letters requesting, 138–140
Recommendation reports, 233
Recommendations, 274
Redundant words, 78
Reference list, 440–442
Reference request, 405–406
Refusing claims, 201
Refusing requests, 198–201
Rejection follow-up letter, 407
Repetition of key ideas, 62
Repetitious words, 77
Report/report format, 30, 223. *See also* Formal reports; Informal reports
Request for proposal (RFP), 254, 255
Research, 50–52
   e-mails/memos, 96
Resolving business problems, 193
Résumé, 361–377
   action verbs, 366–368
   awards/activities, 368
   capabilities/skills, 367–368
   career objective, 364, 366

chronological, 361–362, 374
combination, 364, 365, 373
computer-friendly, 369–376
cover letter, 377–383
e-mailing the, 377
education, 366
enhanced (desktop publishing features), 372
faxing the, 377
final touches, 376–377
functional, 361–364
inflated, 371–376
keywords, 370–371
main heading, 364
personal information, 368–369
persuasive, 361
references, 369
résumé-writing services, 377
scannable, 369–370
work experience/employment history, 366–367
Résumé follow-up letter, 406
Résumé fraud, 371–376
Résumé-writing services, 377
Revising, 28, 74–91
   abstract nouns, 80
   cliches, 79
   conciseness, 75–79
   concrete nouns, 80
   e-mails/memos, 96
   fillers, 77
   jargon, 78
   long lead-ins, 76
   needless adverbs, 77
   outdated expressions, 76
   overuse of articles, 77
   precise verbs, 79
   proofreading, 81–83
   redundant words, 78
   repetitious words, 77
   reports, 238
   sentence structure, 74
   slang, 79
   verbs, 79
   wordy prepositional phrases, 76
   See also Grammar
RFP. *See* Request for proposal
Ribau, Jose, 162
Round numbers, 500
Routine letters, 124–160
   claim request, 127–128
   customer claim response, 135–138
   customer order response, 133–135
   information request, 125–127
   information response letter, 131–133
   order request, 130
Royal Bank of Canada, 370
Rule of seven, 341
Run-on sentence, 56
Russell, Nicholas, 56